Learning Conversations In Museums

Learning Conversations in Museums

Edited by

Gaea Leinhardt
Kevin Crowley
Karen Knutson
University of Pittsburgh

LEA
LAWRENCE ERLBAUM ASSOCIATES, PUBLISHERS
2002 Mahwah, New Jersey London

Lawrence Erlbaum Associates, Inc., Publishers
10 Industrial Avenue
Mahwah, New Jersey 07430

Cover design by Kathryn Houghtaling Lacey

Library of Congress Cataloging-In-Publication Data

Learning conversations in museums
p. c.m.
ISBN 0-8058-4052-4
1. Museums—Education Aspects. 2. Museum exhibits—Social aspects. 3. Museum visitors—Education. 4. Museum techniques—Study and teaching (Higher). 5. Museums—Study and teaching (Higher). 6. Non-formal education. I. Leinhardt, Gaea. II. Crowley, Kevin. III. Knutson, Karen.

AM7.L43 2002
069'.071—dc21

2002024253

Books published by Lawrence Erlbaum Associates are printed on acid-free paper, and their bindings are chosen for strength and durability.

Printed in the United States of America

10 9 8 7 6 5 4 3 2 1

Dedicated to

Sam, Zoe, and Lucille

Joseph E. and Mary V. Crowley

Les and Anne Knutson

Acknowledgments

We would like to thank the funders of the Museum Learning Collaborative, the Institute for Museum and Library Services (IMLS), National Science Foundation (NSF), National Endowment for the Humanities (NEH), and the National Endowment for the Arts (NEA). We appreciate the support and cooperation of our museum colleagues at the Carnegie Museum of Art, Carnegie Museum of Natural History, Senator John Heinz Regional History Center, Birmingham Civil Rights Institute, Exploratorium, Connor Prairie, Henry Ford Museum and Greenfield Village, Indianapolis Children's Museum and Pittsburgh Children's Museum. Finally, we thank our colleagues at the Learning Research and Development Center at the University of Pittsburgh.

Contents

Preface

Museums are among our preeminent cultural institutions for learning. Museums are where society gathers, preserves, and displays visible records of social, scientific, and artistic accomplishments; where society supports scholarship that extends knowledge from paleontology to meteorites; and where people of all ages turn to build understandings of culture, history, and science. People visit museums for a wide variety of reasons: to pass time with friends, to find a moment of calm in a hectic life, to come to know a particular locale and its values, or to learn. People visit as individuals, families, school groups, or groups of friends. Some people visit museums regularly, others rarely. Some visitors track particular art forms or events whereas others just find themselves with time on their hands and choose to spend it at a museum.

What do people learn from visiting museums and how do they learn it? We approach this question by focusing on *conversations* as both the process and the outcome of museum learning. People do not come to museums to talk, but they often do talk. This talk can drift from discussions of managing the visit, to remembrances of family members and friends not present, to close analyses of particular objects or displays. This volume explores how these conversations reflect and change a visitor's identity, discipline-specific knowledge, and engagement with an informal learning environment.

The question of how to consider learning in museums has long been of interest to museum developers, directors, curators, educators, and funders. There have been many prior studies of museum learning, although many of these studies have differed in what they considered learning to be. Approaches to learning in museums have ranged from information accumulation and time-on-task (e.g., Anderson & Lucas, 1997; Borun, Chambers, Dritsas, & Johnson, 1997; Cone & Kendall, 1978; Sandifer, 1997; Serrell, 1995, 1977), to affective responses and emotional reminiscences (e.g., McManus, 1993; Stevenson, 1991), to meaning making and constructivism (e.g., Doering & Pekarik, 1996; Falk & Dierking, 2000; Gelman, Massey, & McManus, 1991; Hein, 1998; Silverman, 1993).

It is natural that in an emerging field such as museum learning there should be a rich variety of meanings assigned to the notion of learning. Unlike other areas of social science research, studies of museum activity are conducted for the most part in a piecemeal, private, and proprietary fashion. It is often the museums themselves that seek out and pay for evaluations of visitor behavior, and they need the answers to very practical, immediate questions: Are visitors using the exhibits? Do visitors understand the label copy? Do they enjoy the experience? What programs are needed to align the exhibit content with local curriculum standards for visiting school groups?

The potential of this interesting yet isolated museum learning research prompted calls for a more focused, theoretically grounded, and publicly shared research agenda (Friedman, 1995; Hein, 1998). In 1997 the Museum Learning Collaborative (MLC) was funded as a research project to study the meaning of learning in museums and the ways in which it occurs. The MLC was funded by the Institute for Museum and Library Services, the National Science Foundation, the National Endowment for the Humanities, and the National Endowment for the Arts.

To guide our approach to museum learning, the MLC has focused on three themes. The first, *identity, motivation, and interest,* is a construct located within the visitors. Included in this theme are notions of the role of museums in the longer trajectory of family and group life. The second theme, *explanation, interpretation, and meaning,* represents the interface between the museum and its visitors. This theme is concerned with questions about how visitors construct knowledge, explanation, and informal theory through an asynchronous dialectic with curatorial messages. The third theme, *learning environment,* is focused on how museums as designed spaces influence visitor experience. This theme incorporates notions about how specific design features support specific kinds of learning and how the larger setting of the museum as location and institution sets the stage for learning. These three themes offer a broad, multidimensional framework in which to explore visitors' conversations in museums.

Public and observable, the study of conversation offers a reflection of the intertwining of social and cultural processes (White, 1995). Sociocultural theorists see this intertwining as a primary activity of knowledge co-construction and appropriation (Rogoff, 1990; Wertsch, 1991). The chapters included in this volume are part of a family of research deliberately designed to help sharpen our core questions, refine our definitions, and explore a range of methodologies. These studies were conducted across the country in a variety of venues and with a variety of methods. We have studies in science museums and art museums, from Birmingham to San

Francisco; we have studies that make use of experiments, discourse analysis, and ethnographic methods. All of the studies are grounded in an integration of sociocultural and cognitive approaches to considering learning and meaning making in social settings. The majority of the studies use small groups as the unit of analysis.

We have chosen to cluster the studies in this volume using the lens of time as an organizing construct—moving from a year, to an afternoon, to a moment. Part I of the volume, *Conversations: A Year of Learning*, emphasizes a longer time frame and tends to explore more deeply issues of the learning environment of the museum. The volume begins with "Creating a Space for Learning: Curators, Educators, and the Implied Audience," in which Knutson traces, through a detailed ethnography, the year-long evolution of an international art exhibition, jointly curated in Pittsburgh and Amsterdam. In the second chapter, "Two Docents in Three Museums: Central and Peripheral Participation," Abu-Shumays and Leinhardt examine how highly knowledgeable docents interact over several months with three very different exhibitions: In one case they are central participants; in another they have substantial knowledge but are not central participants; and in the third they have no special connection to the exhibit. Taken together, these two chapters examine conversations behind the scenes in museums and conversations in the layer of mediation between the museum's representation and the visitors. The third chapter in this section, Ellenbogen's "Museums in Family Life: An Ethnographic Case Study" explores the ways in which a particular family defines and uses museums over the course of a year in the pursuit of education and learning. It invites the reader to explore the nature of boundaries and definitions in institutions that deal with learning. The final chapter by Leinhardt, Tittle, and Knutson, "Talking to Oneself: Diary Studies of Museum Visits," acts as a counterpoint to the studies of groups and their conversations by exploring the conversation with self as expressed in a series of 40 diary entries by eight diarists over 9 months.

Part II, *Conversations: An Afternoon of Learning*, emphasizes the interactions that surround visitor conversations at a single exhibition. These chapters emphasize the explanatory engagement of visitors as they appropriate, struggle with, or reject major ideas in each exhibition. In Part I of the volume, the dialectic tension is between exhibitions. In Part II, the dialectic tension is between elements of a single exhibition. "Burning Buses, Burning Crosses: Student Teachers See Civil Rights," by Leinhardt and Gregg, examines the impact of a visit to the Birmingham Civil Rights Institute on the personal knowledge and small group discussions of a class of student teachers. The chapter by Fienberg and Leinhardt, "Looking Through the Glass: Reflections of Identity in Conversations at a History

Museum," focuses on the way in which the identity of group members interacts with the nature of what is talked about in a glass exhibit. Catherine Stainton's chapter, "Voices and Images: Making Connections Between Identity and Art," explores how deep expertise and personal connection affects the discussion of artistic features of a challenging exhibit. In "Looking for Learning in Visitor Talk: A Methodological Exploration," Allen considers which aspects of a science exhibition provoke conversation. Part II concludes with "Conversations Across Time: Family Learning in a Living History Museum." Museum curators and educators Rosenthal and Blankman-Hetrick analyze how first-person narrative discourse inhibits or facilitates visitor discussion.

In Part III, *Conversations: A Moment of Learning,* the time frame is shortened and the examinations are more fine grained. In the previous sections the emphasis was on examining identity and explanatory engagement. The chapters in Part III emphasize visitor connections to particular features of an exhibit. The section opens with Crowley and Jacobs' "Building Islands of Expertise in Everyday Family Activity." This chapter describes how parent-child conversations create shared interest and knowledge about scientific topics. In "Negotiations of Biological Thematic Conversations in Informal Learning Settings," Ash analyzes a conversation to show how families use the content of an exhibit as a springboard for extended reasoning. Paris and Mercer describe experimental studies of visitor identity issues in "Finding Self in Objects: Identity Exploration in Museums." Part III concludes with "Supporting Science Learning in Museums" in which Schauble and her colleagues investigate instruction, support, and learning around an exhibit designed to support collaborative family activity.

We felt that the notion of time created a particularly useful way of organizing the book, but we could have grouped the chapters by museum type or by visitor type. If we had organized the chapters by museum type, we would have had five chapters on science museums, three chapters on art museums, four chapters on history museums, and one chapter on multiple museums. If we had organized by type of visitor, we would have had five chapters focused on families, two on individual visitors, five on friendship groups, and two on museum professionals.

The volume, *Learning Conversations in Museums,* is both consequence and prologue. It is the result of 3 years of research conducted under the auspices of the Museum Learning Collaborative. The MLC took this time to work through concepts, approaches, and methods for the systematic study of learning in museums. But the work in this volume is more than a series of "tests" or pilot studies; each chapter contributes to larger discussions of informal learning, museum learning, and learning in families and among peers. The volume is prologue in that it sets the stage for the second phase of work in the MLC. With a clearer sense of understanding how people converse in museums, how those conversations impact learning, and how we as researchers can study this, we are poised to launch our next wave of research in museums. We report these results in a second volume of work.

REFERENCES

Anderson, D., & Lucas, K. B. (1997). The effectiveness of orienting students to the physical features of a science museum prior to visitation. *Research in Science Education, 27*(4), 485-495.

Borun, M., Chambers, M. B., Dritsas, J., & Johnson, J. I. (1997). Enhancing family learning through exhibits. *Curator, 40*(4), 279-295.

Cone, C. A., & Kendall, K. (1978). Space, time and family interactions: Visitor behavior at the Science Museum of Minnesota. *Curator, 21*(3), 245-258.

Doering, Z. D., & Pekarik, A. J. (1996). Questioning the entrance narrative. *Journal of Museum Education, 21*(3), 20-22.

Falk, J., & Dierking, L. (2000). *Learning from museums: Visitor experiences and the making of meaning.* Walnut Creek, CA: AltaMira Press.

Friedman, A. J. (1995). Creating an academic home for informal science education. *Curator, 38*(4), 214-220.

Gelman, R., Massey, C. M., & McManus, M. (1991). Characterizing supporting environments for cognitive development: Lessons from children in a museum. In L. Resnick & J. Levine (Eds.), *Perspectives on socially shared cognition* (pp. 226-256). Washington, DC: American Psychology Society.

Hein, G. (1998). *Learning in the museum.* New York: Routledge.

McManus, P. M. (1993). Thinking about the visitor's thinking. In S. Bicknell & G. Farmelo (Eds.), *Museum visitor studies in the 90s* (pp. 108-113). London: Science Museum.

Rogoff, B. (1990). *Apprenticeship in thinking.* New York: Oxford University Press.

Sandifer, C. (1997). An examination of time-based behaviors at an interactive science museum: How much learning is really going on? *Science Education (Informal Science Education-Special Issue), 81*(6), 689-702.

Serrell, B. (1995). The 51% solution research project: A meta-analysis of visitor time/use in museum exhibitions. *Visitor Behavior, 10*(3), 5-9.

Serrell, B. (1997). Paying attention: The duration and allocation of visitors' time in museum exhibitions. *Curator, 40*(2), 108-125.

Silverman, L. (1993). Making meaning together. *Journal of Museum Education, 18*(3), 7-11.

Stevenson, J. (1991). The long-term impact of interactive exhibits. *International Journal of Science Education, 13*(5), 521-531.

Wertsch, J. V. (1991). *Voices of the mind: A sociocultural approach to mediated action.* Cambridge, MA: Harvard University Press.

White, H. C. (1995). *Where do languages come from?—Switching talk.* Unpublished manuscript, Columbia University, New York.

Part I

CONVERSATIONS: A YEAR OF LEARNING

The first section of *Learning Conversations in Museums* uses a wide lens and a broad brush to describe museum learning. Part I moves from the voices behind the scenes at museums, to the voices that mediate between exhibits and visitors, to the voices and thoughts of the visitors themselves. The chapters take as a point of contrast more than one exhibition or one version of an exhibition, and place that within the overall lives of the visitors. The chapters focus less on the specific objects of a particular exhibition and more on the role of museums, responses to the learning environment of the museum, and the impact of exhibitions.

Part I opens with the year-long ethnography of the construction of a temporary art exhibition. In this chapter, Knutson traces a portion of the design process, following the planning and installation of one complex and innovative show. By moving through the different perspectives of four of the major actors, Knutson traces the transformation and emergence of converging goals. She documents the classes of experiences afforded by the exhibition, how visitors are perceived by museum staff, and concludes with an extended example of decisions and compromises surrounding the installation of one key element in the show.

The second chapter, by Abu-Shumays and Leinhardt, explores the particular responses of two docents to three different exhibits. The chapter examines the structure and function of their conversations in light of the centrality or distance of the docents to the content and setting of each exhibit. The conversations are analyzed by noting how the language of these friends changes from short, list-like, evaluative exclamations in some circumstances to longer, more engaged explanations in others. The authors present a model of object based reasoning whose central components are identification and interpretation.

The chapter by Ellenbogen describes a family that home schools their two children, making extensive use of museums as one of several key learning environments. In the process of documenting the family's use of a local science museum and other learning environments, Ellenbogen expands our understanding of how museums might be used as educational environments. She explores the definitional tensions between formal and informal learning and traces how shared interests and learning agendas are negotiated across place, person, and time. The chapter challenges us to reconsider concepts of formal and informal, and learning and play.

The Leinhardt, Tittle, and Knutson chapter focuses on diaries written by eight frequent museum goers. By exploring these intra-individual conversations, the chapter provides a counterpoint to the more traditional sense of conversation as inter-individual activity. Four constructs were used to interrogate the diaries: purposes of the visit, institutional frames, core experiences, and cognitive tools. Younger diarists tended to visit museums for open-ended or floating purposes, while senior diarists were more focused. Younger diarists tended to use tools of identification and narrative while senior diarists more often used tools of analysis.

Sociocultural theory reminds us to remain cognizant of the many layers in which a particular activity is embedded (Rogoff, 1998). To use the analogy of a camera, as researchers, we can focus with a wide angle and try to see as much of the full picture, historically and interactively, as possible. Alternatively we can focus closely on the minutia of one exchange. Regardless of the level of the grain size we choose, we must be mindful that there is detail overlooked in the broad picture and intertwining settings overlooked in the narrowly focused picture. This first section of the book contains chapters that take the wide-angle view. But we use that wide-angle in several different ways. In the chapter on designing an exhibition, we emphasize development over time. In the chapter based on visitor diaries, we emphasize variation and examine the cumulative effects of museum visits over time. In the chapter on families' uses of museums, we see how the museum takes its place among a number of cultural and intellectual resources over time.

REFERENCES

Rogoff, B. (1998). Cognition as a collaborative process. In D. Kuhn & R. S. Siegler (Eds.), *Handbook of child psychology: Vol. 2. Cognition, perception, and language* (pp. 679–744). New York: Wiley.

Chapter **1**

Creating a Space for Learning: Curators, Educators, and the Implied Audience

Karen Knutson
University of Pittsburgh

One of the major insights gleaned from studies of museums within the last decade is the notion that museums and museum exhibitions are not neutral—that, in fact, exhibitions are ideologically based and rhetorically complex arguments (Bal, 1996; Bennett, 1995; Hooper-Greenhill, 1992). This recognition is beginning to impact studies of museums, and some preliminary work on museums has explored the ways in which museum mission (Duncan, 1995; Gurian, 1991), architecture (Yanow, 1998), and even label copy (Coxall, 1991) might affect the reception of resulting exhibitions. These studies suggest that "presentation is more than window dressing" (Roberts, 1997), yet at this point researchers know relatively little about the decision making that happens behind the scenes and how beliefs about the nature and goals of museum experiences, exhibitions, and audiences impact, directly and indirectly, resulting exhibitions.

Research on museums, and on art museums in particular, has tended to focus on visitor interaction with specific exhibit features, or on analyzing the effectiveness of innovative educational programs. These are important studies, but I suggest that a closer examination of the curatorial framework—the intentions, strategies, and beliefs that inform the development of exhibitions—may provide valuable insight into our understanding of how art museums construct learning experiences.

This chapter has two goals: to provide a rich description of the process of the development of a major temporary art exhibition, and to analyze the curatorial framework for this show—the ways in which museum professionals and the consultants involved in the process imagine their audience. What impact do the collection, layout, signage, and visitor services have on the experiences of visitors? Given the complexity of the informal learning environment of a museum, the "free choice" learner (Falk & Dierking, 1992), and the varied agendas that visitors bring to the museum (Doering, 1999), research on museum visitors has had, by necessity, to consider the museum messages at their most gross level. What we tend not to see, or to explore in our museum research, is the fact that exhibitions are, in fact, designed. Exhibitions are not the hapless combination of objects within a space, but rather they are complex rhetorical events that operate on many levels. They are the result of a long and careful process of decisions and deliberation, of solutions devised in response to explicit goals and agendas, mediated by practicalities, unforeseen events, implicit beliefs and values, and the limitations of time and budget. The decisions made during the creation of exhibitions reflect foundational beliefs about what it means to educate and what it means to know.

This chapter reports on an ethnographic study that examined the conversations and decision-making process as a curator works with other museum staff, including an architect, the installation staff, and museum educators, to create an art exhibition. Through the course of developing this exhibition, the conversations that evolved reflected these professionals' beliefs and values about art and about learning about art in museums. Later, when we, as museum researchers, listen to visitors' conversations, there are traces and echoes of these originating curatorial conversations. The process of listening in and tracing the conversations of museum professionals during the design of an art exhibition sheds an interesting light on how museums function as learning environments.

With these issues in mind I began a yearlong ethnographic study of the design process for an art exhibition that opened April 7, 2001 in Pittsburgh. *Light! The Industrial Age 1750–1900, Art & Science, Technology & Society* was jointly curated between Louise Lippincott of the Carnegie Museum of Art in Pittsburgh and Andreas Blühm of the Van Gogh Museum in Amsterdam, as a special exhibition to be shown only at these two venues.[1] The show was a large-scale project for the Carnegie Museum, and it represented four years of research by the curators. *Light! 1750–1900: The Industrial Age, Art & Science, Technology & Society*, was, as the name suggests, a broadly based and complex exhibition. As the curators put it:

[1]The objects were gathered from world-renowned collections, and the high cost of insurance for the expensive and fragile scientific instruments and art works was a major factor in limiting the show to just these two venues.

> Light itself doesn't change physically. Therefore a history of light is really a history of the human perception, understanding, and manipulation of light. (Blühm, Lippincott, & Armstrong, 2001, p. 11)

Consisting of over 300 works, including both scientific objects and blockbuster paintings (e.g., works by Turner, Van Gogh, Monet, and Toulouse-Lautrec, among others), the show presented a novel and multifaceted approach to the subject of light. In addition to dealing with the complicated notions of the science and technology of light, the show also considered broader themes about society and the impact of technology on daily life during this historical period.

From the beginning, staff felt that the combination of art and science put forth in the show's content called for a new and innovative approach to the design of the installation and to the development of programs. The subject matter was envisioned as providing an opportunity to blend the intellectual story of the history of light told from an artist's point of view with the kind of discovery-learning experiences usually found in science museums. To this end, the show in Pittsburgh included five illustrative displays that presented scientific principles or concepts concerning the developing understanding of light in this period. For example, a prism showed refraction and the spectrum, and a Rayleigh tube illustrated how the atmosphere's particles affect the color of the sky. Elsewhere in the show visitors could use a hand-held camera obscura or a photometer,[2] two scientific devices that artists used to help them with their goal of more accurately representing the world. Large sandwich-board signs explained the science behind these displays.

I was fortunate to have had the opportunity to follow the development of this unique exhibition. I became involved in the process as work on the catalogue was ending and plans for the physical show were just beginning. At the time, I had been working with the Museum Learning Collaborative at the Carnegie Museum of Art conducting research on visitors to the *Aluminum by Design: From Jewelry to Jets* exhibition and asked if I might observe the development of the *Light!* exhibition. The curator graciously agreed. She felt strongly about the potential for this exhibition, with its ambitious aims, diverse objects, and hands-on activities. She believed the exhibition would be challenging, both for the institution and for the art museum world in a broader sense. The curators created a story that looked across disciplinary boundaries. The inclusion of hands-on elements *within* the exhibition space challenged traditional notions of art exhibitions that deal with historical art.

---

[2]Due to technical difficulties these photometers were later removed from the show.

Art critics gave the show very positive reviews first in Amsterdam, where the *London Telegraph* reported that it was "the show to see" during the season (Dorment, 2000). The Pittsburgh installation received similar reviews (i.e., *The Wall Street Journal*), and the catalogue was also celebrated with an American Association of Museum Publications Design award. The show's attendance figures, both in Amsterdam and in Pittsburgh, reflect these accolades.

My interest in studying the *Light!* show does not, however, primarily concern the content of the show, but rather the ways in which the exhibition was crafted, and how the various staff members contributed to its successful final result. Staff members had particular goals concerning the learning experiences offered in this show, and this I felt would offer an interesting opportunity to conduct research on education within an art museum context. Art museums, I suggest, offer particular challenges to the museum learning community, where research has, thus far, focused primarily on science museum exhibits (e.g., ASTC, 1993; Borun, Chambers, & Cleghorn, 1996).

Art museums pose special challenges for the museum researcher. What we need to keep in mind is the fact that, unlike the case of educational science museum exhibits, which convey extant science knowledge to the public, the temporary exhibitions presented in art museums contribute to the discipline of art history even as they share "known" information with the public. Art curators are active and central participants in the academic discipline. Temporary exhibitions are a valued way in which knowledge is generated for the field of art history. And so, although the educational role of art museums is vitally important, curators must also speak to a scholarly audience. This fact, coupled with the historic elitism of museums as preserves for the enlightenment of the upper middle classes (Bennett, 1995; Hooper-Greenhill, 1992), can result in exhibitions that speak primarily to an educated audience, while those without the relevant background knowledge are left feeling excluded and alienated by the experience (Bourdieu & Darbel, 1991). In a large-scale study of art museums conducted in 1986, Elliot Eisner and Stephen Dobbs pointed out the resistance to more visitor-friendly measures in art museums, and while changes are happening, this paradoxical relationship between art museums and the visiting public still exists (Rice, 2001). Speaking of museums in general, Roberts (1997) suggested, "one of educators' biggest challenges has been to deal with the fact that even visitor-friendly interpretations only reach those visitors to whom those interpretations are indeed friendly" (p. 74). In the art museum, this point rings especially true and there is a need to better understand the art museum as a particular set of problems in museum education research. With this study, I am interested in exploring more closely how art museum professionals deal with the tension between providing a challenging curatorial message and inviting and accommodating diverse audiences. Although the *Light!* show posed particular and unique challenges for staff, the story outlined in this chapter illustrates common issues and standard phases of practice that art museum professionals might face at any institution.

We currently understand more about the function of science museums as learning environments than we do about art museums. We have documentation of how exhibit designers and content specialists collaborate to create instructional environments that are informative and compelling for the visitor (see Schauble et al., chap. 13, this volume). In science museum exhibits, the goal is explicitly educational in its focus and researchers study the affordances for learning or perform task analyses to gauge just how precisely the desired outcome is reached (i.e., Allen, 1997; Boisvert & Slez, 1995). Increasing emphasis placed on the accountability and educational role of museums has resulted in more expensive and comprehensive exhibit projects that utilize a team-based approach, with specialists and consultants contributing to what was once seen primarily as a curatorial project that would later be supported by educational programming (Toohey & Wolins, 1993). Ethnographic studies of museum practice (in botanical gardens and history museums) have highlighted the team-based approach (see Roberts, 1997; Ames, Franco, & Frye, 1992, respectively). Roberts suggests that the team approach is bringing the museum educator to a position on par with the curator, whereas authors in the Ames, Franco, and Frye volume demonstrate the need for specialized curatorial consultants for the development of successful interpretive history exhibitions. The *Light!* exhibition employed consultants and a team of staff members; I was curious to explore the nature of their roles, and how they perceive the audience.

Methods

Between April 2000, and May 2001, I attended more than 40 meetings at the Carnegie Museum of Art and conducted interviews with key staff members.[3] I conducted semistructured interviews with the head of education, the architect, the head of exhibitions, the lighting consultant, the publications editor, and two members of the media communications staff.[4] Beginning in September 2000, meetings were held at least once a week and generally lasted 1 to 2 hours. The majority of the meetings were "design meetings," where the architect, lighting consultants, curator, and two mem-

[3]All of the staff members encountered in any of the meetings were informed about this ethnographic study and signed consent forms. They were also informed of the study via email memos from the curator, and a discussion of the study at an all-staff meeting.

[4]These interviews included questions about their role at the museum, their work on the exhibition, and their hopes for visitors' experiences of the show.

bers of the exhibition design staff met to discuss the development of the installation plans and architectural design. Other staff members and consultants appeared at these meetings as needed, including registrars, conservators, marketing, and education staff. Many of the meetings were so-called "nuts and bolts" meetings, where a broader cross-section of staff convened to discuss details and progress on their specific individualized schedules. Other meetings that I attended included education departmental meetings, general docent training sessions, docent training on light-specific scientific concepts, and a focus group meeting with members of a special college arts and sciences program at Carnegie Mellon University. I also traveled to Amsterdam to view the initial installation of the *Light!* show at the Van Gogh Museum. While there I attended the curatorial walkthrough provided for the international press, and later toured through the exhibition with both curators, asking them to reflect and cross-examine one another about the Amsterdam installation. This ethnography, while based on conversations with many different staff members and their varied perspectives, is more strongly filtered through the eyes of the Pittsburgh curator. I worked most closely with the curator and met with her on a regular basis to discuss the evolving process, unexpected events, and her response to meetings we had both attended (see Table 1.1).

During the meetings I took detailed notes of the conversations. Several of the meetings were tape-recorded and transcribed.[5] I also gathered artifacts of the production process: the catalogue, memos, media releases, layout plans, lighting plans, object lists, label copy, schedules, and drafts of program ideas. I made extensive notes during the meetings, transcribed interview tapes, and made observation notes throughout the process, analyzing the cumulative record for recurring and emergent themes.

These notes and documents provide a very rich source of data that was used for three different studies. This study concerns staff perceptions of the audience; another explores the notions of practice, expertise, and innovation; a third study examines how visitors respond to the show, using taped visitor conversations that were gathered as part of Museum Learning Collaborative research. This data provides a comprehensive look at factors influencing the development of art museum exhibitions and the communicative processes of museums.

As a team was gathered to develop and install this art exhibition, and over the course of the process, it became clear that very distinct divisions of

[5]All of the interviews were tape-recorded and transcribed. I took notes during most of the meetings, as staff felt more comfortable with notes being taken than with having an audio recording of the meeting. I used the audio recorder sparingly during meetings, asking permission to use it, and only if there were extenuating circumstances that would make it difficult for notes to be accurately taken (i.e., during discussions of the list of objects or during meetings that happened while moving through the museum).

TABLE 1.1
Types of Meetings Attended

Meetings	*Types of Activities*	*Number*
Design meetings	-development of the layout and hands-on activities	19
Schedule meetings	-Nuts and Bolts meetings—update other departments on object status, and design meeting decisions -Organizational committee meetings—interdepartmental schedule planning across exhibitions	6
Education department meetings	-development of programs for *Light!* show	1
Update meetings	-meetings with the curator to discuss progress -meeting with both curators in Amsterdam	10
Special meetings	-focus group with university students -docent training sessions -special interest group meetings (joint lecture series) -press tour (Amsterdam)	6
Programs attended	-gas lighting demonstration -curators' lecture -art historian lecture -docent tours	5
Interviews	-role, beliefs, and values about practice	8

labor were maintained. To provide a context of the working environment and process surrounding the development of the *Light!* show, I first discuss the roles and activities of four key members of the exhibition development team: the curator, the architect, the head of exhibitions, and the educators. Next, I examine prevalent beliefs and assumptions about the nature of the "implied audience" for this exhibition, as the team members gathered together to discuss the installation of the show. Finally, I provide an extended example of discussions and events surrounding the installation of one element of the show. This example illustrates the complexities of the issues discussed throughout the installation process, as it also points out the resulting interconnected and multifaceted narrative of the exhibition. By providing a variety of approaches to the reporting of this data, and by including a sense of the passing of time, I hope to remind the reader of my role as observer and analyst of this process. I encourage the reader to observe the points at which I have made choices about the routes taken through this data with the belief that the meaning of research results "is not independent of the process that produced them" (Polkinghorne, 1997, p. 9). This chapter documents one possible path through the data, the two later studies provide different perspectives of the process, but all three reflect my own interests in coming to understand the particular tensions surrounding the interpretation of art for the general public.

CREATING AN ART EXHIBITION—*LIGHT!*

The *Light!* exhibition, like all scripto-visual displays, provides a complex message (Blais, 1995). An art show might be experienced solely through the appreciation of beautiful objects, in a fundamentally aesthetic presentation (think "white-cube," single artist); but in this case the visual combinations of objects were chosen to convey a story, and explanatory labels provided contextual information about the individual objects. Paintings were selected for the *Light!* show not primarily for their aesthetic appeal, but rather as Goode's "well-chosen specimens to illustrate a story"—to stand in as points in a persuasive narrative about the history of light (Goode, 1889). The *Light!* show was a thematic exhibition, and to this end there were detailed object labels, group labels that made connections between several objects, one-word section headings, and large-scale room level explanatory labels. The themes of the show were explicit, and important points were repeated in different ways throughout the exhibition. The show was a complex rhetorical event, an argument put forward at a visual and cognitive level. The argument was supported at an affective level as well. It was not a dry and didactic thematic exhibition, but instead, theatrical elements were called in to provide a context for the works, evoking a feeling about the curiosity and wonder that scientists and average people alike must have felt when seeing these new discoveries for the first time.

The installation of the *Light!* exhibition in Pittsburgh was divided into five thematic sections: Rays of Light; The Light of Nature; Makers of Light; Personal Lights; and Public Lighting. The entrance of the show featured a case of sparkling, dazzling objects, including an incredible faceted crystal candelabrum, juxtaposed with an imposing painting showing a prism nicely, but incorrectly, radiating the spectrum. A large specially designed prism hung overhead, throwing a large and brilliant spectrum on the side wall, and "demonstrating" the scientific experiment depicted incorrectly in the painting. These elements—the candelabrum, painting and prism—highlighted the overarching themes of the show: the science of lighting (Newton's theory of the refraction depicted in the painting), changes to daily life during the time (represented by the candelabrum), and demonstrations of the work of scientists (alluded to by the prism overhead).

The first section of the show, "Rays of Light," discussed optical theories circulating in the 18th century, with objects illustrating the theories of Newton, and the notions of reflection and refraction. Scientific objects such as mirrors, lenses, microscopes, cameras, and prisms were shown with artworks that demonstrated the impact of theory on artistic practice (e.g., Chardin's *Glass of Water and Coffee Pot*). The science behind this section was demonstrated by the prism at the entrance and further explored with a hands-on area where visitors could use a camera obscura to look at a dramatically lit statue. Many of the reflective surfaces of the objects in this section were situated so that they too reflected the statue in the center of the space. Visual connections between the various objects and the concepts of the show were thus made explicit for the visitor.

The second section, "The Light of Nature," looked at how artists have grappled with the depiction of natural light. Two versions of Monet's *Cathedral at Rouen* illustrated the Impressionists' interest in capturing the changing effects of light on their subjects, while three landscapes, Van Gogh's *Trunks of Trees and Ivy,* Signac's *Place des Lices, St. Tropez,* and Bierstadt's *Light and Shadow,* showed a variety of approaches to the depiction of light filtering through trees. A hands-on activity was provided to show how artists used light meters, "photometers," to calculate the relative light values of a scene. Artists could then create the same light values in their paintings, with the hope of creating more light effects that were true to their landscape subject matter.

The third section, "Makers of Light," focused on the ways that meaning has been ascribed to light, by institutional forces—the church, the state, and various capitalist enterprises. Allegorical paintings of state processions were combined with illustrations of world expositions and their newest lighting inventions. The fourth section, "Personal Lights," combined candleholders and lamps with paintings depicting scenes with artificial lighting. These art works show how life was impacted by the quality of light available after dark, as in Van Gogh's *Potato Eaters,* which shows a poor family crowded around the light of a small kerosene lamp. The final section, "Public Lighting," included paintings of evening street scenes and evening events illuminated by gaslight. Early light bulbs and lamps equipped for both electric and gas were also displayed. The final room of the gallery featured a demonstration of the vastly different qualities of different types of lighting. A painting by Van Gogh, *Gaugin's Chair,* was alternately illuminated by gas, arc, and natural daylight, and the resulting difference in the appearance of the painting was remarkable.

ROLES AND ACTORS

In this section I look at the roles of four of the key groups of actors involved in the creation of the *Light!* exhibition. The process of developing the show was a multifaceted project that entailed both the independent and joint work of the exhibition team. Like most other museum exhibitions, the process included researching and writing the catalogue, securing the objects, creating a layout plan, writing the label copy, and installing the objects. Other departments worked to market the exhibition and to create supporting educational programs. The objects themselves required care to ensure that they were properly conserved, displayed, and protected with adequate security measures.

I include these four descriptions to provide an outline of the processes and nature of the roles required to develop art exhibitions, as well as to provide a context for understanding this particular case. Each of these four sections describe a particular set of problems and reveal something of the nature of the perceived roles and hierarchy of professional practice in this institution and among this particular set of museum professionals. The curator worked to provide the intellectual framework for the exhibition, selecting and combining objects, and creating the vision for the exhibition. Specifically hired for *Light!*, the architect worked with the curator and then with other staff members to create the look of the show, with a layout plan of the space and specifications for all of the cases and interior walls to be built by Carnegie staff. The architect also suggested a graphic design consultant and a firm of lighting specialists to assist in the design process. As advocates for the many diverse audiences the exhibition was expected to serve, the educators created special programs to support the curatorial messages of the show. They also worked with the design team to make the exhibition more intellectually accessible and physically functional for visitors. The exhibitions staff coordinated among different staff departments, such as security and conservation. They kept track of the overall schedule and focused on the practical concerns of the physical space and objects, always with an eye on the budget.

Within each of the four descriptions, I highlight a key aspect of work for the show that occupied this particular person, situating these overlapping and complicated decisions within a roughly chronological frame, providing a fragmented narrative of the show's development along with an analysis of the actor's role within it.

The concept for the *Light!* exhibition emerged in both Pittsburgh and Amsterdam. Louise Lippincott, the Pittsburgh curator, had become intrigued by the history of gas lighting. At the same time, in Amsterdam, science museum curator James Blackburn and Van Gogh Museum curator Andreas Blühm were talking about creating a joint exhibition that would explore science and art themes around the concept of light. Blühm and Lippincott were introduced by a mutual acquaintance, and an international collaboration began. From 1997 to 2000, research on the show was conducted. The catalogue reached its final stages in April 2000 with much of the research and collaborative writing of the catalogue taking place via email.

Curator

I have created a simplified timeline using several of the Curator's[6] recurring metaphors to describe the state of the exhibition's development at

[6]For clarity, from this point I use a capital letter to indicate the identity and role of key individuals in the study (i.e., the Curator, the Architect, the Educator, the Head of Exhibitions).

each stage. In April 2000, for example, she talked about "going public" with the show, that is, presenting the exhibition idea and content to the staff, and the world, via the marketing department and the catalogue. From May to August 2000, she was concerned with "making it real," figuring out how to translate the catalogue into a three-dimensional exhibition, using a particular selection of objects from the catalogue. From September through to November, as the plans for the exhibition began to gear up, she was concerned with what she called "hammering." During this period, she was working hard to ensure that other staff departments had begun to think about the work they would need to do for the *Light!* exhibition. She felt that this exhibition, with its combination of art works, scientific instruments, and science concepts, offered a challenge to traditional ways of working at the museum. And she wanted the key design staff to have clear thoughts about the show before going to Amsterdam in November to see that version of the show. In December, January, and February, work on the exhibition became quite intense, and there was an overarching metaphor of "being on the top of the roller coaster." In the midst of tightening schedules and important decisions the Curator knew that a wild ride was ahead, and she hoped she had done enough planning to make sure the installation would run smoothly. Finally, in March, the Curator described her current feelings as "execute, execute, execute," meaning that many decisions had been made and it was now just a matter of following the schedule. The team was still busy, but had no more creative decisions to make.

Table 1.2 provides a general overview of the way in which I've chosen to divide the timeline and situate the metaphors. The shaded bars indicate the areas of the process and timeline that I discuss shortly. I discuss the Curator's work on the conceptual framework of the show, the Architect's development of the layout plan, the Educator's planning of supporting programs, and the Exhibitions staff work on the budget and installation details. Most of the highlighted activities occurred throughout the development process, the shaded areas suggest the times during which these activities occurred most intensively.

April 2000, my first visit to the Curator's office. She said that she was just at the point of "going public" with the show, and would soon begin to "make it real." The search for grant money for the *Light!* exhibition required that substantial work on the show be finished much earlier in the exhibition timeline than for other exhibitions (Curator interview, April, 2000). At this point then, the Architect had already produced a version of the plan and a virtual computer generated walkthrough of the show. The Curator provided a 10-page narrative "walkthrough" of the exhibition in order to apply for these grants. Although some preparatory work had therefore already been completed on the show, the Curator saw it as an important moment, when she officially relinquished the catalogue, object list,

TABLE 1.2
Overview of the Exhibition Development Process

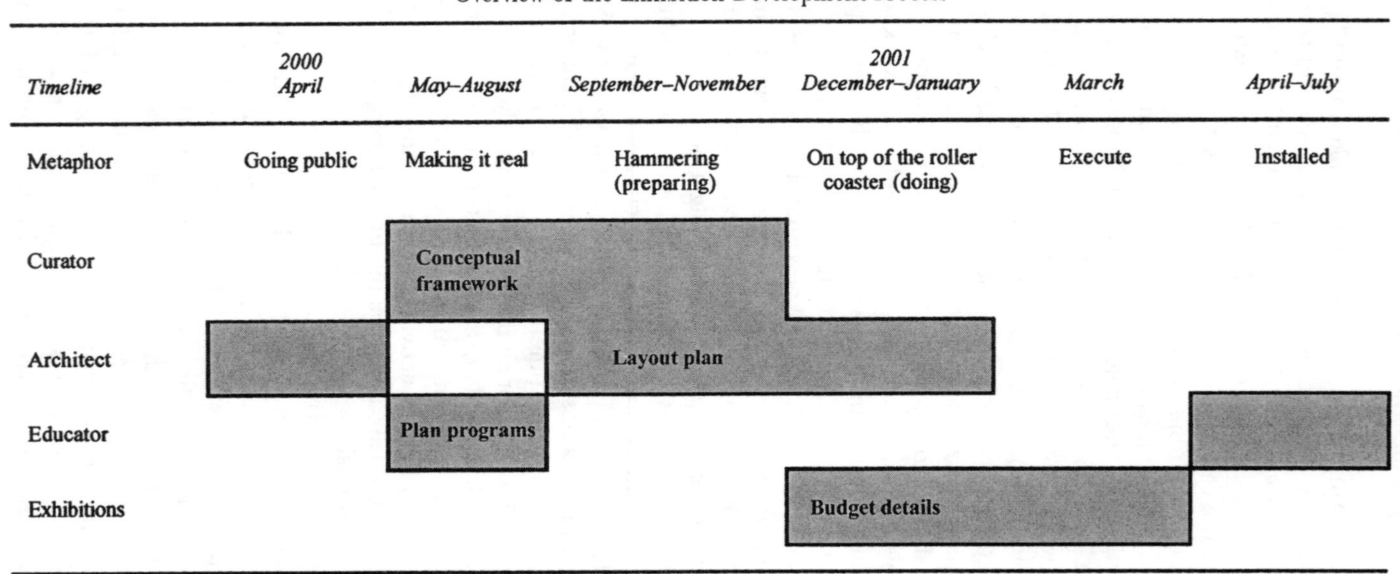

Timeline	*2000* *April*	*May–August*	*September–November*	*2001* *December–January*	*March*	*April–July*
Metaphor	Going public	Making it real	Hammering (preparing)	On top of the roller coaster (doing)	Execute	Installed
Curator		Conceptual framework				
Architect			Layout plan			
Educator		Plan programs				
Exhibitions				Budget details		

and walkthrough to the rest of the staff, including the marketing department who would use this material to begin the process of sending out press releases.

> Based on her belief in the notion that people like to shop, she said she'd put way more information and objects out there knowing that people won't look at all of it. The show won't be based on the book directly—but recreated from "scratch" on the big entry wall to her office. (Field notes, March 22, 2000)

Having finished the catalogue, the Curator now needed to figure out how the objects would come together in the physical space—the five rooms called the Heinz Galleries used for large temporary exhibitions at the Carnegie Museum of Art.

The Curator's office: To the right of her desk was a large wall-size window with a low bookcase piled high with books and auction house catalogues. Another row of low bookcases behind her were also stacked high with resource books she'd collected to write the *Light!* catalogue; on her left behind her computer, the wall was decorated with her sons's drawings and cards. The fourth wall of the room, the wall that she faces as she works at her desk, was blank, and covered from floor to ceiling in white cork. Next to her computer, this wall was perhaps the most important part of the workspace. This is the wall where the Curator visualized the exhibition.

Freshly removed from the wall, in piles lying on the ground in front of it, were hundreds of pieces of paper—photocopied images of the objects she had assembled for the catalogue. The piles marked a fresh start, both physically and mentally. The wall would soon be covered again, as the Curator began to sort out, in her mind and on the wall, how the rooms of the Heinz Galleries would be filled with the three-dimensional version of the story told in the catalogue. At the same time, thousands of miles away, the Amsterdam curator, a bit further ahead in his schedule—because his show would open in less than 6 months—was similarly hard at work creating his version of the story. Over the course of the next 12 months the Pittsburgh curator would continue to work on the corkboard, mapping out the rooms of the show. The corkboard wall is where the conceptual laying out of the exhibition took place. A semipublic display of the exhibition in progress, staff members could survey the wall and discuss the emerging plans for the show with the Curator (e.g., two lengthy discussions about the layout on the wall took place September 6, and December 1, 2000). The Curator provided staff members with more formal information about the show, circulating drafts of the catalogue essay, and an exhibition walkthrough, and later giving a lecture to all staff members. But it was the wall where the most up-to-date versions of the content of the show were seen.

To create the wall, the Curator used black and white photocopies of the individual pieces that she had copied from other resource books and catalogues. The photocopies, or when these were not available an artist's name or a title, were tacked onto the corkboard and arranged, and rearranged, until a conceptual scheme began to form. Small sticky notes in different colors reminded the Curator of various types of problems: which version of a painting would be borrowed, which loans were not yet secured, or where the location of an object within the conceptual plan was not yet fixed. Other colored strips of paper were later added to suggest different types of labeling and headings to be used in the galleries. The photocopies and labels were arranged, and rearranged, augmented and culled, until a conceptual scheme, and then a layout idea, began to take shape.

This time consuming process was not the same as that used by the Architect later, as he created the layout plan. On the corkboard there were no physical correlations to the actual spaces of the galleries. The wall and the photocopies were not divided according to scale but rather the five rooms haphazardly filled the space on the wall, with only a small label to indicate the beginning of "Gallery 12," or "Gallery C1." In some cases there were multiple photocopies, showing different versions of the same object, or alternate choices that could stand in to make the same point. On the wall a 7-foot-high sculpture seems the same size as a tiny print. The Curator called it a place to represent the contents of her brain on the subject. This was the preliminary step in the process and the place where the thematic divisions would be made to serve the Pittsburgh version of the story. (The two curators had different points of view about how the story should be told, and somewhat different collections of objects with which to work.)[7] The first version of the Pittsburgh story emerged in August, with subsequent alterations occurring up to the second week of September 2000, and some other minor changes taking place much later in the process.

The outline of the exhibition's thematic divisions suggests the vast range of both objects and concepts with which the Curator grappled. With its illustrations of scientific principles, discussions of lighting technology, and lighting's impact on society, the show was not a typical art exhibition. For example, the exhibition installation paired a Turner landscape with a Rayleigh tube experiment. While it made an illustrative point central to the show, the Curator found the pairing somewhat shocking and counter to her art historical training (May 4, 2001). Although the Curator said that she enjoyed the challenge of venturing into other disciplines and using different types of objects, at its heart, the exhibition remained true to its art historical roots. Speaking about one section of the show to the Educator, the Curator acknowledged:

[7]The Amsterdam show was divided across three floors of the Van Gogh Museum. The first floor dealt with science and technology, the second with art and artists, and the third with "amusements" such as light used in portable theatres, or to illuminate narrative scenes on lampshades.

> *Curator:* [Gallery] C1 is, I call it "Makers of Light" at the moment. This is the really, the whole symbolic section and . . .
>
> *Head of Education:* How big are those?
>
> *Curator:* About this big [using arms to indicate size].
>
> *Head of Education:* Oh that's not so bad.
>
> *Curator:* And this is quite big . . . then I go into state—fireworks, public illumination, military search lights. . . . This can move over here. But the idea is that only the state can really afford to do this on a big scale. State makes a huge spectacle of light. "Beacons." Statue of Liberty, and then we're going on to . . . world's fairs, showcase for the technology [pointing out smaller concept groupings of objects]. It's a fairly standard argument. Industrial argument. . . .
>
> *Head of Education:* And that's [Gallery] C1.
>
> *Curator:* I've moved a few. These pictures used to be in "Streets" but otherwise it's pretty much the same as it was before. And then what I changed. And they still may not go there. Now, [Gallery] C2 starts here and goes down this way. And [Gallery] C3 starts here and goes down this way [gesturing at arrangement on wall]. And basically there's the history of artificial lighting told through the different fuels that came into use. (September 6, 2000; author notes in square brackets)

Within the show there are also discussions about how the knowledge of light's actions impacted artists' work, like this text panel about *Turkish Bath,* a painting by Alexandre-Gabriel Decamps:

> Critics of the period admired Decamps's subtle handling of light and shadow. In this painting, he depicts a ray of light hitting a wall and glancing into the corner, illuminating the space with its reflection. A 19th-century physicist measured Decamps's work with a photometer (an early light meter) and found him to be one of the few to paint light with an accuracy that met scientific standards.

The text panels asked viewers to pay particular attention to the light effects captured in the art works, and offered information about the scientific thinking about light during the period.

The complexities of finding and securing the loans of various objects for the show had an impact on the process of creating the thematic divisions of the show. Many of these problems originated outside of the Curator's control. She hoped that some important works in the Van Gogh Museum's version of the show might also travel to the Pittsburgh exhibition, and waiting for confirmation kept the layout plans from being finalized. On the other hand, the constant search for an elusive or excellent object also impacted the show's development. For example, a collection of historically significant light bulbs from the Henry Ford Museum, in Dearborn, Michigan, was among several instances of objects secured late in the design process, further complicating the arrangement of cases in the layout design. The conceptual framework and list of objects were created far in advance of the exhibition's opening, yet the layout plan continued to change up to (and beyond) the opening of the show, frustrating the other members of the design team who needed to make decisions based on a final count of objects. The Curator's never-finalized object list became a standing joke among the team, including the Curator. She was aware of the hardships this indecision placed on the team, but couldn't resist late additions to the show. During one meeting late in the process, she told the design team that although the list of objects was basically complete, she'd located some unusual and highly tempting light bulbs on the auction website, "E-bay." After a smiling groan, exhibitions staff suggested that they would have to get online and bid against her! (February 8, 2001).

The Curator realized early on in the process that the security requirements surrounding this exhibition layout would be difficult for her. Most of the object locations needed to be finalized well before the show's opening. This would temper her natural predilection for what she called her "stage managing" approach to the installation process, where objects could be tested in various locations (August 15, 2000). The time spent developing the layout plan probably contributed to a very smooth installation time (moderate days and no overtime), but she still managed to make room for some last-minute additions to the show. An Edison light bulb was added to the show just before the opening-night party, and a large Sinumbra chandelier was added after the first weekend of the show.

Architect

The Curator's process of developing the thematic layout of the show was both preceded and followed by the work of the Architect on the design of the exhibition space.

> *Architect:* My goal is to create an evocative space that allows the visitor to have an unencumbered experience with the object, which must be respected. Too much in our lives comes to us in a mediated way, and the opportunity to have a direct experience with a real work of art is important to my work as an exhibition designer. (Interview, March 14, 2001)
>
> In contrast with his work on an earlier art exhibition, the Architect noted that the quality of the art in the show demanded a certain kind of respect and that he couldn't have the same artistic freedom that he had previously had in designing the exhibition space. (Field notes, April 13, 2000)
>
> He outlined the traffic pattern through the show, highlighting that he wanted visitors to have an unencumbered experience with the objects and that the in-

> formation was all to be provided along one side of the space. (Field notes, April 13, 2000)

During an interview on March 14, 2001, the Architect for the *Light!* show (Paul Rosenblatt, with the firm Damianos+Anthony) spoke at length about the particular challenges for this exhibition design. The above quotations reveal the tensions underlying of the craft of designing art exhibitions. The design of an art exhibition must first and foremost respect and highlight the works on view, while at the same time the design is used to support the messages of the show. Accomplishing a balance between these two goals is a complicated task. As the Curator noted:

> I think the challenge of a curator . . . is to find the point of connection between the experience the maker of the work of art is trying to convey and the experiences that visitors can share. [In other words] where is the contact between that past experience that's lost and some experience in the present that [visitors] can connect with? It's nice to think in terms of experience rather than information or background, or aesthetic training; I think experience is a little more democratic. And it also suggests that there are more ways to get that experience than looking at a picture. (Interview, May 4, 2001)

The Architect's consultation process involved both historical research on the objects and ideas of the show, and discussions with the Curator about the nature of the experience that she wanted visitors to have.

The Curator's organizational scheme had to be transferred into the physical space of the gallery. Months before she had finished the catalogue or started the organizational scheme on her office wall, the Curator began work with the Architect to discuss the key ideas of the show and how they might influence the design of the gallery space. Experimenting with a new process, the Architect created a computer model: a virtual exhibition space including simulated people and models of the artworks to scale within a potential layout design of the galleries. This virtual tour allowed the Curator and potential exhibition sponsors to see what the exhibition space might actually look like with different arrangements of objects, styles, and colors of walls and cases.

The Architect had completed a significant portion of his work before the design team began to meet in September 2000. The Architect had worked to combine the notion of scientists and their laboratories with the historical style of the world's expositions, where many of the lighting innovations were first shown to the public. In addition to thinking about the conceptual framework of the show, the Architect also had to consider some challenging practical issues, such as the inclusion of hands-on display areas in galleries that were already targeted for a maximum number of objects and cases. The Architect also knew that the show would feature a number of blockbuster paintings, as well as fragile scientific instruments and books. After spending time reading the catalogue and studying books about the development of light and lighting technology, the Architect developed the notion of Newton and the prism as an orienting device in the space. He began to "do some sketching, and it was those initial drawings that were sort of inspired by the path that light was [taking and] the way that the angle of the light changes as it passes through the prism" (Interview, March 14, 2001). He designed the floor plan with a path suggestive of a beam of light bouncing from one area to another through the space. "Sometimes it's defined by the edge of walls, sometimes it's defined by the angle of the axis of a pedestal or a platform in the space. Sometimes it's not quite as well defined as other times, but it's always there" (Interview, March 14, 2001). Built walls were angled through the space, creating a back and forth traffic pattern suggestive of angled beams of light coming through a prism (see Fig. 1.1—Layout Plan Gallery 12).

The process of collaboration between the Curator and Architect is instructive. Unlike the work of other staff members on the show, the work of the Architect retains the mark of its creator in its contribution to the Curator's vision. Recognizing the artistic domain of the Architect, the Curator was careful to preserve, wherever possible, elements that were central parts of the design that was originally presented. At the same time, however, the Architect was similarly deferential to preserving and supporting the Curator's vision. Finally, the Architect applied his knowledge of other design issues, like graphics, and lighting. He suggested the hiring of the lighting consultants and graphic designers that became involved in the project in December 2000. While he tried to preserve the overall vision of the show, the Architect valued his role as facilitator of the design process. He actively

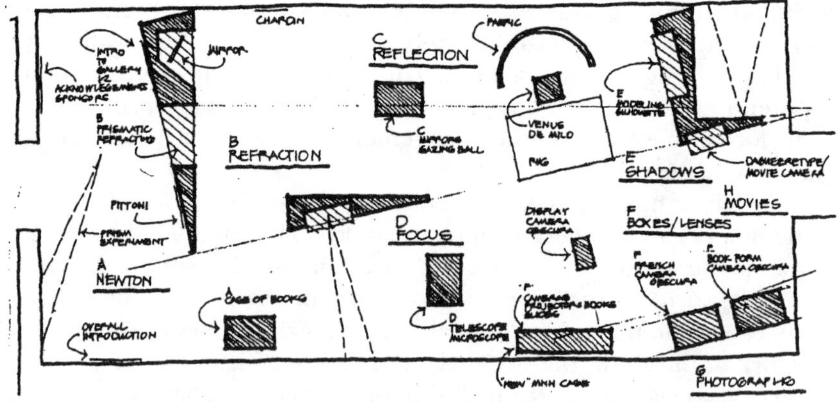

FIG. 1.1. Schematic Layout Plan Gallery 12, December 19, 2000. Reprinted with permission from Paul Rosenblatt AIA of Damianos+Anthony.

generated solutions to emerging problems, working closely with the design team and the Head of Exhibitions to devise practical solutions in light of a changing budget. The resulting design combined the Architect's interpretation of the Curator's vision impacted by the collaborative solutions of the design team to practical and budgetary constraints.

Educators

> . . . we're assuming that we'll do daily free tours—walk-in tours. We're assuming that we'll have "Ask me about Art" interns at this point, and that we'll do an education resource center. . . . We should add here that we'll do adult group tours as well, meaning tours that groups call and make arrangements, and there's someone on hand to do them, so we should add group tours on there. . . . under group tours, let's say, we'll do . . . local, regional, distant and we'll do college. . . . The timing is not good for college and university but we'll want to think of that as an audience to pursue with whatever connection we can. (June 8, 2000)

The educators' conversations surrounding the development of the *Light!* show reveal three strong points of interest: a commitment to serving diverse audiences; a desire to broaden their awareness of, and to collaborate with, other cultural agencies in the city; and a commitment to ensure that the exhibition would adequately support the experiences of a general visiting audience.

In June 2000, educators at the Carnegie held their second departmental meeting about the *Light!* show. They gathered around the long table in the library, and the Head of Education asked each member to report on their progress with the programming for the show (e.g., see Fig. 1.2). The education department was able to implement the plans they had originally devised for the show, nearly a year in advance of the opening. The department serves a wide variety of audiences, and this priority is evident in an examination of the conversations from this meeting. Each member of the group was in charge of representing a particular audience (general adult, families and school-aged children, or teenagers). After presenting progress of the program ideas, the Head of Education further focused the conversation on whether or not they had provided for each type of audience.

Light! programs were particularly diverse and well-attended. Academic types were accommodated by a lecture series that included well-known 19th-century art historian, Robert Rosenblum. The two curators discussed their joint creation of the exhibition. Two docents paired up to give special Thursday night tours of the show that highlighted the show's science and arts perspectives. Seth Riskin, a performance artist who works with light, did a "light dance" and talked about his methods. There was a performance by a traveling Magic Lantern theater group. The Rushlight Club spoke about

EXHIBITION TOURS
Drop-in tours (daily at 1:30)
Gallery attendants (at hands-on experiments)
Adult and Student Group tours (pre-registered, docent-led)
Gallery Brochure (annotated floor plan)

LECTURES/ DEMONSTRATIONS
Dan Mattausch, Rushlight Club
Aaron Sheon, Art History University of Pittsburgh
Leonard Shlain, Surgeon, writer, inventor
Robert Rosenblum, Art History, New York University
Andreas Blühm, Louise Lippincott, Curators of *Light!*
Seth Riskin, Artist, MIT (performance)
Larry Schaaf, University of Glasgow

WEB SITE/ CD-ROM/ ACOUSTIGUIDE
Web site for the exhibition
CD-ROM sold with catalogue
Acoustiguide tour for the show

ADULT PROGRAMS
Perspectives Gallery Talks-art and science perspectives
Adult Classes—art history, Lunch and Learn, studio classes, elderhostel
Downtown Lecture Series
Outreach Talks (by appointment)

PROGRAMS FOR KIDS AND FAMILIES
The American Magic- Lantern Theater (performance)
ARTventures –studio activities in the Hall of Sculpture gallery
Kids labels-Art Cat (throughout the exhibition)
Summer Art Camps (week long)
Homeschooler workshop: Art and Science

TEACHERS AND STUDENTS
Light Teacher Consultation (group of teachers to discuss exhibition content and curriculum ideas)
Tours and Curriculum Materials
Teacher event –special evening to hear about the exhibition and pick up materials for classes
Teen Ambassadors –high school students to work in galleries as attendants

FIG. 1.2. "Bright ideas for Light! programs" CMA internal memo draft 1/17/01.

history of gas lighting and lighting fixtures, while lighting up a series of historic lamps.[8] Finally, in addition to these special events, the education staff implemented their regular daily docent tours. Saturday hands-on activities were planned. Unlike most large-scale shows at the Carnegie, little empha-

[8]Watching the constant tending of the lamps, the relative brightnesses of different styles of lamps, and the overpowering smell of fuel oils provided an increased appreciation of lighting technology and its impact on daily life.

sis was placed on developing school programs, because school would be in session for only part of the run of the show.

Unlike the Curator and Architect, much of the Educators' work on exhibitions comes after the opening of the exhibition, when the implementation of special programs begins. Yet the Educators were involved in the development of the *Light!* show itself, and with the Head of Exhibitions and the publications director, they acted as audience advocates. For example, responding to a presentation of an outline of the show by the Curator, the Head of Education replied:

> Yes, we need the arrangement [of objects] to speak loudly but you also need to provide information. Because some people will get it and they won't read the labels and the people that don't get it will need the labels. (August 15, 2000)

Due to their prior commitments to work on other shows that were already running, members of the education department did not attend all of the design meetings but came in, as invited, at key moments in the process. For example, Educators met with the Curator and design team to discuss such things as the graphic design and text style for the exhibition and to go section by section through the organizational structure of the exhibition. In these venues, they worked hard to argue for the visitors, asking that more explicit directions and tools be provided in the exhibition space. As a result, a series of special labels for parents and children were installed in the show, and a comprehensive take-home gallery guide was designed. The child-oriented labels, indicated by a cartoon character "Art Cat," provided simplified explanations and posed questions about key features of the show. For example, next to William Jennings' *A Thunderbolt* (containing a photograph and a stylized sketch of lightning), an Art Cat label asked:

> Do you like to watch thunderstorms? Do you close your eyes and cover your ears? Before photography was invented, no one knew the true shape of lightning because the flash happens so quickly. Compare the photograph of lightning to the drawing. Which one says 'lightning' to you?

The glossy, colored gallery guide identified locations of audio tour stops, the children's labels, and key sections of the show on a layout map of the exhibition. Both of these measures, the labels and the guide, were seen by staff as new and important ways in which to help visitors interact with the exhibition's somewhat challenging content.

Head of Exhibitions

> [The Head of Exhibitions] talks about built walls. The built walls are 12–14 ft high. He estimates about $100.00 a foot plus $50.00 an hour labor. With the extra finishes that [the Architect] wants, the cost runs to $200 or $220. There are 34 feet of walls in the first gallery. They should really try to cut the costs a bit. [The Architect] wants tops and bottoms for the walls, so that they really have style, and look like real walls, to give it a historical feel. The show in Amsterdam had a modern style and it just didn't create the right feeling. So they discuss and decide that maybe [the Curator] will settle for tops only. No bottoms, but she really wants tops. [The Architect] suggests the first wall could be done in the style he wants and then the others having a reduced style element, to lower costs. (November 8, 2000)

So far I have discussed the conceptual planning that was involved in creating the show. The foregoing passage from my field notes illustrates some of the detailed planning work that involved the Head of Exhibitions. The Head of Exhibitions and his Assistant were in charge of handling the specific details concerning the physical installation of the show. The exhibition posed particular challenges for Carnegie staff, including the layout and security, as well as standard concerns like setting a timeline and controlling the budget.

Unlike many of the shows done previously at the Carnegie, the precise layout of the show needed to be completed before many of the objects even arrived in Pittsburgh. The value of the objects on loan to the museum meant that many of the objects would arrive with a courier, a representative from the loaning museum, in tow. The courier would stand by as the object in his or her command was installed in the gallery space, according to the demands of the loaning institution. The demands ensure the safety and security of the objects. No couriered object could be moved without the courier present. The objects would be set up, and a security device, such as a protective case or an alarm, would be installed. The objects could arrive at any point in the installation process, and so it was essential to predetermine the exact location of every object in the show. A painting fastened in the wrong location could throw off the measurements for the rest of the room, meaning that the rest of the paintings to hang in a particular group would no longer fit the space.

The Head of Exhibitions and his Assistant were in charge of scheduling and planning the installation of all the shows in the Museum. For any show, various types of installation meetings would occur. "Design Team" meetings primarily involved the Curator, Exhibitions staff and outside consultants (i.e., Architect, lighting designers, sometimes the graphic designers) in the conceptual planning of the *Light!* show. Occasionally, other museum staff (e.g., educators, registrars, publications staff) were also present. "Nuts and

Bolts" meetings were a means for museum staff members of the design team to report to, and hear reports from, other staff, including conservators, registrars, and security, about their respective progress on issues for the *Light!* show. "Organizational Committee" meetings looked more broadly at scheduling issues, determining schedules and deadlines for all of the shows at the museum. Several staff members referred to these meetings by their colloquial term, *organized chaos* meetings, as these meetings involved the creation of interdependent and contingent deadlines across shows. When disagreement about deadlines was intense, the Assistant to the Head of Exhibitions threatened to make a "scary schedule," a schedule across exhibitions showing *all* of the deadlines. While Exhibitions staff kept a 3-year overview calendar of key installation weeks in their office, most staff preferred to keep only their own most pressing deadlines in view. Any other view of schedules and deadlines was indeed a "scary" and overwhelming sight.

The *Light!* exhibition encountered some difficult scheduling problems. The previous show in the space, *Aluminum by Design: From Jewelry to Jets,* would require an especially lengthy de-installation due to the number and size of objects in it. (The show included a car and a full scale replica of a building façade.) The unusually valuable objects for the *Light!* show required that a layout plan be finalized earlier than usual. The hands-on scientific experiments, lighting challenges, and funding requests also required a longer lead time than most exhibitions. The Curator was concerned about the scheduling and pressed other departments to engage in their work on the *Light!* show far in advance of their normal lead time. She referred to this time as one of "hammering" away at the staff.

Finally, the Head of Exhibitions was in control of the budget for the show. As the opening section of transcript illustrates, the Head of Exhibitions had a firm grasp of the ultimate costs for different configurations of the space, and throughout the process he was the unfortunate one who had to step in and curtail excited brainstorming sessions about different possibilities for the show suggested by the Architect or lighting consultants.

THE VISITOR EXPERIENCE

Throughout the design process the Curator operated with beliefs that resonate with those expressed by museum educator Danielle Rice, who sees the goal of art museums as "pleasure through enlightenment. For in revealing the rich, abundant world of ideas behind objects, we encourage people to rediscover . . . delight, curiosity and wonder" (Rice, 1987, p. 19). The conversations that surrounded the development of the *Light!* exhibition reflected a concern for presenting the information and narrative of the show, couched in the desire to help viewers get a sense of the impact that light innovations had on society in the industrial age.

TABLE 1.3
Dominant Themes of Talk Through Design Process

	Themes			
	Aesthetic	*Affective*	*Physical*	*Practical*
Specific Issues	Concern for proper placement and lighting	Concern for attracting, impacting perception of work through environmental cues	Concern for visitor movement and safety through space	Scheduling, measuring, technical concerns, lighting

Although this chapter provides a general overview of the intentions the Curator had for this exhibition, a closer examination of the conversations that took place among staff members reveals certain assumptions they had about the audience and the nature of visitor experience in this exhibition. The conversations that took place over the course of the design development process reveal common and recurring issues that fall into four thematic areas: aesthetic, affective, physical, and practical. Of these categories, shown in Table 1.3, I discuss three: aesthetic, affective, and physical. Practical issues, although a dominant area of concern for the design team, are not a focus of this chapter.

Providing an Aesthetic Experience

As I described in the section concerning the role of the Architect, there was a strong desire to respect and support the aesthetic power of objects. For the creation of the *Light!* exhibition, and across art museums more generally, the concern for "the aesthetic" forms a point of tension. In art museums, works are displayed to encourage reverence, pleasure, or wonder; to highlight the attractive qualities of the objects; and to document the realness, or authenticity, of the objects. These are primary goals of putting works of art on display. Yet, the Curator and the rest of the design team also believed that the historical works of art and scientific objects needed a context. The Curator was primarily responsible for deciding how the exhibit should tell the story of light and technology during this period, and so conversations about the design primarily concerned the aesthetic experience. The Architect, for example, hoped that visitors would be able to have "an unencumbered experience" with the objects that they found compelling (April 13, 2000). During the design conversations, the Curator's message took a back seat to the consideration of the aesthetic power of the objects. When pressed by educators to move beyond her comfort zone in terms of mediating the objects, the Curator would respond: "as long as a visitor has one meaningful interaction with one object in the show, then our work is done," or "if they choose to ignore all of this information, that's fine with me." Clearly, with the amount of work she put into the thematic layout of the show and the research and selection of these objects, the Curator was working to tell a particular story about the objects on display. But for this particular part of the process, the emphasis in the conversations was on how the works would be viewed and appreciated by visitors. This was to be an art show, after all, displayed in an art museum, and design choices were made to reinforce this point.

A painting by Chardin, for example, was the subject of a long conversation about proper placement. The work, although small, was considered an important piece; it was an excellent work of art and one that came from the Carnegie's own collection. It needed to be hung in such a manner that it would receive an appropriate amount of attention in the space. On the layout plan, it was situated close to a group of glittering crystal objects and reflective lenses, and these, it was thought, would distract from the painting. However, because the work was small, it might be lost if hung with other paintings.

> [The Head of Exhibitions] says we want the environment near the Chardin to be calm. The mirror there is kind of boring. [i.e., the Chardin might work next to the not so glittery Italian mirror]. [Head of Exhibitions] says having one little one there is compelling. More so than 2 paintings. (December 15, 2000)

In the end, this arrangement was implemented and the painting was hung alone on a dark wall with dramatic lighting. The team agreed that the aloneness and isolation from competitors would help to highlight the painting (see Fig. 1.3). In case visitors failed to notice the dramatically lit, wonderful little painting, its importance would also be signified by situating a bench nearby and by including it on the audio tour. The Curator added that the small symbol used to mark the items on the tour would be noticed by audio tour users as well as by the general public and would be seen as an important part of the show (May 28, 2001).

The aesthetic experience of the show was considered on a variety of levels, from the proper placement and lighting of the works, to the characteristics and placement of the label copy. During one lengthy conversation about the labeling of the show, the Curator concluded with the stipulation that, where possible, label copy and object should not be in the same field of vision. Instead, the viewer should be made physically aware of moving from an aesthetic viewpoint to an information gathering one (August 15, 2000). As a result, the labels were, where possible, placed along a label rail set along the edge of cases and not on the wall. The physical shape of the la-

FIG. 1.3. Installation photograph of Gallery 12. (Chardin Painting at center of photograph visible through the case holding the Gazing Ball). From Carnegie Museum of Art, Pittsburgh, PA. Richard A. Stoner, photographer. Reprinted with permission.

bels was also considered and the decision was made to have square shaped object and group labels, so that when placed on the wall they would not "read" at a distance as objects (i.e., like the rectangular framed prints) in the show (February 8, 2001). This concern, to have reading and looking happen on two different planes, shows the care and consideration taken to promote and preserve the quality of the aesthetic experience of the works on display.

Creating an Affective Experience

Although the aesthetic experience of the visitor was an important consideration throughout the design process, the Curator was keenly interested in finding ways to help visitors have something more than an aesthetic experience. She was concerned to find ways to help visitors connect with the distant time period in which the works were created, and to help them experience a sense of the wonder that these new lighting technologies had on society in the 18th and 19th centuries. While these contextual issues are most commonly addressed through the use of text panels accompanying the objects, in fact, the design of the exhibition space itself was envisioned as a means to help create a context for understanding the works and the narrative of the show. The layout, lighting, color choices, and even the design of the object cases were thoughtfully selected in order to help create these effects.

In terms of museum research, the notion of the psychological influence, or the affect, of a physical space remains an unexplored issue. Of the impact of the physical environment in museums, John Falk and Lynn Dierking note, "often these influences are at once the most subconscious and the most powerful, the hardest to verbalize but the easiest to recall. For this reason, the role of the physical context upon learning has been one of the least-studied most-neglected aspects of learning (1995, p. 11). Museum research commonly considers the selection of objects in a show, examines the impact of the label copy, or measures how long visitors spend in front of each object; however, the effects of exhibition design on visitor experience are deeply felt but remain somewhat elusive to capture. In this section I discuss the ways in which aspects of the *Light!* show were debated, selected and chosen, in order to provide a compelling affective experience for visitors—an experience designed to support and enhance visitors' appreciation of the qualities of light, and the role of lighting technologies during this historical period.

> [The Curator] notes that she's not so keen on having a curtain threshold between galleries because she likes the naked one-word signs overhead. [The Architect] says, well the curtains are theatrical and a sign of the times. [But the idea is shortly thereafter struck down.]
>
> The [Head of Exhibitions] talks about the effect of the brick wall above the skylight in the second set of galleries. It changes the color of the light. [The Curator] agrees and says that in the first gallery the light is really cold and she doesn't like the effect. That skylight is near a museum wall made of stone. So [the Lighting Consultant] says well we can compensate for it. It will look cooler at night but during the day we can compensate for it with gels [filters on the lights]. (Field Notes, January 3, 2001)

These two examples, selected from hours and hours of similar discussions, show a range of concern with elements of affect in the *Light!* exhibition. From elements suggestive of a historical context, to the quality of the light in the galleries, the design team has considered, debated, and decided upon the details of the exhibition, from the brand and fittings of the lighting equipment, to the colors of the walls, the style of the font, and the details of the cases. With the Curator presiding, and the Head of Exhibitions (in control of the budget) assisting, all of these decisions were subject to intensive discussions in the design meetings, and these discussions focused on the effect of these decisions on the visitors' experience of the exhibition.

The color choice for the walls, and the lighting of the galleries were critical to create the right ambience for the show. The first room was painted a dark brown, and dramatic spotlighting emphasized the glittery objects placed there (see Figs. 1.3 and 1.4). The dark brown was also selected for its

FIG. 1.4. Installation photograph Gallery 12. (Showing brilliantly lit *Pallas Athena* and Camera obscura station). From Carnegie Museum of Art, Pittsburgh, PA. Richard A. Stoner, photographer. Reprinted with permission.

historical connotations—it relates to the Victorian period. A light blue helped to emphasize the feeling of daylight in the room with works by the impressionists. A covered skylight was opened overhead in the gallery to add to the effect. Lighting consultants located special equipment and used filters to help make the objects glitter, shine and glow, or flicker (to simulate the candlelight in which some objects were originally used or seen). Throughout the design process staff returned to key concepts, looking to make each room visually support the thematic content areas. The first room was dark and dramatic, the second brilliant and light, moving toward evening, the third powerful and dramatic, the fourth and fifth rooms more calm and neutrally lit.

> [The Head of Exhibitions] liked the taxonomy and comparison of the lamps and the exposition idea will come out in that style too. [The Curator and Architect agree]. (Field Notes, December 15, 2000)

The Architect worked with the Curator on the design for the show, with the idea of creating a sense of the historical style of the period between 1750–1900. By suggesting this historical context, the design of the show would help to provide visitors with a richer experience of the objects on display. As he created the design, the Architect worked with the ideas of an old scientific laboratory, or one of the world expositions that took place around the turn of the century. The Curator also suggested that the paintings be hung with a middle line of 65 inches, which is higher than normal. Although this was primarily a decision made in response to large numbers of predicted visitors to the exhibition (who would be better able to see the paintings when the galleries were crowded), she noted that it would also subtly add to the historical effect, because paintings were often hung higher than eye level in the 19th century.

A look around the Carnegie Museum of Natural History (which is adjacent to, and institutionally integrated with the Carnegie Museum of Art) suggested another way to add to the historical context for the exhibition. Scattered throughout the Museum are beautiful old cases that reflect another age. The carved wooden details, angled tops, and carefully turned legs are quite different from the standard art museum case used today—that common, unadorned, square or rectangular column covered in a plexiglass cube. Several of these old cases were found in the basement of the Museum, cleaned up, and used in the *Light!* exhibition as another subtle yet important way to augment the historical and affective feel of the show.

Imagining a Physical Experience

Conversations that took place in December 2000 and January 2001 are particularly useful for insight into the ways in which visitors' physical experience was conceptualized by museum staff. The creative decisions made within the aesthetic or affective areas were checked against staff understandings of how visitors might actually encounter and interact with the planned installation. Three main categories of concern recurred throughout discussions about the layout. Staff were interested in using the power of attraction to support key aspects of the show. This concept reflects a belief in the individual will of visitors to select the areas of the show to which they might attend. Navigational issues formed a second area of concern, with staff discussing the potential flow of visitors through the space; a third component of discussions focused on accommodating the special physical needs of visitors.

The Curator often made connections between the museum audience and shoppers. This metaphor recurred at numerous points through the development of the show, and evidence of this belief can be seen in the resulting final product. The Curator was interested in the work of Paco Underhill (1999), a shopping researcher, hired by several Fortune 500 companies to surreptitiously examine how shoppers are helped and hindered by the layout of merchandise in a store. Underhill advises companies where to place targeted items for quick sale, and how to arrange entryways and check-out areas for shopper comfort (the more comfortable they are, the longer they shop) and for shopper enticement (how to capitalize on impulse buying). Drawing from this work, the Curator believed that people like to shop, that they would pick and choose what they want to attend to. The Curator, convinced that visitors would not read everything provided, wanted to put "way more out there," with the realization that visitors would not see everything. This belief system resulted in a very complex exhibition space with far too much to absorb in a single visit. Using the metaphor of visitor-as-shopper meant that the Curator was also aware of the need to provide the same information in slightly different ways throughout the exhibition space. The average visitor should not come out of the exhibition without having gained some small appreciation for the vast changes brought about by the development of lighting technology during the Industrial Age. The metaphor of visitor-as-shopper helped the design team to think about ways to ensure that visitors would be drawn to the most essential works in the show. At a global level, they used dramatic lighting and vista locations for key works. For example, a platform of stunning miniature lighthouses (4 feet high) was placed directly opposite a gallery entrance to draw visitors in; an altar-like setting was created in the center of the final gallery to hold an important lighting demonstration. This display, a room within a room with a black velvet curtain backdrop, shows a Van Gogh painting *Gaugin's Chair*, under different types of lighting. As the Curator noted, however, visitors will also choose to notice items that have audio guide labels, or other special labeling, understanding that this special treatment indicates a "don't miss" highlight of the show.

> [The Curator] says we could put the sign next to the books. [The Head of Exhibitions] says and that's the holding area. [The Architect] says there's nothing over there. [Installation] says yeah that's fine. And [The Curator] says we'll put a bench there. [The Architect]: What about an experiment there? [The Curator]: No it'll stop the flow. I think the entrance is traditionally supposed to be sparse, get them in and moving. I like the glittering objects and the Pittoni there just fine. (Field Notes, December 19, 2000)

> [The Head of Exhibitions] says he's glad that the introduction is around the corner now. He says, we'll need to figure out the passageway; people will be going slowly here; there's lots of info and they need space to get oriented too. We need to keep people moving. But there are good hooks to get them moving. (Field Notes, December 19, 2000)

In addition to discussions of creating an attractive layout, staff also imagined what the flow of the exhibition might be like when the exhibition was installed, and how they might improve upon the design. As projected numbers for the exhibition rose, changes were made to the exhibition plan. Questions about bottlenecks in the traffic patterns arose, and stanchions would be placed in front of all the paintings to protect them from visitors' reach. During these types of conversations, visitors were seen as masses to be moved efficiently through the space. Although visitors were sometimes seen as a large mass to be efficiently moved through the space, they were, at the same time, imagined as shoppers, having their own interests and desires to follow through the show. The Architect noted that he did not believe in guiding the visitor through from one point to the next; instead, the traffic paths should be more open and visitors should be able to exercise their own options in moving through the show (April 13, 2000).

As the installation plan neared completion, educators began to discuss the ways in which the show might be adjusted in order to assist the viewer in relating to the Curator's message. Signage plans were developed to indicate thematic areas in the show, with individual object labels and room level text panels helping to explain the visual connections between the different types of objects displayed. In addition to this integral means of mediating the objects, other supportive measures were taken. Resource areas were planned, and catalogues were situated in the spaces between galleries. A random-access audio guide was designed, a series of child-friendly "Art Cat" labels created, and an elaborate gallery guide was produced, all to help visitors access the type and level of information they desired.

Marilyn Hood (1993) has shown that museums in general have not been proactive in accommodating their visitors' most basic needs, such as wayfinding and providing adequate seating. The Curator and the design team considered these types of needs, making adjustments to label copy and placement based on their knowledge of American Disability Association (ADA) Standards for Accessible Design. They also created elements in "human scale," focusing on the size and spatial requirements for visitors. The height of the label rail and sandwich board kiosks that explained the scientific activities were debated, as the design team wanted to ensure a comfortable reading height for the average visitor. But staff also discussed the placement of labels "so that elderly visitors would not have to bend over to read them." (December 19, 2000). Benches were also provided at several places: inside the entrance and in front of works deserving special contemplation, (e.g., at the Chardin, at a powerful set of three landscapes showing different treatments of light and shadows, (by Bierstadt, Van Gogh, Signac), and at Van Gogh's, *Gaugin's Chair,* with the lighting demonstration that took almost 5 minutes to view). The design team also considered basic wayfinding issues, as the Heinz Galleries are difficult to locate within the large art/natural history museum complex.

HAPPENSTANCE: THE STORY OF VENUS

> "Time to stop." The Curator signs and dates the note, in large letters with a Sharpie pen on a 3-foot-high board. "March 9." And it means no Venus de Milo for the Pittsburgh installation of the art exhibition *Light! The Industrial Age 1750–1900.* (Field Notes, March 9, 2001)

This final section of the chapter looks at the events and decisions surrounding the installation of one key element in the *Light!* exhibition, providing insight into the practical complexities surrounding the installation of a major art exhibition. By focusing on the installation of one object, I hope to capture a sense of the time and contingency that underlies this design process. In addition this extended example illustrates how objects function in this exhibition, exposing aspects of the conceptual roles, physical installation, interpretation and labeling that surround this single object in Gallery 12. March 9th marked a disappointing end for the key work, a statue of Venus, designed to be in the first room of the show. A plaster cast of Venus had been used in the catalogue, shown in the Amsterdam version of the show, and even used in the promotional videotape. With the show opening in less than a month, and many leads for other statues turning into dead ends, the Curator would have to find a solution, and fast.

Plaster casts of famous sculptures have long been an important part of the training of artists. Before budding artists were allowed to sketch from life, they traditionally spent hours sketching collections of plaster casts of famous sculptures like the Venus de Milo, or the Victory of Samothrace. With this history in mind, the curators of *Light!* imagined an installation of a Venus statue, illuminated in such a way as to dramatically affect the light cast on the planes and angles of the sculpture. The cast was to be shown alongside an 18th-century painting of artists working in a studio sketching a cast of Venus; both displayed near a case containing other artists' accoutrements including a cast of a foot, and a poseable jointed 2-foot high wooden human model.

In the Amsterdam installation of the show, a cast of Venus was theatrically shown on a rotating round platform in front of a corner window overlooking the courtyard of the Van Gogh Museum. A wall backed part of the platform so that she was not visible for part of the rotation. The light entering the window cast sharp shadows across Venus, highlighting the planes and shapes that artists would have focused on in their drawings of the sculptures. The rotating Venus conveyed a sense of the modeling, the play of light and shadow on a three-dimensional object that artists think about in their work. In addition to illustrating the concept of modeling, the rotating Venus was a theatrical element in the show. Visible from the courtyard, the Venus, situated on a platform used in automobile showrooms, served as a signpost for the exhibition, and stood as a spectacle and a playful gesture on the part of the Amsterdam curator. The gesture pointed toward the unique interplay of science and art in this exhibition, and marked a departure from the ways in which art from this period is typically shown.

For the Pittsburgh show, a statue of Venus was desperately needed. In the Pittsburgh installation, the Venus would also be used to illustrate scientific principles, to show how a camera obscura works. Visitors would be invited to use a simple camera obscura that would project a tiny and blurry image of the Venus upside down on the screen inside the box. Other reflective lenses in the gallery area would also pick up the Venus, creating a funhouse effect, where Venus would appear contorted in a garden Gazing Ball or upside down in various lens apparatuses.

The Curator had found it difficult to locate a statue of Venus de Milo for the show. She had pursued numerous leads, but for a variety of reasons no one was willing to lend their copy. Months earlier, the Curator was excited about a lead on a copy in Maryland (December 1, 2000). She had done the initial groundwork and spoken with registrars at the potential lending site. She was assured that the Venus copy was in good condition, with only a few minor scratches. The Curator was pleased and waited for the photo to arrive. When it did, she was surprised and dismayed to note that in spite of the registrar's attention to recording the minute details of the condition of the Venus, the registrar had neglected to note that this copy of the Venus actually had no head. A statue that stands for beauty with no head! Hmmmm. No.

And so, running out of options, the Curator looked at the Carnegie Venus. The Carnegie Museum of Art has a wonderful collection of casts, from the Parthenon to Venus, standing as they were installed about 100 years ago in the spectacular "Hall of Architecture." But the Curator knew that the Venus in the Carnegie was not her best option. While artworks on loan to the museum took a direct path from freight elevator to temporary exhibition space, this Venus would have to be moved from one end of the museum to another. And this Venus was mounted on a solid-looking base with a marble baseboard, and it didn't look like she would be moved easily. Now forced to try and use the local cast, the Curator was certain that it could somehow be done, and she worked hard to find a way. The Carnegie registrars had dissuaded her from pursuing the Venus cast in the Carnegie collection but they now hesitantly supported her work to detach it. However, after sending a consultant to excavate the base of the sculpture, and finding a concrete core with heavy lathe work and a thick plaster finish, the Curator conceded. The process would be expensive, difficult, time-consuming and it would put the sculpture at risk, even as Venus looked safe, but rather undignified, wrapped in protective sheeting tied with black strapping tape while her base was being excavated. Venus would have to stay put. But perhaps another cast could serve the same purpose? A look around the cast collection revealed another candidate.

A bust of Pallas Athena was selected instead. Heavy, yes, but this one was much smaller and not attached to the base. It would have to do. Instead of a long elegant Venus body, the show would have a head.

So after all this work, decision making, and problem solving, it was disappointing for the Curator to write, "Time to stop" beside the Venus sculpture. But it was deemed not worth the time, energy, and engineering to sever Venus from her historic and indestructible base, or to use up more valuable time, money, and the cooperation of staff to get this particular sculpture up into the *Light!* show. The Pallas Athena was selected instead. Smaller and not fixed to its base, the Athena required just a little bit of preparation time. At some point, someone seemed to think that it was not Athena after all, but rather "Steff's brother," which was inscribed onto a flat space on the front of the statue. The removal of graffiti was far easier than moving a large and unwieldy Venus. The decision was made and Athena replaced Venus, wisdom replaced beauty, the practical replaced the ideal.

Obtaining the sculpture was only part of the problem. The texts, and promotional video, and the audio guide had to be altered to reflect the new element in the show. And while the Venus issue remained yet undecided, the design team was hard at work figuring out how to make the camera obscura that visitors could use to see the Venus sculpture upside down. A number of these cameras needed to be available for visitors to use in the show. This hands-on activity illustrates how lenses work. This concept is central to many of the contraptions displayed nearby that artists used to more accurately depict their subjects. The directions to make such an item were not difficult to find, but to actually make the object work in practice proved to be another story.[9]

A local science teacher was consulted and asked to build a prototype. A camera made out of foam core and a small vellum screen inside arrived a few months later (November 2000). But the correct distance between the screen and the pinhole lens proved tricky to calculate. Many trial-and-error sessions led to the identification of the correct distance for the camera to function, but museum staff noticed that the camera needed an extremely brightly lit object in order to work (February 9, 2001). The camera actually worked best outdoors, and the lighting in the gallery was going to be far too low to make the camera work at all. The lighting consultant was called in and he brought in a number of high powered lamps. Lamps were focused on Venus, still in the Hall of Architecture, and she was "blasted" with increasing amounts of light, until her image began to faintly emerge inside the camera prototype.

However, the Architect and lighting designers noted that all of this light focused on Venus would need to be contained in some way. Some of the other objects in the room required low light, and the room was meant to have a dramatic effect, high lights and low lights, with objects glittering and glowing. The amount of light needed to make the camera work would de-

---

[9] The creation of this exhibition offers interesting insight into disciplinary knowledge, practice, expertise, and innovation as these art museum professionals encountered many challenges as they learned to "do science."

stroy the ambiance of the rest of the room. There was talk about having some kind of a light sponge to absorb the light bouncing off the Venus. The idea of having felt or velvet behind her was raised. The idea was considered. The cost was perhaps too high; but no, they could use mill ends, and a local low-cost supplier was suggested. A velvet curtain behind Venus would work as the light sponge needed, it would intensify the effect of the camera, *and* it just might work to enhance the aesthetic effect of the galleries, adding to the drama and the historical context desired to support the content of the show. The idea was expanded to include large curtains hanging in between the rooms of the show, reflecting Victorian parlor room taste. And the velvet curtain could be repeated in the last room of the show behind Van Gogh's painting, *Gaugin's Chair,* that would be a dramatic focal point near the end of the show. The technical effects of changing light sources on the colors in that painting would also benefit from the light sponge qualities of a velvet curtain behind it. The Venus curtain and the *Gaugin's Chair* curtain stayed in the design, while the room divider curtains were later omitted for reasons of cost and for the simplicity of design.

Now work could begin on other aspects affecting the display of the Venus. How many camera obscuras would be needed? Where would they be displayed? How would visitors be guided to pick them up and use them? Could visitors be blinded by the strong light falling on the Venus? Would a barrier be required to keep visitors from going behind the curtain? Did the whole area need a special cue to help define the hands-on nature of this area?

Staff hypothesized about the flow of the space and the number of camera obscuras required. It was thought that visitors might carry them throughout the show. Should this behavior be discouraged? The Curator felt that it was fine for visitors to wait to use the cameras and to carry them around the show (August 15, 2000). Twelve to twenty cameras would be provided, and they would be stored in a sandwich board "kiosk" designed by the Architect. Instructions would be provided on one side of the sandwich board, and the cameras would be stored in cubicles on the other side. Potential problems were raised. Discussion centered on the wayward visitor who might miss the instructions: Would they stand puzzled with the camera? What if the instructions were blocked by lots of other visitors? It was decided that simple "look here" "point this end toward the sculpture" instructions could be placed right on the cameras. A gallery attendant would also be available during peak times to further assist visitors (February 9, 2001). What if visitors went behind the curtain somehow? What if they were blinded by the light and fell into the sculpture? Could this happen? A rug was added to the design, set in front of the sculpture, to help demarcate the space and to keep visitors safe in some way. The rug had the added benefit of absorbing more of the spill light, reducing possible glare.

The Statue in the Exhibition

The sculpture of Athena reflected in the camera obscura, in the gazing ball, and in the assorted lenses displayed nearby. The curtain draped beautifully in a semicircle behind her and in this dramatic setting, she looked quite stunning (see Fig. 1.4). As the foregoing story suggests, the design team—Educators, Curator, Exhibitions staff, and Architect—came together to ponder choices that would affect visitors' physical experiences of the Athena statue and the camera obscura activity. Yet these decisions did not reflect the didactic elements of the display—the arrangement and texts created by the Curator to explain and support the concepts underlying the show. Next, I provide a discussion of the space where the statue was situated, along with the text panels that made direct reference to the statue, to offer a sense of how the themes and concepts and works of art interacted with one another within the exhibition space.

The Pallas Athena was situated in the first room, along with "Light of Day" text. The section in which she stood was marked overhead with a sign, "Shadows." A thematic level text panel (serving a small group of related objects), read:

> Modeling, the use of light and shadow to create the illusion of three-dimensional form, is a technique developed in western Europe and used by artists since the Renaissance. By the 18th century, the practice had been codified in art schools and was an established convention of drawing and painting. Artists practiced their modeling skills by drawing sculpture under different lighting conditions. Monochromatic plaster casts, such as this reproduction of the Pallas Athena, were especially suited to the study of light effects in black-and-white drawings.

A book nearby showed a picture of Venus and a gazing ball, Venus carefully contorted on the surface of the ball, a print showed Venus being examined in a gallery at night by a crowd, with some people holding torches up to illuminate her. Across the room, a camera obscura was located in a case. The text panel said:

> This device is focused on the statue of Pallas Athena. Its image is projected onto the translucent screen at the back of the camera obscura. A second lens inside the box makes the statue appear right side up on the screen.

A daguerreotype camera also referred to the Athena statue:

> This camera is focused on the statue of Pallas Athena. The image is projected upside down on the translucent screen at the back of the camera. The pho-

> tographer would focus the image on the screen, then insert a light-sensitive metal plate to make a photograph.

An odd brass model of an eye was accompanied by the text:

> Scientists believed that the human eye operated on the same principle as the camera. The lens, or cornea, admitted light and projected it upside-down on the opposite surface, or retina, at the back of the eye. This model of the eye has a lens on one side and a translucent glass screen on the other side, where the upside-down projected image of the Pallas Athena can be viewed.

An activity area was situated to the right of the statue, with a sandwich-board shaped kiosk holding 20 long rectangular camera obscuras, sitting on the edge of an oriental rug in front of Athena. The text on the back explained:

> Each box is a simple camera obscura. To make it work, point the end with the pinhole toward a brightly lit object, such as the Pallas Athena, nearby. Look through the opening at the end opposite the pinhole, and you will see a small, upside-down image of the statue on the translucent paper inside the box. An 18th-century diagram of how the camera obscura works can be seen in an adjacent case, along with examples of a camera obscura used by an artist, a model of the eye, and an early photographic camera that all work on the same principle.

These objects and texts suggest the ways in which connections were made between the various objects on display, and the degree to which the scientific concepts were discussed.

CONCLUSION

This chapter illustrates some of the complex negotiation and team work that is involved in staging a large-scale temporary art exhibition. Although current trends are leaning toward team-based exhibitions, several art museum educators have noted the difficult tensions inherent in this approach, as curators and educators battle for somewhat different ends (Roberts, 1994; Toohey & Wolins, 1993). Watching the *Light!* exhibition develop from a conceptual plan into a realized installation revealed a design team that had clearly defined boundaries, and a leader (the Curator) who maintained a clear focus on an ultimate goal for the show. Ames, Franco, and Frye (1992) emphasized the importance of strong leadership and a focused vision to the success of history exhibitions, and in this case, the Curator's sense of leadership was similarly important. Early on in the installation phase, the Curator, with her metaphor of "hammering," indicated this leadership, and with 4 years invested in the project, it is easy to see why she was insistent that other staff try to find time in their schedules to think about issues, that they make time in their schedules to deal with the *Light!* show.

Although the sense of leadership was therefore a key element in the success of the show, it also reveals the traditional tensions between the different members of the team, most importantly those between the Curator and the Educators. The development of this particular show follows a fairly traditional model of art exhibition planning. It is the Curator's vision that is handed down as a completed project to the Educators, who are then invited to support the exhibition's materials. (For example, in many cases, as in this one, exhibition label copy is primarily the creation of the Curator that receives some copyediting.)

And, as I have suggested in this chapter, each member of the design team has a slightly different notion of what it is that the visitor should experience. The process of designing art exhibitions, then, is quite different from the design of science museum exhibits, where a team might work more directly on learning outcomes, and might try to develop a more unified sense of what it is that visitors should learn in the exhibition. Through the development of the *Light!* exhibition there were a variety of conceptions of the visitor. They were envisioned as a physical mass, as individuals with different interests and ways of learning or as a shopper—deciding which parts of the exhibition to examine. This variety of targets resulted in an exhibition that defined visitor experience and visitor learning in very different ways, although the kinds of learning expected by the Curator received perhaps the most attention. This chapter suggests some of the ways in which learning in museums is considered by staff. It also reveals the fact that the consideration of "learning" remains for the most part an implicit construct, institutionally, and occupationally defined.

Although strongly bounded by the Curator's notions of experience, the Educators were allowed the freedom to explore new areas of practice. "Art Cat" labels were designed and written by the Educators to help younger children make sense of a daunting array of scientific concepts and instruments. The extensive gallery guide was also an opportunity for Educators to mediate the Curator's message, and to assist the visitor in navigating through the complicated show. Additive, supportive, and perhaps secondary, Educators' roles in the development of the exhibition were nonetheless essential, and members of the design team deferred to Educators' judgments about accessibility or audience behavior.

Given the current and common structure of art museums, moving toward a fully team-based approach to exhibition design remains a daunting challenge. Unlike curators, educators traditionally work across all of the exhibitions on the schedule, whereas curators might focus on one or two at a time. Research suggests that successful exhibitions require strong project leaders and the traditional curator/educator role reflects this type of organization. Interactions during the development of the *Light!* show at the Carnegie reflected a symbiotic relationship, where boundaries were clearly defined, and specialized expertise valued. In spite of this, the particular novelty of this exhibition offered participants the opportunity to perhaps engage in more team-based decision making than in other shows. And it seemed clear that the institution was moving toward more experimentation in specifically educational initiatives, with new approaches to label design, experiential components, and to the accommodation of a diverse public. After this yearlong process of observation, they note that they have focused more closely on how they envision experiences for their visitors. By bringing the exhibition design process to light, museum professionals might begin the process of examining, and perhaps, reconciling, sometimes conflicting notions of their audience, as museum researchers consider a broader range of factors that were designed to influence visitor experiences in museums.

ACKNOWLEDGMENTS

The research reported here was supported in part by the Museum Learning Collaborative (MLC), Learning Research and Development Center, University of Pittsburgh. The MLC is funded by the Institute for Museum and Library Services, the National Science Foundation, the National Endowment for the Arts, and the National Endowment for the Humanities. The opinions expressed are solely those of the author and no official endorsement from the funders should be presumed.

The author would like to thank Joyce Fienberg for her editorial assistance, Gaea Leinhardt for her encouragement, and members of the design team and staff at the Carnegie Museum of Art, especially Louise Lippincott, Marilyn Russell, Chris Rauhoff, Paul Rosenblatt, Heidi Domine, Patty Jaconetta, Lucy Stewart, Tey Stiteler, and Rich Tourtellott, Arlene Sanderson, and Haldane Hilbish, for their openness and generosity.

REFERENCES

Allen, S. (1997). Using scientific inquiry activities in exhibit explanations. *Science Education* (Informal Science Education–Special Issue), *81*(6), 715–734.

Ames, K., Franco, B., & Frye, L. (Eds.). (1992). *Ideas and images: Developing interpretive history exhibits.* Nashville, TN: American Association for State and Local History.

Association of Science-Technology Centers. (Ed.). (1993). *What research says about learning in science museums* (Vol. 2). Association of Science-Technology Centers. Washington, DC: Author.

Bal, M. (1996). *Double exposures.* London: Routledge.

Bennett, T. (1995). *The birth of the museum: History, theory, politics.* London: Routledge.

Blais, A. (Ed.). (1995). *Text in the exhibition medium.* Quebec: La Societé des Museés Quebeçois.

Blühm, A., Lippincott, L., & Armstrong, R. (2001). *Light!: The Industrial Age 1750–1900, Art & Science, Technology & Society.* London: Thames & Hudson.

Boisvert, D. L., & Slez, B. J. (1995). The relationship between exhibit characteristics and learning-associated behaviors in a science museum discovery space. *Science Education, 79*(5), 503–518.

Borun, M., Chambers, M., & Cleghorn, A. (1996). Families are learning in science museums. *Curator, 39*(2), 124–138.

Bourdieu, P., & Darbel, A. (1991). *The love of art: European art museums and their public.* (First published in French in 1969). Cambridge: Polity Press.

Coxall, H. (1991). How language means: An alternative view of museum text. In G. Kavanagh (Ed.), *Museum languages: Objects and texts* (pp. 85–99). London: Leicester University Press.

Doering, Z. (1999). Strangers, guests or clients? Visitor experiences in museums. *Curator, 42*(2), 74–87.

Dorment, R. (2000, November 22). Intensely illuminating. *London Telegraph.* [On-line]. Available: www.telegraph.co.uk.

Duncan, C. (1995). *Civilizing rituals: Inside public art museums.* New York: Routledge.

Eisner, E., & Dobbs, S. (1986). *The uncertain profession: Observations on the state of museum education in twenty American art museums.* Los Angeles: J. Paul Getty Center for Education in the Arts.

Falk, J., & Dierking, L. (1992). *The museum experience.* Washington, DC: Whalesback Books.

Falk, J., & Dierking, L. (Eds.). (1995). *Public institutions for personal learning: Establishing a research agenda.* Washington, DC: American Association of Museums.

Goode, G. B. (1889). *Museum-history and museums of history.* Papers of the American History Association, *3,* 253–275.

Gurian, E. (1991). Noodling around with exhibition opportunities. In I. Karp & S. D. Lavine (Eds.), *Exhibiting cultures: The poetics and politics of museum display* (pp. 176–190). Washington, DC: Smithsonian Institution Press.

Hood, M. (1993). Comfort and caring: Two essential environmental factors. *Environment and Behavior, 25*(6), 710–724.

Hooper-Greenhill, E. (1992). *Museums and the shaping of knowledge.* New York: Routledge.

Polkinghorne, D. (1997). Reporting qualitative research as practice. In W. Tierney & Y. Lincoln (Eds.), *Representation and the text: Reframing the narrative voice* (pp. 3–21). Albany: State University of New York Press.

Rice, D. (1987). On the ethics of museum education. *Museum News, 65*(5), 13–19.

Rice, D. (2001). Looking into seeing: What people learn in the art museum. In C. Davidson (Ed.), *The museum as a place for learning* (pp. 42–49). Ithaca, NY: The Herbert F. Johnson Museum of Art, Cornell University.

Roberts, L. (1994). Educators on exhibit teams: A new role, a new era. In J. Hirsch & L. Silverman (Eds.), *Transforming practice: Selections from the Journal of Museum Education, 1992–1999* (pp. 89–97). Washington, DC: Museum Education Roundtable.

Roberts, L. (1997). *From knowledge to narrative: Educators and the changing museum.* Washington, DC: Smithsonian Institution Press.

Toohey, J., & Wolins, I. (1993). Beyond the turf battles: Creating effective curator-educator partnerships. In J. Hirsch & L. Silverman (Eds.), *Transforming practice: Selections from the Journal of Museum Education, 1992–1999* (pp. 98–103). Washington, DC: Museum Education Roundtable.

Underhill, P. (1999). *Why we buy: The science of shopping.* New York: Simon & Schuster.

Yanow, D. (1998). Space stories: Studying buildings as organizational spaces while reflecting on interpretive methods and their narration. *Journal of Management Inquiry, 7*(3), 215–239.

Chapter 2

Two Docents in Three Museums: Central and Peripheral Participation

Mary Abu-Shumays
Gaea Leinhardt
University of Pittsburgh

Museums are complex and unique social communities. On the one hand they are made up of clearly identifiable subcommunities, each with their own agendas: directors, curators, scientists, designers, educators, docents, volunteers, security personnel, and marketing staff (Linn, 1983; Roberts, 1997); on the other hand these distinct, and sometimes contentious, subcommunities organize themselves around their shared resources (the museum's holdings) and their shared function of helping strangers (visitors) enjoy and appreciate the environment of the museum itself. If the museum is to operate effectively, these various subcommunities must understand each other and at least to some extent appreciate each others' particular concerns and functions. The communities must come together from their different perspectives, to focus on the visitor and on how the visitor is either attracted to, indifferent to, or repelled by the museum experience. Moreover, just as all members of the museum community can play out their own roles within the museum they also can take on the role of visitor and see the museum as a visitor might. Granted, museum staff are not typical visitors, but they can be considered visitors nonetheless.

Not only are museums complex communities in general, but each museum type, and each museum, has its own ecology of communities within it. Natural history museum communities, for example, have the common goal of collecting, preserving, understanding, displaying, disseminating information, and fostering an appreciation of the natural world: from natural environments (flora and fauna) to diverse culture groups (ancient and modern, near and far, large and small). The members of the natural history community share a discourse that reflects their goals and communicates to visitors their thinking about the natural world.

Taking into account this need to communicate to visitors, much research on museums and their visitors has focused on the typical visitor and typical behavior. Such research is conducted because museums want to know exactly what the general public experience during their museum visits and what they take away from the visits. Among the experiences that researchers have documented are those of enjoyment, attitudinal changes, socialization, enduring memories, and learning (e.g., Erätuuli & Sneider, 1990; Falk & Dierking, 1992, 1997; Gottfried, 1980; McManus, 1993; Stronck, 1983). Learning as an outcome has become a particular interest to researchers who examine museums as informal learning environments, and to those who investigate school group field trips (e.g., Boggs, 1977; Borun & Dritsas, 1997; Feher, 1990; Hilke, 1988; Kindler, 1997; Lewin, 1989; Sykes, 1992). Yet, although these studies rest on the typical *behavior* of the typical visitor they do not tend to offer a clear consensus of what *learning* might mean for museum visitors. In our research we consider learning to be more of a process and less of a possession than do other approaches to museum studies (Leinhardt & Crowley, 1998; Schauble, Leinhardt, & Martin, 1998). Our notion of learning as a process is that it allows one to participate more centrally in any given community. Thus, a casual group of visitors to an exhibit of African art might, if they engaged in learning, expand the ways in which they could talk about this art so that they could discuss and critique what they saw in a way that could be recognized by others who had more experience and had participated more regularly in exhibits of that kind. These visitors would develop not shared values or opinions but a vocabulary for expressing those values and opinions.

A long tradition of research in anthropology and sociology entails the use of an informant. An informant is not a "subject," that is, an anonymous individual divorced from his or her personal social roles; rather, an informant is a known individual who has a particular window into a community, its practices, and its values. Any individual or group is a member of several formal and informal communities, each with its own set of practices and unique discourse patterns. Any given informant can be considered as a central or peripheral participant in a particular activity for a particular community (Lave & Wenger, 1991; Sfard, 1998). In the museum world, visitors are a particular kind of potential informant; it is because of this that some of the work of the Museum Learning Collaborative (MLC) engages with and makes use both of visitors who are known to the researchers and visitors who are not (see chapters by Ellenbogen; Fienberg & Leinhardt; Gregg & Leinhardt; Knutson; Leinhardt, Tittle, & Knutson; and Stainton, chaps. 3, 6, 5, 1, & 7, respectively, this volume).

One type of visitor who can be particularly helpful in informing us about the experience of learning in a museum is the visiting docent. Within the museum community it is the subcommunity of docents who are most directly concerned with the visitors. Docents are at the very center of the museum–visitor interface. They are responsible for sharing the fundamental intent of the curatorial staff, a staff that remains largely invisible and anonymous to visitors. It rests with them to prompt visitors to see the careful design decisions that are made, and to support an understanding and appreciation of the specific objects or the concepts that are being shared (Grinder & McCoy, 1985). Thus when docents tour their own and other museum exhibits we assume that they move back and forth between their role as a visitor and their skills as a docent. We assume that they view exhibits through the lens of their practice, the activity of docenting. Thus there is much to be gained from looking at some carefully selected docent visitors because they have a particularly strong connection to museums by virtue both of their high level of museum experience and their high level of participation in a particular community of practice within the museum world (Carr, 1991, 1998). Their central position within the museum community, together with their expertise in exhibit content and in communicating with visitors makes them worthy of study. We consider docents to be ideal museum visitors because they are trained to ask questions about museum exhibits and about the curatorial intent that informs exhibits; assuming this critical stance enables them to demonstrate a remarkable level of visitor engagement. Looking at the discourse of these people during their visits to museums enriches our understanding of the potential for learning in a variety of museum environments.

In this chapter, we document and analyze conversations carried on in three different museum settings by a visitor group that consists of two docents, Julia and Elsa (pseudonyms). Julia and Elsa are experienced docents from the Carnegie Museum of Natural History in Pittsburgh, Pennsylvania. This study considers these two people as they participate in two different ways: as central community members, docents, and as more peripheral members, visitors. The study traces the ways that these visitors with experience in the natural history setting engage as central members of one discourse community. We also examine how they engage in two other settings in which they are less central members.

DOCENTS AS LEARNERS AND TEACHERS

Different members of the museum staff community emphasize some of the shared general goals and activities more than others. Museum docents emphasize the instructional activities of the museum world. The docent community tends to attract intelligent and articulate people who are also highly motivated lifelong learners. Like museum visitors, novice docents join the museum community as peripheral participants. Docents, however, follow a learning path that differs from that of most visitors. The docents participate in training, practice their roles, and gradually gain experience that moves them from being peripheral participants to occupying a central position in the daily activity of the museum. However, because each kind of museum has its own community and practices, the deep knowledge of one's own museum does not place one at the center of participation in another museum.

One important feature of the learning process for the docent is the formal training period (often 2 years in duration) that supports the novice docents as they increasingly understand the activities and goals of other members of the community, including curators, exhibit designers, and educators. Through their interactions with curators, docents become aware of the institution's collecting and research interests which are reflected in what the museum offers to the visitor in the form of public exhibits. Through interactions with exhibit designers, they see how the curators' agendas and insights are translated into exhibits of objects and themes that foster an appreciation of the natural world. Through interactions with museum educators and fellow docents, they begin to understand how they can use their own knowledge to transform their own insights about museum practices into an interpretation of museum exhibits for the public. They move, then, from the role of visitor to the role of docent. Ultimately, their goal is to help visitors both appreciate the museum's goals and also begin to participate in the discourse of this museum community. The formal training for novice docents includes meeting established criteria, such as completing formal written exams, and making coherent, interesting, and age-appropriate oral presentations in the galleries in front of their peers and supervisors (Grinder & McCoy, 1985). The docents' most privileged set of interactions, then, is with the visiting public, where they take on the role of teacher. They, thus, assume a dual role within the community, that of learner vis-à-vis the museum staff, and that of teacher vis-à-vis the museum visitor.

It is the activity of teaching that is perhaps the most challenging for the docents. One aspect of this teaching activity is engaging the visitor through the use of museum tools in the forms of objects, text, and exhibits. The docent uses these tools to interpret the museum with the visitor. When docents study a gallery in preparation for interacting with visitors, they use a shared set of information to create their own unique lesson plan. At the core of this plan are the overarching themes that curators, designers, and educators have formulated for the gallery, sometimes articulated as goals for the visitor experience. It is important to remember that some galleries have long histories, histories that predate the personal experience of a given docent. In these situations the docent "learns" the gallery history from other docents, curators, and even guards. The docents customize the experience that they plan for visitors by selecting particular objects or exhibit cases they will use to illustrate the general themes. During their preparation they immerse themselves in written resources, such as label copy, lecture notes, videotapes, curators' catalogues or essays, and docent manuals prepared by education staff. They also rely heavily on discussions with other (sometimes more experienced) docents about the identification, meaning, appeal, or importance of museum objects, and they may model their own interpretation of a gallery on that of another docent they have observed in action. Indeed, one of the requirements of their formal training is that they follow along and observe experienced docents guiding groups of visitors through the museum. All of these activities, formal training, informal observations of museum practice, and practicing the activities of docents, prepare docents for assuming their role as teachers.

The most salient aspect of the docent's teaching activity is direct interaction with visitors. In general, docents are highly motivated as learners themselves to become full participants in the life of the museum; yet as teachers they may be faced with visitors whose interest in the museum is minimal, or with visitors whose knowledge of museum practices and discourse is at a high level. Successful docenting requires that the docents quickly evaluate visitors' experience, interest, stamina, and the likelihood of visitor engagement with the exhibits; the docents must also smoothly adjust the level and intensity of interaction between themselves and their audience. Through training and practice, both with museum objects and with museum visitors, docents assume their central role as teachers.

TWO DOCENTS

Our two docent informants work at the Carnegie Museum of Natural History (CMNH) in Pittsburgh. The CMNH is a part of a complex of institutions built by Andrew Carnegie, a local hero and villain, a member of the group of people known as the "robber barons" (Kinard, 1995). Carnegie's institutions included the Carnegie Institute of Technology (now Carnegie Mellon University), Margaret Morrison College (named after Andrew Carnegie's mother and now a part of Carnegie Mellon), the Carnegie Library of Pittsburgh, and the Carnegie Museums of Art and Natural History. These institutions are located within a half mile of each other and within sight of each other, and their histories, mission, and structures are known to our two docents.

Julia and Elsa are clearly central participants in the activity of the museum. They are both over 75 and both began their careers at the museum more than 25 years ago, after completing what they viewed as their first career, that of raising a family. They regard their tenure at the museum as a second career, for which they and their colleagues receive minimal compensation. Elsa and Julia have participated continuously in the life of the museum for a combined total of more than 50 years. Their experience has spanned five directors, the construction and opening of the Scaife wing of the Carnegie Museum of Art, and the development and installation of more than 10 permanent and dozens of special exhibits in the Museum of Natural History. Julia and Elsa have shaped the character of the docent community because they participate in the formal training and supervision of novice docents. They have been both formal course-based teachers and field supervisors as well as informal mentors.

Elsa and Julia fit the profile of highly motivated lifelong learners because they approach every learning experience in the museum with enthusiasm and purpose. This characteristic is especially visible with respect to their deep interest in minerals, a topic that many other docents, novice and experienced alike, find very challenging. The fact that these docents both have college degrees in chemistry has supported their affinity for understanding and appreciating minerals and helps to explain why many of the other docents look to them for guidance in how best to understand and interpret minerals for visitors. The museum's curatorial staff also recognize and appreciate their expert skills, often consulting them on issues of emphasis, sequence, and philosophy as new exhibits are planned and older ones updated. Although there are no externally recognized standards for measuring expertise among docents—such as one might have for expertise in chess—the experience and reputation enjoyed by Elsa and Julia make it clear that they are expert, central participants in the docent community and the museum's natural history museum community as well. Elsa and Julia are also good friends. They spend time together at work, on professional trips to other museums several times a year, and share a similar social and philosophical background.

To summarize, Elsa and Julia are on "home turf" in the CMNH. They are central participants in the physical, intellectual, and design history of the museum. They are central participants in the social interface between the docent community and the curatorial, design, and educational communities. They are models of communicative skill with the visiting community. They are model visitors in their museum when new exhibits are developed. Much of their shared knowledge is situated in the textures, sounds, and objects of "their" museum; but they can carry the intellectual tools of understanding and appreciating the museum into other settings where they play a less central role.

THREE MUSEUM ENVIRONMENTS: NATURAL HISTORY, HISTORY, ART

To gain a better appreciation of the relationship of the highly skilled, anchored activity of seeing the CMNH and the skilled but less anchored activities of seeing different museums we asked Elsa and Julia to visit three distinct museum environments, including an exhibition hall in their own museum, so that we could see whether and how they carried their experience and practice in the natural history museum to other museum environments. The three environments we selected were the Hillman Hall of Minerals and Gems at the CMNH, the *Glass: Shattering Notions* exhibition at the Senator John Heinz Pittsburgh Regional History Center, and the *Soul of Africa,* a temporary exhibition at the Carnegie Museum of Art.

The first setting, Hillman Hall of Minerals and Gems, is a place at the center of Julia and Elsa's practice as docents. They have walked through Hillman Hall, examined its specimens, and talked about them hundreds of times. Indeed, they assisted curators in the preparation for the opening of the hall in 1980. They know how and why the various displays are organized as they are, and exactly where particular mineral specimens are located. They clearly understand the intentions of Henry Hillman and the Hillman Foundation, whose vision and financial support were responsible for creating the hall. Hillman's vision was to present to the public the finest possible collection of minerals displayed in aesthetically pleasing surroundings. Accordingly, although text in the hall does give scientific information about minerals, the primary aim is to allow visitors to see the beauty of minerals, many of which are encased and lighted as if they were gems in a jewelry store, with a minimum of explanatory labeling. When they guide visitors through this gallery, our two docents see their task as assisting visitors both in appreciating the beauty of minerals and in understanding how the minerals formed. To that end they have acquired a repertoire (consisting of scientific information and understanding of visitors' interests) that allows them to create a story about minerals, a story illustrated by the specific objects they choose to focus on as they walk through the exhibition.

In contrast to the Hillman Hall of Minerals and Gems, we chose two environments in which Elsa and Julia played no active development role and appreciate less completely. The first of these, the *Glass: Shattering Notions* exhibition opened to the public in 1998 at the Heinz History Center (Madarasz, 1998). The exhibition is organized around a dual purpose: featuring the beauty of the individual pieces of glass, and telling the story of the Pittsburgh glass industry. This dual curatorial message mirrors the duality of the Gems exhibits with the emphasis on aesthetics and history. The exhibits feature glass pieces that can be appreciated primarily for their craftsmanship and beauty as well as glass that illustrates the diversity of designs available. The process of glass-making is illustrated through graphics, text, video, and actual industrial equipment. Artifacts from labor, history, and marketing complement the glass on display and afford the visitor a comprehensive look at the history of the industry in Pittsburgh and surrounding regions. Interactive features include quizzes on identifying which objects are made from glass, matching historic events to particular glass designs, matching chemicals to the colors they produce in glass, and manipulable exhibits that demonstrate polarized glass and heat resistance.

The History Center where the exhibition is located opened to the public in a renovated industrial building in 1996. Although the History Center is a newly opened museum, its parent organization, the Historical Society of Western Pennsylvania, which in the past also housed a smaller Pittsburgh glass collection, was previously located a few blocks from the Carnegie Museums. As longtime Pittsburgh residents, our docents were familiar with the Historical Society, the move to and opening of the new museum, and with the fact that 19th-century Pittsburgh was home to a large glass industry. Because Carnegie Museum of Natural History also once displayed a glass collection, and because both Elsa and Julia are chemists by training, they have an understanding and interest in glass as a material, and in the process of making glass. What they lack, however, is an intimate knowledge of the specific pieces displayed in *Glass: Shattering Notions*, of the curatorial intentions, design compromises, and physical layout of the exhibition (for greater detail see Fienberg and Leinhardt, chap. 6, this volume).

The third exhibition that we selected, *Soul of Africa*, was a traveling show that was on exhibit at the Carnegie Museum of Art for several months during 1999. It included 200 pieces of Central and West African art, culled from a much larger collection that was assembled in the early 20th century by the Swiss collector, Han Coray. The collection consists for the most part of masks, jewelry, stools, neckrests, musical instruments, and funerary figures fashioned out of wood, brass, ivory, and cloth (Szalay, 1998). A particularly dramatic feature of the exhibition was the minimal use of glass cases to present the art. Most pieces, whether hung on the walls or displayed on risers, could be viewed directly without any intervening medium. The low placement of labels also facilitated the viewer's direct experience with the pieces. A section of one gallery was devoted to a resource table where visitors were invited to peruse the exhibition catalogue and other books on African art, and to record their reactions to the exhibition in a public comment book provided.

The primary aim of the show, consistent with the mission of the art museum, was to offer a collection of artworks of high quality that could be appreciated on their aesthetic merits. Realizing that many American museum-goers are unfamiliar with African art, curators at a previous venue had organized the artworks under several thematic headings such as "Rank and Prestige" and "Music in the Service of Spirits and Kings," and had written text panels for each heading, and label copy for individual or small groupings of objects. There is no evidence, however, that the original collector, Coray, collected the pieces with these ideas in mind. The Carnegie Museum of Art utilized this text and labels as well as maps to help visitors appreciate the artwork in the context of the African cultures that produced them. The exhibition thus offered both an aesthetic and an anthropological entree to the pieces (for greater detail see Stainton, chap. 7, this volume).

Because the Carnegie Museum of Art and the Carnegie Museum of Natural History share the same building, our two docents have visited the art museum many times, and know many of its staff members. Although they may be familiar with its physical space, they are very much on the periphery of its practice. They have no formal experience with art, and have limited interest in looking at art exhibitions of unfamiliar material. Nevertheless, they do have a tangential knowledge of the art of some non-western cultures. The Carnegie Museum of Natural History's anthropological halls feature exhibitions of non-western cultures (ancient Egypt, central Canadian Inuit, and several North American Indian tribes), and some of the artifacts produced by these cultures are considered to be works of art. Indeed, the curator of the CMNH's Walton Hall of Ancient Egypt chose to illustrate the difference between anthropological and art methods of display. In this hall most of the artifacts are organized under headings that illustrate a particular aspect of ancient Egyptian culture. By way of contrast the curator decided to exhibit one of the artifacts, a sculpture entitled, "Head from a Nobleman's Statue," as a work of art. It has been placed by itself in a glass case, apart from other artifacts, with only an art-style label.

Our docents' knowledge of and ability to interpret non-European cultures, and their appreciation of the difference between art and artifact provided them with a connection to the *Soul of Africa* display of non-western art. Yet in comparison with the history museum and its glass collection, the art museum's offerings were farther away from the docents' personal and professional experience. These three museum environments, natural history, history, and art offered our docents the opportunity to draw on their repertoire developed in the natural history museum to assign meaning and value to museum objects in history and art collections that they were viewing for the first time.

CONVERSATIONAL ELABORATION

We expected that, when acting as visitors to the various exhibitions, Julia and Elsa would engage in a number of activities that are common to museum goers (Falk & Dierking, 1992). Once inside the museum, they would locate the exhibition of interest to them and then orient themselves within the exhibition space, partly by reference to objects that attracted their attention, and partly by wall text and labels that gave them clues as to content. Their route and pace through the exhibition would be guided by the designers' organization of the show, including spacing and pathways as well as objects and text. In the choice of a route, Elsa and Julia's social relationship would play a role as well. We would expect that as they found their way and managed various aspects of the visit, as well as when they actually engaged with the substance of each exhibition, they would talk. In order to understand the activities of Julia and Elsa in these three contrasting museum environments, we look at this talk in two different ways. First, we analyze their conversations in terms of a structure that is relatively independent of content. For this purpose we employ the construct of conversational elaboration as described in the introduction to this volume. Second, we examine the content of their talk in terms of how they make sense of the exhibitions as docents. For this purpose we examined their conversations with reference to the Object Based Activity Model (OBAM).

During any museum visit, observable external activities take place, while at the same time, less observable, more internal activities take place. One way that we can trace both of these activities is by monitoring the discourse of visitors to the museum. Language becomes both the means by which many of these activities are accomplished and the evidence for them. In order to trace the ways in which meaning grows and develops while visitors are engaged with an exhibition we need to build both a general language descriptor and one that is sensitive to the specific tasks, content, and context of the exhibits. The general discourse activity that we have chosen to examine involves the depth and analytic level of the conversation.

Conversational elaboration points to the ways in which visitors participate in a discussion of a museum exhibition's offerings (Leinhardt & Crowley, 1998, and in the introduction to this volume). We use four components of such discussions, namely the activities of listing, analyzing, synthesizing, and explaining. We consider these activities to be common types of conversational responses to objects in a museum. For the purposes of this research, *listing* is the naming of objects, and answers the question, What is it? *Analyzing* describes the features or qualities of an object, and answers the question, What is it like? *Synthesizing* compares a particular object or a feature of an object on view to another object, whether the second object is in the same exhibit or is known to the visitor through a previous experience. This activity answers the question, How is this object like (or unlike) that object? Finally, *explaining* builds up a coherent and satisfying (to the visitor) account of the object, and answers such questions as, Why is this here? How does this work?

We have presented these activities in a sequence that ranges from less to more complete in terms of the sophistication with which discussion of museum objects is conducted. Thus *analyzing* the features of an object demands a more involved degree of engagement than does *listing*, merely naming the object. Likewise, *synthesizing* goes beyond listing in elaboration, but not necessarily beyond analyzing, since a synthesis may require the prior (either explicit or implicit) activity of analyzing each object that is involved in a synthesis, or it may simply compare the total object to a similar one already encountered. In the same way, *explaining* is more involved than analyzing or synthesizing because it requires (either explicitly or implicitly) that the speaker identify an underlying query and then make use of the tools of listing or identifying, analyzing or examining, synthesizing or comparing, to construct an explanation.

Visitors generally engage in these four discourse activities in an informal and unconscious manner as they view museum objects; that is, they do not expressly list, analyze, synthesize, and explain with reference to every object or exhibit component that they approach, but their overall discussion within a particular exhibition tends to contain all four kinds of conversational elaboration. Visitors will utilize any or all of these discourse activities in their visit. Thus when Julia and Elsa engaged in conversation while playing the role of visitors in museums, they participated in the way that most visitors do, albeit at a rather more sophisticated and intense level. We use this structural trace of the discourse of our docents to help examine the impact of their more or less central roles in each of the museums on the content of their conversation. We also use this set of analytic tools to help us uncover the more general skills that they may be able to import to the less familiar and meaningful environments. Thus, we would expect to see rather more explanation in the exhibit of Minerals and Gems and less listing; whereas we would expect to see more analysis and synthesis in the other two exhibits because the lack of familiarity of purpose and content may not support explanations but the skill of careful thoughtful examination may support analysis and synthesis discussions of objects.

OBJECT BASED ACTIVITY MODEL

Our second examination of the docents' conversation focused on the content of the discourse. We organize this content with respect to the Object Based Activity Model (OBAM). In order to consider the ways in which Elsa and Julia examined these different exhibits we developed a conceptual model of their activity in the museum. We assume that objects and the docents' responses and connections to them are at the heart of their experiences. The model focuses on the ways in which our docents engaged with objects as they made meaning from them: by this we mean the way they responded to specific objects in an exhibit and connected those objects to each other and to the exhibit as a whole in a way that made sense to them. We assume that while typical museum visitors respond to objects and make sense of exhibits, the particular training and practices that have shaped Julia and Elsa's experience make their museum activity unique. We believed that their participation as docents in their own museum would alter the ways in which they engaged in any museum. If that proved to be the case, then features of the OBAM would be present in each museum visit, albeit at different levels.

The OBAM is derived from a model that analyzes the activities of practicing historians as they read familiar and unfamiliar historical texts (Leinhardt & Young, 1996). That research recognizes that historians are unusually skilled readers and re-readers of texts, and that written texts are one of the primary objects with which historians engage as they construct a narrative of the past from various records. Thus, documents are often the "objects" in an historical world. The model of reading developed by Leinhardt and Young (1996) showed how historians sought to identify the document and its author, and locate it in time and space. Historians compared the text to similar texts and tried to understand its purpose and significance. Historians interpreted documents through their own perspective on history. These activities were more explicit and therefore visible when historians read a text that was unfamiliar to them. However, when historians approached a text that they already knew, these activities became implicit, because the explicit processes of identifying and interpreting the document had already occurred during previous readings. Having historians respond to texts that differed in their level of familiarity helped to highlight implicit practices as well as to point out the practices that were general across different levels of prior experience and familiarity.

For our study we viewed our natural history docents as central, expert "readers" of the familiar "text" of the Minerals and Gems exhibition; we asked them to "read" the text of an exhibition in which both the exhibition itself and the subject matter, African art, were unfamiliar; we also asked them to *read* the text of a history exhibition that was unfamiliar to them, but whose subject matter, glass, was somewhat familiar. The purposes of an art museum are more distant from those of a natural history museum than they are from those of a history museum. We are using the term *text* in a broad sense to indicate everything in the exhibitions, and not just written material; likewise we are using the term *read* in an extended sense to indicate the activity of following a route, looking at displays, reading labels and wall text, and talking about objects in each of the three exhibitions. We realized that the underlying analogy of reading documents, one chosen by the historian and one not, can only be taken so far. A series of objects collected together to form an exhibition is not the same as a series of words forming a single document. Size, time, and complexity are all quite different. However, from previous research we do have a good general picture of visitors' behavior, just as we have a good picture of the typical readers' response to a short passage. What we lack is a deeper understanding of the potentials and nuances of the visitors' behavior, just as we initially lacked an understanding of the reading of those who read as a central part of their activity. We can better understand those potentials and nuances through analyzing exactly what it is that expert visitors do.

The model for reading and understanding the *text* of a collection-based exhibition involves two primary activities: identifying individual objects or sets of objects, or processes,[1] and interpreting these objects or processes. Our two docents engage with an object or an exhibit to *identify* it, stating conversationally what it is, and what distinguishes it from other things. They may also *interpret* the object, in other words, discuss its meaning and importance or respond to its visual features. The assumption we are making is that central levels of participation as a docent require a rich repertoire of actions surrounding specific objects in specific displays. Further, we assume that the overriding purpose of the activity is to position the docent to explain to and share the objects with visitors. Although even the most casual visitor can engage in some level of identification and interpretation, docents participating at the center of museum practice call into play increasing layers of specificity. They also make use of a particular set of transformational actions that support them as they prepare to share their own interpretations or to prompt the visitor's engagement with interpretive behavior, *because* what makes a museum experience meaningful is the potential of sharing that experience. Figure 2.1 shows the OBAM. In the model each node represents an activity cluster of responses. The activities Identify and Interpret are shown as the primary nodes. These primary activities build from several other activities, each of which is shown as a node connecting to Identify or Interpret.

Identify

Identify is connected to three secondary nodes, Classify, Source, and Contextualize. Each of these nodes represents a set of activities that helps to identify an object or exhibit. For example, if a docent were looking at some glass on display, there are several ways she might identify it. First, she might *classify* it, either as an individual *object,* as an *instance* of a type of glass, or as the product of a particular *process.* Each of these three classify activities—object, instance, and process—are shown in Fig. 2.1 as tertiary nodes that connect to the secondary classify node. The *classify* activity is illustrated by the statement, "Look at the bottle." Here, the docent *classifies* the *object* by assigning it to the category of bottles. She might go into more detail, and mention the color or say that it is a ketchup bottle. In that case, she is *classifying* the object according to one of its *properties* (color) or according to its *purpose* or *function* (why it was made or how it was used). On the other hand,

[1]We include processes here because in science and technology museums the process that the object demonstrates is of more cultural value than the object itself.

rather than saying, "Look at the bottle," she might say, "There's some pressed glass." Here, she is not classifying the object as an individual bottle, but as an *instance* of one type of glass. A third way of classifying focuses on processes rather than objects or instances. If the docent says, "They made that by pouring hot molten glass into a mold and letting it cool," then she is classifying the *process* by which it was made.

A second tool used to support identification can be seen in the *sourcing* node. In this case, the docents seek to establish identity by determining the origin of something. The question, "When was that made?" is an attempt to source it by *date.* The statement, "That bottle was made in Pittsburgh," sources the object by *location.* The docent might also be interested in *authenticating* the object by determining who was the *collector* of the object, or the *curator* of the exhibit. These various activities are shown as tertiary nodes that link to the secondary sourcing node.

Identifying might entail a third tool, shown in the *context* node. Here the docents identify an object by making a comparison to *similar objects,* as in the statement, "That dish is just like the one Aunt Jane has." Other means of contextualizing are by comparisons to *similar places,* "That was made by the same company as the pop bottles over there"; *similar times,* "That dates from the same period as the ketchup bottle"; or *similar functions,* "I remember using a celery dish just like that." These four activities are shown as tertiary nodes that are connected to the *context* node.

Classifying, sourcing, and contextualizing are all activities that support the identification of a museum object or exhibit. In a conversation a visitor might go through all three activities associated with Identification, or he or she might take turns with another visitor or might alternate across objects. But docents do more than identify; they also interpret exhibits, and do so at the same time as they are identifying the exhibits.

Interpret

Just as identifying is accomplished by various activities, so, too, is the activity of interpreting. Each of the major interpreting activities, *direct response* and *transformational communication,* is shown as a secondary node that links to Interpret in Fig. 2.1.

These activities reflect a response to the visual features of an object, or serve to establish its meaning and importance. Thus, a docent's *direct response* to an object, shown in Fig. 2.1 as a secondary node linked to Interpret, involves constructing meaning through reacting to the object. A direct response might involve *describing* an object; that is, characterizing or giving details that go beyond what the museum label offers, as in, "Oh, boy! Look at

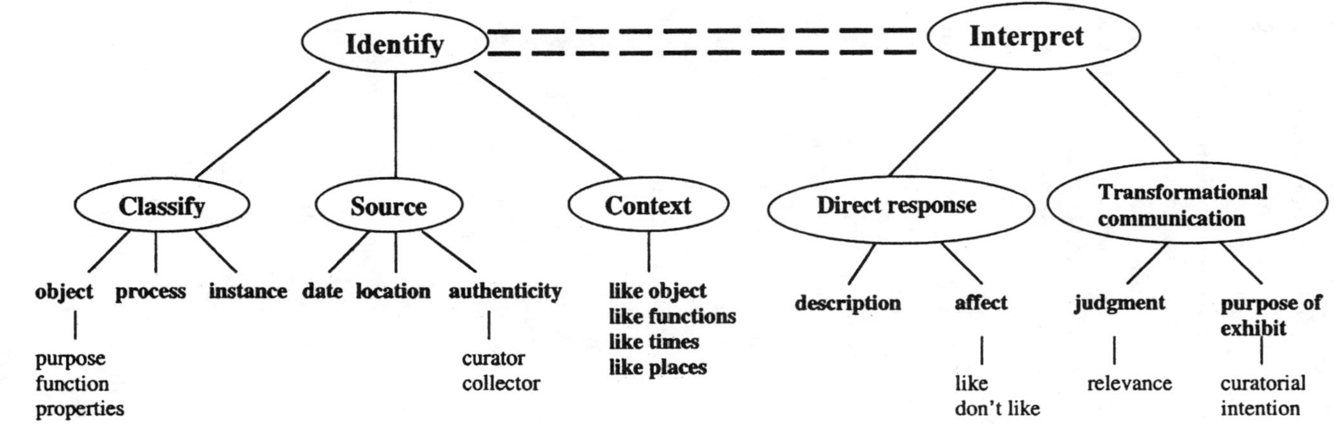

FIG. 2.1. Object Based Activity Model (OBAM).

how intricate, the way they've got the leaves pressed."[2] Or the response might be an emotional reaction, or *affect,* either *positive* ("That tumbler is gorgeous") or *negative* ("I don't care for that pink glass setting"). Both description and affect thus link to the secondary direct response node.

Transformational communication, the second node linked to Interpret, is another component of the docents' interpretive activity. Using this tool, which we believe is unique to docents, they filter their own visiting experience through the lens of their identity as experts in the task of transforming the sometimes disparate museum objects and text that make up a museum exhibition into a coherent and meaningful experience for visitors. Their understanding of objects, exhibitions, themes, curatorial intentions, and public programming, derived from their central participation in their home museum, gives them a standard by which to interpret exhibitions in other museums. They have certain expectations about a museum or its exhibitions that are either realized or frustrated during their visit. They have varying levels of knowledge and interest in each museum's offerings. They continuously evaluate the affordances of all museums, whether their own or others. They notice and evaluate informally the quality of displays, the amount and validity of information offered, the physical comfort, ease of wayfinding, and adequacy of the space available for docents to guide groups through galleries. Participation in training and practice has helped them to develop a particular kind of museum repertoire that assesses museums and museum exhibitions from the perspective of their own identities as well as from the perspective of a potential docent-tour group experience. In any museum that they visit, they tend to ask themselves: If I were a docent in this particular space, how would it work? How would this particular setting support my role as a guide for the visitor? How would it support the visitor's comfort, enjoyment, and learning? It is this perspective on museums that supports their *transformational communication* of a museum's offerings.

The docents' *transformational communication* impacts interpretation in two ways: through understanding the *purpose of the exhibition,* and through passing *judgment* on the exhibition. Both of these activities appear as secondary nodes that connect to the transformational communication node. The first activity, understanding purpose, may be straightforward, as in, "This exhibition emphasizes the importance of the glass industry to Pittsburgh"; or it may invoke *curatorial intention,* as in, "I wonder what they mean by *Shattering Notions.*"

In the second activity, *judgment,* the docents assess an exhibit through the lens of their identity as exhibit guides. Judgment may be expressed in a statement such as, "This display about glass blowing really helps the visitor

[2]This comment was coded as a visitor's description only if the label does not use the same description.

understand the process," where the docent *judges* the *relevance* of the exhibit to the visitor. When the docent says, "This exhibit ought to focus more on glass companies," she is *judging* the *appropriateness* of the exhibit for visitors. The question, "Why don't they tell us what chemical produces that blue color?" is a *judgment* on the amount or lack of *information* provided. Finally, the comment, "If they placed a mirror under that plate, we could really see the design," is a *judgment* on the *display* of the object. Each of these four types of judgment—relevance, appropriateness, amount of information, and display—can be seen as a tertiary node that supports the secondary transformational communication node.

Transformational communication as a cluster of activities is more than just another action in the model. It is the distinguishing activity cluster that reflects self-awareness and the layeredness that is the complexity of docenting. Docents share their informed perspectives to help visitors gain greater insights and meaning from the exhibits.

We use the general structural approach to analyzing the conversations of our two special visitors in combination with the OBAM model of the activity of engaging with and making meaning from the objects in the exhibition to help us understand the docents as visitors. In the next section we state in more detail the specifics of the study and its methodology.

METHODOLOGY

Procedure and Data Collection

We asked Elsa and Julia to visit together one exhibition in each of three different types of museums in Pittsburgh: *Soul of Africa*, a traveling exhibition of African art at the Carnegie Museum of Art; *Glass: Shattering Notions*, a permanent exhibition on the history of Pittsburgh glass at the Senator John Heinz Pittsburgh Regional History Center; and the Hillman Hall of Minerals and Gems, a permanent installation at the Carnegie Museum of Natural History. We asked Elsa and Julia to choose their own route and to go at their own pace through each exhibition. We asked them to carry on a natural conversation with each other and with the researcher(s); that is, they were asked to say whatever came to mind as they viewed each exhibit. The first author, herself a docent at CMNH, acted as a participant observer whose task was to accompany the docents throughout their visit, and to occasionally prompt them to clarify or to elaborate on their comments. Both before and after they toured each gallery, we asked them a set of questions that were designed to elicit talk about the exhibitions and to uncover various aspects of the docents' background and identity. All of the tours and pre- and postinterviews were audiotaped, and two of the tours were videotaped as well.[3] A second researcher followed the conversational group and took notes on their route and their comments, which were recorded on floor maps of the exhibitions. The total time for each museum visit and interview ranged between 60 and 90 minutes. The audiotapes were transcribed into verbal protocols, and videotapes were used to annotate the verbal protocols with action information where relevant.

Coding

We divided the protocols into conversational segments, which are defined as sections of transcript about one topic. These segments correspond, in general, to the exhibit components at which the docents stopped; the segments usually begin as a response to the exhibit, but they may continue after the docents leave one component and walk past or visit other components. All the conversational segments were the location for our analysis, and were coded in two ways. First, we coded for conversational structure, that is, for the conversational elaboration elements of listing, analysis/synthesis, and explanation. Second, we coded each segment for conversational content, that is, for the presence of the OBAM elements of identify and interpret and in this analysis we paid particular attention to the presence of the interpretive activities of describing and transformational communication. Under the transformational communication node we singled out requests for information. We coded something as transformational either when the docents referred specifically to the way they would present the object to visitors or when they explicitly stated that they needed more information in order to make such a presentation.

When we coded for conversational elaboration, we assumed that the elements should be treated as hierarchical and cumulative in nature; that is, as the docents' conversation moves from listing to analysis/synthesis and from analysis/synthesis to explanation, it is moving from less complex to more complex discourse activities. An analysis/synthesis contains either explicitly or implicitly the activity of listing; similarly an explanation contains either explicitly or implicitly the activities of listing and of analysis/synthesis. Therefore, when we coded a segment that contains more than one of these elements, we count only the more complex element. Thus, if listing occurs in a segment along with explanation we coded it as explanation. The intercoder reliability for coding the structural and OBAM features of the segments in the transcripts was 87%.

Because these codings form the core of our analyses we provide examples of both structure (conversational elaboration) and content (OBAM)

[3]We were unable to videotape the traveling African art exhibition because of copyright issues.

frameworks below. We begin with structure and give examples of each element of conversational elaboration: listing, analyzing, synthesizing, and explaining. The first example comes from a display of drums in *Soul of Africa*:

Elsa: Goblet drum? What kind of drum is this? Hourglass, . . . Luba. Ok, it's the Congo.

Here, Elsa is reading label copy for drums; she determines which of the drums is the goblet drum and also that it was made by the Luba people of the Congo. Because there is no further engagement with the object beyond this naming activity, we code this instance as *listing*.

The foregoing listing activity contrasts with the following *analysis* that occurred at a large freestanding panel of glass that is located just inside the entrance of the *Glass: Shattering Notions* exhibition:

Julia: I know a friend came in and was fascinated with this. And you see, the name of it is "Shattered Glass."

Elsa: A crazed material, isn't it? Is the other side smooth like that too? Well, feel it.

Julia: (from other side of crazed glass) It feels, it feels-

Elsa: It's crazed?

Julia: -No!

Elsa: (simultaneously) No, smooth!

Julia: No, it feels smooth.

In this instance, Elsa and Julia go beyond the naming of the exhibit object, a panel of "shattered glass" (*listing*),[4] to describe a feature of the panel, its surface texture. They find that although the panel looks "crazed," both sides of it are in fact smooth. Hence, we code this instance as *analyzing*.

The docents' *synthesizing* activity is seen in the following example where Julia is looking at ceremonial staffs and whisks in the *Soul of Africa* exhibition:

Julia: Well . . . these are staffs from Africa obviously of importance . . . You notice in Egypt that the gods there all have their staff? . . . You remember the Indians, the prairie Indians . . . their staff?

Here Julia is standing in front of a display of African staffs. There are no Egyptian artifacts in the exhibit, nor any textual reference to Egypt. Neither are there any American Indian artifacts, or reference to them. Yet Julia calls

[4]*Shattered glass* is Julia's name for this exhibit. The glass is not labeled as such. The heading in the glass panel, *Shattering Notions*, is actually the subtitle for the whole exhibition.

upon her knowledge of these two cultures, both represented in the CMNH, to make a comparison between the African staffs she is looking at and the importance of staffs in two other cultures; that is, she *synthesizes.*

Finally, an example of *explaining* from the visit to *Glass: Shattering Notions.* In this example the docents' conversation encompasses two exhibit components, a piece of cullet and an exhibit called Miracle Material. These two exhibits stand opposite each other in the second gallery of the exhibition. The cullet, a lime-green translucent piece of unformed glass about a cubic foot in size is displayed in a glass case. The label copy reads:

> In this raw, unformed piece of glass you can still see ingredients of the batch that did not melt in the furnace.

The Miracle Material exhibit consists of wall text above a table on which are placed three cones of differing sizes that represent the proportions of the ingredients used in making glass. The wall text reads as follows:

> Who when he first saw the sand or ashes . . . melted into a metallic form . . . would have imagined that, in this shapeless lump, lay concealed so many conveniences of life?
>
> —Samuel Johnson, 1752

> What is glass?
> Glass, usually hard and smooth to the touch, begins as grains of sand. To sand is added ash, which helps the sand to melt, while lime acts as a stabilizer. These are the three raw materials of what is known in the industry as a batch of glass. Other additions give the glass color or assure its brilliance.
>
> To transform the batch into glass, the materials are heated in a furnace pot or tank to approximately 2,400° F. From this molten liquid, the miracle material of glass is formed.

The text on the table next to the three ingredient cones—labeled sand, ash, and lime—reads:

> Miracle Material
> What is glass?
> Glass is about 75 percent sand (silica), 15 percent potash or soda ash, and 10 percent lime—melted together.

And here is Elsa and Julia's conversation at these two exhibits:

Elsa: Oh my goodness! What's this, Julia? Quartz?

Julia: This is what they call "cullet."

Elsa: Oh, ok.

Julia: I don't think their label-

Elsa: Oh!

Julia: -explains enough.

Elsa: No. I don't either. There's lots of information I'd like to have from about these things.

Julia: (moving to Miracle Material) Because, over here, they're . . . telling you: sand-

Elsa: -the ingredients.

Julia: -and soda ash, and lime, all of which were available here. But what they DON'T tell you . . .

Elsa: Is how to . . .

Julia: . . . is they add cullet in this place. At least at Kopp Glass, they had these big bins—I'll bet they had sixty of them—stored with different kinds of broken-up glass that they saved from all of these. And it was sorted as to what kind, what color, what formula of glass. And that was the cullet. And that was put in as a flux. Now it didn't . . . have anything to do with the actual reaction of this, but it was the flux. It made it much easier to melt . . .

Mary: So, so that cullet isn't always a big piece like that?

Julia: No. It was broken up-

Elsa: Broken up.

Julia: -in pieces, and you see them, some places that they toss in what they cut off from the end they'll—you see them tossing it aside. Well, that was all collected and SAVED for the next batch. And, you see, this-

Elsa: (reading Miracle Material wall text) No, they don't mention it in the label copy . . .

Julia: They don't mention the cullet. And really it had nothing to do with the reaction from it . . .

Elsa: No. . . . It just made it easier to happen.

In this example, Elsa and Julia play off each other to construct an explanation about the importance of cullet in the process of making glass. Julia notes that although cullet is not strictly speaking an ingredient in glass, cullet is added to the batch as a flux, which makes it "much easier to melt." Although this particular explanation contains the elements of listing ("cullet," "soda, lime, and ash"), analyzing ("broken up glass"), and synthesizing (Julia's knowledge of glassmaking from previous visits to Kopp Glass: "at Kopp Glass they had these big bins"), we code it for the more complete activity of *explaining*.

Each of these structural elements of conversational elaboration are naturally occurring instances of museum talk. These same segments of conversation also carry content as reflected by the OBAM. Since we do not see the

OBAM as a hierarchy we coded each element as it occurred in a segment. This means that when we report our results the OBAM will be from a different system of "counting" than the Conversational Elaboration. We begin with the *Identify* portion of the model, and introduce a segment from *Soul of Africa* where Elsa is looking at necklaces:

Elsa: Now look it, see, they've got all this neat stuff down here. Wood, seeds, glass beads, animal teeth? Do you think those are animal teeth? . . . Yeah . . . bone. And, and look at that, that thing in the center.

Kate: I think that's the whistle.

Elsa: Hmm. I, you know, I really know practically nothing about the heritage of these people other than, you know, where they came from and that sort of thing. Hmm. Alright, got all these things I gotta look up when I go home (chuckles).

This comment, taken from Elsa's conversation about necklaces in the *Soul of Africa* exhibition can be coded as *identifying.* Elsa *identifies* by *classifying* an *object,* a necklace, with respect to the property of its materials.

Another synthesizing segment at a case in *Soul of Africa* displaying ivory pendants illustrates the activity of *identifying* by other means:

Julia: One of my friends had a figure like that-

Mary: -like these amulets?-

Julia: -from Africa, it came from Africa . . . and it was a fertility figure.

Mary: Ah.

Julia: That's what I was wondering if those were . . . for fertility figures.

Here, Julia makes a connection to an ivory pendant by recognizing its similarity to an object owned by her friend; in terms of our model, she *identifies* the pendant by *contextualizing* it. She compares it to a similar *object,* and also wonders whether it has the same *function,* a fertility figure, as the one belonging to her friend. In addition she *identifies* the pendant by *sourcing* it, albeit very generally: it comes from Africa.

We coded *interpretative* action as well. In the following analytic segment Julia makes a *direct response.* In our example, taken from *Glass: Shattering Notions,* Elsa and Julia are viewing glass celery containers at an exhibit entitled "Old or New?" where various criteria for dating glass objects are discussed and illustrated. A 19th-century celery vase and an early 20th-century celery tray are shown, with this accompanying text:

Clue Four—Form

The form of an object indicates its use—certain objects were used in certain periods. In the early 1800s celery was expensive, and was displayed on the table in a special celery vase. In the 1900s as celery became more common, it was served in relish dishes or celery trays.

Celery Vase, 1820–45
Probably Pittsburgh; colorless lead glass; blown with cut decoration.
Museum Purchase, Brendel

Partition celery tray, c. 1925
McKee Glass Co., Jeannette, Pa.; green glass, pressed in the "Lenox" pattern.
Gift of Paul G. Sailer

Here is the docents' talk about the celery containers:

Julia: They used to serve celery that way; modern is this way. I never saw that used as a celery. But, again, notice the change in intricacy of pattern . . . -think if I were picking out glass today, I would pick the plainer pattern.

Elsa: I would too! It's easier to clean (chuckle)!

Julia: Well . . . they would appeal to me more.

In this segment, there are two types of *direct response.* First, Julia offers a *description* of the celery dishes, "the change in intricacy of pattern." This comment is coded as *description* because it originates with the visitor, and is not based upon the exhibit label. In addition to a description both Elsa and Julia have an *affective* response to the objects: both docents "would pick the plainer pattern," "they would appeal to me more."

In the following explanatory segment Julia and Elsa engage in *transformational communication* in the Hillman Hall of Minerals and Gems:

Elsa: (at the large amethyst geode) Ok, if I'm gonna be following the quartz, this is something I like to work with because now after I have given my spiel a couple of times then they'd be able to identify that exactly.

Mary: And how would they identify-

Elsa: -the shape of the crystal.

Mary: Ok. They wouldn't think it was fluorite, 'cause of the color?

Elsa: No, because of the shape of the crystal you can see that if you've got points on there and also then, why is it purple, because all quartz is not purple. It's varying colors, what determines what color it's gonna be, and that depends upon . . . what impurities have gotten involved there.

In this instance Elsa *interprets* the geode exhibit by assuming her docent role. She implicitly asks herself how she would interpret this exhibit if she were actually leading visitors through the gallery ("this is something I like to work with because now after I have given my spiel a couple of times . . .") and thus we code it as *transformational communication.* The transformational communication is accomplished through Elsa's *judgment* on the exhibit; she assesses its *relevance* for a putative tour group audience.

In another kind of *judgment* the docents assess the amount or quality of *information* given in an exhibit. In this type of *transformational communication* activity the docent asks whether the text attached to a particular object or exhibit offers enough information for her to give a satisfactory explanation of the exhibit. The following example of that kind of judgment is taken from the docents' visit to the *Soul of Africa,* where Elsa is looking at wooden neckrests.

Elsa: No, they don't tell you what this stuff is made out of.

Kate: [-]

Elsa: I assume it's some kind of wood.

Kate: Oh sure, but uh-

Elsa: -but uh, you know look at, look at the color of that versus the color of that.

Kate: Maybe they don't know and maybe to determine it would hurt the piece-

Elsa: Well uh I, I don't think it's directed to someone like Julia or myself because that's the first thing you know: where'd they get the copper from to make the brass tools and what kind of wood do we have here, what kind of trees are predominant in that area that they would use to make these things? They're gorgeous. Ok. (pause) This is the difference between the Museum of Natural History and the Museum of Art. Exactly! Obviously I'm looking at wh-, what's it made out of (chuckles) and that kind of thing and they're telling you what the symbolism is and that kind of thing.

In this example, Elsa complains that the exhibit labeling does not provide the necessary information about the particular type of wood used to make the headrests. Hence, we code this as *interpretation—judgment—*request for *information.*

Analyses

The three transcripts were all segmented and each segment was coded with respect to its structural and OBAM features. There were 27, 44, and 54 segments in the CMNH, CMA, and the History Center respectively. In the case of the structural features only one code was assigned per segment; in the case of the OBAM one code was made for each feature of the model per segment. The first level of analysis consisted of examining the distributions of the kinds of talk across museums. We did this by examining the percentage of talk for each segment in relation to the total that we saw in each category by museum. We also examined the ways in which the structural features of the talk related to the OBAM. We did this through a more qualitative examination of specific examples throughout the three visits. Finally, we returned to our initial question about the ways these special visitors contribute to our understanding of how people learn in a museum.

RESULTS

Two experienced natural history docents visited three museum settings. In each of these settings their relationship to the exhibited material varied in three respects. First, it varied with respect to their perceived role in each museum. In the history and art museums they were true visitors, outsiders, to the exhibition in question; in the mineral exhibition, they performed the same tasks of touring through and talking about the material, but they spontaneously assumed the role of teacher, or insider. Second, their relationship varied with respect to their interest in the material offered. They had a high level of interest in both minerals and glass, and although they engaged with the material in the art museum, they were much less interested in it as art. Finally, their relationship varied with respect to their knowledge of the material. With respect to the mineral exhibition, the docents knew a great deal both about minerals in general and about the specifics of the exhibition, that is, the individual objects, the arrangement of pieces in the hall, and the curatorial premises that informed the hall. In comparison, they had substantial knowledge of glass products and glassmaking, but little specific knowledge of the glass exhibition. With respect to the art exhibition, they had neither background knowledge about African art, nor knowledge of the exhibition itself.

We consider first the simple distributions of the kinds of talk that went on in each museum. Then in a more detailed way, we interpret why and how Julia and Elsa behaved as they did.

Distributions of Types of Talk

We assumed that there would be differences in the kind of talk that Elsa and Julia engaged in depending on which museum they were visiting. As we stated earlier we expected that there would be more explaining and less listing in Minerals and Gems because there Elsa and Julia are knowledgeable practitioners and explaining is what they do as docents. Hampered by a lack of knowledge in the other two exhibits we expected somewhat more listing, considerably more analyzing and synthesizing, and less explaining. Results of that analysis are shown in Table 2.1. The percentages given for each museum setting (row) add up to 100%, except for rounding.

Table 2.1 shows that the distribution of the listing, analyzing/synthesizing, and explaining activities varied as the docents moved from one museum environment to another. In Minerals and Gems, Julia and Elsa constructed an explanation in 85% of the conversational segments, and that explaining, which we consider to be the most complex conversational activity, was their predominant discourse in this setting. Their rate of explaining in Minerals is considerably higher than in History and Art; 11% and 14% respectively. If our docents are not explaining in these other two museums what are they doing? When we look at the distribution for the activities of analyzing/synthesizing we find that their conversation contains 78% and 68% in History and Art respectively. Analyzing/synthesizing is the predominant activity in these two settings, and compares to the low 7% rate in Minerals. We interpret this finding to mean that the docents, as experienced museum-goers, are using their general tools of analyzing and synthesizing with respect to museum objects and exhibits to engage with objects and exhibits in less familiar settings, in essence to help them move towards an explanation. Finally, when we look at the activity of listing, we see a low of 7% in Minerals compared with a much higher 18% in Art. We take this difference as confirmation that the docents were able to engage in a more complex level of meaning construction as reflected in their discourse in Minerals because they had rehearsed and practiced that activity. Even though they were visiting and not actually leading a group, they had all of their tools ready and available. It is interesting to note, however, that listing is not a predominant behavior in any of the museum settings. Julia and Elsa are still engaged in complex behaviors even in unfamiliar environments.

Our second analysis examined the content of conversational segments for the degree to which they seemed to be using the Object Based Activity Model, more specifically the degree to which they engaged in the two primary activities of Identifying and Interpreting and the degree to which they engaged in the two subordinate interpretive activities of describing and transforming. We also distinguished between those situations in which the

TABLE 2.1
Comparison by Museum of Percent of Segments That Contain Different Kinds of Conversation

Museum setting (# of segments)	*List*	*Analyze/Synthesize*	*Explain*
Minerals & Gems (27)	7	7	85
Glass (44)	11	78	11
African Art (54)	18	68	14

TABLE 2.2
Comparison by Museum of Percent
of Segments That Contain the OBAM

	Identification	*Interpretation/ Description*	*Interpretation/ Transformational Communication*	*Interpretation/ Transformational Communication/ Information*
Minerals & Gems	96	93	81	0
History	93	22	26	22
Art	84	36	34	28

docents transformed information and when they asked for information so that they could make the transformation. We took the presence of three elements in any one segment, namely identifying, interpreting/describing and interpreting/transforming, to signify a substantial adherence to the engagement model. Results of that analysis are shown in Table 2.2. Percentages for each museum add up to more than 100% because we counted identification, interpretation description, and interpretation transformational communication (TC) separately for each segment, and the docents engaged in more than one activity in many of the segments.

The first row in Table 2.2 shows the docents' activities in the Mineral exhibition. A very high percentage of the conversational segments involves the entire model. In 96% of the segments, the docents identified what they were looking at, in 93% of the segments they offered a description, and in 81% of the segments they engaged in the activity of transforming the material for potential visitors. In no case did they ask for additional information so that they could transform the information. As expected, these results suggest that in the exhibition with which they were most familiar, the docents engaged at a very high level in all areas of the model.

The first column of Table 2.2 shows a consistency across three museums for the identifying portion of the model. With percentages of 96%, 93%, and 84% for the three exhibitions, it is clear that Elsa and Julia identified in some way almost every exhibit that they visited and discussed, and that their tool kit for visiting exhibitions in varying environments involved both directly looking at museum objects and using museum labels. This level of engagement with the objects is common for most visitors. (See Fienberg and Leinhardt, chap. 6, this volume, to note a similar rate of identification among less specialized visitors.)

Although Julia and Elsa consistently identified objects and exhibits in the three venues, they were less consistent in interpreting the objects. In 22% of the History and 36% of the Art conversational segments they described the material. Similarly, in 26% of the History and 34% of the Art segments they engaged in the activity of transforming the material for potential visitors. When we compare these figures to the much higher figures for describing (93%) and transforming (81%) in the Mineral segments, and to the much higher figures for identifying in all three museums, we see that the model applies most completely to the docents' activity in the environment where they are central members of the community. It is in a familiar environment that they fluently interpret objects, whereas in less familiar environments their activity is more focused on identifying.

It is worth asking how much of the docents' transforming activity is either a comment on the amount of information offered, or a direct request for more information (the last column in Table 2.2). Whereas the docents do not comment or complain about the amount or lack of information offered in the Minerals exhibition, the request for more information represents a substantial percentage of their talk (22% and 28% respectively) in both History and Art. These figures show that more than 1 in 5 of the conversational segments in the environments in which they are not central participants as either docents or visitors contained a request, either explicit or implicit, for more information. In these instances, like the historians described earlier, the docents expressed their frustration that they had insufficient information to permit them to construct a satisfying account of the exhibit (see Leinhardt & Young, 1996). Even in unfamiliar settings, Elsa and Julia attempt, in many cases, to engage in the docent action of transformational interpretation. It is in fact how they go through an exhibition and make it make sense to themselves.

Understanding the Talk as Conversation for Developing Meaning

Julia and Elsa do not talk in precoded segments; these are artifices placed on their conversation by us as researchers. Clearly, there is a connection between the structural features of their conversation and the way they toured the different museums and discussed the objects as valued representations of ideas and symbols. We can analyze these connections by looking at a complete segment from the sedimentary rock exhibit in Hillman Hall of Minerals and Gems. The exhibit consists of four objects, a large specimen of sandstone and three small specimens of the minerals selenite, kernite, and clay. The accompanying wall text reads:

> Formation of Sedimentary Minerals
> Sedimentary rocks account for 5% of the Earth's crust, while covering about 75% of the surface in a thin veneer. They are formed in layers at or near the Earth's surface by the processes of erosion, deposition and lithification. Parti-

> cles of pre-existing rock are eroded by both mechanical and chemical weathering. These are carried by water, wind and glacial ice and deposited elsewhere as clays, muds, shales, and sandstones, called clastic sedimentary rocks. Chemical sedimentary rocks are deposits of altered organic material, such as coal and chalk, or chemical precipitates from a solution, such as limestone. Cave deposits of limestone are familiar as stalagmites. Both clastic and chemical deposits become solid rock by lithification—compacting of the particles and cementing them with mineral material.
>
> Clay and quartz are the most common clastic minerals. Chemically precipitated minerals include calcite, dolomite, gypsum and halite (rock salt). Gypsum and halite are two of the many evaporite minerals that are precipitated when a lake without an outlet evaporates, or when a body of sea water becomes isolated from the ocean.

Here is the complete segment of the docents' conversation at this exhibit:

Julia: . . . you'll have to tell me if you think this is worth using. I never use this . . . but I wonder if it should be used. Basically you're deep into sedimentary rocks before you get to this. You know how they're formed, different kinds of rocks, but here we're talking about rocks, sedimentary rocks in existence now, what's happening to them. And sandstone is soaking up water.

Mary: So you think the presentation here of the sedimentary rocks is different from the presentation of the igneous?

Julia: Yes, because this basically doesn't tie into anything else, but yet there's a very local story here in that we are a sedimentary rock region, we have a lot of sandstone, it holds a lot of water. When I moved to this area I was surprised, every farm has a spring house. I didn't know about those things, and that's because of the water that's back in all of this sandstone and if there's water in there, what does water do? It dissolves. So that that water becomes laden with minerals, different kinds of minerals, and here are some of the minerals. This is a borate-

Mary: -the Kernite is a borate?

Julia: -a borate, which is very soluble. It's been dissolved out of that. Selenite is a crystalline gemstone; now that's not as soluble as this but it is still, if you give it time it'll dissolve in water.

Mary: Now you're saying in Michigan where you came from there was not that amount of sedimentary rock?

Julia: It was a gravel pit.

Mary: Oh, from the glaciers-

Julia: -from the glaciers-

Mary: -yes, yes.

Julia: But the important thing is the clay. That's the basis of a lot of the original economy of this region. Where there was clay or claystone you had china down along the Ohio rivers. Around here you had tile, ceramic tile. You remember when all our tile was ceramic tile? You had cement being made from the clay, you had concrete block being made, you had bricks, all of which came from this. But I've never used this in a tour. I just didn't have time.

If we look for the conversational elaboration in this segment we find Julia giving an explanation on two levels. First, she explains why she does not use this particular exhibit when she leads tours: "you're deep into sedimentary rocks before you get to this," "this doesn't tie into anything else," and "I just didn't have time." In other words, she does not generally use this exhibit because it is poorly placed within the gallery. Her second explanation relates to the minerals and rocks in the exhibit itself: "there's a very local story here in that we are a sedimentary rock region." She gives both a geological and a historical explanation: several of the minerals on display are formed when water dissolves them out of sandstone, a sedimentary rock common in Pennsylvania; and several of the minerals displayed formed the basis for local industries. In this segment, Julia's explanations work in two ways. She makes sense of the objects on display by relating the sedimentary minerals and rocks to each other and to the economic history of the Pittsburgh region, and she explains that this particular exhibit is not optimally placed within Hillman Hall to become part of the coherent story about rocks and minerals that she constructs when she guides visitors through this gallery.

Having highlighted a conversational segment that is very rich in explanation, we ask whether this same segment also shows the docents deeply involved in the OBAM. We do find that the primary activities of Identify and Interpret are present; and that the secondary interpretive activities of description and transformational communication are also present. In the first place, Julia *identifies* both the display as a whole, "sedimentary rocks," and several components of the display. She *identifies* by *classifying objects* such as sandstone, selenite, and clay, and by *classifying* kernite as an *instance* of a borate. She also *describes* objects and processes: Sandstone "holds a lot of water," water "dissolves . . . becomes laden with minerals," borate is "very soluble," selenite is a "crystalline gemstone," clay is the economic basis for the local manufacture of china, tile, cement, concrete blocks, and bricks. Finally, interpretation through *transformational communication* is a prominent feature of this segment; calling upon her extensive experience in Hillman Hall, Julia passes *judgment* on the *relevance* of the sedimentary rock exhibit to visitors' understanding of the entire gallery. As we pointed out above in our discussion of her explanations about the sedimentary rock display, she does not find this particular exhibit very useful when she leads tours: "you're deep into sedimentary rocks before you get to this," "this doesn't tie into anything else," and "I just didn't have time."

When the docents converse in a way that supports explanations, they are also deeply engaged in the model of docent activity that is anchored around object interpretation. That is, transformational interpretation generally occurs in the context of an explanation, but it can also occur during analyses and syntheses. Consider the connection between the analyzing and synthesizing elements of conversational elaboration and OBAM. The "Early Glass" exhibit in *Glass: Shattering Notions* consists of some fifteen utilitarian glass objects, ranging in color from green to aqua green to amber, and all made in the Pittsburgh region during the early to mid-19th century. The accompanying text reads:

> Early Glass
> Window glass and bottles were the primary products of the first glasshouses. The same green glass used for those objects was sometimes fashioned into simple utilitarian goods such as bowls, pans, jugs, and jars.

Here is the complete segment of Julia and Elsa's talk at the "Early Glass" exhibit:

Elsa: See, now, here, wouldn't you like to know why it's green, or why it's yellow, or why it's blue?

Julia: Well . . .

Elsa: They don't TELL you that!

Julia: You're, you're putting out an exhibit for the general public . . .

Elsa: (chuckles) Are you telling me I don't belong in the general public?

Julia: (chuckles) Well . . .

Elsa: Well, no, I understand.

Julia: I don't think-

Elsa: But I think that's an automatic question: Why is it green? And don't the kids ask you in Mineral Hall—How come if you're talking about quartz if it's pure it's clear . . .

Julia: Yeah, I guess so.

Elsa: And why is it purple and you get amethyst? And why is it rose and you get rose-colored quartz? That's why . . . the kids ask you, and that's a natural question, I think (chuckle).

Here we see the two of them analyzing and synthesizing but also trying to interpret by requesting additional information so that they could engage in their roles as docents. Later, in the same visit they view a Stained Glass display that features a trade sign from Rudy Bros. Co., well-known makers of stained glass in early 20th-century Pittsburgh. Along with the sign, the display includes photographs, watercolor studies for glass design, and stained glass panels. The docents have the following exchange:

Elsa: (at Stained Glass display) Oh, look. Rudy Brothers must have made a lot of stained glass stuff, too. Look at the beautiful windows! Now where did Tiffany get his stained glass for his Tiffany lamps?

Mary: I don't know.

Elsa: Did he get them from Rudy Brothers? I wonder, if that's where he got his stained glass from. I never even thought about that . . .

Julia: Well, a lot of stained glass—this was something I noticed moving from Michigan to Pennsylvania—very ordinary houses had stained glass. Particularly the window where—on the turn of the stairs, would be a stained glass window. And you didn't have to curtain it, then. And the entryway would either have stained glass panels at the side or over the top. And that- and ordinary houses around Pittsburgh were that way, but I didn't see that in Michigan.

Mary: You're right. I mean not about Michigan, but about Pittsburgh.

Julia: Well, that was one of the things I noticed . . .

Elsa: Yeah.

Here we see synthesis since Elsa and Julia extend the description of the specific piece they are looking at to describe where in the local community stained glass is used (in the stairwells where you would not need to use a curtain). They are also identifying the pieces and interpreting them by describing them. However, in this segment they are not engaged in the activity of transforming the information for the "other" nor are they explaining.

In the next segment we see Julia and Elsa deeply engaged in explaining a display of plush textiles in *Soul of Africa,* in part by analyzing it. Together they attempt to figure out exactly what the cloth is. They question each other and the first author. Moving back and forth between each other as resources and the text they jointly construct a satisfying explanation of how the material and design are made but they do not have the resources or motivation at least at this object to transform that information for a visitor audience. Here we sense they are playing the role of visitors only, as opposed to the role of docents as visitors.

The label copy for the cloth display reads as follows:

> The plush textiles of the Kuba result from the artistic cooperation between men weavers, who produce the plain base cloth, and women embroiderers who decorate its surface with vibrant patterns and create the plush texture. The raw materials for both men and women are fibers from the raffia palm tree.

And here is the docents' conversation:

Julia: Is plush a native weave?
Elsa: Plush I think is a terminology . . . -
Julia: -or is that is, that is the type of its uh . . . no, this is raffia.
Elsa: It's a it's a kind of weave.
Julia: Oh. (after reading the label copy) Men are the weavers, the women do the decorating which is applied after the weaving.
Elsa: Oh, ok. Congo.
Julia: Designs are all geometric.
Elsa: What are they made of?
Mary: Does the uh-
Elsa: It doesn't say in there I don't think-
Mary: -it's called raffia cloth.
Elsa: Uh, oh it doesn't say that here uh Mary. That, that's alright, I . . . well.
Mary: Uh here Elsa.
Elsa: Oh ok.
Mary: (reading label copy) Says the raw materials used by both men and women are fibers from the raffia palm tree.
Elsa: Ok. (pause) I don't know anything about this. Ok. (pause) Ok.
Elsa: Mary.
Mary: Yes?
Elsa: Are the patterns painted on by the men after the cloth or is-
Mary: I think the women uh-
Elsa: No the, I mean-
Julia: -the women put the design on.
Elsa: Oh, ok. Yes, I'm sorry, yeah. But they're painted on, it's?-
Julia: -No I don't think so-
Elsa: -I don't know-
Julia: -it looks as if they're stitched on.
Mary: I believe it's stitching.
Elsa: Well, yes, that-
Mary: Don't touch! Sorry, I know you want to touch. (chuckles)
Elsa: Well that's what I was trying to figure out, if it-
Julia: -Well look at that picture. Doesn't it look as if she is is stitching?
Elsa: Yeah! Ok.
Mary: Yes.
Julia: Yeah, I think it's stitching-
Elsa: -The, the pattern is stitched, ok. That's what I needed to know.

This conversation clearly shows Elsa and Julia trying to *identify* the textile by *classifying* it in several ways. They classify it as a type of native weave, discuss the process by which it was made, and figure out that the material used is raffia from a palm tree. They also *identify* the cloth by *sourcing* it according to its origin; they mention that it comes from the Congo. Woven into these identifying activities during the conversation is an activity of interpretation. Julia and Elsa *interpret* the exhibit through a *direct response*, the observation (not taken from label copy) that the designs are geometric.

SUMMARY AND CONCLUSIONS

We have seen two docents who act as central players in the activities of one museum setting as they visit two other museum settings in which they are more peripheral players. As we would expect, they act more like docents in the environment in which they routinely engage in that activity. But even in the unfamiliar settings, their general museum docenting stance, which they have developed along with their specific natural history line of inquiry through years of practice, comes into play. Julia and Elsa use their museum-going tool kit to engage with museum objects in a thorough and intense manner, although not always to their own satisfaction. They are aware of the differences among the museums they visit.

When touring museum exhibitions, Elsa and Julia consistently engage in the activity of interpreting the exhibit for a potential audience—acting out two roles, that of a visitor, and that of a docent. In the Minerals and Gems gallery, they go so far as to re-play the interpretation of the exhibition that they give to visitors. We sense that the activity of docenting has been woven into the fabric of their museum experiences and has become a lens for questioning, exploring, and experiencing all of the museums that they visit. Anecdotally, we have seen this same stance in other docents, both those whom we have observed in the Carnegie Museum of Art (see Stainton, chap. 7, this volume) and those who have written of their experiences (see Leinhardt et al., chap. 4, this volume).

Our discussion of the docent stance raises the issue of how this insight can be helpful to other visitors as they make sense of their museum experience. It is important for visitors to develop a sophisticated identity as museum-goers. By this we mean that they approach museum exhibits with a critical interpretive stance. We want to distinguish between this stance and a direct affective response to objects. We know that visitors do identify objects, they do describe objects, and they do have affective responses to objects, the latter being the "Wow," "Neat," or "Gee-whiz" approach to museum objects. Although identification and affective response may be necessary first steps for museum visitors, we believe that visitors are capable of a deeper engagement.

We have demonstrated with the OBAM that the docents' interpretive stance took the form of transformational communication; that is, they practiced or re-played their role as docents in each exhibition they visited. It was this assumption of their docenting role that enabled them to come to terms with unfamiliar objects and to make sense of unfamiliar exhibits. We do not suggest that visitors need to become docents in order to learn in museums. Rather, we mean that a critical interpretive stance of some kind will serve to anchor visitors' engagement with museum material. If visitors are able to pose questions such as "What do I think of this object?" or "What does this object mean to me?" or "Why has this object been placed next to that object?" then they are engaged in active interpretive behavior. That sort of activity is learnable and can help draw the visitor from the periphery of the museum world into a more central conversation with it.

However, if visitors are to truly learn from museums, that interpretive activity needs to be coupled with content knowledge. The docents' response confirms our sense that it is always helpful to bring to the fore background knowledge when visiting a museum exhibit. This is true whether the background knowledge is about museums per se or about the content of the exhibits. The more one knows about a given topic, the more one can engage with the objects in an exhibit. We recommend that museums and museum educators consider how they can enable visitors to develop an interpretive stance toward the museum, a stance that incorporates both content knowledge and a position related to the visitors' own identity. Such enablement will help visitors to enhance both their enjoyment of and their learning from the museum.

ACKNOWLEDGMENTS

The research reported here was supported by the Museum Learning Collaborative (MLC), Learning Research and Development Center, University of Pittsburgh. The MLC is funded by the Institute for Museum and Library Services, the National Science Foundation, the National Endowment for the Arts, and the National Endowment for the Humanities. The opinions expressed are solely those of the authors and no official endorsement should be presumed.

The authors thank the two docents at the Carnegie Museum of Natural History who willingly participated in the study. They also wish to thank Catherine Stainton, Joyce Fienberg, and Karen Knutson for their help with data analyses and manuscript editing.

REFERENCES

Boggs, D. L. (1977). Visitor learning at the Ohio Historical Center. *Curator, 20*(3), 205–214.

Borun, M., & Dritsas, J. (1997). Developing family-friendly exhibits. *Curator, 40*(3), 178–196.

Carr, D. (1991). Minds in museums and libraries: The cognitive management of cultural institutions. *Teachers College Record, 93,* 6–27.

Carr, D. (1998, April). *Museum use and the problems of information.* Paper presented at the annual meeting of the American Educational Research Association, San Diego.

Erätuuli, M., & Sneider, C. (1990). The experiences of visitors in a physics discovery room. *Science Education, 74*(4), 481–493.

Falk, J., & Dierking, L. (1992). *The museum experience.* Washington, DC: Whalesback Books.

Falk, J. H., & Dierking, L. D. (1997). School field trips: Assessing their long-term impact. *Curator, 40*(3), 211–218.

Feher, E. (1990). Interactive museum exhibits as tools for learning: Exploration with light. *International Journal of Science Education, 12*(1), 35–39.

Gottfried, J. L. (1980). Do children learn on field trips? *Curator, 23*(3), 165–174.

Grinder, A. L., & McCoy, E. S. (1985). *The good guide: A sourcebook for interpreters, docents and tour guides.* Scottsdale, AZ: Ironwood Press.

Hilke, D. D. (1988). Strategies for family learning in museums. In S. Bitgood, J. Roper, & A. Benefield (Eds.), *Visitor studies—1988: Theory, research and practice* (Vol. 1, pp. 120–134). Jacksonville, AL: Center for Social Design.

Kinard, A. D. (1995). *Celebrating the first 100 years of The Carnegie in Pittsburgh, 1895–1995.* Pittsburgh, PA: The Carnegie.

Kindler, A. (1997). Aesthetic development and learning in art museums: A challenge to enjoy. *Journal of Museum Education, 22*(2 & 3), 12–16.

Lave, J., & Wenger, E. (1991). *Situated learning: Legitimate peripheral participation.* Cambridge, England: Cambridge University Press.

Leinhardt, G., & Crowley, K. (1998). *The Museum Learning Collaborative: Phase 2* (Tech. Rep. LRDC). University of Pittsburgh, Pittsburgh, PA. http://mlc.lrdc.pitt.edu/mlc/Research.html

Leinhardt, G., & Young, K. (1996). Two texts, three readers: Distance and expertise in reading history. *Cognition and Instruction, 14*(4), 441–486.

Lewin, A. W. (1989). Children's museums: A structure for family learning. *Marriage and Family Review, 13*(4), 51–73.

Linn, M. C. (1983). Evaluation in the museum setting: Focus on expectations. *Education Evaluation and Policy Analysis, 5*(1), 119–127.

Madarasz, A. (1998). *Glass: Shattering notions.* Pittsburgh, PA: Historical Society of Western Pennsylvania.

McManus, P. M. (1993). Memories as indicators of the impact of museum visits. *Museum Management and Curatorship, 12,* 367–380.

Roberts, L. (1997). *From knowledge to narrative.* Washington, DC: Smithsonian Institution.

Schauble, L., Leinhardt, G., & Martin, L. (1998). A framework for organizing acumulative research agenda in informal learning contexts. *Journal of Museum Education, 22*(2 & 3), 3–8.

Sfard, A. (1998). On two metaphors for learning and the dangers of choosing just one. *Educational Researcher, 27*(2), 4–13.

Stronck, D. R. (1983). The comparative effects of different museum tours on children's attitudes and learning. *Journal of Research in Science Teaching, 20*(4), 283–290.

Sykes, M. (1992). Evaluating exhibits for children: What is a meaningful play experience? In D. Thompson, A. Benefield, S. Bitgood, H. Shettel, & R. Williams (Eds.), *Visitor studies: Theory, research and practice* (Vol. 5, pp. 227–233). Jacksonville, AL: Center for Social Design.

Szalay, M. (Ed.). (1998). *African art from the Han Coray collection 1916–1928.* Munich: Prestel.

Chapter 3

Museums in Family Life: An Ethnographic Case Study

Kirsten M. Ellenbogen
King's College London

The study presented in this chapter is part of a larger, ongoing research project that examines the lives of families who go to museums[1] frequently. The larger research project has three goals: (1) to lay a foundation for conceptualizing the agendas of frequent museum-goers from a sociocultural perspective; (2) to make visible the ordinary social processes of family learning in museums; and, (3) to offer a systematic, theoretically grounded approach to the study of the role of museums in family life.

The current study extends the existing body of literature on the characteristics and motivations of families who visit museums (see reviews by Borun, Cleghorn, & Garfield, 1995; Dierking & Falk, 1994; McManus, 1994). The study focuses on a frequent museum-going family over the course of 6 months using an ethnographic perspective in an effort to describe the role of museums within the larger context of the family culture. This study complements the detailed analyses of conversations reported in other chapters by examining a broader view of museum identity and culture based on observations that span contexts and time.

This study is a story of tensions—tensions among multiple definitions of the terms *museum, education,* and *learning environment*; tensions between the museums' agendas and the family's agendas; and tensions between describ-

[1]In this chapter, the word *museum* is used as a generic term to refer to a variety of educational institutions, including art, history, and natural history museums, historic homes and sites, science, technology, and nature centers, botanical gardens, aquaria, and zoos.

ing learning as a group activity when confronted with the unique experiences of an individual in the group. The resolution and consequences of these tensions form the concluding questions about the role of museums in the educational infrastructure.

Museums have not always seen themselves as educational institutions. The mission of American museums has evolved from one of collecting and preserving to one of educating the public (Falk & Dierking, 2000; Hein, 1998; Roberts, 1997). This evolution has been driven in part by the American Association of Museums' (AAM) commissioned reports, *Museums for a New Century* (AAM, 1984) and *Excellence and Equity* (AAM, 1992), which spotlight education as the central focus of museums' public service. This new focus on education and public service has led museums to reexamine their place in the country's educational infrastructure (Inverness Research Associates, 1996). Museums are just one of many resources for learning that include other institutions (e.g., libraries and schools), organizations (e.g., community, church, and scouting groups), and media (e.g., books, newspapers, magazines, television, film, radio, and the Internet). However, the actual position of museums within the multilayered educational infrastructure, and the very nature of the museum as a learning environment is contested.

FORMAL AND INFORMAL LEARNING ENVIRONMENTS

Developmental psychology research on human development has tended to focus first on preschool children learning in family contexts and second on older children learning in school (Gleason & Schauble, 2000). There is also a "third leg" of human development—informal, or out-of-school environments (Schauble, Beane, Coates, Martin, & Sterling, 1996). Examinations of informal learning environments may both enrich our understanding of learning and force a re-examination of typical in-school environments. Efforts to define informal and out-of-school learning (Bunch, 1997; Crane, 1994; Greenfield & Lave, 1982; Resnick, 1987) have generally resulted in lists of characteristics (see Table 3.1).

One of the most common characteristics to emerge from these lists is structure. In-school learning is described as mandatory, dictated by formal curriculum at local, state, and national levels, as part of a highly organized system of activity. Informal or out-of-school learning is described as voluntary, unencumbered by curriculum or standards, and open-ended. These descriptions are based more on a traditional view of schools and museums than a research-based description of learning environments. Ironically, research on the design of museum exhibitions (Vallance, 1995) and on the

TABLE 3.1
Comparing Characteristics of Formal and Informal Learning Environments

Formal/In-School Environments	*Informal/Out-of-School Environments*
De-contextualized (Greenfield & Lave, 1982)	Embedded in daily life activities (Greenfield & Lave, 1982)
Symbol manipulation (Resnick, 1987)	Contextualized reasoning (Resnick, 1987)
Pure mentation (Resnick, 1987)	Tool manipulation (Resnick, 1987)
Reliance upon teacher communication and verbal symbols (Bunch, 1997)	Reliance upon objects and exhibitions (Bunch, 1997)
Teacher is responsible for imparting knowledge and skill (Greenfield & Lave, 1982)	Learner is responsible for imparting knowledge and skill (Greenfield & Lave, 1982)
Mandatory participation as part of a credited school experience (Crane, 1994)	Voluntary participation (Crane, 1994)
'Lock-step' scheduling and formal curriculum (Bunch, 1997)	Open-ended exploration (Bunch, 1997)
Lack of social motivation (Greenfield & Lave, 1982)	Motivated by social contribution of novices and their participation in the adult sphere (Greenfield & Lave, 1982)
Individual cognition (Resnick, 1987)	Shared cognition (Resnick, 1987)
Generalized learning (Resnick, 1987)	Situation-specific competencies (Resnick, 1987)

activities of people participating in informal learning activities (Henze, 1992) points to a "hidden curriculum" that structures learning in informal environments.

FAMILY LEARNING IN MUSEUMS

Inasmuch as families comprise more than half of all visitors to museums, there have been a large number of research projects on families in an effort to better understand and serve them (e.g., Borun et al., 1998; Crowley & Callanan, 1998; Diamond, 1986; Dierking, 1987). Families are also of great interest to museum researchers because they represent a unique learning group with mixed ages and backgrounds who attach great importance to social interactions. Their social interactions are interconnected to a complex shared system of past experiences, beliefs, and values (Heath, 1991; Leichter, Hensel, & Larsen, 1989). Family members are accustomed to interacting and learning together, and they are equipped with an extensive array of personal and cooperative learning strategies that facilitate the museum learning experience.

Research on family behavior in museums has shown that families' actions follow predictable patterns (Dierking, 1987; Falk, 1991; Hilke, 1987). Most of the actions of family members in museums are related to acquiring or exchanging information and involve interaction with an exhibit. Individuals prefer to acquire information for themselves, and then exchange information with family members, usually with an intergenerational partner (Hilke, 1987). Extensive observations of families' interactions and conversations show that parents take on the role of teachers during the museum visit (Diamond, 1986; Leichter et al., 1989). Families interact in predictable patterns because they come to museums with specific agendas, ranging from entertainment to convenience to family traditions (Hood, 1983; Moussouri, 1997; Rosenfeld, 1980).

Further research on museum visitors' agendas (Falk, Moussouri, & Coulson, 1998) argues that families not only have underlying motivations or agendas for their visits, but that these agendas directly influence what is learned during the museum visit. The growing body of research on the relationship between museum agendas and family agendas points to the potential for deeper understandings of family agendas which could in turn, contribute to the design of more effective programming and learning environments. Museums should not only be aware of themselves as resources for family learning, but also aware of the need to recognize and accommodate families' agendas and resources in order to create a museum environment that the visitors can call successful.

DESIGN

This study was prompted by an interest in how families use museums over an extended period of time, and was driven by an effort to gather a rich description of the role that museums play in family life and the educational infrastructure. The driving question of the study is, "What resources play a role in a family's free-choice learning activities?" Other questions include, but are not limited to

1. How does the family's use of museums relate to their use of other educational resources?
2. What role do free-choice learning activities play for different family members and how are those roles negotiated?
3. How do family members define "learning" and "museum," and how do those definitions vary from their definitions of other activities and learning environments?

Methods

The study reported in this chapter is based on the growing body of literature emerging from the use of ethnographic perspectives in educational research. Educational researchers have adopted ethnographic techniques as a way of getting at the culture of learning environments (e.g., Barton & Hamilton, 1998; Curry & Bloome, 1998; Fine, 1991; Gilmore & Glatthorn, 1982). This study adopts an ethnographic perspective in that it is designed to describe parts of a culture. Unlike an experimental project, this study begins not with a hypothesis, but with a question. It is not an effort to make generalizations; it is an effort to gain knowledge by building cases and generating hypotheses.

Observations began in November 1998 and continued for 6 months. This study consisted of three phases: grand tour, specific investigation, and triangulation. Data collection focused on museum visits, but also included observation in the home and other leisure sites. The museum visits were to be planned according to the family's normal schedule; no additional visits were planned for the study. Research began with a grand tour phase in which participants were interviewed about their past museum visits and other leisure activities. I also accompanied them on their museum visits, writing field notes immediately after the visit. This phase was designed to capture a broad picture of the museum-going family life and indicate specific issues to focus on in the next research phase.

The second research phase was the specific investigation of key issues identified during the grand tour phase. During this phase, I took field notes and made audio recordings during the family visits to museums in an effort to capture both the physical and verbal interactions of the family. Addendum to the field notes were completed at the end of each visit. Conversational interviews at museums and other sites were used to follow up on the museum visit and other interactions. Interviews were audiotaped, with supplementary fieldnotes.

In order to investigate the meaningfulness of the museum visit, the families were also observed while they were at home. These observations were focused on shared social moments, such as dinner time or homework time and generally lasted a portion of the day that included a meal (e.g., 11 A.M. to 1 P.M.). Home observations were audiotaped or recorded in the field notes, as appropriate. The participants were observed in other leisure environments, such as an outdoor festival, in an effort to contrast the unique aspects of the museum when compared to other leisure environments. These visits were recorded using videotape, audiotape, or field notes, as appropriate.

During the final phase, triangulation, the participants were asked to confirm findings. During exchanges in the home and via phone and email, I shared findings and asked participants for their feedback. In some cases, data were discussed in specific detail through an interview where participants gave feedback on my observations of their activities in museums and at home.

The participants were not required to go to a systematically distributed variety of museums; the study is not designed to make conclusive generalizations across museum types. Over the course of 6 months, data were collected in multiple visits to science and art museums, concert halls, rehearsal halls, an international fair, the home, and in the car. Interview data included reflections on all of these environments as well as botanic gardens, history museums, historical societies, historic reenactments sites, an agricultural center, libraries, scout camp, and public spaces like airports and building lobbies.

Analysis

Fieldnotes, interviews, and recordings of visits to museums and other leisure sites were transcribed and analyzed (see Table 3.2). Analysis was facilitated by the software program NUD*IST, which allows coding categories to be added or changed as they emerge from the data. This characteristic allows the researcher to be as emic as possible, recognizing and adopting terms as they appear in the data, after preliminary coding has already begun. Codes were layered, allowing for the same data to be analyzed for different issues (such as conceptual and descriptive issues) facilitating a comparative perspective.

TABLE 3.2
Corpus of Data and Analysis

Actors/Events/Environment	*Data Gathering Method*	*Analysis*
Observations of family visiting museums	Field notes Videotape	Parse by turn at talk and code by topic & activity (e.g., different content and types of talk and activities)
Interviews with family about museum visits	Audiotape	Parse and code by topic (e.g., motivations, role of museums)
Interviews with family about learning and learning resources	Audiotape	Parse and code by topic (e.g., what counts as education, motivations)
Home life or leisure activity observations	Field notes Videotape or audiotape as appropriate	Parse by turn at talk and code by topic and type (i.e., comparing types of talk at home to types of talk at museums)
Interviews with family about leisure experiences	Field notes Audiotape	Parse and code by topic (e.g., cultural and institutional roles of leisure environments, what counts as a museum)
Informal conversations with family about museums, learning, learning resources, and leisure experiences	Audiotape	Use for triangulation with other data analysis

Coding included terms from past museum research as well as terms that emerged from the family's conversations, interviews, and their own examination of the data. Categories from past research included agendas for museum visits: place, education, life cycle, social event, entertainment, and practical issues (Falk et al., 1998). Other categories from past museum research focused on the types of conversations: identifying, describing, and interpreting–applying (Borun et al., 1998). Coding categories emerged from the data within the framework of

Definitions (e.g., defining museums or defining educational activities)
Locations (e.g., where learning activities take place or locating educational resources)
Actors (e.g., who is participating, directing, influencing)
Context (e.g., when is the activity occurring and what proceeded it).

Categories within the framework were multilayered and interconnected. For example, an activity in the home would be coded for what was occurring, where it was taking place, what took place before and after it, and who was involved (although not necessarily physically present). Some categories were created at the beginning of the study with the expectation that they would be present in the data, only to find that they did not naturally occur in the family's activities and conversations. For example, I created the categories "school-learning" and "museum-learning" with the expectation that the family would categorize types of learning based on where it occurred. Although the family did talk about types of learning, a distinction strictly based on where the learning occurred never appeared in the data.

Conversational interviews were used to follow up on the coding themes, or to clarify interactions at the museums and other sites. Thematic analysis was directed toward building cases that represented the family's participation in free-choice learning activities in order to examine how the themes played out throughout the study, leading toward a description of the shared cultural models involved.

Participants

Contacts at the local science center identified four families who were regular visitors. The criteria for selecting participants was that they went to museums six or more times per year (i.e., frequent museum goers). The museum staff members were the first to approach these families, describing the study and passing on contact information only after the families gave their permission. Two families consented to participate in the study, although only one—the Parker[2] family—participated for the entire 6 months.

A Case Study: The Parker Family

The Parker family goes to museums frequently—sometimes as much as once a week. They live outside of the city in an unincorporated area that is fast becoming a suburb. Tipper and Mark, both around 50 years old, have two children at home: Rachel, who is 14 and David, who is 12. Mark, who has a masters degree in science, owns his own electronics business that primarily installs security systems. Tipper, who has a bachelors degree, stays home and educates Rachel and David. Mark comes from a "farming family," and Tipper grew up in an affluent area of the city. Both thought buying farmland sounded like a good idea, so 12 years ago they bought a house in a rural area outside of the city.

As you get off the main road and on to the winding roads of their neighborhood, there are horse farms next to newly built houses with large yards. The Parkers live in an old farmhouse that is still known in the area by the name of its original owner, Miss Lilly's Farmhouse. A wooden playscape that Mark built is adjacent to the house. To the side is a small henhouse where they keep about a dozen egg-laying hens, and four dogs roam the yard. Next to the henhouse is a small stall where they keep miniature horses—a self-described hobby that they started recently after meeting a retired couple that raises miniature horses professionally.

The house is filled with books, musical instruments, and projects in varying states of completion. The back room of the house, which is heated by a wood stove, is a cramped, but frequent gathering spot for the family. One entire wall is covered in shelves containing books, kits, and projects, such as a tiny plastic greenhouse with plants in different stages of growth. The upstairs main room is also a frequent site of family activity. There is open space for Rachel to do ballet spins, a drum set and numerous other musical instruments, a couple of desks, a computer, and many books. In the dining room, the table is used as a study area where books and projects are spread out. Eating often takes place at the smaller table in the kitchen. There are folding card tables for other activities. When talking to the Parkers in their home, they constantly refer to resources around the house. A comment about a music report includes gestures to all of the books that were used for it. A reference to a particular book as the source of inspiration requires a run to the next room to retrieve the book. There are always physical examples to illustrate the discussion topic.

---

[2]All names are pseudonyms

Extended observations of the Parkers' activities during their visits to museums, family time at home, and other leisure activities began to frame an image of their family culture. Following, I have selected five components of their family life that serve to define the role that museums and other resources play in the educational aspects of their lives: Education in the Parker Family; Rachel and David as Learners; The Parker's Use of Museums; Rachel's and David's Use of Museums; and David's Free-Choice Learning Activities. Within these five components, I summarize the data that typified their activities, and provide quotations to highlight the exact nature of their experiences.

Education in the Parker Family

Tipper and Mark talked about home schooling Rachel and David long before they were born. Tipper relates a story of being suprised when she found out that her "suburban, station wagon-driving soccer mom neighbor (M.1.2)" home schooled her children. The idea was intriguing. Tipper and Mark were drawn to home schooling because it was "different" (M.2.1); they never expected it to become the large movement it is today. Tipper and Mark do not have antiestablishment feelings, nor do they dislike public schooling. They see their choice to educate their children at home as an alternative, not as an antischool activity.

Tipper and Mark fit some of the typical characteristics of a home-school family (Lines, 1999): They are a White, two-parent family that is more affluent and educated than the national average. They are atypical of home school families in many other ways: They have only two children, they are not devoutly religious, and they are not politically active. The Parkers have participated in home school organizations in the past, but no longer choose to do so because they were uncomfortable with their conservative and religious emphasis.

Instead of using home school organizations as a source of educational information and resources, the Parkers rely on an informal network of friends who also home school their children. Friends and acquaintances are frequently mentioned as sources of information or inspiration. Tipper warns me that I also play an educational role in the family, specifically as an influence on Rachel, because, "Girls didn't go getting Ph.D.'s when I was your age" (P.1.1). As I gain more access to the family's friends and acquaintances, I see that details about travels, family history, or interests in the conversations may end up a topic of study later that month.

There is, however, a filtering process to determine which topics are introduced into the children's education. Tipper has very specific ideas about what is and what is not educational. She has to think about this issue for home schooling—they are required to engage in educational activities 4 hours per day for 180 days. Tipper distinguishes educational activities from everyday life and from entertainment. She gave an example of getting home after an all-day Saturday ballet practice and an evening performance of the symphony and falling into bed at 11 P.M. saying "We didn't do anything educational today" (M.5.2). The ballet practice and symphony performance do not count because they are the children's hobbies. If they go to an afternoon symphony performance and then spend the rest of the day at the downtown public library looking up composers and museum theory, however, it "counts" as educational.

Tipper believes in letting the children's interests drive their education. She comments, "It is so interestingly motivating to let children pursue their interests instead of forcing them into an education" (P.4.2). Tipper explains that she tries to create educational units around the children's interests, and uses their energy for education. One month, they worked on the Declaration of Independence, James Watt, and time zones while continuing to work on a Mozart family scrapbook that was started the month before. Tipper specifically described the rationale for the Mozart assignment, explaining that it was a broad study that would not be appropriate for a report format, so they were making a scrapbook.

Rachel and David as Learners

Tipper and Mark talk about their children as learners. But from our very first conversation, they characterize Rachel and David as different types of learners. Rachel is a "slow learner" and David is a "fast learner and self-starter" (M.3.2). Tipper and Mark point to specific skills of Rachel's: she is very kinetic and she has an ability to notice design details and make connections based on them. "Rachel loves details like buttons, styles of clothing, or materials (M.3.1)" as well as architecture and textiles, such as cloth. Tipper described Rachel's learning activities: "[She] makes historical connections at other museums or in other situations based on details, not based on a label or something she read" (M.3.2). Rachel is a very focused child who has devoted herself to ballet for years. She has taken a number of master ballet courses over the years and has been offered private lessons, but has always preferred to take group lessons with other girls instead.

In contrast, Tipper explains that "David sometimes just picks up on something while I am teaching it to Rachel" (M.3.2). Mark describes David as "self-entertaining, which is not common for a boy" (M.15.2). Mark occasionally brings David to work, and Mark will find him hours later talking with one of the adult staff, or working on an electronic project. David is interested in a wide variety of activities. He takes violin lessons, drum lessons, participates in Boy Scouts, practices juggling, takes tap dance lessons, and likes to invent things. He has high goals in many of these activities. In Boy Scouts (where Mark is a troop leader), David hopes to progress from Star Scout to Life Scout to Eagle Scout within 2 years. If he does this, he would be one of the youngest boys to reach the Eagle level. Tipper and Mark talk to David about choosing one activity over another—something that is difficult for him. During each of my visits to his house, he talks about a different hobby and shows me a new project. David's career aspirations reflect his varying interests. He does not talk about choosing one career; instead, he talks about his first career, and then a second, and then a third.

The Parkers' Use of Museums

Tipper describes museums as an important part of the children's education: "They bump into information there" (M.8.1). Tipper also speaks about the children and herself getting more interested in museums around October or November. "We get more interested in museums at this time of year. We like to just hang out with stuff. Museums don't require parent preparation. We can leave the books behind. Every year, in the fall, we start with textbooks, and then decide they don't work so we fall back on museums" (P.3.2). But visiting museums is not just an educational activity for the Parkers.

At times, the Parkers go to the local science museum once a week and meet another home-schooled family there. This weekly meeting at the museum is scheduled for Mondays for convenience, because the Parkers always come in to the city on Mondays for Rachel's ballet lessons. The Parkers live outside of the city, but drive in often for the children's classes (e.g., ballet and music lessons). Tipper, Rachel, and David often leave the house in the morning and do not get back until the evening.

Museums are good places to stop and fit in some educational activities: "[We go] during wait time or because it is on the way to something else" (M.2.1). The motivations of practicality and education are sometimes difficult to distinguish. For example, dress rehearsals for Rachel's ballet performance are in the same large performance complex as a museum. Tipper seizes upon this as an opportunity: "During [Rachel's] intensive Nutcracker ballet rehearsals is a good time to go to the State Museum since we can go on the same parking tab" (P.3.1). Choosing a museum to visit may have as much to do with its location as its exhibitions. One friend of the Parkers keeps museum information in her purse. If she and her children are out and have an hour to fill, they find the nearest museum. When Tipper lists local museums she reflects the notion of the museum as a convenient stopping place (although she never uses the word convenient). She includes public spaces, such as hospitals, airports, and office lobbies, as well as more traditional, but obscure museums such as galleries at local universities and community colleges. The Parkers and their museum-going friends fit Hood's (1983) profile of the frequent museum-goer: they place a high value on doing something worthwhile in their leisure time.

The first time I met the Parkers at a museum, it was for a meal. The Parkers had been out of the house since early that morning, and they would not return home until early that evening. Their day included everything from running errands to music lessons, as well as ballet and tap classes. This was not an uncommon day for the Parkers. When Tipper realized that she was spending $150 per week on drive-through lunches without even liking the food, she began packing lunch on their busiest days to eat at a suitable location during the day—often at a museum. Consequently, she now believes that, "Museums are sometimes places to sit and eat lunch" (M.7.2). The Parkers frequently have lunch at the cafeteria of the local science museum, a practice allowed by the museum, and encouraged by the wonderful panoramic view of the city visible only from the cafeteria.

The Parkers first bought a membership to the local science museum because they loved the train exhibits there. They had a membership to the local botanical garden and art museum, but they did not renew it when the museum started charging an additional fee to get into the most popular yearly special exhibition, Trees of Christmas. They go to the local science museum most frequently. They also go to the local historical museum frequently. They will go to see a specific exhibition more than once, explaining that the first visit was with friends, and more social. On more than one occasion Tipper justifies a repeat visit to an exhibition by pointing out that one visit was not sufficient: "We saw it before but it was just a quick walk through" (M.9.1). There is a sense of different intensities involved in exploring an exhibition.

The Parkers also go to museums while on vacation. Tipper checks the reciprocal entrance list that comes with her local museum memberships to see if there are museums that will admit them without a charge in the city they are visiting. The Parkers will even stop at a city known to have a good museum along the way to their destination city. They take yearly business trips to Florida and return to a botanical garden there every time.

Tipper also reminisces about museums. She talks about going to the blockbuster traveling King Tut exhibit in a nearby city before the children could walk, carrying them in their "pack" (M.7.1). Tipper also speaks about small local museums: "Everything has a museum" (M.3.1). She lists examples like a small tool collection at a suburban agricultural center, art displays in downtown business lobbies, and historical sites throughout the area. Tipper notes that her daughter Rachel particularly likes historical museums and historical reenactments; David likes everything.

Rachel's and David's Use of Museums

Rachel and David have very different ways of visiting museums. The Parkers go to a museum as a group, with one or occasionally both of their parents. I have observed Mark and David at a special exhibition opening in the evening, but typically Rachel and David go to museums during the day with Tipper. Upon entering a museum the family has a very brief orientation period (Falk, 1991) as they generally take very little time to decide what to do and where to go. As they approach an exhibition, Tipper usually asks one of the children to choose where to start. There is some talk like 'What is that?' or 'Is that one really softer?' or 'That one is just like the one you made at home,' all consistent with the identifying, describing, and interpreting conversations typical of museum visitors (Borun et al., 1998). The family quickly splits into smaller groups, or individuals. This is consistent with research that shows that museum visitors prefer to acquire information for themselves first before discussing it with others in their group (Hilke, 1985). But the consistency and pacing of their groupings varies among family members.

Rachel changes groups often, pairing with Tipper or sometimes her brother, and sometimes alone. Rachel also chooses to talk to people outside of her family. In contrast, as the rest of the family goes through an exhibition, David immediately falls behind. He reads every label, sometimes more than once. David takes notes in a small notebook that he keeps in his pocket during these visits. He rarely socializes outside of his family group, even when a stranger at the same exhibit talks to him. He is not rude, but he does not engage the person in conversation. This is not to characterize David as a nonsocial person—he is very talkative and engages in conversations with peers and adults alike. He simply chooses not to use museums in a very social way.

Tipper and Rachel usually have to wait for David to get to the end of an exhibition. They are willing to wait for him and do not urge him to go through the exhibition at a faster pace. As they wait, Tipper and Rachel critique the exhibition, comparing it to previous ones they have visited. Like other parents during a museum visit, Tipper takes on the role of teacher (Diamond, 1986). But Tipper's questions are generally more directed toward interpreting and analysis than simple "show and tell." After seeing one traveling exhibition based on multiple science topics around the theme of a television show, Rachel shrugs when her mother asks her what she learned, and replies, "There was a lot of different stuff" (M.10.2). Tipper agrees and they talk instead about a geology exhibition they preferred, eventually agreeing that it was better because it was all one topic. On another museum visit, David's critique of an exhibition was that it looks empty, or too brief. Tipper, Rachel, and David are all very comfortable critiquing exhibitions, comparing them to the many others they have visited.

When the Parkers visit the local science museum, they generally spend part of their visit in the museum's computer room. They usually do not sit together. Instead, they use a variety of software (e.g., Sim Ant and Mavis Beacon Typing). The computer room staff person knows the Parkers by name and is quick to point out any new software or websites she has found that she thinks will be of interest. Tipper often uses this time at the computer to look up ordering information about books or curriculum kits she has heard about, sometimes calling on David to help her negotiate her way around on the Web.

In the computer lab, Rachel uses the software for brief periods of time, moving on to different programs quickly. She spends more time talking to the people sitting on either side of her, both peers and adults. Rachel uses the computer as part of the social interaction, looking up websites related to the conversation. For example, after talking to a younger girl next to her about dancing in the Nutcracker, she searches for websites about the Nutcracker and looks to see if her ballet school has a website. David, when not helping his mother, uses some of the same programs as his sister, but for extended periods of time. On one visit, David spent an extended period of time on a computer game that I did not recognize. When I asked him what he was doing he replied that he was "learning problem solving skills" (M.11.1). Similar to his activities in exhibitions, David spends extended periods of time on a limited number of software programs.

David's Free-Choice Learning Activities

David's activities at the museum contrast with his sister's activities, but are consistent with his participation in other free-choice activities. One activity, however, seems different. David has become more and more interested in conducting since last summer. His interest is very focused on a conductor, Kathy Dean, who has been working with David in a mentor-like relationship. David's interest in conducting grows in an apprenticeship-like manner, as he attends rehearsals and concerts, and studies scores that Kathy recommends. Miss Kathy—as they now call her—also has an influence on David's nonconducting activities. She happened to mention she had been to Belize, so David and Rachel did a report on the country. Kathy has also started to give David and Rachel specific assignments, asking for reports on various conductors.

David's interest in conducting is intricately related to his interaction with the conductor, Kathy. Based on my observations, how he chose conducting and how he pursues it is different from how he chooses and pursues other free-choice learning activities. I thought I would examine this as a contrasting representative case (i.e., it is representative of how David does not usually choose and participate in free-choice learning activities). One interview was designed to elicit a more extensive description of how he chose to focus on conducting and how he has continued to learn about it. The interview was surprising. How David chooses and participates in conducting activities seems, in fact, representative of how he chooses and participates in many learning activities. Instead, it seems that museums are the anomaly.

In an effort to compare how David came to choose and participate in conducting to other free-choice learning activities, I ask him if he always learns things in the same way. He responds that "you just become interested in a subject (H.5.1)" and describes his interest in flight as an example.

> D: Well, um. Me and my neighbor got into some pretty interesting ideas. One was we just built a giant kite and pulled it behind our go-cart with one of us attached to it. That idea we kind of decided not to do because we have a lot of trees in our yard, and we figured that would be just a really stupid idea. And so, then we, I went on to doing a glider, with kind of like a go-cart attached to it with a motor in the back. With a propeller. I've seen those kind of airplanes before, and I just always, I just kind of wanted to build it. And I was just like making designs here and there. And, I actually made designs for gliders that you actually pedal. But I never actually got to build any of these, but. Probably because they were going to be like in the thousands, and I have like two hundred dollars to my name. And, so. But it was a lot of fun to think about doing that.

David describes a series of flight-related activities he and his neighbor pursued designing gliders, propeller-based flying machines, and other contraptions. His flight-related activities are described as social and spatial; similar to his conducting activities, but in notable contrast to his museum activities. Later in the interview when I ask David to describe other projects, his accounts are still social and spatial. For example, he reports on building a clubhouse with his neighbor, detailing their work with pulleys to make a sign and other features. When pressed to directly compare his conducting activities to other free-choice learning activities, David connects his interests and participation in activities to social interaction.

> K: Does that . . . so in the flying situation you met someone, well, she's your neighbor, so you started talking about the flying and working on that. And in the conducting you met [the conductor]. Is it usually that you meet someone and you start talking to them about these ideas, or do you . . .
>
> D: Sometimes I come up with these ideas and then I just talk to them about them, and it just turns out that they have the same interest, and we'll just go off from there.

This is a moment where David's museum way of doing things that I have observed is challenged by his discourse. He does not talk about his ideas with other people at museum exhibits; he takes notes. Yet interest and social interaction drive David's other learning activities. This is consistent across disciplines (music, science, history) and environments (home, outdoors) with the exception of museums. David's activities in museums most resemble descriptions of formal learning activities: They are individual (Resnick, 1987), and there is a lack of social motivation (Greenfield & Lave, 1982). Outside of the museum environment, David's activities resemble descriptions of informal learning: They are embedded in daily life activities, the learner is responsible for imparting knowledge and skill, and the activity is motivated by social contribution of novices and their participation in the adult sphere (Greenfield & Lave, 1982). Additionally, David's nonmuseum activities involve contextualized and shared reasoning (Resnick, 1987). In museums, the informal learning environments designed for social activities, David is a formal learner.

DISCUSSION

What Counts as Education

Because the Parkers educate their children at home, I had a biased expectation that their educational activities at home would resemble school-based activities and would be driven by an educational framework established by Tipper and based on state educational mandates. Instead, freed from the constraints of national or state curriculum-based definitions of education and learning, most of Rachel and David's home-based activities are interest based. Tipper does distinguish between learning and nonlearning activities. But her definition of learning leads her to incorporate interest-based activities into their state-mandated educational time. The Parkers do not differentiate between free-choice activities and mandatory educational activities. The benefits of allowing educational activities to be based on the learner's interests has already been well researched and applied to school and museum settings (Csikszentmihalyi, 1990; Csikszentmihalyi & Hermanson, 1995). Participation in interest-based activities that are intrinsically rewarding can push a person to higher levels performance and even lead a person to discover things about himself as a learner.

Places for Learning

The Parkers see many environments as resources for education—including environments that would not typically be classified as educational. The tension between definitions of educational activities and environments signals a possibility that people's limited use of public educational resources (Miller, 1992) may be due to tensions between the publics' definitions of what is and what is not educational and the definitions held by the supporting organizations and government bodies.

Research has already shown that people who visit museums just once or twice a year differ from frequent museum visitors in their belief that the leisure attributes they desire are not available in sufficient quantities in museums. The Parker's firm belief in the worth of museums as a leisure environment extends to the point of feeling a sense of ownership. The Parkers are comfortable going to museums for short or long periods of time, even using their practical facilities (e.g., the cafeteria) instead of the educational facilities on some visits. Their confident use of leisure environments extends even to their definitions of what counts as a museum: They include office lobbies and university lounges as educational resources. An examinaion of people's perceptions of educational activities and institutions may reveal a much stronger effect of perception than previously realized. This only reinforces the need to re-evaluate and re-present museums to address visitors' agendas.

Institutional Versus Personal Agendas

For David, choosing and participating in most activities is a social and spatial experience. The interview about conducting indicates a distinctive social and spatial driven pattern in his participation in free-choice learning activities. Yet there is a tension in David's use of free-choice learning environments. My observations of David in museums—an environment designed for free-choice learning and social interaction—point to almost a complete lack of socially driven participation. David, who has never attended a school, turns to museums as a formal learning environment, carefully taking notes in silence as if there is a teacher lecturing. When is the museum a formal learning environment? When the visitor treats it as one.

David is not the only one differentiating his learning; his family and the very design of the exhibitions are allowing it. Physical and unspoken cues mediate David's use of museums. Tipper and Rachel willingly move ahead through exhibits, allowing him to stay behind taking notes. The design of the museum also mediates this interaction. Research on the design and use of museum exhibitions shows that they can interfere with group use and interaction (Borun et al., 1998; Hensel, 1987). Borun has shown that exhibits can be redesigned to accommodate and encourage group use and interaction, but how do we redesign the museum culture to accommodate social learning?

CONCLUSIONS

Frank Oppenheimer, the founder of The Exploratorium, is reputed to have said that people cannot fail museums. David's interactions in museums and other free-choice learning environments show that perhaps museums can fail people—that is, they can fail to meet the agendas and needs that people bring to museums. If these same expectations and needs are met in other free-choice learning activities, it is not suprising that these people may not choose to go to museums. The nonmuseum visitor does use other leisure environments, just not museums. David does go to museums with his family, but he uses them in an isolated manner in sharp contrast to his other learning activities. Research has shown that visitors can use information presented in museums to draw conclusions that are opposite to the museum's intended outcome. David's case suggests that visitors can use the very learning environment of a museum in a manner that is opposite to a museum's intentions.

Our understandings of how museums are used will be heightened by including the complex interconnected network of learning resources that make up our educational infrastructure. The Parkers see museums as just one of many educational resources, and they are not restrained by the borders established by institutions. The public's identity of museums may be inexorably intertwined with the larger educational infrastructure. A willingness to expand our research boundaries to other free-choice learning environments may reflect a more realistic view of the public's view of the educational infrastructure.

Research that expands, or even ignores the institutionally defined boundaries of learning environments has shown promising results. One extreme example is Howard Gardner's (1991) suggestion that schools should be more like museums. Another suggestion is that museums may be a good place for schools to test innovative educational programs (Schauble et al., 1996). Universities and museums have worked together to do just that, using the museum as a laboratory to test university-developed prototypes.

Perhaps the most interesting research will come from programs and environments that occur at the boundaries of different types of learning environments. Consider these examples: the *Fifth Dimension* literacy consortium of technology-supported after-school programs (Cole, 1996); the *Cheche Konnen* program, ("search for knowledge" in Haitian Creole) providing an alternative approach to science education in language-minority classrooms (Rosebery, Warren, & Conant, 1992); *Schools for Thought*, an integration of social structures for supporting learning, authentic problem solving, and computer-supported knowledge building (Bruer, 1993); and, the growing number of museum schools in the United States (Science Museum of Minnesota, 1995). A willingness to cross the institutionally established boundaries of learning environments will afford a better model, and ultimately, a better understanding of our complex educational infrastructure.

ACKNOWLEDGMENTS

The research reported here was supported in part by the Museum Learning Collaborative (MLC), Learning Research and Development Center, University of Pittsburgh. The MLC is funded by the Institute for Museum and Library Services, the National Science Foundation, the National Endowment for the Arts, and the National Endowment for the Humanities. The opinions expressed are solely those of the author and no official endorsement from the funders should be presumed.

This study would not have been possible without the generous participation of the Parkers (pseudonym), who welcomed my presence in their family as an opportunity to give back to the museum community that they enjoy as an integral part of their life.

REFERENCES

American Association of Museums. (1984). *Museums for a new century: A report of the commission on museums for a new century.* Washington DC: Author.

American Association of Museums. (1992). *Excellence and equity: Education and the public dimensions of museums.* Washington DC: Author.

Barton, D., & Hamilton, M. (1998). *Local literacies.* London: Routledge.

Borun, M., Cleghorn, A., & Garfield, C. (1995). Family learning in museums: A bibliographic review. *Curator, 38*(4), 262–270.

Borun, M., Dritsas, J., Johnson, J. I., Peter, N. E., Wagner, K. F., Fadigan, K., Jangaard, A., Stroup, E., & Wenger, A. (1998). *Family learning in museums: The PISEC perspective.* Philadelphia, PA: The Franklin Institute.

Bruer, J. T. (1993). *Schools for thought: A science of learning in the classroom.* Cambridge, MA: MIT Press.

Bunch, J. (1997). Educational philosophy and program planning; Applying learning theory and research in youth museums. In M. Maher (Ed.), *Collective vision: Starting and sustaining a children's museum* (pp. 79–89). Washington, DC: Association of Youth Museums.

Cole, M. (1996). *Cultural psychology: A once and future discipline.* Cambridge, MA: Harvard University Press.

Crane, V. (1994). An introduction to informal science learning and research. In V. Crane, H. Nicholson, M. Chen, & S. Bitgood (Eds.), *Informal science learning: What research says about television, science museums, and community-based projects* (pp. 1–14). Dedham, MA: Research Communications, Ltd.

Crowley, K., & Callanan, M. (1998). Describing and supporting collaborative scientific thinking in parent-child interactions. *Journal of Museum Education, 23*(1), 12–17.

Csikszentmihalyi, M. (1990). *Flow: The psychology of optimal experience.* New York: Harper & Row.

Csikszentmihalyi, M., & Hermanson, K. (1995). Intrinsic motivation in museums: Why does one want to learn? In J. H. Falk & L. D. Dierking (Eds.), *Public institutions for personal learn-*

ing: Establishing a research agenda (pp. 67–77). Washington, DC: American Association of Museums.

Curry, T., & Bloome, D. (1998). Learning to write by writing ethnography. In A. Egan-Robertson & D. Bloome (Eds.), *Students as researchers of culture and language in their own communities* (pp. 37–58). Cresskill, NJ: Hampton Press.

Diamond, J. (1986). The behavior of family groups in science museums. *Curator, 29*(2), 139–154.

Dierking, L. D. (1987). Parent-child interactions in free-choice learning settings: An examination of attention-directing behaviors. *Dissertation Abstracts International, 49*(04), 778A.

Dierking, L. D., & Falk, J. H. (1994). Family behavior and learning in informal science settings: A review of the research. *Science Education, 78*(1), 57–72.

Falk, J. H. (1991). Analysis of the behavior of family visitors in natural history museums. *Curator, 34*(1), 44–50.

Falk, J. H., & Dierking, L. D. (2000). *Learning from museums: Visitor experiences and the making of meaning.* Walnut Creek, CA: Altamira Press.

Falk, J. H., Moussouri, T., & Coulson, D. (1998). The effect of visitors' agendas on museum learning. *Curator, 41*(2), 107–120.

Fine, M. (1991). *Framing drop-outs.* Albany, NY: SUNY Press.

Gardner, H. (1991). *The unschooled mind: How children think and how schools should teach.* New York: Basic Books.

Gilmore, P., & Glatthorn, A. (1982). *Children in and out of school.* Washington, DC: Center for Applied Linguistics.

Gleason, M. E., & Schauble, L. (2000). Parents' assistance of their children's scientific reasoning. *Cognition and Instruction, 17*(4), 343–378.

Greenfield, G., & Lave, J. (1982). Cognitive aspects of informal education. In D. Wagner & H. W. Stevenson (Eds.), *Cultural perspectives on child development* (pp. 181–207). San Francisco: Freeman.

Heath, S. B. (1991). "It's about winning!" The language of knowledge in baseball. In L. B. Resnick, J. M. Levine, & S. D. Teasley (Eds.), *Perspectives on socially shared cognition* (pp. 101–124). Washington DC: American Psychological Association.

Hein, G. E. (1998). *Learning in the museum.* London: Routledge.

Hensel, K. A. (1987). Families in a museum: Interactions and conversations at displays. *Dissertation Abstracts International, 49-09.* University Microfilms No. 8824441.

Henze, R. C. (1992). *Informal teaching and learning: A study of everyday cognition in a Greek community.* Hillsdale, NJ: Lawrence Erlbaum Associates.

Hilke, D. D. (1985). The family as a learning system: An observational study of families in museums. In B. H. Butler & M. B. Sussman (Eds.), *Museum visits and activities for family life enrichment* (pp. 101–129). New York: Haworth Press.

Hilke, D. D. (1987). Museums as resources for family learning: Turning the question around. *The Museologist, 50*(175), 14–15.

Hood, M. G. (1983). Staying away: Why people choose not to visit museums. *Museum News, 61*(4), 50–57.

Inverness Research Associates. (1996). *An invisible infrastructure: Institutions of informal science education, Vol. I.* Washington, DC: Association of Science-Technology Centers.

Leichter, H. J., Hensel, K., & Larsen, E. (1989). Families and museums: Issues and perspectives. *Marriage and Family Review, 13*(3/4), 15–50.

Lines, P. (1999). *Homeschoolers: Estimating numbers and growth. Web edition.* Washington, DC: U.S. Department of Education, Office of Educational Research and Improvement [online]. Available: www.ed.gov/offices/OERI/SAI/homeschool/homeschoolers.pdf

McManus, P. M. (1994). Families in museums. In R. Miles & L. Zavala (Eds.), *Toward the museum of the future: New European perspectives.* London: Routledge.

Miller, J. D. (1992). The public use of science and technology museums: Is science-technology museum attendance decreasing? *Association of Science-Technology Centers Newsletter 20*(2), 11–12.

Moussouri, T. (1997). *Family agendas and family learning in hands-on museums.* Unpublished dissertation, University of Leicester, England.

Resnick, L. B. (1987). Learning in school and out. The 1987 AERA Presidential Address. *Educational Researcher, 16*(9), 13–20.

Roberts, L. C. (1997). *From knowledge to narrative: Educators and the changing museum.* Washington DC: Smithsonian Institution Press.

Rosebery, A., Warren, B., & Conant, F. R. (1992). Appropriating scientific discourse: Findings from language-minority classrooms. *Journal of the Learning Sciences, (2),* 61–94.

Rosenfeld, S. B. (1980). Informal learning in zoos: Naturalistic studies of family groups. *Dissertation Abstracts International, 41*(07). (University Microfilms No. AAT80-29566).

Schauble, L., Beane, D. B., Coates, G. D., Martin, L. W., & Sterling, P. V. (1996). Outside the classroom walls: Learning in informal environments. In L. Schauble & R. Glaser (Eds.), *Innovations in learning: New environments for education* (pp. 5–24). Mahwah, NJ: Lawrence Erlbaum Associates.

Science Museum of Minnesota. (1995). *Museum school symposium 1995: Beginning the conversation.* St. Paul, MN: Science Museum of Minnesota.

Vallance, E. (1995). The public curriculum of orderly images. *Educational Researcher, 24*(2), 4–13.

Chapter **4**

Talking to Oneself: Diaries of Museum Visits

Gaea Leinhardt
University of Pittsburgh

Carol Tittle
City University of New York

Karen Knutson
University of Pittsburgh

Museums are fundamentally social and cultural institutions. They are cultural in that museums are where our society gathers and preserves valued and visible records of social, scientific, and artistic accomplishments. They are social in that the collector, curator, designer, and educator are in tacit and sometimes explicit dialogue with the visitors. They are also social in that they are places where groups go together to visit exhibitions. The study we are reporting in this chapter serves as a counterpoint to the studies of conversational groups represented in the rest of this volume in that it focuses on the private and interior conversations of the individual as he or she experiences and records the museum encounter. The record is written instead of spoken and is distinctly authored, edited, and selected. At first glance it might appear that the idea of an inner conversation is an artificial extension of the concept of a socially produced audible (or visible) act of communication between two or more people. But as recent studies of electronic conversations (Aleven & Ashley, 1997; Schofield, 1999) and older theories of dialogue with the self (G. H. Mead, 1934) have shown, the critical features of conversation, namely an awareness of social context, self-monitoring and reflection, a strong sense of other, are often preserved in these non face-to-face settings.

By adding the diary study to the interconnected web of studies presented in this volume, we intend to illuminate some of the ways in which more completely developed elaborations of meaning unfold. In studies in which we follow participants as they experience the exhibitions and interview them afterwards we have the advantage of the intensity and immediacy of the experience. In this study we have the advantage of reflection and selection of experiences; what is reported as significant in the diaries are presumably the more memorable aspects of the visit. Memory studies add to the contextual picture of museum learning (McManus, 1993; Stevenson, 1991). The resulting diaries portray socially constructed semantic and episodic memories (Cobb & Bowers, 1999; McManus, 1993; Neisser, 1982; Tulving, 1983). In discussing learning in museums many of us have referred to the "conversations on the way home." We know what we mean by this (or think we do) but we are frustrated by not being able to capture the language and thoughts by which the unique and special experience is folded into, and becomes a part of, the visitor's larger sense of self—the manner in which the details become appropriated by the visitor and the results of that appropriation (Wertsch, 1997). In this study we have laid out before us the results of imposing a sense of meaning on an experience. The simultaneous crackling of events and experiences are drawn out into the forced linearity of prose. The odd personal mixture of the trivial and profound have all been re-weighted by the diarist's own hand.

Here we trace the ways identity and personal history play themselves out in interpreting the museum experience. Forty diary entries from eight individuals, each having visited five museum exhibitions, are studied for the ways the diarists approached the institutions, their sense of the environment, and the ways that they built meaning out of engagement.

Visits to museums have been described at a variety of levels of detail from broad brush strokes of the experience (Falk & Dierking, 1992) to more fine-grained examinations (Silverman, 1990). In Silverman's (1990, 1995) discussions of meaning making in the museum she emphasized the contributions of the individual's identity and experiences to the museum encounter. At a more observational level Pekarik, Doering, and Karns (1999) emphasized the role of specific classes of experiences and patterns of behavior in the museum. To these researchers we owe the recognition of not only specific museum experience but of the more general categories of expectations about the objects to be seen, the kinds of cognitive potentials, the introspective experiences that the museum affords and the social opportunities that museums in general support. In work not directly related to museums Wertsch (1997) has discussed the ways that historical narratives are appropriated and mediated by groups in the former Soviet Union. In a similar sense our diarists molded and formed their museum experiences by melding knowledge and values with curatorial presentation in a private conversation (Rogoff, 1990).

At times these recollections of museum visits illustrate aspects of Dewey's notion of "aesthetic experience." The experience with the object includes completeness and uniqueness, and,

> the underlying emotion that permeates an experience has . . . ups and downs and may . . . undergo . . . transformation. . . . Those changes, however, form a coherent whole . . . the emotional history of the experience. . . . Dewey wants us to understand that emotional unity is fundamentally aesthetic. (Jackson, 1998, p. 11)

What makes the transactions with the object an *experience* as distinct from description, is that the diary has integrity, coherence, informal structure, attachment to an object, and it is cumulative. The narrative (text) provides a framing of the experience, its meaning and interpretations, and the viewer is giving shape to the experience. The "object" of an experience could be a single work of art, an exhibit, or even the museum itself.

These strongly singular "experiences" tempt us, at one level, to simply reproduce the diaries and exclaim, "Look! Aren't these marvelous!" Pulling apart, counting, and reconstructing what has already been done with thought and care by these diarists seems almost destructive. However, studying the diaries as text and discourse opens up a window onto insight. Through these texts we can do two things: First, we can understand the general construction of the visit and the critical features that impact it; second, we can examine the diaries to see which cognitive tools are used as the diarists interpret and enfold their experiences, we can note the mediating features of the museums that the diarists themselves note, and we can examine which of the many possible ideas and themes become appropriated by the diarists and woven into their identities. We can explore the ways in which the specifics of the experiences in different types of museums change or do not change the interpretations of the diarists and the ways in which these diaries show or do not show development over time.

DESIGN

Population

Ten women and eight men, all of whom were acquaintances or friends of at least one of the authors, who were known to visit museums regularly, and who were known to naturally do some level of writing were approached and asked to participate. The approach was quite simple, usually an email or telephone call explaining the overall MLC mission and the role of the diary study. If the person agreed to participate they were given a series of tasks and a promise of payment upon completion of the overall task. Each participant was then asked to write a personal description; to agree to visit five museums in the subsequent 4 to 6 months; and to write up a diary account of each visit. Any museum was acceptable and any spacing of the visits was acceptable. Eight of the women and seven of the men agreed to participate. All of the women who participated handed in all five entries within 7 months and one man handed in one entry (a second man sent in his diary 4 months later and the data are not included).[1]

The diarists ranged in age from 21 to 67 years. Three of our diarists were under 33 and five were over 55. Their educational level varied from college student to Ph.D. Their occupations included opera singer, university advisor, educator, university professor, docent, TV producer, and insurance investigator. Their frequency of museum visits ranged from once a year to 48 times a year with one going approximately 120 times a year. Of the three under age 33 the average number of visits per person was six visits per year, whereas the average number of visits to a museum for those over 55 was 21 (not including the docent who was in a museum at least 120 days a year). Their personal interests in museums ranged from very little interest to deep subject matter curiosity and study to personal fulfillment and expansion. The diarists were clustered on the two coasts of the continent (Portland, Seattle, San Francisco, New York, Boston), with one across the Atlantic in London.

Task

The diarists were free to visit any museum that they wanted to for any purpose. Each diary entry was to be written as soon as possible after the visit and was to be between three and five typewritten pages in length. All of the entries were at least three pages although some were longer than five pages. Diarists were asked to include any pictures, cards, flyers, or catalogues that they felt would help us understand what they were writing about. The diaries were sent to the first two authors. Upon completion of the five diaries each diarist was paid 500 dollars. The diarists made a total of 40 visits. The diarists made 28 visits to art exhibitions—in art museums and other museums; 10 visits to history or natural history exhibitions—these included historical reconstructions, historical surveys of instrumentation or scientific ideas, and history museums; and two visits to live exhibitions—a zoo and a forestry center. We asked that each diary include the purpose and circumstance of the visit. We did not encourage nor discourage people taking notes or using any other device for remembering their experiences. In the sections that follow each quotation will be followed by a pseudonym and a number, for example, (Molly, 7.4). This means that the seventh diarist was writing about her fourth visit. Thus, the reader can always tell both which

[1]Follow-up conversations and emails with the men who had agreed but subsequently did not write the diaries did not turn up any clear pattern—the men were distributed geographically and demographically in almost identical patterns to the women. Each individual had a slightly different reason for not sending in the diaries.

segments come from the same diarist and which diary in the sequence of five it represents.

Analysis

Each diary was read at least five times by the three authors. We then worked on parsing the general structure of each diary in the following way: We located and interpreted the purpose of the visit; located and interpreted the diarist's response to the general layout, orientation, or environment of the exhibition; and identified at least one central connecting interpretive concept on the part of the diarists—that is, the main big point or elaboration (sometimes there were several). We then considered the kinds of cognitive tools that were used by the diarists as they built up meaningful interpretations of their visits and the ways in which the mediating features of the museum interacted as the diarists appropriated messages and meanings of their own.[2] These separate structures and the specific codes within them described below all emerged from our joint readings of the diaries. The structures and codes are consistent with the sense of mediation and appropriation present in sociocultural theory—our processes and analyses were emergent.

Coding

In order to describe the purpose of the visit we developed three codes that seemed to capture the various reasons that the diarists gave in their writing. *Floating* meant that the diarist appeared open to any experience and had few preconceived ideas as to what the exhibit was about or would mean to them. *Focused* meant that the diarist had a clear purpose in going to a particular show, usually to expand her understanding of a particular art form or to learn a specific thing; frequently these visits were prompted by seeing articles in a local paper. *Challenging* meant that the diarist wanted to stretch herself or force herself into an unfamiliar situation. Each diary was coded for one and only one purpose.

In order to describe the environmental impact we considered whether the diarist made any particular mention of the museum environment at all; if not then the environment was coded as *neutral.* If the environment was described mainly as a context or a setting for the exhibit then we coded that environment as *frame.* If the environment was melded into a part of the exhibit and became as much a part of the discussion or analysis as any object then we described that as *content.* Finally, in some cases where we felt that the environment was described as disruptive or unpleasantly confusing, we

[2]We use the concept of cognitive tool here in the way that Greeno (1991) uses it.

labeled it as *conflict.* Each diary was coded for one and only one environmental impact, although parts of some diaries clearly reflected multiple responses.

In order to describe the kinds of cognitive tools that our diarists used as they constructed meaning in their writing we made use of four categories. These categories all treat the diary and the diarist as if there were, at least at some level, an awareness of self as diarist and an awareness at some level of us as readers. The first tool is *description.* The diarist recounts in a fairly complete fashion most of the objects in the exhibit. A second tool is *analysis.* When diarists use analysis they focus on a few objects and inspect their component parts in great detail, often elaborating on those details as seen in other settings. Another tool is *narrative identification.* When using narrative identification as a tool for making meaning from objects in a museum our diarists spun out a small (one or two paragraph long) story usually attached to an analytic feature but sometimes attached to themselves as possible players in the scene. Diarists deliberately blurred the lines between the objects in the exhibit and themselves—sometimes drawing the meaning or interpretation of an object out into their own lives, or at other times imagining themselves in the metaphorical situation completely. Finally, some diarists *wove* several strands of analysis together, moving from large panoramic images to very small fine-grained components as they examined a specific piece. This was not very common but was very noticeable when it occurred; it was a kind of intertextuality in which personal travel experience, a particular object, and detailed textual descriptions were merged. Two other tools that we did not retain because they were diarist specific were *argument*—in this case the diarist argued against the curatorial decisions, and *docent*—in this case the diarist imagined herself to be conducting a tour.[3] The diaries were coded for the predominant cognitive tool, although most diarists used several. Intercoder reliability for codes was 83% on a 30% sample of the data.

RESULTS

> The paintings are not beautiful. It is the light in them that is overwhelmingly beautiful. I look at these paintings and ask: "how *does* he do that?" . . . the next room was a study in the light present in storms lashing open fields and roads, and three or four paintings of the fires in eastern Washington a few years ago, the light in the fire being the subject. These paintings are dark, grey, wet, foggy. They look like the wet, charcoal grey days all too familiar in Northwest winters, and make you grab metaphorically for the gore tex jacket. The light in the storm pictures is present yet subtle. If the light on the mason jars is focused, laser beam-sharp, the light in these pictures is diffused, hopeful, want-

[3]See Abu-Shumays and Leinhardt (chap. 2, this volume) for discussion of this latter stance.

ing to be, but uncertain. I am reminded of how Northwesterners look at grey wet skies and say, hopefully, "look it's lightening up." We have a finely nuanced range of greys that substitutes white grey for sun yellow in our winter psyches, allowing our sun-starved winter souls to be satisfied with the high, white grey of a wispy overcast, and not the clear, sky blues and yellows of a New England winter day. (Megan, Art, 1.2)

. . . a raven standing on top of a giant clam shell. . . . The carving is situated on a carpeted pedestal in a sort of rotunda, surrounded by carpeted benches so that people can walk or sit all the way around the carving . . . it is meant to depict the Haida story of how the Haida people . . . came to be . . . there was a big flood that covered the earth for a long time. After it receded, Raven was walking along the beach, looking for something to break the monotony. Finally he came upon a huge, half-buried clam shell. He bent closer to examine it and saw that the shell was full of tiny, frightened looking creatures. He leaned towards them and "with his smooth trickster's tongue, coaxed and cajoled and coerced them to come out and play in his wonderful new shiny world." . . . I really enjoyed this piece, although whether it was because of the art itself or the story behind it I'm not sure. I suspect that as usual it was the mixture of the two. . . . The people inside the clam shell were really great—they were in all sorts of scared and topsy-turvy looking positions, and of some you could only see pieces, like a hand or a rear end, poking out from inside the shell. The raven on top was covered with all kinds of intricate carvings, including a big, upside down face on the top of its tail. . . . Mostly . . . I loved the way everything—the roundness, the lighting, the simplicity of the pale yellow wood, and that chaos of what it depicted—combined to catch an instant in time and freeze it for anyone and everyone to see. It was so completely unto itself, and yet it represented the creation of humanity. Somehow the wholeness of it really worked for me. (Jane, History, 3.1)

The first thing I saw when I got to the third floor was a bunch of muted green rectangular objects attached to the wall near the elevator. Each object was attached directly above the next in a stack formation, almost like rungs in a ladder, and the caption next to it said "Green Stack" (in case we couldn't figure that out). Even though the title was rather uncreative and the rectangles could have been a brighter green, I thought this piece looked pretty cool. The squares looked good on the wall, and I thought it was a creative idea to put them there. (Molly, Art, 7.4)

As these three quotes show, our diarists, in describing objects in the various exhibits, wrote richly and responded deeply. Some diaries show a continuous connection to a larger frame of reference and embedding of the experience in the world at large. The discussion of light and grey in the first segment by Megan shows, we think, how this diarist responded to the messages of the curator and the artist to enhance or expand her own experiences of Northwestern winter skies and to interpret the specifics of the painting. The next segment offers a rather detailed description of an object and Jane's responses to it. In this passage we see the diarist drawn completely into the work and sounding detached from the rest of her own or the museum's world. In the last passage we see Molly considering the effectiveness independent of the construction effort, and with less engagement. In some senses she is trying to "get" the message of the museum and the modern art.

How did our diarists come to see what they did? Was it a simple matter of who they are? Was it a matter of their intentions and plans? Was it the skill and insight of the curatorial staff involved? In the next sections we examine the varying purposes and intentions that each diarist had on each visit, the ways in which they responded to the overall environment, and then examine the major message that emerged from a sample of diaries. We examine these major messages in terms of the cognitive tools used, the mediating factors clearly present, and the kinds of appropriations being made.

Purposes

At some level the purpose for all of the museum visits was to help fulfill the obligation of participating in this study. That is, we, as authors, can never be sure that any one of the diarists would have gone to a particular exhibition on a particular day if they had not been a part of the study. However, beyond that reservation, all diarists expressed personal and convincing reasons for the visits they made.

We did notice patterns among the purposes. On some occasions the purpose was clearly to pass the time or to enrich a portion of a day—we call these *floating* purposes because the sense we got in reading the diaries was that the individual was open to whatever the experience might have to offer—purposes of these types ranged from almost aimless: "Often I find myself going to museums to 'find out' without having planned to do so. This lack of planning gives me a sense of relaxation and adventure. And rarely do I read anything beforehand about exhibits—I like the freedom of discovering things on my own in museums" (Celine, 4.1) to introspective and almost metaphysical, "I almost always go into the museum at Lincoln Center for that solace of the soul it provides," (Anne, 2.3) or simply social, "this visit was an opportunity for us to spend time together at the Metropolitan Museum of Art. We enjoy being able to do something we both like, and usually have lunch together afterwards" (Sara, 6.3).

On other occasions the purpose for the visit was intensely *focused* and intellectual. We considered visits in which the diarist wanted to see a specific object, examine a particular feature of a display, or was responding to an analytic piece of writing that she had read to be of these "focused" types. "I decided to visit Tibet House and this exhibit since I am currently trying to learn more about Tibetan art after a visit to Tibet in June 1999. I expect to see Thangkas from different periods of Tibetan art and perhaps from different traditions in Tibetan art. I plan to expand my understanding of the iconography, probably not styles of individual artists, but perhaps some differentiation based on the century (time) of the art" (Sara, Art, 6.2).

Finally, some purposes were what we call *challenging* in the sense that the diarist was pressing herself to be expansive; the diarist seemed to sense that there was more to learn in a general way about her immediate environment. "Mostly, I'm going to this museum because it's different from the types of museum I usually visit, and because now and then I like to get a dose of what it means to be part of something larger than yourself, which is really, for all of its individual achievement and athlete-heros, what sports is all about" (Jane, History, 3.5).

When we hear the diarist's voice in these ways we can see that these purposes can either strongly shape the experience—as in the case of the focused visit to Tibet House, or simply leave the visitor open for whatever comes by as in the visit to Lincoln Center. What Pekarik et al. (1999) referred to as satisfaction would likewise be quite different depending on the initial purposes. Thus, a visit to a museum that included a gruff and unhelpful guard might cloud the experience if the purpose was closer to that "solace of the soul" than if the purpose was to "see Thangkas from different periods of Tibetan art." In the former case part of the purpose was a calming experience, whereas in the latter the clarity of focus might provide a kind of immunity from the disruptions of daily life.

Of the 40 diaries we soon saw that the purposes for the visits were neither a single property of the diarist nor of a museum type. That is, each diarist had a range of purposes, and each museum provoked a range of purposes. We judged that 10 of the diaries were of the floating type, 20 were of the focused type, 10 were of the challenging type. Were these different purposes evenly distributed among our diarists? Did our youngest and oldest, least experienced and most experienced, share evenly the different purposes? If this distribution held evenly for each of our visitors we would expect that out of the five visits 1 would be a floating type, 1 would be challenging, and two or three would be focused.

Our three younger diarists made a total of 15 visits. The purpose of seven of these visits we viewed as floating, 1 was focused, and 7 were challenging. What this suggests is that our younger diarists who were less engaged in museum visits (but probably far more than the average public) tended to go to the museum for less focused and structured purposes than did our senior diarists who were more engaged with museum going in general. Our five senior diarists visited museums for floating purposes four times, 18 were focused, and 3 were challenging. If the visits had been proportionately distributed among purposes we would have expected that out of the 25 visits 13 would have been focused, 6 would have been floating, and 6 would have been challenging. Thus, this group had a focused purpose approximately 30% more than would have been expected overall. Purposes did not seem to be influenced by the kind of museum visited.

Figure 4.1 shows the rather striking difference between the percentage of visits with a focused agenda and those that had a more personally challenging agenda. Our three younger diarists went to museums to challenge themselves in about the same proportion as they went to just have an experience. Our four senior visitors went far more frequently to a museum for a focused purpose. We noticed that our middle-aged visitor seemed to combine the features of the younger (under 33) and more senior (over 60) diarists.

We do not consider one purpose to be superior to another, nor, as we mentioned, do we sense that purpose is a consistent characteristic of an individual; rather it is a characteristic of the individual in interaction with the particular museum and exhibition and the particular time. We do consider that the intentions and purposes probably influence what the diarist ultimately felt about the visit and the meanings that they made from it. It is not obvious whether this pattern of differences between younger less experienced and older more experienced is a consequence of age and knowledge or whether it is a more subtle consequence of cultural change: shifts in interpretation about what a museum is and is for, or a shift in the role and view of authority and information. It does seem that there is quite a distinction between our senior and more frequent museum goers (four over 60) and our younger less frequent museum goers (three under 33); what makes this even more compelling as a consideration is that our one diarist in the

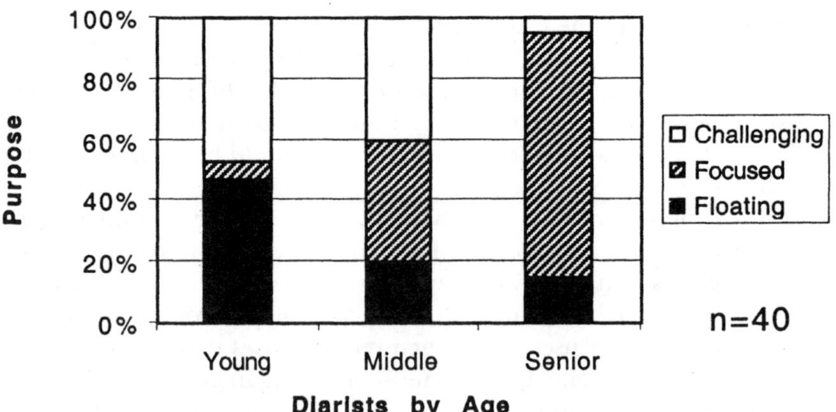

FIG. 4.1. Percentage of diaries coded by purpose: floating, challenging, or focused.

middle (55) is indeed in the middle. We see her diaries as having some of the focused feel (two of them did), some challenging (two did) and one floating. Her words, too, have a feel of self-exploration and discovery found more commonly among our younger visitors; but we also hear the respect and notice of the curatorial effort that has gone into the exhibits, a voice that tends to be silent among our younger diarists. We return to these issues at the end of the chapter.

Responding to the Environment

Our diarists may have each had unique and special reasons for selecting the exhibitions that they did. But these intentions could have been foiled, redirected, or enhanced by the specifics of the physical space. For most of the diarists it seemed natural to move from a brief description of the nature of the visit to some sort of discussion of the general layout of the exhibit and its environment. In some cases, of course, the environment was the visit. To give the sense of the range of ways in which the diarists responded to the environment we arrange the descriptions from the outside of the buildings to the inner layouts.

> When I first saw the Met. I was struck by the beauty of the building itself, especially the two beautiful fountains and the enormous staircase out front, with all the people sitting on it sunning themselves. They somehow reminded me very much of seals I saw in San Francisco harbor who were always lounging and playing in the sun. I think it was because these people seemed happy to be sitting on the steps . . . and that left me with the impression that the Met was a fun place to be. (Molly, Art, 7.1)

What is especially interesting about this reaction is not only does it resonate with those authors who incorporated the Metropolitan Museum into our adolescent New York City lives but how contrary it is to the more common academic postmodernist take on the meaning of the Metropolitan's overall layout. Here we do not see the visitor in front of the "Temple" diminished in stature and importance, overwhelmed by the grand scale of the architecture (Duncan, 1995; Duncan & Wallach, 1980). We see a visitor reminded of seals sunning themselves on rocks; a place of fun and relaxation. Becoming a part of that group does not require special expertise or badges of knowledge, rather the environmental setting is perceived as almost beckoning. Other museum environments are more challenging but also more informative with respect to their contents. In some cases the environment sets a calming mood, in other cases it jars the visitor into a unique setting. Sometimes the entrance is seen as part of the aesthetic experience as both context (the first quote below) and content (the second quote below):

The entrance is now up a ramp beside a large reflecting pool to double burnished copper doors. It is very understated and lovely. One enters into a small two story rotunda, with daylight pouring down through the skylights. The rotunda is Shaker simplicity itself, with a waxed colored stone floor and a single bench along the wall, thus the light plays an important role in setting the aesthetic ambiance . . . (Megan, Art, 1.2)

I entered the tower through a very narrow spiral set of stairs surrounded by old brick walls. There was a thick rope to hang on to as I made my way upstairs-no rails. . . . I felt like I was embarking up into a hide-away in a castle during a harsh Medieval conquest! As I made my way into the attic, I noticed some huge oak logs constituting the walls, the ceiling and support beams for the ceiling. Right away there was a flair of the "old" in the atmosphere, along with a mix of real herbs that were being displayed around. (Celine, History, 4.5)

In the second passage the diarist, who is visiting a museum of medieval medicine located in a 19th-century operating theatre in London, quite literally enters into the sense of the museum by reenacting the daily passages of the doctors who had worked in the operating theatre and apothecary shop. She responds to the authenticity and oldness of the place. In this environment size and scale is appropriately oppressive, not grand and intimidating, nor sweeping and inviting, but authentically crowding and pressing in, almost secretive.

Once inside the museum some of our diarists responded to the building as frame and setting for the objects within. They recognized the ways in which the buildings set a tone and set off the pieces being viewed but also how the totality created mood and ambiance.

Although *The Treasury of Saint Francis* [exhibit] contained but a modest number of objects, its setting in two large, wonderfully proportioned rooms to the right and left of the central, marble foyer, immediately gave it importance and grandeur. Both of these rooms have soaring creamy ceilings and heavy mouldings, while the walls, painted a subdued medium brown, perfectly set off the paintings and other artifacts. Taped Gregorian chanting added an ecclesiastical note. (Sally, Art, 8.4)

But not all of the responses to this framing were so completely positive. For some the fit between either the objects and their surrounds or the intentions of a museum and its surrounds were in some type of collision. Diarists noticed most clearly the situations of collision but as can be seen from the quotes that follow also sensed when the environment supported their activity of viewing and interacting with the contents.

The American Craft Museum has turned its entry into a bazaar. . . . Entering the museum for *Spirits of Color* was to be plunked into a scene of hot, active

> color and pattern. . . . There is always a sense of grandness in climbing or descending the Craft Museum stairs. The curve is gentle but emphatic. The pitch is high yet broad risers at the banister edge give the feet secure comfort. And at the head of the stairs in this exhibit was a large, stunning, blue-green patchwork piece. (Anne, Art, 2.2)

> The Berkeley Art Museum is an aggressively harsh modern building, built of concrete and steel. Its harsh, tent-like interior consists of a large central space that is broken up by great gravity-defying walls and slashes of glass windows admitting intense Californian light . . . the paintings had carried me into another world, and when I turned to go down, I again was assaulted by the aggressive architecture: diagonal concrete, slashes of light and a red painted steel automaton relentlessly hammering, the centerpiece of the floor below. I was filled with admiration that the curator of *Genji* had managed to create such a different mood in a space of quite another sensibility. (Sally, Art, 8.3)

In some cases there was either an ambiguity or duality with respect to the fit between environment and exhibit. If an historically recreated house is the "museum" is it the house itself or the objects in the house that are the museum or is it the integration between the two? If a zoo artfully displays animals in "their own habitat" but also places those habitats in the larger habitat of the park in which the zoo is located how do visitors respond? In the next two segments from diaries we see how these issues played themselves out as the diarists responded to being a part of and in some senses inside the exhibit itself.

Here Molly begins her description of a visit to the home of Paul Revere in Boston:

> As we got closer to the house, however, we entered an area of Boston that had very narrow streets, some of which were still partly paved with cobblestones. There were no side walks. The shadows from the buildings completely covered the streets, obscuring the sunlight. I know Paul would have been familiar with these streets. Somehow, it was a little unnerving to look at this part of the city, because it made me understand how cramped and claustrophobic the whole city would have been, and poor sanitation and wood smoke hanging over everything would have made the problems much worse.

> When we first saw his house I was filled with awe because Paul Revere actually lived here. This was the house he returned to after staying up all night chopping open chests and dumping tea into Boston Harbor. This was the house he left to make his famous night ride, and this was the house the many spies who reported things to him in the months leading up to the war came to. . . . Only the roof covered with wooden [shingles] and a sort of fragile look the house had showed that it was in fact very old. . . . not only was Paul's house still in tact, some of his old yard on the other side of the house was there too. (Molly, History, 7.2)

We can see quite literally that the diarist moves back and forth between the real modern world and the assumed historical world that is still present with its narrow sidewalkless streets before she plunges herself into the fantasy of Paul's daily life. Another, highly reflective, diarist both responds to the design features of the large-scale setting of the zoo and appreciates them as acts of design. She explores how the design works just as she had asked, how does the painter do that?

> The zoo is so beautiful. It really is a park and not just a bunch of animal habitats. The paths between habitat areas are richly landscaped to guide you naturally to the next viewing area. Viewing areas are either openings in the vegetation surrounding habitats, or lean-to enclosures with glass separating you from the habitat and animals. You feel very much a visitor to the animal's home because of this. . . . The pool is crossed by a small bridge on which you can just lean over and watch the water and feel like you're a thousand miles from a major urban area. (Megan, Zoo, 1.1)

Examples of the Fit Between Purpose and Environment

In addition to playing a role as a part of the exhibit, the environment was also a facilitator or impediment to the visit. All of our diarists commented at least to some extent about the layout within each museum, or the setting of the museum in its larger surround. Our docent commented extensively at a meta-level on each museum or exhibit area in terms of its probable feasibility for a docent guided tour. For her some layouts were clear and crisp and the general plan of the exhibition easy to find and follow, for example the Korean gallery of the Asian Art Museum. Although other visits, especially the one made to the Berkeley Art Museum, she described as both frustrating physically and confusing intellectually—that is, a chronological route through the exhibition was hampered by physical and design layout.

Overall, the environment interacted strongly with what for lack of a better term we will call the management of the visit. Most of our diarists were either clearly in control of how to manage the visit (going early, cycling through backwards, and getting maps to plan the visit) or were able to make use of the physical tools such as maps or the social ones such as helpful museum store clerks to design a path that in turn afforded them the opportunity to engage with the intent of the exhibition. Rarely, the combination of intention and museum environment combined to create a less than productive tension surrounding the visit. An example of the kind of confusion that did occur came from Celine's visit to a retrospective of Kurt Weill in London. Celine did not know who Kurt Weill was and did not automatically look for a chronological organization. In an attempt to avoid physical objects and people she worked through in a somewhat backward and roundabout fashion. This in turn led her to be confused about some of the assumptions of the exhibition.

Her purpose: "In sequence of buildings along the river, Royal Festival Hall was next. I went in. Quite randomly as most of my museum visits tend to be . . . Often I find myself going to museums to 'find out' without having planned to do so. This lack of planning gives me a sense of relaxation and adventure."

Her orientation and visit:

> The posters were mounted on display panels of about 1m × 2m arranged in a circle with both sides showing some aspects of Weill's life. At the entrance to the circle, there was a TV monitor with headphones as well as some brochures. I came into the circle from the right and walked initially counterclockwise. The first poster I saw was titled "I am an American." It consisted of a big black and white photograph of Weill covered up in cigarette smoke, reproductions of his identity cards, and some quotes about his sentiments—extremely positive—for the USA. This poster drew my attention fast since I am currently evaluating my own sentiments of the same country where I have spent the last 12 years of my life.
>
> Before going on to see the rest of the posters, I went back to the TV station and put a headphone on to listen to some of Weill's music. I don't know why. Maybe I was hoping there would be something special about him filtering through his music. The TV didn't work.
>
> At this point I realized that maybe the exhibit was to start from the other side of the circle and the posters were to be followed clockwise, eventually leading to his life in the US. I didn't care nevertheless. (Celine, Art, 4.1)

Other museum visits, in contrast, proved quite fruitful, where the subject matter was personally meaningful, the environment comfortable, and the objects intriguing. Anne, a quilter by hobby, visited an exhibit of contemporary quilts where the environment and the objects on display combined to create a resonant experience, which started, as we quoted earlier, with the sight of an particularly stunning quilt displayed at the top of the museum's magnificent staircase:

> Then I mounted the curving stairs. . . . And at the head of the stairs in this exhibit was a large, stunning, blue-green patchwork piece. To a quilter this was a marvel.
>
> The gallery is small by most standards. And yet to stand, to contemplate and to appreciate the works took me over an hour. Some of the time I spent listening to a docent give a class of children inside tips on how the quilt was made and why the design took the form it did.

> I will carry the image of those children sitting on the floor in front of various quilts and slowly warming to the lure of the cloth, the design, the stories. They did get involved. They did understand the ideas the quilts were picturing. They made me understand ever more surely that the quilting carries a tradition that is beyond the traditional bed covering. They are a way to make art that touches the soul. (Anne, Art, 2.2)

The diaries show us how the intentionality of the visit, the environments of the museum, the planning and orienting behavior of the visitor combine to support the activity of carrying out a particular museum visit. When the intention is highly focused and something in the environment is less than facilitating—large crowds for example, or confusing instructions—then quick tricks such as starting from the back, or going through an exhibit very fast and returning to one or two pieces are extremely helpful. On the other hand, when the intention is less focused and more generally experiential then the environmental features of format and display can either support, as in the case of the zoo, or inhibit the activity as in the case of the Kurt Weill exhibit.

Figure 4.2 shows the ways our diarists used the overall environment of the museum. Note that our younger visitors never treated the museum space as neutral and considered it as content 30% of the time. In contrast our senior visitors never treated the museum as content and tended to treat the environment as neutral more than 40% of the time. Fortunately, both younger and older diarists sometimes visited the same museum (the Metropolitan, for example) and indeed, they did treat that environment differently. Our middle diarist treated the museum as frame somewhat more than the younger diarists or our older ones and treated the environment as content more than our older diarists but less than our younger ones. Of

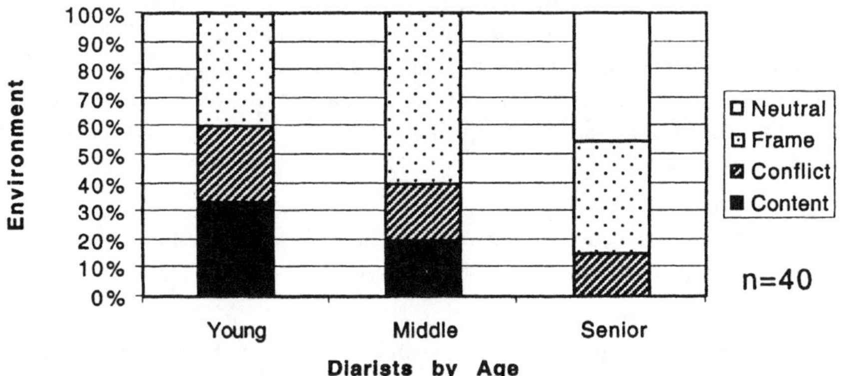

FIG. 4.2. Percentage of diaries coded by environmental effect: neutral, frame, conflict, or content.

course as with the diarists' purpose we can ask if it was the age of the diarist or the type of museum itself that influenced the sense and response to the environment. Appendix A shows there is very little difference by museum type. However, the historical museums are seen as content more frequently than art; on the other hand, art museums are seen as frame a disproportionate amount of the time.

A Core Experience

Up to this point we have presented the edges of the diarists' experiences. We have described their general purposes, their responses to the environment, and the ways in which they manage their visits. We turn now to a sharper focus on eight diaries, one from each diarist. We use these examples to develop the idea of a "core experience." Table 4.1 identifies the dia-

TABLE 4.1
Samples of Core Visit Experiences

Identity	*Museum Type*	*Purpose*	*Core Idea*	*Tool*
Molly (21) College/opera 7.2	Historical House	Challenging	What life would have been like for Paul Revere	Narrative Identification
Jane (23) Writer 3.1	Anthropology	Floating	Curatorial effort, discussion of *Raven and the first men*	Weaving
Celine (33) Educator 4.4	History	Focused	Chemistry display lacked coherence	Analysis
Megan (55) Undergraduate advisor 1.2	Art	Focused	Connection of art and life via discussion of northwestern skies	Narrative Identification
Anne (61) Writer, producer, quilter 2.2	Art	Focused	Aesthetic quality of quilts	Analysis
Beth (60) Retired professor 5.5	History	Focused	Varied understandings of Rosetta stone	Descriptive
Sara (66) Educational psychologist 6.2	Art	Focused	Analysis of Tibetan art	Weaving
Sally (67) Docent 8.5	Art	Focused	Imagining tour of Korean art exhibit	Analysis

rist by pseudonym, identifies the museum, categorizes the purpose, and briefly describes the core idea of the selected diary. We describe the diary topics in greater detail next and then turn to an analysis of essential meaning that was constructed, trying to point out the ways in which various features of the identity of the diarist, the tools available to her, and the museum supports were used. We start with Molly, an aspiring opera singer, visiting the reconstructed house of Paul Revere briefly noted earlier. She had gone there with her parents in part because she had liked reading about Revere as a child.

> When I saw the house's front entry, which was barely big enough for one person to stand in, and the stairs which were incredibly small and cramped and delicate, I realized the house was much too small to have held all of Paul's children (I was told he had sixteen, but probably only about six were living with him at one time) and his wife and mother comfortably. It occurred to me that he could not have had any privacy back then. The only way that a person could stand not having any privacy was if she didn't mind displaying intimate details of her life for everyone to see. I suppose people back then weren't shocked by much. Paul was such an easy going person I'm sure it never occurred to him to worry about what people saw him doing. . . .
>
> The upstairs further convinced me Paul had no privacy, his bedroom doubled as an upstairs living room where he entertained friends, and the only way to get to the back bedroom was to walk through his room . . . but back then space must have been more important than privacy . . . the bed looks so incredibly uncomfortable and hard on the back. Apparently two of his children slept in this bed. I doubt they ever expected to sleep through the entire night without waking up. . . .
>
> The thing I noticed most about the house was the almost total absence of entertainment and "impractical" things. . . . The biggest impression I received from seeing Paul's practical house was that in Paul's time enormous stress was laid on practicality and usefulness. . . . Basic things like cooking took up so much time and effort that "impractical" things like the arts were probably thought of as empty wastes of time. Paul Revere was by all accounts an extremely competent and practically-minded person, so he would have fit in well. However, I doubt I would have fit in to his time very well. I don't think I would have had a very high opinion of myself if I lived then, because I would have had little opportunity for mastery, and I might never have known that I have certain skills. . . . I also have extremely little patience for repetitive tasks, but "women's work" was filled with them . . . If I had been Paul Revere's daughter I would have learned to read and write a little, and I am good at those things so I would have taken pride in that . . . I would still be able to sing well, although I would never be able to sing as well as I do now because I wouldn't have had singing lessons. . . . Of course I never would have been sent to college back then. Girls had absolutely no choice about what they would do when they grew up. . . . All men back then were sexist, but I don't get the impression Paul was especially so. . . . After touring the house and dis-

> covering how dreadfully practical life was in Paul Revere's day, I was shocked to see some of his silver work. . . . His work took my breath away because of the sharp contrast between it and the no-frills environment he lived in. It was delicate and intricate down to the last detail. . . . Paul wanted his work to be as beautiful as he could make it. I'm sure he would never have allowed an apprentice or a journeyman working with him to do sloppy work. He would have been just as excited or perfectionist as any artist. . . . So this practical man got his greatest joy out of making something impractical. He was a lot more like me than I thought. (Molly, History, 7.2)

Here we have a young woman caught in a time warp. She imports herself intact to the past and imagines all of her talents, desires, and limitations to be carried with her—as they were in her visit. In a prefeminist time women's lives were narrow and prescribed; Abigail Adams, first lady, abolitionist and ahead of her time, has no presence in Molly's picture of Revolutionary America. Molly would have wanted the kind of spacious privacy she has been raised with and imagines everyone suffering without it. Her beliefs about the social independence of interests and competencies ring quite loudly. She *identifies* with Paul Revere's daughter and develops a narrative of practicality and female oppression that is then up-ended when faced with the delicacy and art of Paul's silver work. What is remarkable about the diary is that the diarist has retained in the retelling the same contradiction she experienced. She has simultaneously braided a story of what her life would have been like, how as a girl she would have been deprived, and placed in an almost unbearably practical public environment and recognized the contradiction of Revere's work so clearly impractical and artistic.

Jane, a talented writer, visiting the Museum of Anthropology in British Columbia is likewise connected to a portion of the museum. She, too, is visiting with her parents but with some trepidation. She does not usually enjoy this type of museum, she is a bit burnt out from visitors, but she had been reading Annie Dillard's *The Living* which was set near Vancouver, so she was hopeful. In addition to the Raven by Bill Reid that is described in a quote opening the results section, this diarist was drawn to a room that had been curated by a group of college students for an anthropology class:

> In addition to the exhibit materials itself, there was also a binder in the middle of the room in which students had recorded their learning process with photos and a step-by-step explanation of how the physical exhibit had come to be. I really enjoyed looking through the binder, especially because it called my attention to many details about the exhibit that I wouldn't have noticed otherwise, including the color of the walls (a greenish turquoise)—along with an explanation of why they had chosen that color over the initially favored bright magenta, the brightness and direction of the lighting, the font used in the exhibit text, and the difficulty of condensing weeks, or even months, worth of research into a single short and understandable paragraph that visi-

tors will want to read. In addition to learning about the process of exhibit-building, I was also fascinated by the exhibit itself. The prints and drawings were all from either Baker Lake or Cape Dorset. . . . The students had broken up into five groups of about three students, and each group had chosen a subject to research, such as Inuit economy and the printing press, the place of myth and story in Inuit culture, hunting and so on. . . . A short explanation written by the instructor . . . said that although most outsiders think of the Arctic as a bleak and colorless place, there is a time once every year when the ice breaks up and melts away and amazing colors spring forth. . . . I don't know what attracted me most to the "Break in the Ice" exhibit. It could have been that, unlike the rest of the museum, there was some small amount of explanatory text in this exhibit that made me more able to relate to the pictures. It could have been the fact that it was created by students, and that their sharing of the learning process made me look at it from a slightly different perspective. (Jane, History, 3.1)

Here again we see a diarist drawn into a particular relationship with the museum. In this case the connection is not with the material of the exhibit but with the college-age curators. The diarist appreciates the difficulty and success of the task and recognizes the narratives of the students and the metaphor of the exhibit and relates to them. The insight gained from this section of the museum spills over into her description of the Raven sculpture and the details of its placement that opened this section. What she has come to realize is that the material she gets to see is the consequence of myriad decisions and cuttings. In her own work of writing she too has to struggle with what to keep in and what to leave out so she appreciates and responds to the details of the decisions and the effort that went into them. She does not place herself in the narrative as strongly as the previous diarist, rather she is drawn both to the narrative of constructing the display and to the narrative of the Raven as creator of the Haida. Her *weaving* consists of movement between the objects, the text, and her sense of her own experiences.

We move next to Celine who wears a fairly critical lens most of the time. A scientist by training, and a Turkish Cypriot, she completed her Educational doctoral work in the United States and has moved to England. Her stance in viewing the Science Museum in London was one of concern for her discipline and how the public might be viewing it. She visited the museum with a focused intention. "As someone with a background in chemistry, I wanted to start with the chemistry exhibits. I am always curious to see how chemistry is 'displayed' to the public . . . (4.4)" Although she is not directly looking at the exhibit as if she herself is being examined, her close identification and appreciation of chemistry presses her to not simply look at the objects but to look at how those objects might be understood and judged by others.

> Walking past the exhibit area on chemical analysis, we ended up in a section of display panels consisting of old weighing equipment. Of course if you knew a bit of chemistry, you'd find some meaning in the role of weighing in chemistry. Linking changes in matter with mass of matter, the ground for the chemical revolution of the 18th century. Discovery of oxygen. Phylogiston and negative weight. The whole room was filled with balances, made in Egypt to China, some looking crude, some beautiful and meticulously decorated, which makes one think of a blur of art and science.
>
> I noticed a piece that was labeled as one that was made in the Ottoman Empire in the 17th century. I suppose due to my ethnic background, I'm always drawn to anything that touches on Turkish history so I studied the label of this piece a bit more closely. There was reference to a weighing unit, "oke," from this time which surprised me. Nobody in Turkey these days would utter anything close to this term to denote weight. But in Cyprus Turkish, there is an unit, "okka" which I always assumed was a word of Greek influence because of the way it sounds. The word could still be of Greek origin, I suppose, since there were many Greeks living under the Ottoman rule. But more importantly, the prospect that this word was brought to the island and survived after almost 500 years when it didn't in the mainland, I found quite fascinating. . . .
>
> I enjoyed the exhibit on balances even though on the surface it might have looked boring. It was a gallery of balances. One gets the point after seeing just one balance! However, the diversity of cultures depicted and the ambition to measure—for trade, for science, for whatever purpose it might have been—was interesting to witness. The question in my mind at this point was why the exhibit was not organized the other way around—chemical analysis techniques to come later not first—if the exhibit was to tell a story about the history of chemistry and how these techniques played a role in the development of this science. What I mean is that I would not put a polarometer equipment in front of anyone before a balance! If the aim of this part of the museum is to inform people about chemistry, then there needs to be some logical coherence in the way that the information is presented . . . (Celine, History, 4.4)

Celine, about 10 years older than the other two young diarists, stays firmly outside the exhibit as an *analytic* critic but seeks a logical narrative in the organization of the exhibit. What was developed first, what made a difference first historically should be presented first. But, at the same time she holds this rather dispassionate stance, she is drawn into the origin of a word and its power to survive, and to survive on "her" island. She delights and marvels in the discovery at the same time she critiques the rest of the display. Her concern and assumptions about other visitors are likewise quite interesting. She assumes that "others" will not see the inherent beauty in the mix of design and function of the balances; even though many who may have little interest in armament look at the armor of the Middle Ages and examine its beauty and refinement. Likewise she assumes that the logical temporal order of first to last is more sensible than near to far—an ordering that unpacks the present in terms of the past. What comes through as subtext is a desire that the presentation of her domain, science, and her field, chemistry, be one whose logic and aesthetics are visible and interpretable to a larger public.

We turn now to Megan whose quotes about the grey skies opened the results section of the chapter. Her various analyses show an acute awareness of self and environment. In terms of her identity she moves back and forth between being drawn into the exhibit, analyzing it from a more distanced eye, and taking it with her. Originally an historian by training, a person clearly formed by the 1960s, she advises young people at a university and so stays very much in touch with their perspectives. She had a focused purpose in going to this exhibit.

> One painting, in particular, "Still" by Thomas Shields with the salt marsh in the foreground, the slough winding through it into the sea and the mountains in the background, caught my eye. I could feel my blood pressure going down just looking at this print, for it was still, indeed. It was a hard edged painting, with the marsh and slough stylized, but representational and the mountains in silhouette, the colors fairly muted bronze oranges, pale dawn yellows, greys, indigos, and black. Realistic in a lithographic sense, not a photographic sense. When I am at the top of a mountain, or at the edge of the sea or a lake in the wilderness, my mind empties out all of the urban images, chaos, and deadlines into the view. They don't necessarily disappear, but they become faint memories. . . . I don't mean this to sound like a trite child of nature essay—I still recognize and appreciate the inventions of humans—indoor plumbing and heat, good clean water, a good movie or book, a beautiful flower vase . . .
>
> Tony Angel . . . has long been a favorite of mine. An environmental educator . . . his sculptures of birds are particularly well known. The museum did a nice job of juxtaposing a sculpture of a hawk owl by Angel next to a painting of a hawk owl by one of the artists. A nice curatorial touch. My favorite sculpture was of a small bird, I'm not even sure of its name, now, carved out of a piece of light brown marble. The sculpture was no more than six inches tall, a large flat piece of marble out of which rose the small bird as if flying. The bird was horizontal—only its body and wings fully visible in the marble. While the bird was highly polished, the rest of the marble was left rough and unpolished. The tactile nature of the sculpture-finely polished and smooth-made us all want to rub our hands over the bird, which the museum guard was conscientiously telling us not to! The contrast between the polished bird and the unpolished marble was especially compelling for the polished stone was not beautiful. Whereas one longed to stroke the smooth curve of the bird, the flat rough marble out of which it rose didn't invite one to touch it. A long crack went through the piece of marble, and through the carved bird, slightly distracting but also in a strange way, adding to the beauty of the small bird. It was

a piece, which if you had it at home on your table, you would constantly pet as you came by, the way you might pet a cat sleeping in the sun. Just for the pure pleasure of the feel of the warmth and smoothness. (Megan, Art, 1.2)

For this diarist, 20 to 30 years older than our previous three, *identification* and interpretation means allowing one to be transported to other experiences that are reminiscent but it also means appropriating the very objects and figuratively taking them home. There is a strong interplay between the relaxation in viewing the paintings that allows this diarist to recapture other experiences of similar environments, to the strong analytic descriptive discussion of one sculpture, to finally imagining that piece in her own home. She is aware of herself as a member of the museum public in tension with the social rules governing all art museums DON'T TOUCH and of the tacit rebellion of many visitors. But she is also deeply conscious of the social messages of the exhibit itself as well as the curatorial effort and decisions.

Anne, one of the senior diarists, is a writer, TV producer and, among her many talents, she is a quilter who teaches homeless women quilting. She went to see the American Craft Museum's quilt show with several identities: in a sense to pay homage, in a sense to study what is being done and how it is being appreciated, and, finally as a member of the quilting community. Her diaries are different from the others in that for the most part she selected a rather long list of objects and elaborated on each one. The other diarists tended to focus on two or three major objects or topics and emphasize one aspect. Anne in all of her diaries had a more reportorial style—her facility with the computer also meant that for each object *analyzed* she clipped in a picture of it or a similar object.

A psychologically disturbing quilt was the fractured traditional piece called Transitions by Sandra Smith. About six feet square, this piece whirls and jumps, shouts and screams. I felt under attack by the color, the energy, the undiluted power of it. Red triangles in light medium and dark shades made a tumbling effect in sharp under-tie shapes. They flew around the space on a grey, also fractured, ground. It was as if Hollywood special effects were incorporated into the cloth. And I did not stay long. Violence unnerves me.

And so to my favorite piece [quilt] in the show, *Crystalline Fantasy* is a wonder of wonders. Made by Gwendolyn A. Magee, she must have had the patience of Job and then some. The notes indicate that this is based loosely on the forms of plants and flowers, but it takes the viewer beyond simple imagery into a fantasy worked of sparkling embroidery and applique. My favorite size, 34 1/2″ X 40″ it is a marvel in that every centimeter is covered with a layer of sequins. It sparkles. It shimmers. It scintillates. The fronds and tendrils of the fantasy plants, which look only distantly like anything real, seem to float in their own sea of gold and light. I suspect that the plants were appliqued onto the golden ground, then the entire piece was covered with the crystal sequins.

> Once more I am awed and warmed that the human mind can conceive and execute such wonders. I relate more easily to the beautiful but can comprehend the unpleasant. This show showed many sides of the human condition. The quilts themselves let the artist makers tell their side of the story. They were able to inject the energy and enthusiasm that reaches out of the piece into the mind of the viewer. (Anne, Art, 2.2)

On several occasions one or another of our diarists went to an exhibit because they were in some sense a member of the producing community: a photographer, a costume designer, a quilter. Anne was perhaps most involved with the actual production of the contents of this exhibit. Not only did she know many of the quilters personally but she could appreciate the kind of skill and effort required to produce a particular piece. Like Celine in the Chemistry exhibit Anne wore a double hat, one which allowed her to see a part of herself and her personal interests in the exhibit, but she could also watch how that exhibit was appreciated by others.

In contrast to Anne, Beth visited a specific object, one she knew a considerable amount about but in no way identified with. Beth chose to visit the British Museum to see the Rosetta Stone with a good friend with whom she had first seen the stone nearly 30 years earlier. Her intention was quite focused. Other than noting some structural changes she barely mentioned the larger environment of the museum. Perhaps initially intended as a visit to an "old friend" the visit instead became a rather thorough and somewhat scholarly activity.

> I was thrilled to see the Rosetta Stone, a fragment of a dark stone stela, now in a glass case with lights shining on it. For many years the Rosetta Stone had been encased in a metal cradle and I remember that it had been much more difficult to see all sides of the stone. The inscription on the stone had been fully conserved and redisplayed for the exhibition. The commentary indicated that the inscription on the stone is a decree for King Ptolemy V Epiphanes dating from March 196 BC which is repeated in hieroglyphs, demotic and Greek and that by using the Greek section as a key scholars realized that hieroglyphs were not symbols but that they represented a language. Special displays also emphasized the important work of Thomas Young . . . and Jean-Francois Champollion . . . on deciphering hieroglyphics. Jean-Francois Champollion was an outstanding scholar who realized as early as 1822 that the hieroglyphs represented a language which was the ancestor of Coptic, the known language of medieval Christian Egypt.
>
> As I walked through the exhibit I found that I had to read the accompanying commentary and study the charts carefully to fully understand the items on display. While in many cases I was initially attracted to the appearance of an item I still had to read more about it to truly appreciate its importance . . . (Beth, History, 5.5)

In no sense was Beth overwhelmed by the authority of the curatorial voice; she was, however, very attentive to it in her detailed *description.* Her diary showed a shift from rather casual visitor to a known object, to a serious museum-goer, ready and prepared to respond appreciatively to the scholarly aspects of the museum. She was disciplined, not simply content to be attracted to objects for their aesthetics, nor facile with respect to the trust of her own intuitions—she was there to learn and learn quite rigorously and formally. For her, this growth in knowledge and competence is the fun of visiting a museum.

Sara, our next diarist, presents the most focused set of diaries of the set. She had a clear set of motives and goals, even when those are social as opposed to intellectual. She went to Tibet House in New York City to see some thangkas as a way of continuing her developing understanding of Tibetan art following her recent visit to Tibet. Her diary is highly structured: She wove her use of the catalogue with her own rich set of experiences and personal knowledge, she described the content of the exhibit and then focused on a few pieces for greater discussion.

> The first two thangkas that I looked at in depth were from I and III, of the Bodhisattva Maitreya (#32) and the Green Tara (#38). The bodhisattva thangka was of modest size . . . harmonious, bright colors, enchanting, and beautifully mounted as a scroll hanging—with dark brown suede framing the picture. . . . According to the catalog it was probably painted in central Tibet (Tsang) the first half of the 15th century. . . . He is surrounded by 28 lamas above and down both sides, the top seven with yellow hats and the bottom seven bare headed . . .
>
> My trip to Tibet in June 1999 included the Gyantse Kumbum (The Great Stupa of Gyantse) in which the richness and beauty of the paintings are extraordinary. The paintings in the Kumbum represent the full pantheon of Tibetan religious art of the 15th Century. . . . The Kumbum paintings have influences of the Nepali . . . style, and so does this painting particularly in the expression and grace of the hands and body. The painting reminds me again of the wonderful art in the Kumbum, evokes the spiritual world of Tibetan paintings, and is emotionally engaging—in the beauty of the painting and appreciation for the unknown master artist. My feeling for and understanding of the painting is expanded with the description provided in the exhibit catalog. I felt happy and excited that I could be in a situation where I could both study the painting and have the detailed description of the iconography in the painting. I also felt that although there is more for me to understand about these paintings, this visit provides a unique and welcome study in detail . . .
>
> I was intrigued by a painting from the Celestial Visions section. This painting was drawn on heavy silk . . . from the central region of Tibet, and from the 12th- early 13th century. . . . The title was Eleven faced Avalokiteshivara with footprints. The painting intrigued me because . . . the huge footprints appear

> in Buddhist sites and Tibetan works in several ways. Early on there were no images of the Buddha. At Sanchi (a site in India I visited last January) there are stupas and archways from about 200 BC. The carvings on the columns of the arches include a number in which there are large footprints to represent the Buddha. In present day Tibet many monasteries have large cotton "flags" or hangings over outside entrances to the main halls; and these hangings are up on the ceilings and have two large footprints. These flags also indicate the continuity of the symbols in Buddhist art. (Sara, Art, 6.2)

Here we see the diarist studiously engaged in and *weaving* between the fine-grained detail of the catalogue for the show from which she reads and quotes and the specific objects in the show; and between these specific objects and larger personal travel experiences. She used the show both to expand her understanding and to connect a series of ideas and experiences. Like Beth her pleasure in the object is related to her pleasure in gaining competency and a rather rigorous level of learning.

Like Sara, Sally, a docent in training for the Asian Art Museum in Berkeley (she had previously been a docent on the East Coast), was deeply knowledgeable about Buddhist artistic traditions and appreciative of the many types of artistic expressions found throughout Asia. She began her diary by contextualizing her visit, describing her previous visits to similar exhibits in the early 1990s. Her diary was then structured around her own movement through the gallery and her sense of how it could be handled by a docent.

> It seems that the NamGoong images have never been shown publicly before, nor have they ever been professionally studied. I was fascinated by that fact and formulated my own opinions utterly without guidance. I was struck by the fact that the two reliquaries were far more refined and delicate in their craftsmanship than the images and wondered why that should be. In contrast to those wonderfully meticulous little house forms of the reliquaries, the images seemed quite chunky—heavily proportioned and with minimal detail in the rendering of features or drapery. I was also struck by the differences in alloy—some of the images had a distinctly pink cast while most were more yellow . . .
>
> The Koryo dynasty . . . was a period of both great Buddhist power and incredible artistic refinement. Its excellence in painting, as well as its celadons, has never been surpassed in Korean art. The fourteenth century "Buddha Amitabha with the Eight Great Bodhisattvas," a hanging scroll done in ink, mineral colors, and gold on silk, is a splendid example of this courtly refinement found in paintings of this period. Made for daily worship in a monastery, it depicts the Buddha of eternal life and boundless light, who promises his believers rebirth in his Pure Land paradise. Severely static in composition, it is rendered in remarkable detail—most especially the fabrics with their intricate patterns finely painted in gold.
>
> The work is beautifully placed in the gallery being the first work you see on entering, and if I were to tour the gallery, as it now stands, I think I would be-

gin my tour with this hanging scroll. After describing its sophistication and elegant refinement, I could then easily move on to investigate the origins of such an art and begin with the early pieces. (Sally, Art, 8.5)

Sally *analyzed* the reliquaries with the eye of a docent and the skill of a collector. Her analysis drew on her background knowledge of the Koryo dynasty. Her eye was drawn both to the small details of fabric folds on a hanging scroll and to the larger context of the position of the object in the gallery itself.

The eight segments from our different diarists each show how the individuals engaged with the material in a way that allowed them to build up an interpretation and meaning in the context of their own expectations and their understandings of the significance of what they were seeing. Thus, our last two diary segments reflect the profound appreciation by Sara and Sally of Buddhism and Buddhist-inspired art. They are not looking at that as a form of national expression in the way Jane did for the Haida or Molly did when visiting Paul Revere's house. Nor are they imposing a Western aesthetic sense of mood arousal and connectedness that we saw with Megan's discussion of light and the bird carving.

Figures 4.1 and 4.2 contrast our diarists by age with respect to their purpose for the visit, and the way the environment of the museum was seen, whereas Fig. 4.3 shows four cognitive tools that all of the diarists seemed to be using as they constructed meaning in their museum diaries. It is important to note, of course, that writing itself is a meaning constructing activity and that that no doubt affected all of our diarists. There are two notable differences among the diarists. First, in the use of what we called narrative identification, our younger and middle-aged diarists used this tool more

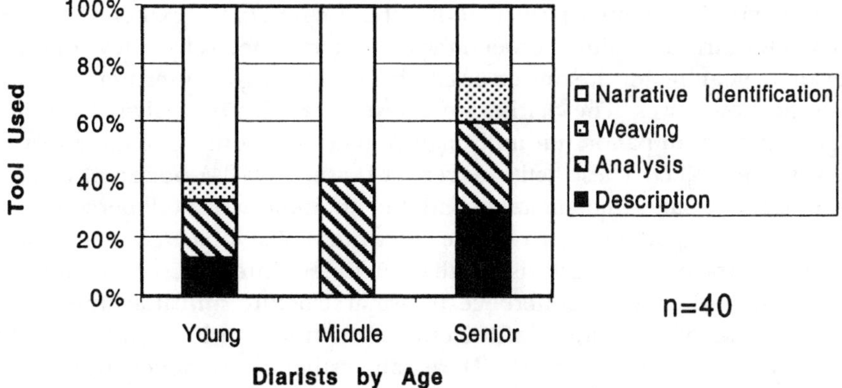

FIG. 4.3. Percentage of diaries coded by cognitive tool used: narrative identification, weaving, analysis, or description.

than 50% of the time whereas our senior diarists used it only 25% of the time. On the other hand, our senior and middle-aged diarists used what we called analysis between 30% and 40% of the time, whereas our younger diarists used it only 20% of the time. The main cognitive tools being used by the different populations are different although both our younger and senior diarists used all of the tools we identified. Again Appendix A displays these same categories of tool use by museum type.

SUMMARY AND CONCLUSIONS

When we designed this study we wanted to have a wide range of people participate as diarists. We certainly had no hypothesis with respect to age or development as a critical dimension, given that all of our diarists were adults. Naturally, if one is a fairly steady museum-goer—say 10 visits a year from age 18 onwards, then the difference in actual numbers of museums visited between our youngest and oldest visitor would be almost 500 museum visits. The point is that we have three reasons all of which might be convincing explanations for why younger adult museum goers might differ from our senior ones: It is a matter of personal development; it is a matter of museum experience and exposure; it is a matter of a subtle and ongoing changes between the generations concerning what a museum is for, how the society views the role of museums, and how one takes advantage of that personal experience. We tend to favor the latter, namely, that the differences reflect an evolving sensibility about museums, with a serious consideration for the cumulative differences in experience level.

We examined the diaries to see how the diarist's background and purposes influenced the choice of tools and reflect the personality of the diarists. But these segments also illustrate points at which the diarists had a distinct or intense experience with a particular object or themes of the exhibit. They deliberately blurred the lines between the exhibit and themselves, developing a personal meaning for the object, or exhibit, or drawing an interpretation out into their own lives. The diarists wove several strands of analysis together, highlighting both panoramic and small-grained components of the encounter with the object. These activities reflect Dewey's (1934) notion of experience, as the expansion of meaning and the "attainment of a full perception." This expansion goes beyond a simple description of an object. In many cases we found instead characteristics that included integrity, completeness, uniqueness—there was a coherence, informal structure, and attachment that allowed some of the features of the environment to stand out and others to fade away. To reach this kind of Deweyian aesthetic experience, the viewer has to appreciate the artist's and curator's accomplishments, culminating in appreciative understanding. In these diary excerpts, we see evidence of this engagement with the "object" per se, as the diarists reflect upon the significant aspects of their visits. In the diaries we are led to these moments, where the description of the visit deepens, and where an extended reflection on the aesthetic elements of the artwork takes place, where an interpretation is made, or where the curator's message is drawn into the discussion. An initial attraction to a particular object might be supported by the diarist's own memories, or background knowledge, and the museum's contextualization of it. The combination of tools, purpose, and environment come together to provide a coherent, engaged response to a museum object, and one that comes together in the retelling of the museum visit.

What we have seen in the diaries overall is the finely honed skill of perspective taking and appreciative imagination displayed by our younger diarists coupled with a sharp, precise, analytic skill more frequently displayed by our senior diarists. What we are seeing is human beings in a social setting bringing to bear their own identities and responding to a particular context. Museums are cultural institutions multiply defined by a public that finances their existence; by curatorial "experts" who make decisions about collections, content, and display; and by visitors who visit with a complex array of cognitive and social tools. Visitors shape and reshape their own personal activity of museum going and each museum visit—be it a novel experience, or checking in with an old friend—adds to the identity of who that visitor is. Our diarists have provided a completely unique window into that process and its meaning.

ACKNOWLEDGMENTS

The research reported here was supported by the Museum Learning Collaborative (MLC), Learning Research and Development Center, University of Pittsburgh. The MLC is funded by the Institute for Museum and Library Services, the National Science Foundation, the National Endowment for the Arts, and the National Endowment for the Humanities. The opinions expressed are solely those of the authors and no official endorsement from the funders should be presumed.

The authors wish to thank the participants of the diary study for their insights and their commitment to completing the diaries. They also wish to thank Mary Abu-Shumays, Joyce Fienberg, Catherine Stainton, and Kevin Crowley for their invaluable assistance with coding, analysis, and editing the manuscript.

REFERENCES

Aleven, V., & Ashley, K. (1997, June). Evaluating a learning environment for case-based argumentation skills. *Proceedings of the Sixth International Conference on Artificial Intelligence and Law, ICAIL-97. Melbourne, Australia* (pp. 170–179). New York: Association for Computing Machinery.

Cobb, P., & Bowers, J. (1999). Cognitive and situated learning perspectives in theory and practice. *Educational Researcher, 28*(2), 4–15.

Dewey, J. (1934). *Art as experience.* New York: Minton, Balch & Company.

Duncan, C. (1995). *Civilizing rituals: Inside public art museums.* New York: Routledge.

Duncan, C., & Wallach, A. (1980). The universal survey museum. *Art History, 13*(4), 448–469.

Falk, J. H., & Dierking, L. D. (1992). *The museum experience.* Washington, DC: Whalesback Books.

Greeno, J. G. (1991). Number sense as situated knowing in a conceptual domain. *Journal for Research in Mathematics Education, 22*(3), 170–218.

Jackson, P. W. (1998). *John Dewey and the lessons of art.* New Haven, CT: Yale University Press.

Mead, G. H. (1934). *Mind, self & society from the standpoint of a social behaviorist.* Chicago, IL: The University of Chicago Press.

McManus, P. M. (1993). Memories as indicators of the impact of museum visits. *Museum Management and Curatorship, 12,* 367–380.

Neisser, U. (1982). *Memory observed: Remembering in natural contexts.* San Francisco: Freeman.

Pekarik, A., Doering, Z., & Karns, D. (1999). Exploring satisfying experiences in museums. *Curator, 42*(2), 112–129.

Rogoff, B. (1990). *Apprenticeship in thinking.* New York: Oxford University Press.

Schofield, J. W. (1999). Goals, computer use and education: A sociocultural issue. *Journal of the Learning Sciences, 8*(1), 171–179.

Silverman, L. (1990). *Of us and other "things": The content and functions of talk by adult visitor pairs in an art and a history museum.* Unpublished doctoral dissertation, University of Pennsylvania, Philadelphia.

Silverman, L. H. (1995). Visitor meaning-making in museums for a new age. *Curator, 38,* 161–170.

Stevenson, J. (1991). The long-term impact of interactive exhibits. *International Journal of Science Education, 13*(5), 521–531.

Tulving, E. (1983). *Elements of episodic memory.* New York: Oxford University Press.

Wertsch, J. V. (1991). *Voices of the mind: A sociocultural approach to mediated action.* Cambridge, MA: Harvard University Press.

Wertsch, J. V. (1997). Narrative tools of history and identity. *Culture and Psychology, 3*(1), 5–20.

Appendix A

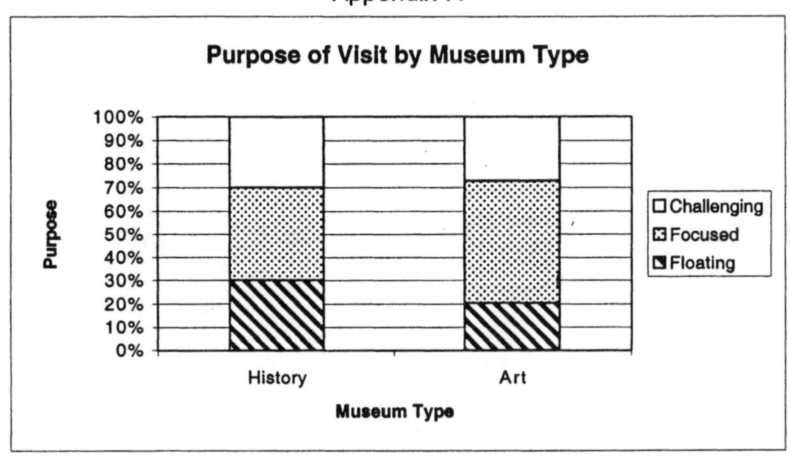

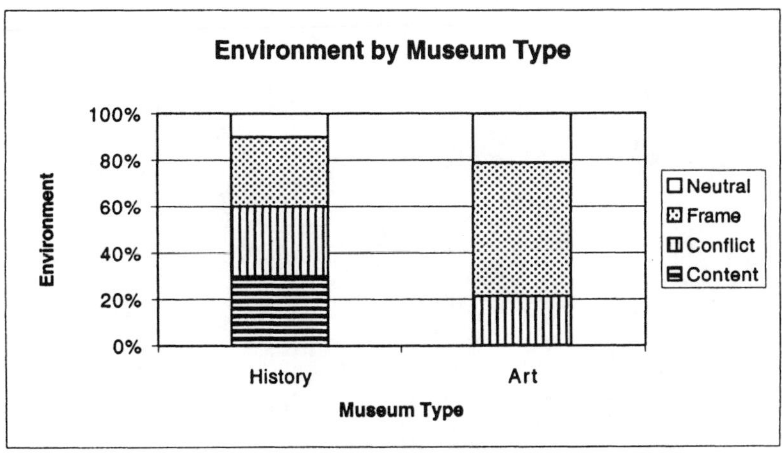

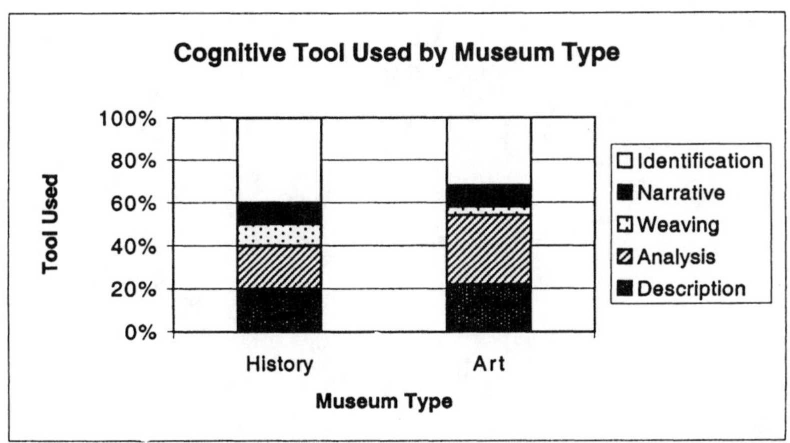

APPENDIX A

Part II

CONVERSATIONS: AN AFTERNOON OF LEARNING

To revisit the analogy of the camera, in Part II of *Learning Conversations in Museums*, we are focusing at midrange, and we trace visitors over the course of one entire visit to an exhibition. Chapters in this section emphasize visitor identity and how it is reflected in actions and conversations. Chapters address issues ranging from challenges to identity faced by visitors to a civil rights museum, to issues of who has permission to talk and who decides what they should be talking about, to practical methodological issues surrounding the capture and interpretation of conversations as visitors move through an exhibition. These chapters share more tightly than elsewhere in the book a similar methodology of tracking conversation, although conversations are tracked in a variety of both museums (history, art, science, and living history) and visiting groups (families, teachers, and friends).

Part II begins with Leinhardt and Gregg's study of a group of student teachers who are learning how to design an educational experience around an informal environment. The research explored the ways in which cultural institutions can play a role in the expansion and development of content knowledge, emotional connection, and social insight for future teachers. This chapter examines the impact of a carefully designed visit to a civil rights museum by a group of preservice teachers. Analysis of changes in these teachers' individual understandings and of their small group conversations revealed that the visit had a profound impact on levels of knowledge and appreciation of the complexity and meaning of the Civil Rights era.

The chapter by Fienberg and Leinhardt emphasizes the ways in which particular visitor identities influence what is noticed and how. In this study of a glass exhibition in a Pittsburgh history museum, visitors included those with architectural knowledge, former glass factory workers, and international visitors who assumed the city of Pittsburgh was solely a steel town. Variation within the groups prompted different depths and types of conversation. Among those groups in which there was both a fairly large disparity in knowledge and a socially constructed permission for teaching, conversations were more elaborate.

Stainton's chapter describes visitors to an African art exhibition who began with very different levels of understanding about African art. An interesting aspect of this exhibition was that accessing the aesthetic aspects of the show was particularly difficult for visitors given the tendency to assume an anthropological stance about African material and the fact that the art museum is physically connected to a natural history museum. Stainton traces aspects of the content of conversations and signage to identify ways in which visitors make meaning from the material.

The Allen chapter examines which types of exhibits are more or less likely to evoke different classes of conversation. Allen reviews different ways in which learning can be considered and then develops a set of conversational codes that capture those various meanings. Using the codes as a database of information about visitors, the chapter then explores differences in conversations as a function of exhibit and dyad type. The chapter gives both a detailed explanation of the methodology that evolved, and also traces the process by which it was developed.

In the final chapter of this section, Rosenthal and Blankman-Hetrick examine how conversations are influenced by the exhibition type and by the use of first-person interpretation. They note that visitors do not establish their own conversational space while in the presence of a speaking interpreter, but instead they will join or prompt the interpreter. After the encounter, visitors developed their own conversational channel. By following a number of groups through one portion of a living history museum, the authors establish that there is in fact this duality and note that conversational elaboration takes place after the encounter with the interpreter and not during it.

All of the chapters in an Afternoon of Learning follow groups of visitors over a period of time in which they experience a complete exhibition. The time frame is between ½ hour and 2 hours. The chapters here emphasize the actual construction of meaning and learning in real time rather than the ways in which the event of going to a museum fits into a larger context that we saw in the first section. The outside world pokes its way into the museum experience in these pieces through visiting groups' identity, prior knowledge, and dialectic stance toward the curatorial message.

Chapter **5**

Burning Buses, Burning Crosses: Student Teachers See Civil Rights

Gaea Leinhardt
University of Pittsburgh

Sr. Madeleine Gregg, fcJ
University of Alabama

The research reported here grows out of the pursuit of the goal of understanding how the use of cultural institutions, such as museums, can play a role in the expansion and development of content knowledge, emotional connection, and social insight of future teachers. The research was conducted in and around the Birmingham Civil Rights Institute. The expectation was that preservice teachers might expand their specific knowledge of events, attitudes, and social conditions during the Civil Rights Era. Further, they might, in small conversational groups, expand and develop a social awareness that had not been present before the visit. Before they visited the museum and again after their visit, 50 undergraduate preservice education students developed individual concept webs of their understanding of the Civil Rights Era and in small groups they discussed ideas and issues related to that time and the uses of the museum to portray the period. Analyses of the webs and transcripts reveal that the visit to the BCRI had a profound impact on the preservice teachers not only in terms of their individual levels of knowledge but also in terms of their appreciation of the complexity and meaning of the era and their willingness to connect to the period emotively as well as intellectually.

The research reported in this paper emerged from a dialogue between the two authors. The dialogue itself shared two goals: first, to understand more precisely how non-school environments such as museums might be understood as unique learning environments; second, to continue to develop ways that preservice teacher education experiences could improve the knowledge and understanding of future teachers. This chapter reports our findings with respect to the first goal. A second paper (Gregg & Leinhardt, in press) reports the results of the second goal. In the pursuit of our own improved level of understanding we chose to focus both our discussions and the activities of the study in two ways. First, we selected a topic of personal and national importance, the Civil Rights Era. The struggle for civil rights is not only a part of our national past but is a vital segment in all U.S. history curricula, a topic that future teachers need to understand in deep and engaged ways. Second, we selected the Birmingham Civil Rights Institute (BCRI) as a location and museum of unique significance. The BCRI is situated in the heart of the locale of the Civil Rights struggle and it is also a particularly well-designed and provocative institution. Our exploration weaves together three issues not always associated with each other: direct and indirect invitations to student teachers to move closer to their own community of practicing teachers by learning new material; the particular role of museums as privileged settings for making connections to the world outside of the classroom walls; and the meaning of a particular moment in our nation's history.

Moving from the periphery of the teaching world into the realm of practice requires the new teachers to engage in a complex and multifaceted set of activities (Ball & Rundquist, 1993; Lave & Wenger, 1991). The affordances that these activities provide are dependent on how teachers perceive the activity and its goals. As Borko and Putnam (1996) noted, "teachers' existing knowledge and beliefs are critical in shaping what and how they learn from teacher education" (p. 674). In visiting a local museum, preservice teachers may consider the trip an "enrichment" or "motivational" activity. They may, in other words, have a schema of the fun-filled field trip and expect that they will experience an outing in the way their future students will. They are less likely to imagine a museum visit as an occasion for fundamental belief change or challenge.

The research reported in this chapter centers on the responses of preservice teachers to a visit to a local history museum, the Birmingham Civil Rights Institute. The study is unique because it was conducted in the Deep South with undergraduate students of both European and African American descent enrolled in elementary teacher education programs at the University of Alabama.[1] Much of the Civil Rights drama was enacted within the living memory of the parents and grandparents of these preservice teachers and much of the drama actually took place at the very doorsteps of their homes, churches, and schools. Whereas the rest of the country can treat

[1]After careful consideration we believe we can not discuss the results of this work in terms of the racial identity of the participants. The work was not designed to help us understand similarities or differences and we did not inform our participants that we would analyze the data in a way that highlighted distinctions.

this era with a respectful sense of distance, objectivity is very difficult for many young people in Alabama. Although there are frequent references in the South to the Civil Rights Movement, the effect of constant attention to "The Struggle" has been to trivialize, for many Southerners of European descent, the very real legacy of racism in this area of the country. For many Southerners of African American descent, the way the Civil Rights Era is formally taught in schools, in some cases, ignores, obscures, or mystifies the specifics of the period. Because the topic is addressed in an artificially neutral language and with an emphasis on the political as contrasted with the personal one that African American students have learned from their families, many of them discount and distrust the information contained in formal school accounts of the struggle for civil rights (Epstein, 1998).

Preservice teachers, regardless of race, need to learn not only about the history of the Civil Rights Era, but about how perceptions of the Movement influence race relations among Southern school children and their parents today. However, it is very difficult for many preservice teacher educators to address issues of race and racism directly. The beliefs preservice teachers bring to their professional studies, beliefs resulting from their personal histories in particular socio–cultural–historical contexts, influence how receptive they will be to ideas encountered in their courses (Banks, 1998; Holt-Reynolds, 1992).

Student resistance to discussions of race and racism has been, for many teacher educators, a formidable barrier (Banks, 1995). Rather than overcome the resistence, many teacher educators have unwittingly colluded in the silence (Schofield, 1989). In the context of hypersensitivity to long-standing issues of racial inequality, one might suppose that a simple trip to a Civil Rights museum would have little impact on the preservice teachers' appreciation for the details of the Civil Rights Movement and its role in the history of the United States. In this chapter, we argue that such a trip, when coupled with thoughtfully designed experiences, can actually have a rather dramatic impact. In good preservice programs, teacher educators try to connect the content of learning to teach with the real-life experiences of the preservice teachers in order to model for them the types of linkages they will want to provide for their future students (Larkin et al., 1995). When the context is emotionally charged, as is the case we are describing, real-life experiences are precisely what the beginning teachers may want to avoid discussing.

One of the less studied aspects of learning to teach is the ways in which that learning can be connected to the world outside of the school setting. Although a great deal has been written about the non-school setting and informal learning, less has been written about direct curricular efforts to broaden and connect the larger world to student learning (Carraher, Carraher, & Schliemman, 1985; Heaton & Lampert, 1993; Resnick, 1987).

Making these connections can be facilitated by the use of community resources such as a museum. Museums store and exhibit the artifacts and symbols of greatest value for a particular culture (Leinhardt & Crowley, 1998). This is true whether it is a museum of historical memorabilia, such as Ivy Green, the home of Helen Keller (Tuscumbia, AL) or The Paul Bear Bryant Museum, shrine to The University of Alabama's famous football coach (Tuscaloosa, AL); a reconstruction of pioneer times, such as Tannahill State Park (Tuscaloosa County, AL); or an interactive science museum, such as the McWane Center (Birmingham, AL). Visiting these museums immerses the visitor in an intense experience of the content presented in the museum. How the content is understood and appropriated by visitors is a consequence of their own sense of identity, prior knowledge, and explanatory engagement, as well as their use of the devices and tools built into the museum environment (Koroscik, 1993; Leinhardt & Crowley, 1998; Short, 1993). In coming to understand these cultural resources, the preservice teacher learns content, but is also pulled toward the center of a larger cultural community.

However, a museum visit, as research has shown, is not in and of itself a guarantee of a meaningful experience. In late spring, teachers often plan museum visits as fun-time filler or rewards for a year of hard work. The lack of explicit connection to the curriculum results in many teachers and students failing to attend to the museum as a unique learning environment. In the fall, by contrast, the museum is often used as an "out of school" school. Students come burdened with pages of worksheets to fill out in the uncomfortable setting of the museum. The workbook-like pages usually could have been better completed with the aid of a text or library book (e.g., Falk & Dierking, 1992, 1997; Price & Hein, 1991; Stronck, 1983). Other museum visits occur as the culminating activity of a unit of study. After the museum visit, the content may not be discussed or referred to again because the class has finished learning about that topic. If using museums effectively with elementary school students is challenging, how might we use them effectively with preservice teachers?

BCRI

The Birmingham Civil Rights Institute is an historical museum that focuses on the Civil Rights Era as experienced in Alabama. It is located several blocks west of City Hall and directly across the street from the 16th Street Baptist Church on one side and Kelly Ingram Park on the other. Built in the early 1990s, the BCRI museum makes an effort to connect the historical struggle for Civil Rights in the United States with contemporary struggles for human rights around the world. Visitors to BCRI follow a clearly prescribed path through the exhibits. Although they can slow down and spend more time at particular points in the museum, the only evident exit to the museum passes though all of the exhibits. A thoughtful but direct route through the museum will take an average visitor a little more than an hour.

Visitors enter the museum by walking up a long, tree-lined stairway to a rotunda. They are directed into a small theater where they view a 12-minute film that recounts the political and economic history of Birmingham from its beginning in 1871 through the 1920s. Tensions between the Black and White communities are highlighted in the film. The wall on which the film is projected then opens onto the first gallery, which shows aspects of everyday life for Black citizens of Birmingham during the years preceding the Civil Rights Movement. This gallery shows the legal and cultural barriers to equal rights embodied in the Jim Crow Laws and the political, economic, and social organization of Birmingham. The next gallery focuses on the confrontations that grew from the *Brown vs. the Board of Education* lawsuit and the increasing violence of the Ku Klux Klan. The following galleries document the progress of the movement itself. In chronological order, supplemented by large timelines detailing events in the Nation and State of Alabama, the exhibits focus on the Montgomery bus boycott, the Freedom Riders, the Voter's Registration Drive, Dr. Martin Luther King, Jr.'s incarceration in the Birmingham Jail, the Birmingham Children's March, the March on Washington, and the Selma to Montgomery March. These galleries end at a large picture window which frames the 16th Street Baptist Church. Text panels and photographs around the window tell the story of the four young girls who died when the church was bombed on a Sunday morning in 1963.

The museum is rich in providing textual materials that support the exhibits. These materials are varied: timelines, newspaper articles, captions, hand-outs, and text panels on the wall. Visitors can also stop to listen to and watch one of the many multimedia presentations contained in the exhibits. Among the most important of these are a tape of Dr. King reading his "Letter from a Birmingham Jail," and videos of the Freedom Riders, the Children's March, the March on Washington, or Voter Registration. Across the street from the museum is a small park that displays a number of provocative sculptures that relate directly to the Civil Rights Struggle. One sculpture, for example, consists of a pair of parallel walls from which realistic statues of snarling dogs lunge out toward the visitors as they pass between them.

Our study was designed to examine the impact that visiting the BCRI and the adjacent park had on preservice teachers' appreciation and understanding of the Civil Rights Movement. We softened the direct discussion of racial issues by embedding them in the task of designing meaningful instruction for young children. By pressing preservice teachers to analyze the content presented in the museum for the purposes of transforming it pedagogically, we tried to provide a context in which preservice teachers could investigate their knowledge, their attitudes, and their assumptions. The research was designed to go beyond simply adding information to the preservice teachers' knowledge base and instead to support both an increase and a rearrangement of fundamental concepts relevant to the topic. We examined this aspect by measuring their knowledge about the Civil Rights Era and the organization of that content. The research was intended to show how visiting the museum supported conversations with peers about issues central to the Civil Rights Era. We examined this aspect by measuring the depth and nuance of personal conversations among them about Civil Rights and race-related topics. In summary, we examined "impact" at two levels: the personal and the social. A third aspect of their learning, professional growth, is reported in Gregg and Leinhardt (in press). Because of the strong personal connections people often make between historical sites and their own interest and previous experiences, BCRI is an ideal site for research on learning.

METHODS

The research was done in the context of preservice education. The preservice teachers visit BCRI and other museums as a regular feature of the social studies teaching methods course.

Population

The participants were 50 preservice teachers who were enrolled in elementary teacher education programs at The University of Alabama in Tuscaloosa. Ninety-six percent of the preservice teachers were female and 12% were of African American descent. The median age was 20; most of them were born after the end of the Vietnam War, and 10 years after the assassination of Dr. Martin Luther King, Jr. Thus, the Civil Rights Era is part of the historical past for these students. The preservice teachers were enrolled in two different sections of a social studies teaching methods class.[2]

Procedures

In anticipation of the visit to the BCRI, we asked the preservice teachers to engage in a number of activities. We asked them to repeat some of those activities after their visit and it is the difference between their responses to

[2]One is a traditional elementary–early childhood program. The other is an innovative program that merges elementary, early childhood, and special education teacher preparation. The discussion of these differences is reported in Gregg and Leinhardt, in press.

these activities that constitute our main data. The activities were planned to help the preservice teachers think about their upcoming museum visit. Their responses would reveal to us their understandings about the Civil Rights Era, their attitudes toward issues of race as it related to that era, and their sense of how to design such a visit for young students. We deliberately structured the activities to include both individual and small group experiences. We did this because we believe that there is a real difference between what an individual can generate when asked a specific set of questions and what results from a group discussion or planning activity as a form of professional practice. We needed to understand both.

In order to determine the effect of the museum visit on the preservice teachers' knowledge of the Civil Rights Movement and how they structured that knowledge in memory, each preservice teacher drew an initial web diagram showing what he or she thought of when considering the Civil Rights Era. The web was created by writing "Civil Rights Movement" in a circle in the center of a blank piece of paper, the teacher then proceeding to elaborate on the topic as much as he or she could or wanted to.

When the preservice teachers had finished their webs, they were asked to discuss with a small group of colleagues their opinions and knowledge of the Civil Rights Movement, its connection to racism, and ways in which teachers can use field trips as powerful learning experiences. Questions to guide the discussion were printed on slips of paper, which were turned face down in a stack on the table. The preservice teachers were asked to give everyone a chance to discuss the ideas and then go on to the next topic. The discussions were audiotaped and transcribed for analysis.

When the small group discussions were over, the preservice teachers participated in a whole class lesson on how to prepare for, design, and manage field trips. Although the lesson dealt with many practical issues, the emphasis of the lesson was on how to make a field trip a powerful learning experience by situating it within a coherent sequence of learning experiences.

As a part of the lesson, the preservice teachers were assigned the task of designing their own set of activities for using the community resource of a museum for the purpose of facilitating children's construction of meanings of democracy (a State mandated competency). From the preservice teachers' point of view, the museum functioned as a unique learning environment to which they could take their own future students. A field trip to the museum could help the children begin to assign meaning to moments and episodes from the Civil Rights Era while learning about "knowledge of democracy, democratic institutions, democratic values, or democratic behaviors which foster respect for self and others." The preservice teachers worked in small groups to produce field trip guides that focused on one of the episodes exhibited in the museum. The guides, for the purposes of this study, are considered the motivating context for the trip.

Preservice teachers visited the museum with the second author in groups of 25 on a Saturday morning. They spent up to 4 hours at the museum. The second author moved back and forth among the groups, facilitating the visit in multiple ways. During the next class session, the postvisit information was collected. Data thus consist of: pre- and postvisit webs of the preservice teachers' knowledge about the Civil Rights Movement and audiotapes of pre- and postconversations about the museum.

Data Analysis Procedures

Webs. Each web consisted of the words "Civil Rights Movement" written in a circle in the center of the web. Connected to that circle were additional ideas. In order to see if the level of information had changed, we counted *the number of ideas* displayed on each person's pre- and postweb. We treated each node (entry) as a single idea.

To go beyond the simple measure of how much information people put on their webs, we analyzed *the structure of the webs* to see if the organization of the information had changed. In this analysis, the levels of entries were examined. Entries directly connected to the center circle were considered Level 1 ideas; entries that connected to Level 1 ideas were considered Level 2 ideas, and so on. The complexity analysis compared the number of levels on the pre- and postwebs, the number of entries per level, and the extent to which the entries were connected to each other. This measure was thus an indication of both the breadth and depth of the preservice teachers' knowledge about the Civil Rights Movement before and after the museum visit.

The third web analysis compared each subject's webs to determine if the postvisit web showed *a reorganization of the information* about the Civil Rights Movement or if it simply showed an accumulation of more information. We defined reorganization as having occurred when:

1. fewer Level 1 entries were present on the postwebs with a corresponding increase in other levels of entries,
2. Level 1 entries showed a conceptual pattern, such as organization by event, person, or theme, or
3. preservice teachers rearranged the ideas shown on the previsit webs to display a pattern at another level of the web, often Level 2.

These three analyses ignore the content of the webs. A fourth web analysis examined *the content of the entries.* Each entry was coded as one piece of information, even though, quite often, entries contained more than one idea. The content codes were comprised of: people, organization names, events, details, themes, and error (incorrect ideas). The details category referred only to facts, clarifications, or specifications about people, organizations, or events. Themes referred both to generic events (sit-ins) and to larger ideas (racism). When more than one idea was expressed in an entry, the order of assigning a code was: people, organization name, and then event. The content analysis focused on the actual information expressed on the webs, the number of ideas in each category of information, and the new ideas that emerged in the postvisit.

Audiotapes of Group Discussions. The discussion transcripts were analyzed by examining changes in conversational elaboration (Leinhardt & Crowley, 1998) to understand how the preservice teachers' discussion about the Civil Rights Movement changed as a result of visiting the museum. The coding of the transcripts focused on four aspects:

Listing of museum elements that related to Civil Rights was coded when the discussion simply made mention of the existence of something they saw or might experience at the museum.

Analysis of museum elements was coded when the discussion of a museum exhibit was analyzed by giving detailed description of aspects within one or another of the exhibits.

Synthesis was coded when the discussion related something in the museum experience either to something else within the museum or to something related but external to the museum.

Explanation was coded when the discussion provided a causal answer to an implicit or explicit question; these usually included both analysis and synthesis.

RESULTS

Before turning to the specific results of our analyses, we describe briefly what we observed both in the data and in the interpersonal comments. In the space of 1 week, which included one visit to BCRI, we saw substantial changes in the preservice teachers. Individual levels of knowledge increased, as did the fluency with which the preservice teachers were able to discuss complex and difficult issues with their peers. In addition, the preservice teachers began to move toward competency in designing appropriate museum-based activities for their future students. In the following sections, we summarize the quantitative results for the collection of preservice teachers and follow each of those up with more detailed examples of a specific teacher or group.

Individual Changes

We start our discussion of how individuals changed in their personal knowledge of the Civil Rights Era by looking at the general change in information. As Table 5.1 shows, the preservice teachers more than doubled the number of entries on their postvisit webs. This difference is significant ($t[49] = 11.28$, $p \leq .00$).

A closer look at the extent of the web changes shows that nearly two thirds of the preservice teachers at least doubled the amount of information displayed on the webs. The percent of preservice teachers who added information in their postvisit webs is shown in Table 5.2. Figure 5.1 shows a contrast of two hypothetical web structures. Both share the real mean values of all pre- and postwebs combined with respect to nodes, links, and depth. What the figure helps us to see is that greater detail, depth, and complexity is present after the visit as contrasted to before the visit.

In order to show something of the nature of how one preservice teacher's webs changed with respect to *content*, consider Figs. 5.2 and 5.3. Figure 5.2 shows a previsit web that contained 13 entries. This web shows little conceptual organization; it appears that the student simply wrote down all the information that she could find in her memory as bits of isolated facts and attached these equally around the central node. The information ranged from people (Rosa Parks, George Wallace, and Martin Luther King) to events (church bombing in Birmingham) to groups of participants (military involvement and hate groups protested) to a node that indicated when the Civil Rights Movement occurred. Thus, no overarching conceptualization of the Civil Rights Movement seems to have guided the selection of the information found on the web. Four of the Level 1 nodes have one other idea associated with them; two have no other idea associations, and one has two Level 2 ideas. But there seems to be no specific method by which the

TABLE 5.1
Number of Nodes (entries) on Webs

N = 50	*Previsit Webs*	*Postvisit Webs*
Average number of entries per web	12.9 (5.3)	27.6 (11.1)

TABLE 5.2
Changes in Information From Pre- to Postwebs

No New Information	*Some New Information*	*Doubled the Information*	*Tripled the Information*	*More Than Tripled the Information*
6%	30%	28%	14%	22%

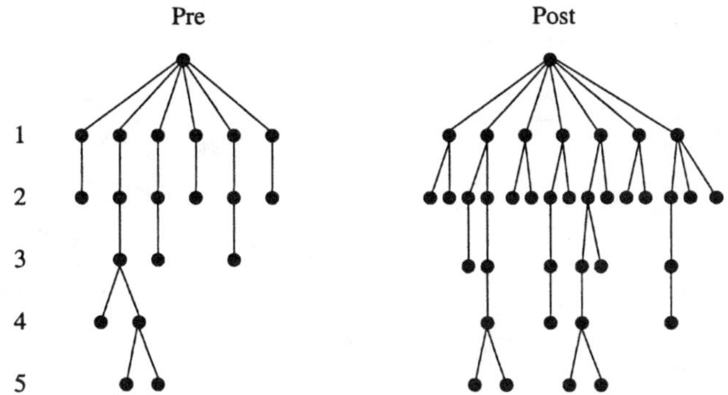

FIG. 5.1. Average pre- and postweb structures.

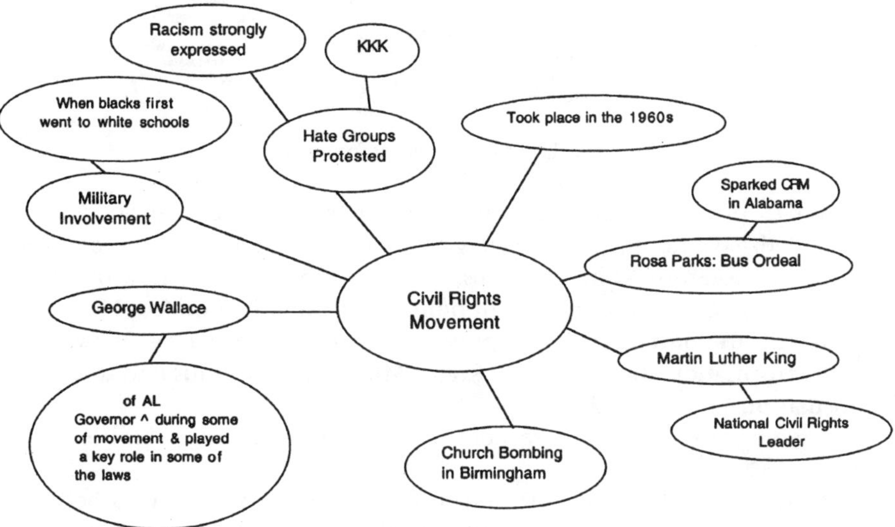

FIG. 5.2. Previsit—information.

preservice teacher generated the associations. For example, the jobs or roles of Wallace and King are indicated; for Parks, the web states, "sparked CRM (Civil Rights Movement) in Alabama." Finally, none of the Level 1 or 2 ideas are connected to each other, which is another way that a conceptual organization could be expressed.

Figure 5.3 shows the same student after her visit. This web shows a similar lack of organization seen in Fig. 5.2. However, there is considerably *more information* on the postvisit web. For example, on her previsit web, she created a node for the "Church Bombing in Birmingham." After her visit, she not only created a node that identified the event as the "16th St. Church

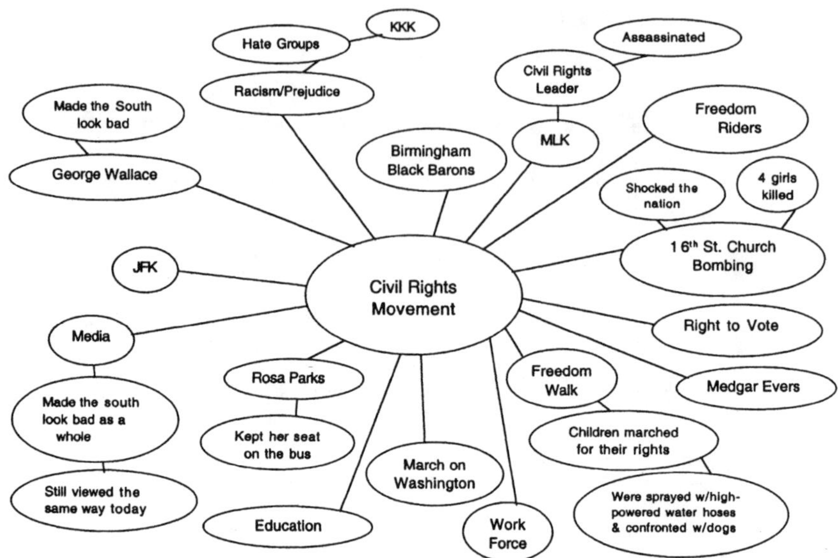

FIG. 5.3. Postvisit web—information.

Bombing," but she connected to it nodes for "shocked the nation" and "4 girls killed." We do not want to exaggerate the importance of some of the changes between pre- and postwebs; certainly, not all of the new information focuses on the most important points that could be noticed. However, we do want to point out that this preservice teacher now expressed twice as much information about the Civil Rights Movement and thus had twice the information to work with.

To get a sense of how these webs were coded, examine Tables 5.3 and 5.4.

The data in Table 5.3 show that this preservice teacher's web became more complex after visiting the museum, that is, she added more first-level information (from 7 to 15 entries) but also increased her Level 2 entries

TABLE 5.3
Sample Coding of the Webs in
Figures 5.2 & 5.3 With Respect to Levels

Levels	*# of Entries Previsit Web*	*# of Entries Postvisit Web*
1	7	15
2	6	8
3		4
Total	13	27

TABLE 5.4
Sample Coding of the Webs in
Figures 5.2 & 5.3 With Respect to Categories

Content	*# of Entries Previsit Web*	*# of Entries Postvisit Web*
People	3	7
Events	1	3
Organizations	1	3
Details	5	7
Themes	3	7
Errors	0	0
Total	13	27

and added a third layer not present initially. The information presented at Levels 2 and 3 was no more systematic or organized than was the information on the previsit web. But it did add to the amount of specific information expressed. Looking at Table 5.4, the nature of the web changes becomes apparent; each content category gained new information.

Another way that a preservice teacher might add to his or her web is to add specific details about the people, organizations, events, or themes on the webs. Figures 5.4 and 5.5 are examples of such webs. Most striking is the

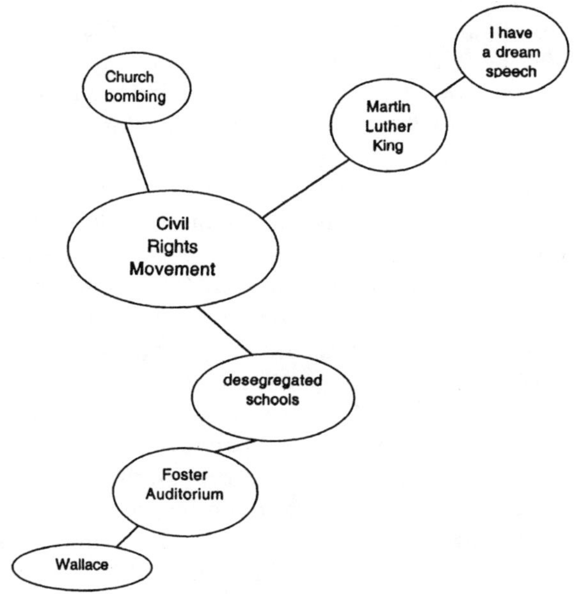

FIG. 5.4. Previsit—details.

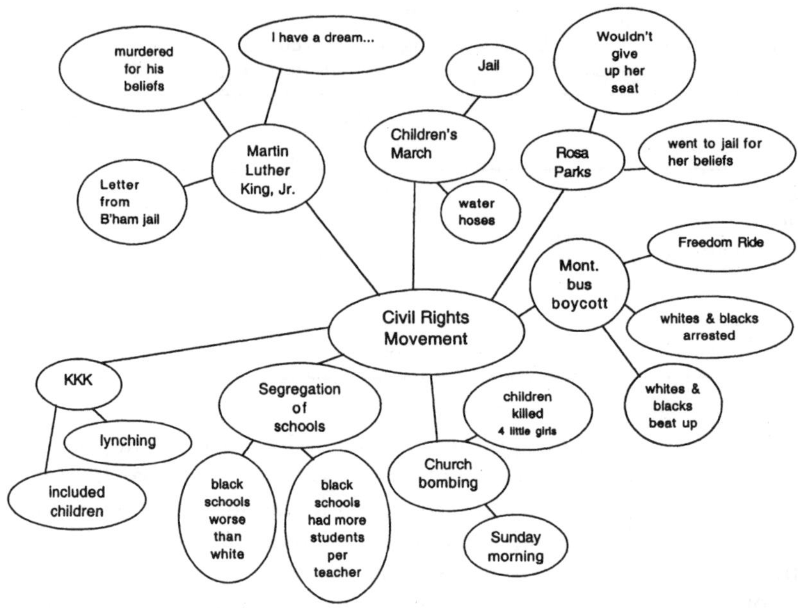

FIG. 5.5. Postvisit web—details.

fact that on the previsit web, none of the entries consisted of detailed information; on the postvisit web, 13 details are coded.

Examine, for example, the two nodes starting with Martin Luther King Jr. On the previsit web this preservice teacher associated only one idea with this node, "I have a dream speech." As shown on the postvisit web, Martin Luther King Jr. was now linked in her mind with his authorship of the Letter from the Birmingham Jail, as well as the "I have a dream" speech. In addition, she included the information that he was murdered for his beliefs. Note also the parallel between this detail and the fact that on the postvisit web, the "Rosa Parks" node is linked to "went to jail for her beliefs." Before the visit there was no node for the Children's March, whereas after the visit, the "Children's March" node is attached to nodes for jail and water hoses.

Not all the information reported on the postvisit webs was precisely accurate. For example, this young woman linked the "Montgomery bus boycott" node to the "Freedom Rider," "Whites and Blacks arrested," and "Whites and Blacks beat up" nodes. A case can be made for associating the Freedom Ride with the Montgomery bus boycott although the two actions were of different kinds, one being a boycott and the other being a deliberate decision to ride busses. The arrests and beatings were associated with the Freedom Riders, however, not the bus boycott, as indicated on the web. That this arrangement of nodes actually indicates mistaken information rather than being the result of careless web-making is indicated by the fact that there

TABLE 5.5
Patterns of Change from Previsit to Postvisit Webs

Same Level of Details	*Some More Details*	*Doubled the Details*	*Tripled the Details*	*More Than Tripled the Details*
10%	16%	14%	2%	58%

was plenty of space available for nodes to attach to the "Freedom Ride" node.

The percentage of preservice teachers who added varying amounts of detailed information to their postvisit webs is shown in Table 5.5.

Besides simply adding more information, another way in which some webs changed was by a reorganization of the information. Such reorganization indicates that the preservice teacher came to think about the Civil Rights Movement not simply as a collection of facts about people, organizations, and events, but in some more conceptual way. Figures 5.6 and 5.7 are the pre- and postvisit webs of a preservice teacher who reorganized the information on her web.

The web in Fig. 5.6 is very like the webs of most of the preservice teachers: It showed a relatively unelaborated set of ideas about the Civil Rights Movement. Even the information associated with the "segregation" node is generic and does not specifically name either places or events that instantiated segregation. The three people, three events, and one structure shown as Level 1 ideas seem to have been placed on the web as they occurred to the preservice teacher, in a haphazard order. The postvisit web of Fig. 5.7, by contrast, has completely reorganized the information. Now the Level 1 ideas are categories of information, not merely labels. Each category is elaborated with Level 2 nodes. The only Level 3 node shown is an elaboration of

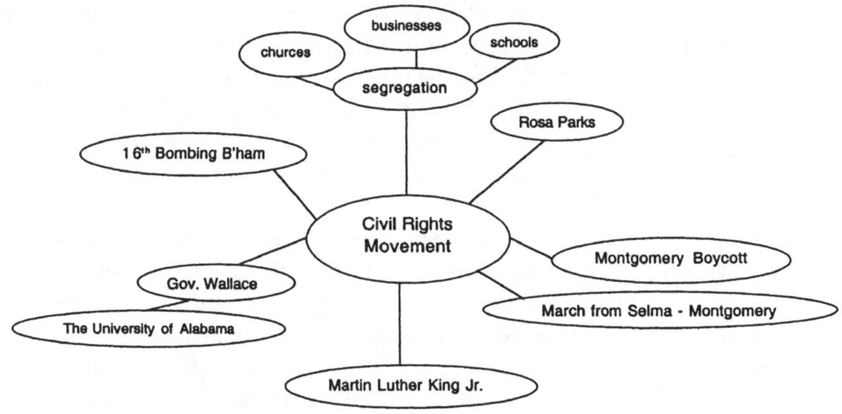

FIG. 5.6. Previsit—organization.

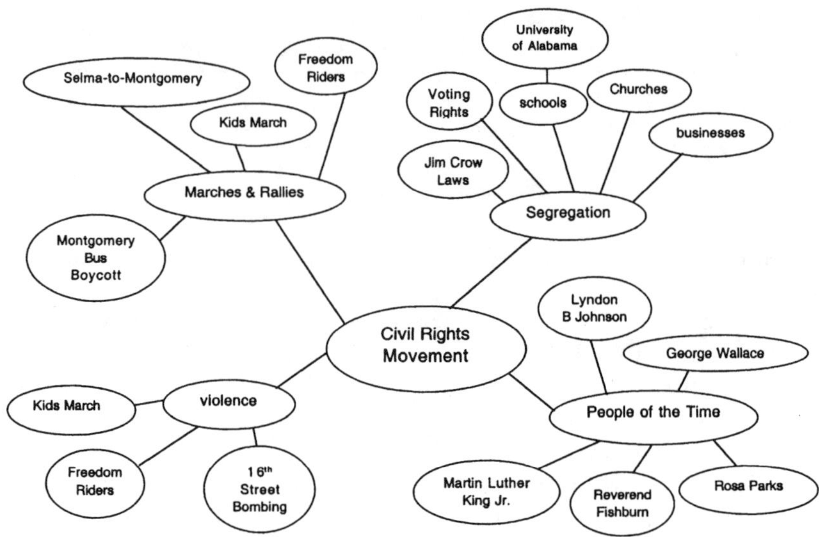

FIG. 5.7. Postvisit web—organization.

the "segregation" node. It is an instantiation of a segregated school, "The University of Alabama."

The organization of web information by category allows the preservice teachers to express a more nuanced presentation of information. Notice in the "People of the Time" category that Lyndon Johnson and Reverend Fishburn have been added to the information on the previsit web. The three people shown on the previsit web are all "State of Alabama" level figures. Lyndon Johnson, as President, adds the national perspective. "Reverend Fishburn" is meant to identify a person at the local level. Almost certainly, this preservice teacher was trying to remember the name of the local Black minister who was the driving force behind many of the Civil Rights actions that took place in Birmingham. His name actually was Reverend Shuttlesworth. Because she had never heard of him before, she was unable to retrieve the actual name. But the inclusion of "Reverend Fishburn" indicates that this beginning teacher now has added, if not quite correctly in all its particulars, as yet, the knowledge of specific local people involved in the Movement.

The content coding of these webs does not necessarily or explicitly show the reorganization of information that occurred. Often, however, a decrease in the number of Level 1 nodes on the web is an indicator of such reorganization. However, this decrease does not always indicate reorganization: Sometimes university students are less engaged in the research than one would like; their agenda is to get the postvisit webs "over with." When reorganization has occurred in the minds of these students, their webs are likely to have fewer "main" (Level 1) ideas, but these ideas are more elaborated than they were as Level 1 ideas on the previsit web. Forty percent of the preservice teachers reorganized the information on their postvisit webs.

The web information represents a conservative data source in that the preservice teachers could undoubtedly have provided more extensive information about the Civil Rights Movement had they been responding to a list of specific questions. Or, had they been prompted in a discussion with knowledgeable others, they could have discussed even more (Vygotsky, 1978). But even as it is, a conservative, brief estimate of readily accessible knowledge, the analysis shows that these preservice teachers gained in the density of ideas and facts, in the ways in which those ideas were organized, and in understanding what was important about the Civil Rights Movement.

Small Group Discussions

It would be possible for the museum experience to be an extremely powerful, personal experience and yet not influence preservice teachers' social behaviors as exhibited in a discussion. That visiting the museum is a powerful experience is evidenced by the behaviors of preservice teachers during their visit. The significance of the museum can also be attested to by the fact that many preservice teachers take advantage of the invitation to bring family or friends to the museum for the field trip. In addition, many of the preservice teachers spend in excess of 4 hours at the museum, even though they would only need about 1½ hours to complete their assignment. This is in contrast to the research findings that visits to museums are comprised of very brief (30 second) encounters with the museum exhibits (Falk & Dierking, 1992, 1997).

The series of questions to which the preservice teachers responded as a group were designed to prompt discussion about the Civil Rights Era, including issues of racism, pedagogical concerns associated with teaching about the Civil Rights Movement, and organizing and conducting a field trip. At a general level there is substantial evidence that these young people became more fluent and articulate about all of these issues. In the previsit discussions the average number of lines of substantive talk during discussions across all groups was 149; the average number of lines of discussion after the visit grew to 194. This is approximately a 30% increase. Clearly, they were able to talk more because they had more to talk about. But the nature of conversations themselves also changed. Before their visit their conversation often included a listing of elements or ideas, with little elaboration. Approximately 34% of their talk consisted of these lists, which bore little resemblance to conversation. After their visit their discussions included only 8% of these kinds of lists.

If the preservice teachers talked more, but listed elements less, then what was the discussion like? Before their visit about 57% of the discussions were presented as analyses, syntheses, or explanations. After their visits about 82% of the discussions were of this type. That is, the preservice teachers used their increasing levels of knowledge and the reality of their experiences to form coherent conversations. We refer to this change as conversational elaboration (Leinhardt & Crowley, 1998). To get the flavor of the kinds of changes we are describing, we share some parts of the discussions.

A fairly typical response to the previsit query, "What would you expect to find in a museum about the Civil Rights Movement?" was given by one group:

-- different articles
-- yeah, and, um, like the "I have a dream" speech playing in the . . .
-- lots of pictures of the big events, like the march and the beatings
-- desegregation of schools
-- Parks on the bus
-- standing in the school house door
-- Yeah. George Wallace.

Several features are evident in this portion of the discussion. First, the images that are called up for these young people are sparse, iconographic, and disconnected. Then, there is no sense of conversational exchange in this segment. The apparent operating rule is that one must come up with a label different from the labels already mentioned. This brief list thus suggests these preservice teachers had, at best, a rather impoverished vision of what the museum might be like.

To develop further a sense of the kind of limited listing that preservice teachers engaged in before their visit, consider the answers of a different group to the prompt, "What about the Civil Rights Era could possibly take up enough space to fill up an entire museum?"

-- Dr. Martin Luther King
-- Martin Luther King
-- (laughter, chuckles *[in the context of being unable to think of other ideas]*)
-- anything
-- segregation
-- how many years of slavery and then it ended? I mean-
-- I don't think of slavery
-- I don't either. I think of segregation, I don't think of slavery, though.
-- Me neither. . . . I think there'd be a lot of stuff to fit in the museum.

In this discussion, the impoverished, list-like feature is still present, but there is the beginning of something that looks like a conversation. The speakers are speaking to each other and even disagreeing over the issue of whether or not slavery would be part of the museum. Other groups imagined that the BCRI would be filled with newspaper clippings that reported on the events. But all of the discussions were characterized by isolated bits of information coupled with energetic attempts to say something about the topic.

We believe that there is ample evidence that the visit had a rather dramatic effect on these young people. Next we share some portions of the discussions the preservice teachers held after visiting the museum. We believe they show first, an increase in the conversational sense of the exchanges and then, the development of analytic, synthetic, and explanatory features in their discourse. Finally, we share an unanticipated outcome that shows how the visit prompted further exploration.

One group responded to the prompt, "What did you see that surprised you?" by starting the following discussion:

-- The statues of the Ku Klux Klan, and the voices, all those clear patches of people that voices came out of when you were walking through.

-- Very scary

-- That scared me

-- Um, just the impact of how they set up the whole Institute. When you saw the film of Martin Luther King's speech, "I have a dream," and you felt like you were in the crowd with all of those people around you. Um, with pictures of people. And they were talking about all those people getting sprayed by fire hoses and the water was coming down from the display.

-- Yeah, actually seeing it, like we've always learned about like in history and stuff but to actually see pictures of it. And like seeing the bus and the freedom riders—

-- What about that burned up bus?

-- The burnt bus

-- Yeah

-- Yeah the bus—and actually to see the church across the street. Like I had always heard about it but to actually see it, even rebuilt, it really affected.

-- I thought the Freedom Walk was um, that we went on Saturday was really, had a lot of impact on me. When you walked through and you had dogs jumping out at you and . . .

-- Walking through the jail part

--And pictures of actual hangings of people. That scared me
--Yeah.

The preservice teachers are continuing to list to some extent people, events, places; but we also see them listening and supporting each other, repeatedly saying "yeah" and acknowledging the topic of the burned bus, things that had frightened them, and the realism of the experience. The segment that describes the effectiveness of the voices in pulling the visitor into the time and place suggests a new-found meta-awareness. They describe to each other both their reaction and the design features that produced that reaction. This is both conversational, in that information is being shared, and it lays the groundwork for future discussions with young students. We would hope that these future teachers might explore the content of museums as well as discussing the role and mechanisms of museums. By sharing awareness of both their own reactions and what produced them, they are in a position to begin such a discussion.

In fact, the previous discussion does begin to sound like a conversation in its connectedness and richness of detail. It is conversational too in that it focuses on an abstract idea of "realism" that can only be understood by shared reference to a specific experience. In this next exchange, also given in response to the prompt to discuss what surprised them, we can see even more elaboration:

--Uh . . . I remember the, um, that Ku Klux Klan outfit. I came around the corner and saw it and I just about fell down. I mean, I've never seen any, you know, I've never seen one of those except in pictures and movies and whatever. And it was very-
--Evil
--Evil, yeah. And I was very shocked.
--Something that surprised me was to see how Blacks were portrayed in negative stereotypical ways in the advertisements.
--Yeah
--And those pictures of Aunt Jemima. And something called the Gold Dust Twins, like you could clean your house with the Gold Dust Twins powder. And the Blacks were portrayed in really odd-shapen faces and hands and features. I never really thought of that before.
--Something that surprised me was the picture, there was a picture of a lynching or a—
--Oh
--Too many had been killed. And there, people turned around for a picture and they were all smiling, they looked so happy like they were just

so excited to be there at this lynching. And V. and me just died. And it really surprised me.

--I was surprised at the treatment of the children. You know, I've always heard of the Children's March. And the statues outside with the attack dogs. But I had the Children's March topic. And I actually watched the video where the water hose actually would raise the kids up off the ground

--Oh. Really?

--And they would turn it off. Yeah. And the children would fall.

--Oh

--But the children, like their—they would sing gospel songs through the whole thing. And I was really amazed at how strong and determined they were.

--And brave

--Ummm . . .

In this discussion can be seen both a conversational linkage and a level of analysis. The segments of the conversation have evolved away from lists and toward richer descriptions. The elaboration of detail and irony of juxtaposition is clearly discussed. The idea of stereotyping is brought up for group consideration and then elaborated with details about the specifics of the stereotyping. Again, an abstract idea is posted for the group and then specified. It is likely that many of these students had read about stereotyping, but they had little detail to attach to the concept. The museum visit provided the detail that they could recognize as instantiations of stereotyping. The analysis of what it was about the Children's March that made it so remarkable, namely the contrast of the young people's courage and the brutality of the police against them, is developed in the discussion. The displays and the emotional impact that the displays had on them as viewers are acknowledged in ways totally absent in the previous discussions.

Both before and after the visit, we asked the question of who the museum was for. One group explored at some length the issue of exactly whom the museum was geared to and for what purposes. Before the visit almost every answer to this question was quite similar—it was a museum for Black people to learn about and honor "their" struggle. Afterwards the discussion was far more nuanced.

--I think it was geared to adults—You know, you can definitely take children and definitely as far as me as an adult, it was a powerful experience for me

--I don't know who it was—I don't know if it was, I don't know if it was created—I think it was created to, to evoke feelings in people. And I don't know that it was created to be geared toward anybody in particular. I mean, maybe you know, maybe it was—I don't know. (laughs) Maybe it was geared to me. I mean White, middle-class America. Maybe that's who it was geared for. I don't know. But I know that, I mean, you know, like that picture we saw that we were talking about and stuff, I mean, you saw things there that you never, ever, would have seen. And I mean, if we had not gone there we would never have ever known some of that stuff. Never. So, why? (laughs) I mean it's like this big . . . I mean, why is not talked about? Why is it not discussed?

--I don't know, you know, I didn't learn about it in school. I mean, I was really unaware of what happened. I mean, I was shocked, you know. And I talked to my husband about it. And I was shocked. And what I learned that day by going to the field trip. I mean I worried. "What did I learn in school?" But you know, it really showed me how important it is to teach children, you know, in my class, about it. And I will. And it really changed my view.

--But see, I think the reason we didn't learn about it, I mean, it's like this big conspiracy! (laughs) And that sounds kind of crazy! Like, to hide it and cover it up because it's you know, I mean it's like—

--It's uncomfortable for everyone

--Doesn't make us feel good talking about it.

--No, it doesn't make you feel good to talk about it. But I mean, I think a lot of it was, you know, like those pictures that we'd never seen. Where have those pictures been? I mean, they've been somewhere. But they've not been where we could see them. I mean, I think it's like this big . . . I mean, that sounds like kind of crazy, like a big conspiracy to cover it up. But maybe it's not. Maybe purposefully it has been covered up all these years.

As dispassionate scientists we are expected, we suppose, to report these statements as a simple advancement in the knowledge base of these young people. But in truth, neither author was fully prepared for the impact and depth of these reactions on the part of the university students. Naturally, not all of the preservice teachers expressed the same level of emotional reaction or depth of self-analysis, but most seemed to have had a powerful learning and eye-opening experience. In the foregoing voices, we literally hear a kind of honesty and sincere inquiry that is typical when preservice teachers discuss the details of their teaching, but is often absent when they approach substantive issues that are controversial such as race. Here is a group quite comfortable before their visit with simple answers to questions of race. After their visit, they acknowledge how uncomfortable it is to talk about injustices that their families and communities were involved with (on either side) but they also realize they need to see the "pictures" and by implication "hear the story."

One of the more interesting, serendipitous findings was that none of these young people had realized that both Blacks and Whites were involved in the Civil Rights Struggle; almost all of them mentioned that discovery as a surprising result of their visit. We close this section with a second bit of serendipity. We assumed that most of the visitors would be moved and provoked by what they saw, but we did not anticipate a prompt to further exploration. The same group of preservice teachers quoted above engaged in a lengthy discussion of Dr. King's "Letter from a Birmingham Jail" written in response to clerical criticism. Readers are reminded that in this section of the United States, religion plays a profoundly important and public role. That religious leaders would have attacked Dr. King, even verbally, is nearly incomprehensible to these young people. The fact that the clergy had not supported Dr. King disturbed them greatly.

> --In the jail cell. You know, like, in the part where it was a jail cell and a bed. And you could hear?
>
> --But see I looked it up, I looked it up on the Internet and go I mean I got a copy of the letter. And I read it. And I didn't, I mean I remember hearing that, him saying that until your first name becomes ____ and your second name becomes "boy" and until your wife or your mother is never addressed as "Mrs.," or whatever, that you know, you can't understand. But like I went back and read the letter. Like, his response to them. And it was . . . I mean, that was something that was completely new to me. That, I mean, you know, that government leaders and that stuff didn't support Martin Luther King and don't support the rallies and marches and stuff. But you would think that religious leaders either would stay out of it or would not condemn him. So that was very . . . I mean, to me it was heartbreaking.

The analyses of the discussion data uncover the complexity and dynamism of the ways in which preservice teachers spoke about Civil Rights issues before and after visiting the museum. We have seen how the discussions expanded from abbreviated, embarrassed, list-like structures to rich, genuine conversations that were both self-expressive and nuanced. That this degree of conversational elaboration could result from such a brief encounter with the museum speaks of the power of a museum as a unique learning environment, one that should not be overlooked by teachers or by teacher educators.

DISCUSSION

The analyses of the webs and discussions showed changes in the beginning teachers' knowledge about the Civil Rights Movement and in their ability to discuss issues associated with it. What conclusions can be drawn from this?

The field trip to the BCRI was a powerful learning experience for the preservice teachers that directly affected their ability to discuss issues of race and racism in substantive, conversational ways. The preservice teachers moved from halting, list-like utterances to actual discussions of Civil Rights topics as a result of visiting the museum and producing a field guide. In a very short period of time, the preservice teachers greatly increased their knowledge of the people, organizations, events, and themes of the Civil Rights Movement. In particular, their knowledge of detailed information about this important period in U.S. history increased.

The results of this study, however, go beyond simply increasing preservice teachers' knowledge: There is evidence that the preservice teachers altered their social historical sense of the Civil Rights Era and of themselves. There is evidence, too, that this learning experience caused a substantial number of them to reorganize the information in their memories. We argue that this reorganization is an index of the preservice teachers' changing conceptions and attitudes about the Civil Rights Movement. The extent of the change we have documented highlights the importance of crafting authentic experiences for preservice teachers, assignments that stretch them beyond their comfort zone and expose them to information and ideas they may resist. The added context of the trip, producing a field trip guide, required the preservice teachers to focus on the museum exhibits, not in terms of their own learning, lack of knowledge, and confrontation of racist or negligent attitudes. Rather, they were looking to find out how to help elementary school-aged students learn from the museum.

As is the case for almost all teacher education assignments, this museum learning experience was an invitation to the preservice teachers to move from the periphery of practice toward the center of practice by learning how to handle one of the common places of teaching (Lave & Wenger, 1991; Leinhardt, 2001; Lortie, 1975; Schwab, 1978). Designing and leading field trips is a regular feature of elementary school teachers' lives. The work they did in the context of creating field trip guides allowed the preservice teachers to appropriate, to make their own, knowledge and even language that was previously not part of their repertoire. Such appropriation influences what teachers will do once they have moved from periphery to practice.

The issue of the periphery is twofold. On the one hand, these preservice teachers are moving from the periphery of practice into the center. At the center, we have a vision of expert highly engaged teaching, but also a notion of very vivid engagement with issues critical to helping children develop a self-identity within a racially diverse society and culture. One goal of teacher education is to bring these students into that engagement. However, the preservice teachers also occupy a peripheral stance with regard to that critical part of our national dialogue and self-identity that comes into play around issues of race. It is not that they don't know as a society we need to understand that race is problematic—they know about it as well as any other 20-year-old, undergraduate teacher education students. However, they have managed to remain distant from discussions of complex social issues in general. Through the BCRI visit, they are brought closer to a place where they can have honest conversation among themselves about some of their own history because they have come to understand something of the pain and importance of the Civil Rights Era.

Before the museum visit, the stance of preservice teachers of European descent was akin to, "There was a terrible injustice inflicted on African Americans by European Americans, but now all is well. It's time to move on." The stance of African Americans seemed to be that they held a personal and private pain resulting from discrimination and lack of equal opportunity. They simply did not want to participate in a more elaborated discussion and they didn't know how. After visiting the museum, these preservice teachers understood that the injustices and cruelties of so many years have left emotional wounds that can not be eliminated by silence or merely passing laws and deciding to put the unpleasantness behind us. Rather, their ability to talk specifically about a bus, a church, or the jail cell assigned to Dr. Martin Luther King, Jr. allows all of them to enter into conversations about what those wounds might be and how they might be healed. They can look beyond the museum exhibit to discern the humiliation of a man in jail, under the eyes of guards day and night, confined to a very small space in which he would eat, sleep, pray, and even wash or go to the bathroom. They can better understand how the lack of privacy violates a person's sense of human dignity. They can especially imagine the pain that Dr. King must have felt when he read in the newspaper the rebuke written by White clergymen toward his "untimely action" and the anger and anguish that prompted his "Letter from a Birmingham Jail." As these students move toward full participation as teachers, they will be receiving a teaching license that will entitle them to 40 years of teaching, allowing them to influence many of our nation's young people. We want these teachers to be full participants in our society. We want them to be fully alive to this sense of who we are and where we have come from and to. Only thus will they be able to place future events into that context and help children of the future face the new challenges that will continue to come to those living in a pluralistic, racially diverse society. Such participation is an essential aspect of teaching expertise.

We think we have evidence from the webs and discussions that some of the preservice teachers were changed by the experience. From being dispassionate and standing outside the Civil Rights Movement, they appropriated parts of it into their own sense of who they are (their identity) and their understanding of what their tasks are as teachers, to make them better (Wertsch, 1997). We made these preservice teachers aware that, even though they will be elementary education teachers, the substantive knowledge that they have needs to continue to be expanded, in contrast to their assumption that they knew enough. We nudged them toward understanding that pedagogy and knowledge are intertwined (Shulman, 1987). These preservice teachers saw that dynamic in operation.

We have built a case for a museum as a powerful learning environment. When teachers are aware of what scale, three-dimensionality, realism, intensity, and intertextuality can bring to their students' learning, they are more able to exploit these characteristic features of museum exhibits, both during museum visits, and in the classroom. We have discovered a way to work with the "taboo topic" (Schofield, 1989) of race, which people are acutely uncomfortable discussing beyond either platitudes or polemics. Although our approach was oblique, we tried to create a context in which to address these issues directly and not let the preservice teachers keep putting it off to the side.

We have evidence that these preservice teachers engaged deeply with emotionally laden content and successfully analyzed difficult material. They grappled with a problem that they had never actually understood before. In the museum, they saw the problem of segregation, the emotional wounds that resulted from it, and the violence associated with dismantling it. They saw various instantiations of discrimination and injustice. Our hope is that their teaching will be informed and even transformed by the experience.

ACKNOWLEDGMENTS

The research reported here was supported in part by the Museum Learning Collaborative (MLC), Learning Research and Development Center, University of Pittsburgh. The MLC is funded by the Institute for Museum and Library Services, the National Science Foundation, the National Endowment for the Arts, and the National Endowment for the Humanities. The opinions expressed are solely those of the authors and no official endorsement from the funders should be presumed.

The authors thank the Elementary Education students of the University of Alabama for their generosity and sincerity in participating in the work. We thank Joyce Fienberg and Catherine Stainton for their help with data analyses and manuscript editing.

REFERENCES

Ball, D. L., & Rundquist, S. S. (1993). Collaboration as a context for joining teacher learning with learning about teaching. In D. K. Cohen, M. W. McLaughlin, & J. E. Talbert (Eds.), *Teaching for understanding: Challenges for policy and practice* (pp. 13–42). San Francisco: Jossey-Bass.

Banks, J. A. (1995). Multicultural education: Historical development, dimensions, and practice. In J. A. Banks & C. A. M. Banks (Eds.), *Handbook of research on multicultural education* (pp. 3–24). New York: Macmillan.

Banks, J. A. (1998). The lives and values of researchers: Implications for educating citizens in a multicultural society. *Educational Researcher, 27*(3), 4–17.

Borko, H., & Putnam, R. T. (1996). Learning to teach. In D. C. Berliner & R. C. Calfee (Eds.), *Handbook of educational psychology* (pp. 673–708). New York: Macmillan.

Carraher, T. N., Carraher, D. W., & Schliemann, A. D. (1985). Mathematics in the streets and in schools. *British Journal of Developmental Psychology, 3*, 21–29.

Epstein, T. (1998). Deconstructing differences in African-American and European-American adolescents' perspectives on U.S. history. *Curriculum Inquiry, 28*(4), 397–423.

Falk, J. H., & Dierking, L. D. (1992). *The museum experience.* Washington, DC: Whalesback Books.

Falk, J. H., & Dierking, L. D. (1997). School field trips: Assessing their long-term impact. *Curator, 40*(3), 211–218.

Gregg, M., & Leinhardt, G. (in press). Learning from the Birmingham Civil Rights Institute: Documenting teacher development. *American Educational Research Journal.*

Heaton, R. M., & Lampert, M. (1993). Learning to hear voices: Inventing a new pedagogy of teacher education. In D. K. Cohen, M. W. McLaughlin, & J. E. Talbert (Eds.), *Teaching for understanding: Challenges for policy and practice* (pp. 43–83). San Francisco: Jossey-Bass.

Holt-Reynolds, R. D. (1992). Personal history-based beliefs as relevant prior knowledge in coursework: Can we practice what we teach? *American Educational Research Journal, 29*, 325–349.

Koroscik, J. S. (1993). Learning in the visual arts: Implications for preparing art teachers. *Arts Education Policy Review, 94*(3), 20–25.

Larkin, M. J., Colvert, G. C., Ellis, E. S., Iran-Nejad, A., Casareno, A., Gregg, M., Rountree, B., & Schlichter, C. L. (1995). Applying whole theme constructivism in the Multiple Abilities Program (MAP): An integrated general and special education teacher preparation program. *Canadian Journal of Special Education, 10*(1), 67–86.

Lave, J., & Wenger, E. (1991). *Situated learning: Legitimate peripheral participation.* Cambridge, England: Cambridge University Press.

Leinhardt, G. (2001). Instructional explanations: A commonplace for teaching and location for contrast. In V. Richardson (Ed.), *Handbook of research on teaching* (4th ed., pp. 333–357). Washington, DC: American Educational Research Association.

Leinhardt, G., & Crowley, K. (1998). *Museum Learning Collaborative revised phase 2 proposal.* (Submitted to the Institute for Museum and Library Services, Washington, DC, November, 1998.) Learning Research and Development Center, University of Pittsburgh, Pittsburgh, PA.

Lortie, D. C. (1975). *Schoolteachers: A sociological study.* Chicago: University of Chicago Press.

Price, S., & Hein, G. E. (1991). More than a field trip: Science programmes for elementary school groups at museums. *International Journal of Science Education, 13*(5), 505–519.

Resnick, L. B. (1987). Learning in school and out. *Educational Researcher, 16*(9), 13–19.

Schofield, J. W. (1989). *Black and white in school: Trust, tension or tolerance?* (rev. ed.). New York: Teachers College Press.

Schwab, J. J. (1978). The practical: Arts of eclectic. In I. Westbury & N. J. Wilkof (Eds.), *Science, curriculum, and liberal education: Selected essays* (pp. 322–364). Chicago: University of Chicago Press.

Short, G. (1993). Pre-service teachers' understanding of visual arts: The reductive bias. *Arts Education Policy Review, 94*(3), 11–15.

Shulman, L. (1987). Knowledge and teaching: Foundations of the new reform. *Harvard Educational Review, 57*(1), 1–22.

Stronck, D. R. (1983). The comparative effects of different museum tours on children's attitudes and learning. *Journal of Research in Science Teaching, 20*(4), 283–290.

Vygotsky, L. (1978). *Mind in society: The development of higher psychological processes.* Cambridge, MA: Harvard University Press.

Wertsch, J. V. (1997). Narrative tools of history and identity. *Culture and Psychology, 3*(1), 5–20.

Chapter 6

Looking Through the Glass: Reflections of Identity in Conversations at a History Museum

Joyce Fienberg
University of Pittsburgh

Gaea Leinhardt
University of Pittsburgh

This study is one of several that have been designed under the auspices of the Museum Learning Collaborative (MLC) to inform a model of how learning occurs in museums (Leinhardt & Crowley, 1998). The MLC takes a sociocultural perspective on learning, one in which the conversations people have as members of a cohesive conversational group during a museum visit are seen as places where ideas are brought forth for public sharing in a way that allows group members to build on each other's knowledge and understanding. Studying conversations provides a window into this joint meaning-making activity (see Silverman, 1990; Wertsch, Hagstrom, & Kikas, 1995). The MLC takes *conversational elaboration* as a measure of learning and presumes there are three interconnecting elements that contribute to conversational elaboration: the nature of visitors' *identity*, the structure of the *learning environment*, and the degree of *explanatory engagement* (Leinhardt, 1996; Leinhardt & Crowley, 1998; Schauble, Leinhardt, & Martin, 1998). In this study we focus on one part of the model: the connection between a cluster of background characteristics and interests that visitors bring to a museum—what we call visitor identity—and the nature of visitor conversation during a museum tour—what we call explanatory engagement. We suggest that the conversations visitors have with friends or family members as they tour a specific exhibition both reflect certain aspects of the identity of those visitors and mediate visitors' engagement and understanding. In turn, various levels of explanatory engagement are indicative of, and related to, learning. The main purpose for conducting this study was to trace and understand the connections between visitors' identities and the structure and content of their conversations in a museum.

The study involved audiotaping conversations among small groups of visitors in a history museum and examining those conversations in light of what the visitors told us about themselves in interviews prior to the tour. We analyzed their conversations in terms of both the structure (the pattern of talk as visitors toured) and the content (thematic emphasis) in order to understand connections between various background characteristics of group members and the conversations that evolved in each group. We looked for evidence of some recurring structural patterns in the talk that showed increased conversational elaboration on certain thematic topics depending on the presence of particular identity characteristics in the group.

One common conception of identity is that it is comprised of a set of demographic characteristics such as age, gender, socioeconomic status, race, and ethnicity, characteristics that influence people's attitudes and behavior and sometimes influence how they are treated by others in the society. Another conception of identity is that it includes the kinds of knowledge and patterns of experience people have that are relevant to a particular activity. This second view treats identity as part of a social context, where the prominence of any given feature varies depending on which aspects of the social context are most salient at a given time.

Museum researchers have typically examined the role of visitor identity as part of evaluative studies undertaken to understand the demographic characteristics of the population the museum had successfully attracted or to ascertain what kinds of exhibits would attract repeat visitors. These efforts have primarily served a marketing goal rather than a goal of improving visitor understanding or learning (e.g., Falk, 1998; Mintz, 1998). A few other museum researchers have explored the concept of identity in more in-depth ways. One such line of work is that of Doering and Pekarik (1996), who proposed that visitors have "entrance narratives" comprised of their "interest in the subject" and "knowledge and opinions about it." For Doering and Pekarik, the background interest and knowledge that visitors bring with them to a museum exhibition provides them with an "internal storyline" that guides them through their visit. Although Doering and Pekarik do not use the phrase "visitor identity," they invoke elements that we consider part of visitors' identity, namely, background knowledge and experience. Unlike those who view knowledge as a finite entity that people have in varying measures, which needs to be augmented or transformed in specific ways for learning to occur,[1] Doering and Pekarik take a broader view that

[1]An alternate, developmental approach to visitor identity is found in the work by Housen (1980), who classified art museum visitors into one of five categories based on which of five different hierarchically organized "modes of aesthetic understanding" they possess. Housen's categories provide a useful tool for considering the kinds of support an art museum might offer to less well-informed visitors to help them move to the next level.

includes attitudes and predispositions (e.g., the propensity to be a knowledge-seeker). From a sociocultural perspective, this broad view of the role of visitor identity supports the expectation that visitors touring a museum exhibition in the company of friends or relatives will talk among themselves in ways that reflect their joint identities—they will seek to make meaning from the museum content based not only on what the museum provides but also on what they as a group know about each other and value. We consider visitor background knowledge and experience to be intertwined with interest and motivation.

When people visit a museum as part of a socially cohesive conversational group there are, in addition to the influences of the content and organization of the museum displays, both explicit and implicit social influences that shape, support, or perhaps curtail their conversation. These influences come primarily from the nature of the relationship among the group's members—the degree to which they are familiar with each other and the ways in which they normally handle subtle social issues such as turn-taking, topic control, or—in a museum setting—who gets to choose the pathway, the length of time at each stop, the together-time versus apart-time, and so forth. Much of these "social dynamics" have been worked out by family members and close friends before a specific museum visit. In some cases a novel situation affects the way the group interacts, or the presence of a less-close family member or friend in the group introduces the need or an opportunity to adjust the "rules." We believe that some of these social influences are bound up in the joint identity of the visiting group and thus influence the nature of the conversations that evolve.

Another component of the MLC's overall model of learning in museums is one that reflects visitors' interaction with the information or message the museum is providing and with the information visitors are exchanging with each other in order to make meaning for themselves and their companions. Whether the museum presents information in a didactic way or in a way that fosters visitor inquiry, and whether one or another visitor tends to do more of the talking, the conversations that evolve give us a sense of the way the visitors are "engaged." We call this component explanatory engagement (Leinhardt & Crowley, 1998; Schauble, Leinhardt, & Martin, 1998). Engagement is a measure of the degree to which visitors become involved in particular explanatory opportunities, whether those opportunities exist at specific exhibit stations or in some overarching exhibition theme.

We can describe explanatory engagement in several ways, one of which emphasizes physical interaction and another that emphasizes verbal interaction as a way of inferring the depth and degree of intellectual connection with the material. In using the latter framework, four levels of engagement are discernable:

1. People may engage in a simple, unidimensional, response to the content in the form of a phrase that identifies an object or a list of features, but seldom extends further. We call this Listing.
2. The conversation may include analyzing underlying features of an object, a process, or an abstract concept. We call this Analysis.
3. The conversation may integrate multiple ideas across knowledge sources (e.g., from outside the museum or from other exhibit stations within the museum) in order to support an idea. We call this Synthesis.
4. Some combination of analytic and synthetic discourse may be brought to bear on the task of helping one or another member of the group (including oneself) understand how or why something exists as it does, works the way it works, or happened the way it happened. We call this Explanation.

(For a more detailed discussion of these levels of explanatory engagement, see Leinhardt & Crowley, 1998.[2] For a slightly different take on these dimensions see Abu-Shumays & Leinhardt, and Leinhardt & Gregg, chaps. 2 and 5, this volume.)

Throughout a museum tour, as visitors are talking among themselves, they may exchange *brief* comments or they may *expand* on an idea that is triggered by some aspect of a museum display. In terms of the levels of explanatory engagement outlined earlier, we expect listing, analysis, and synthesis to be present in their brief comments—that is, a single phrase can reflect analysis ("That vase is etched not molded"). Although analysis and synthesis are expected to occur within the expanded talk as well as the abbreviated talk, explanations require more expanded talk; therefore we expect explanations to be found only in the expansions. Thus, although the length of a conversational utterance may vary from a phrase to a paragraph in this study, we were primarily interested in those portions of the conversations that exhibited some noticeable expansion that was recognizable in terms of both length and depth. We argue that *expansions* indicate some level of increased knowledge and/or interest on the part of one or another member of the group.

---

[2]Explanations as an indication of learning in museums were also considered in the work by Borun and her colleagues in the Philadelphia-Camden Informal Science Education Collaborative (PISEC), where an increase in behaviors such as "explain the exhibit" implied increased learning at specific exhibit stations that had been enhanced in some way (see Borun, Chambers, Dritsas, & Johnson, 1997). The MLC is attempting to provide a less goal-referenced examination of museum visiting, one that values personal meaning making.

Heinz History Center

The study took place at the Senator John Heinz Pittsburgh Regional History Center in Pittsburgh, Pennsylvania, in a permanent exhibition—*Glass: Shattering Notions*—completed by the museum in 1998 (see Madarasz, 1998). The museum itself is housed in a 19th-century former ice warehouse situated between the downtown business and convention area and a busy narrow piece of land known as "The Strip" (bounded as it is by cliffs on one side and railroad tracks and the Allegheny River on the other). The Strip is dominated by wholesale vendors, bustling warehouses, and railroad tracks. Many Pittsburghers go to the Strip early on Saturday mornings to buy their week's produce from wholesale foodstores that reflect the rich cultural diversity of the city. Within these surroundings, the six-story museum building, which was used originally to store blocks of ice for both commercial and private ice boxes prior to the advent of electric refrigeration, provides a kind of historical context for much of the temporal and physical content the museum portrays.

In its structure, location, and focus, the museum speaks to the working people of the region and provides a unique sociocultural milieu. Set neither on a grand boulevard nor on palatial grounds high on a hill, the museum sits in the heart of the wholesale warehouse district where it resonates with the working-class people who have toiled in the region for generations. The huge old ice-house has been carefully restored and re-directed to a different yet fitting role. It now houses collections of artifacts and documents, some precious and some common, that tell the stories of people both great and small, familiar and unknown, with whom everyone can communicate at some level.

On entering the museum, visitors find themselves in a large ground-floor gallery with high ceilings, thick rough wooden support beams, walls of exposed brick, and giant aluminum air ducts coming down from the ceiling. This expansive gallery space features historic modes of transportation that were used in the region, including a covered wagon, an antique motor car, and an electric trolley that people can climb onto and pretend to ride. In striking contrast to these authentic historic vehicles, a mobile robot is often present and actively engaging visitors with information (both spoken and available on its screen) about exhibits to be found throughout the museum. At the back of the ground-floor gallery, visitors come to an open steel staircase that leads to the upper floors, which are also accessible via one of two freight-size elevators located behind the staircase.

Glass: Shattering Notions, a 4,600-square-foot permanent exhibition that portrays the history of glass making in Western Pennsylvania, is located on the fourth floor of the museum, along with three or four other permanent and temporary exhibitions. An expansive "foyer" on the fourth floor by the elevators contains an atrium-like opening that has been retained from the building's original warehouse function and which reveals the sights and sounds of exhibits on the floors below. A sign near the elevator points across the way to a glass door and a hallway leading to *Glass: Shattering Notions* (as well as two other exhibition halls beyond it).

On entering this hallway, visitors can see the clear glass facade of the *Glass: Shattering Notions* exhibition on their right, with a central, semicircular portal bordered dramatically in glossy, opaque, black glass. Within that semicircular black frame, a pair of tall clear glass doors are flanked by glass shelves that display both artistic and functional glass objects. The remaining facade of floor-to-ceiling window-walls provides a "window" on the exhibition, through which can be seen a large model of the Statue of Liberty.

From this hallway, visitors move through the pair of glass doors to the exhibition's own entrance foyer where they see ahead of them a wall of "shattered" glass engraved with the title of the exhibition and a general introduction. To their left is a display of modern, abstract, hollow glass sculptures in swirls of vivid primary colors, created by a Pittsburgh-area glass artist, Kathleen Mulcahy. To the visitors' right is a glass-block partition on which are mounted photographs of famous structures in other cities that contain glass made in Western Pennsylvania (e.g., glass tiles in the Lincoln Tunnel and glass windows in the crown of the Statue of Liberty in New York) and famous people using glass products from the Pittsburgh region (e.g., President Harry Truman dining at the White House). Like the view from the hallway, the entrance foyer of the exhibition fosters the theme of the importance of the glass industry in Western Pennsylvania and the varied nature of glass products made in this region.

The exhibition has historical, aesthetic, and technological themes woven throughout. It is a densely packed hall with roughly 70 exhibit stations, containing art objects, historical documents, cultural artifacts, maps, and interactive exhibits as well as video presentations. According to the chief curator of the museum, the exhibition title was chosen to reflect the museum's goal of correcting two common misconceptions: that Pittsburgh is only a "Steel City," and that aesthetics is "the sole criterion for inclusion of glass in museums" (Rosenthal, 1998, p. iii). Both of these misconceptions are addressed by the exhibition's emphasis on glass production and related industrial issues, although examples of strikingly beautiful glass objects are prevalent as well. The gallery consists of thematically grouped exhibits arranged in room-like areas that allow for multiple pathways through the exhibition. Textual information is provided in the form of large section headings (at least 19, including Miracle Material, Why Pittsburgh?, From Craft to Industry) that are in turn supported by subheadings, wall panels, case labels, and object labels. Throughout the exhibition, object names (e.g., egg cup, rolling pin, microscope, stained glass) in faint cursive writing serve as borders along the bottom of some of the large, wall-mounted, text panels, reflecting multiple uses of glass.

How Do Visitors Construct Meaning?

In conducting this study in *Glass: Shattering Notions*, we were interested in how visitors touring in small groups build meaning for themselves. In particular, we had two underlying questions: (1) What is the pattern or structure of visitor conversation as groups tour through an exhibition; that is, how exactly do people talk among themselves as they tour through an exhibition in the company of friends or family members? and (2) How are visitors' conversations influenced by their identities; that is, how do visitors' background knowledge, interests, and experiences influence the nature and focus of their talk? We hypothesize that visitors with high levels of knowledge about or experience relevant to the content of the exhibition (in this case, glass—either its collection or production), with high levels of museum experience (whether at history or other types of museums), or with strong ties to Pittsburgh or Western Pennsylvania (long-term enough to have been exposed to some of its history and to feel a connection to it), will engage more deeply with those aspects of the exhibition than will people who have lower levels of such background characteristics. This means we expect to see places in the tour conversation where there are conversational elaborations or expansions of talk beyond the content provided by the museum, and that the location of those expansions or elaborations will differ depending on the multiple identity characteristics of the conversational group.

METHODS

Data Collection

The data for this study come from conversations among small groups of visitors while they toured the exhibition and from interviews with these small groups before and after their tours. All conversations and interviews were audiotaped and transcribed, and all visitors were assigned pseudonyms.

In total there were 10 visitor groups involved, 5 observed during the fall of 1998, and an additional 5 during the fall of 1999.[3] The first 5 groups consisted of preselected visitors with particular background characteristics that were expected to be relevant for their response to the exhibition; that is,

[3]The two phases of this study bracketed the study conducted in *Soul of Africa* at the Carnegie Museum of Art (see Stainton, chap. 7, this volume). Together with that study, this one

people known to the researchers were chosen based on their having either a high or low level of three attributes—(a) knowledge of glass (as a maker, professional user, or collector), (b) familiarity with the Pittsburgh/Western Pennsylvania region, and (c) prior museum-visiting experience. All participants were asked to sign informed-consent forms at the outset of their participation. The Pre-Selected visitors were interviewed in depth 1 to 3 days prior to their museum visit. They participated in another very brief preinterview on location immediately prior to entering the exhibition and a postinterview at the end of their tour. All interviews and tours with this set of participants were audiotaped by means of a portable tape recorder held by the researcher who conducted the interviews and who accompanied the visitors as a participant–observer. An additional one or two researchers followed behind the touring group, taking field notes on their route, recording a fragment of their talk at each location, and timing the duration (in seconds) of each "stop," in order to later annotate the audio transcripts with location information. Among our Pre-Selected visitor groups, two were dyads that consisted of one participant and one participant–researcher whose role was intentionally subordinated in order to give voice to the target participant. Those groups are identified by a single name—the pseudonym of the target participant.

The second set of visitors (On-Site) was randomly sampled from the naturally occurring museum population over the course of 3 weeks, including both weekdays and weekends. Researchers stationed themselves outside the entrance to the exhibition for 3 or 4 hours,[4] and visitor dyads or small groups who walked toward the entrance were approached and invited to participate.[5] For those who agreed to participate, two members of the group were asked to sign consent forms and to wear small microphones that transmitted their talk to remote tape recorders held by observers. The target members of each group were asked to participate in a self-admin-

---

sought to explore substantive issues at the same time as it worked to develop a methodology that would serve for research in multiple types of museums and with multiple types of visitor populations. Thus, observational and interview techniques evolved across the two phases of *Glass: Shattering Notions*, influenced by our experiences in the art museum. Similarly, the first phase of the glass study influenced the design of instrumentation for *Soul of Africa*.

[4]Research times were decided in conjunction with the museum education staff in order to avoid times when large tour groups would be going through this tightly packed exhibition.

[5]For the On-Site visitors, records were kept on the number of groups approached and the number of refusals. Visitors touring alone or as part of a large group were not approached. The rate of acceptance among those approached was 45%. Some people declined for vague reasons ("don't want to do that") whereas others were more specific ("old friends with too much personal catching up to do"). A mother in a family with two pre-teen boys said "You don't want us . . . not THESE kids!" implying she felt they would do or say things that would embarrass her (or us).

istered preinterview that was designed to foster discussion.[6] For these On-Site visitor groups, the researchers functioned as observers. Each group sat at a small table outside the entrance to the exhibition and talked among themselves in response to a set of previsit questions that were printed on 5 × 8 index cards. As with the Pre-Selected visitors, interview discussions among members of the On-Site groups were audiotaped.

Following a preinterview with the target participants, the full group of sometimes three to six people would proceed on their tour and would engage in conversations with various members of that group either all together or in subgroups. Although we often could not hear the dialogue of unmiked group members, we could detect that something was being said to a target participant and we understood the response given by one of the microphoned participants to be relevant to what was being said by other members of that group. Those conversational episodes were included in our data.

During the On-Site tours, observers again took detailed field notes on the visitors' progress through the gallery. For these visitor groups, information about the sequence of their stops, as well as their opening and closing fragments of talk at each stop, was recorded on a small-scale floor map of the exhibition. Following the tour, all On-Site visitor groups were asked to participate in a postinterview discussion that was conducted just outside the exhibit hall using card prompts in the same manner as the preinterview, with researcher–observers monitoring at a distance.

All the interviews and tours were transcribed and then coded. We used information from the preinterviews to establish identity characteristics for each group; the tour transcripts provided data on the group's museum conversations.

Participants

Based on information from visitors' discussions about their backgrounds during the preinterviews we rated each group as being either *high* or *low* with respect to their connection to glass, their relationship to Pittsburgh, and the frequency of their museum experiences. Visitors were given a high glass-knowledge rating if they indicated background experiences such as having worked in a glass factory, having made glass themselves, or having studied or seriously collected glass objects. A high rating on the relationship-to-Pittsburgh dimension was given to visitors who had lived in the region most of their lives. A high rating on the museum-experience dimension was given to people who indicated they either worked in a museum or visited museums routinely. We also used observer notes that contained estimates of basic demographic characteristics of the visitors in order to build a

[6] The use of written prompts to foster discussion was implemented after this methodology was successful in another MLC study (see Leinhardt & Gregg, chap. 5, this volume).

"profile" of our visitor groups. A summary of each group's characteristics and identity ratings is shown in Table 6.1. Because it turned out that most of the visitors had a high connection to Pittsburgh, we do not consider that dimension further.

Coding

Episodes

To understand the structure and focus of the conversations that evolved during the museum visit, we examined the tour transcripts. Transcripts were segmented into conversational episodes that could be seen as having a natural start and end in that they focused on a coherent topic. Episode boundaries usually corresponded to the move from one exhibit station to another; therefore, the number of episodes for each group tended to be close to the number of exhibit stations at which they stopped, although some conversational episodes continued across two or more exhibit stations. In other cases, there was more than one conversational episode at a given exhibit station, because the variety of content on display, or a related idea offered by one of the visitors, fostered two or more different mini-conversations. The demarcation of conversational episodes served as a means of identifying the primary unit of analysis for many of the issues with which the study is concerned. The mean number of episodes for a tour was 46, with a range of 23 to 59.

Within each episode we coded all conversation that was in any way related to the content of the museum exhibition, and excluded all talk pertaining to self-monitoring of the overall museum enterprise. Thus any talk related to such activities as general route-planning ("Should we go to the left now?"), keeping track of companions ("Where's David gone?"), or monitoring of time ("Do we still have time to get to the Byzantine exhibit?") was not considered in our analyses.[7] The remaining talk was coded for evidence of structural patterns, explanatory engagement, and content emphasis.

Pattern of the Talk Across Episodes

Within each episode we examined the conversation among the members of the group to determine the general pattern of talk. We noticed a tendency for many of the episodes to have a cyclical pattern of conversation that contained some recurring elements, not always in the same order and not always present in every episode, but recurring enough to warrant coding for their presence. We therefore coded each episode to determine whether one or more of the following elements were present:

---

[7]These self-monitoring and management comments occupied an average of 4.2% of the talk during the tours, ranging from a high of 8.1% to a low of 0%.

TABLE 6.1
Background Characteristics of Groups[1] and Their Classification as High or Low on Three Identity Dimensions

Group	*Relationship*	*Gender & Age Range*	*Education*	*Glass Background (Level & Source)*	*Pittsburgh Connection*	*Museum Experience*
Pre-Selected Visitor Groups						
1. Riley & Clara	2 spouses & 1 friend*	1M, 2F 60–70	university	HIGH -serious collectors -1 worked in glass factory	HIGH	HIGH
2. Minsu & Yuri	acquaintances*	1M, 2F 20	university	LOW -1 chemistry -1 public health	LOW	LOW
3. Jason	acquaintances*	1M, 1F 40–50	university	HIGH -architecture	HIGH	HIGH
4. Julia & Elsa	friends*	3F 60–80	university	HIGH -chem. lab & docenting	HIGH	HIGH
5. Armand	friends*	1M, 1F 40–60	high school	HIGH -worked on glass factory floor	HIGH	LOW
On-Site Visitor Groups						
6. Sarah & Pat	cousins	2F 50–60	1 high school 1 not avail.	LOW -grandma collects	HIGH	HIGH
7. Kimiko & Herbert	sister- & brother-in-law	1M, 1F 60–70	1 university 1 not avail.	HIGH -1 worked in glass industry	HIGH	LOW
8. Jasmine & Yvette	friends	2F 50–60	1 university 1 high school & nursing	LOW -nursing -some collecting	HIGH	LOW
9. Brenda & Amelia	cousins	2F 30–40	1 university 1 high school	LOW -some collecting & grandma collects	LOW	HIGH
10. Pauline, Andy, & Kyle	family (mother, father, son)	2M, 1F 10–50	2 university 1 grade 6	LOW -some collecting -1 works in steel industry	HIGH	HIGH

[1]All names are pseudonyms. An asterisk indicates the presence of a participant-researcher in the group.

1. *Identification*—either a statement that identified something, such as an object, place, or process; or some indication that the visitor was trying to identify an object, place, or process (e.g., "That's a cut glass vase." "Which company used to be in Coraopolis?" "What is that?"). Identification queries could be explicitly in question form or they could be implicitly embedded within a statement (e.g., "I wish they would say the names of these companies; they say only where they were located").
2. *Evaluation*—either positive or negative comments about the aesthetic quality of an object (e.g., "I like that one." "That's so pretty" or "You could find that at any flea market"), the overall appeal or usefulness of an exhibit station ("a wonderful movie"), the level of skill involved in producing an object or engaging in a type of work ("There's a whole lot of talent in that"), or the quality of an exhibit at another museum ("They have a fabulous collection of glass at that museum in New York"). These statements indicate some level of opinion or judgment along a continuum.
3. *Expansion*—an extended form of interaction with museum content or with an idea stimulated directly or indirectly by the exhibition, which indicates a level of visitor engagement beyond a simple or direct comment or response and which is lengthy enough to occupy at least three lines of transcript. Expansions consisted of rich pieces of conversation that either reworked the given information or added to it (e.g., "When we had to blow glass in chemistry lab we . . ."). Expansions may take the form of a story that is called up in response to an idea the museum display has triggered (e.g., "Oh my gosh! We used to have one of these . . . and one time we were playing football and we knocked it off . . . and broke it") or it may take the form of more analytic talk in support of an idea (e.g., "These molds revolutionized this industry. Can you imagine? One hundred dollars worth of cut glass there—looks the same at a distance and it's made for a few pennies by pressing it."). We identified all expansions in a transcript and then counted the number of episodes that had at least one expansion in them.

Within those episodes that had identification or evaluation activity, there might or might not be expanded talk, although there could be some brief analytic or synthetic conversation that did not become an expansion. However, as stated earlier, we did not expect to find an explanation in any episode that did not have an expansion; thus we focused considerable attention on the expansions. Those portions of the conversations that contained only unexpanded talk were used to identify or confirm the episode boundaries and the topic of focus as well as to determine the presence of identification activity and evaluation comments in an episode.

Explanatory Engagement in the Expanded Talk

Within the expansions we examined the level of explanatory engagement that was present and classified each expansion as belonging to one of three categories:

1. *Analysis*—an explicit or implied comparison of the features of something to something else (e.g., "Look at these three canes. One is . . . fluted. That one is a spiral . . . This is also spiral but it's inferior, it's hollow . . .")

2. *Synthesis*—a drawing together of ideas that have been noticed across exhibit stations (e.g., "This jar looks like the one we just saw around the corner . . . I think they were used by storekeepers for . . ."), or ideas that visitors bring into the discussion from their outside knowledge or experience (e.g., "Times have changed [for apprentices] . . . in terms of signing an indenture. I served a 3-year apprenticeship . . . It's a little different . . . You can move around. You're not stuck studying under one person . . .")

3. *Explanation*—a more comprehensive exploration of how or why something is (or was) done, works, or happens (e.g., "They've done a really nice job here and they're showing us shattered notions here with the tempered laminated glass. They shattered the glass in between two layers of regular glass and we can see . . .").

Content of the Expanded Talk

We wanted to see whether there was a link between visitors' identities and the location of the expansions in their museum conversations—that is, whether the places where they tended to engage in expansions were located in, or were focused on, topics where they had a special interest or some form of background knowledge, or whether expanded conversations were randomly distributed throughout a museum visit. Thus we also coded each expansion according to the content of the talk, which we classified in terms of six major thematic topics that emerged from the data. These themes reflect ideas that were present in the exhibition and also present in varying degrees throughout the conversations of most visitors. Each expansion was classified as belonging to one of the following thematic categories based on the content that was dominant within it:

Technology—features of a scientific or manufacturing process, including methods or materials used.

History/Pittsburgh—discussions of people, places, events, dates, social conditions, and change over time, as well as Pittsburgh area institutions such as sports teams or companies other than glass manufacturers that are tightly identified with the region.

Aesthetics/Value—the visual attributes of an object (such as color, pattern, shape), the visual appeal of a display; or the intrinsic or monetary value of something (including notions of rarity).

Work—the tasks involved in or the skills needed for certain jobs, including those for artists and laborers.

Museum—the way objects or ideas are organized or displayed in this or other museums, including individual exhibit stations or overall museum characteristics.

Function—the way an object is used, or the attributes of a material that make it suitable for certain functions.

After the transcripts were segmented into conversational episodes and coded for the presence of type of talk, thematic focus, and level of explanatory complexity by one researcher, another researcher independently segmented and coded a subset of transcripts for purposes of obtaining a measure of reliability. Reliability was 92% for segmenting the transcripts and 88% for coding them.

Relationships Within Groups

In addition to examining the pattern and the thematic content of the talk, we watched for intragroup social interactions that indicated some influence of the relationship among the members of the group on the way the conversations evolved in that group (here too we excluded the general self-monitoring or management talk that was not tied to the exhibit in some way). We noticed instances of social moves such as dominating the conversation, curtailing gossip, pedagogical moves with a school-aged child, in-jokes between friends or family members, and so forth. However, one feature of particular interest for this study was the degree to which one or another member of a group had and was considered by the group to have particularly relevant knowledge or experience about certain aspects of the content of the exhibition or about museums in general. We expected that in such cases there would be a tendency for that person to feel empowered to offer expansions on some aspect of the content for the other member(s) of the group. Doing so implied some understanding among the others in the group that yielding the "floor" to that speaker was appropriate. Sometimes this acknowledgment of expertise or authority to speak is understood among groups members prior to the visit, sometimes a member of a group has authority that comes from power relationships unrelated to knowledge or expertise, and sometimes the authority or acknowledgment of expertise evolves as the group moves through an exhibition. Allowing or even encouraging a group member to offer expanded talk during the tour affords other members of the group the opportunity to have a richer experience than they otherwise might have. The group members, then, can add their companion's experiences to their own repertoire of experiences and they can expand on that with their own ideas, thereby enriching the group experience further. Although not all visitor contributions to museum conversation are enlightening or even accurate, we felt that expansions in the talk were an indication of at least a certain increased level of interest and this interest is bound up in their identity. We also examined the data for information about the relationship among members of each group with respect to the presence of a difference in knowledge or experience within a group, or a kind of gradient, that might be expected to prompt the giving of more expanded talk by one member or another at different places along the way. Groups were classified as having or not having this differential (or gradient) among its members in the area of glass knowledge.

Analysis of the Data

Analysis focused first on the structure of the talk in each *episode*. Results from coding the structural pattern of talk were tabulated and used to determine the prevalence (expressed as a percentage of all episodes) of identification, evaluation, expansion, and explanation that occurred in the conversations of all groups as they toured the exhibition. (Because anywhere from one to four structural elements could be present in a given episode, the percentage values represent overlapping measures and thus will sum to more than 100.) To see whether the pattern of conversations differed among groups with different identities, the data were examined in two different ways—first according to the groups' connection to glass and then according to their level of museum experience. For this comparative analysis we again focused on the relative proportion of episodes (expressed as percentages) that contained at least one instance of identification, evaluation, expansion, and explanation.

Following the analysis of the episodes, we looked more closely at those places in the tour conversations where *expansions* occurred, this time taking into account every instance of an expansion and determining both the level of explanatory engagement involved and the dominant thematic topic of focus in each. Results from this dual coding of all the expansions were used first to see which levels of engagement and which topics were most prevalent among visitors in general. The data on the expansions were then cross-tabulated to see which kinds of thematic topics generated the largest proportion of each level of explanatory engagement—that is, whether visitors were more likely to engage in explanation-level talk when they were considering historical versus aesthetic themes, for example. To see how groups who were rated high on the connection-to-glass dimension reacted relative to those rated low, we examined the expansion data separately for the Highs and Lows to determine the trends in their thematic emphasis, levels of explanatory engagement, and then the interaction of those two dimensions. In summary, what we are trying to understand from this data is the kinds of talk people engage in as they tour an exhibition and have conversations in a small group. We want to describe that talk in terms of its structural features, its subject-matter focus, and its level of engagement. Further, we want to examine the degree to which certain identity characteristics that people bring with them, such as background knowledge relevant to the exhibition content, and certain social relationships within the groups are related to the observed patterns.

RESULTS AND DISCUSSION

Pattern of the Talk—Overall

To understand the overall pattern of the talk that visitors engaged in, we examined the structure of conversational episodes of all the visitor groups combined. A summary of these results is shown in Fig. 6.1, which is in the form of a Venn diagram that displays the overlapping categories of talk (identification, evaluation, expansion, and explanation) and the percentages of all episodes that contained various combinations of these talk elements. Of the 460 total conversational episodes (represented by the largest oval), we found that 98% contained talk that reflected some form of identification activity (see light grey large oval).[8] Almost half of these episodes (46% of all episodes) contained evaluations as well (see checkered oval). Also within the portion of episodes containing identification, there was a subset of episodes (see right oval) in which some form of expansion occurred (52% of all episodes). Some of the episodes with expansions also contained evaluation—27% of all episodes (see overlapping ovals in center). Nested within the episodes that contained expansions were the set with explanations—10% of all the episodes (see smallest oval)—some of which also occurred in episodes containing the full cycle of identification-plus-expansion-plus-evaluation.

What is most noticeable about the results of coding for type of talk across all visitor groups is that there is an overwhelming tendency for visitors to engage in some form of identification activity at almost every stop in their tour. Clearly conversations need an agreed-upon target, but what is also clear is that much visitor energy is expended in trying to identify the objects on display or the features of a display that are relevant for their understanding. The 2% of the episodes that did not have any identification activity consisted primarily of nonspecific evaluation-type comments (e.g., "that's really beautiful"), where visitors may have been communicating the focus of their comment via gesture.

Figure 6.1 also shows that episodes containing evaluation in combination with identification represented a major proportion of the talk. The cy-

---

[8]All percentage values are rounded.

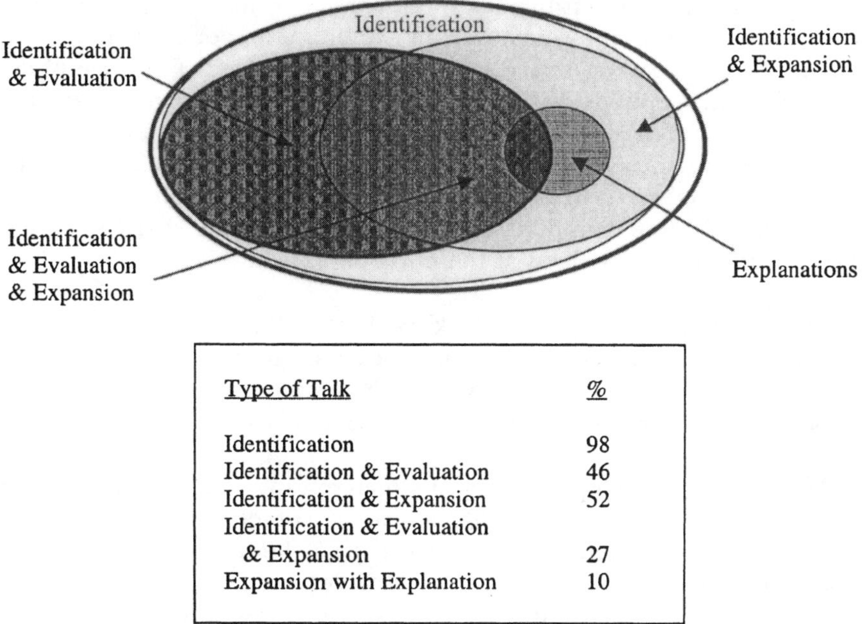

Type of Talk	%
Identification	98
Identification & Evaluation	46
Identification & Expansion	52
Identification & Evaluation & Expansion	27
Expansion with Explanation	10

FIG. 6.1. Percentage of episodes ($n = 460$) with different combinations of talk type.

cles within those episodes varied with respect to whether the identification happened prior to or following the evaluation ("That's a cut glass vase. Isn't it magnificent?" versus "I like that! Look at the dark green. That's pretty, isn't it? Monongahela Valley, olive green glass . . ."). Sometimes an evaluative comment acted as the conclusion of the episode and indicated a move to the next topic or exhibit case (e.g., ". . . so it's quite a mixture here, leading from the sublime to the mundane"). Some evaluative comments were primarily affective (like/dislike), whereas others were more analytic, but their prevalence in nearly half the episodes indicates how important they are to visitor conversations. If nothing else, they were likely to stimulate a response from a companion, even if that response was simply "Mm-hm." Thus, even if these comments provided little in the way of substantive exchange of ideas, they supported conversation generally. At times they led into or wrapped up a more detailed conversation at an exhibit station.

Figure 6.1 further shows that more than half the episodes contained a combination of both identification and at least one expansion. This means that more than half the time visitor groups engaged in conversations that added to or reworked the material in the exhibition, either by analyzing some aspect of an object or idea in an exhibit, synthesizing information from elsewhere with information in an exhibit station, or explaining some feature or idea in a way that was not already explicated. The cycle of talk that occurred in episodes with an expansion sometimes began with an identification activity or an evaluative comment prior to the expansion, but at other times began with a rush of enthusiastic expanded talk on an idea sparked by something in the museum, which was then followed by a focused identification comment, as in the example below, where Sarah and Pat are viewing glass objects at the entrance facade:

Sarah: Did you know Monica is a glass blower? . . .

Pat: It's amazing to watch someone who's really good at this . . . (whispering) You take deep breaths because the glass is [very precious].

Sarah: And there's a glass [globe] . . . (Group 6, lines 8–27)

Whether or not an episode contained an expansion or an evaluation, it often contained instances of *brief* analytic or synthetic information; some episodes also contained attention moves (e.g., "Look at this over here!"). Some contained explicit comments about learning or wanting to learn more (e.g., "I didn't know that!" or "They don't tell us how the color is put in."); and occasionally there was some comic relief, where people teased each other or shared inside jokes, which seemed to relieve the intensity of inquiry that so often leads to museum fatigue. Although some of the "work" in building understanding from museum exhibits in conjunction with companions could take place within the unexpanded talk, we were more interested in the expansions because that is where explanations could occur and where we expected to find the strongest links between visitor identity and conversational elaboration.[9]

Pattern of the Talk in Groups with High Versus Low Glass Knowledge

Beyond the issue of identifying a general pattern of visitor conversation in *Glass: Shattering Notions*, we also wanted to know the effect of different backgrounds and experiences on the pattern of group conversations. We have already indicated that visitors' Pittsburgh identity was not considered in our

[9]In some cases a pair of visitors would query each other (or the invisible curator) but be unable to resolve their query with the information available. The sense of query, however, could be quite strong, as could the sense of curiosity and interest; so the level of involvement could be considered high even though the level of explanatory engagement did not extend very far and there was no notable *expansion* in the dialogue. (See Abu-Shumays & Leinhardt [chap. 2, this volume] for an example of Julia and Elsa's unresolved queries on how glass is made in different colors.)

analyses because so few groups were rated Low on that dimension that we could not construct a meaningful comparison. For the Museum identity dimension we found that there was no particular pattern in the data; thus we do not discuss the museum dimension further. We did see a difference for groups with a High connection to glass as opposed to those rated Low on glass. By separating the results for High glass groups ($n = 5$) from those for groups with a Low connection to glass ($n = 5$), we were able to see where the pattern of their talk was similar and where it differed. Figure 6.2 shows two Venn diagrams that illustrate the pattern of talk for the High and the Low glass groups based on the percent of episodes that contained each of the following talk elements: (a) identification; (b) identification plus evaluation; (c) identification plus expansion, including the overlap with b; and (d) those episodes within the expansions that also had explanations.

Overall, the High groups had 25% more episodes than the Low groups. As can be seen in both the chart and the schematic Venn diagrams of Fig. 6.2, groups with a high connection to glass had the same percentage of identification activity throughout their tours as groups with a low connection to glass; they had similar percentages of episodes with evaluative commentary; but the High groups had a noticeably higher percentage of episodes that contained expansions (59% vs. 43%) and also a much higher percentage of episodes (five times greater) that contained explanations. (The percentages for episodes with explanations [3% and 15%] correspond to six episodes for the Low glass-knowledge groups compared to 38 for the High knowledge groups.)

The findings from this analysis indicate that in general visitor groups who came to a museum exhibition with prior knowledge or experience relevant to the content of the exhibition had a greater likelihood of engaging in a more expanded way than did those with less connection to the content. A more detailed examination of the thematic emphasis of those expansions and the instances of explanation-level talk that were generated in certain expansions will help us see how visitor identity affected the content and depth of the conversations.

Thematic Focus of the Talk

In listening to the tour audiotapes, we became aware that visitors generally engaged in meaningful discussion at places where they paused and expanded on the museum presentations in some way. Thus, to understand more about the nature of visitors' conversations we looked closely at the content of those expansions. Because more than one expansion could occur within a single episode,[10] we used expansions rather than episodes as

[10]Of the 460 conversational episodes, 9.3% had multiple expansions in them.

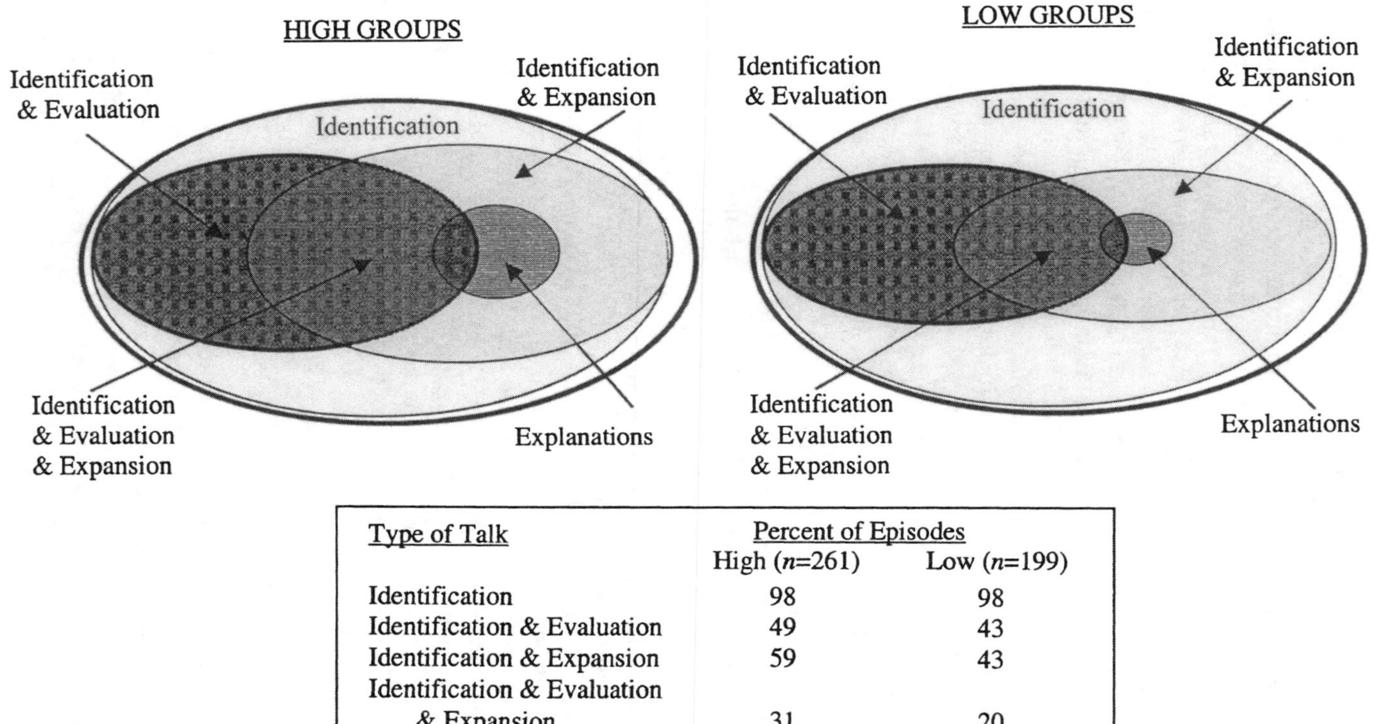

Type of Talk	Percent of Episodes High (n=261)	Percent of Episodes Low (n=199)
Identification	98	98
Identification & Evaluation	49	43
Identification & Expansion	59	43
Identification & Evaluation & Expansion	31	20
Expansion with Explanation	15	3

FIG. 6.2. Percentage of episodes with different types of talk for groups with high versus low glass knowledge or experience. (Note: Venn diagrams are not to scale.)

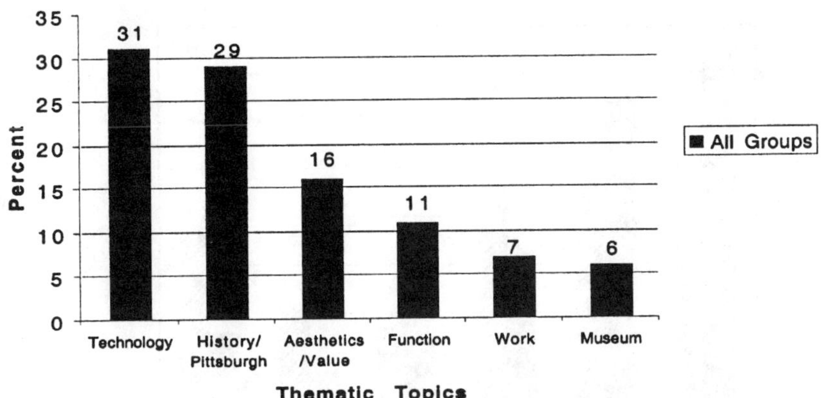

FIG. 6.3. Percentage of expansions by theme.

the unit of analysis here. The purpose of this part of the analysis was to see whether visitors with certain identity characteristics were more or less likely to engage in expansions on particular thematic topics or to engage in more or less sophisticated levels of explanatory dialogue on certain topics. As stated earlier, each expansion was coded as belonging to one of the six thematic categories (Technology, History/Pittsburgh, Aesthetics/Value, Work, Museum, or Function); and each expansion was also classified according to whether the talk was primarily Analyzing, Synthesizing, or Explaining. The percentage of expansions falling into each of those thematic categories and levels of engagement was tabulated for all visitor groups combined.

Across all groups, there were a total of 290 Expansions. As Fig. 6.3 shows, most of the expanded talk emphasized either Technology (31%) or History/Pittsburgh (29%), with each of the other thematic topics receiving smaller percentages of the expanded talk. This thematic emphasis in visitors' expanded talk in part reflects the dominant themes of this exhibition, in which texts, artifacts, and displays tell the *history* of the development of a *technologically* based manufacturing industry in the *Pittsburgh*/Western Pennsylvania region. We wondered, however, whether some visitor groups emphasized certain thematic topics in their expanded talk more than other groups did, and whether the group-specific thematic emphases were related to any identity characteristics of those groups. We therefore examined the data on thematic emphasis in terms of how groups with a high connection to glass compared to those with a low connection and the results of that analysis are shown in Fig. 6.4.

As Fig. 6.4 shows, groups with a high rating on glass knowledge or experience generated expansions that focused more on technology than did those groups with a low rating on glass (37% vs. 20%) and the High groups also focused considerably more of their expanded talk on the History/Pitts-

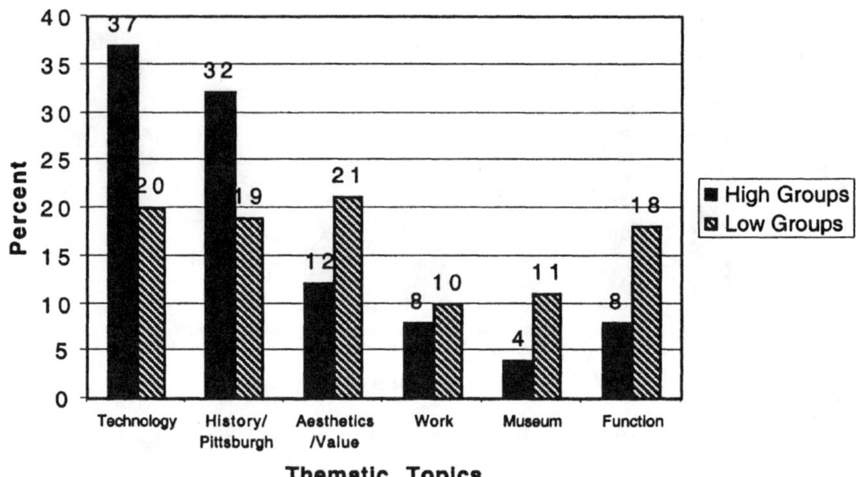

FIG. 6.4. Percentage of expansions on each theme by groups with high vs. low glass knowledge.

burgh theme than did the Low groups (32% vs. 19%). Taken together these findings suggest that groups with high levels of experience with glass could make use of the affordances in the museum exhibits in more detailed and specific ways than could those with less background experience. Conversely, these findings suggest that visitors with *less* sophisticated connections to glass were more likely to expand on those features of glass that are more readily accessible and require less technical depth. But it also shows that even without sophisticated access to the material, visitors engaged. Examples of expansions on three specific themes are shown next—two that occurred in the conversation of a High group and one in a Low group.[11]

Technology Theme/High Group

The first example is a technology expansion that occurred in the conversation of a High glass group at an exhibit area called "Handmade." This exhibit consisted of a display of traditional tools for making glass by hand as well as a series of large photographs showing a glass blower at three stages in the process of making a glass pitcher.

Riley: For example, see, he's blowing a bubble . . . then he puts his pipe on here, and he rolls it back and forth and spins a flat plate. Then they

[11]Ellipses in all these transcript excerpts indicate portions of dialogue omitted here for reasons of clarity or brevity. Square brackets indicate an inaudible word or phrase. One small dash indicates dialogue interrupted by or interwoven with a companion's comment.

mold the plate into what they want . . . say, a salad bowl with frets. . . . The fascinating thing about glass is it never melts. You see it's always being worked like taffy. See them cutting it with this pair of shears there.

Mary: Yes.

Riley: Then they'll bend it over and . . . touch it to here and that's how they make the handle.

Mary: Oh, I see.

Riley: See, lift it up here at the lip . . . Guide it with a stick . . . and it would bond because everything is the same temperature. (Group 1, lines 704–761)

History/Pittsburgh Theme/High Group

The second example of a thematic expansion is one given by the same High glass group at an exhibit of old glass flasks, where the visitors' experience as collectors provided the background for the following historical commentary:

Riley: Here are the old flasks. A fascinating history on them. Back in the early 1800s people couldn't read. So when they wanted to identify the liquor that they were drinking, they identified it by the-

Mary: the shape . . .

Riley: -by the bottle . . . some would be in the shape of a log cabin. Remember the old Log Cabin maple syrup?

Mary: Yes.

Riley: . . . you knew you were getting maple syrup if it came in a log cabin can or bottle.

Mary: I see.

Riley: The same way here. Your bottles were all indicating the type of, of liquor that was in them. (Group 1, lines 595–621)

Function Expansion/Low Group

The third example is an expansion on the theme of Function, given by a group with a low connection to glass. This discussion by Amelia and Brenda occurred at the glass-block partition early in the tour and it provides an example of how visitors drew on their outside experiences to help them connect to the museum content—in this case the function of a particular glass product.

Amelia: These block glasses are nice. A lot of people do these in basement[ways] and [things]

Brenda: What did you say? Oh, these—Yeah, they're arranged interiors, over in England now, if people buy them . . .

Amelia: Yeah. (Group 9, lines 30–38)

Levels of Explanatory Engagement

In examining the expansions that visitors engaged in, we looked not only at the thematic emphases of those conversations but also at the depth of their engagement; that is, we wanted to know the extent to which groups engaged in expansions that were analyses, syntheses, or explanations. Figure 6.5 shows that the expanded talk came in the form of analyses, syntheses, or explanations at the rate of 42%, 40%, and 18% respectively.

What these results help us to see is that most visitors were able to formulate substantial analytic contributions to the information available in the exhibition and to an even greater degree most were also able to elaborate on ideas they drew in either from outside the museum or from exhibit displays elsewhere in the exhibition to enrich their understanding of what the museum was offering. To a lesser extent, visitors were able to elaborate on the museum's presentation to the level of what we call explanation. Within these general trends, however, there was considerable variation between groups in terms of the degree to which they were likely to engage in analysis, synthesis, or explanation. An examination of the performance of High versus Low glass groups reveals how visitors' backgrounds influenced their level of explanatory engagement (see Fig. 6.6).

As Fig. 6.6 shows, the High and Low groups differed little with respect to the percentage of their expanded talk that was at the level of analysis. Low groups, however, engaged in a greater percentage of expansions at the level

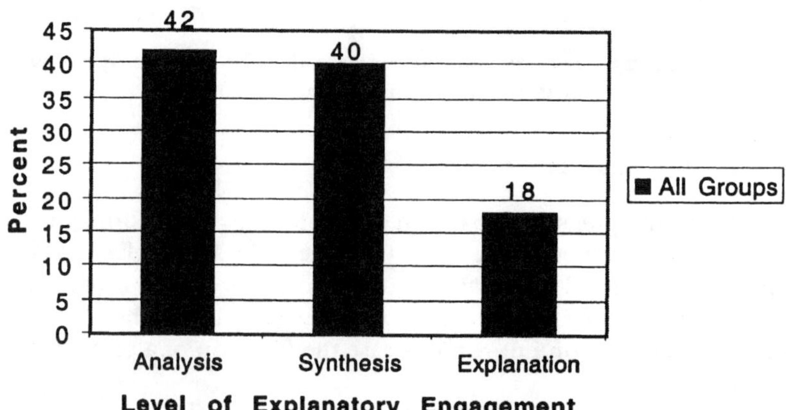

FIG. 6.5. Percentage of expansions that are analysis, synthesis, or explanation.

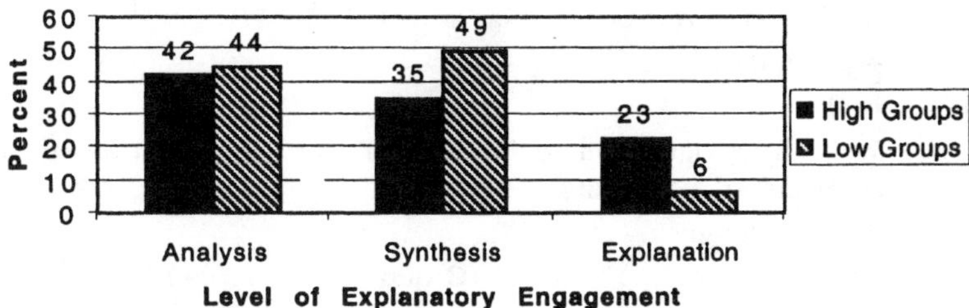

FIG. 6.6. Percentage of expansions that are analysis, synthesis, or explanation for groups with high vs. low glass knowledge.

of synthesis. (It should be noted that a large proportion of these syntheses in the Low groups' conversations came in the form of personal stories about people they knew or about events in their lives.[12] High groups had a smaller percentage of their expansions in the form of syntheses than did the Low groups, and fewer syntheses that were quite so grounded in personal stories about friends and relatives.) The greatest difference between the High and Low groups was found in the percentage of explanation-level expansions, as shown on the right-hand side of Fig. 6.6. To give a sense of how expansions at these three levels sounded, examples of visitors expanding in the form of analysis, synthesis, and explanation are provided next, some from groups with high connections to glass and some from groups that were low.

Analysis/High Group

The following example of an expansion in the form of analysis was given by Jason as he considered the aesthetic features of a jar at the exhibit for Print Advertising, where some of the items featured in old advertisements mounted on the wall are also displayed in a case of glass objects. The specific object of focus here was a tall, cylindrical, clear glass container with a lid. Deep blue rings of glass that protrude slightly from the surface of the jar provide decorative markings at approximately one third and two thirds of the way down. Jason, the architect, was interested in the use of glass for both its structural and aesthetic qualities and was drawn to unusually designed objects in this exhibition, as can be seen in his analytic focus on the aesthetic qualities of the jar's rings:

Jason: It's a, it's a jar with cobalt rings around it. . . . covered jar. 'The addition of blue rings of glass makes this utilitarian object beautiful.' I agree, I think you know-

[12]Unlike McManus (1989, pp. 183–184) we found overwhelming evidence of visitors using personal stories in their museum conversations as they responded to exhibits.

Joyce: -Yeah, you were, your eye was attracted to-

Jason: -sometimes it's the little [—]

Joyce: [—]

Jason: Well, that's right. You could, yeah. [Don't know] that it's just the color either, I think it's -

Joyce: -It's the design-

Jason: It's the, it's the . . . Yeah . . . (Group 3, lines 1363–1375)

Synthesis/High Group

The following expansion was in the form of a synthesis that was provided by Jason at an exhibit on Polarized Glass. The exhibit included three back-lit photographs of famous Pittsburgh professional athletes set behind rotatable lenses of polarized glass, such that in certain positions the photographs could be clearly seen and in other positions the polarized lens blocked all light and the images disappeared. Jason's expansion at this exhibit was a synthesis that drew on his outside experience as an architect who uses glass in his profession in a way that requires a deep understanding of various glass products and their properties and also requires him to be up-to-date on technological advances in his profession anywhere in the world. Here he tells about another usage of this feature of glass in a different setting that is architecturally relevant.

Jason: What's happening here? Polarized glass. Oh, this is great stuff. The Japanese have been using, uh, electronics with polarized glass. (*synthesis*)

Joyce: Uh-huh.

Jason: Press a button and electronically the glass polarizes and so you have this jet-clear glass all around you in the conference room, and when you want privacy, you press a button, and the glass polarizes, and you can't see through it- (*synthesis continued*)

Joyce: Ooh!

Jason: -electronically, and they're doing that in the outside of buildings as well. . . . It's blackout shades for conference rooms, and-

Joyce: -privacy-

Jason: Yeah . . . Polarized glass is a filter. So we have here, we can't see a darn thing, but when we turn it 90 degrees, we watch the Pirates play ball. (Group 3, lines 747–768)

Synthesis/Low Group

The following synthesis occurred in the conversation of a group with a low connection to glass. As with many stories told by visitors who were less connected to glass, this one recalls a personal experience that reveals an authentic but peripheral connection to glass. In this synthesis, Sarah and Pat were looking at a display of intricate glass tubes and containers at Lab Glass and Sarah describes a time when she ordered objects like this for a school district.

Pat: Oh, [these are the old-]

Sarah: [—].

Pat: Yeah. "Gulf Research, Harmarville."

Sarah: When I worked in the schools in St. Louis, I used to call Fisher Scientific.

Pat: Did you?

Sarah: All the time. To order our beakers . . . and all the stuff for the chemistry department. And we use to order the frogs for the dissection . . . [P— —]

Pat: [Petrie tray]. (Group 6, lines 120–131)

Explanation/High

The following expansion was in the form of an explanation given in a High group where one member, Herbert, had experience working in a stained glass factory. At the Stained Glass exhibit, Herbert provided the following lengthy explanation for his group about how stained glass is repaired. They are looking at two back-lit stained glass windows mounted on the wall under the sign of a local manufacturer, Rudy Brothers, accompanied by text and photographs from that factory. There is no information given in the exhibit about full antique glass, about how stained glass is repaired, nor even that a repair is involved in the display. This transcript excerpt is annotated (in parenthetical italics) with indications of various conversational moves that build toward the explanation.

Herbert: This is, this, this is as full antique as they make at Blenko . . . (*identification*) and there's hardly any place in the country that makes full antique anymore.

Kimiko: Oh.

Herbert: I had a repair job that had . . . six different kinds of full antique and I hear you can't replace 'em. (*synthesis/personal*)

Kimiko: What did you do with it? Just to [get] the color close to it? (*query/prompt*)

Herbert: [Just put what is close as you could. Whatever color takes.]

Kimiko: Is this, umm, a design behind the glass that, what is that–

Herbert: No, no, this is little chips-

Kimiko: Oh-

Herbert: -of glass, and they put it on a piece of clear glass or whatever color you want on there– (*explaining how it's done*)

Kimiko: Um-hum.

Herbert: -and then you fuse it in the kiln. Stick it on there. (*explain actions*)

Kimiko: What, what, I don't get this. Down here. (*prompt to continue*)

Herbert: Oh that's just painted on.

Kimiko: Oh, looks like toes.

Herbert: Well, you paint it, well, that's what it is, but I mean you paint it and put it in the kiln. (*explain actions*)

Kimiko: Of course.

Herbert: Yeah, that's why it looks like feet.

Kimiko: (laughs)

Herbert: You put it in the kiln . . . and cook it. And that fuses the—The paint is mixed with fine, fine, fine, ground glass . . . You see here, there's a whole bunch of repairs on this. (*explanation continues*)

Kimiko: Are there? How can you tell? (*prompt for further explanation*)

Herbert: Well, see these should match. And these pieces that they've got now cross pieces- (*starts new explanation of stained glass repair*)

Kimiko: Uh-huh.

Herbert: -of different levels.

Kimiko: I see.

Herbert: . . . [There's a cross there . . .]

Kimiko: I see. So they mi- repair it where it needs it.

Herbert: They can't replace the piece-

Kimiko: Uh-huh.

Herbert: -so they put a piece of lead-

Kimiko: I see.

Herbert: -there on the other side, that same level-

Kimiko: Uh-huh.

Herbert: -that covers the crack. (*explanation continues*)

Kimiko: So, the- these two should match, you're saying.

Herbert: Yeah.

Kimiko: And this, this should match. I see.

Herbert: No, this is covering a crack in the glass . . . they can't get a piece like that. So they just covered the crack.

Kimiko: I see. Hmm. (*explanation understood*)

Herbert: And they put a piece on the other side-

Kimiko: Um-hum.

Herbert: -matching it so it looks like it's part of the picture there. (*explanation ends*) (Group 7, lines 831–911)

In each of these examples we see visitors having conversations about objects or ideas in the exhibition by expanding on what the museum has provided and making meaningful connections between the museum content and their own backgrounds. In each case the museum display prompted visitors to engage their companions in discussions that included details or points of view that were sparked by the exhibit and this prompt often called up into active memory an idea that had lain dormant for some time. What these examples failed to show clearly was the dominant tendency among Low groups for much of their syntheses to come in the form of a personal story that helped to make a feature of the exhibition more meaningful. These story-like syntheses seemed to help visitors to connect to the exhibition by means of recollections about objects they owned, people they knew, places they had been, or events in which they had participated. If their companions were familiar with some element in the story, the story served to call up a familiar and shared idea for the group and made an immediate link to the museum content for everyone. If the story was more individually sourced, it became, in the telling of it, a shared expansion on the museum content, whether the story was about a collectible object or a technological process. Their prevalence reflects one of the intentions of the exhibition curator, who says in the catalogue:

> Clearly the American public feels a special connection to the substance, as glass collectors form one of the largest group of collectors in the country. Many more people also identify with a single piece or group of objects that has special meaning to them alone. . . . Glass [may become] infused with personality when it is passed person-to-person by those who share a relationship. The object's form and being are unchanged, but its value increases because it reminds one of the previous owner . . . Use and shared understanding [of all forms of glass] have created a cultural construct whereby the material is assigned symbolic meanings. By looking at the glass in our lives and in the past we can begin to unlock those meanings. (Madarasz, 1998, pp. 12–14)

Among the stories told during conversations in this exhibition about glass objects and people who owned them, many were shared by members in the two groups whose expansions contained no explanations, but which often took the form of personal reminiscences used to support an idea at the level of analysis or synthesis. In their pre- or posttour discussions, both groups talked about the nostalgic pleasures of viewing such an exhibition, and this nostalgic thread can be seen in the stories they tell. Although their expansions were often anchored to a personal reminiscence, the stories they shared were relevant to particular thematic topics being portrayed by the exhibition, most often in the Aesthetic/Value, History/Pittsburgh, or

Function strands. Examples of some of these more narrative, story-like syntheses are shown next.

In the first example, Yvette and Jasmine were looking at decorative glass objects in the Handmade section of the exhibition, which included a display case of "Cut and Engraved" objects. Something in the display triggered recollections of the aesthetic qualities of a special glass vase owned by someone Jasmine knew, and which she described eagerly to her companion.

Yvette: I used to—I can remember watching them, umm, do the etching on the glass up at Washington, I was so fascinated with it. (pause) Hmm. (*synthesis/reminiscence*)

Jasmine: B____'s mother has a vase that comes out real nice with big fluted edges, and when you put the flowers in . . . the edges flop out all over . . . Oh, it makes the prettiest arrangement you ever want to see. Just gorgeous. (laughs) (*synthesis using reminiscence of personally relevant object's aesthetic qualities*) (Group 8, lines 237–249)

The second example of a synthesis in story form comes from Sarah and Pat as they viewed a display of objects at "Pressed Glass." Something in the display case makes Pat recall a favorite object used by their mutual grandmother on special occasions. Their shared reminiscence of those events seems to be imbued with a sense of fond nostalgia as Pat provides details to enrich the memory.

Pat: I remember . . . Grandma [had] a relish tray . . . On holidays she had . . . celery and carrots and all the vegetables. You know the relish tray? (*synthesis using reminiscence of personally relevant object and its function*)

Sarah: Oh, I remember that too. (*shared reminiscence*)

Pat: . . . this glass, let's see . . . It's the same shape . . . (*identification*)

Sarah: It's exactly the same, yeah. Awww.

Pat: She always had carrots and celery and pickles and olives and onion . . . For holidays she always got that out. (*synthesis/personal story continues*)

Sarah: It's so fun to see all this . . . (Group 6, lines 380–399)

The third example comes from Yvette and Jasmine again when they were at the Stained Glass exhibit and Jasmine was reminded of a moment in her life when she realized that not everyone shared her sense of the value and aesthetic qualities of stained glass windows. She told that story to her companion with the element of "shock" that she felt at the time.

Jasmine: It's just so beautiful. (*aesthetic evaluation*)

Yvette: Hmm.

Jasmine: . . . Y'know, the people that bought our house in Pittsburgh . . . the first thing they did was take the [stained glass] windows out . . . (*synthesis/personal story*)

Yvette: Oh!

Jasmine: It was like, (laughs) I was shocked! I don't know what they did with them. I wish I would have known. I would have bought them from them! (*synthesis/story continues/aesthetic-value theme*)

Yvette: Yeah. (Group 8, lines 403–421)

Explanatory Engagement Within Thematic Topics

Although our results from analyses of thematic emphasis and levels of explanatory engagement are interesting on their own, one additional question is whether certain levels of explanatory engagement were more or less likely to be associated with certain thematic topics; that is, whether visitors tended to engage in expansions at the *explanation* level on aesthetic/value issues, for example, more than they did on issues of the nature of work. We cross-tabulated the results from the coding of thematic topics and levels of explanatory engagement (shown separately in Figs. 6.3 and 6.5) in order to see which levels of explanatory engagement were likely to be associated with each topic. Figure 6.7 shows the percentage of expansions by thematic topic and level of talk for all groups combined.

What Fig. 6.7 lets us see is that people synthesized information across all types of thematic talk. The largest proportion of expansions occurred as syntheses within the thematic strand of History/Pittsburgh (21%). As indicated earlier in this chapter, much of the expanded talk in the History/Pittsburgh strand involved personal stories about objects, people, places, or events in people's lives that allowed them to make a personal connection to

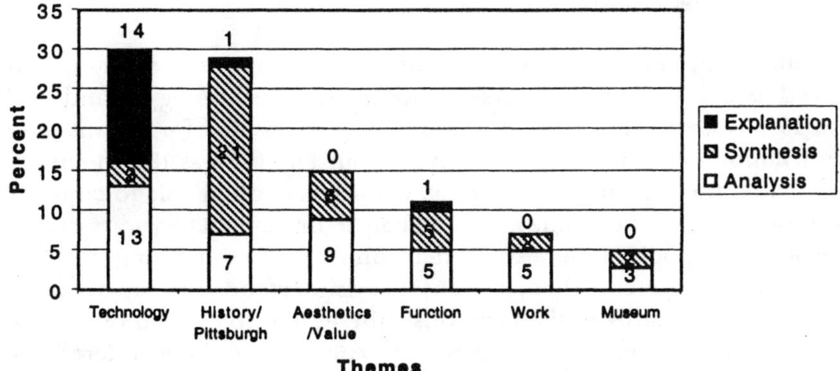

FIG. 6.7. Percentage of expansions by theme and type.

some historical idea that was present in the exhibition. In the earlier examples we focused on personal reminiscences and stories invoked by groups with a low connection to glass, but groups with high glass backgrounds did so as well, as the following excerpt from Julia and Elsa's tour demonstrates. Julia and Elsa were at the "Cut and Engraved" exhibit, looking at the display case of intricately carved objects. Julia expanded on the idea of the popularity of cut glass at a certain point in time, based on her recollection of her mother's ownership of it. Although there is a personal story underlying this history synthesis, it also contains an analysis of the cost and affordability of glass based on what Julia knew about the "poor people" who owned it.

> *Julia:* Well, see, there is cut . . . glass. . . . At the time my mother married, cut glass must have been a very popular wedding gift, because many women of her age had many pieces of cut glass. And I don't think it was expensive, 'cause they were poor people. (Group 4, Julia & Elsa, lines 507–517)

Some of the personal stories people invoked and used to expand on an idea were social in nature, such as those calling up memories of family gatherings where a particular object was used long ago. If a companion shared a family connection with the speaker, then the social event became a jointly constructed recollection of a family event or a family member, as in the case of Sarah and Pat's discussion about their grandmother's relish tray cited earlier. Occasionally visitors engaged in a form of synthesis that allowed them to expand on a more fundamental, historical idea, such as change over time, as in the following example from Yuri and Minsu:

> *Yuri:* By the way, I think the mirror was produced not so long ago. Is the mirror also antiquated?
>
> *Minjung:* I know that Cleopatra used mirrors.
>
> *Yuri:* At that time mirrors [were] bronze . . . (Group 2, Minsu & Yuri, lines 91–94)

Returning to Fig. 6.7, we see that the next largest sets of expansions occurred as explanations and analyses within the Technology strand (14% and 13% respectively). What this finding suggests is that for expansions in the technology strand, which we know from Fig. 6.3 was the theme that dominated the expanded talk overall, visitors were often able to target features of the exhibit content in more analytic or explanatory ways because they found a "hook" in the exhibit that connected to something they knew more about. In general, then, it seems that visitors tended to expand on history themes primarily in the form of syntheses and to expand on technology themes in the form of analyses and explanations. We wondered what features of the museum experience might account for that trend and in particular whether the level of explanatory engagement in each thematic strand was influenced by visitors' backgrounds. We suspected that these results reflect particular areas of competence that our visitor groups brought with them, which enabled them to connect with the affordances of the museum exhibition in particular ways. We have already seen that those visitors who came with a strong background in glass, especially those who were involved in the production or professional uses of glass, were much more likely to engage in expansions in the technology strand than were other visitors. If we focus more directly on those expansions that were explanations and compare explanations given by High versus Low glass groups we can delineate the differences more clearly.

Connections Between Visitor Identity and the Conversations

We focused on the explanations that groups engaged in because that is the most complex level of engagement. The percentage of explanations for groups rated High versus Low on the glass dimension is shown in the right-hand portion of Fig. 6.6, where we see that 22% of the High groups' expansions come in the form of explanations compared to only 5.4% of the Low groups'. This roughly fourfold difference in explanatory behavior indicates that visitors who came to the exhibition with a high connection to the content were more likely to engage in conversations that extended the information provided by the exhibition than were less knowledgeable visitors, and to do so at a more complex, sophisticated level. The elevated rate of explanations among High glass groups was true whether they had a high level of educational attainment (e.g., Herbert & Kimiko) or a low formal education level but personal glass-making experience on the factory floor (i.e., Armand). An example of an explanation by Armand early in his tour helps to illustrate the way a specific type of experience or knowledge relevant to the content of an exhibit can foster the offering of explanations that embellish the museum exhibit. In this instance, Armand was looking at a display of small glass objects of mostly bird and animal shapes that were set on shelves inside a tall metal cage and labeled "Glass Menagerie." Although Armand had not been to a museum for more than 40 years, and although he continually expressed dismay at his inability to adequately describe the many beautiful objects he was encountering as he toured, he was in fact able to engage at the level of explanation on the content of the exhibition in ways that none of our other visitors were able to do.

Armand: Look at the, look at the colors in this . . . candy dish . . . All very, very beautiful stuff that's individually made. What a talent they had to make this stuff, to put the colors in there . . .

Kate: How do you . . . think they would make the birds lighter than the back part?

Armand: There's a dye, there's certain, they put like, a dye in and—I've seen it done where they know exactly how to pour that. It's like a liquid dye is what I remember. . . . They know where they're putting the dye or the painted sections in it. And they just roll it. They keep rolling and rolling it. They get it on the table, it goes back and forth on the table and . . . Amazing. Amazing. Now what I, where I worked at it was just simple. You just put the glass on a pipe and put it in the mold . . . you open the mold, put the glass in, you close the mold. And after it cools down, you open the mold and pull your item out. That was . . . a job, but it wasn't a talent like really rolling the glass to get the colors and different designs in. (Group 5, lines 96–111)

Although Armand had not produced glass objects with color embedded in the design himself, he repeatedly had observed first-hand how it was done and was able to describe that in detail to his companion. Of Armand's 25 expansions, five (20%) were explanations either on the theme of technology or the theme of work. This percentage is slightly higher than the mean percent of expansions (18%) that were explanations for all groups combined, as shown in Fig. 6.3.

Social Factors in Museum Conversations

In addition to considering the effect of visitors' identities, especially with respect to their background knowledge in and experience with glass, we considered other factors that might account for the relative presence or absence of explanations within each conversational group. One of the features of the groups rated High with respect to their connection to glass was that there was also a gradient in the knowledge level among individual members of those groups. That is, within each High group, one or another member was acknowledged by the group to be more expert with respect to glass. For Riley and Clara, for example, who were both keen glass collectors, Riley had in addition to that knowledge base a very strong technical understanding of the processes involved in making glass. For Julia and Elsa, both of whom had been chemistry majors, which required them to blow glass in the lab, and both of whom had provided extensive docent support at a natural history museum where glass had once been a featured exhibit, Julia was considered to be more expert for two reasons—she had visited and observed at the Kopp Glass factory on numerous occasions thanks to a friend who worked there, and she had toured the *Glass: Shattering Notions* exhibition previously. Kimiko and Herbert (and their other companions) were visiting the exhibition in large part because of Herbert's interest in glass. Although they did not specify the nature of his connection to glass during the pretour conversation, evidence of his expertise emerged during the tour as Kimiko and other group members listened to and queried him about things he knew. In a sense, then, the gradient in levels of knowledge and expertise was what motivated this group to come to the exhibition in the first place.

In a similar vein, one of the groups with a Low rating on connection to glass—Group 2 (Minsu and Yuri)—had a greater percentage of their expansions that were explanations (13%) than the other Low groups. Many of Group 2's expansions and explanations evolved in conversations prompted by Yuri's interest and expertise in epidemiology. Unlike visitors in our other groups, Yuri saw health and public policy issues embedded in several displays and she shared these insights with the members of her group as she engaged them in historical discussions of the impact of industry on workers' health. Thus, it was the difference in *areas* of expertise, not simply levels of expertise, which may have accounted for the presence of more explanations in that group than in other Low groups. In other words, the gradient in knowledge among members of Group 2 resided largely in the domain of public health rather than in glass, and although that pushed the level of their explanatory talk, their lack of experience in glass limited the percentage of their expansions that were explanations relative to the High glass groups.

Among the other groups with a Low connection to glass, Group 10 (Pauline, Andy, and Kyle) had the next highest percent of their expansions as explanations (10%). Those explanations were prompted, we believe, by the parent–child relationship within the group. This family had no particular connection to glass and although they were knowledgeable about Pittsburgh they were not life-long residents. They did describe themselves as regular museum-goers and we suggest that in part it was this aspect of their identity that led them to engage in expansions and explanations about the museum. Clearly the parents were providing for their child a way of understanding how museums work. They told him, for example, that the reason why there was a model of the Statue of Liberty included in this exhibition was *because* there were glass windows in the statue's crown, although the two-dimensional, matte-finished, monochromatic, wooden cut-out model of the statue's head and crown did not make that feature obvious. Many other visitors wondered why a seven-foot replica of this famous American icon was included in the exhibition and was placed in such a prominent position. Although the Statue of Liberty is instantly recognizable to visitors from around the world, the fact that there are windows in its crown is not as well known, and the sense that there were glass panels in the crown was not supported by the dull green façade of this replica. Pauline, the mother in this family, discovered the glass connection for this piece by reading the wall text and then she told the other members of her group about it. The statue's relevance to the Pittsburgh region made sense once one knew that there were windows in it.

A few moments later in this tour, the father and son began to engage in an extended analysis of the meaning of a display in the Glass-as-Metaphor case. One pair of objects in this case consisted of two half-filled drinking glasses that were set side by side and partly "filled" to illustrate the common metaphorical phrase "half full or half empty." In this instance, the case label (Metaphor) was perhaps overlooked or was overshadowed in the father's mind either by the overarching exhibition topic (glass) or by the object label that was expressed in the form of a question (Is the glass half empty or half full?). The father took the question literally and debated with his son for some time about whether there were different amounts of white "stuff" in the two glass tumblers, or if perhaps one of the glasses had a thicker base. The father called the son back to this case a couple of times from other exhibit stations where the boy and the mother were looking at something else, and at one point the father actually got down on his knees in order to examine the bottoms of those tumblers at eye level. The subliminal cultural message here for the child was that museum displays are organized the way they are for a reason and it's partly the visitor's obligation to figure out the meaning.

Thus we can see that there are various ways in which different levels of expertise can emerge among group members so as to produce more expansions in the form of explanation than occur among groups with a balanced level of expertise among its members. In the case of Pauline, Andy, and Kyle, we suggest that their expansions reflect the presence of another kind of gradient—where a difference in social roles provided the stimulus for much of the explanatory behavior as this family "rehearsed" their parent/child roles in the museum setting.

Conversely, the absence of a gradient in levels of expertise could account for the absence of explanations in the talk of two of our Low glass-knowledge groups. This notion of a gradient (or lack thereof) in acknowledged levels of expertise could also account for extreme cases where there is an overall suppression of talk between visitors who are highly knowledgeable about exactly the same things and do not need to share their thoughts in much detail with their companion—a simple phrase will call up a whole network of unspoken ideas. (See Stainton, chap. 7, this volume, for a discussion of a dyad where both members had high knowledge backgrounds, were familiar with each others' backgrounds and experiences, and thus spoke in a truncated–abbreviated fashion to each other during their tour of *Soul of Africa.*)

Recurring Issues

There were other ways that conversations were prompted by the social dynamics of the group or by the way the group was organized. We could see, for example, that people played out social roles in the course of dealing with an idea that was of special concern for them and became a recurring issue in their tour. For many of the groups there were one or more of these special issues or concerns that recurred throughout a tour, weaving in and out and appearing in places where the particular exhibit station did not seem to directly prompt that kind of response. Some of these issues surfaced as repeated brief mentions and did not show up in the expanded talk. (See Young & Leinhardt, 1998, for a similar phenomenon that was found in the use of analogical language in history classrooms, where repeated brief mentions of a thematic construct tended to accumulate weight over time.) In other cases the repeated discussions of a particular concern came in more expanded form. We saw earlier some examples of a recurring concern for the family group (Pauline, Andy, & Kyle) to convey to the child a sense of how museums work. We discuss three other examples of recurring issues next, two from Group 2 (Minsu & Yuri) and one from Group 6 (Sarah & Pat).

There were two different recurring threads through Minsu and Yuri's tour. One thread involved their shared Korean background that provided them with a particular lens for viewing certain parts of the exhibition. While examining the Model-T Ford replica, with its decorative embellishment in the form of an external bud vase, Minsu was reminded of the way modern-day Korean taxi drivers decorate their vehicles ("In Korea, taxi drivers usually decorate the gear handle . . ."). Near the end of their tour, as they looked at a wide array of glass objects on display in a reconstructed hotel room that represented the annual glass show held in Pittsburgh years ago, he wondered why they, as Koreans, had never heard anything about Chinese glassmaking, although they knew about many other Chinese innovations.[13]

Minsu: I have a question. Um, most civilization or cultural development originated in China, at least in my knowledge. We knew [about] a lot of inventions [such] as pottery (china) and gunpowder (explosives) but I've never heard [about the] glass of China before. China had at most crafted Sam-chae[14] that was colored production [on the] surface. I remember [the] Koryo dynasty had imported glasses from elsewhere. Why did China have no glass in [the] pre-modern period . . . ?

Minjung: Where did they import it from?

---

[13] This discussion reflects the influence of China on Korean culture over many centuries (Kim, 1991, pp. 125–126; Macdonald, 1988, p. 11).

[14] Sam-chae is a form of painting on pottery developed in China in the 10th century that allowed three colors to be used together (Minjung Kim, personal communication, November 2, 2000).

Minsu: A trade took place with Arabic merchants, so we exported papers and Chinese ink stick instead.

Minjung: I know Ginseng was exported too.

Minsu: Sure. (Group 2, lines 591–604)

Although Minsu's query essentially went unanswered, the issue was clearly an important one to the group. Not only were they using China as the anchor for their historical comparison but also they were identifying with China as the exemplary Asian cultural leader and technological innovator.

The other recurring thread for this group stemmed from Yuri's public health background, which prompted her to engage her companions in discussions of public health issues at various exhibit stations where no other groups did so. At an exhibit called "Pittsburgh Lights the World," which was part of the Machine Made section of the exhibition, they had the following discussion:

Minjung: I think lead glass blowing must be harmful to glass makers' health.

Yuri: Definitely, you know they would suffer from mercurial poisoning . . .

Minsu: But did they understand the dangerous effects of lead?

Yuri: [Many people died!] Its cumulative effects were understood [only] after several decades and required people to actually start to study it. And finally relevant laws were passed.

Minsu: I wonder if people had enough of an understanding about it.

Yuri: It needed, of course, a long time to be recognized.

Minjung: I think the desire for mass production caused [this].

Minsu: However, crystal glass was blown as before, wasn't it?

Minjung: It was. There is some apparatus to control it for workers' health.

Yuri: So certain laws to regulate it were made but actually didn't work well.

Minsu: I have heard of it before, so, I mean, are lead vapors seriously dangerous?

Yuri: Absolutely . . . (Group 2, lines 267–289)

Later, at an exhibit on Labor, this group viewed a life-size picture of the "Glass House Boys"—children who worked in a glass factory—as Yuri introduced another epidemiological discussion. The exhibit station actually was a semitransparent scrim that showed two different images depending on the light source. In one image the young boys were present among adult men in the factory; in the alternate image, men held fancy glass canes and displayed glass chains or other decorative glass objects that they showed off in the annual glass makers parade. As this group considered the working conditions of the boys, Yuri expanded on the exhibit with the following information:

> *Yuri:* 'They employed kids from 8 through 13' . . . I can find many episodes related with glass industrial and labor union history here. One of the most famous studies is about cleaning chimneys, which needed small tiny kids to climb up. At the end, they had suffered from pneumoconiosis or silicosis. Do you know the well-known case study about those little kids? . . . (Group 2, lines 360–368)

As the image on the scrim changed to reveal the alternate scene, this group built on their discussion of adverse working conditions to understand a particularly sophisticated curatorial message:

> *Minsu:* Maybe, it seems to give meaningful message to us. There is something behind the apparent scene.
>
> *Minjung:* We could see a gorgeous front, but couldn't perceive those sacrifices . . .
>
> *Yuri:* To noble man who used glasses . . . Yes, consumers just enjoyed glass [but] these workers were screened. (Group 2, lines 371–377)

Another recurring idea appeared in the conversations between Sarah and Pat. Throughout their tour, they made repeated references to Sarah's niece, an artist who loves to blow glass but cannot make a living at it. (The first reference occurred at the Entrance Façade: "Did you know Monica's a glass blower? . . . She can't make a living at it full-time, so she has to do something else, but . . . that's what she likes to do." The second reference occurred at the display of artistic Mulcahy pieces: "Monica just loves all kinds of things like this . . . but she can't really make a living. She works for a company there that . . . hand paint[s] wallpaper . . ." The third reference came while they were moving from Bottles by the Billions (a ceiling high stack of green glass bottles), to Women Workers, to the Video showing how flat glass has been manufactured for more than 100 years: "Where did [she] learn glass blowing?" "In college . . . That's what she wanted. She was an art major, and that's what she loved doing, but. . . .") The third time this issue came up for discussion, it was the focus of their conversation across multiple exhibit stations with little mention of the objects or ideas on display at those exhibits. After a brief glance at the video, which showed pictures of men blowing giant glass tubes and swinging them over an open pit—which riveted the attention of our other groups—Sarah and Pat moved on, although they indicated they would like to come back to see the video "some time."

Clearly, this issue of a "starving artist" was a concern for these visitors. Although the financial plight of would-be glass artists was not an issue addressed by the museum, this topic was not extraneous to the exhibition—the visitors' concern about the life of a would-be glass artist was triggered by the exhibition on glass in ways that it would not have surfaced in another kind of exhibition. Thus it represents an example of how visitors' connection to the content may get called up in response to the overall context of a museum exhibition in ways that a museum could not possibly anticipate. Sarah and Pat's discussions of the niece, which were based on personal connections to someone they both knew, enriched their thinking about the nature of "work" in a way that other visitors would not be able to do based on the exhibition information alone.

In a way, these recurring issues represent one type of agenda people have as they tour in small groups and continue a social dynamic from before the visit that will likely continue afterward. These social dynamics support not only the large-scale structural features of the conversations people have during their visit (in terms of topic control, turn-taking, route-choosing, and so forth) but also the content of the talk as group members respond to the interests, concerns, or areas of expertise within the group.

CONCLUSIONS

We started this chapter with a set of questions that are designed to help inform the larger model of learning in museums. The model considers learning to be influenced by visitors' identity, their explanatory engagement, and the nature of the learning environment. In this chapter we looked closely at locations for elaboration in the course of a visit to *Glass: Shattering Notions* and at the identities of the visitors who made those elaborations. We found a general pattern in all the conversations and then focused on visitors' expanded talk in order to examine conversational elaboration more closely.

From listening to and analyzing the conversations in *Glass: Shattering Notions* we found that visitors tended to talk in similar ways as they moved through the exhibition, revealing a pattern to visitor conversation; that is, most episodes in the transcripts contained some form of identification activity, almost half included some evaluative commentary, and a large proportion of the talk (more than half) consisted of expansions on what the museum offered. Within the expanded talk we found that there was a distinct influence on the nature of museum conversations depending on the identity of the people who were visiting. Groups with high glass knowledge and interest, especially those who approached glass from a technical viewpoint, tended to engage in more expanded "explanation level" talk than did others. The increased incidence of explanations was also associated with a gradient in the acknowledged *levels* of expertise among group members, and sometimes with a difference in the *areas* of expertise. These differences within a group seemed to provide an opportunity for the explicit expressions of information or reaction. Furthermore, the presence of certain social roles, such as those in a parent–child relationship, were likely to be associated with an increased level of explanatory talk within groups that did not necessarily possess high levels of content knowledge.

One of the features we noticed about the museum conversations was that within all groups some talk was narrative-like and personal whereas other talk was more content-based or expository in nature. The presence of both these kinds of talk across topic boundaries and levels of explanatory engagement reflects our sense that people make meaning from a museum exhibit in more than one way. Some groups came to the museum with deep knowledge of the content being offered there, whereas others came with an interest that was fostered more by informal experience or simply an openness to new ideas (see Leinhardt, Tittle, & Knutson, chap. 4, this volume). The entrée for visitors with more informal knowledge was often a personal experience that was prompted by a specific museum display; and that personal experience often evoked a narrative-like response. Furthermore, we sensed that people who were touring the museum in the company of friends or relatives were in a social situation that predisposed the offering of stories about people they knew or events they had shared or about people or events that others could imagine because they knew something about the teller. Some of the stories were tangential to the museum topic, whereas others connected directly to the content and helped build shared meaning for the group. Visitors also exhibited in their conversations a tendency to repeat ideas that were of concern to them—questions they wished to have answered or issues that worried them—and these were very specific to each group. Only the prevalence of such recurring issues was common across groups.

As a final note, we offer an illustration of how members of a group can support each other's museum experience through conversation. Kimiko and Herbert were two adult visitors touring together with four other adults, forming varying combinations of dyads as they moved through the exhibition. Because Kimiko and Herbert were often in the company of a nonmicrophoned member of their group rather than sticking with each other, they often viewed specific exhibit stations at different times and in a different order. Toward the end of their visit, as Kimiko and one of the other members of their group finished watching the videotape showing changes in how glass has been manufactured over the past 100 years, Herbert rejoined them from another exhibit station around the corner. Herbert did not know exactly what they had seen on the video, but he did know a great deal about glass manufacturing processes and he wanted to share his knowledge with Kimiko. She, in turn, wanted to share her new-found knowledge with him. A portion of their exchange follows:

Kimiko: We saw the film! That's very interesting how they made plate glass.
Herbert: Yeah.
Kimiko: Yeah.
Herbert: I didn't watch the film—
Kimiko: I had no idea that it was rounded and they cut it off and put it back in the furnace and flattened it.
Herbert: Well, well what they do they, they, they blow it in a big, long tube.
Kimiko: Yeah.
Herbert: They used to make tubes *way* large.
Kimiko: Yeah.
Herbert: Then they cut off both ends and they put it in a, in a kiln. In a layer.
Kimiko: Yeah, that's what we did see.
Herbert: And then it heats up and they-
Kimiko: Right, right! That's amazing.
Herbert: -cut it and then they lay it flat.
Kimiko: So, it's the same evenness around.
Herbert: Yeah.
Kimiko: That's how they do that. I never knew that.
Herbert: But now they don't.
Kimiko: That's the old way.
Herbert: Right.
Kimiko: Now, yeah they were saying that-
Herbert: Now, now they just–
Kimiko: -umm, that you can do it all mechanically, uh.
Herbert: Yeah, it's, it's amazing. (Group 7, lines 687–719)

This conversation continued with Herbert elaborating further on the specific process for making "full antique glass," which he knew about from his experience in the manufacture of stained glass. He has Kimiko's full attention, including a very clear indication that she feels she is learning something new from this part of the exchange ("I see. That makes it antique, then . . .")

Herbert: When we saw it at [Blenko], when we were down there, in, in Milton—
Kimiko: Yeah?!

Herbert: They had some of that stuff.

Kimiko: Um-hum.

Herbert: And they still make the full antique glass; that's what they call it when they mouth blow it and then flatten it.

Kimiko: Oh I see, that makes it antique, then. Because it's hand done.

Herbert: Um-hum. Full antique is-

Kimiko: I see.

Herbert: -mouth blown.

Kimiko (simultaneously): Huh! Uh-huh. (Group 7, lines 719–733)

This exchange shows how a group conversation in a museum can build on the joint experiences of visitors to create a much richer experience than any individual could have alone. As such, it supports our sense that conversations among members of a small, socially cohesive group of friends or family members is privileged and offers each member of the group a special opportunity for enrichment.

As part of our efforts to capture the experiences visitors had in *Glass: Shattering Notions*, we were concerned about the extent to which the groups understood the main story the curators intended to convey. Although we did not discuss these data in terms of our groups' connection to Pittsburgh, we were nevertheless interested in seeing how these groups in general understood the overarching curatorial message about the importance of the glass industry to the Pittsburgh region. From the tour transcripts and from the postinterviews, we found that all groups "got" the overarching message. Some people indicated that they knew the importance of this industry before coming to the museum; others seemed pleased to be reminded ("I'd forgotten Western Pennsylvania is really the . . . home of glass, isn't it, with Pittsburgh Plate Glass . . ."); and the newcomers (Minsu and Yuri) declared that they would now adjust their image of the region as a steel-dominated one to an image of Pittsburgh as an "industrial city," although they felt steel was still dominant. Given that the curators had avoided providing any explicit or direct comparisons between the steel and glass industries—in terms of numbers of employees or amount of corporate earnings, for example—it is safe to say that all visitors did interpret the overarching curatorial message, regardless of the strength of the visitors' connection to the region, as well as adding their own take to that message.

What we found from our study of small-group conversations at the Heinz History Center was that more than half the time groups tended to engage in expansions, sometimes lengthy and substantial expansions, on what the museum provided. In cases where there was at least one group member who had specific experience with, or knowledge about, the content, those groups engaged in more expansions and more of their expansions were at the level of explanation. Groups with less formal connection to the content tended to make meaningful connections by means of syntheses in the form of personal stories about people they knew, places they had been, or events in which they had participated, although all groups engaged in this form of personal meaning-making to some extent. The social roles operating within a group—its social identity, so to speak—also influenced the structure and content of visitor conversations, fostering or inhibiting certain emphases or patterns of talk, which in turn influenced the levels of explanatory engagement in that group.

This study suggests that the nature of visitors' backgrounds—the knowledge, experience, and social dynamics they bring with them to the museum visit—constitute an important element in the combination of influences on what people can "take away" from their museum visits. Museums provide a platform on which meaningful conversations can be built, using the tools that people bring with them to extend and enrich the knowledge among group members by expanding on features that one or another group member is prompted to introduce for discussion. These expanded, more elaborated conversations support a sense of connectedness of visitors to the museum content and to each other. Museums, then, should look to ways of increasing the opportunities for visitors to expand ideas with companions during a museum visit. Visitors, in turn, should consider seeking opportunities to go to museums with friends and family members of varying backgrounds so that the press to expand for each other is enhanced.

ACKNOWLEDGMENTS

Support for the research reported in this chapter was provided to the Museum Learning Collaborative at the University of Pittsburgh, Learning Research and Development Center, by the Institute for Museum and Library Services, with funding from the National Science Foundation, the National Endowment for the Arts, and the National Endowment for the Humanities. The ideas expressed are solely those of the authors and no official endorsement from the sponsoring agencies should be presumed.

The authors wish to thank Catherine Stainton and Mary Abu-Shumays for their support in designing and conducting the study and helping to analyze portions of it. We are grateful to the staff of the Senator John Heinz Pittsburgh Regional History Center, especially Ellen Rosenthal who was Chief Curator at the time, and Anne Madarasz, Curator of the exhibition, for their unfailing generosity and cooperation in this undertaking. We are also indebted to John Levine for his helpful discussions about the meaning of identity in social situations. We thank Minjung Kim for her participation in the data collection and her considerable translation endeavors.

REFERENCES

Borun, M., Chambers, M. B., Dritsas, J., & Johnson, J. I. (1997). Enhancing family learning through exhibits. *Curator, 40*(4), 279–295.

Doering, Z. D., & Pekarik, A. J. (1996). Questioning the entrance narrative. *Journal of Museum Education, 21*(3), 20–23.

Falk, J. H. (1998). Visitors: Who does, who doesn't and why. *Museum News*, March/April, 38–43.

Housen, A. (1980). What is beyond, or before, the lecture tour? A study of aesthetic modes of understanding. *Art Education, 33*(1), 16–18.

Kim, B. Y. (1991). *A content analysis of the treatment of Korea in contemporary social studies textbooks used in Connecticut high schools.* Unpublished doctoral dissertation, University of Connecticut, Storrs.

Leinhardt, G. (1996). *Museum Learning Collaborative* (proposal submitted to the Institute for Museum and Library Services, Washington, DC, August, 1996). Pittsburgh, PA: University of Pittsburgh, Learning Research and Development Center.

Leinhardt, G., & Crowley, K. (1998). *Museum Learning Collaborative revised Phase 2 proposal* (proposal submitted to the Institute for Museum and Library Services, Washington, DC, November, 1998). Pittsburgh, PA: University of Pittsburgh, Learning Research and Development Center.

Macdonald, D. S. (1998). *The Koreans: Contemporary politics and society.* Boulder, CO: Westview.

Madarasz, A. (1998). *Glass: Shattering notions* (catalogue for the "Glass: Shattering Notions" exhibition at the Senator John Heinz Pittsburgh Regional History Center). Pittsburgh, PA: Historical Society of Western Pennsylvania.

McManus, P. M. (1989). Oh yes they do! How visitors read labels and interact with exhibit text. *Curator, 32*(3), 174–189.

Mintz, A. (1998). Demographic trends, strategic responses. *Museum News*, May/June, 47–67.

Rosenthal, E. (1998). Preface. In A. Madarasz, *Glass: Shattering notions* (catalogue for the "Glass: Shattering Notions" exhibition at the Senator John Heinz Pittsburgh Regional History Center; pp. iii–v). Pittsburgh, PA: Historical Society of Western Pennsylvania.

Schauble, L., Leinhardt, G., & Martin, L. (1998). A framework for organizing a cumulative research agenda in informal learning contexts. *Journal of Museum Education, 22*(2&3), 3–8.

Silverman, L. H. (1990). *Of us and other "things": The content and functions of talk by adult visitor pairs in an art and a history museum.* Unpublished doctoral dissertation, University of Pennsylvania, Philadelphia.

Wertsch, J. V., Hagstrom, F., & Kikas, E. (1995). Voices of thinking and speaking. In L. M. W. Martin, K. Nelson, & E. Tobach (Eds.), *Sociocultural psychology: Theory and practice of doing and knowing* (pp. 276–290). Cambridge, England: Cambridge University Press.

Young, K. M., & Leinhardt, G. (1998). Wildflowers, sheep, and democracy: The role of analogy in the teaching and learning of history. In J. G. Voss, & M. Carretero (Vol. Eds.), *International review of history education: Vol. 2. Learning and reasoning in history* (pp. 154–196). London: Woburn Press.

Chapter 7

Voices and Images: Making Connections Between Identity and Art

Catherine Stainton
University of Pittsburgh

Art museums are environments that offer visitors both a challenge and an opportunity that other kinds of museums do not: the occasion to engage deeply with works of art that have been selected and presented according to particular standards and motives. Through the very act of going to visit galleries with curated displays, visitors are challenged to develop or refine a sense of meaning for themselves that is connected to particular kinds of artwork. Curators enter a tacit dialogue with the visitor that shapes this experience by presenting exhibitions that carry multiple messages. These messages are determined both by the particular goals of the curators, be they political, educational, or historical, and by the constraints imposed by the material to be displayed. Museum visitors come to view these exhibitions with their own "entrance narrative" that allows them to make meaning from exhibitions as they look through the lens of their own personal experiences and identity (Doering & Pekarik, 1996; Falk, Moussouri, & Coulson, 1998; Silverman, 1995). What visitors bring with them adds to their experience in the museum and helps to supply their side of the tacit dialogue.

Although curators may be experts in their field or competent at the business of putting on successful shows, museums have little information about what visitors are experiencing while they tour. There are solid descriptions of general visitor experience in museums of various types (Falk & Dierking, 1992; Gennaro, 1981), and other studies have focused on more tightly defined issues. Visitor studies, designed and implemented by museum staffs to answer specific queries or resolve particular "local" issues, often take by necessity a narrow, problem-driven approach to understand what visitors experience. Some studies have timed the seconds visitors pause in front of an exhibit as a way of inferring their engagement with it (Serrell, 1992). Others rely on pre- and posttests of exhibition fact retention to rate how much visitors "learned" from their experience. While timing and testing are important components of research that are indicative that some kind of learning has occurred, these methods do not tell the entire story of visitor interaction with museum exhibitions. Although these and other approaches supply very useful information about general visitor behavior it is incumbent on the field to engage deeply by asking questions and conducting research that takes on the larger issue of what and how visitors learn in art museums.

The extant research on issues of visitor experience and learning specifically related to art museums is similarly uneven in its focus. Studies that focus on the cognitive aspects of learning about art hold that learning is facilitated by a preexisting knowledge base, appropriate search strategies, a disposition toward wanting to learn, and verbal cues to set learning in motion by helping a person looking at art make connections (Koroscik, 1997; Koroscik et al., 1992). Considerable work has been done to develop stage theories of aesthetic appreciation which characterize the responses of people looking at art according to their developing intellectual levels and experience (Housen, 1996; Parsons, 1987). By definition, stage theories look at only one side of an issue, which they define using a single metric. Our approach is to consider visitors to be in dialogue with each other and with the museum and through that process to be developing a sense of meaning about their experiences of objects they are viewing.

This study takes a sociocultural approach toward defining and determining what learning in a museum might encompass (Leinhardt & Crowley, 1998; Schauble, Leinhardt, & Martin, 1996). Seeing a museum through a sociocultural lens considers the visitors as people who are in conversation, literally and figuratively, with the artwork on display and with the curatorial intent (Hooper-Greenhill, 1992; Worts, 1991), not as the "uninitiated" who come to the museum to have curatorial information inserted into their heads, a view of the visitor held by some art museums (Eisner & Dobbs, 1986a, 1986b; Ripley, 1969). We consider one key to understanding visitors' experience as being their conversation as it unfolds, rather than in constructing a checklist or quiz to determine what they may have noticed. Capturing the conversational construction of meaning by visitors with respect to aspects or features of the artwork gives the researcher critical insights about the visitor experience as it happens. Collecting an after-the-fact summary from the visitor is certainly useful, but we must recognize that such a distillation of a visit may be very different from knowing about the particular aspects or features of artwork s/he noticed or other associations made while in the gallery.

Museums are learning environments that raise different challenges than school or other formal settings; they are "free" environments in that visitors choose what they engage with (Birney, 1988; Ramey-Gassert, Walberg, & Walberg, 1994; Schauble, Beane, Coates, Martin, & Sterling, 1996; Scribner & Cole, 1973). The combination of curatorial interpretation of exhibition content, visitor experience, and their prior knowledge generates very complex conversational meanings. Using an art museum as a setting for trying to determine what learning means, we must thus define learning more broadly than as a set of facts that could be captured by a checklist. In this chapter, as in the other chapters in this volume, we thus consider the meaning-making that comes through visitors' conversational elaboration to be a form of learning. We are interested in examining *what* visitors talk about as well as *how* they structure their comments and explanation to each other. We believe these analyses may reveal more completely how learning occurs when people engage with art in a museum setting.

This study investigated 26 visitors' interactions with messages of curatorial intent by examining their conversations about an exhibition of African art called *Soul of Africa*; these conversations were recorded online in the galleries of Pittsburgh's Carnegie Museum of Art (CMA) during the summer of 1999. We were particularly interested in understanding which elements of the curatorial intent behind the exhibition visitors noticed and resonated with, as well as the other kinds of connections they made with the art they were viewing. In addition, we wondered how visitors' identities influenced their meaning-making.[1] Further, we considered the sociocultural context of an art museum as a useful place to see how visitors are in dialogue with museums. Thus, we chose several objects from the exhibition and compared what they had to "say" to visitors in terms of appearance, available information, and placement in the exhibition, with what visitors had to say about the objects.

Background of the Exhibition and Visitors

The *Soul of Africa* exhibition, a traveling show that originated in Zurich, consisted of 200 pieces of 19th and 20th century African art: wooden masks and figurative sculpture, chairs and stools, jewelry, textiles, ivory carvings, and musical instruments. The pieces were amassed between 1916 and 1928

[1]While tackling the issue of the relationship between visitors' entrance narratives—their identity—and curatorial intent, this study also sought to work on three methodological issues we felt would be useful to the museum research field. First, we collected data from two kinds of visitors, people known to us and visitors who happened to show up to see the exhibition. Second, we used two conditions for the pre- and postinterviews. The third issue we explored was how to effectively capture visitor conversation and tour routes without overly interfering with the visit.

by a Swiss collector, Han Coray, and they represent the work of various West and Central African tribes. Coray, interested in Dada and Surrealism, was attracted to the exoticism of Africa and the objects' abstraction and bought more than 2,000 pieces in a milieu of artistic and intellectual rejection of the tenets of Western art. The original premise of the collection was to inform a new kind of artistic expression. By Western standards, the body parts of the figures are elongated and distorted, their facial expressions peculiar. Some figures are assemblages of many different materials and others are studded with nails. Coray never visited Africa; he bought the pieces because of their striking aesthetic qualities, not because of any particular anthropological interest.

As Rice (1992) noted, looking at art contemplatively and analytically can be difficult, particularly for people who are untrained in aesthetics, art history, or the process of making art themselves. We chose to focus on *Soul of Africa* in part because the aesthetics of this artwork are uniquely challenging for the average American to grasp. Compared to other artistic traditions, the newness of Western museums' interest in exhibiting African art means that many people are unfamiliar with it (Vogel, 1991). In addition, particularly for White Americans, knowledge of African history and culture is cursory and often based solely on media accounts of wars and humanitarian disasters, or impressions from popular culture rather than from academically elaborated sources. Although the museum-going population tends to be better educated than nonvisitors (Falk, 1993), we still assumed that the general knowledge of Africa and its anthropology possessed by the people in our study would be fairly incomplete. Capitalizing on this unfamiliarity, we believed that the *Soul of Africa* would be a challenging exhibition along several dimensions and that the process of seeing it would thus prompt visitors to display a wide range of reactions and meaning-making activities, more so, perhaps, than would seeing a more familiar genre such as Impressionist painting.[2] Visitors viewing unexpected, unfamiliar art will have a very different experience from that of visitors for whom the art is familiar and comfortable. We also believed that this show might possibly attract more than the usual number of African American visitors and thus offer us an opportunity to add to the limited amount of scholarship on this visitor population (Falk, 1993).

Another compelling reason to study *Soul of Africa* had to do with this art museum's own process of mounting the show. The CMA sought to serve the Pittsburgh community by offering what they viewed as a valuable show that

[2]Indeed, a museum director notes that all the highly attended, "blockbuster" museum shows in this country are of 19th century European painting/antiquities (J. H. Dobrznski, "Blockbuster shows lure record crowds into U.S. museums," New York Times, 2/3/00, page B5.)

might interest members of the African American community, a population that seldom utilizes this institution, as well as its regular core visitors. While the museum made special efforts to advertise the exhibition and make African American visitors feel welcome, they did not presume that all African Americans would necessarily be interested in it. During the curation and design process, the museum was faced with the same issues and dilemmas encountered by other museums when presenting a collection as both art and artifact (Karp, 1991; Riegel, 1996; Vogel, 1991). The issues of exoticizing non-Western cultures and presenting their effects out of context are extremely problematic; even terminology can provoke strong criticism of museum exhibitions (cf. Rubin, 1984). In this case, the museum decided on an approach that combines both strands: It chose to display the artwork in such a way that its aesthetic qualities could be appreciated while at the same time presenting it with supports and materials[3] that would support visitors who have little or no background knowledge of African art, all without "dumbing it down" for knowledgeable visitors. In many instances, there was not a clear delineation in label copy and wall text between the messages of curatorial intent devoted to aesthetics and those of anthropology, a conflict of sorts that the curators freely admit. The CMA's curatorial decisions were driven by their view of the visitor as closer to intellectual sparring partner than empty vessel to be filled by curators' expertise. Even though the objects that comprised the show were pre-assembled and the explanatory text was developed elsewhere the CMA continued the tone of accessibility in the exhibition's design. Because of the complexities involved for both museum and visitor, we felt that studying a show like this would thus be particularly valuable.

We defined the two overarching messages of the show as aesthetic and anthropological.[4] These messages were sometimes supported in different ways. The objects were displayed in typical art-museum manner in that they were arranged both thematically and in a visually exciting way on stands and walls, spot lit with boutique lighting. Several visually striking pieces were showcased by being placed by themselves on enormous walls or by having a lot of empty space around them. Others were placed so that they were framed by doorways as the visitor surveyed the galleries. Vitrines were used sparingly; visitors were able to see most of the artwork at close range without the interference of plastic. There were no railings. Labels were unobtrusive and low so as not to overwhelm the eye. The walls had been painted

---

[3]The CMA chose to use the exhibition themes and label copy that had been developed by the Munson-Williams-Proctor Institute in Utica, NY, one of *Soul of Africa's* prior venues.

[4]To establish the curatorial intent of the exhibition we conducted interviews with exhibition curators and designers, examined the catalogue, docent training tapes and tours, and wall and label copy. From these sources, a set of core messages was developed. A curator indicated that our set was compatible with what she viewed as the CMA's curatorial intent for this show.

saturated shades of cool colors (not the browns and reds Westerners often associate with Africa) while African music played in the background. There was a wall panel devoted to "African Art Aesthetics."[5] A resource table provided an array of books on African art as well as a comment book for visitors to record their impressions. These exhibition design decisions helped convey the museum's aesthetic intent to show these objects as examples of high art, worthy of space in an art museum, not as natural history objects. The anthropological intent was expressed through the arrangement of the objects within themes: "Art and Leadership," "Rank and Prestige," "Life Transitions," "Communication with the Supernatural World," "Remembering the Dead," and "Music in the Service of Spirits and Kings." Wall text and label copy supported the themes. Maps on the wall and on each label showed where in Africa the artwork had originated. Some exhibits had small color photographs, placed next to the label copy, showing similar objects in use by modern Africans. These photos gave visitors a cultural context in which to view objects with which they may have been completely unfamiliar.

But much of this two-stranded curatorial intent was tightly entwined. A portion of the wall and label content contained aesthetic ideas as well as the useful and culturally sensitive anthropological information and are recognizable as "standard" museum copy. The color photographs also gave a sense of the aesthetic as well as cultural tradition shared by the object in the photo and the similar object in the exhibition. In short, the CMA curators intended the aesthetic and anthropological ideas about the art work on display to support and complement each other; they would disagree with the usefulness or even possibility of considering them separately. Our decision to pull apart these two strands is in the service of better understanding exactly what visitors resonate with as they engage in the often difficult task of looking at and making meaning about unfamiliar art.

The two broad categories that comprise the central curatorial intentions of the exhibition—aesthetics and anthropology—are defined in specific ways for the purposes of this study. Aesthetics refers to the art objects' appearance (including features such as materials, form, construction, design, patina, detail, balance, pattern, beauty) without reference to situating the objects in the larger context of other African art. Anthropology refers to the information provided by curators that describes the art objects' practical and symbolic functions in the particular culture that produced it.

---

[5]The CMA's highly trained docent staff gave regular gallery tours that emphasized the aesthetics of the artwork by giving visitors features to look for throughout the exhibition. There was also a videotape and a CD-ROM station on African art and culture for visitors. We did not include these affordances in our study.

Model of a Visit to the *Soul of Africa*

One way of thinking socioculturally about what is involved in a visit to an art museum involves consideration of the curators' voice as providing one side of a conversation about a work of art and the visitors as providing the other side (see Fig. 7.1). The objects themselves become the focus of activities—judgment, interpretation, appreciation, and meaning-making. The wide end of the top angle represents the full breadth of scholarship that informs wall and label copy, thoughts about exhibition design and object placement, and the specific ideas about what could be told about the artwork that curators draw upon. As their thinking and the work of putting on the exhibition progresses, the range of all possibilities is distilled into the final plan of the exhibition (the narrow point of the top angle). The wide end of the bottom angle represents visitors' background knowledge, life experiences, and identity characteristics they bring with them to the museum. Visitors employ relevant ideas from this repertoire as they focus on the art in order to make meaning of it (represented as the narrow point of the bottom angle). The curatorial intent and visitor experience come together when the art work is viewed in the context of the museum-provided supports, the point of intersection represented by the African mask at the center of the figure. The art objects act as catalysts for the "conversation" be-

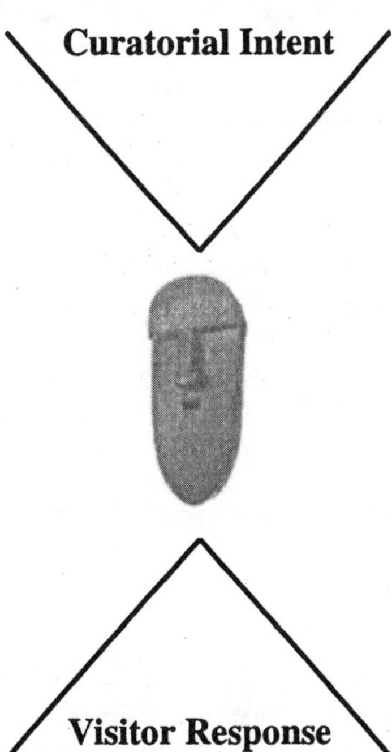

FIG. 7.1. Model of curatorial intent and visitor response. Mask from *African Art from the Han Coray Collection 1916–1928* (p. 65), by M. Szalay, 1998, Munich: Prestel-Verlag. Copyright 1998 by M. Szalay, Völkerkundemuseum der Universität Zürich. Reprinted with permission.

tween visitor and curator. We imagine this model might also apply to other museum exhibits whose curatorial approach is similarly organic (i.e., takes the visitor into account), as opposed to didactic (represents the authority of the museum).

The physical or environmental supports for this conversation lie in the way the gallery space is utilized and in the design of the exhibition. The open plan for movement through the gallery allowed multiple pathways and a kind of "free range" access to the artwork (see Fig. 7.2). As shown in the exhibition floor plan, visitors entered through the main door and found themselves in the exhibition's central room, which featured a broad expanse of empty central floor space, several large masks, and a long wall. The sound of African music could be heard from behind the wall. In general, visitors started their tour by reading the exhibition's introductory wall text and then they proceeded toward an area on their left, right, or behind the wall according to their own preference, not by any curatorial (or researcher) directive. In each area, after approaching an object visitors would typically read the label copy, identify it, make additional remarks about its appearance, function, or meaning, and then move on (see Fienberg & Leinhardt, chap. 6, this volume).

In order to describe and understand visitors' experience of *Soul of Africa* and the influence of visitors' identity on that experience we examined their conversations both for the curatorial messages being reflected there and for visitors' personal perspectives on the art work. We wanted to know how visitor conversations in an art museum were reflective of the multiple, entwined messages of curatorial intent being conveyed—in this case both aesthetic and anthropological strands. Within the aesthetic and anthropological thematic tension of this exhibition of African art, how much of the visitor conversation seems to reflect curatorial messages directly and how much seems to reflect visitors' own personal "take" on the curatorial messages based on their identity—their background and experience with respect to Africa, art, and museums in general? To explore these issues we examined visitor conversations as they toured through the exhibition, compared reactions at specific pieces of art, and examined two particular visitor groups.

METHODOLOGY

Visitors, Selected and On-Site

Data were collected from two kinds of visitors, "selected" and "on-site" (cf. methodology in Fienberg & Leinhardt, chap. 6, this volume). Six groups of selected visitors (totaling 13 people) were personally known to the researchers. All already had a personal relationship with the other mem-

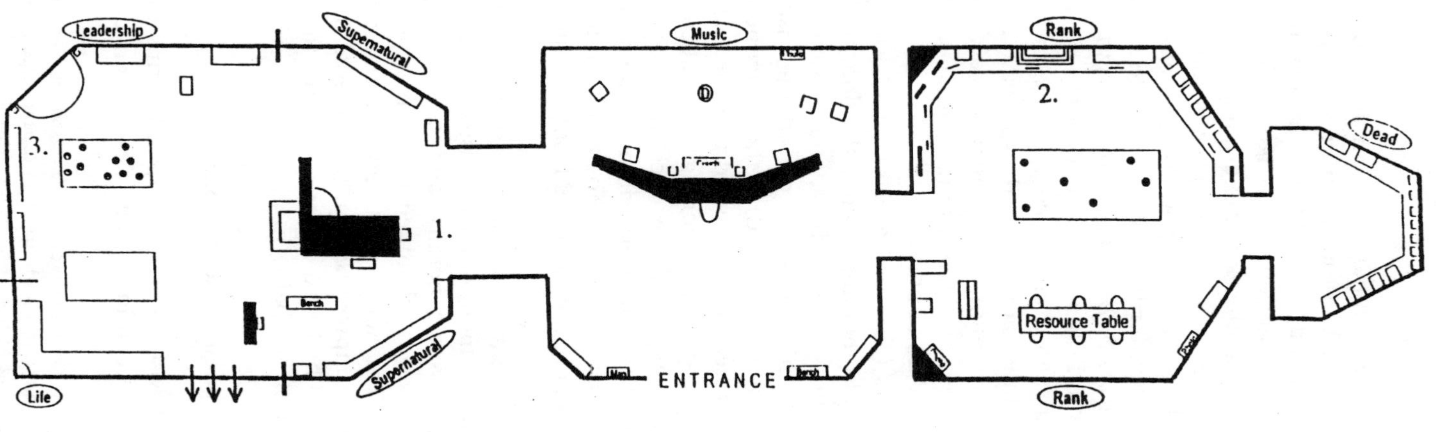

1. Nailman
2. Neckrests
3. Poro mask

FIG. 7.2. Plan of *Soul of Africa* galleries, showing exhibition themes and placement of specific objects.

ber(s) in their group. We invited them to participate in the study because they had a background that pertained to one or more aspects of visitor background in which we were interested; that is, they each had some particular and high level of art, Africa, or museum experience. These experiences included collecting African and other kinds of art; making, teaching, and writing about art; living in Africa; having close friends and coworkers with a high level of knowledge about Africa; and working in museums. We viewed these visitors as being special informants who could add a great deal to our understanding of what *Soul of Africa* had to say to visitors who are not necessarily well represented in the Pittsburgh museum-going population. Thus, inviting these visitors who had a known competence to converse thoughtfully within these three dimensions allowed us to have a basis of comparison for analyzing the conversations of a potentially very different population, on-site visitors who were not known to us. The on-site visitors are representative of the "random" museum-goer.

The six groups of on-site visitors (also totaling 13 people) who participated were recruited for the study as they approached the door to the *Soul of Africa* galleries. Their backgrounds in art, Africa, and museum experience were initially unknown to us. Criteria used in considering visitors for the study included an indication (by word or deed) of their intention to see the exhibition, expressed before researchers revealed that they were conducting research; and their membership in a visiting group that contained between two and four people, including families with children of preschool age or older. We did not include those who were willing to participate but expressed a worry about time pressures, or those who turned out to be subsets of a large group tour. Visitors were not excluded from the study if they had visited the exhibition before.

All potential on-site visitors were invited to participate; the acceptance rate was approximately 33%.[6] Recruitment of on-site visitors and data collection for all 12 groups of visitors were generally conducted during times of the day when the galleries were not scheduled for regular docent-led tours or tours by school groups. This was done to avoid congestion and high noise levels that might have compromised our participants' ability to move about the galleries freely and be heard on tape. None of the participants were given any compensation for being in the study.

Data Collection: Pre- and Postinterviews, Gallery Tour

After agreeing to participate, all visitors signed consent forms that described the research and promised confidentiality. Researchers attached

---

[6]Those who declined cited time pressures or a preference for not sharing their museum visit with strangers. The researchers involved in this study are all European American; acceptance rates for both European American and African American visitors were comparable.

small cordless microphones to one or two members of each group and then conducted a preinterview with the group or handed them a set of pretour questions on cards and asked the group to respond to the questions together without the researcher. The preinterview questions and those printed on the pretour cards were identical, except that the card "questions" were phrased in "Talk about __" form rather than question form as a way of fostering a more natural conversation.[7] Both instruments queried visitors about their museum visiting habits, what they expected to see that day, connections they may have had to Africa and its art, and whether they made art themselves. During this activity, regardless of interview format, visitors sat outside the gallery; when using cards, researchers stood apart from the visitors, taping and monitoring the conversation through headphones.

After completing the preinterview, visitors toured the exhibition at their own pace, following their own route. They were told they could talk about anything they cared to and could stop to rest whenever necessary. Two researchers followed at a distance, making notes and recording visitors' movements on maps while audiotaping and monitoring the conversation through headphones. By annotating each "stop" with opening and closing dialogue, researchers were able to later match the recorded conversation to the corresponding stations of artwork in the galleries. The wireless microphones allowed researchers to hear and observe at long distances without undue intrusion on subjects' personal space.

Although every visitor did not necessarily examine every piece of artwork in the exhibition, all the visitor groups toured some portion of all five of the gallery spaces. The tour lengths ranged from 28 minutes to 77 minutes, with the average being 43 minutes.[8]

When visitors indicated they had completed their tour of the exhibition they were asked to participate in a postinterview, using the same type of methodology as they experienced for the preinterview. The posttour questions or prompts asked visitors to describe anything that had surprised them, what they had noticed about the artwork, what the exhibition had caused them to think about in terms of their own culture, and what they would tell others about the exhibition. For this activity, visitors were invited to sit either in the galleries or just outside the door. The audiotapes of the pre- and postinterviews and the tours were transcribed; pseudonyms were assigned to all participants.

---

[7]These two techniques allowed us to explore any difference in talk between visitors who were interviewed and those who conducted their own conversation about the same topics.

[8]Not surprisingly, the average length of the selected visitor tours (51 minutes) was slightly longer than the on-site visitors' average (36 minutes). We attribute this difference to the selected pool's agreeing to participate ahead of time, and their level of comfort with the researchers.

Coding Visitor Identity

We believe visitors' interests and background knowledge influence what they engage with as they tour. To narrow down the myriad aspects of life experience for the context of understanding this art exhibition we chose visitors' degree of experience with the three dimensions of Africa, art, and museums as the aspects of their identity we felt were pertinent for this study. Some of our visitors were rated high on all three, others low, and many had differing amounts of experience with these dimensions. Information from the pre- and postinterviews (which was occasionally supplemented from comments made during the tours) was used to rate the visitors as having high, medium, or low experience with Africa, art, and museums. The criteria for rating visitors is shown in Table 7.1. Children were rated according to the same criteria as adults and could thus be considered "high" in a proportional sense.

Coding the Conversations

We were interested in understanding which aspects of the curatorial intent were included in conversation as well as what visitors themselves supplied to their discussions of the artwork. The visitor tour transcripts were segmented and coded for the content of the talk mentioned while they toured the exhibition. A segment of talk was an idea unit that consisted of at least

TABLE 7.1
Criteria for Rating Visitors' Africa, Art, and Museum Identity Dimensions

Rating	*Africa*	*Art*	*Museums*
High	Growing up/living in Africa and/or expressing a keen interest or high knowledge of Africa	Being an artist; making/looking at art frequently; collecting art as a hobby; or having a degree in art	Frequently visiting museums (several times a year) and/or working in a museum
Medium	Visiting Africa; having close friends or relatives who are African or who live there; or studying Africa in school	Making art occasionally and/or expressing an enjoyment of art	Visiting museums occasionally but expressing enjoyment
Low	Never visiting Africa and expressing no interest in or knowledge of Africa	Never making art and/or expressing no particular interest in art	Seldom visiting museums

one line of transcript; breaks to the next segment coincided with conversational shifts to either a new curatorial topic, or a shift from "museum" to "visitor" talk about a curatorial topic, or both. Table 7.2 defines the seven distinct categories used in the first level of coding of the transcripts. For all categories, talk was prompted by three actions: visitors looking at the artwork, reading wall or label copy, or reacting to other visitor conversation. This coding scheme allowed us to account for all visitor vocalization, except for sneezing, coughing, laughing, and any accompanying "Bless you's."

Figure 7.3 shows the second level of the coding of visitor conversation; this coding pertained to the segments of visitor conversation that fell into the first four categories of talk described in Table 7.2; there was no further coding of the Personal, Management, and Other talk. Figure 7.3 shows that, for each segment of visitor conversation that was prompted either by museum affordances or by the visitor's personal take (the ovals), the content could be either about aesthetics or anthropology (the top row of four boxes). Below these two curatorial strands for each kind of talk are boxes in which are listed the curatorial submessages that pertain to aesthetics and anthropology. Coding for the submessages allowed us to see which and to what extent specific curatorial ideas and messages within the aesthetic and anthropology strands were discussed by visitors.

The submessages for aesthetics and anthropology are listed and defined in Table 7.3. Although the coding of "aesthetic," "visitor/aesthetic," "anthropological," and "visitor/anthropological" remarks by visitors was based on the same sets of curatorial ideas, they are actually quite distinctive be-

TABLE 7.2
Coding Categories of Visitor Talk and Definitions

Category of Talk	*Definition*
Aesthetic	Talk that pertained to aesthetic ideas supplied by label copy or prompted by visible features of the artwork.
Anthropological	Talk that pertained to anthropological ideas supplied by label copy or prompted by visible features of the artwork.
Visitor/Aesthetic	Talk that contained visitors' own "take" on the aesthetic ideas or features.
Visitor/Anthropological	Talk that contained visitors' own "take" on the anthropological ideas or features.
Visitor Management	Talk that referred to spatial orientation on the visit, feeling tired, having trouble reading labels, interactions with guards and other visitors, and any other talk pertaining to the museum as an institution.
Visitor Personal	Talk not pertaining to the above five categories of African art, anthropology, or the museum.
Other	Talk that was inaudible, unintelligible, or too fragmented to assign a meaning.

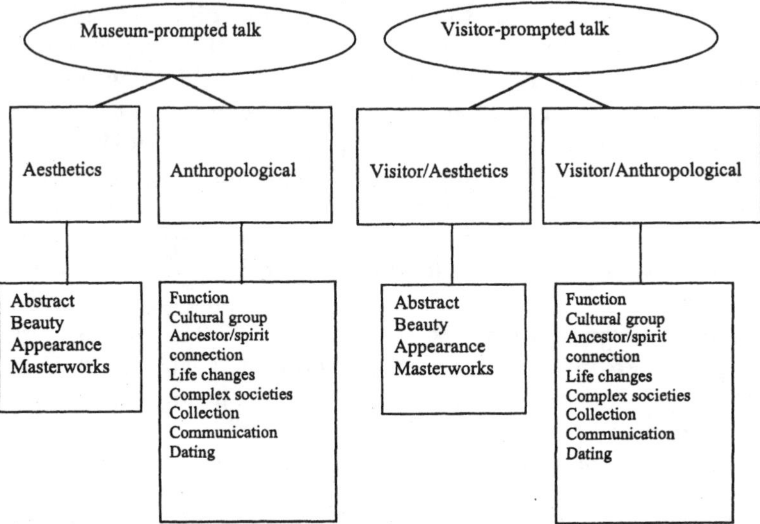

FIG. 7.3. Structure of coding categories within the two dominate curatorial strands.

cause they represent very different kinds of talk. The following two examples of the submessage of "function" illustrate this difference in the origin (whether it is museum or visitor prompted) of a segment's content. The following remark was coded as "anthropological/functional" because the visitor talked about an object's function with museum-derived information gleaned from the label copy:

Elaine: Cosmetic boxes and bark boxes. I wonder if it says what they put in them. Oh, held personal ornaments, the bark boxes. Special clothing. They used at home or while traveling. (Selected 1, tour)

A different piece of conversation about a large wooden mask was coded as "visitor/anthropological/functional" because this visitor used some personally derived information from her own experiences living in Africa when commenting to her touring companion.

Isoke: It's funny that a lot of people don't realize that those {masks} were made to be worn, and when they're worn they really come to life. Have you ever seen anybody with them on?

Vera: No.

Isoke: In Ife I've seen them actually in, you know, daily rituals and the dancers, even the picture doesn't portray it because the dancer moves, you know, to go along with the [—]. And they have to be totally cov-

TABLE 7.3
Aesthetic and Anthropological Submessages With Definitions

Aesthetic Submessages	*Anthropological Submessages*
Abstract concepts—African art is created according to ideas and concepts; objects are semi-abstract representations of abstract concepts, such as fertility, ancestry, life transitions, power.	**Functional**—Objects are functional, designed to be an active part of daily, ceremonial, and political life, not admired from afar.
Beauty—Objects are well-crafted, classical and formal; they continue a corpus of established, elegant, traditional designs.	**Cultural group**—Objects represent 48 cultural groups from specific geographical locations.
Appearance—Objects range from jewelry to sculpture to masks and are planned, simple, elegant, patterned, contained, balanced, proportioned, geometric, figurative (includes mentions of/attempts to articulate features of a piece [e.g., figures, animals, carving, materials]).	**Ancestor/spirit connection**—Objects allow the living to remain connected to spirits and ancestors by maintaining their memory; spirits and the dead participate in the lives of the living by blessing, protecting, and influencing them.
	Life changes—Objects facilitate the marking of life changes with ceremonies, secret societies, initiations, funerals, weddings.
Masterworks—Objects are masterworks made by talented artists.	**Complex societies**—Objects reflect highly organized, stratified, complex societies by indicating rank, status, social and moral values, aesthetic achievement.
	Collection—Objects were collected by Han Coray in the context of European avant garde/Dada rejection of Western art.
	Communication—Objects show the importance of music and art as a means of communication in African societies.
	Dating—Dating of these objects is imprecise.

ered. You can't see any part of the body of the dancer. (Selected 4, tour)[9]

Similarly, this difference between museum-inspired talk and visitor-take is evident in the following exchange about a wooden neckrest. Elaine's comment was considered to be "aesthetic/appearance" because she described the visible features of the piece with a phrase from the label copy (shown in italics). Lorna's response represents a shift to "visitor/aesthetic/appearance" because, from looking at the object she makes a comment that expresses her own feeling; in essence, she makes a personal value judgment based on the visual attributes of the decorative carving on the neckrest:

[9]Square brackets in these transcript excerpts indicate an inaudible word or phrase. Ellipses indicate portions of dialogue omitted here for reasons of clarity and brevity. A dash indicates dialogue interrupted by or interwoven with a companion's comment.

Elaine: It's a *full-bodied woman with her hands on her hips.*

Lorna: I relate much more to the African women than to [—] when you think of the American, they've got these skinny mini models! (laughs) These are real people. (Selected 3, tour)

After coding the transcripts, the number of lines of talk in each category and each submessage were summed and the percentage each represented of the total talk was computed for each visitor group and for the selected and on-site visitors. The latter two totals were then combined to describe the conversation among all groups with respect to each category and submessage.

Use of the Pre- and Postinterviews

The pre- and postinterviews were used as reference points to supply information needed to give the on-site visitors a rating on the identity dimensions of Africa, art, and museum. We assessed the tour conversations of the low and high visitor groups using the interviews as benchmarks of meaning making. The interviews were used to supplement our understanding of the ideas visitors expressed during their tour about specific pieces or about their overall impressions of the exhibition. We compared the pre- and postinterviews carefully for evidence, as expressed by visitors, of learning.

Data Analysis

After coding the conversations for the curatorial messages they reflected we were able to show the varying amounts of talk devoted to each category and each submessage. We then juxtaposed the amount of talk about each submessage with the identity characteristics of our visitors. To further examine the nature of the talk we selected specific pieces from the exhibition and considered each of them from three perspectives: the museum support provided for each, the direct message the object imparts, and what visitors had to say about the pieces through their museum-prompted and visitor-take comments.

RESULTS AND DISCUSSION

Results of Coding Visitor Identity

Visitor responses to the questions in the preinterview pertaining to the Africa, art, and museum identity dimensions allowed us to have a way of knowing a bit about the identities of our on-site visitors and to form a basis for comparing them to the selected visitors who were already known to the researchers. Additional information gleaned from the pre- and postinterviews and researcher observation during the tours was used to form more complete portraits of the visitors. This sometimes anecdotal additional information included visitors' ethnicity, relationship, education, and sometimes occupation. Table 7.4 shows the visitors' pseudonyms, personal within-group relationships, ethnicity, residence, identity dimension rating, and education. Of the 26 visitors in the 12 groups, 12 (46%) were African American and 14 (54%) were European American. One group was rated high on all dimensions, one was rated low, and most others were a mixture of ratings. All the selected and half of the on-site visitor groups lived in Pittsburgh; the others were visiting the museum from elsewhere in the United States (Florida, Texas, and Las Vegas).[10]

In order to compare the backgrounds of selected to on-site visitors on the three identity dimensions we assigned point values to the identity dimension ratings (high = 3, medium = 2, and low = 1) and computed the means. Figure 7.4 shows a set of parallel lines that display the means and ranges for both kinds of visitors for each dimension. For the Africa dimension, the first two lines of the figure show that the selected groups were entirely between the medium-high rating of 2 and 3, while the on-site groups were rated low-medium, between 2 and 1. The medians (2.6 and 1.6) are a full rank apart. This represents the biggest difference in the backgrounds of the two kinds of visitors. The third through sixth lines, representing the art and museum dimensions, indicate that both groups of visitors had members with ratings that ranged from low to high. The medians show that the selected visitors in general were rated higher on art (2.4) and museum (2.3) than were the on-site visitors (1.8 and 1.9); however, the differences between these medians are not as great as in the Africa dimension. Although we expected that the selected visitors would come to the museum with more knowledge about and experience of these topics than visitors chosen randomly, we believe the gaps between the two groups are small enough to feel comfortable combining their conversations into one data set.

---

[10]Experimenting with methodology was rewarding: The card condition was less intrusive than was the interview (particularly for the on-site visitors who did not know the researcher interviewers) and in most cases rewarded us with reasonable conversation under the rather forced circumstances of a research study. Visitors said they liked having the questions visible on the cards to refer to as they formulated their answers. Collecting data using remote microphones permitted sufficient privacy for visitors while they toured, but also permitted researchers to hear their conversation. Visitors tended to ignore the researchers and were not encumbered by the microphone. These techniques worked well, but the down side of producing a set of protocols suitable for coding for this degree of richness is that the time/labor factor is prohibitive for anything but a small study. Finally, having the opportunity to compare the conversations of selected vs. on-site visitors revealed the limitations of interpreting the comments of complete strangers.

TABLE 7.4
Pseudonyms, Personal Relationships Within Group, Age, Ethnicity, Identity Dimension Rating, and Education of Selected On-Site Visitors

Selected Visitors	*Relationship*	*Age*	*Ethnicity*	*Identity Dimension Rating (Africa, Art, Museum)*	*Education*
01 Elaine & Bella	friends	70s, 60s	AA,[1] AA	H, M, H/H, H, M	MA, Ph.D.
02 James, Bonnie, Jake	family	40s, 40s, 9	EA, EA, EA	M, L, L/M, H, M/M, H, M	Ph.D., BA, Grade 3
03 Elaine & Lorna	coworkers	70s, 40s	AA, EA	H, M, H/H, M, H	MA, BA
04 Isoke & Vera	advisor/mentee	40s, 20s	AA, AA	H, M, L/M, L, L	Ph.D., MA
05 Bunny & Jared	coworkers	70s, 70s	EA, EA	H, M, H/M, H, H	MA, MA
06 Tobias & Donald	friends	70s, 70s	AA, AA	H, H, H/H, H, H	BA, MA
On-Site Visitors	*Relationship*	*Age*	*Ethnicity*	*Identity Dimension Rating (Africa, Art, Museum)*	*Education*
01 Tina & Chrissie	mother/daughter	30s, 9	AA, AA	M, L, L/M, L, L	Unknown, Grade ?
02 Jennie & Doug	couple	50s, 60s	EA, EA	L, L, L/L, L, L	HS, BA
03 Harold & Camilla	couple	50s, 50s	AA, AA	M, M, L/M, M, H	MA, BA
04 Janice & Kenneth	friends	50s, 40s	EA, AA	M, M, H/L, L, L	MA, HS
05 Bliss & Dinah	mother/daughter	50s, 20s	EA, EA	L, M, M/L, M, M	BA, BA
06 Nora, Alfie, Randie	mother/daughters	30s, 7, 9	EA, EA, EA	M, H, H/M, H, H/M, H, H	MA, Grade 1 & 3

[1]AA means African American, EA means European American.

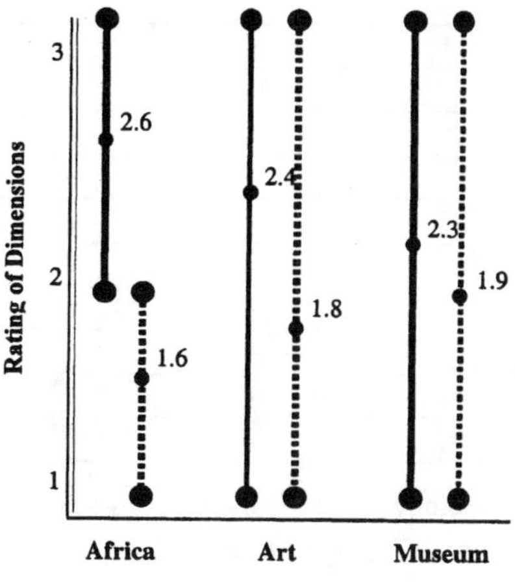

FIG. 7.4. Ratings of selected and on-site visitors on three identity dimensions.

Results of Content Coding—Level 1

Figure 7.5 shows the results of the first level of content coding of visitor conversation for the broad categories of aesthetics, anthropology, management, personal, and other. The first two bars of Fig. 7.5 show the combined percentage of both museum-inspired and visitor-inspired talk devoted to aesthetics and anthropological aspects of the artwork (i.e., "aesthetic" and "visitor/aesthetic" have been combined, as has "anthropological" and "visitor/anthropological"). As can be seen in the figure, for most visitors there were slightly more aesthetic comments than anthropological ones. Although the exhibition provided a two-stranded curatorial message, visitors' talk reflected more resonance with the aesthetic messages; and although the museum strongly supported the aesthetics of the exhibition, this finding is somewhat surprising for two reasons. First, the label copy was primarily anthropological in content and supported anthropological talk because it supplied the vocabulary and ideas for visitors to use as they conversed. Supports for the aesthetic strand of curatorial intent were, by comparison, much more abstract—signage did not support language, for example. Furthermore, although the lighting, wall color, background music, and the arrangement of art objects may have prompted strong reactions, they did not supply words to visitors. Evidently, the aesthetic aspects of the art objects in

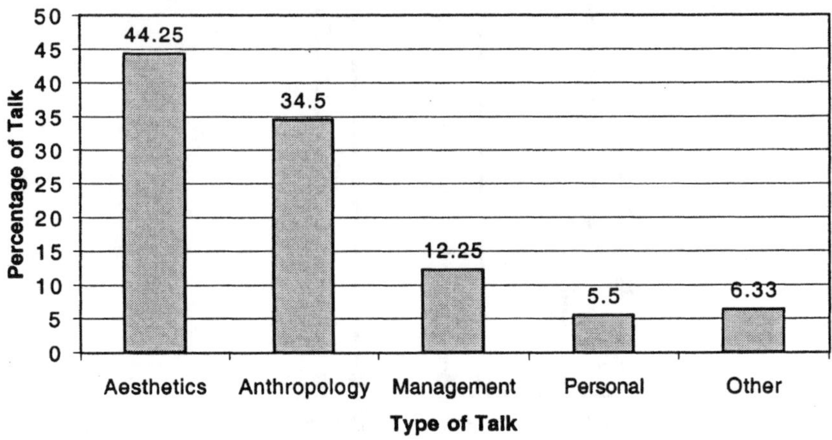

FIG. 7.5. Percentages of visitor talk about first level of content coding.

the exhibition had much to say to visitors, and prompted slightly more talk than did the anthropological aspects.

Bars three and four of Fig. 7.5 show the percentage of talk devoted to visitor management and the extraneous, museum-content-free visitor personal comments. The consistently low number of personal comments across groups suggests that both kinds of visitors mostly attended to the activities of looking at and reading about the artwork without socializing by engaging in tangential discussion. It is possible that visitors unconsciously considered the visitor-take side of their museum conversation as a vehicle that carried the social, recreational side of their museum visit. Or, it may be that recruitment into a research study influenced these visitors to perceive their task as one that promoted a particular pattern and flavor of conversation.

There were larger variations in the management category that resulted from differing group circumstances. The highest (for on-site group 4, 39%[11]) was due to an unfortunate, personal intrusion by a guard during the tour; the next highest (for on-site group 6, 26%) represented a parent's efforts to keep her two young daughters focussed on the artwork. Excluding these two highest numbers, the average of the remaining visitor groups' management talk is 8.2% devoted to issues like orientation and label legibility. This number indicates the importance of museum navigation issues to our visitors; possibly the "random plan" (McLean, 1993) of the exhibition prompted more talk about routing and what to look at next than might have occurred in a "direct"-planned exhibition. There were small variations

[11]This group also had the smallest number of codable lines of all the transcripts, which had the effect of enlarging the percentage of talk that included the guard incident and other orienting talk.

across visitor groups in the amount of talk coded as "other" (i.e., the conversation that was inaudible or fragmented). These variations were due to fluctuating noise conditions in the galleries and visitor mumbling during the taping.

These results are regrouped in Fig. 7.6 in order to show the percentages of talk prompted by the museum's voice as opposed to visitor-take talk. In Fig. 7.6's third bar, management, personal, and other talk has been merged. (The means of these combined percentages for both selected and on-site visitors is similar [20.5/21.5%].) The first bar shows the percentage of all groups' conversation that reflected the anthropological and aesthetic messages from museum-supplied label and wall copy and visually obtained features of the artwork. The second bar shows the percentage of talk about the same anthropological and aesthetic messages that reflected the visitors' take on them. This graph shows that about half the discussion is a direct reflection of the museum's message while half reflects the influence of a larger social history.

Results of the Coding—Level 2, Curatorial Submessages

Figure 7.7 shows the results of the coding of the curatorial submessages for the aesthetics and anthropology strands. For this graph all the submessage talk was considered as being 100% (i.e., personal, management, and other talk was thrown out). Only the submessages for which there was 4% or more talk were included on the graph. The bars show that visitor talk about the different submessages was very concentrated into just a few categories, with 14 categories having less than 3% of the talk for both kinds of visitors. For all visitors, the consistent pattern of talk, whether museum-based or visi-

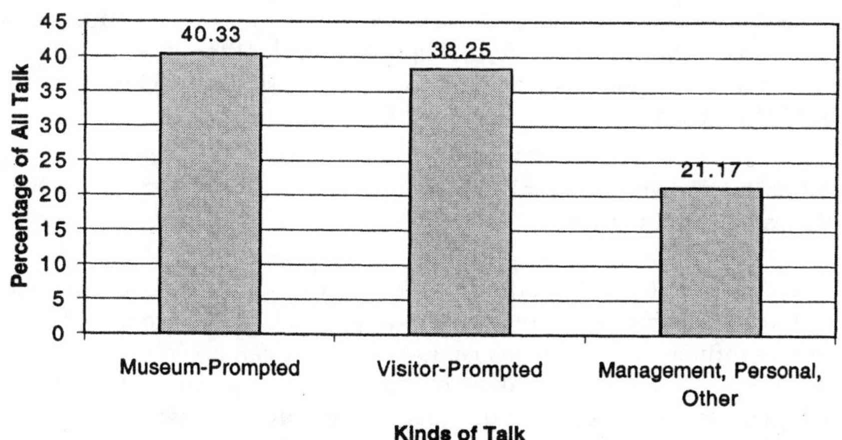

FIG. 7.6. Percent of museum-prompted and visitor-prompted talk.

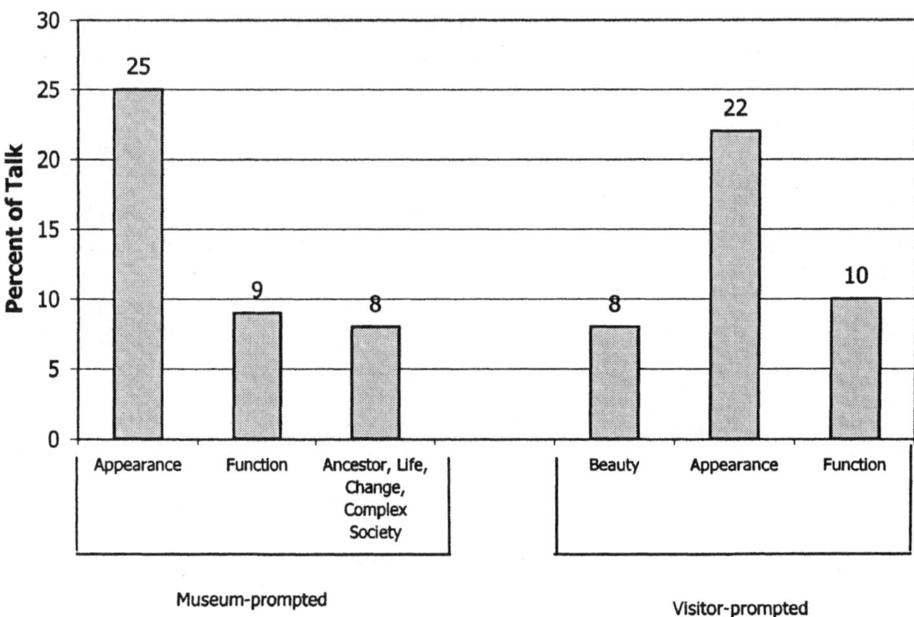

FIG. 7.7. Percentage of curatorial submessage talk by both visitor groups' museum- and visitor-prompted talk.

tor take, was a concentrated focus on two submessages: Aesthetic/appearance and Anthropological/function. (See the "appearance" and "function" bars in both parts of Fig. 7.7.) Visitors were more likely to talk about the appearance and function of the pieces of artwork than about any other of the submessages. This pattern of concentration recalls the curators' contention that aesthetics and anthropology are inextricably linked. The appearance and function submessages evidently supported each other in terms of being reflected in visitor conversation and provided a basis for attachment of the other submessages.

Relationship Between Visitor Identity and Content Coding Results

Based on the results of the coding and from the qualitative perspective with which we considered each conversation as a whole, we believe that visitors' identities influenced their conversation about African art in two ways. The first way was through visitors taking on the challenge of viewing the artwork and making meaning of it by drawing in part on their own background knowledge and experience. This was revealed by different people mentioning in their conversation different curatorial submessages than other people did; not all messages resonated conversationally with all visitors. Because the talk about the submessages was taking place in the sociocultural context of an informal, recreational event, it may be that, for certain visitors, certain curatorial messages leant themselves to conversational integration more readily than did others. (Although every visitor did not read every label, the subcategory messages were distributed throughout the exhibition and we believe that even visitors who may have only "sampled" label copy most likely encountered all the messages.)

The second way that identity and meaning-making are related is in the finding that visitors did such a large amount of meaning-making through their own personal comments about the aesthetic and anthropological submessages about the artwork. As indicated previously (see Fig. 7.6), about half of the talk was visitor-prompted; the other half, museum-prompted. Identity is thus a fertile source for supplying ideas about unfamiliar art and the idea that these visitors of different ethnic and experiential backgrounds conversed in a similar way is compelling (cf. diarists' seeing what they cared to see in a museum exhibition and using what they saw in their meaning-making, not the museum's messages of curatorial intent in Leinhardt, Tittle, & Knutson, chap. 4, this volume).

Analyses of Visitor Conversations

The results of the coding for the kinds of talk our visitors engaged in and the curatorial messages that were reflected in these conversations allowed us some quantitative, structural understanding of visitors' experience of the *Soul of Africa*. However, counts and percentages have more meaning in human terms when the conversations they represent are analyzed in a more sociocultural light. To this end, we undertook several comparative analyses: examining multiple perspectives on single objects; considering visitors' tours in terms of the visitors' levels of experience with Africa, art, and museums; and exploring the implications of visitors' ethnicities on their conversations.

Discussion of Visitor Conversation About Specific Objects

As a different, qualitative way of understanding the richness of the interplay of museum-prompted and visitor's personal take comments we analyzed the array of conversations visitors had in front of several pieces from the exhibition that, judging from the attention they received, attracted and particularly interested visitors. The array of different conversations about the same object allowed us to consider the influence of visitor identity. These pieces of art were chosen as sites for examination also because of their strongly aesthetic or anthropological message. Each object is discussed as a way of presenting what occurs, conversationally, when visitors encounter a piece of artwork and go about interpreting it and the messages of curatorial intent associated with it. (See Fig. 7.2 for the gallery placement of the specific objects.)

Nailman. A photograph of this "Oath-taking figure" and its accompanying label copy and label map is shown in Fig. 7.8. The piece, nicknamed "Nailman" by curators, researchers, and some visitors, is a striking wooden figurative sculpture that stands approximately 3 feet high. The features of the carved face are well-developed in comparison to the body; its expression and the posture of the crudely defined torso and limbs impart a sense of urgency and tension (although this is a 21st-century interpretation). The body is studded with an assortment of several hundred iron nails and blades that bristle at all angles.

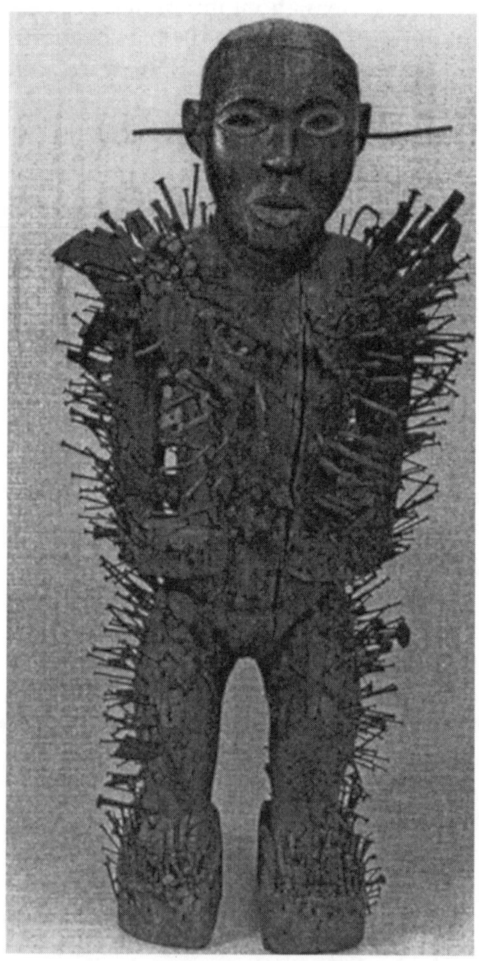

FIG. 7.8. Nailman. From *Nkondi Art from the Han Coray Collection 1916–1928* (p. 125), by M. Szalay, 1998, Munich: Prestel-Verlag. Copyright 1998 by M. Szalay, Völkerkundemuseum der Universität Zürich. Reprinted with permission.

The exhibition curators displayed the piece in a way that highlighted its arresting aesthetic qualities by placing it alone on a tall stand against its own wall and by spotlighting it; further, the curators indicated that the aesthetics of this figure are important by framing it within the doorway between the room it occupied and the central, entrance gallery. Thus, the piece was both showcased and used as aesthetic bait to attract visitors to the next room and to give them a starting focus for considering the other pieces that were grouped under the "Communication with the Supernatural World" theme. The label copy indicated Nailman's geographic/cultural origins and provided some information about how it functioned: as an object that officiated over oaths, contracts and legal decisions, as well as acting as a healing force. The act of driving in the nails activated the supernatural power it represented and served to change the appearance and ultimately to "finish" the piece.

All the visitor groups commented on Nailman; the tenor of many comments indicated that its appearance shocked most of them, prompting a range of reactions:

> Whew!
> Oh, this guy must be in pain.
> Oh, my goodness! Incredible.
> I wonder what made them do that?
> He had to be *dead* though!
> What they should have done to Clinton.
> This is the result of the first Home Depot in Africa.
> Talk about "Ow!"
> Why did they put nails in him?
> God!

These exclamations show the personal, visitor-take in operation. Likewise, these reactions are considered aesthetic because they are responses to the physicality of the piece itself.

Though not shocked themselves, one pair of selected visitors who are natural history museum docents and who also collect African art, recalled similar reactions to a similar piece in another museum:[12]

Elaine: We used to have a piece like this on display downstairs. When the school children would pass by, it just kinda blew their minds that somebody would actually make something like that.

---

[12]The Carnegie Museum of Natural History.

Lorna: Well I had a kid, we were walking through Sculpture Hall, and she looked up and saw the statues and she said, "Why do you have them there if children are walking through?" (chuckles) (Selected 3, tour)

Nailman's provocative appearance prompted visitors to seek information from the label copy to help them understand it. Despite the straightforward, unemotional, largely anthropological explanation given by the label, visitors nevertheless had difficulty rationalizing the figure's function with their own emotional reactions to its appearance. Visitors used a lot of "text echo" (McManus, 1989; shown in italics) to annotate their reactions and subsequent personal comments as a way of making sense of the object, as did this visitor (Tina) and her 9-year-old daughter:

Tina: Wow! Look at that! What's this one?

Chrissie: That's a figure with nails.

Tina: *Oath-taking figure.* Look at all those nails! (Gasp) Ooooh. Wow! This is from the Republic of Congo.

Chrissie: Congo!

Tina: Mm-hm. . . . It's a *power figure in which iron nails and blades have been driven. This process calls the attention of the supernatural*—It looks like a Voodoo doll too.

Chrissie: Mm-hm.

Tina: . . . *It calls the attention of the supernatural power. It represents and arouses it to action to witness oaths, contracts, and legal decisions.* So, whenever they make a really, really big decision—

Chrissie: Mm-hm.

Tina: —then they would bring this doll out. Or this figure out. Okay? *It is therefore an agent of justice, but also of punishment and revenge.* Okay? But it also has the power to heal. *The large number of nails and blades in this figure attest to its efficacy.*

Chrissie: What's efficacy?

Tina: Its effect. It's very effective. So it must have gotten a lot of powerful things done around this figure. (On-site 1, tour)

In addition to using text-echo, this exchange shows visitors using their self-generated idea about Voodoo to explain the figure's appearance and perhaps, function. Voodoo was salient to the visitors in three other groups who mentioned it, even though the label copy did not. Visitors had difficulty getting over the idea that this figure was not an example of a Voodoo artifact and that Nailman was not meant to represent a person being persecuted. The visitor-take notion of Voodoo seemed to represent the most plausible explanation to visitors for impaling a figure with nails, possibly their best African referent for explaining an alternate scenario to the St. Sebastian-like predicament of the Nailman figure.

The references to Voodoo are indicative of a general trend we noticed about visitor-take comments, that of making associations between the aesthetics or anthropology of the objects on display and ideas from their own background. After noticing many such comparisons within visitor-take talk we termed them *cross-cultural comparisons.* These kinds of comments occurred when visitors were reminded of something similar (in appearance or function) to the piece that came from another culture. For example, Donald and Tobias[13] each made different cross-cultural comments on Nailman's function and appearance:

Donald: Now, what's fascinating about this is that, people would drive these nails in when they were suffering from something, like a sore foot or something like that. And in Greece they still do the same thing with statues there . . .

Tobias: And the amazing thing about the head, it's almost Aztec or Oriental, sort of . . .

Donald: And what's marvelous is the difference in the nails . . .

Tobias: Makes you think of our friend Wolf! (laughs)

Donald: It does! It makes me think—I was just thinking about Wolf.

Tobias: Yeah. (laughs) Started to think of his [—]. (Selected 6, tour)

Donald talked about a functionally parallel statue in Greece; Tobias noticed what he interpreted to be Aztec and Oriental qualities of the face. Both of these are cross-cultural associations. Their final association, between this piece and pieces of nail-studded wooden sculpture made by a mutual friend, we termed *cross-personal associations.* We noticed that other visitors made similar personal associations as they looked at the artwork, such as comparing a piece in the exhibition to one in theirs or a friend's collection, or being reminded of friends or other personal memories.

Neckrests. On display were several wooden neckrests, grouped on a stand, that were located in the exhibition's "Rank and Prestige" thematic section (see Figs. 7.9 and 7.10).

All these pieces were identified in the label copy as serving the same function (providing a neck support to protect an elaborate hairdo during sleep). Each was carved in the shape of an animal or human figure and was designed so that the parts of the body (whether horns, tail, or arms) did the

[13]These visitors represent the high end of our visitors' connections to art and Africa, based on researchers' knowledge of their many achievements regarding the study's identity dimensions. A relevant sampling of these includes: exhibiting their own artwork, having it in museum permanent collections, curating shows, collecting different genres of art, writing books about art and artists, teaching students in the art center to university setting, and receiving numerous awards and recognition for their accomplishments.

Neckrests
Luba, Democratic Republic of Congo
Wood, glass beads, fiber string
Cat. Nos. 156, 157, 158

Among many African people, a tid coiffure is a sign of civilization as wel as a status indicator. Among the Luba peoples, hairstyles can identify a person by gender, marital status, and profession. Elaborate hairstyles were preserved through the use of neckrests which elevated the head above the sleeping mat. Wealthy members of Luba society might own figurative neckrests such as these, including two with supporting figures illustrating the coiffures of elites.

FIG. 7.9. Neckrests with accompanying label copy. Neckrests from *African Art from the Han Coray Collection 1916–1928* (pp. 196–197), by M. Szalay, 1998, Munich: Prestel-Verlag. Copyright 1998 by M. Szalay, Völkerkundemuseum der Universität Zürich. Reprinted with permission.

supporting work. The appearance (including patina, carving, and beadwork) of the figures themselves reflected the societies' high standards of beauty (e.g., glossy skin, scarification, bead ornamentation, hair design) that the objects sought to help the user to attain and maintain for themselves. Each neckrest uses symmetrical elements to achieve a sense of aesthetic as well as structural balance.

While conversing about the neckrests visitors attended less to the aesthetic features than to the anthropological ones. Many attended to the

Neckrest with Female Caryatid Figure
Yaka, Democratic Republic of Congo
Wood
Cat. No. 93

Neckrests are personal items of furniture that support the head and preserve an elaborate hairdo during sleep. Among the Yaka people, neckrests are the prerogative of elder heads of households, although they may also be used by religious specialists in the ritual interpretation of dreams. This example depicts a full-bodied woman with her hands on her hips.

FIG. 7.10. Neckrest with label copy. Neckrest from *African Art from the Han Coray Collection 1916–1928* (p. 144), by M. Szalay, 1998, Munich: Prestel-Verlag. Copyright 1998 by M. Szalay, Völkerkundemuseum der Universität Zürich. Reprinted with permission.

complex society submessage of high social status that was afforded by the idea of someone needing and owning such an object. But the majority of visitors, including those with high knowledge of Africa, were more intrigued by how neckrests were used and were skeptical of the comfort they could provide. Representative comments of this general consensus from two different groups are shown next.

Isoke: I can't imagine how those neckrests actually were ever used. They don't seem very comfortable. But they must be, they use them a lot. (Selected 4, tour)

Nora: That looks really uncomfortable. (On-site 6, tour)

Visitors made a lot of cross-cultural comparisons in their neckrest conversations referring to Japanese and Egyptian cultures, who also use wooden pillows, as well as Westerners who use feather pillows; these cross-cultural comments may have helped visitors imagine how neckrests might actually be more comfortable than they appear.

From the tenor of the visitor conversation, the *Soul of Africa* was a particularly challenging collection for most viewers. We focused on visitors' conversations about Nailman and the neckrests because these were objects that represent extremes of the aesthetic and anthropology strands of this exhibition. From our examination of visitor meaning-making here, we see that differences in visitor identity can explain some difference in conversation, but clearly not all. There are compelling aspects of the ideas available in the exhibition that affected everyone, regardless of background.

Poro *Mask.* We chose to examine two visitors' comments about this piece as a way of illustrating more about how visitor identity and conversation are related. The *Poro* mask (pictured in Fig. 7.1) is a simple but elegantly abstract mask that served as a vehicle for the spirit world to communicate with the living. It was one of an array of masks hung on a wall, and did not receive the "universal" visitor attention that Nailman and the neckrests did. The almond-shaped face is long (approximately 2 feet) and mostly smooth-textured, with parallel lines carved across the top. Tiny eyes look down from the overhanging forehead over the huge nose. The mask imparts a lot of expression given the economy of the design.

This mask prompted interesting responses from two visitors with different backgrounds. On the basis of its simplicity and aesthetic vocabulary, Donald called it, "The great one" and, in the postinterview said it was among his picks for the exhibition's three best pieces. Bonnie and Jake, a mother and son subset of a selected family group, also noticed the mask. Bonnie observed to Jake that the mask looked like Jay Leno. Herein lies the crux of the identity and sociocultural issues. Donald had a firm basis from his life-long interest in Africa, art, and museums to make an informed judgment on this mask's aesthetic efficacy. Bonnie, with a BA in studio art and an on-going interest in aesthetic issues, was certainly poised to comment in a more sophisticated way. However, unlike the other parents in the study who relied heavily on the information in label copy, Bonnie made this Jay Leno comment in the service of placating her hungry and disgruntled 9-year-old touring with her. Using her visitor-take comment to compare the artwork to a figure from popular culture was a device to help Jake engage and, potentially, see other aspects of the exhibition. In fact, recognizing Jake's bad mood, this family framed most of their tour conversation around

Jake's identification of aesthetic features of the artwork that reminded him of *Star Wars* characters, one of his passions. The legitimacy of comparing an African mask to Jabba the Hutt may strike some as a stretch, but we believe that a visitor's ability to view art of a completely alien genre in terms of characters that typify archetypal narrative forms (Campbell, 1999) shows an idiocyncratic but deep appreciation of curatorial effort.

The African American Versus European American Visitors' Experience

Thus far, we have considered the visitors in this study as a single population without making any distinctions between the comments of the 12 African Americans and 14 European Americans. In terms of the identity rating of Africa, art, and museum experience we assigned to all visitors, the European American and African American visitors had similar levels of familiarity and association with Africa. Both kinds of visitors made comments indicating personal connections to the curatorial messages. One European American, Lorna, commented, "Most of the things that I saw I related to my culture; the initiation rites, my son just had his Bar Mitzvah this week and it was a rite of passage. But I just, to me, it shows how similar everybody is" (Selected 3, postinterview). What was different about most African American visitors' tours was not revealed by coding but by our examination of the tone and personal content of their comments. Although all visitors of both ethnicities who toured with their children (whose ages ranged from 6 to early 20s) made explicit efforts to engage and teach them about African art and culture, several African American visitors expressed, through their visitor-take comments, a sense of pride in sharing the heritage that the artwork represented. For example, as an African American parent, Tina made comments that further connected the anthropological information and artwork to the particulars of her and her daughter's African American culture, such as comparing a mask's cowrie shellwork to shells brought from Africa by Chrissie's great-great grandmother. Tina also related the funerary pieces of the "Remembering the Dead" section of the exhibition to their family's Kwaanza ritual of toasting the ancestors:

> *Tina:* So that's a tradition that came from Africa—that you always, always hold very, in high esteem, your ancestors, because those are the people who came before you and made it possible for YOU to be here. So it's still very, very, very important. Our grandmas, and grandpas, and uncles and aunts [are] very important to us. (On-site 1, tour)

But being an African American did not guarantee a connection necessarily. For example, in the postinterview, Kenneth criticized what he described as the exhibition's lack of background information and summarized his experience with, "I didn't get much out of it." Although the European American visitors indicated their admiration of the aesthetic achievement and cultural sophistication represented by the artwork, these comments were made from the perspective of being the "other."

The Effect of Identity on Conversational Elaboration

Selecting half of our visitor groups based on our knowledge of their often high level of experience with the study's identity dimensions allowed us to have a contrast case in terms of their conversational elaboration for visitors with considerably less such experience. Comparing portraits of two visitor groups, one *low* and one *high*, gives a sense of the range of experience and differing elaboration that took place during *Soul of Africa's* tenure.

Low Group. Jennie and Doug, a pair of European American on-site visitors from Florida, were rated low on all dimensions. According to their preinterview, both had "No clue" as to what they expected from the exhibition. They conducted their tour as a team effort: Thinking she would not need her reading glasses for her visit to the museum, Jennie had to rely on Doug for help reading the label copy. Doug did a lot of text echo for her benefit, and their museum-prompted talk (65%) outweighed their visitor-take talk (35%). These visitors relied heavily on the museum's supports for a way in to looking at the artwork, and talked a bit more about anthropological issues (48%) than aesthetics (39%). They made efforts to discover how the pieces functioned in a practical way (e.g., how masks were worn, how the wearer saw through them, what scale the bow harps were tuned to) and limited their aesthetic comments to admiring the carving detail and matching the materials identified in the label copy to the pieces.

From comments made during the tour and in the postinterview, Jennie and Doug entered the exhibition as visitors who were profoundly uninformed about African art and culture. When looking at some carved ivory pendants they commented:

Jennie: I just can't get over this detail on their sculpture and stuff.

Doug: Yeah, y'know, it's all by hand.

Jennie: I know! But it's beautiful! And I mean, they couldn't have had, y'know, like, tools per se. (On-site 2, tour)

Later, at a display of raffia cloth textiles, they commented:

Jennie: Can you imagine the time it took them to sit down and make something though?

Doug: Well, they didn't have to go to work.

Jennie: Well, that's true.

Doug: They didn't have an 8:00 to 5:00 job, you know. . . . They just did what had to be done. (On-site 2, tour)

These were two of several tour instances where it is evident that the art work and label copy challenged Jennie and Doug's paradigm of African society as primitive and unstructured. Their responses in the postinterview revealed that they had noticed several messages from the anthropological strand, such as the centrality of religion, the frequent use of initiation rituals, and the importance of motherhood and childbirth for continuing society. They also noticed the curators' message that the art work was produced by complex, hierarchical societies:

Doug: African culture, more organization, than I . . .

Researcher: In what way?

Doug: Uh, as, as far as the status and, and, and the government, and the, uh . . . Well, I, y'know, I probably always just thought before, "Well, they all just did their thing, they went out and killed whenever they needed to eat, and they all brought it in here and ate it." But there was definitely a hierarchy in there, that, and a government, and, and, uh, crime and punishment. (chuckles) . . . Which probably parallels every soc-, civilization that there ever has been. (On-site 2, postinterview)

In terms of the exhibition's usefulness to students, Doug suggested,

> That they need to see it to, to see how other cultures and other civilizations lived, and probably how their ancestors at one time lived, even though they may not have been on the same continent. . . . They may have very well, and probably did, live very much the same way. . . . It's just that some civilizations advanced faster than others did. (On-site 2, postinterview)

These glimpses into visitor reasoning about unfamiliar aesthetics and anthropology are quite revealing. They show the power of the conceptualization of 19th and 20th century Africans as uncivilized and backward to prompt a visitor to make some misinformed statements. It is certainly disheartening that these visitors in their 50s, with high school and 5-year bachelor's degree backgrounds, could hold such deep misconceptions about an entire continent. Nevertheless, the hour they spent in *Soul of Africa* was entertaining for them and the exhibition clearly affected their thinking by expanding their knowledge of anthropological specifics and by making them reconsider some of their beliefs. The tone of their tour and interview conversation was not defensive. Given their lack of experience with art and museums, their inability to articulate much about the aesthetic messages of the artwork is not surprising. They cited "*National Geo*" as being their closest exposure to African art and also said that their own social culture was not receptive to it anyway:

Jennie: I—, Well, I'd just definitely tell him he missed something—or that they missed something—'cause it is very, very—

Doug: Yeah.

Jennie: It's beautiful!

Doug: We're going to see friends tonight and they'll say, 'I'm not going to go see that!' (chuckle)

Jennie: (chuckles) Yeah. They probably wouldn't want to.

Doug: (chuckles)

Jennie: I don't think, unless you came in and seen it (*sic*), if you just heard about it, that's one thing you would say: 'No—'

Doug: Yeah.

Jennie: —'I don't want to go see that.' But once you get in, it's—, I really enjoyed it.

Researcher: Got your attention.

Jennie: Yes.

Given the misinformation these visitors were touring with it seems very probable that the authority of the museum played a part in impressing them that African art has merit and thus gave them permission to engage with it in a way that was not threatening. These visitors seem to have gotten a lot out of the show, in spite of the impediments they carried into the museum.

High Group. By contrast, Tobias and Donald were African Americans who both felt deeply rooted connections to African art and culture. As we noted earlier, both were artists and teachers who had received recognition for their artistic accomplishments. Both were avid museum goers who traveled regularly to see art that interested them. Touring the exhibition with this immersed perspective permitted these visitors to transcend conversationally the need to "figure out" what each piece was in terms of the anthropological messages (19%) about it and concentrate on their main interest, aesthetic issues (70%). Neither relied much on the label copy, as reflected by the difference in the amount of their museum-prompted talk (15%) and their visitor-take talk (82%).

Tobias and Donald's tour conversation reflected their high degrees of experience in art, Africa, and museum in terms of the abstract ideas they expressed about the exhibition as a whole, and their culturally and aesthetically based observations about individual pieces. They roamed the exhibition, pointing out particular features and favorite pieces (both had seen the show previously but not with each other). As old friends who knew each other extremely well they often spoke in a kind of short hand, using short phrases that had iconic meaning to both of them.

Tobias: This I thought was very sculptural.
Donald: Yeah. It's amazing.
Tobias: It's a pipe.
Donald: Look at that vocabulary. It's amazing.
Tobias: Yeah.
Donald: Wow.
Tobias: Yeah, that is—
Donald: That's something, isn't it.
Tobias: Chokwe.
Donald: Angola again. (Selected 6, tour)

These visitors were familiar with African geography and were able to fluidly connect different locations, cultural groups, and aesthetic features. Because *Soul of Africa* was arranged thematically, not geographically, these visitors had an enhanced ability to view the art work as it stood in dialogue with a theme because so much other information was already in place. They referred often to the pieces' cultural affiliation, echoing this curatorial message more than any of the other visitor groups.

They also made a lot of cross-personal connections between the exhibition's pieces and those of their own and friends' collections by comparing the aesthetic features of each (cf. Nailman discussion).

Tobias: Well now, is your Luba stool larger than that?
Donald: It's different, because it's bigger in the body.
Tobias: Yeah.
Donald: It's about the same height. And the legs are bent back just like that but they're tucked in [—] much bigger body.
Tobias: And the seat part is wider too, isn't it?
Donald: Yeah. But I think they varied from village to village.
Tobias: Um-hum. Yeah, that's a great stool. (Selected 6, tour)

At times they were literally in dialogue with Han Coray ("He's got a lot of things from right next door to where the um, the Luba . . ."). Intimate familiarity with looking at African art (in and out of the museum context) moved Donald to comment on the aesthetic taste of the collector.

> I see the hand of a single collector here. Somebody who has a consistent understanding of {aesthetic} language. We all have language. . . . And this person had a language too, I mean, within himself, whoever put this thing together. And that remains consistent all the way. . . . So you can go from one object to the other object to the other object and you can see the consistency of the person who put it all together, besides seeing the individual objects. That's what struck me about this. It wasn't like other museums where, you know, they've collected this, they've got that, they've got that, one's a bequest, one's an auction sale, one's something else. And here, it's one person who's guided it all the way through. (Selected 6, postinterview)

This comment echoes the curator's message about the aesthetic premise that prompted Coray to assemble the collection. Tobias and Donald also understood the historical context of the aesthetic ideas that had so excited Coray:

> *Tobias:* But, like I tell students, one of the most important things about African tribal art you have to remember, that it changed what we think of as Western art. . . . that's the significance of tribal artists to me. When all the artists at the turn of the century like Picasso and all these people that were forerunners of contemporary art, this changed their [view], changed our attitude about art and I think this the significance. And when you're looking at, at, some of the tap root, if you will, of the contemporary art, modern art, and looking at this and turning around the corner, and going to the contemporary wing of the museum, and say, "Well, this is a springboard for a lot of what I'm seeing now." And understanding that idea, I think, is a very important idea. (Selected 6, postinterview)

Selected and On-Site Visitors' Learning in *Soul of Africa*

So what did visitors learn? Returning to our definition of learning as being conversational elaboration, in this case visitors' thoughts on curatorial ideas about African art and culture, we now examine the changes in visitor thinking by comparing the pre- and postinterviews. The preinterviews revealed that, except for the two men who had seen the show previously, visitors had either no preconceived ideas of what they might see or some very general expectations, such as, "Animals, masks, carvings." All visitors had much more to say in the postinterviews than in the preinterviews. The finding that most of what visitors talked about was directly related to the objects and ideas in the exhibition suggests a high level of engagement with the exhibition. Further, visitors worked hard to make connections collaboratively by exchanging curatorially supplied information they thought interesting or worthwhile filtered through their cross-cultural and cross-personal connections. To give a flavor of the learning that was experienced in the *Soul of Africa* we present a discussion of visitor comments. Our analysis of these responses to the questions in the pre- and postinterview indicate that what visitors took away with them can be summarized into five general aspects of learning:

1. Mentioning and referring to specific ideas and themes regarding anthropology that were derived from label copy.

Most of the visitors in this study made extensive use of the label copy in order to understand the exhibition.

> It would have been horrible without information.
>
> Yeah, we read as much as we looked. (Bliss & Dinah, On-site 5, postinterview)

Visitors' postinterview comments explicitly recalled the curatorial intent regarding a number of anthropological ideas they had read, thought about, and discussed with each other while touring. This anthropological aspect of learning was reflected in a wide range of comments given the differing experience and prior knowledge held by both groups of visitors. For visitors like Jennie and Doug, who had so little information in place upon which to draw, almost everything they saw or read was something of a revelation. But they, and the visitors who enjoyed richer backgrounds, selected and conversed about anthropological ideas they had found intriguing, often by drawing parallels. Janice noticed two anthropological ideas and compared the African and American versions of them:

> In the part of the exhibition where it displayed the objects that people acquired in order to show their status, I thought immediately of expensive cars. You know, and the other kinds of things that people in our culture acquire probably more in order to show other people who they are than because the item has any usefulness or intrinsic value. So, maybe to some people it's an ivory mask and to somebody else it's a Mercedes. It's pretty much the same thing. The other thing that surprised me was the use—And this we only read about. The use of secret societies to control social behavior. And I wish I understood more about that because I don't know whether that means they're similar to the KGB or the CIA or whether they're more like the Ku Klux Klan. You know what I mean? Whether they're official and legal or whether they're, some of them were really just gangs. (On-site 4, postinterview)

The theme of social status and its trappings had been mentioned by the labeling in various places in the exhibit, and was echoed here by Janice. The issue of the legitimacy of secret societies had not been addressed by the curators and serves as an example of how visitors pressed on the information available to them. Visitors mentioned other curatorial themes in their postinterviews; one that resonated with several groups was the idea that in African societies objects of art were created for everyday consumption, not as rarified objects. Almost everyone commented on the on-going and important relationship Africans maintained with deceased relatives and how this belief system plays out so differently in Western society.

2. Mentioning and referring to specific ideas and themes regarding aesthetic features that they noticed.

Despite their generally professed ignorance of an ability to appreciate African aesthetics, visitors showed that they had noticed a great deal by readily recalling and describing the aesthetic features of specific pieces from the exhibit. Numerous comments were made recalling the complexity of the carving; the variety of shapes and forms; and other details, such as the use of a variety of materials like mirrors in the eyes of some of the figures. The look of specific pieces was compared to the art of other cultures. Most wondered about how many of the masks and necklaces were worn, given the tremendous weight of the carved wood. The foreigness and difficulty of African aesthetics was still in evidence for several visitors; building on the aesthetic information they derived from the label copy the exhibit raised new aesthetic questions for them. Elaine and Lorna chuckled, "I guess in most African art they're not afraid . . . To show people! Their bodies. The body's parts." Another pair continued their tour debate about their interpretation of some of the funerary figures' breasts and gestures representing fertility into their postinterview.

> This concern about fertility that comes through in so many of them . . . the women grabbing their breasts as a symbol of being, I think we said, nurturing . . . It's sort of an interesting symbolism . . . I never would have thought of that as a nurt— I mean, I understand that breasts are nurturers, but grabbing the breast wasn't exactly what I would have thought . . . (Bunny & Jared, Selected 5, postinterview)

Similarly, another visitor observed,

> I remember seeing a statue of a woman holding a baby. And made the comment that the baby was like, a totally detached thing from the mother, that it wasn't a mother holding a baby but it was just like an ornament on her. Hmm, I noticed that. (Bonnie, Selected 2, postinterview)

3. Evidence that visitors were actively engaged in considering their role of being in dialogue with the curatorship and learning environment of the museum itself.

Visitors' consciousness of their position vis-à-vis the curator was expressed in comments that ranged from their appreciation of the nuts and bolts of the set up of the exhibit to deeper philosophical issues. Some griped about the label copy being too small or too low to read without having to bend over; others found the information curators provided invaluable ("I liked the maps. I always appreciate maps to see where things came from in relationship to the rest of the world." [Nora, On-site 6, postinterview]). Visitors made comments that indicated their awareness of the curator/collector's hand in shaping the exhibit. In her preinterview, Isoke wondered,

> And with the "Soul," I don't know what they mean by that, whether they're talking about the spiritual arts in Africa or by the "Soul of Africa" meaning the core, I don't know . . . And it's also interesting to see what they, how they, what they mean by Africa. They usually mean Sub-Saharan Africa—and often West Africa, East Africa. South and North don't come in so it'll be interesting to see how they define Africa. (Selected 4)

Several said that they compared this exhibit (the pieces and thus the decisions made about displaying them) to other African exhibits they had seen at the CMA and elsewhere.

> It was probably the best collection of African art I've ever seen. That it's a collection from a lot of different places in Africa as opposed to from Kenya or Nairobi, the places where tourists from here tend to go. And from the turn of the century in contrast with the probably contemporary African art that I've seen around. (Nora, On-site 6, postinterview)

Others mentioned more specific curatorial issues that they noticed:

> They're probably wanting if know if people are offended by sex organs or something like that. But it didn't bother me, did it you? No. (Bliss & Dinah, On-site 5, postinterview)

4. Mentioning and referring to examples they had seen in the exhibition of new, different, or finer examples of objects or ideas already familiar to them.

The African art collectors among our visitors made comparisons between what they saw in the *Soul of Africa* collection and their own collections or exhibits they had seen previously. Tobias, the artist, reported feeling very moved by seeing a particular mask:

> You know, like I was talking about the Yaka mask back there. I've seen [—] in books, they're in every book. But coming face to face with one the first time in the 50 years I've been looking at art, that's a totally new experience. (Selected 6, postinterview)

And others who had less experience of African art similarly found their sensibilities refined. Several visitors raised an important issue related to African art being viewed by Americans—that they were aware of a difference existing between "tourist art" and museum-quality works but did not feel aesthetically equipped to understand it. In his preinterview, Jared mused:

> I sometimes become very tangled up with what I consider to be real art or fraud. . . . I cannot, by my skimpy knowledge, authenticate. Is that object related to some ritual? I don't know. All I can do is look at it. I'm at a loss to try to place some kind of importance or value on it.

Bunny's response to his comment echoed this sentiment:

> . . . because cultures like this which have made objects which are part of their everyday life and their rituals, once they get involved in the market system realize, Oh, they can make money by making this to sell. And this changes their art. And certainly that's true of the native American art. (Selected 5)

The exhibit's "pedigree" (as indicated by the introductory panels) was reassuring for many visitors. The process of seeing the show allowed visitors to compare their previous aesthetic impressions or experiences of African art with the Coray collection and understand the differences between mass produced pieces and masterworks.

> You see African art, it's real rough and primitive. Like, you know [the] antelope figures in the other room? That reminded me of two figures that my friends have. But they were real plain and they looked like they could have come from Pier One. But these were just so detailed and the carvings and like, mirrors and shells. And, the way the, even the dried leaves were just so deliberately put on. (Bonnie, Selected 2, postinterview)

Ideas as well as aesthetic appreciation extended visitors into new territory when they made comments that indicated the exhibit's label copy had supplied information that had augmented their prior knowledge of African culture.

> Ancestral worship was extremely important and I had known that but in looking at some of the artifacts that we saw today, it just reinforced how important ancestral worship was and how they felt the ancestors controlled their destiny and what was going on. Even today our ancestors still continue to control part of our destiny but not to the extent we find in the African culture. (Camilla, On-site 3, postinterview)

5. Connecting of aesthetic and anthropological ideas to their identities/personal lives.

At one level, the positive tone and richness of the visitor responses indicates a high degree of personal engagement. No one discussed the pieces or ideas in reporting style; many anecdotes and cross-personal comparisons were woven through the postinterviews. Initiation ceremonies reminded visitors of family bar mitzvahs and confirmations, mother and child carvings brought to mind the sentimentality of motherhood. The artists among the visitors seem to have felt the strongest connection to the exhibit. Tobias' identity prompted him to recall specific pieces that were special to him as an artist who sought inspiration in others' work:

> And the Slit drum because I'm a great, one of my inspirations is Brancusi and Noguchi. And the Slit drum has such a contemporary sculptural feeling. And I think, while my things don't look like that, but there is a feeling, that sort of very pure form, pure shape that has come out of this type of thinking through Brancusi, through Noguchi, through many contemporary artists, including myself. (Selected 6, postinterview)

It is illuminating to compare what was said in the online tours to the summative responses to questions in the postinterview. Our data reveal that visitors sometimes describe pieces or ideas as particularly meaningful after the fact that they barely mentioned while in the gallery with the art work or label before them. While looking at the ceremonial weapons, Bliss commented, "Oh. I love those weapons. Gosh!" (On-site 5, tour) without the further elaboration she had given about other pieces. When asked in the postinterview what she particularly enjoyed, she said, "I liked the weapons the best, I guess. I guess that's cause we're from a hunting family" (On-site 5, postinterview). This example shows the schism in visitor thinking and talking that can occur between viewing and after the fact questioning. However, this is not to say that a lack of talk about a piece or idea during the tour meant that visitors were unable later to make thoughtful and sophisticated syntheses. Similarly, visitors tended to do more describing of the specific aesthetic features of an object, particularly of its beauty, while they were looking at it, than afterward. Because label text supplies words to visitors and aesthetic features do not necessarily do so, it stands to reason that anthropological issues are easier to talk about in a deeper way.

As we described earlier, several of the curatorial messages barely received a conversational nod in terms of the percentage of talk they represented. Possibly, these messages had no particular meaning to the visitors in our study. What is likely, however, is that visitors internalized some of these messages without indicating so in their talking, either in the tours or postinterviews. Certainly, the composition of the tour groups influenced the tone and tenor of conversations. A family's conversation, with its high management component and explanation for children, sounded considerably different from that of two old friends spending an afternoon together. Further, touring the exhibition with a different person might open up or close down a visitor's potential for discussing different ideas or noticing different features.

The African American visitors' conversations revealed an added dimension of identity at work. Even those who considered themselves to be art and museum neophytes said they were not surprised by what they saw in *Soul of Africa.* Nevertheless, the exhibition was deeply meaningful to most of the African Americans because it gave them an opportunity to engage with objects of their shared culture and heritage, writ large ("I felt a kinship . . ."). The postinterviews revealed two sides to this engagement. Some African American visitors, whose relatives had an active interest in African art and culture, used their tour as an opportunity to compare the ideas and objects of the show with past discussions with family members ("Grandaddy had a cane like that"). Others mentioned having relatives who had refused to talk about their African heritage because its loss to them was so painful. These visitors found the exhibit very meaningful because it gave them a nonfamilial, more neutral forum to view, talk, and learn about a part of themselves that could be difficult to discuss elsewhere.

None of the African American visitors expressed any discomfort with seeing this collection of objects, some of which had played extremely important, sacred, and secret roles, out of the African tribal context from which they had been produced and functioned. The collection and display of some of the objects, arguably, could have struck certain visitors as offensive (e.g., the *minganji* mask which in Pende society was so secret that women and children were forbidden to look at it; or the hourglass drum, that was supposed to be destroyed upon a chief's death because it represented his voice, and thus his power). Several visitors said they were grateful to be able to see these objects directly, as opposed to in books or on television, and without having to travel to Africa. The high visitor pair applauded Coray's removal of the artwork "from the flies and the mud" because it could be shared around the world in a state of excellent preservation. But other comments gave a subtle sense that the African American visitors' view of themselves was as the other in terms of the ostensibly European American museum presentation.

CONCLUSIONS

Results of the first level of content coding have given us an empirically based sense of the different subjects that these museum visitors talk about as they tour an art exhibition. In this case of *Soul of Africa,* the majority of talk concerned exhibition content, but a consistent amount of management talk showed that visitors with all levels of museum experience were concerned with issues of orientation and were always aware that they stood in dialogue with museum issues.

Whether or not visitors resonated with all the curators' submessages about *Soul of Africa*, their conversations reflected the influence of their own knowledge and experience that served to help them in making connections between the information and meanings that were museum-supplied or visitor-supplied.

Some art museum curators who labor long and hard to create thoughtful and informative label copy and sensitive exhibit design might feel dismayed and misunderstood if they were to hear the large amount and seemingly tangential nature of visitor-take talk going on in their galleries. We believe that this result should actually be seen as very encouraging for curators. There was a paucity of talk that was completely off subject (personal talk). The finding that visitors used so much of their personal take to make meaning shows that *Soul of Africa's* curatorial supports created a rich art environment in which people felt sufficiently comfortable to make many different associations. Their visit could be informative as well as personally meaningful, not solely an occasion to absorb new knowledge about unfamiliar aesthetics and anthropology. In addition, that visitors were so interested in the aesthetics of the artwork showed that they were not distracted or overwhelmed by the anthropological affordances. The curators seemed to have balanced the strands nicely: Visitors appreciated the anthropology but did not forget that they were in an art museum.

ACKNOWLEDGMENTS

The author wishes to thank Mary Abu-Shumays, Joyce Fienberg, Marilyn Russell, and Lucy Stewart for their conceptual and editorial assistance. Thanks also to the visitors in this study who were so generous with their time and their thoughts.

REFERENCES

Birney, B. (1988). Criteria for successful museum and zoo visits: Children offer guidance. *Curator, 31*(4), 292–316.

Campbell, J. (1999). *The hero's journey: Joseph Campbell on his life and work.* Boston: Element.

Doering, Z. D., & Pekarik, A. J. (1996). Questioning the entrance narrative. *Journal of Museum Education, 21*(3), 20–22.

Eisner, E. W., & Dobbs, S. M. (1986a). Museum education in twenty American art museums. *Museum News, 65*(2), 42–49.

Eisner, E. W., & Dobbs, S. M. (1986b). *The uncertain profession: Observations on the state of museum education in twenty American art museums.* Los Angeles: J. Paul Getty Center for Education in the Arts.

Falk, J. H. (1993). *Leisure decisions influencing African American use of museums.* Washington, DC: American Association of Museums.

Falk, J. H., & Dierking, L. D. (1992). *The museum experience.* Washington, DC: Whalesback Books.

Falk, J. H., Moussouri, T., & Coulson, D. (1998). The effect of visitors' agendas on museum learning. *Curator, 41*(2), 106–120.

Gennaro, E. A. (1981). The effectiveness of using pre-visit instructional materials on learning for a museum field trip experience. *Journal of Research in Science Teaching, 18*(3), 275–279.

Hooper-Greenhill, E. (1992). *Museums and the shaping of knowledge.* New York: Routledge.

Housen, A. (1996). *Studies on aesthetic development.* Minneapolis: American Association of Museums Sourcebook.

Karp, I. (1991). Other cultures in museum perspective. In I. Karp & S. D. Lavine (Eds.), *Exhibiting cultures: The poetics and politics of museum display* (pp. 373–385). Washington, DC: Smithsonian Institution Press.

Koroscik, J. S. (1997). What potential do young people have for understanding works of art? In A. M. Kindler (Ed.), *Child development in art* (pp. 143–164). Reston, VA: National Association for Education in the Arts.

Koroscik, J. S., Short, G., Stavropoulos, C., & Fortin, S. (1992). Frameworks for understanding art: The function of comparative art contexts and verbal cues. *Studies in Art Education, 33*(3), 154–164.

Leinhardt, G., & Crowley, K. (1998). *Museum Learning Collaborative revised phase 2 proposal* (Submitted to the Institute for Museum and Library Services, Washington, DC, November, 1998). Learning Research and Development Center, University of Pittsburgh, Pittsburgh, PA.

McLean, K. (1993). *Planning for people in museum exhibitions.* Washington, DC: Association of Science-Technology Centers.

McManus, P. M. (1989). Oh yes they do! How visitors read labels and interact with exhibit text. *Curator, 32*(3), 174–189.

Parsons, M. J. (1987). *How we understand art: A cognitive developmental account of aesthetic experience.* Cambridge, England: Cambridge University Press.

Ramey-Gassert, L., Walberg, H. J., III, & Walberg, H. J. (1994). Reexamining connections: Museums as science learning environments. *Science Education, 78*(4), 348–363.

Rice, D. (1992). Visions and culture: The role of museums in visual literacy. In S. K. Nichols (Ed.), *Patterns in practice: Selections from the Journal of Museum Education* (pp. 144–151). Washington, DC: Museum Education Roundtable.

Riegel, H. (1996). Into the heart of irony: Ethnographic exhibitions and the politics of difference. In S. Macdonald & G. Fyfe (Eds.), *Theorizing museums: Representing identity and diversity in a changing world* (pp. 83–104). Oxford: Blackwell Publishers/The Sociological Review.

Ripley, D. (1969). *The sacred grove.* New York: Simon & Schuster.

Rubin, W. S. (Ed). (1984). *"Primativism" in 20th century art: Affinity of the tribal and the modern.* New York: Museum of Modern Art.

Schauble, L., Beane, D. B., Coates, G. D., Martin, L., & Sterling, P. (1996). Outside the classroom walls: Learning in informal environments. In L. Schauble & R. Glaser (Eds.), *Innovations in learning: New environments for education* (pp. 5–24). Mahwah, NJ: Lawrence Erlbaum Associates.

Schauble, L., Leinhardt, G., & Martin, L. (1996). *Museum Learning Collaborative proposal* (Submitted to the Institute for Museum and Library Services, Washington, DC, August, 1996). Learning Research and Development Center, University of Pittsburgh, Pittsburgh, PA.

Serrell, B. (1992). The 51% solution: Defining a successful exhibit by visitor behavior. In *Current Issues in Audience Research and Evaluation, 6,* 26–30. Jacksonville, AL: Center for Social Design.

Scribner, S., & Cole, M. (1973). Cognitive consequences of formal and informal education. *Science, 182*(4112), 553–559.

Silverman, L. H. (1995). Visitor meaning-making in museums for a new age. *Curator, 38,* 161–170.

Vogel, S. (1991). Always true to the object, in our fashion. In I. Karp & S. D. Lavine (Eds.), *Exhibiting cultures: The poetics and politics of museum display* (pp. 191–204). Washington, DC: Smithsonian Institution Press.

Worts, D. (1991). Visitor-centered experiences. In A. Benefield, S. Bitgood, & H. Shettel (Eds.), *Visitor studies: Theory, research, and practice, Vol. 4* (pp. 156–161). Jacksonville, AL: Center for Social Design.

Chapter **8**

Looking for Learning in Visitor Talk: A Methodological Exploration

Sue Allen
The Exploratorium
San Francisco, CA

When the Exploratorium was asked to conduct one of the early studies to contribute to the Museum Learning Collaborative (Leinhardt & Crowley, 1998), I considered it a rare opportunity to contribute to both of the professional communities that I currently straddle.

As an educational researcher, I embraced the chance to study in-depth learning in the public space of the Exploratorium. One of my continuing goals at the museum is to explore and refine fruitful methods of collecting and analyzing evidence of learning in an environment that is highly challenging from a research perspective. In addition, I wanted to use the lens of visitor conversations to gather baseline research data about what visitors learn while visiting an Exploratorium exhibition. Few exhibitions are ever studied in this way, and the Exploratorium's recent temporary exhibitions are of particular theoretical interest because they combine elements from different museum traditions. For example, the *Frogs* exhibition that was the focus of this study contained hands-on interactive elements typical of a science museum, terrariums of live animals typical of a zoo or natural history museum, cases of cultural artifacts such as fetishes and musical instruments typical of a cultural history museum, and two-dimensional elements that could be read or looked at, such as maps and examples of froggy folklore. Such diversity is unusual in the museum field, and gave me an opportunity to make comparisons among the kinds of learning experiences visitors have with different types of exhibit elements.

As an exhibit evaluator active in the field of Visitor Studies, I also had an additional goal for the study. I wanted to explore possible methods for data gathering and analysis that might be of practical value to exhibit evaluators. There are both political and practical reasons for assessing the kinds of learning that happen in informal environments. In the face of increasing pressure to prove their effectiveness as educational institutions, more and more museums are conducting summative evaluations of their exhibitions. Such evaluations usually include tracking and timing studies of visitors' behavior (summarized in Serrell, 1998), often combined with a fairly tightly structured exit interview or questionnaire. It seems to me that these evaluations would benefit from including a component that assessed visitor learning through more naturalistic or open-ended study of visitor conversations, particularly those that happen "in real time" during the visit. In order to make this kind of study feasible, we need to develop methods that do not demand the resources of time, money, and research expertise that characterize large research efforts. To that end, this study had a pure research focus, but also explored some possible avenues for bringing a more sociocultural definition of learning to standard evaluation practices.

BACKGROUND

It is commonly accepted by museum evaluators and visitor studies professionals that school-based methods of assessing learning, such as conceptual pre- and posttests, do not transfer well to the study of learning in informal environments (e.g., Bitgood, Serrell, & Thompson, 1994; Crane, 1994; Falk & Dierking, 1992; Hein, 1998; Jeffery-Clay, 1998; Munley, 1992; Serrell, 1990). It is also well known that learning in museums is highly social in nature, and museum researchers are beginning to embrace sociocultural perspectives to describe learning (e.g., Crowley & Callanan, 1998; Falk & Dierking, 2000; Guberman & Van Dusen, 2001; Martin, 1996; Matusov & Rogoff, 1995; Silverman, 1990; Uzzell, 1993). However, most of the methods used to study visitors' experiences still rely on the responses of individuals rather than groups, and visitors' feedback is most often gleaned after they have left the exhibition.

One promising way of looking for the subtle, moment-by-moment learning that characterizes learning in museums is by analyzing visitors' conversations as they move through the public exhibit space. Although conversational analysis is not a routine part of most evaluations, a number of researchers have conducted such studies (e.g., Borun et al., 1998; Crowley & Callanan, 1998; Diamond, 1980; Guberman, Emo, Simmons, Taylor, & Sullivan, 1999; Hensel, 1987; Hilke, 1988; Lucas, McManus, & Thomas, 1986; McManus, 1988, 1989b; Silverman, 1990; Taylor, 1986; Tunnicliffe, 1998).

Of these, Silverman was unusual in focusing on exhibitions; other researchers have studied exhibit elements primarily, or have focused on an entire visit. I believe that the exhibition is a particularly interesting unit of study for several reasons. First, it is coherent conceptually, given that most exhibitions have a fairly well-defined and articulable scope and set of objectives; this gives a relatively clear curatorial framework with which to compare visitor experiences. Second, exhibitions are logistically suitable for conversational analysis, because they are large enough to show repeating patterns of visitor behaviors, but not so extensive as to require an entire day just to gather the data on a single family, as is often the case with whole-visit studies (e.g., Diamond, 1980). Lastly, exhibit development projects (such as those funded by federal agencies) usually generate exhibitions that require summative evaluations, so there is an opportunity to gather data that may serve both research and evaluation purposes.

Another key feature of the foregoing studies is their analysis schemes, which vary considerably. Stubbs (1983) pointed out that "discourse analysis is very difficult. We seem to be dealing with some kind of theory of social action" (p. 3). Indeed, I would argue that visitors' conversations as they move through an exhibition are particularly complex, because they involve such close ties between situation, knowledge, action, and language. Stubbs also notes that discourse analysis encompasses a wide variety of techniques and stances toward natural language, as researchers grapple with problems such as the multiple meanings that utterances can have. For example, he distinguishes between discourse acts, which are defined according to their function within the discourse itself (such as initiating, continuing, and terminating exchanges), and speech acts, which are defined according to psychological and social functions outside the ongoing discourse (such as naming, thanking, promising). From this perspective, the studies by McManus and Diamond focused more on discourse acts, such as "elicitation," "summons," "reply," "tell to read," and so forth. For the purposes of the *Frogs* study, I wanted to focus exclusively on speech acts, and in particular, those acts that functioned to advance the visitors' learning as defined next.

Whereas Hilke and Diamond devoted considerable attention to the differences in roles and relationships among members of a group, I preferred to make the simplifying assumption of treating all group members as collaborative learners, with a focus on the joint advancement of understanding. Also, based on my secondary goal of exploring practical discourse analysis methods for evaluators, I wanted to keep my utterance categories few in number and highly generalizable across different exhibitions. This was in contrast to Hilke and Tunnicliffe, each of whom devised a coding scheme with more than 70 categories of utterance, and in contrast to Tunnicliffe, whose analysis scheme involved specific content-specific categories at the more detailed levels (e.g., "mentions reproductive organs").

THEORETICAL FRAMEWORK AND RESEARCH QUESTIONS

My fundamental research goal was to characterize and quantify evidence of learning in the conversations of people visiting this exhibition. Further, I wanted to know whether "learning-talk" could be reliably identified as falling into different categories, and how common the various categories would be. Lastly, I wanted to characterize any differences between the patterns of learning-talk elicited by different types of exhibit elements, or between the conversations of groups that include and exclude children. Answers to all these questions would contribute to basic research on learning in informal environments, and would also inform museum practitioners who are in the business of designing learning experiences for diverse audiences, using a variety of exhibit-design strategies.

In defining "learning" for the purposes of this study, I used the following general framework:

1. I embraced the set of categories, generally attributed to Bloom (1956) which includes affective, cognitive, and pyschomotor learning. These categories are frequently used by museum studies professionals because they map well onto the kinds of experiences visitors usually have in museums: thinking, feeling, and interacting with objects.

2. I took from the sociocultural perspective a focus on learning as an interpretive act of meaning-making, a process rather than an outcome, and a joint activity of a group, rather than being attributable to one of the people only. For this reason, I did not attempt to analyze the learning of individual visitors, but rather to characterize learning by the group.

3. I wanted to be sure that my definition was not so tied to formal learning assessments that it would exclude the kinds of learning that are most prevalent in informal settings. In particular, research has shown that museum learning tends to be affective, personal, sporadic, concrete rather than abstract, and associational rather than deductive. Even explanations tend to be brief, partial, and nonhierarchical (e.g., Crowley, Galco, Jacobs, & Russo, 2000).

4. In terms of the scope of the content, I wanted to define *learning* quite narrowly to refer to discussion of the exhibits and the exhibition, and its topic area. In other words, I excluded learning-talk that related to other parts of the museum visit. I also excluded navigational talk such as beckoning over, or noting that an exhibit has been missed. This choice was made partly for political reasons, to respond to the recurring comment, "Yes, visitors have fun in museums, but what do they really learn?" By starting with a definition of learning that constrains content, I hoped to put the museum in a stronger position to make claims about its efficacy as a learning institution.

My definition of learning did not require intentionality on the part of the speaker or listener (which would have been very difficult to infer, and is also not a necessary condition for advancing meaning-making). Also, learning did not require explicit expression of awareness or acknowledgment, although such statements did end up being coded as a subcategory (metacognition) of the learning-talk.

Throughout the study, my bottom-line question was always: Is this evidence of learning? From a cognitive science perspective: Is it likely that one or both of these people have just acquired new knowledge or ability from what was said? Or, from a more sociocultural perspective: Has this utterance advanced the dyad's collaborative process of making meaning from the exhibition? If so, I tried to include it somewhere in the coding framework.

OVERVIEW OF THE *FROGS* EXHIBITION

The context for the learning study was *Frogs*, a temporary exhibition built by Exploratorium staff in collaboration with several consultants who had expertise in amphibians, exhibition design, and exhibitions involving live animals. It was open from February 1999 to February 2000, and occupied approximately 4,000 square feet of museum floor space.

Front-end evaluation studies conducted early in the development process revealed that Exploratorium visitors thought frogs to be an interesting topic, but most knew little about them. Many visitors reported having had some contact with amphibians from high school biology classes, and had listened to frogs calling on spring or summer evenings. Some visitors knew about malformed frogs.

Informed by these data, the development team created the following goals and conceptual outline: (a) to present scientific, social and cultural aspects of people's relationship to frogs, (b) to engender respect and appreciation for the animals in the museum's visitors, (c) to create something that would be beautiful, intriguing, and informative for the museum's age-diverse audience.

In terms of content subdivisions, the exhibition included: an introductory area that defined frogs and toads and amphibian development, sections on eating and being eaten, frog and toad calls, a showcasing of amphibian anatomy, a close-up observation area, a cluster of exhibits showing "amazing adaptations," an area that discussed the declining status of frogs worldwide, and a section on frog locomotion.

As already mentioned, the final exhibition contained an unusual diversity of different *types* of exhibit elements, in an attempt to illustrate the broad variety of ways humans have understood and connected with frogs, as well as to engage visitors with different learning styles. In all, there were:

- 10 hands-on interactive elements typical of a science museum,
- 23 terrariums of live frogs and toads, typical of a zoo or natural history museum,
- 5 cases of cultural artifacts such as fetishes, baskets and musical instruments typical of a cultural history museum,
- 18 two-dimensional elements that could be read or looked at, such as maps, excerpts from children's books, and renderings of froggy folklore from many cultures,
- 3 cases of organic material, such as preserved frogs or frog food,
- 3 videos of frog activities; 2 windows to the "Frog Lab" where frogs were allowed to rest and breed,
- an extended entry bridge, and
- an immersion experience of sitting on a back porch at night and listening to a chorus of frogs.

METHODOLOGICAL CHALLENGES

Studying conversations, especially at a highly interactive museum such as the Exploratorium, is a logistically difficult and expensive undertaking. The environment of the museum floor presents a set of challenges beyond those inherent in most laboratory or school settings.

First, the acoustics of the public spaces are very poor, and there is a huge amount of ambient noise. Major sources of sound include background hubbub from distant visitors, screams from excited children, conversations by nearby visitors (easy to mistake for members of the study group), and the myriad of sounds that interactive exhibits make when in use, such as bangs, dings, music, ratcheting, splashes, music, and prerecorded speech.

Second, visitors move around a great deal, and the groups they arrive in keep changing and reforming on short time-scales. This means that microphones in static locations can only catch conversations over small intervals of time (typically a minute), and researchers wanting to record extended conversations have to use cordless microphones, with their potential for interference and other audio problems. The fluid movements of visiting groups also complicate the decision of which visitors should be asked to wear a microphone, because the parties to a conversation keep changing, so that different conversations might take place simultaneously among different members of a group.

Another logistical difficulty is that much of the visitor activity involves interacting with the specific objects in the environment, so it is almost impossible to make sense of an extended audio stream without corresponding video or observation data.

Once the conversations have been recorded, transcription is expensive and time-consuming, and the recordings are particularly challenging to decipher because visitors speak with a great variety of accents and styles, and bring a huge diversity of previous experiences that might be referred to at any time.

Even if visitors' words are audible, coding of the conversations is difficult because much of the discourse is fragmented, ambiguous, or lacking clear referents. One reason for this is that in conversation, speakers seldom articulate what is obvious to listeners: the details of the physical situation they are in, what they are attending to, the set of common experiences they have shared over the years, the "short-hand" words and phrases they have come to use together. As Garvey (1984) put it, "in conversation . . . if something can be taken for granted, it usually is" (p. 12).

Finally, interpretation of the results is especially challenging because the museum environment is dense and complex, with many variables that can influence what visitors say and do not say. For example, conversations are likely to depend on visitor variables (such as demographics, psychographics, previous experiences, interests, attitudes, expectations, group dynamics, and current state of comfort and energy), exhibition variables (such as location within the museum, degree of orientation provided, lighting, seating, ambient noise, and current crowdedness), and variables in the detailed design of individual exhibit elements (such as height, coloration, physical accessibility, interface, display style, label content and tone). It is seldom easy to draw conclusions about what kinds of exhibit environments lead to what kinds of conversations.

Addressing the Audio Challenge

Recording extended visitor conversations has been historically difficult to achieve in the noisy, open, fluid environment of a hands-on science museum (e.g., Borun et al., 1998). However, recent advances in audio technology have made it possible to buy high-quality cordless radio microphones at a reasonable cost. We used two such microphones, putting them in "fanny packs" which the visitors could wear around their waists. At a convenient remote location (just behind a high wall bordering the public space), we mixed the signals together and recorded the conversations onto regular audio cassettes. We also made backup cassette recordings of the components of the conversation, directly from the receiver and before mixing.

The quality of the sound was generally high, and limited mainly by the degree of clarity of the speaker. Only one tape was rejected from the study because of inadequate audio quality, and this was a tape of visitors who were speaking extremely quietly to each other, almost as if they were whispering. Given the extremely high level of ambient noise in the Exploratorium, and the high degree of crowdedness of the exhibition, we were very satisfied with the audio quality achieved.

Gathering Synchronous Movement Data

We wanted to know where visitors were when they were speaking, so that we could relate their conversations to the 66 specific exhibit elements comprising the *Frogs* exhibition. We considered videotaping to get the most precise information about visitors' movements, but eventually dismissed this as unfeasible, mostly because it would have taken a large number of fixed cameras to cover the 4,000 square-foot exhibition, with its many twists and turns. A tracker carrying a camera would have had to keep very close to the visitors in order to get good enough video to code, which we thought would be highly intrusive. Furthermore, it would have been very difficult to maintain a video stream that is at once steady enough to be useful, and fast-moving enough to record the positions and behaviors of two people who may be moving somewhat independently of each other as they explore the exhibition.

Instead, we obtained information on visitors' locations by having a "tracker" follow them discreetly, noting their movements and behaviors. In order to get synchronicity of this information with the conversations, we used a system of three microphones: two worn by the visitors, and one by the tracker. The tracker's audio stream was recorded onto the Right channel of a tape, while the mixed signal from the two visitors was simultaneously recorded on the Left channel. The result is a set of tapes that contain accurate information about where visitors were when they spoke, to an accuracy of a few seconds, assuming the tracker was alert to all movements. This technique proved to be a successful way of keeping the two audio streams synchronous, although (as described later) we ended up tolerating some looseness in the timing of the tracking call-outs.

Visitor Selection

Based on our pilot observations of visitor groups moving through the *Frogs* exhibition, we decided to conduct the study using only groups of two visitors (dyads). Part of the reason for this was our concern that the tracker would not be able to monitor more than two people simultaneously. In addition, we noted that larger groups tended to split up and reform in different combinations, yielding the possibility of different simultaneous conversations, which would result in a garbled sound on the recording. During the analysis phase, we discovered yet another reason for excluding larger groups. Because they frequently split up and reform, the visitors in these groups are much more likely to talk or ask each other about what they have previously seen or done at other exhibit elements. Such talk adds to the complexity of the coding scheme because it introduces new categories of talk that are about the exhibits but have a reflective aspect (e.g., descriptions of exhibit features remembered but not currently visible).

We thus simplified the study by inviting only dyads to participate. Our complete list of criteria for participants was as follows:

1. The visitors were in a party of two.
2. They spoke English as their first language, ensuring that their conversations would be understandable to the coders, but also normal and comfortable for them.
3. It was their first visit to the *Frogs* exhibition, so that we would be studying conversations about real-time experiences rather than the more complex case of real-time experiences combined with reflections.
4. Both visitors were 18 or older, or a child[1] was accompanied by a parent or guardian, so that they could give informed consent to be recorded.

Of the 118 dyads we approached, 45 (38%) declined our invitation to participate. Most of these gave no specific reason for their decision, and we did not ask them to justify it. The most common reasons that were spontaneously given were lack of time (6), other arranged meetings within the museum (6), or the difficulty of making it work with a fast-moving, young, or reluctant child (12). We ourselves refused a further 24 dyads (20%) who expressed initial interest, but proved to be ineligible to participate. Of these, the largest group (14) were visitors who had already seen the exhibition. We decided to exclude this group for simplicity, to avoid the complications of having a subgroup of visitors who might only re-visit parts of the exhibition, and whose talk would be an ambiguous combination of real-time experience and reflection. The remaining 49 dyads (42%) were both eligible and willing to participate in the study.

We felt that the use of dyads was an excellent way to study conversations and keep the complexity of the situation at manageable levels. The only major drawback to this method was the amount of time it took to recruit participants. Our constraints on group size and age meant that we spent relatively long periods simply waiting for an appropriate group to approach, and this was sometimes disheartening for a recruiter. Even with an acceptance rate that was much higher than expected, it took us about 20 days of data collection to record and interview 49 visitor dyads. We found that we could collect data from an average of 3 to 4 dyads on a given weekend day, and 0 to 2

[1]We experimented with the minimum age of child participants. We succeeded in recording (and later interviewing) children as young as four.

on a weekday afternoon, once the school fieldtrip groups had left the museum. It was unfortunate that the exhibition was near the rear of the Exploratorium, so that it took about an hour for visitors to begin arriving there. We also found that we could not recruit any participants in the last 90 minutes of the museum's open hours, because visitors expressed anxiety about getting through the exhibition in time to see other things before closing time. These constraints left a productive period of perhaps 4½ hours each weekend day, and 2 hours each weekday.

To recruit a higher number of participants, we tried letting larger family groups participate by designating two people to carry the microphones. This met with limited success. Some families did act on our requests to go through the exhibition in two groups (the dyad separate from the rest) without all talking together, but in most cases the excitement of the exhibition was too much for them not to share what they were seeing with family members on the other side of the gallery. This created serious problems in the transcription, because family members who mingled in this way seemed even more likely to compare reflections on what they had already seen and done, which complicated later coding considerably. We recommend using this technique only if data-collection time is severely restricted, and even then, suggesting strongly to the family that the two groups look at different parts of the museum while the study is underway.

Obtaining Informed Consent

When recruiting visitors at the entry to the museum, we told them that we would be recording their conversations so that the museum staff could learn more about visitors' experiences in the exhibition. We also told them that we would be watching them to see where they went within the exhibition. We did not ask them for written consent, however, until they had finished seeing the exhibition, and after the interview had taken place. There were two reasons for delaying the signing of consent forms. First, we found that visitors were much more relaxed at the end of seeing the exhibition than at the beginning, and took time to consider what we were saying or to ask questions. The recruitment point, being at the most inviting entry point to the exhibition, was a place where visitors tended to be focused on getting into the exhibition, especially when the dyads included children.

Second, at the end of their visit visitors were in a better position to assess how comfortable they were with what they had actually revealed during their conversations. Had anyone refused to give their consent at that point (and nobody did), we would have given them their audiotape to take home with them. We also offered all dyads a choice in whether to let their tape be available for use at conferences and larger professional settings beyond the museum, and one dyad decided not to allow this.

Tracking Visitors

We had already told visitors that we would be following them to see where they stopped. Nevertheless, we felt it was important to track them unobtrusively, so as to influence their behavior as little as possible. The tracker dressed in dark colors so that her own cordless microphone (pinned so as to be near her mouth) would be inconspicuous, and she spoke in low tones as she followed behind the dyad, concealing herself behind exhibit elements where possible. The only times this technique proved ineffective were on the rare occasions when the exhibition was empty; in one such case, a visitor being tracked actually approached the tracker and attempted to start a conversation. The best solution to this problem, if staffing allows, is for the person who recruits to be different from the tracker; this minimizes the chance of the visitors becoming conscious of the tracker while moving through the exhibition.

The most important thing the tracker did was to note where the two visitors were at all times, irrespective of whether they were talking or not. The tracker's audio stream went something like this: "She stops at Jungle . . . he joins, he moves on . . . to . . . Spadefoot . . . she joins . . ." We defined a "stop" as happening whenever someone's two feet come to a halt in front of an element, and their eyes are on the element. Unlike the case in many tracking studies (e.g., Serrell, 1998), we did not wait for a minimum of several seconds before counting something as a stop; reporting two simultaneous movements was too taxing for any further judgments about minimum time, and in any case, we wanted to include everything they saw (however briefly) in case they talked about it later.

One key behavior we overlooked was interactions with other visitors. When the museum is busy, many people may be crowded around an exhibit element, and some of the audiotapes include voices that we can't unambiguously identify as belonging to our tracked visitors. For this reason, we would recommend for future studies that the tracker attempt to record the presence of nearby visitors, and, in particular, the moments when they seem to be talking.

How Authentic Are the Visitors' Conversations?

One of the main concerns that museum professionals have about microphoning visitors is that this may affect the nature of the talk and behavior in unpredictable ways. Although a full assessment of such impacts was beyond the scope of this study, we did make some attempts to assess the most obvious kinds of impact.

When coding the visitors' transcripts, we created a code for verbal evidence that visitors were aware of the microphones or the fact that they were acting as research subjects. Of the 30 dyads whose conversations were transcribed in detail, 9 (30%) mentioned something about the research as they first entered the exhibition. These initial comments included expressions of pleasure and support for the research, suggestions about dealing with the microphones, and jokes about talking in code or not swearing.

Once they had entered the exhibition, 14 of the 30 dyads (47%) made some reference to the microphones or audiotaping. Most commonly, parents encouraged children to keep their microphones on but not to play with them (6 dyads), individuals talked about removing their microphones to participate in a jumping activity (6 dyads), and dyads who were visiting with a larger group explained what they were doing (6 dyads). Although such comments were more frequent than we had hoped, in most cases it was a single incident, took no more than a few seconds, and did not result in any obvious derailment of activity (such as an explicit decision to move somewhere or do something). The majority of dyads never mentioned the research or the microphones at all.

We attempted to minimize visitors' awareness of the recordings by keeping out of their view as much as possible and by using fanny packs that they could "strap on and forget." However, there is a limit to how unobtrusive we can be, because our ethical policies require that we tell visitors what we are about to do, and ask for their consent to be recorded. During the pilot phase of the study, we also experimented with different recruiting locations in an attempt to lessen the impact of visitor awareness, but this strategy proved to be laughably unsuccessful.[2]

There was at least one dimension of visitor behavior that was significantly affected by the methods used in our study. The dyads who participated stayed much longer in the exhibition than visitors who were unobtrusively tracked. A study of the *Frogs* exhibition by Contini (1999) showed that the average time spent in the exhibition was 10.9 minutes, and the median time 9.0 minutes. By contrast, the average time spent by visitors in the conversa-

---

[2]We hoped that we could find a way to make visitors less self-conscious by giving them the microphones without them realizing that the *Frogs* exhibition was the focus of our interest. We anticipated some kind of exponential drop-off in visitors' self-consciousness, so we reasoned that the ideal situation would be for the visitors to forget about the microphones just around the time they happened to enter the *Frogs* exhibition. We explored this option by asking 20 groups of visitors who were entering *Frogs,* where they had been about 20 minutes previously. We then recruited visitors at the point that seemed the most popular "upstream" location, and gave them microphones, telling them that we would catch up with them at a later time, probably about 45 minutes hence. This technique proved disastrous, when visitors happily moved in tantalizingly different directions from the *Frogs* entrance, and we were forced to sit in the audio room, waiting impatiently and hoping for our true study to begin. The experiment ended abruptly, and we resigned ourselves to recruiting at the entrance to the exhibition for the sake of efficiency.

tion study was 25.4 minutes, and the median time was 24.1 minutes (more than twice as long). Even so, the longer times do not necessarily imply that the visitors in the study were behaving unusually. At least part of the time difference may be due to a selection effect. Visitors who chose (for a variety of possible reasons) to take a "quick look" at the exhibition would have been included in the tracking study, but would probably have refused to participate in an extended study. Moreover, McManus (1987) found that the constituency characterized by the briefest stay at exhibits at the British Museum (Natural History) was the "singletons" (groups of one), and this constituency was entirely excluded from our conversation study.

We take the view that every powerful research method yields insights and creates distortions, so that we would use this kind of method in combination with others that complement it. For example, the standard tracking methods that are common to museum evaluations give a much better sense of how long visitors stay in exhibitions, where they stop, and for how long; we would not propose to compare our timing data directly with that collected unobtrusively, nor would we calculate quantities such as "sweep rates" or "percentage diligent visitors" (Serrell, 1998). However, standard tracking methods leave us wondering about visitors' interpretations of what they are seeing, and how they think about it, moment by moment. In understanding these kinds of learning processes, analysis of conversations is an appropriate and powerful tool.

Perhaps it is most appropriate to compare recording visitors to conducting a "cued interview," one of the more common techniques in visitor studies. It has the same qualities of alerting visitors to the fact that they are under scrutiny, so one might expect them to pay closer attention to the exhibits, to try harder, talk more, or generally be "on their best behavior." For this reason, we cautiously take the position of regarding the conversations as a probable "best case" display of visitors' authentic behavior.

Transcription

One of the most time-consuming aspects of analyzing the conversations was getting them transcribed. With a modest transcription budget, we were only able to get 15 tapes transcribed professionally. Thereafter, we put a call out to museum volunteers, who were enthusiastic but limited in the amount of time they could commit to the project. We ended the study with a total of 30 transcripts.

On the whole we were disappointed with the quality of the transcriptions, both professional and done by volunteers. Even after sampling a range of different companies, we found that we always had to review the entire tape and make many edits. We found that we could hear almost everything the visitors were saying, but the transcribers obviously struggled.[3] We suspect that this difference was due to the transcribers' complete lack of familiarity with the exhibition. We did notice an increase in our own ability to hear visitors after we printed out the entire label text of the exhibition and became very familiar with its contents as part of the coding process, so we conclude that familiarity with the exhibition is a key requirement for good transcription.

Suggestions for Obtaining Intelligible Audio Recordings Without Video

At this point I wish to respond to the challenges raised at the beginning of this chapter, by summarizing our solution for obtaining intelligible audio recordings without video, even in a very active and noisy public space:

- Get a set of at least three high-quality cordless microphones, and test that they give a strong signal over all parts of the museum.
- Recruit visitors who arrive in groups of two, speak English as their first language, and are at least 4 years old. The reduction in complexity will be worth the extra wait.
- Document the exhibition in fine detail so that you can refer to labels and exhibits later, as questions arise in the analysis.
- Employ a transcriber who is intimately familiar with the exhibition.

With all of these in place, we felt able to make sense of almost everything visitors said in the tapes, without the need for video. We should say, however, that one of the reasons for our success may be that the commonest type of exhibit in the *Frogs* exhibition was the terrarium containing live animals, rather than the hands-on interactive exhibits for which the Exploratorium is well known. It may be that visitors were forced to communicate with each other using language, in part because there were reduced opportunities for them to communicate via more physical means.

Coding Visitors' Locations

We were pleased to discover, on listening to the Right and Left channels of the tapes, that most of the time visitors' talk was about the exhibit that was currently in front of them. Most of the exceptions were due to a "movement

[3]For example, "What frogs and toads eat, insects" was transcribed as "Can frogs and toads mate? It's sex."

lag," during which visitors would notice another exhibit, walk toward it, and start to comment on it before they came to a stop in front of it (e.g., a visitor might say, "Wow, look, orange frogs! Aren't they gorgeous" before coming to a stop). Because we wanted to know what kinds of learning were *evoked* by what types of exhibit elements, we chose to assign such statements to the exhibit that visitors were focusing on, rather than the one they were about to leave. Thus, our coding for location was based primarily on the exhibit element that visitors were talking *about*, but informed by the tracking information, which told us where they were when they were static, and which exhibits they were moving between.

For this step in the coding (parsing the transcripts based on exhibit element discussed), the straightforwardness of the task was reflected in our high intercoder reliability. We measured a 100% level of intercoder agreement about which exhibit elements were discussed, and a 90% level of agreement about which exact word in the transcript signified the start of the next exhibit element. In a similar study, Silverman (1990) also reported ease with this part of the coding: "With the aid of observation notes indicating where in the exhibit the pair was, as well as the pair's own comments, conversations were fairly easily broken down into object-related interactions for coding."

We also used the tracking information to create a list of exhibits that the visitors stopped at, but did not speak about ("silent stops"). We did this because we wanted to know all the exhibits visitors had seen, partly to get a measure of how common talking was compared to stopping, and partly to inform us of their total experience when it was time to do the exit interviews.

To our surprise, we found that we did not need a code for visitors "between exhibits" because it was very rare for conversations to happen between exhibits that were neither about the exhibit just left nor the one being approached. Perhaps it was partly due to visitors' awareness of the microphones, or partly due to the strength of the exhibition, but we found that visitors' conversations were tightly coupled with what they were seeing; so much so, that we were often able to guess movement information for the bulk of a written transcript, prior to hearing the tracking audio channel. The only times we ran into the problem of visitors talking about exhibits they were not near was with dyads that were part of larger families. In two such cases, the larger group met up with our dyad in the course of visiting the exhibition, and began talking with each other about what they had seen and done at remote exhibits. This behavior confirmed our preference for recruiting only true dyads in future studies, so that such family retrospectives would not arise. We found that when true dyads split up and rejoined, they tended to beckon each other over to see what was of interest, rather than talking about it later in the exhibition.

Creating a Specific Coding Scheme

In creating a framework by which to code the conversations, I combined approaches from sociocultural and cognitive science perspectives. I took a sociocultural approach when we decided not to categorize the conversations by individual speaker, but instead took verbal expressions of noticing, thinking, feeling, and acting, all as evidence that learning was taking place within the pair of companions. On the other hand, the specific categories of talk I used were mostly based on cognitive concepts such as attention, memory, declarative knowledge, inference, planning, and metacognition. I also included the categories of "Affective" and "Strategic," both of which have generally been regarded as fundamental areas of strength in informal learning environments, and which extend the assessment of learning beyond the strictly cognitive realm.

Within the basic framework already outlined, I tried to let the details of the categories and subcategories be "emergent," that is, shaped by the nature of the conversations themselves. To do this, coder Marni Goldman and I had to iterate on the coding scheme many times until we reached a stable and reliable set of categories that seemed to span the space of all types of learning talk. Ultimately, our coding system consisted of 5 categories and 16 subcategories of "learning-talk," utterances that we took as evidence of learning.

The Coding Scheme in Detail

Figure 8.1 shows the hierarchical structure of the final coding scheme, with 5 main categories and 16 subcategories of learning-talk.

1. Perceptual Talk. This category included all kinds of talk that had to do with visitors drawing attention to something in the sea of stimulus surrounding them. We regard it as evidence of learning because it is an act of identifying and sharing what is significant in a complex environment. The category included four subdivisions:

(a) Identification = pointing out something to attend to, such as an object or interesting part of the exhibit (e.g., "Oh, look at this guy," or "There's a tube.")

(b) Naming = stating the name of an object in the exhibit (e.g., "Oh, it's a Golden Frog.")

(c) Feature = pointing out some concrete aspect or property of the exhibit (e.g., "Check out the bump on his head," or "That's loud, huh?")

(d) Quotation = drawing attention to exhibit text by reading aloud part of a label. Needs to be an exact quote or a very close paraphrase (also

Perceptual	**Conceptual**	**Connecting**
Identification	Simple	Life-connection
Naming	Complex	Knowledge-connection
Feature	Prediction	Inter-exhibit connection
Quotation	Metacognition	

Strategic	**Affective**
Use	Pleasure
Metaperformance	Displeasure
	Intrigue / Surprise

FIG. 8.1. Coding scheme, with 5 categories and 16 subcategories of learning-talk.

known as "text echo," McManus, 1989a), (e.g., "One of the most common frogs in North America, and a typical jumping frog.")

2. Conceptual Talk. This category captured cognitive interpretations of whatever was being attended to in the exhibit. To classify as a "cognitive interpretation," an utterance did not necessarily have to be abstract, have multiple steps, or reach a profound conclusion. We wanted our coding scheme to capture the breadth of small, individual, literal inferences that seemed far more typical of the conversations elicited by exhibit elements. The subcategories of conceptual talk were:

(a) Simple inference = single interpretive statement or interpretation of part of an exhibit (e.g., "They eat mice" after seeing a jar containing a mouse in a display of frog food, or "See now it looks like it's swimming" after successfully using a zoetrope to simulate the motion of a swimming frog)

(b) Complex inference = any hypothesis, generalization of exhibit information, or statement that discusses relationship between objects or properties (e.g., "That's a lot of body for them skinny legs to carry around," or "That would be hard to carve, wouldn't it?") Although we used the term *complex* to distinguish this from the very simplest kind of inference, it should be borne in mind that these were often single words or phrases rather than a formal series of deductions. The key criterion was that visitors draw some kind of inference about the exhibit element, beyond correctly interpreting what has been explicitly displayed.

(c) Prediction = stated expectation of what will happen, including what visitors are about to see or do (e.g., "I think it's going to be 'kwaa kwaa

kwaa' " when anticipating the sound of a particular frog call, or "Yeah, you'll start to grow legs" when viewing a tadpole.)

(d) Metacognition = reflection on one's own state of current or previous knowledge (e.g., "I didn't realize they could get that big," or "I can't remember, but I recognize him.")

3. Connecting Talk. This included any kind of talk that made explicit connections between something in the exhibition and some other knowledge or experience beyond it. Although we assume that all learning-talk involves previous knowledge to some degree, we felt that some types of utterance were distinct in that visitors were using the exhibits as a stimulus to share a personal story or previously learned information that was not directly coupled to what they were looking at. Subcategories were:

(a) Life connection = story, personal association, or likening of exhibit element to something familiar (e.g., "Yeah, my grandmother loves to collect stuff with frogs all over it" or "It looks like a brick, a floating brick.")

(b) Knowledge connection = declaration of knowledge gained prior to visiting the exhibition (e.g., "In Florida the dogs eat poisonous toads and die" or "Frogs, when it lays their egg, their egg floats to the top.")

(c) Inter-exhibit connection = any kind of link between exhibit elements, including the bringing of information gleaned at a previously visited element to the discussion of the current element. (e.g., "That's what I said. It eats anything as long as it fits in its mouth" when referring to the label from a previous part of the exhibition.)

4. Strategic Talk. Strategic talk (talk about strategies) was explicit discussion of how to use exhibits. It was not limited to hands-on exhibit elements, but was defined so as to include descriptions of how to move, where to look, or how to listen to something. Subcategories were:

(a) Use = statements about how to use an exhibit (e.g., "You're supposed to play this like that" when playing a wooden instrument that sounds like a frog, or "Okay go down to the water . . . and then go towards the back. See that little leafy type thing?" when searching for the leaf frog.)

(b) Metaperformance = expressions of evaluation of one's own or partner's performance, actions, or abilities (e.g., "I don't think I did a very good job of it.")

5. Affective Talk. In this category, we tried to capture all expressions of feeling, including pleasure, displeasure, and surprise or intrigue. Subcategories were:

(a) Pleasure = expressions of positive feelings or appreciation of aspects of an exhibit (e.g., "beautiful," "wonderful," "cool," "I like that one,") This subcategory also included laughter.

(b) Displeasure = expressions of negative feelings or dislike towards aspects of an exhibit, including sadness or sympathy (e.g., "poor thing," "ugly," "eeew," "gross," "yuck.")

(c) Intrigue = expressions of fascination or surprise (e.g., "wow," "gosh," "woah," "ooooh.")

Two caveats are worth mentioning with respect to the *affective talk* category. First, these verbal measures are, at best, crude indicators of the affective impact of an exhibition. However, we think it is worth making an attempt to capture affective learning-talk as best we can, and the prevalence in the conversations of words like those listed previously does suggest that they carry some significant aspect of visitors' shared experience. (A helpful review of some other approaches to affect is given in Roberts, 1990). Second, expressions of displeasure by visitors are not necessarily criticisms of the exhibition. In the case of the *Frogs* exhibition, some of the displays of organic material were deliberately graphic, and many children responded to videos of frogs eating such things as maggots with cries of "Ewwww!" yet seemed highly engaged and almost delighted.

Last, we note that the coding scheme we developed does depend quite sensitively on the detailed content of the exhibition, and the labels in particular. A single statement, such as "These are declining in California" could be a quote, a simple inference, a complex inference, a knowledge connection, or even an inter-exhibit connection, depending on what is written in the label-text at that exhibit element.

Counting Instances of Learning-Talk

As described earlier, we broke each conversation into segments of speech based on which exhibit element was being discussed. For each block, we then coded for the presence or absence of each of the 16 subcategories of learning-talk. This resulted in a coding matrix of 1's and 0's for each dyad, covering all types of learning-talk at all exhibit elements stopped at.

We did explore the possibility of coding the *frequency* of each kind of learning-talk for a given exhibit element, but decided against it based on the difficulty of determining what constituted different cases of a certain type of talk. Visitors' conversations often included repetitions, with slight variations or elaborations of each other's comments; these would have been quite difficult to count. For example:

Adult: Oh, I like them, these ones I like. Look at them.

Child: Oh, there's a whole bunch!
Adult: These are from Texas.
Child: Mom there's a thousand of them in there!
Adult: Those are from Texas, they're Texas ones. They look dry.
Child: They're everywhere, look.
Adult: And if they're from dry land, would they be frogs or Toads, John?
Child: Toads.
Adult: If they're from Texas, would they be frogs or toads?
Child: Toads.
Adult: Toads, yeah.

This kind of echoing was especially prevalent in the conversations of child–adult dyads, but was also quite common among adult–adult dyads. It made counting frequencies extremely difficult, and led to our decision to code only for presence or absence of each type of talk for each exhibit element. In spite of its coarseness, our "digital" approach nevertheless yielded a detailed profile of each dyad's conversation, owing to the large size of the coding matrix, and the fact that visitors tended to talk relatively briefly at a relatively large number of exhibit elements. We note that Silverman (1990) coded her conversations the same way, although she did not elaborate on the reasons behind this choice.

In combining the different subcategories of talk into the five larger categories, we used the logical "OR" function for each individual dyad. In other words, we coded any given dyad as having expressed "strategic learning-talk" at a given exhibit element if their conversation included at least one example of any of the subdivisions of strategic talk: use-talk, metaperformance talk, or both.

Intercoder Reliability

The coding process consisted of two steps: (a) parsing each transcript into segments of talk, one for each of the exhibit elements talked about, and (b) for each exhibit element, deciding which of the 16 types of talk were present. Because the two steps are not independent, we assessed intercoder reliability for both steps together.[4] Overall, we found our coding to be 78% reliable. We noted that this figure rose to 84% if we let go of the distinction between the subtly different categories of *simple* and *complex* cognitive talk.

[4]In the matrix of exhibit elements by talk subcategories, we ignored all cells that both coders assigned a "0" to; in other words, the large number of "absent" types of talk were not counted as agreements. We then counted as agreements all cells which both coders assigned "1" (i.e., cases where both agreed that a certain subcategory of talk was present in the conversation of a particular dyad at a particular exhibit element.) To determine the inter-coder reliability, we divided this number of agreements by the total of agreements plus disagreements

Specific Questions Driving Conversational Analysis

As outlined earlier, my principal goal for this study was to characterize the kinds and frequencies of learning, as revealed by visitors' conversations in the *Frogs* exhibition. In addition, the multifaceted nature of the exhibition gave me an opportunity to use these conversational assessments to compare the learning patterns of visitors at different types of exhibit element. More specifically, I had the following questions regarding the conversation data:

- What was the average frequency of learning-talk, albeit in a situation where visitors were cued? Was it something generally rare or common?
- What categories and subcategories of learning-talk emerged from the data, and what were their relative frequencies?
- Did different types of elements within the exhibition (e.g., hands-on, live, readable) tend to elicit different kinds of learning-talk?
- Were there any differences between the learning-talk of adult–adult (AA) and child–adult (CA) dyads, either in frequency or type?
- Given that one of the goals of the exhibition was to engender respect and appreciation for frogs, did visitors express any intention to take personal action or change their behaviors, based on the exhibition?

RESULTS

Here I present the key results of the conversational analysis, beginning with the number of stops made by dyads at the various elements in the exhibition. The data on stopping are important because they were used as a normalization factor in subsequent analyses. In other words, every frequency of learning-talk was calculated as a percentage of the elements where each dyad chose to stop, because I regarded these "stopped" elements as the only ones providing real opportunities for learning conversations to occur.

Number of Stops

On average, the visitor dyads stopped[5] at 34 exhibit elements (51% of the total on display), and spent an average of 25.4 minutes in the exhibition.

(the Jaccard Coefficient of similarity). In counting disagreements, we included every mismatch in every cell of the coding matrix, even though this meant that a single coding of a single utterance by two coders could result in as many as two disagreements in the count, but could lead to one agreement at most. For this reason, we consider our reliability measure to be somewhat conservative.

[5]An element was considered to be a stop if either one of the visitors in a dyad, or both, stopped there.

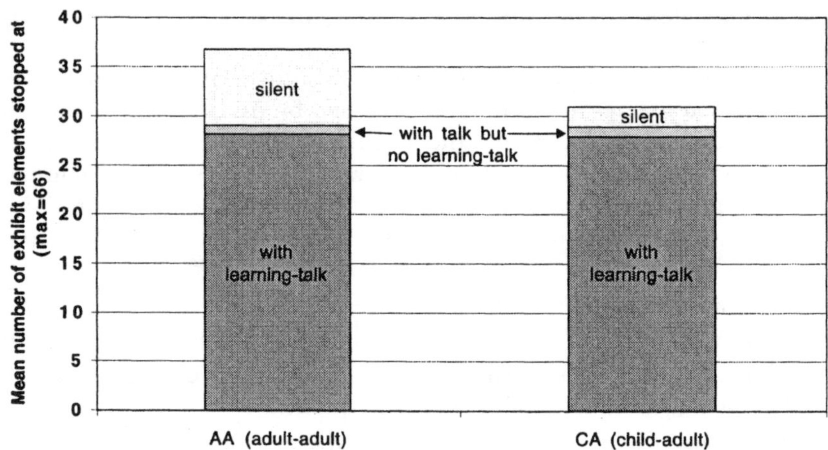

FIG. 8.2. Mean number of exhibit stops by AA and CA dyads.

The AA dyads spent slightly longer than CA dyads (27.1 minutes vs. 23.8 minutes), though this difference is not statistically significant. The AA dyads also saw significantly more elements (37 vs. 31; $t_{27} = 2.52$, $p = 0.02$), as shown by the total column heights in Fig. 8.2.

Figure 8.3 compares the frequency of stopping across the four most common types of exhibit elements in the exhibition. The most attractive exhibit type was the Live Animals; on average, dyads stopped at 74% of the 23 live animals in the exhibition. This was followed by Hands-on and Artifacts (not significantly different from each other). Far less attractive were the Readable elements; dyads stopped at only 14% of these 18 elements which involved reading or looking, but no live or hands-on component.[6]

Overall Frequency of Learning-Talk

On average, dyads engaged in learning-talk at 83% of the exhibit elements at which either person stopped (28 out of the 34). This figure is impres-

[6]The figure does not show stopping frequencies for any of the exhibit types which were only represented by two or three physical examples. These types included Videos (multiple clips of frogs eating or moving), Cases of Organic Material (such as frog foods and dissected or deformed frogs), and Labs (rooms containing many live animals resting or in breeding chambers). These have been omitted from the analysis of exhibit types because each type presents such a small number of opportunities for visitors to stop at them, that we consider the stopping frequencies to be unreliable. However, we can get an idea of their relative attractiveness from their ranking as individual elements. The Videos were intermediate in attractiveness, ranking 24, 33, and 46 out of 66 elements. The Cases of Organic Material were fairly high, ranking 11, 13, and 27. The Lab windows ranked 4 and 14, which made them comparable with the most attractive type of exhibit elements, the Live Animals in smaller terrariums.

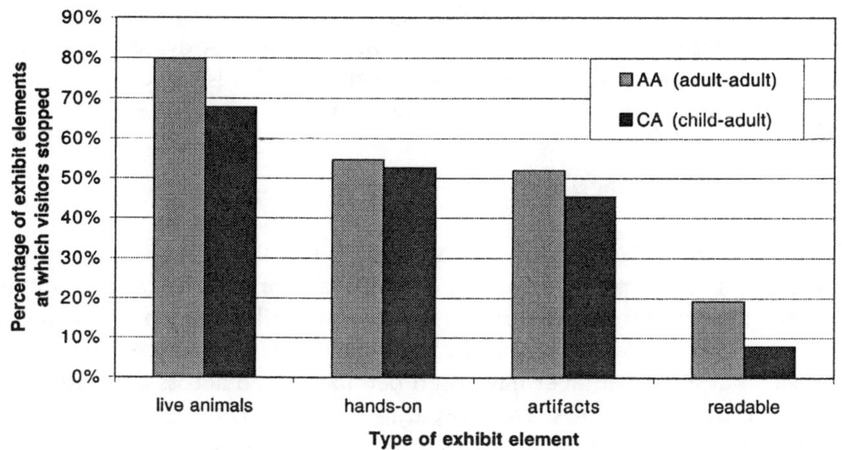

FIG. 8.3. Types of exhibit elements where visitors stopped.

sively high, considering that the visitors in a dyad were free to split up and view exhibit elements alone, if they chose. They had only been instructed to "do whatever you'd normally do," and indeed, many of them did split up for periods during their visit. The high frequencies of learning-talk for both AA and CA dyads (shown in Fig. 8.2) indicate that a broad range of visitors repeatedly chose to engage in this kind of communication with their companion, even in a noisy and stimulating environment where conversation requires some effort.

At the remaining 17% of stops, then, no learning-talk occurred. In the majority of these cases (14% of stops) there was no talk at all; the stop was a silent one. Usually, this reflected a situation where the dyad under study had temporarily split up to pursue individual interests in moving about the exhibition. More importantly, it was quite rare (occurring at the remaining 3% of stops) for a dyad to talk while at an exhibit element but say nothing that could be coded as learning-talk. A closer look at the nature of these "learning-free" conversations reveals that most were expressions of a navigational nature, either beckoning someone to come over, or noting some area of the exhibition that had been missed. Only one case by one dyad could be considered "off-task" in terms of attention to the exhibition. In this single case, a woman said to her adult companion, "I think I hear the girls," which was shortly followed by their exit from the exhibition.

Figure 8.2 compares the occurrence of learning-talk by AA and CA dyads. Learning-talk by AA and CA dyads occurred at almost exactly the same absolute number of stops (28.2 vs. 27.9). Also very similar were the number of stops where there was talk, but no learning-talk (0.9 vs. 1.0). However, AA dyads had significantly more silent stops (7.7 vs. 2.0; $t_{27} = 2.14$,

$p = 0.04$), which may account for the slightly longer times of adult dyads in the exhibition overall. It seemed, then, that AA and CA dyads engaged in learning-talk to a similar extent, but that the AA dyads took a little more time to browse some additional exhibit elements, mostly silently.

Categories of Learning-Talk

Figures 8.4 and 8.5 show the frequencies of the five major categories of learning-talk: perceptual, affective, conceptual, connecting, and strategic. For each dyad, the frequency of each category of talk has been calculated as a percentage of the total number of exhibit elements where either visitor stopped. These percentages have then been averaged across all dyads (Fig. 8.4) or across AA and CA dyads separately (Fig. 8.5).

Overall, the most common categories of talk are perceptual, affective, and conceptual. Pairwise comparisons of the frequencies in each category (summing over all dyads) show significant differences between all but the affective and conceptual categories.

Particularly interesting is the high frequency of conceptual talk. This is heartening news: Museum professionals are constantly looking for evidence that learning is occurring during regular museum visits, yet such evidence is often hard to find if learning is assessed with outcome-based tools imported from the school environment. In this study, we found that visitors engaged in some type of learning-talk at 83% of the exhibit elements they stopped at, and in specifically conceptual talk at 56%.

Also noteworthy is the lower frequency of connecting talk, which includes connections among exhibit elements, connections to previous

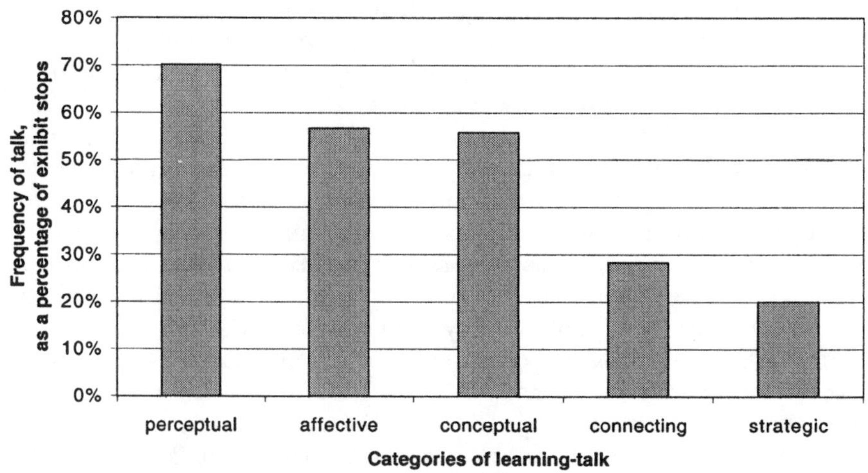

FIG. 8.4. Frequencies of different categories of learning-talk (30 dyads).

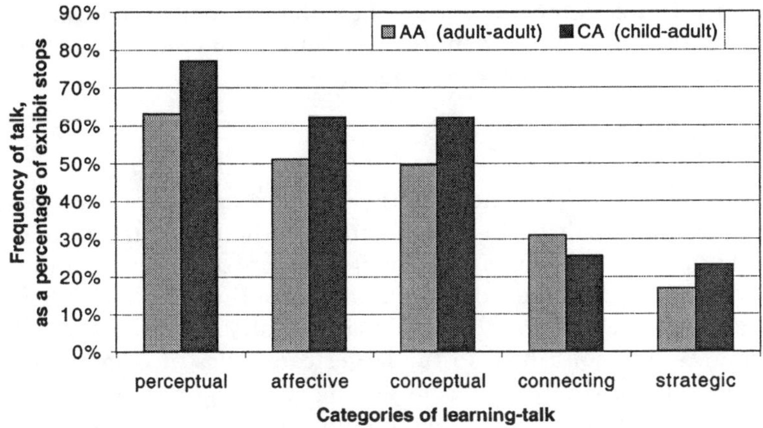

FIG. 8.5. Frequencies of categories of learning-talk for AA and CA dyads.

knowledge, and personal stories or associations. These kind of connections are often regarded as a powerful and ubiquitous means of learning in informal settings, so it is interesting that the category was much less frequent than the "Big 3" (perceptual, affective, conceptual), and was present at only 28% of the exhibit stops overall.

Finally, Fig. 8.5 shows that CA dyads engaged in learning-talk slightly more frequently than AA dyads in four of the five categories. However, this difference was spread almost uniformly across the different categories, and probably reflects the general tendency of AA dyads to view more elements alone, thus lowering their percentage of talk per exhibit stops. The exception is the category of connecting talk, the only one in which AA dyads engaged more frequently than CA dyads. Although the difference is not significant ($t_{27} = 1.17$, $p = 0.25$), the deviation from the pattern in other categories suggests a true (if slight) tendency for adults to make more connections to their prior experience and knowledge than child–adult dyads. It is interesting that this effect was limited to connecting talk, and did not apply to conceptual talk. Perhaps parents felt that the stimulating environment of the exhibition supported immediate inferencing rather than storytelling.

MORE DETAILED ANALYSES

In order to explore the learning-talk data in more depth, I conducted three types of more detailed analysis. First, I divided the five categories of learning-talk into their 16 subcategories, and analyzed their relative frequencies over the whole exhibition visit. Second, I used the main categories to compare the impact of two different types of exhibit element within the exhibition. Third, I ranked the 66 individual exhibit elements according to frequencies of learning-talk, to identify some outstanding individual examples and highlight some of their design features.

1. Subcategories of Learning-Talk

Figure 8.6 shows the frequencies of the 16 subcategories of learning-talk, averaged over all dyads. As in Figs. 8.4 and 8.5, the percentages are out of the total number of elements where visitors stopped, rather than the total number of elements in the exhibition, to remove the effects of differential attracting power. The figure shows a detailed analysis of the different kinds of utterances that contribute to the larger categories of conversation. In this graph, all pairwise comparisons among subcategories give significant differences except for those between identification and quotation, intrigue and pleasure, and simple and complex inferences.

The most common subcategories of learning talk were: identification (44%), quotation (43%), complex inferencing (37%), intrigue (37%), pleasure (36%), simple inferencing (36%), and feature (35%). By contrast, predictions (3%) and inter-exhibit connections (5%) were the least common, and much rarer than we would have expected for a thematic exhibition in an inquiry-based learning institution. These findings are discussed further in the Discussion section later in the chapter.

Voiced Intentions. One of our research questions was: Is there any evidence that the exhibition might affect visitors' attitudes or behaviors once they return to the world beyond the museum? Of course, this is not an easy

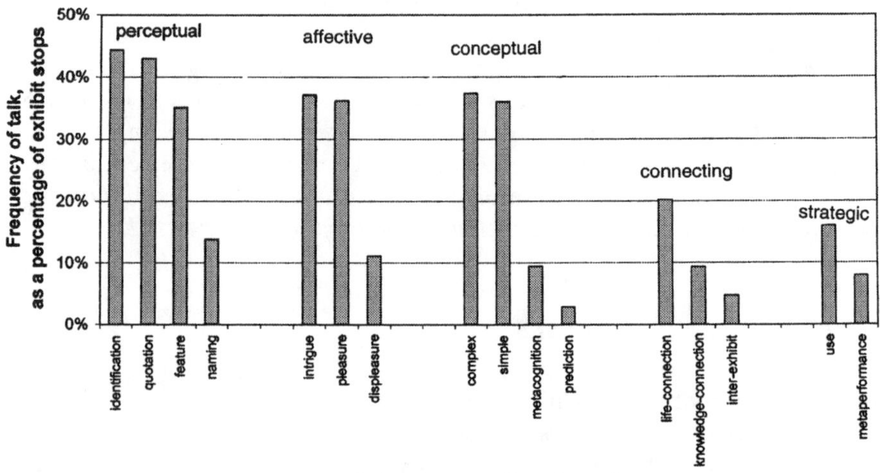

FIG. 8.6. Frequencies of different subcategories of learning-talk.

question to answer, but we were able to code conversations for visitors at least expressing their *intent* to take some action beyond the walls of the exhibition.

In all, 7 different dyads expressed an intention to carry out a total of 10 actions. Of the 10 actions visitors spoke about:

- 3 were intentions to share something from the exhibition with others in some way:

  "I'm going to tell Alice there's a Surinam Toad here."
  "We should take our drawings home."

- 3 were joking expressions of whimsical or teasing intentions that seemed unlikely to happen in reality:

  "In case we meet a frog on the way home, we'll steer clear of his tongue!"
  "I'll buy a load [of frogs] and keep them in the apartment."

- 4 were actions that seemed seriously intended, inspired by different aspects of the exhibition. They were:

  "I should go to Tompkins County when I'm in New York."
  [at an immersion exhibit element where visitors sat on a 'porch in Tompkins County' and listened to frog sounds]

  "Don't eat frog legs any more."
  [at a label about the different animals that eat frogs]

  "You need to keep your frogs at home near water, to keep them from dehydrating."
  [at an element showing the thinness of frog skin and the threat of dehydration]

  "We should get that."
  [to a fellow scientist, after watching a time-lapse sequence of frog embryos]

Although such instances were very rare, it is at least encouraging that they were aligned with the curatorial goals of inspiring visitors to appreciate and protect frogs.

2. Comparison of Exhibit Types

One of the research questions driving our study of the *Frogs* exhibition was: Is there any difference between the patterns of learning-talk that happen at different types of exhibit elements? We thought *Frogs* would provide an excellent opportunity to study this, because the Exploratorium had taken the unusual step of designing an exhibition that combined elements from different museum traditions.

Our original research plan was to compare the patterns of learning-talk at as many of these exhibit types as possible. However, when we began to code and analyze the data, we became aware that our ability to do this would be severely curtailed, due to insufficient numbers of visitor stops at most of the exhibit types. Because our coding scheme allocated a score of 0 or 1 to each exhibit element, we required numerous examples of any given exhibit type in order to generate a distribution of scores by different dyads. The exhibition itself had four types of exhibit element represented by five or more examples: live animals, hands-on exhibits, cultural artifacts, and readable elements. However, two of these types (viz. cultural artifacts and readable elements) were so underused by visitors that the average number of stops at each of these was only 2.4 by each dyad. This made any comparative analysis of little use, because visitors had effectively reduced their own exposure to these types to a point where the frequencies of different types of learning-talk were unreliable.

These limitations were not entirely predictable ahead of time, as they depended in part on the specific choices visitors would make about where to stop in the exhibition. Counting frequencies in a free-choice environment is inevitably susceptible to such disappointments.

We did, however, have two exhibit types (live animals and hands-on elements) that had high enough stopping frequencies to warrant comparison of the learning-talk they elicited. On average, dyads stopped at 17.0 live animals and 5.4 hands-on exhibits.

Averaging over all dyads, visitors engaged in learning-talk at 88% of the live animal exhibits they stopped at, compared with 75% of the hands-on exhibits they stopped at. This difference is significant under a paired t test ($t_{29} = 3.99$, $p < 0.001$), and suggests that even in a hands-on museum such as the Exploratorium, exhibits do not necessarily have to have a manipulative quality in order to evoke widespread learning-talk among visitors. In this exhibition, "hands-*off*" exhibits, in which physical interaction was limited to the search and observation of live animals, elicited slightly higher rates of learning-talk among both AA and CA dyads.

Figure 8.7 shows a more detailed analysis of the differences between learning-talk at live animals and hands-on exhibit elements. All pairwise differences between the two exhibit types were significant. The graph shows that strategic talk was the only category in which visitors engaged more frequently at hands-on elements than live animals. This difference is primarily due to a difference in the subcategory of "metaperformance," in which visitors reflect on their own skill or accomplishment.[7] In every other category,

[7]Strategic talk also includes utterances about how to use an exhibit. Although it might seem almost inconceivable to have a "use" category for live animals, the coding scheme for strategic talk included any reference to *how* to look at something, where to stand, how to locate it, etc. There were no significant differences between exhibit types on the "use" subcategory.

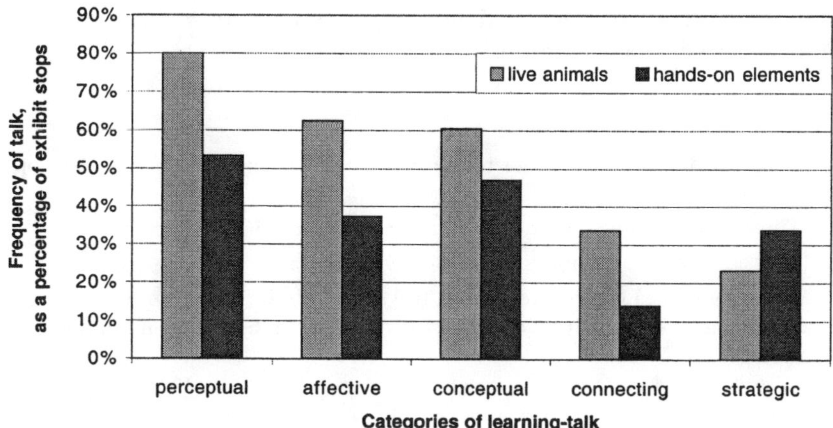

FIG. 8.7. Frequencies of categories of learning-talk at two exhibit types.

live animals evoked more frequent learning-talk than hands-on exhibit elements. In the perceptual category, live animals evoked significantly more talk in the following subcategories: identification, naming, and noting features. In the affective category, live animals evoked significantly more positive affect, and more surprise/intrigue. In the conceptual category, they evoked more simple inferences, complex inferences, and metacognition. And in the connecting category, live animals evoked more life connection and knowledge connection. These findings show that, at least in this exhibition, live animals not only stimulated more frequent learning-talk overall than hands-on elements, but that the differences were much more widespread than purely perceptual modes of learning.

3. Outstanding Individual Exhibit Elements

In addition to providing overall patterns in the conversation data, the coding scheme can be used to identify individual exhibit elements which were outstanding in terms of their tendency to evoke certain subcategories of learning-talk. We highlight some of them here to give texture to the data, and also to highlight key design characteristics that we think may have led to the success of each one as elicitors of learning-talk. In each case, we have selected the exhibit element (out of 66) that gave the highest frequency of talk by all the dyads who stopped there.

Quotation. The most-quoted label was that of "Frog's Eggs," an element designed to show the embryonic development of fertilized frogs' eggs up to the time of hatching. This exhibit element displayed a series of jars containing real frog embryos at different stages of development, as well as a timelapse video that condensed two days of development into a continuous sequence lasting one minute.

Examples:

"Look through the magnifier to see frog's eggs in several stages of development."

"Three days, and at the end it's five days . . . these are frog eggs."

"That's 21 hours, 27 hours . . . 2 days, 5 days . . ."

"Frog's eggs . . . Look at the African frogs mate in the fall. Hundreds of eggs are laid and then it only take them 3 or 4 days to hatch . . . they use time-lapse photography."

"In 3 months."

We hypothesize that this element was particularly likely to elicit quotations because it contained luminous displays of compelling organic material without narration, so that visitors who were initially drawn to the visual stimuli wanted a reference or explanation of what they were seeing. Also, the series of jars invited comparison by visitors, but the dimensions of comparison were fairly technical in nature (e.g., "21 hours: developing backbone visible"), thus leading to a tendency to quote verbatim from the label. Finally, the fact that this was one of the earliest elements in the exhibition may have made visitors more likely to read the label aloud; museum researchers (e.g., Falk, Koran, Dierking, & Dreblow, 1985; Gilman, 1916) have noted the robust phenomenon of "museum fatigue," in which visitors view exhibits more cursorily after a period of time, and this effect may apply to an exhibition as well as a whole visit.

Complex Inference. The element evoking most frequent complex inferencing was "Frogs and Toads." This was a large open tank containing a miniature ecosystem, including a small stream, stony beach, and dense vegetation. It also contained 17 marine toads that, being nocturnal, were notoriously difficult to locate during the day. Typically, visitors searched for the toads for some time, and then generated hypotheses for why the toads might not be visible. In our coding scheme, all hypotheses were regarded as complex inferences.

Examples:

V1: Would they bury themselves?

V2: Perhaps, yeah, or they may be really camouflaged too.

"Maybe it's just showing where they like to live."

"Something must be under here because, see, the water is moving."

This element was also very early in the exhibition (usually the first live exhibit visitors encountered), and this may be partly responsible for its success in eliciting inferences. However, it is striking that the most frequent complex inferencing was at an exhibit where the phenomenon described in the label was often impossible to see; it seems that the lack of obvious frogs served both to slow visitors down, and to generate a mystery or challenge worthy of discussion. In this sense, the element facilitated learning in an unexpected but fruitful manner.

Prediction. A silent, 90-second video called "Mealtime" showed a series of clips of frogs catching and eating a variety of foods, including insects, maggots, and even a live mouse. Most visitors who stopped at the video stayed for a complete cycle, and it was not unusual for them to stay until a favorite clip came around again.

Examples:

"Oh, they're going to start it again."

"See, they're gonna catch their food."

"Beetle, bet you it spits it out."

The repeating nature of the video seemed to encourage visitors to make predictions, especially when only one member of the dyad had seen the footage the first time. Also, the label invited them to "see what happens when a frog accidentally eats something nasty," implicitly inviting them to make a prediction.

Metacognition. The Mealtime video was also the element most likely to evoke a metacognitive comment from visitors.

Examples:

"Well, I would be surprised that it ate a whole mouse."

"I never would have believed."

"I didn't realize they got them with their tongue. Did you?"

I believe the success of this element was due to its surprising, articulable content message, and its strong graphic presentation. Visitors were not aware of the size or variety of foods that frogs eat, and the nature of the video footage (colorful, high-speed and suspenseful) made this point so powerfully that visitors were eager to share their surprise with each other.

Life Connection. The most frequent personal connections were elicited by a graphic reproduction of a leaf from the children's book, *Frog and Toad are Friends.*

Examples:

"Oh, this is, oh, look, it's Frog and Toad. I remember that one. That was your favorite book when you were little."

V1: 'Cos here's the story, Mom. I used to have these books a lot.

V2: Oh you're right. Oh, you're exactly right. That's Toad and Frog.

The success of this particular element reflects the use of evaluation studies to inform the choice of popular book. By choosing a well-known children's book, the development team hoped for exactly this response, that visitors would be reminded of their own personal connection to frogs and froggy stories.

Knowledge Connection. The element most likely to generate connections to previous knowledge was a bulletin board of current events called "Frogs and Toads in the News." Most of the articles on the board concerned the scientific debate about whether declining frog populations were caused by human activity such as the use of carcinogenic chemicals. Although few visitors stopped there, most were highly informed about frogs, so this element had the highest ratio of knowledge-connection talk per stop.

Examples:

V1: I thought they found that they don't believe there's any type of carcinogen or anything that, because it's . . .

V2: Well, it depends on where it is though.

V1: it occurs so naturally and so frequently.

V2: Oh, I see what you're saying. That I don't know.

V3: So it splits the developmental field at a time when it can regenerate PTA.

V4: I guess at some point it prevents two groups of cells from talking to each other while one is, they are supposed to form one thing, they form three things. Most split . . .

V3: Because they form two out of the same, but, that . . .

V4: Yes. There's some little undergrad who did it at Stanford.

It is interesting that a bulletin board displaying current science articles should elicit more of visitors' own declarative knowledge (n = 4) than quotes from the articles (n = 0).

Inter-exhibit Connection. The only element that evoked more than three inter-exhibit connections was the live "Poison-Arrow Frog." In all, the *Frogs* exhibition contained three terrariums of live poison-arrow frogs, which were not all the same species, and had a variety of colorations. Nine visitor dyads made explicit or implicit reference to the fact that they had already seen a poison-arrow frog in a previous terrarium.

Examples:

V1: Oh Mum, look at this frog.

V2: Oh, poison-arrow. These are my favorite ones.

"Those are more poison-arrow frogs."

"That's a poison-arrow too."

Clearly, visitors made this kind of connection because different frogs had the same common name on their label. While being a tribute to careful label reading by visitors, this type of inter-exhibit connection was probably more superficial than the development team would hope for.

Use. The sound exhibit "Croak like a Frog" generated the highest frequency of utterances about how to use an exhibit. In this exhibit, visitors could listen to a variety of prerecorded frog calls, and record their own attempts to imitate these calls.

Examples:

"You gotta record your own, honey. Now, you push the record button."

"You have to do it before the red line disappears, or it doesn't record."

I believe this exhibit elicited most use-talk because it had a combination of a clear, appealing goal, and a fairly complex interface. The title, "Croak like a Frog," along with the installed microphone, probably served to give visitors easy access to the main point of the activity, and engaged them enough to help each other through the subtleties of the push-button interface.

Metaperformance. "Croak like a Frog" also generated the highest frequency of reflection on skills or performance.

Examples:

V1: What do you think, Jill, close or not close?

V2: Not close.

"That's not too bad, try this one."

"See, look at the difference . . . It's different. Okay! This was right, except I made it too long."

As well as playing the sound of a frog or human imitator, this exhibit included a graphical display of the volume, frequency, and timing of the sound on a computer screen. For this reason, it afforded (and explicitly encouraged) both visual and aural comparison of the authentic frog song with one's own attempt. In other words, metaperformance was a central design goal of this element, and visitors' conversations verified its success in this regard.

Pleasure. The exhibit that generated the most frequent expressions of pleasure was "African Clawed Frog," a spectacular large tank of swimming *Xenopus laevis.* Visitors' laughter accounted for many of the coded examples.

Examples:

"They're funny."

"That's hilarious. I want to hug you . . ."

"Cool!"

"I like this one. Yeah, that is so cute."

I would speculate that the main reason for visitors' widespread pleasure with this element was due to its unusually lively inhabitants. For most of the exhibition, terrariums contained frogs at rest, but this huge tank contained frogs that were alternately perfectly still and actively swimming. In addition, the swimming frogs displayed a particular behavior that many visitors noticed and found endearing: they stretched one arm out in front of them as they swam, as if to warn them of unexpected obstacles.

Displeasure. The exhibit that elicited the most frequent expressions of displeasure was a plastinated dead frog displayed to show the internal organs. It was labeled "What's Inside a Frog?"

Examples:

"Eeww! Oh my gosh, okay. Eeww."

"Yuck, where's his brain?"

"Don't care to see the insides."

"Poor frog. Eew."

Perhaps this negative affect was the most predictable of responses, because the exhibit element combined graphic organic material (brightly colored organs) with the context from which it came (the surrounding frog, roughly intact). Thus we recorded visitors who found the exhibit either gory or sad, or both. The development team had previously argued about whether to include dissected frogs in the exhibition, given its focus on respect for these beautiful living animals. The final decision was made to include a plastinated frog for the scientific value, and to make the point that frogs and humans have so much in common.

Overall Diversity. By counting the number of codes assigned to individual exhibit elements, it was possible to determine which element elicited the largest number of different subcategories of learning talk, on average. The video element called Mealtime evoked an average of 6.1 different subcategories of learning-talk. This seems a particularly impressive total, given that the exhibit is neither live nor hands-on, nor does it even have an audio component. This finding shows that it is possible to use video to elicit a broad range of learning conversations among visitors.

Although a detailed analysis of rankings is beyond the scope of this chapter, we note that, after the Mealtime video, the following 14 top-ranking elements in terms of diversity all included live animals (either in individual terrariums or in the two laboratory windows). The hands-on elements were intermediate in the diversity of learning-talk they elicited, and the readable elements (including the exhibition introduction, maps, bulletin boards, and highlights of books and stories about frogs from a variety of cultures) ranked extremely low. All 18 readable elements fell within the lowest 25 rankings out of the 66 elements in the exhibition, in terms of diversity of learning-talk by those visitors who chose to stop there.

DISCUSSION

Similarities to Findings From Previous Studies

Frequency of Learning-Talk. Overall, learning-talk in *Frogs* was extremely frequent, occurring at 83% of the elements where either member of a dyad stopped, and fully 97% of the elements where some kind of talk occurred. Comparable figures were obtained by Hilke (1989), who reported that 86% of all events undertaken by families concerned the exhibits, and that 64% of all behaviors (including nonverbal behaviors) were exhibit-related behaviors that would classify as learning-related in the current study. Our data supports Hilke's general conclusion that families are "pursuing a clear agenda to learn while in the museum." Even more strikingly, we found an extremely low percentage (3%) of exhibit stops where visitors discussed something that did not contribute to exhibition-related learning. Although it must be acknowledged that the effect of cueing visitors may have had an effect here, I believe it unlikely that a dyad could stay "on-task" to this degree for nearly half an hour unless it was close to their natural behavior. Our data support McManus's (1989a) conclusion that "Conversations were about the topic established by label-writers. Instances where visitors shifted from the exhibit topic to introduce an unrelated topic were exceedingly rare in the transcripts" (p. 181).

Frequency of Quotations From Labels. We found that label-reading was common: On average, visitors quoted from labels (or closely paraphrased them) at 43% of their exhibit stops. Although many of these cases were simply a few words, it shows that visitors were attending to labels to a high degree. McManus (1989a), whose study dispelled the common notion that "visitors don't read labels," found an even higher rate among four exhibit elements at the British Museum (Natural History): an average of 71%. Diamond (1980), on the other hand, reported an average closer to 10% of exhibit elements stopped at, but she used a narrower definition of "read aloud" that excluded paraphrasing, so we would expect her frequencies to be considerably lower than those in our study.

Comparability With Exhibitions From Art and History Museums. Although developed independently, our coding scheme turned out to be surprisingly compatible with Silverman's (1990) earlier analysis of visitors' conversations in an art and a history museum. Silverman used very similar methods to those we used to gather conversational data from dyads of visitors, and proposed five broad categories of interpretive speech acts: establishment, absolute object description, evaluation, relating special knowledge, and relating personal experience. Her categories correspond closely to our categories of: perceptual talk (excluding the "feature" subcategory), feature talk, affective talk, knowledge connection, and life connection.

Disparities and Unexpected Findings

High Frequency of Conceptual Talk. In our greatest divergence from Silverman's coding scheme, we identified Conceptual Talk as a major category of learning-talk, and one of the three most common in visitors' conversations. This category included the subcategories of prediction, metacognition, simple, and complex conceptual talk. The most common subcategory was "complex inferencing" involving hypotheses, generalizations, or relational thinking. This occurred at 37% of exhibit elements where either visitor stopped, and shows that even inferential reasoning, though often brief and informal, is not uncommon in visitors' conversations.

Silverman's coding scheme does include two categories where conceptual talk could be counted.[8] However, in both cases the inferences and hypotheses are treated as minority members of a larger category with a differ-

[8]The categories are: a) "interpretation," a subset of "evaluation," where visitors share a message, meaning or conclusion derived from an object; and b) "absolute object description" which includes not only perceptual aspects of an object, but elaborations and deductions about their function and subject matter.

ent focus. This divergence in coding schemes may reflect subtle differences in the researchers' epistemologies and areas of interest. Alternatively, it may reflect a true difference in visitors' conversations in the different types of museums represented. Perhaps visitors to a hands-on science museum are more likely to engage in verbal acts of reasoning, prediction, and self-reflection than visitors to either an art or history museum, by virtue of the different missions and natures of these institutions.

Perhaps Hilke (1989) comes closest to including a conceptual category, which she names "pure-info" and which contains "action-events that involve direct attempts at acquiring or exchanging information" (p. 110). However, Hilke's subcategories for this code include nonverbal behaviors such as "gaze at" and "manipulate," which, while evidence for engagement with the exhibit, would fall outside our narrower definition of verbal evidence for learning.

I would argue that learning-talk of a conceptual nature should be highlighted in museum research, especially because it is the category that comes closest to traditional definitions of learning from school and laboratory settings. While museums may have unusual strengths in facilitating learning of the affective or sensory kinds, it is also important to recognize that visitors engage frequently in cognitive learning-talk during their exhibition visits.

Strategic Talk. We also identified the category of Strategic Talk, incorporating talk about how to use an exhibit element, and reflections on one's degree of success in using it.

Several other researchers have coded this kind of talk somewhere in their scheme, but have coded it together with all kinds of comments about an exhibit (e.g., Borun et al., 1998) or with metacognitive statements such as "I understand it" (e.g., Diamond, 1980). Hilke (1989) included the category of "Say what to do," which may have coded talk about how to use an exhibit, or may also have included beckonings and turn-taking kinds of statements, which we did not code as part of "use-talk." Interestingly, Silverman (1990) did not mention any strategic category or subcategory. Perhaps this reflects a real difference between the kinds of learning that happen in a hands-on versus more observational museum exhibition; part of what is learned in a hands-on exhibition is how to interact with the objects it contains, with skill and self-awareness.

I believe that strategic knowledge, about how to interact with exhibition objects, is a category of learning-talk worth recognizing. In attempting to extend its applicability beyond manipulable exhibit elements, we included in this category any utterances related to *how* to see, hear, or otherwise interact with, any exhibit element, even the live frogs in terrariums that needed skill to locate. For this reason, I propose it as a generalizable category of learning-talk.

Rarity of Connections Among Exhibits. Visitors made explicit connections to other exhibit elements at only 5% of the elements (1.6 elements on average). This result is surprising and quite provocative, given the large amount of focused effort that goes into the design and coordination of objects, labels, graphic treatments, and visitor orientation within a typical museum exhibition.

It is interesting that Diamond (1980) did not have "inter-exhibit connections" in her category system, even though she did have "reminisce about exhibit," in which a visitor makes a comment about a previous interaction with the same exhibit. Perhaps it is rarer for visitors to make connections among exhibits than it is for them to make connections among different interactions with the same exhibit.

Hilke (1988) interpreted her own data in a way that may shed light on ours: "The family's primary agenda is not to look for relationships within the content of the show. Rather, family visitors will seek relationships between their own knowledge/experience and the content/structure of the show. The dominant perspective from which the exhibition is interpreted is more likely to be the visitor's own background experience, own knowledge, and own interests than it is likely to be some common thread or theme of the show" (p. 124). Taylor (1986) reached similar conclusions.

It may be argued that visitors did not explicitly state all of the connections they were making among elements, but this argument could be applied to other types of learning-talk as well, and would not explain why inter-exhibit connections were the second-rarest of the coded subcategories. It is true that this subcategory was coded conservatively, meaning that the coder had to feel confident that the visitor was making a connection to an exhibit element rather than to more general previous knowledge. It may even be the case that the design of the *Frogs* exhibition was flawed, making it unusually difficult for visitors to recognize links among its elements. Serrell (1996) made a strong case for having exhibition design be driven by a single "big idea" that should not be vague or trivial. She wrote, "The big idea provides an unambiguous focus for the exhibit team throughout the exhibit development process by clearly stating in one non-compound sentence the scope and purpose of an exhibition" (p. 2). From this standpoint, *Frogs* could perhaps be criticized as having had multiple goals that were difficult to combine into a single coherent idea; the exhibition was much more of a potpourri of interesting aspects of frogs and their relationship to people.

However, even with all these caveats, the frequency of this type of talk is so low compared with other types that I believe it warrants further attention in the research community.

Rarity of Predictions. Visitors made explicit predictions at only 3% of the exhibit elements (an average of 1.0 element). This was the rarest of the subcategories coded, and seems unexpectedly low, especially in a museum that emphasizes inquiry processes and engagement through curiosity and surprise (e.g., DeLacôte, 1998; Oppenheimer, 1986; Semper, 1990).

It may be that predictions were especially low in the *Frogs* exhibition because the live frogs were relatively static, and did not support direct intervention (except tapping on the glass, which was discouraged in signage and by museum staff).

Alternatively, it may be an unavoidable artifact of our methods: our microphones can record speech but not thought. Perhaps museum visitors are predicting at a more kinesthetic or experiential level, bringing unconscious expectations of the way the world works to their evolving interaction with an exhibit. In the fast-paced, social, stimulating environment of a hands-on museum, predictions may simply take too much time or be too effortful to fully articulate. Perhaps visitors' expressions of surprise and intrigue ("Wow!") should serve as better verbal indicators that an unspoken prediction has been disconfirmed. More light could be shed on this issue if we had comparable data from more typical hands-on exhibits.

Comparison of Types of Exhibit Element: Live Versus Hands-On. Our study showed that live animal exhibit elements elicited significantly more frequent and also more diverse learning-talk than hands-on elements. This is another surprising and provocative result, given that the educational lore of museums, backed by an array of studies, gives such high value to interactive experiences. How is it that small, generally inactive animals confined to terrariums in which they could not be touched or communicated with, could elicit more learning-talk in four out of five categories than custom-designed, hands-on exhibits?

I believe the data constitute a challenge to simplistic notions of interactive learning. Several museum researchers have argued against too narrow an interpretation of concepts such as "interactive" or "constructivist." Hein (1998), while listing some of the research on the value of adding manipulative components to museum exhibits, made the strong point that learning is increased by "*meaningful* physical activity." Osborne (1998) pointed out that "experience, of itself, while highly enjoyable, is overwhelmingly a missed learning opportunity without some attempt to encourage the visitor to focus, recapitulate, and review" (p. 9). As McLean (1993) put it, "rows of buttons and levers may exercise some visitors' fingers and arms, but not necessarily their minds" (p. 16).

With the terrariums of living frogs, the developers seem to have achieved the opposite situation: exhibit elements that are "minds-on" but "hands-off." Although almost entirely noninteractive, the living frogs attracted more visitors and inspired more learning-talk than their interactive neighbors. Of course, even without manipulation, the live animal displays still offered visitors a powerful direct experience on which to reflect, an experience quite different from reading a book. The terrariums were designed to look like jewels, full of rich color and texture from the frogs, foliage, pebbles, sand, and curving tree branches. The visual beauty and complexity of these tiny worlds invited visitors to point things out to each other, and to share their surprise and delight on finding a brilliant Golden Frog or craggy Surinam Toad. The hidden quality of many of the small frogs invited visitors to slow down, look carefully, and hypothesize about what they were seeing or not seeing. The labels, after some formative evaluation, answered some of the questions that often arose in visitors' minds. This was fertile ground for learning-talk.

Several of the hands-on elements had an audio rather than a visual focus. For example, visitors could listen to songs about frogs, hear frog calls, or try their hands at imitating frogs. Perhaps the audio experience tended to inhibit visitors' conversations at these elements (audio was noticeably absent from the highly successful Mealtime video). Visitors wearing headphones, even with the same sound piped to each, would have had to put more effort into sharing any kind of response, thought, or feeling. Also common in the exhibition were hands-on elements that involved interacting with symbolic objects that represented frogs in some way. For example: A zoetrope showed the detailed action of frog locomotion; a set of maps could be lifted to show the changing populations of frogs with time; or a set of door-panels could be opened to reveal the inner anatomy of a frog as compared with a human. Perhaps these symbolic frogs were less compelling, less inspirational, and less evocative of associations, than the "real thing."

Frogs was just one exhibition, and the findings may not generalize even to other Exploratorium exhibitions. Nevertheless, this case does show that designing for learning conversations does not depend on a simple variable such as whether or not exhibit elements are hands-on. I hope museum researchers will continue to study the subtleties of effective exhibit design in the exhibition context.

ANALYZING VISITORS' CONVERSATIONS AS A METHOD FOR VISITOR STUDIES

To end this chapter, I offer some reflections on the advantages and drawbacks of the methods used to studying visitors' learning through the lens of their real-time conversations while in an exhibition.

Hearing or reading visitors' complete conversations is a vivid experience that brings one right into the arena where real museum learning occurs. The transcripts are detailed, dense, and at times brutally honest, providing readers (be they developers, evaluators, or researchers) with a gritty sense of what engages and what doesn't. Personally, I found it a striking reminder of the power of choice in informal environments: Visitors are choosing where to spend every second of their time, and exhibits that do not engage or sustain them are quickly left behind, however "potentially educational" they may be.

Following a single group through an entire exhibition provides continuity; over that length of time, one begins to get a sense of the visitors' particular personalities and preferences, as well as their ways of interacting with each other. Falk and Dierking (1992) called this the "personal context" and "social context" in which museum visits occur, and which interact with the "physical context" to create the visitor experience. It is much easier to understand visitors' personal or social contexts when studying a half-hour of their conversation than the few minutes typical of a single-element interaction.

For the educational researcher, visitors' conversations provide raw material for multiple kinds of studies: comparisons between types of exhibits or exhibitions to explore the effects of different learning environments; studies of sequential patterns in the talk; typing or characterization of visitors based on their talk; and search for possible correlations among conversational talk, visitors' answers to structured interview questions, time spent, and physical interactivity.

In choosing an operational definition of learning-talk, a researcher can choose one of two main directions. One can either define learning with respect to visitors' previous knowledge, or with respect to the contents of the exhibition. The former is difficult because of the practical and theoretical challenges of pre- and posttesting visitors on a vast range of possible ideas and associations which they may bring to bear on their visit. The latter is difficult because it requires that coders be intimately familiar with every word and image in an exhibition, in order to determine the nature of the learning-talk which has just occurred. Ironically, this becomes more difficult as exhibit elements become more effective, because when visitors' language and label language mesh seamlessly, it is hard to tell when visitors are quoting.

For the museum evaluator, visitors' conversations provide plenty of detailed summative information on visitors' responses to individual exhibit elements. The original recordings or transcripts provide a wealth of information for anyone on the exhibition team willing to spend the time to get a close "feel" for the different visitors' experiences. With the addition of a systematic analysis into categories, conversation studies can provide comparisons among the impacts of different types of elements. These studies can also identify the most successful elements in an exhibition, based on criteria such as pleasure, intrigue, and life connection, which are often explicit goals of exhibit development teams. Seeing the "winners" in each category is useful both as a reality check for discussions of exhibit design features (even in the absence of a controlled design experiment), and as data for developers who develop intuitions about visitor behavior mostly through induction over many examples and many years of experience. Even more important, these studies bring the focus of the design debates to the real-time visitor experience, and out of the domain of theory, rhetoric, or even simple observation. In doing so, they challenge developers' assumptions about what visitors will find meaningful in their exhibitions.

One disadvantage of this kind of study is that visitors are behaving inauthentically, at least to some degree, because they are aware of the microphones. We have made an argument for regarding visitors' behavior in this situation as "best case," but if that is so, we need to remember it when interpreting the findings, and resist the temptation to over-congratulate ourselves on our success, particularly in the absence of comparative data from other exhibitions.

The main disadvantage of this kind of study is that it is slow and expensive. In spite of my original intention to find a method that could translate into a "quick and easy" form for summative evaluation, I have come to believe that conversations are too complex to allow for speedy yet meaningful analysis. Even at best, our coders took four hours to code each hour of transcript: two to parse it into episodes based on exhibit element (an easy task), and another two to code into the 16 subcategories of learning-talk (much more difficult). This figure excludes time needed for transcription and data gathering, both of which are also slow. Slowest of all was the development of a coherent coding scheme reliable enough to be of use.

Stubbs (1983) was right to warn of the difficulties of any kind of discourse analysis in a complex setting. We found visitors' language to be subtle, ambiguous, and incomplete. Humor, which was a common feature of visitors' conversations, was particularly difficult to code.[9] The status of questions, interactions with strangers, and nested kinds of learning-talk, created additional challenges to the coding scheme. Even counting was difficult: our choice of a binary scheme by which to count learning-talk at each exhibit element, while it simplified coding, made reliability difficult to quantify and limited the kinds of quantitative comparisons we could make.

How could one simplify this situation and make it more feasible as an evaluation strategy? Reducing sample size is not an option, as 30 dyads were already fewer than most evaluators would consider for a summative evaluation. One could simplify the coding scheme to, say, the main five categories of learning-talk, but the findings would suffer greatly in terms of resolution, and coding time would not be reduced by very much over all, because even these require fine discrimination to use reliably. One could also omit the

---

[9]For example, one visitor startled a group of tadpoles when he approached, and joked "Swim for your lives!" Another visitor watched a giant water snail and commented, "Serious escargot." Such comments, while understandable and entertaining, were very difficult to code in our scheme.

transcription step, and code directly from the audio recordings, but our experiments with this suggested that it would result in a critical loss of reliability, with the added disadvantage of losing the opportunity to show a written record with textured examples to the development team.

I would argue that, to really benefit from studies of visitor conversation, the field of visitor studies would need to establish a standardized coding scheme, somewhat analogous to the convergence of tracking and timing methods following the comparative analysis of exhibitions by Serrell (1998). This would save the large amount of time required to develop a coding scheme for each exhibition. It would also allow for a much clearer comparison of exhibition data across sites, designs, and times than is currently possible, allowing both researchers and evaluators to learn much more from our initial investments of time and effort. I am hopeful that this may emerge from the Museum Learning Collaborative, which has been exploring a variety of methods and coding schemes to adopt for a larger multisite study. Even with such standardization, however, there would be much work to do to train individual coders to use the scheme reliably.

In short, this study leads me to the view that analyzing real-time visitor conversations in exhibitions is a fertile but costly complement to more traditional methods from visitor studies, such as tracking and interviewing. Its strength is in bringing the researcher into the heart of the learning "action" of the museum visit, and emphasizing learning as process rather than merely outcome. Visitors' raw transcripts are rich and revealing, but transcription is difficult and readers tend to drown in detail or be overinfluenced by anecdotes. On the other hand, creating summaries of learning-talk, averaged over many visitors, requires careful coding and counting, with no obvious short-cuts.

ACKNOWLEDGMENTS

This research was conducted as part of the Museum Learning Collaborative and was funded by the Institute of Museum Services, the National Endowment for the Arts, the National Endowment for the Humanities and the National Science Foundation.

I would like to express my thanks to Marni Goldman, Joshua Gutwill-Wise, and Isabel Halm for valuable assistance with many aspects of the data-gathering and coding, and to an enthusiastic team of volunteer transcribers: Helen Allen, Karen Dodson, Ruth Erznoznik, Christine Keppler, Ralph Kerwin, Kanani Lee, and Rebecca Lee. My appreciation also goes to Joshua Gutwill-Wise, George Hein, Kathleen McLean, Beverly Serrell, and Raycyn Wright for their thoughtful comments on earlier drafts of this chapter.

REFERENCES

Bitgood, S., Serrell, B., & Thompson, D. (1994). The impact of informal education on visitors to museums. In V. Crane, H. Nicholson, M. Chen, & S. Bitgood (Eds.), *Informal science learning* (pp. 61–106). Washington, DC: Research Communications Ltd.

Bloom, B. S. (Ed.). (1956). *Taxonomy of educational objectives: The classification of educational goals, Handbook 1, The cognitive domain, Handbook 2, The affective domain.* New York: David McKay.

Borun, M., Dritsas, J., Johnson, J. I., Peter, N. E., Wagner, K. F., Fadigan, K., Jangaard, R., Stroup, E., & Wenger, A. (1998). *Family learning in museums: The PISEC perspective.* Philadelphia: Philadelphia/Camden Informal Science Education Collaboration.

Contini, H. (1999). [A tracking study of the Exploratorium's "Frogs" Exhibition]. Unpublished raw data.

Crane, V. (1994). Understanding the dynamics of informal learning. In V. Crane, H. Nicholson, M. Chen, & S. Bitgood (Eds.), *Informal science learning* (pp. 107–191). Washington, DC: Research Communications Ltd.

Crowley, K., & Callanan, M. (1998). Describing and supporting collaborative scientific thinking in parent-child interactions. *Journal of Museum Education, 23*(1), 12–17.

Crowley, K., Galco, J., Jacobs, M., & Russo, S. R. (2000). *Explanatoids, fossils, and family conversations.* Paper presented as part of a paper set, Museum Learning Collaborative: Studies of Learning from Museums, at the annual meeting of the American Educational Research Association, New Orleans.

Delacôte, G. (1998, June). Putting science in the hands of the public. *Science, 280,* 2054–2055.

Diamond, J. (1980). *The ethology of teaching: A perspective from the observations of families in science centers.* Unpublished doctoral dissertation, University of California, Berkeley.

Falk, J. H., Koran, J. J., Dierking, L. D., & Dreblow, L. (1985). Predicting visitor behavior. *Curator, 28,* 249–257.

Falk, J. H., & Dierking, L. D. (1992). *The museum experience.* Washington, DC: Whalesback.

Falk, J. H., & Dierking, L. D. (2000). *Learning from museums: Visitor experiences and the making of meaning.* Walnut Creek, CA: AltaMira Press.

Garvey, C. (1984). *Children's talk.* Cambridge, MA: Harvard University Press.

Gilman, B. I. (1916). Museum fatigue. *The Scientific Monthly, 12,* 62–74.

Guberman, S. R., Emo, K., Simmons, S., Taylor, J., & Sullivan, G. (1999). *Parent-child conversations in a natural history museum.* Paper presented at the annual meeting of the American Educational Research Association, Montreal.

Guberman, S. R., & Van Dusen, A. (2001). *Children's investigations in a science discovery center.* Paper presented at the annual meeting of the American Educational Research Association, Seattle.

Hein, G. E. (1998). *Learning in the museum.* London: Routledge.

Hensel, K. A. (1987). *Families in museums: Interactions and conversations at displays.* Unpublished doctoral dissertation, Columbia University Teachers College.

Hilke, D. D. (1988). Strategies for family learning in museums. In S. Bitgood, J. T. Roper Jr., & A. Benefield (Eds.), *Visitor studies: Theory, research, and practice* (pp. 120–125). Jacksonville: Center for Social Design.

Hilke, D. D. (1989). The family as a learning system: An observational study. *Marriage and Family Review, 13,* 13–34.

Jeffery-Clay, K. R. (1998). Constructivism in museums: How museums create meaningful learning environments. *Journal of Museum Education, 23*(1), 3–7.

Leinhardt, G., & Crowley, K. (1998). Museum learning as conversational elaboration: A proposal to capture, code and analyze museum talk. (Museum Learning Collaborative Technical Report MLC-01). Available at: *museumlearning.com*

Lucas, A. M., McManus, P., & Thomas, G. (1986). Investigating learning from informal sources: Listening to conversations and observing play in science museums. *European Journal of Science Education 8*(4), 341–353.

Martin, L. M. W. (1996). *A Vygotskian approach to the design of a science center.* Paper presented at the annual meeting of the American Educational Research Association, New York City.

Matusov, E., & Rogoff, B. (1995). Evidence of development for people's participation in communities of learners. In J. D. Falk & L. D. Dierking (Eds.), *Public institutions for personal learning: Establishing a research agenda* (pp. 97–104). Washington, DC: American Association of Museums.

McLean, K. (1993). *Planning for people in museum exhibitions.* Washington, DC: Association of Science-Technology Centers.

McManus, P. M. (1987). It's the company you keep . . . the social determination of learning-related behaviour in a science museum. *International Journal of Museum Management and Curatorship, 6,* 263–270.

McManus, P. M. (1988). Good companions: More on the social determination of learning-related behaviour in a science museum. *International Journal of Museum Management and Curatorship, 7,* 37–44.

McManus, P. M. (1989a). Oh, yes, they do: How museum visitors read labels and interact with exhibit texts. *Curator, 32*(3), 174–189.

McManus, P. M. (1989b). What people say and how they think in a science museum. In D. Uzzell (Ed.), *Heritage interpretation* (pp. 174–189). London: Bellhaven Press.

Munley, M. E. (1992). Back to the future: A call for coordinated research programs in museums. *Patterns in practice* (pp. 196–203). Washington, DC: Museum Education Roundtable.

Oppenheimer, F. (1986). *Working prototypes: Exhibit design at the exploratorium.* Exploratorium Publications, ISSN-0-943451-081-06.

Osborne, J. F. (1998). Constructivism in museums: A response. *Journal of Museum Education, 23*(1), 8–9.

Roberts, L. (1990). The elusive qualitities of "affect". In B. Serrell (Ed.), *What research says about learning in science museums* (pp. 19–122). Washington, DC: Association of Science-Technology Centers.

Semper, R. J. (1990, November). Science museums as environments for learning. *Physics Today,* 50–56.

Serrell, B. (1998). *Paying attention: Visitors and museum exhibitions.* Washington, DC: American Association of Museums.

Serrell, B. (1990). *What research says about learning in science museums* (pp. ii, 30). Washington, DC: Association of Science-Technology Centers.

Serrell, B. (1996). *Exhibit labels: An interpretive approach.* Walnut Creek, CA: AltaMira Press.

Silverman, L. H. (1990). *Of us and other "things": The content and functions of museum talk by adult visitor pairs in an art and a history museum.* Unpublished doctoral dissertation, University of Pennsylvania.

Stubbs, M. S. (1983). *Discourse analysis: The socioliguistic analysis of natural language.* Chicago: University of Chicago Press.

Taylor, S. M. (1986). *Understanding processes of informal education: A naturalistic study of visitors to a public aquarium.* Unpublished doctoral dissertation, University of California, Berkeley.

Tunnicliffe, S. D. (1998). Boy talk / girl talk: Is it the same at animal exhibits? *International Journal of Science Education, 20*(7), 795–811.

Uzzell, D. (1993). Contrasting psychological perspectives on exhibition evaluation. In S. Bicknell & G. Farmelo (Eds.), *Museum visitor studies in the 90s* (pp. 125–129). London: Science Museum.

Chapter 9

Conversations Across Time: Family Learning in a Living History Museum

Ellen Rosenthal
Jane Blankman-Hetrick
Conner Prairie
Fishers, IN

> *Fred opened* The Book. *There was a picture of a guy on a black horse standing on a path . . . dressed from head to toe in black armor . . . "Oh, man," . . . said Fred. "Wouldn't it be great to see knights and all that stuff for real?" Wisps of pale green mist began to swirl around the kitchen chairs.*
>
> —Scieszka (1991, p. 11)

Tales of journeys to dimly known times fascinate us and have made such works as H. G. Wells' *The Time Machine*, C. S. Lewis' *The Chronicles of Narnia*, Edward Eager's *The Time Garden*, and Jon Scieszka's *The Time Warp Trio* favorites among adults and children. Readers observe time travelers as they touch, smell, and taste the past, meeting unusual historic "characters" along the way. They enjoy seeing how ordinary people learn to cope in the past by casting off old assumptions and accepting new "old" ways of doing things. This study also follows ordinary people as they venture to another time via the means of a living history museum. We chronicle the explorations and conversations of five families through Prairietown, a recreated 1836 village at Conner Prairie, Indiana, as we seek to understand and describe the impact of a transporting experience on family learning.

What makes learning in a living history museum different from that which occurs in other museums? At living history museums, historical characters that greet and converse with visitors are the core programmatic element. Studies conducted under the auspices of the Museum Learning Collaborative (MLC), a research endeavor meant to explore the way learning occurs in museums, have posited that when visitors talk about what they have seen, remembered, and explored, they are learning (Leinhardt & Crowley, 1998; Schauble, Leinhardt, & Martin, 1998). According to the theory of Conversation Elaboration, developed by MLC, conversation reveals the product and process of learning (Leinhardt, Tittle, Knutson, chap. 4, this volume). In conducting this study, we wondered what would happen to visitor learning in a museum where they are encouraged to converse. The study, designed by Conner Prairie staff members with guidance from MLC, had two goals. First, we sought to measure interactions between visitors and staff along a number of dimensions and describe the circumstances in which family learning is most likely to take place. Second, we hoped to identify components of learning interactions and use insights to improve interpreter performance at Conner Prairie.

We conducted our examination by following five families as they toured Prairietown, a recreated village of 1836, one of Conner Prairie's historic areas. Located just outside Indianapolis, Indiana, Conner Prairie is internationally recognized as one of the first museums to implement the first-person interpretation technique in which staff "become" people of the past. In Prairietown, costumed museum staff members assume the roles of fictional, yet historically accurate and time-specific characters. These historic "interpreters" never step out of character or time when talking with visitors, or acting out the thoughts, feelings, daily chores, and activities of the past.

Presentation of historical information through impromptu conversation and demonstration is the museum's fundamental goal. The Conner Prairie *Interpreter Resource Manual* (1995), a compendium of research and guidance given to all interpreters, explains:

> The interpreter interprets by saying, "I do." Using this technique, the interpreter role-plays a character, real or contrived, from a different time period while the interpreter actually demonstrates aspects of life he/she, while in character, must relate what is being done without "breaking character." The visitor learns by seeing and *conversing* with an historical character; Conner Prairie becomes a personal time machine. The details of the setting become a major aspect of creating the attitude to facilitate and maximize the learning experience. (Conner Prairie Archives)

This study looks specifically at the impact of the living history environment and first-person interpretation on the family because they make up the largest part of Conner Prairie's general audience (approximately 50%). In addition, the public perceives Conner Prairie as a destination specifically for families. When 600 consumers in and around Indianapolis, Indiana, were asked to characterize Conner Prairie nearly all (95.7%) described it as a place to take your family (Strategic Marketing & Research, Inc., 2000).

For the purposes of this study, we define family as a multigenerational grouping including at least one adult and one child over the age of five.

In looking specifically at the family, we are building on the work of previous researchers on family behavior in museums (Borun & Cleghorn, 1996; Crowley & Callanan, 1998; Hilke, 1988). Researchers Falk and Dierking (2000) noted that "families with children interact, converse and provide information to one another in recognizable patterned ways that are repeated throughout the visit. In fact, the entire visit can be characterized as one single, large-group conversation, even though families engage in numerous small conversations that are constantly beginning and ending" (p. 93). Work by Kevin Crowley and Maureen Callanan (1998) of the Museum Learning Collaborative established that parents can serve as facilitators for learning in a museum environment that supports collaboration if they themselves feel some mastery over the museum's content. Our study is the first to test the MLC theory of Conversational Elaboration in the living history museum setting.

Many museum professionals have supposed that the living history approach enhances learning. "Open-air museums can function as powerful time machines, with the potential to transport visitors mentally and emotionally into the past, where important lessons can be learned" (Anderson, 1984, p. 17). They argue that living history provides visitors with free choice as to what and when to learn, because there are no labels, barriers, or predetermined routes. Visitors are free to ask any question that occurs to them. Interpreters can assess the appropriate level of response at the moment questions are asked and fit the answer accordingly. "By capitalizing on the public's preference to make the study of history an active rather than a passive pursuit, living history museums can turn museum visitors into investigators of the past" (Leon & Piatt, 1989, p. 92). Finally, museum professionals assume that everyone can relate to the activities and objects of everyday life that are presented in living history.

Pedagogical theories of dialogue between teacher and student shed light on how dialogue in a living history setting might enhance learning. In this kind of museum, dialogue is the primary instrument for the transference of knowledge. Interpreters talk to visitors, they do not dramatize historic vignettes as actors, nor present historic lectures. Theorists Burbules and Bruce (2001) examined the pedagogical significance of dialogue by the presence of reflexive and reciprocal interchange between those involved in dialogue, identifying forms of dialogues as inquiry, conversation, instruction, and debate. For dialogue to be truly "dialogical" it must contain "a pedagogical relation" that is characterized by "an ongoing discursive involvement of participants, constituted in a relation of reciprocity and reflexivity." This reciprocity and reflexivity, called a "reciprocal relation" signifies that "the prerogatives of questioning, answering, commenting, or offering reflective observations on the dynamic are open to all participants. Impediments to these capabilities for interaction undermine the quality of the dialogical relation" (p. 1119).

Our study takes a closer look at assumptions put forth by those in both the museum and education fields. By examining how interaction between family and interpreter as a conversational group takes place and when and how instances of learning occur, we have tried to determine by what means living history interpreters might enhance family learning.

CONNER PRAIRIE BACKGROUND

Conner Prairie serves nearly 350,000 visitors annually, including approximately 70,000 schoolchildren. It includes five historic areas, a museum center with exhibit galleries and classrooms, an orchard, fields, pastures, woods, and nature trail. Historic areas consist of 1836 Prairietown, where we conducted our study, 1816 Lenape Indian Camp and McKinnen's Trading Post, 1886 Liberty Corner Rural Crossroads, the William Conner Estate, and PastPort, a hands-on activity area. The outdoor historical components are open from April through November, although the museum center remains open year-round. Located 6 miles north of Indianapolis in one of the five fastest growing counties in the Midwest, Conner Prairie now finds its 1,400 acres to be to be a green oasis amidst burgeoning developments.

In 1934, Eli Lilly, president of the pharmaceutical company by the same name, acquired the property that Conner Prairie occupies today in order to save the home and estate of Indiana pioneer William Conner. After restoring the Conner house for public visitation, Lilly began to acquire and move threatened historic structures from around Indiana to land near the house. Lilly gifted the property to Earlham College, a small Quaker liberal arts school, in 1964, and academic staff began to develop plans for a museum.

When Conner Prairie opened its doors to the public in 1974, Lilly's architectural foundlings, together with additional structures, had been transformed into an entire pioneer village, Prairietown, with approximately 25 buildings. Prairietown was not an "in situ" survival, but rather a collage of previously unrelated houses, workshops, and businesses. Nevertheless, museum developers intended it to interpret the social history of an 1836 central Indiana small town. To this end, they stipulated that presentation within the village would always be:

> (1) with first person, role playing interpreters; (2) with . . . activities [that are] time and site-specific to central Indiana in 1836; (3) with . . . objects (historic and reproductions), landscape features, crops, animals, etc. as accurate as possible for the time period. . . ." (Conner Prairie, 1995)

The presentation of 1836 Indiana lifeways in Prairietown is historically accurate; however the village and its inhabitants are fictitious. Museum developers created a complex and nuanced past for the hamlet, its history beginning with the 1818 Treaty of St. Mary's and the migration of Delaware Indians west of the Mississippi River. As in a true community, each "inhabitant" has a rich personal history and an intricate web of social and familial connections. Each building, called a *post* by staff, has an interpretive focus with goals to convey information about the culture, economics, politics, and lifeways of 1836. Commonly referred to as *post goals*, these guide what is said and done in each building.

Training to become an interpreter at Conner Prairie requires learning post goals, or teaching emphases for each assigned station, the (fictional) history of Prairietown, historical trends in America and Indiana in 1836, and the biographies of each character including personal history, family relationships, and personality traits. Supervisors measure interpreter performance on their ability to adhere to post goals and disseminate required information, to "read" the audience to determine the depth of the historical message they should present, and to present well-organized addresses that "visitors usually grasp" (Conner Prairie, 2000).

In our study, post goals provided a means to distinguish scripted conversation from extemporaneous discourse. For example, at the Golden Eagle Inn, portrayed as an 1836 waystation for travelers, there are separate post goals for the taproom, parlor, and kitchen. The central character in the inn is proprietress Mrs. Martha Zimmerman, a recently widowed Pennsylvania-German woman with two grown sons who manages the Golden Eagle Inn for its owner, the town doctor. Interpreters in the inn's kitchen are asked to cover the following topics: (a) innkeeping, (b) women in business, and (c) food and cooking. An interpreter taking the role of Mrs. Zimmerman's daughter-in-law, Susanna, carried on the following conversation with visitors.

Interpreter: How you folks doin'?

Parent: We're very well today. How are you?

Interpreter: Doing right well. Name's Susanna Zimmerman. My mother-in-law, she runs the inn here for Dr. Campbell. You folks lookin' for accommodations?

Parent: Not today, we're just passing through.

Interpreter: Have you been up to look at the accommodations?

Parent: Oh, we certainly have.

Interpreter: Well, it's one bit for a spot in the bed, two for a meal, if you take your meals with us.

Parent: How much is a bit? 12 cents?

Interpreter: Have ya seen a bit? (yells) Mr. Champion!

Parent (to child): Ever heard of "two bits, four bits, six bits, a dollar?"

Interpreter (to child and parents): Mr. Champion here, he's a guest stayin' with us. He comes from Fort Wayne. He'll come in here to show you a coin.

Mr. Champion hands child coin to examine and explains its worth.

In the first part of this conversation, the interpreter follows the post goals by introducing herself, explaining that the inn is run by her mother-in-law and alluding to how an inn functioned in the early 19th century. In the latter half of the exchange, she uses the visitor's question about the value of a bit to spark an off-the-cuff discussion, even calling in another interpreter. In this instance, the parent prompts the engagement and her child's interest by recalling a familiar line from a nursery rhyme. However, the interpreter carried through by involving the child through firsthand experience with a bit.

How well an interpreter can integrate historical information with character portrayal and visitor interaction depends on several factors: the amount of time they have spent as an interpreter and/or at that particular post, their own personal abilities in the degree to which they adhere to or stray from the post goals, and his or her own style and bias. As one long-time interpreter explained,

> Post goals make it appear pretty one-dimensional too, if you just stick to the book. We know a lot more as human beings [how] they really existed now than what our guidelines are at that post. I think the biography is important because I think that's how everything meshes here, that's how we translate things, we just have to go past it. (N. Allen, personal interview, July 2000)

METHOD

Participants

Five families, representing 23 individuals, participated in the Conner Prairie study, ranging in size from one adult and one child to two adults and five children. Some groups included friends of the family. The nine adults considered were all aged 35 to 45 years and had completed high school. Several had graduated from college or attended college. The 11 children ranged in age from 7 through 14 and included six boys and five girls.

Apparatus

Audiotaping during participants' visits to the village was accomplished with microcassette recorders and clip-on lapel microphones. Video cameras were used to capture both physical and verbal behavior. Interviews and tours were later transcribed by repeated listening and content verified by the C-I-Said program from Scolarie, Sage Publications.

Procedure

The museum asked the families for permission to audiotape them in three contexts: during a previsit interview conducted in the entrance lobby to the museum, during 30 minutes of their tour of Prairietown, and during a postvisit interview conducted immediately after the tour. Conner Prairie was also granted permission to videotape the subjects' tour of Prairietown. Because there are two approaches to Prairietown, visitors were asked to take the left-hand approach, but were left on their own to pace their visit. (One family started their tour from the right.) Most families were able to visit three or four posts of approximately twelve. We stopped the group after 30 minutes and asked them to answer a few questions. After the postvisit interview, we no longer followed the families. They completed tours at Conner Prairie on their own.

Coding

In coding and analyzing dialogue and observing videotapes, researchers examined visitor conversations in four ways. First, we sought to identify if learning, as defined by Leinhardt and others at MLC, took place. Second, we marked when and under what circumstances indicators of learning appeared. We were particularly interested in the role of the interpreter, and therefore measured the levels and depth of engagement between the family and interpreter and interpreter and family. Third, we looked at the relationship between visitor expectations and goals, as expressed in the previsit interview, and in what actually happened on the grounds. Fourth, we looked at the relationship between impressions and understanding voiced in the postvisit interview and what happened on the grounds.

Transcripts were divided into segments defined by interaction and location. In following Burbules and Bruce's definition of dialogue as being an "ongoing discursive involvement of participants" (Burbules & Bruce, 2001) we chose this approach to capture interpreter–visitor engagement over time, as well as a speaker response sequence. References to particular segments in later interfamily conversations were also coded.

Family One, Segment 2, Location; Golden Eagle Porch

Parent to sons: Say good day.
Interpreter 1: How do.
Parent: Hi! How are you?
Interpreter 1: Why I couldn't be better if it were sunny and Saturday!
Parent: That's good.
Interpreter 2: Got a rhubarb pie out there bakin'

Parent: Ok.

Interpreter 2: And ah got a kitchen cook makin' a meal.

Parent: Ok that'll be fine.

Interpreter 2: You folks looking to stay somewhere?

Parent: No, I think we're gonna move on.

Several voices: Well you ought to check the rooms out. Only a halfpence to get you a spot in the bed. You might want to go up and check the beds out. You don't want to buy a pig in a poke.

Parent to family: Wonder how much the rooms are? I wonder how much.

Interpreter 2: Another time passin' through you might want to spend the night.

Parent: Ok.

Interpreter 2: Why don't you check out the rooms and see if you want to stay?

End of segment. Segment 3 begins with interactions in the kitchen area of the Golden Eagle.

Each segment interaction was coded for learning indicators, how and when they occurred, and the depth of engagement. In this example, the interpreter made reference to the post goals (accommodations of a 19th-century inn, sleeping arrangements), interaction was primarily with the adults in the family group with little engagement of the family as a whole, interpreter talk evoked only brief, polite responses, and one learning indicator occurred (the mother's question about the room that was not acknowledged by the interpreter). Segments following the previous interchange showed that the family did not reference this interaction during interfamily conversations later. Segments were also coded for coaching behavior by the adult to child (*Parent to child:* Say good day), and the frequency of questioning by any member of a conversational group.

We coded conversations according to the learning indicators established by the theory of conversational elaboration. At the lowest level, visitors categorize or *list* what they see (e.g., "There's a piano."). Then they *synthesize,* comparing items with reference to prior experiences, knowledge, or other ideas and concepts, "This looks more like the houses we have today." At higher levels of conversation, they seek to *analyze* by discussing how an item, person, or place may have been used or functioned; they also may discuss its qualities "What kind of fabric is that made out of? Feel it." Here, [it] feels like horse or something, [maybe] cow." In the highest level of conversation, visitors bring together old and new to *explain* or draw conclusions, "Look Meg. See that? That [was] once a tree. They had to cut out the center of it to make a trough" (Transcripts, Family Four, 2000).

We measured the level and depth of interpreters' engagement with visitors and vice versa, because we were specifically concerned with the nature of interpreter contact and its relationship to learning. Sometimes the exchange that occurs involves all parties equally; sometime visitors only stop and speak out of common courtesy, but with no real interest. At other times, visitors attempt to initiate a topic of discussion. We needed to be able to describe the nature of the interpreter–family interaction and gauge the level of involvement on both sides. For these measures we relied on dialogical theories posited by Burbules and Bruce (2001), which define engagement as "a relation of involvement among participants." They explain that dialogue

> is not simply a momentary engagement between two or more people; it is a discursive relation situated against the backdrop of previous relations involving them and the relation of what they are speaking today . . . The forms of dialogue may not always even involve active speaking back and forth. In certain cases silence, that is, the choice not to engage in dialogue, can express rejection, intimidation, boredom, irrelevance, etc. (Delpit, 1988; Fine, 1987; Lewis, 1990). It can be a "dialogue move" itself. (p. 1114)

We define the levels of engagement for interpreters as follows, listed from *lowest* to *highest*:

1. *Monologue* is used to indicate when the interpreter "recites" explanations about the post or their character's biography, such as "Now if that should ever happen that I should get married up, Elizabeth would step in my shoes and be the next hired girl here, so Mrs. Campbell is hoping . . ." Monologues can continue for several minutes and sometimes involve conversation between two interpreters. It is as if visitors are watching a play.
2. *Interpreter prompts the entire group* indicates when interpreters question or test the entire group for interest on a particular subject, such as "Now you all lookin' for accommodations for this evening?" The interpreter may be trying to stimulate response or simply repeating a frequently used line.
3. *Interpreter interacts with adults* denotes a situation in which the interpreter speaks only with adults in the family, such as:

> *Interpreter:* This here your wife?
> *Father:* Yes.
> *Interpreter:* You'd be next to each other [in bed at the inn]. Then we put the youngun' next to you and if you needed another one [bed], we'd charge you in addition, cause you'd be takin' up the space.

In this category, children are not involved in the conversation and on videotape could frequently be seen looking or walking around the room, tugging at their parents, or just staring off into space.

4. *Interpreter prompts children* describes a conversation in which reflexivity and reciprocity occurs in the dialogue between child and interpreter. In this example, an interpreter tries to convince a mother and her 13-year-old son that the boy should marry one of his "daughters."

Interpreter: And see my girls wouldn't know the difference probably, see, cause don't tell nobody he's thirteen. Boy, what's the matter with you?

Son: Nothing.

Interpreter: Have you ever been on a hog drive?

Son (laughs): Uh no.

Interpreter: Now he looks like he could pick up two hundred pound straggler, doesn't he?

Interpreter: What do you think Matt?

Son: What, huh?

Interpreter: Should he have to pay Doc Campbell since Doc wasn't able to cure her?

Son: No, I guess not.

Interpreter: Well there you go.

Typically in this level of engagement, the interpreter directs questions and comments to the child in the group, and parent(s) takes silent but attentive stances. Although not part of the conversation, they are engaged in the dialogue between their child and the interpreter.

5. *Reciprocal and reflexive dialogue* designates times when interpreters engage all members of the family through comments, questions and reflections.

Interpreter: Here's a hard one, what's half of fifty cents?

Child: Twenty-five cents.

Interpreter: Nope, it's . . . twelve and a half. That's what this is. It's twelve and a half cent piece. It's called a bit. Here's another hard one, what's half of twelve and a half?

Child: Six.

Father: Six.

Mother: How did they cut the coins? [Why] didn't they come [that way]?"

This situation usually occurred when interpreters engaged children and the parents became involved as well. All members of the family and the interpreter exchange comments, questions, and the dialogue has a reflexive quality to it.

We devised the following scale to indicate the family's level of involvement in dialogue with interpreters.

1. *Utterance.* A family member acknowledges the interpreter by a polite utterance—"hmmm, uh huh" and so on. There is no interaction between the person and the interpreter.

Interpreter: We're just resting a bit. We just finished up the dishes and it was a pretty hard morning for us. . . . Oh it's hot sir. We just let the fire die down and it's still hot. We had to do some cookin' . . .

Father: Hmm . . . Hmm.

2. *One word response.* A family member acknowledges the interpreter with one word, such as yes or no. There is minimal reciprocal interaction between the person and the interpreter.

Interpreter: All the ladies are cooking up things to send down there. So I'm back helping my hired girl getting some things ready to go. So if you want to step back there. . . . I would ask the children to be very mindful of the stove. It's very hot.

Father: Yea.

The three highest indicator levels for involvement reveal the same reflexive dialogue as described in the interpreter indicators for engagement. Therefore, the reader may turn to the previous descriptions for actual examples.

3. *Adult and interpreter dialogue.* An adult or both adults are involved in a reciprocal and reflexive dialogue with the interpreter. Children are not participants.

4. *Child and interpreter dialogue.* Children in the family respond to and interact with the interpreter. There is little interaction with parents or other adults in the family.

5. *Reciprocal and reflexive dialogue between all members.* All family members are engaged in dialogue with the interpreter and express comments, reflections and questions. The highest level of engagement is the same for both interpreters and visitors because it is then that all members of the group are fully engaged in the conversation with no one left out or holding back.

Results

Whereas other learning studies have looked largely at the content of dialogue, our analysis attempts to assess the role of the interpreter in stimulating family learning. We noted the total number of learning indicators and recorded how often they occurred in different situations: during an interpreter's presentation (or monologue), during a discussion with an interpreter, directly after interpreter contact, and independent of interpreter

TABLE 9.1
Frequencies of Conversational Elements per Family

Variable	*Average Occurrence*	*During Interpreter Dialogue*	*After Interpreter Dialogue*
List	30	14.6%	85.4%
Analyze	15	20.7%	77.7%
Synthesize	25	14.0%	58.0%
Explain	25	41.0%	58.0%

Note. N = 248 Conversational Units, containing 1,668 sentences analyzed (five families = 23, 15 interpreters, total 38 individuals)

contact. Table 9.1 shows the average number of occurrences per family of each learning indicator and when they happened.

This analysis makes apparent several findings. Learning indicators occur most frequently after the family has been engaged in discussion with an interpreter. During discussion with an interpreter, families recorded the next highest level of learning indicators although there was a steep drop off. If the interpreter talked too much (monologue) or too little (no interpreter contact), learning indicators were virtually absent. Interpreters usually resorted to monologue when they were attempting to cover post goals and then spoke primarily to adults in the family. In these situations adults would answer with monosyllabic words and children rarely spoke. In fact, as captured on camera, children fidgeted, looked around or even wandered away as interpreters presented information (usually to be pulled back to polite listening stance by their parents). Learning indicators occurred only occasionally during intrafamily conversation without stimulus from an interpreter. Even though parents made repeated efforts to prompt their children to connect to what they were seeing, they usually had limited success.

Table 9.1 provides a snapshot of the impact of engagement with interpreters on family learning indicators. All levels of engagement, save the lowest, have been collapsed to show the impact of interpreters. Although our sampling numbers were too small to reliably correlate the degree of engagement with the frequency of learning indicators, our work suggests that a relationship exists. When the interpreter succeeded in creating a "reciprocal and reflexive dialogue" involving all family members (particularly children), the impact on learning indicators was dramatic. This engagement appears to act as a catalyst, causing a discussion reaction that takes place when the family is alone again.

Furthermore, interpreter engagement appears to stimulate all levels of indicators—listing, analyzing, synthesizing, and explaining. Families identified objects, behaviors, or characters 85.4% within the intrafamily dialogue that directly followed interpreter contact. Families explained a concept, how something was done, or the time period 97% within the intrafamily category that directly followed contact.

Transcripts revealed distinct conversational patterns and distinctions between children and adults, mothers and fathers. Children were more likely to list (26.7%) and analyze (33.9%), than synthesize (20.1%) and explain (11.6%). Adults used analysis, synthesis, and explanation to coach their children (Father or male 29.8%, Mother or female 58.7%) to ask questions, make relationships between past and present, and/or perform a task. Parents whose purpose for being at Conner Prairie was to enhance their children's learning experience used synthesis and explanation to coach their children about a particular topic. For example, a father contrasted the past presented at Conner Prairie with his own childhood and his daughter's life in the following exchange.

Parent: Think of that Meg, in September you'd be picking corn instead of going to school

Child: I know.

Parent: You know your papaw had me picking corn and big potatoes and all that stuff? You do, don't you?

Child: That was harder than it is today.

DISCUSSION

A closer look at the experiences of Family Four with related examples from other families provides a window onto the Conner Prairie experience.

A mother and father, both college graduates in their late 30s, were traveling with their 9-year-old daughter, a third grader, on their way to South Bend. Knowing they would be spending the night in Indianapolis, they explored entertainment possibilities on the Internet. The father explained, "Personally I wanted to go by the Indianapolis 500, but no. We thought it would be a good opportunity for our daughter to experience early . . . life in America." They had never visited Conner Prairie before. Like other parents in the study, the visit was a social outing, but they were attuned to their daughter's interests and previous experiences and hoped to make it educational as well. "She is a very avid reader and has read many of *The Little House on the Prairie* books." They wanted to help her connect and expand upon previous learning. "We live close to the Smokey Mountains in Nashville, Tennessee, so we are close to several . . . museums in the that area. . . . We hope that this will tie in with them." Later, when asked if their family regularly goes to places like Conner Prairie, the father said, "Yes we do. . . . I think it ties in with our daughter's education. It gives her experience of things in school that she can only read about." Their daughter was a willing participant in her own informal education, as she noted that she expected to see "just how the pioneers used to live . . . cause I've always been into pioneer life."

Parents in nearly all the other families described similar expectations of the visit and awareness of their children's previous history learning. Another mother prompted her two sons, seven and nine; "You guys know quite a bit about the history down where we're from, don't you?" And then, "You guys learned about American history at school? Remember, you started back with the pilgrims in Massachusetts and then Mommy came in to do the 'Wagons West' program?" A mother urged her children, ages 10 and 14, to "tell about [that] report. What did you do in school this year?" One child responded, "Oh, we cleared a trail that Robert LaSalle took to get to South Bend." The other added, "He was the first White man to get to South Bend." Parents were quick to suggest that children would enjoy the visit because they already knew something about the topic and that the visit would prove to be a learning experience. "We thought (the visit) would be interesting and educational. We know that the kids . . . follow pioneers so we thought that they would enjoy that too." Asked how they expected to benefit from the visit to Conner Prairie, most parents reiterated the importance of enhancing formal education, particularly for their children. "We are trying to tie things that she is studying in school with actual . . . experience." "Instead of reading in a book at school, you can actually be there . . . you can experience what they have done." There was, of course, the exception to the rule. The mother of the recalcitrant teenage boy asked hopefully, "How did you learn about American history. . . . Reading books?" He quickly responded, "No, not reading books, I don't read books."

Unlike the little girl in Family Four, children were not always as aware of or concerned with the educational side of the visit. When asked about their expectations for the visit, one 7-year-old said he wanted to "see some animals . . . cows, horses, pigs" although his mother quickly followed with "To learn about history . . . to see what it is like in [1836]." One child stated emphatically that she was out to "have fun," wherein her sibling followed that *she* expected "to learn about history." Asked why she comes to places like Conner Prairie, one mother of a 13-year-old son said, "I like it because it's outside. On a nice day like today, you can get outside." Her son added, "I come because I have to."

When Family Four was asked how frequently they go to places like Conner Prairie, they indicated that they visit "lots of places that deal with mountain life in the late 1800s and early 1900s . . . areas [that] have some type of building or museum." Their daughter volunteered, "We also visited in Nashville, Tennessee, the Hermitage house of Andrew Jackson." Other study participants listed places that might be considered attractions, rather than museums, when asked the same question. They mentioned sites such as Chattanooga Park (the Civil War battlefield in Tennessee), Shipshewana, Indiana, Amish Acres (described as a "modern day culture that lives without electricity"), and "Roaring Fort Nature Trail" (probably Big South Fork Park, Kentucky). All of these sites, whether museums or not, were viewed as potential learning experiences for children—places where children might actually experience something they had learned or read about.

As Family Four made their way onto the grounds of Prairietown, and approached the first "post," the Golden Eagle Inn, they discussed their understanding of the basic premise of the museum and first person interpretation.

Mother: Does somebody really live here? (referring to the Golden Eagle)

Father: I don't think so. I think they are in costume. I think that you can get period answers too.

Mother: If you ask questions, you get answers from the period too.

Family Four, like many of the other visitors, were somewhat uncertain about how to understand Prairietown. Did the "inhabitants" actually live there? Was the family to behave as if visiting strangers, by knocking and waiting to be invited in, or should they proceed boldly assuming that their ticket gave them the right to free entry? Conner Prairie offers an orientation film to prepare visitors for the living history experience and provide them with basic rules for their outing. However, many visitors, eager to get outdoors and see the museum, do not take the time to view the film.

Family Four knocked and entered the Inn without pausing. Immediately, the father began to pose questions, point things out to his daughter and prod her to talk to the historic interpreters.

Father: What do you think the bed stuff, mattresses are made of?

Child: Kind of a fill?

Father: Corn husks. Look they have a water pitcher in the bowl 'cause there is no running water.

After an interpreter appeared to offer them, in character, a room for the night and they discussed cost, the mother returned to the subject of the mattress.

Mother (to daughter): Ask him what the beds are made of.

Child: I don't want to ask a question.

Mother: Ask him.

Father: Ask him.

Mother: Ask him. That's a good question.

Father: Do you happen to know what the mattress is made of?

Interpreter: Well sir, in Mrs. Zimmerman's private bed chambers, which is one over there, she has two tics, one stuffed with straw, one of them stuffed with down, bird feathers.

This kind of "coaching" behavior occurred in every family. Parents repeatedly tried to mediate between their children and the museum environment by encouraging their children to ask and answer questions. The parents in a farming family urged their child to take note of historic farming techniques.

Father to child: Ask him if he plows.
Mother: Matt, ask if he plows with the horse.
Mother: Ask if he plows with the horse.
Child: If he what?
Mother: If he PLOWS with the horse.
Child: What is that? I don't know that word. What is it?
Mother: If he plows ground with it.
Child: Oohhhh thaaat.
Mother: Ok; now you can ask him
Mother: Go ahead.

The child eventually succeeded in changing the subject and the question was never asked or answered.

The interest that parents expressed in previsit interviews in connecting the Conner Prairie visit with previous experiences was also apparent on the grounds of the museum. Parents reminded their children of previous experiences and knowledge, such as in the following example from Family Four as they looking in the wash building in back of the doctor's house.

Father: Look at that over there. What's the white stuff? Wonder what that is?
Child: Where?
Father: Over there in that container. Do you know what that is?
Child: What? What is it?
Father: I think it's soap.
Child: Soap?
Father: Yea, it's lye soap. Remember you went to Dollywood and saw them make soap?
Child: Oh yea.
Father: In the pot.

Parents in Family One attempted to remind their young sons of another museum visit.

Mother: Want to touch a rope bed?

Son 2: Yea.

Mother: [They had better] tighten it before the ropes . . . start sagging.

Father: Because they're longer than what they were at Plantation Village. Remember?

Son 2: When were we at Plantation Village?

Father: Sometime ago.

As the tour proceeded, the mother and father in Family Four carried the majority of the conversation. Interpreters directed questions to her occasionally, such as "You know how to sew?" The child replied simply, "No." The interpreter turned quickly to the father, saying, "You've got a lot of work to do sir. You may have some trouble marrying her off." "I know," replied the father, "I have to keep a large dowry."

Although most children resisted their parents pressure to engage, the young girl in Family Four sought to have her questions answered, albeit tentatively at first. In the Golden Eagle Barn, she whispered to her father "Is that horse manure?" He replied, "I don't know. Why don't you ask him?" After his daughter's gesture of shyness, the father said to the interpreter, "Sir, could you tell us what is in this pile?" "It's a manure pile," he replied and the child announced happily "That's just what I thought."

Just once did Family Four became engaged in dialogical conversation in which all family members were engaged with an interpreter. This exchange happened at the Golden Eagle Inn and included 95 exchanged lines. Part of the discussion, related to the meaning of the term bit, was partially quoted previously. The interpreter playing the younger Mrs. Zimmerman explained the cost of beds. When the father asked her to explain a bit, she called in another interpreter who explained the meaning of the term *cipher.*

Interpreter: Well here's . . . Hold on, do you know how to cipher?

Father: Do you know what a cipher is?

Child: No.

Interpreter: You know how to subtract, add, multiply and divide?

Child: Yeah.

Interpreter: [Then] you know how to cipher.

Child: OK.

Interpreter: Your pa must of sent you to school . . . Since you know how to cipher, what's half of a dollar?

Child: Fifty cents.

Following this lengthy exchange the family exhibited listing and other learning behaviors, as shown in the following exchange.

Father: Look how the glass is dimpled.

Father: A churn.

Child: That's how you make butter and milk.

Father: Yes it is.

Child: I know that.

Father: Look, that's a little water pail to wash your hands in when you come inside.

Child: hmm.

Father: I liked how they had all the covers on the foodstuffs in [the] corner [over the] jars.

Child: All the flies.

Father: Well they would keep it covered.

Father: What's that? Look Meg. See that. That once was a tree. They had to cut out the center of it to make a trough.

Child: The horse is real.

This segment of conversation drew to a close with the child's triumphant identification of manure, quoted previously.

Evidence that this conversation made an impact on this family is verified by the postvisit interview. When asked what conversations were their favorites, the mother said, "The guy with the bits." Her daughter confirmed, "Yes, he was probably the best." The family also noted "bits" as something they had surprised them that day.

Father: One thing that I never really had known . . . was the bits. . . . I knew about bits, but I never had experienced what it looked like and how it was created . . . taking the silver dollar and basically and cutting it in pieces.

Child: It's also funny how like now we just use different coins, but they just used sorta the same coin.

Mother: Why do you think that might have been?

Child: They probably didn't make as [many coins].

In 30 minutes, Family Four was only able to visit a few additional areas: Sgt. Hastings cabin, home of an indigent widower, McClure's house, home and workshop of the town carpenter, and the Campbell house and yard, home, and outbuildings belonging to the town doctor. Other families chose other posts to visit, including the Hudsons' Cabin, the home of Quakers, the schoolhouse, and the cemetery (a funeral was taking place that day).

Family Three, a father who farmed and a mother who worked as a teacher's aide, visiting with three of the their own children and two friends, chose to visit the Hudson cabin. According to the Prairietown "history," the

Hudsons are Quakers and abolitionists. On the day of this study, an interpreter, a free Black woman was tending the house. In the dim light of the cabin, She was sewing near an open door. The following exchange occurred:

Father (to child): Want to ask her what she's making?

Interpreter: [They] can't speak—how she's going [to] ask?

Mother (to child): Want to ask her? [If] she's working on the bag?

Interpreter: [inaudible] . . . don't you even worry about it, cause I can [sew] by day.

Mother: Do you have children?

Interpreter: Yes, I have two. These yourin's?

Mother: Three of them.

Father (speaking to Children): She always sews in the sunshine so she doesn't have to burn candles. Right?

Interpreter: . . . burning candles in the daytime, be a [waste]. Candles are [for] nighttime. [For] going out to the barn, out to the outhouse. If I use 'em all up . . . then what are you going to do?

Mother: How many do you usually make a year?

Interpreter: Depends on how many folks are in your family. Gonna need at least three or four hundred.

Mother: Oh wow.

Father (to children): A lot of candles in a year, isn't it?

Child: huh huh.

Interpreter (to children): Gets dark every day, don't it?

In this interpreter–family interaction, the children were nearly silent, yet the videotape shows that they were attentive and watchful. That they were engaged is shown by their conversation after leaving the post.

Mother: She was making a little doll wasn't she?

Child: Yea.

Child: A hanky head doll!

Father: Are you all mute? She couldn't get any of you to talk.

Child: You went in ahead of us.

Mother: You guys better talk the next place!

Child: OK. I'll talk.

Family Two, composed of a 42-year-old mother with a 12th-grade education, a friend of hers (a college graduate) and a daughter, 14, and son, 10, also visited the Hudson Cabin. In this family, the children were similarly quiet, but equally engaged. Their comments in the postinterview discussion reveal that conversation with the interpreter had a greater impact than was reflected in the on-site conversation.

Child: We saw that Black woman over there and we questioned if she was actually a slave.
Adult: Remember, Indiana did not actually have slavery.
Child: She seemed really preoccupied.
Child: Yea, and the Black woman, she was very, very good.
Adult: She was, she was very good. You know [being preoccupied] is probably part of the role.
Adult: Exactly, she would have to be short.

The "funeral," a special program, also served as stimulus for parent–child discussion. Throughout Prairietown, interpreters talked about the reason for the death, preparations that had to be made and the impact on the bereaved family. In the cemetery, a gravedigger prepared the grave. Family One visited the Campbell house, home of the town doctor, and learned from "Mrs. Campbell" that "Mrs. Hawkins passed away, a patient of his (her husband's). And the doctor was called away and was very upset that he can not come to services this sad day. . . . All the ladies are cooking up things to send down there . . ." Afterward, this conversation took place.

Father: My. There's going to be a funeral today.
Mother: I guess it's a sad day, huh?
Father: Yep.
Child: Why?
Mother: Cause someone died.
Child: Is that where they put the lady that died?
Mother: You want to go to a cemetery?
Mother: A lot of women, little kids [died].

Conner Prairie staff have long observed that parents seemed pleased to use the funeral and other events to initiate discussion with their children of difficult subjects.

In their posttour interview, families were asked how seeing life in 1836 may have changed the way they think about life today. All families, including number Four, commented on the amount of work that had to be done, and how fortunate we are today. One family had the following conversation.

Adult: The meals. It takes about an hour. It really is a big ordeal. You have to plan ahead. You can't come home and say, "what's for dinner tonight dear?"

Child: There's no microwave! Or even the chores. Like taking the water out for the sheep.

CONCLUSION

Prior to this study, much had been presumed about learning in living history museums, but little was known. It was supposed that, more than other kinds of museums, living history offered free choice learning and the opportunity for visitors to ask questions and become active investigators of history. In addition, it was presumed that most people relate to the presentation of everyday life, the focus of most living history museums.

Our study suggests that although these may be factors in living history museum learning, they are not the most important factors, at least for families. We found that the nature of family interaction with interpreters had the greatest impact on learning. Learning conversation was more apt to happen between parents and children, if an interpreter had stimulated it. The parents in our study tried earnestly (and repeatedly) on their own to prompt learning exchanges with their children, but more often than not, faced frustrating reticence or outright noncompliance, unless an interpreter had sparked conversation.

The level of engagement with the interpreter seemed to be associated with number and level of learning indicators that occurred subsequently. If both the family and the interpreter became involved in reflexive dialogue involving both children and adults, it became easier for families to talk "among themselves." If only adults were involved in conversation, children were more likely to let their minds and bodies wander, although this was not always the case. If the interpreter directed attention to the child, not only did the child become engaged but the parents were engaged as well; their faces, as captured on videotape, beamed.

These interactions, at their best, can be compared to a dance. The interpreter would "lead" the family in dialogue. At the lower levels of engagement, visitors and interpreters exchanged words and ventured questions but there was little taking place between conversational partners. At the higher stages of dialogue between the interpreter, adult, child, or family as a whole, there was a dynamic, almost rhythmic movement of reciprocity and relational connection between participants in the conversational group. It was this "waltz" of dialogue that seemed to stimulate learning.

In most circumstances, the impetus for active engagement came from interpreters, not visitors. Children, in particular, were loath to ask questions, despite repeated prompting. Adults asked more, but seemed to struggle to find meaningful ways to interact with the 19th century. At their best, interpreters wove the visitor into stories of the time period, subtly contrasting contemporary experience with historical life. For example, in conversing with a teenage visitor, one interpreter suggested that it was time for the boy to marry and offered to match him with one of his daughters. The boy was surprised, and delighted, to find that expectations of him would have been so different in the early 1800s. Our study places the onus for learning far more heavily on the interpreter than previously thought.

What are the implications of this study for Conner Prairie and for the field of living history museums? In brief, our study suggests that interpreters pay more attention to drawing visitors, both adults and children, into the web of the past, and less attention to simply covering topics of information. It also suggests that greater attention be paid in interpreter training to effective ways of interacting with children. It is often assumed that people who are employed as interpreters have natural teaching abilities or a natural ability to engage visitors. This is simply not true in all cases, and often, interpretive staff manages to provide historical content while failing to do so in a way that stimulates visitor discovery. Many interpreters also approach communication with children in the same way they do with adults. Freeman Tilden (1957), an interpretive theorist counseled strongly against this, saying, "Interpretation addressed to children should not be a dilution of the presentation to adults, but should follow a fundamentally different approach" (p. 47). Despite his admonition, museums have not had the expertise, the staffing consistency, or the resources needed to train interpreters to make use of verbal prompts, nonverbal behavior, and hands-on activities that might increase the depth of engagement for children and their parents.

Our study gives support to a trend that gained momentum in the 1990s toward visitor inclusion in presentations, dramatization of historic events, and the creation of opportunities for interaction. Specialists in historic presentation, Stacy Roth (*Past into Present,* 1998) and Roy Underhill (*Khrushchev's Shoe,* 2000) advocate for refining the art of visitor engagement. Their work comes on the heels of a movement among museum professionals to bring greater historical reality to museum recreation. Reacting to criticism that museum restorations presented a cleaned-up, prettified view of the past, devoid of the painful wrongs and blemishes, museum professionals have worked hard to present diversity and portray the darker side of history. Colonial Williamsburg introduced slave auctions and a poor house in this time. Conner Prairie now incorporates funerals, illness, auctions of the poor, discrimination, crime, and substance abuse into its presentation of the past. Perhaps as part of this effort to convey historical truth and complexity, staff became "more interested in providing education opportunities laden in content" (Roth, 1998, p. 121). To emphasize content sometimes meant requiring interpreters to expound, rather than converse.

Our study suggests how critical conversational engagement is to family learning. To date, no one has described the importance of the interpreter's role as conversation catalyst and support for parental attempts to engage children. Researchers on visitor behavior, such as Marilyn Hood, noted the importance of the "togetherness" in family museum outings, stating "Family visitors are primarily interested in social interaction." She suggested that content be kept to a minimum (Roth, 1998, p. 121). Transcripts from our study, however, demonstrate that a substantial part of family conversation at the museum centered on learning. Parents seemed to be modeling excitement about learning, trying to connect experiences at Conner Prairie with previous learning and giving their children a framework for future learning. Understanding this, the museum must see its role vis-à-vis families differently.

Conner Prairie has already begun to change its approach to family interpretation based on this study. Although the museum's interpreter training program rests on a very solid foundation of historical documentation and authenticity, the results of the learning study show there is room for improvement in the areas of interpretive technique, visitor engagement, and family learning. Following completion of the learning study, Conner Prairie created a "Family Learning" Committee. Composed of staff and volunteers from several divisions, including interpreters and program planners, the committee began planning to make broad-based changes to the museum's approach to interpretation. First and foremost, they suggested that because of the time and training required for absorbing content, learning technique, and gathering on-site experience that employment as an interpreter be viewed not as a seasonal activity, but as a profession in its own right. The Committee recommended altering the interpreter infrastructure in order to create full-time year-round "professional" interpreter positions, called "Interpretive Specialists." These positions would be given the responsibility of training interpreters and would be required to develop expertise in such area as educational theory and practice, psychological development, interactive programming, dramatic storytelling, and techniques to improve visitor engagement. They would also be responsible for using evaluation approaches similar to those used in the learning study to assess interpreters' abilities to engage families. The museum plans to de-emphasize expounding on "post goals," and emphasize interpreter training in the many ways they can involve families as a "learning unit."

Results of this study, indicate a need for further study. Conner Prairie will be conducting a full study with a representative population of 60 families to test assumptions during the 2002 season. Research design will encompass the use of control families who are not videotaped, particularly to test family awareness of the camera and its impact on behavior (Lomax & Casey, 1998). Two studies will take place, one at the beginning of the season and at season's end to measure differences and change due to increased interpreter skill training and program enhancements.

Tilden, writing in *Interpreting Our Heritage*, suggests that "Interpretation is an art, which combines many arts. Any art is to some degree teachable" (p. 9). Based on that assumption and the results of this learning study, Conner Prairie plans to teach interpreters how to more effectively engage and involve visitors. The importance of visitor engagement and developing the "art" of interpretation is increased when one considers that 90% of Americans indicated that they associate learning of history more with museums than in the classroom (Rosenzweig & Thelen, 1999). The strength of family conversation and involvement in learning *as a family* has value and reaches far beyond the grounds of our museum. The more we discover how families converse, explore, and learn together, this knowledge can be used in variety of informal learning endeavors both in and out of the museum setting.

ACKNOWLEDGMENTS

The authors would like to thank those whose knowledge, patience, and time made this endeavor possible. Our gratitude to John Herbst, President and CEO at Conner Prairie and others of the staff especially the interpreters and the Program Department for letting us enter their world. Special thanks to Chip Bruce, University of Illinois, Roy Underhill, David Thelen, Indiana University, Greg Reinhardt, Tim Maher, and Phyllis Lan Lin, University of Indianapolis, for encouragement, assistance, and advice. We would especially like to thank Gaea Leinhardt, Kate Stainton, Joyce Fienberg, and Karen Knutson from the Museum Learning Collaborative, University of Pittsburgh, who provided the framework for this project and guidance as it progressed. Special thanks to our families, whose patience and support kept us moving forward.

REFERENCES

Anderson, J. (1984). *Time machines: The world of living history*. Nashville: American Association for State and Local History.

Borun, M., & Cleghorn, A. (1996). Families are learning in science museums. *Curator, 39*(2), 123–124.

Burbules, N., & Bruce, B. (in press). Theory and research on teaching as dialogue. In V. Richardson (Ed.), *Handbook of research on teaching* (4th ed., pp. 1102–1121). American Educational Research Association.

Conner Prairie (2000). *Interpreter handbook*. Fishers, IN: Conner Prairie Archives.

Conner Prairie (1995). *Interpreter resource manual*. Fishers, IN: Conner Prairie Archives.

Crowley, K., & Callahan, M. (1998). Describing and supporting scientific thinking in parent interactions. *Journal of Museum Education, 23*(1), 12.

Delpit, L. (1988). The silenced dialogue. *Harvard Educational Review, 58,* 280–289.

Eager, E. (1999). *The time garden.* New York: Harcourt Brace.

Falk, J., & Dierking, L. (2000). *Learning from museums: Visitor experiences and the making of meaning.* Washington, DC: Whalesback.

Fine, M. (1987). Silencing in the public schools. *Language Arts, 64,* 157–174.

Hilke, D. (1988). Strategies for family learning in museums. In J. Bitgood & A. Benefield (Eds.), *Museum theory, research, and practice* (Vol. 1, pp. 120–134). Jacksonville Center for Social Design.

Leinhardt, G., & Crowley, K. (1998). *Museum Learning Collaborative Revised Phase 2 Proposal* (Proposal submitted to the Institute for Museum and Library Services, Washington, DC, November), Pittsburgh, PA: University of Pittsburgh, Learning Research and Development Center.

Lewis, C. S. (1952). *The Voyage of the Dawn Treader: Book 3. Chronicles of narnia.* New York: Collier Books/Macmillan.

Lewis, M. (1990, April). *Framing, women, and silence: Disrupting the hierarchy of discursive practices.* Paper presented at the annual meeting of the American Educational Research Association, Boston, MA.

Lomax, H., & Casey, N. (1998). Recording social life: Reflexivity and video methodology. *Sociological Research Online,* Vol. 3, No. 2 [On-Line], http://www.socresonline.org.uk/socresonline/3/2/2.html

Leon, W., & Piatt, M. (1989). Living history museums. In W. Leon & R. Rozenzweig (Eds.), *History museums in the United States: A critical assessment* (pp. 64–97). Urbana and Chicago: University of Illinois Press.

Roth, S. (1998). *Past into present.* Chapel Hill: University of North Carolina Press.

Rozenweig, R., & Thelen, D. (1999). *Presence of the past: Popular uses of history in American life.* New York: Columbia University Press.

Schauble, L., Leinhardt, G., & Martin, L. (1997). A framework for organizing a cumulative research agenda in informal learning contexts. *Journal of Museum Education, 22*(2 & 3), 3–8.

Scieszka, J. (1991). *The time warp trio: Knights of the kitchen table.* New York: Viking Penguin.

Strategic Marketing & Research, Inc. (2000). *Conner Prairie: Market and Image Assessment.* Unpublished study.

Tilden, F. (1957). *Interpreting our heritage.* Chapel Hill: University of North Carolina Press.

Underhill, R. (2000). *Khrushchev's shoe and other ways to captivate an audience of 1 to 1,000.* Cambridge, MA: Perseus Publishing.

Wells, H. G. (1988). *The time machine.* New York: Perma-Bound.

Part III

CONVERSATIONS: A MOMENT OF LEARNING

The final section of *Learning Conversations in Museums* looks at museum experiences using a close-up lens. Focusing on either one exhibit or a small segment of an exhibit these authors explore how brief glimpses of talk and thought might cumulate and impact learning, either over time during the exhibit experience or more broadly in the context of family life. The studies in Part III reflect the core themes of the book, with emphases that range from studies concerned with learning environments to those that focus more on explanations or identity.

In the first chapter in this section, Crowley and Jacobs describe the role of museum visits and other everyday activity in the development of children's scientific literacy. The authors document the process by which individual knowledge and interest of different family members are fused in collaborative activity and how everyday conversations build to support collaborative discoveries about links between unknown and known concepts. Finally, Crowley and Jacobs propose a new developmental construct—"islands of expertise"—that emerge gradually over time and serve as a platform for advanced conversations about science.

In a similar vein, Ash explores group learning processes by following families as they visit an exhibit on biology. She considers content features of the learning environment as parents build on children's interest, share expertise, and jointly negotiate their visit. Using a fine-grained analysis of visitor conversations, she also focuses on explanatory features, noting the importance of complex processes where families establish an interactional rhythm. This combination provides insight into the ways in which multiple visits might build up understandings over time.

The chapter by Paris and Mercer explores the role of memory in visitor identity, as visitors view potentially evocative historical objects that might be found in museums. The authors note the idiosyncratic and highly personal responses to the artifacts, and, from an analysis of responses, draw conclusions about the potential influences of identity features such as age and gender. The chapter draws on psychological studies of memory and offers recommendations for ways that the museum community might make further use of such studies in evaluation and design.

The final chapter, by Schauble and her colleagues, reports a portion of a design experiment conducted at a children's museum. Through the design of an interactive exhibit that provides for a range of experiences, from casual to deeply engaged "funneled" experiences, the design process affords the opportunity to study how children behave at the exhibit and how both parents and staff interact with children. The authors analyze the beliefs of both parents and museum staff about the ways in which children's learning should be supported in informal learning environments. They conclude that staff and parents hold different beliefs about how to support learning, but that both groups exhibit somewhat conflicted notions about the nature of informal learning.

Chapter 10

Building Islands of Expertise in Everyday Family Activity

Kevin Crowley
Melanie Jacobs
University of Pittsburgh

How do young children first learn about academic disciplines? Long before they encounter science, history, or social studies in grade school, children begin developing a wealth of informal knowledge about each topic. In science, for example, young children are actively developing nascent scientific reasoning skills, naïve theories for scientific domains, knowledge of interesting science factoids, knowledge about famous scientific narratives, and even some early ideas about what different kinds of scientists do in their professional work. As this everyday academic literacy develops, children are simultaneously developing a sense of identity as individuals who are more or less interested and motivated to seek out opportunities to engage in activities that are related to various academic disciplines. As one focus of our museum learning research, we continue to explore how parents mediate children's experiences in and out of museums to help weave multiple moments of learning into broader informal knowledge about academic disciplines.

In this chapter we introduce the notion of islands of expertise, explore links between related socio-cultural and information processing theory, and overview a study of family conversations while parents and children look at authentic and replica fossils in a museum.

BUILDING AN ISLAND OF EXPERTISE IN EVERYDAY ACTIVITY

An island of expertise is a topic in which children happen to become interested and in which they develop relatively deep and rich knowledge. A typical island emerges over weeks, months, or years and is woven throughout multiple family activities. Because of this, developing islands of expertise is a fundamentally social process. They are co-constructed through the ongoing negotiation of children and parents' interests, children and parents' choices about family activities, and children and parents' cognitive processes, including memory, inferencing, problem solving, and explanation. As children develop deeper knowledge, islands of expertise support conversations and learning that can be more advanced than would be possible in domains in which the child's knowledge is of a more typically sketchy nature. Thus, islands of expertise become platforms for families to practice learning habits and to develop, often for the first time, conversations about abstract and general ideas, concepts, or mechanisms. Even when a child loses interest and an island of expertise begins to fade, the abstract and general themes that used the island's rich knowledge as a launching pad, will remain connected to children's other knowledge.

To illustrate what we mean, consider a child who, on his second birthday, is given a *Thomas the Tank Engine* picture book. In turns out that he likes the book, which is about the adventures of a small steam locomotive on an island railway. In fact, in turns out that he likes the book a lot and asks his parents to read it to him over and over. While waiting for a flight a few weeks later, perhaps the boy's father buys a Thomas the Tank Engine toy at the airport store. Maybe his parents pick up a few Thomas the Tank Engine videos next time they are at the video store. Maybe the mother decides that the boy could be Thomas for Halloween. When planning a Sunday outing, the parents might decide the boy would enjoy visiting a nearby train museum. As the boy's knowledge about trains deepens, the family checks out more advanced train books from the library. The family starts planning side-trips to other train museums when they travel. If they visit Steamtown National Historic Site in Scranton, Pennsylvania, maybe the boy spends a lot of time looking at "Big Boy"—a gargantuan 4-8-8-4 Union Pacific steam locomotive—and maybe, having noticed his interest, the parents stop at the gift shop to buy the boy a T-shirt with a picture of Big Boy on the front and a list of its vital statistics on the back. When he wears the shirt later, it serves as a conversational prompt for the boy, his parents, and others.

If the boy's position on the repeated reading of the same books and the repeated watching of the same videos is anything like that of a typical 2-year-old, the boy (and his parents) would have soon memorized lots of domain-specific knowledge. They would have learned labels such as firebox, tender, boiler, drive wheels, sanding gear, and steam dome. They would have acquired at least some general knowledge about mechanisms of locomotion—for example, that steam, coal, and water are sometimes involved and that diesel or electricity are sometimes involved. They would have learned schemas for a variety of train scenarios, such as firemen shoveling coal, drive wheels slipping on wet tracks, conductors shouting "All Aboard!", passengers eating in the dining car, and (particularly in the case of the Thomas stories) derailments, crashes, and breakdowns of all sorts.

Although the visits to museums have been relatively infrequent, they have provided unique opportunities to attach the well-learned domain-specific knowledge to actual trains. The boy may be able to make some of these connections himself. The parents would probably make many more through explanations, descriptions, and questions intended to help the boy interpret the visit through the lens of their shared prior knowledge about trains. The museum visits may have also opened up aspects of trains that were unavailable from other sources. For example, if the museum has an operating steam locomotive (as many do), the boy may have been surprised to find out that they are much louder, larger, dirtier, and scarier than he might have imagined. Because their previous shared experiences have contributed to a shared knowledge base about trains, family conversations during the museum visit would have been richer and more focused. Similarly, the experience of the visit provides subsequent opportunities to extend and deepen the on-going family conversation about trains as the boy and his parents wait later at a railroad crossing for a freight train to pass, look at snapshots from the museum visit, or read a new book about trains.

By the time the boy turns 3 years old, he has developed an island of expertise around trains. His vocabulary, declarative knowledge, conceptual knowledge, schemas, and personal memories related to trains are numerous, well-organized, and flexible. Perhaps more importantly, the boy and his parents have developed a relatively sophisticated conversational space for trains. Their shared knowledge and experience allow their talk to move to deeper levels than is typically possible in a domain where the boy is a relative novice. For example, as the mother is making tea one afternoon, the boy notices the steam rushing out of the kettle and says: "That's just like a train!" The mother might laugh and then unpack the similarity to hammer the point home: "Yes it is like a train! When you boil water it turns into steam. That's why they have boilers in locomotives. They heat up the water, turn it into steam, and then use the steam to push the drive wheels. Remember? We saw that at the museum."

In contrast, when the family was watching football—a domain the boy does not yet know much about—he asked "Why did they knock that guy down?" The mother's answer was short, simple, stripped of domain-specific vocabulary, and sketchy with respect to causal mechanisms—"Because that's what you do when you play football." Parents have a fairly good sense of what their children know and, often, they gear their answers to an appropriate level. When talking about one of the child's islands of expertise, parents can draw on their shared knowledge base to construct more elaborate, accurate, and meaningful explanations. This is a common characteristic of conversation in general: When we share domain-relevant experience with our audience we can use accurate terminology, construct better analogies, and rely on mutually held domain-appropriate schema as a template through which we can scribe new causal connections.

As this chapter is being written, the boy in this story is now well on his way to 4 years old. Although he still likes trains and still knows a lot about them, he is developing other islands of expertise as well. As his interests expand, the boy may engage less and less often in activities and conversations centered around trains and some of his current domain-specific knowledge will atrophy and eventually be lost. But as that occurs, the domain-general knowledge that connected the train domain to broader principles, mechanisms, and schemata will probably remain. For example, when responding to the boy's comment about the tea kettle, the mother used the train domain as a platform to talk about the more general phenomenon of steam.

Trains were platforms for other concepts as well, in science and in other domains. Conversations about mechanisms of locomotion have served as a platform for a more general understanding of mechanical causality. Conversations about the motivation of characters in the *Thomas the Tank Engine* stories have served as platforms for learning about interpersonal relationships and, for that matter, about the structure of narratives. Conversations about the time when downtown Pittsburgh was threaded with train tracks and heavy-duty railroad bridges served as a platform for learning about historical time and historical change. These broader themes emerged for the boy for the first time in the context of train conversations with his parents. Even as the boy loses interest in trains and moves on to other things, these broader themes remain and expand outward to connect with other domains he encounters as he moves through his everyday life.

What kind of learning is this? First, it is fundamentally collaborative. Everything the boy knows about trains was learned in social contexts co-constructed with his parents. The book reading has obviously been collaborative: The parents read the text, answer the child's questions, ask questions of their own, and point out interesting parts of the pictures that are not reflected in the text. The museum visits have obviously been collaborative: The family goes together to the museum and talks about trains before, during, and after the visit. Watching train videos and playing with train toys may appear less collaborative on the surface because, although he sometimes engages in these activities with his parents, he often does them more or less by himself. However, even this solitary activity is collaborative in the sense that the videos and toys reflect parent choices about what would be appropriate and interesting for the boy.

Second, although some of the learning may be highly planned and intentional, much of it is probably driven by opportunistic "noticing" on the part of both the parent and the child. Recent efforts to consider parent input into children's categorization decisions, for example, have predominately been directed at developing an account for how parents structure a fixed interpretation for children. As Keil (1998) pointed out, casting parents as simple socializers who provide fixed didactic interpretations for children is unlikely to be the right model. There is nothing more annoying then someone who provides you with pedantic explanations that you do not want or that you could not make use of. In reality, however, everyday parent–child activity hinges on a dual interpretation problem. The parents need to decide what is worth noting, based on their own knowledge and interests, their understanding of their child's knowledge and interests, and their current goals for the interaction. Children are making the same calculation simultaneously. Over time, the family interprets and re-interprets activity, bringing out different facets: Sometimes they highlight the science, sometimes the history, sometimes the emotion, sometimes the beauty, and so on. Thus, the family conversation changes to become more complex and nuanced as it traces the learning history of the family and extends through multiple activities.

Finally, and perhaps most importantly, this kind of learning cumulates from many relatively unremarkable moments. As they develop islands of expertise, children may experience a few deep personal insights and powerful moments of discovery. They may receive occasional detailed direct instruction from a parent, teacher, or television show. But most of what they know about a topic they probably learned in smaller moments of practicing, remembering, and exploring. In studies of expertise in adult learners, an often-cited estimate is that it requires about 10,000 hours or about 10 years of practice in a domain before becoming expert (Hayes, 1985). A child's island of expertise around, for example, dinosaurs, is a modest accomplishment compared to what the average paleontologist knows. But the overall point about practice is probably the same: The expertise of both the interested child and adult scientist reflect repeated exposure to domain-specific declarative knowledge, repeated practice in interpreting new content, making inferences to connect new knowledge to existing knowledge, repeated conversations with others who share or want to support the same interest, and so on.

DO ISLANDS OF EXPERTISE EXIST?

Although we do not know much about how children develop scientific literacy and expertise in everyday settings, we do know something about the consequences of such development. Chi and Koeske (1983) described a 5-year-old dinosaur expert who, through repeated reading of dinosaur books with his mother, had developed a well-organized semantic network of dinosaur knowledge that enabled him to categorize and recall novel dinosaurs more accurately when they were related in meaningful ways to his prior knowledge. Similarly, Chi's (1978) earlier work demonstrated that children skilled in chess were better able to recall configurations of chess pieces than a group of college students who were chess novices. Chi's work focused primarily on exploring the role of content knowledge in the development of memory, and findings were interpreted to support the conclusion that the content and organization of children's knowledge played a much larger role in the development of memory than any age-related changes in architectural parameters such as working memory capacity or processing speed.

Despite the fact that Chi's work has now become a familiar staple of textbook chapters on memory development, the field lost interest in what seems to us to be the obvious next set of questions: How did these children become experts? How did they get interested in these domains? What kinds of activities did they engage in? What role did their parents play? Is there anything we could do to facilitate the development of early expertise more generally?

Current approaches to children's development of early theories have often described children as intuitive scientists who instinctively collect evidence and construct theories as they learn about the world (Wellman & Gelman, 1998). A great deal of research has focused on describing the contents and structure of children's theories at different ages. One of the common ways that researchers have assessed children's theories is to present children with a novel instance and to describe the way that children come to identify, understand, and connect that knowledge to their existing theories. Less attention has been paid to the ways that this process occurs in everyday environments and the ways parents might assist children in developing theories.

However, the studies that do exist suggest that spontaneous dialogue between parents and children might provide useful information for building theories, among other things (e.g., Callanan & Oakes, 1992; Crowley, Callanan, Jipson, et al., 2001; Ochs, Taylor, Rudolph, & Smith, 1992). For example, Callanan and Oakes (1992) asked parents to write summaries of parent–child conversations that occurred in response to children's questions about "why things happen" and "how things work." They found that preschool children asked meaningful questions to get information about phenomena they were curious about. Parents provided frequent causal explanations in response to children's questions accounting for a large part of the conversational turns between children and parents (32% with 3-year-olds, 61% with 4-year-olds, 54% with 5-year-olds). These parent–child conversations took place mostly at home during everyday mundane activities such as bathtime, meals, reading, or watching television. They also occurred while riding in the car and to a smaller degree in other activities outside the home. Children's questions encompassed a wide variety of topics including: natural phenomena, biological phenomena, physcial mechanisms, motiviation/behavior, and cultural conventions.

Similarly, Ochs et al. (1992) recorded dinnertime conversation of families with a 5-year-old child and at least one older sibling. They found family conversation to contain the elements and structure of scholarly discourse—a place to posit and challenge theories about everyday phenomena. Families were engaged in conversation in which family members stated evidence for their theories, challenged interpretations of that evidence, and challenged methods used by actors in everyday activities.

In our work we have been interested in exploring the hypothesis that such conversation, and parent explanation in particular, contributes to building islands of expertise in informal learning.

Our interest in explanation as a mechanism is based on research that focuses on the facilitative effect of explanation on adult and children's problem-solving and conceptual change. Among adults, the presence of spontaneous self-explanation has been associated with greater transfer across domains that range from learning how to program LISP (Pirolli, 1991), to learning statistics (Lovett, 1992), to developing accurate mental models from undergraduate physics textbooks (Chi, Bassok, Lewis, Reimann, & Glaser, 1989). Similarly, the construction of collaborative explanations has been linked with problem solving success among dyads working on scientific reasoning microworlds (Okada & Simon 1997) and practicing scientists conducting cutting-edge molecular biology research (Dunbar, 1995, 2001). A number of particular mechanisms have been proposed to account for the facilitative effect of explanations, including proposals that the act of constructing and understanding explanation allows problem solvers to identify impasses in their knowledge, generate new hypotheses, construct new inferences or generalizations, or restructure existing knowledge bases (Crowley, Shrager, & Sielger, 1997; Van Lehn, Jones, & Chi, 1992).

The facilitative effect of explanation also holds for children, although they are less likely than adults to spontaneously generate explanations in the course of exploration, categorization, or problem solving. Laboratory studies of children's thinking suggest that when adults offer explanations as they demonstrate new problem-solving strategies, children are better able to transfer strategies to novel problems (Brown & Kane, 1988; Crowley & Siegler, 1999). Similarly, when adults provide causal explanations as children construct family-resemblance categories from novel instances, children are more accurate in categorizing subsequent instances (Krascum & Andrews, 1998). If adults do not provide such explanations or at least explicitly prompt the child to generate their own explanations, it is unlikely that children will decide to do so on their own (Goncu & Rogoff, 1998; Siegler, 1995). In each of these studies, the adults were experimenters following a script; however, the findings are consistent with the notion that parents giving spontaneous explanations may help shape what children learn from everyday activity.

What does parent explanation look like in the context of everyday scientific thinking? Consider, for example, the kinds of parent explanation identified in a recent observational study of families using an interactive science exhibit during visits to a children's museum (Crowley, Callanan, Jipson et al., 2001). Families were videotaped during spontaneous, undirected use of a zoetrope—a simple animation device with a series of animation frames inside a cylinder that spins. When children spun the cylinder and looked at the animation through the slots on the side of the cylinder, they saw animation due to the stroboscopic presentation of the individual frames.

In more than one third of parent-child interactions, parents were observed to explain to their children. Examples included talk about causal links within the local context ("The horse looks like it's running backwards because you spun this thing the wrong way"), talk that made a connection between the exhibit and prior knowledge or experience ("This is how cartoons work"), and talk about unobservable principles underlying, for example, the illusion of motion ("Because your mind . . . your eye . . . sees each little picture and each one's different from the other one, but your mind puts it all in a big row").

Notice that none of these examples rises to a level that would be considered sufficient to meet formal philosophical or pedagogical definitions of what it means to offer a sufficient explanation of a phenomena or a device. Furthermore, the parent explanations observed were also more simple and incomplete than other forms of situated, informal explanation that have been described in studies of scientific activity in classrooms and professional settings (e.g., Dunbar, 1995; Glynn, Dult, & Thiele, 1995; Lehrer, Schauble, & Petrosino, 2001; Saner & Schunn, 1999).

Although it is undoubtedly true that parents sometimes offer complete and accurate explanations when engaged in everyday family activity, it may be far more common for parent–child conversation to include what might be considered components of a formal explanation: suggestions of how to encode evidence; highlighting individual causal links; offering simple analogies; and perhaps introducing relevant principles and terminology (Callanan & Jipson, 2001; Callanan & Oakes, 1992; Gelman et al., 1998).

To distinguish them from normative definitions of explanation and richer forms of explanation that are sometimes encountered in studies of on-going classroom or workplace discourse, these fragments of explanatory talk have been called *explanatoids* (Crowley & Galco, 2001). Although brief and incomplete, parent explanatoids are well targeted to a moment of authentic collaborative parent–child activity. We hypothesize that parent explanatoids are powerful because they are offered when relevant evidence is the focus of joint parent–child attention and thus they serve the function of providing children an online structure for parsing, storing, and making inferences about evidence as it is encountered. Although each individual explanatoid might be unlikely to catalyze a fully realized moment of strategy shift, conceptual change, or theory development, the cumulative effect of parent explanatoids over time could be one of the direct mechanisms through which parents and children co-construct scientific thinking in everyday settings.

In a second study of everyday scientific thinking in museums, several hundred families with children from 1 to 8 years old were videotaped while using 18 interactive science exhibits representing a broad range of scientific and technical content, including biology, physics, geology, psychology, engineering, robotics, and computers (Crowley, Callanan, Tenenbaum, & Allen, 2001). Replicating the findings of the Crowley, Callanan, Jipson et al. (2001) study, parents were observed to use explanatoids in about one third of interactions. However, this broader study also revealed a gender difference: Parents were about three times more likely to offer explanations when using exhibits with boys than when using exhibits with girls. This finding suggested that, if parent explanation has any effect on children's learning, boys and girls may be learning different things from at least some kinds of everyday scientific thinking and thus may be developing different knowledge or attitudes about science before they encounter science instruction in elementary school. This possibility in part motivated the rationale for the current study's focus on how parent explanation changes what children learn from everyday scientific thinking, although gender differences are not a focus of the current study.

EXAMINING A MOMENT OF LEARNING: FAMILY CONVERSATIONS ABOUT FOSSILS

We now present a study of parent–child conversation while families examined dinosaur fossils together in the Pittsburgh Children's Museum. The study was designed with two goals. First, we wanted to describe family learning conversations while parents and children examined objects that belong to a common domain of early interest and expertise—dinosaurs. Second, we wanted to test whether different patterns of parent–child conversation were associated with different outcomes in terms of what children could remember about the objects they had just seen. As with the other chapters in this section of the volume, this study examines a learning moment in great detail. But we do not do so because we think anything fundamental will be learned about dinosaurs in the few minutes we happen to get on tape. We do so from the theoretical perspective of such common moments being the raw materials through which grander developments such as islands of expertise are built.

Parents and children were asked to interact with both authentic and replicated fossils as they might normally do during a museum visit. Two researchers set up a table with two sets of dinosaur fossils—a set of five authentic fossils and a set of four fossil replicas. The authentic fossils were an eggshell fragment from the Saltasaurus dinosaur, a toe bone, a rib bone fragment, a piece of coprolite (fossilized feces), and a gastrolith (stones thought to aid digestion). The replicas included the hind claw of a Velociraptor, a footprint of an unknown dinosaur, an Oviraptor egg, and a 7-inch tooth from Giganotosaurus. Alongside each object, researchers put an index card containing information on the identity and age of the fossil and the location where it was discovered.

Twenty-eight families with children from 4 to 12 years old were recruited into the study when they approached the table during a visit to the Pittsburgh Children's Museum. The researchers explained the study to the families and, if the parents and children were interested in participating, obtained informed written consent from the parents. Families then examined both sets of fossils (order of the sets was counterbalanced), taking as much time as they liked. After they had finished with both sets, parents filled out a questionnaire while the experimenter asked children to identify each of the fossils. Sessions lasted approximately 15 minutes for each family and were videotaped.

What One Family Said

We begin with an example interaction to illustrate the kinds of conversational support that parents provided. The following interaction took place between a 4-year-old boy and his mother. On the parent questionnaire the mother rated her son's interest in dinosaurs as 7 on a 7-point scale and rated his current knowledge as 3. She rated her own interest as 6 and knowledge as 4. The mother reported that the family had visited the local natural history museum more than 5 times in the last year and had also visited the local children's museum, the science center, and the zoo 2 to 5 times each. She reported that the family engaged several times a week in watching science-oriented TV, reading books about science, and using computer programs or websites focused on science. Clearly, they were well-practiced in informal science settings.

As the session begins, the pair are sitting at the table; the boy on the left and the mother on the right. In front of them are the replicas; randomly laid out from right are the egg, footprint, tooth, claw, and coprolite. The boy (B) reaches across his mother (M) to pick up the Oviraptor egg at the far end of the table:

B: This looks like this is a egg. [He turns it over a few times in his hands.]

M: Ok well this . . . [M picks up the card and glances at the label. She is using a "teachy" tone that suggests that the boy is probably wrong and she is going to correct him and inform him what the object actually is.][1]

M: That's exactly what it is! [She appears surprised, speaking quickly in a more natural and rising tone of voice while turning to the child and patting him on the arm] How did you know?

B: Because it looks like it. [He is smiling and appears pleased.]

M: That's what it says, see look *egg, egg* . . . [pointing to the word "egg" on the card each time she says it and annunciating the way parents do when they are teaching children to read] . . . Replica of a dinosaur *egg*. From the oviraptor.

M: [Turns gaze away from the card towards her child, putting her hand on his shoulder and dipping her head so their faces are closer.] Do you have a . . . You have an oviraptor on your game! You know the egg game on your computer? [M makes several gestures similar to the hunt-and-peck typing that a child might do on a computer keyboard.] That's what it is, an oviraptor.

M: [Turns back to the card and points to text on the card. She again starts speaking in her "teacher" voice.] And that's from the Cretaceous period. [pause] And that was a really, really long time ago.

M: And this is . . . all the way from Mongolia which is way, way, way far away. [Her intonation drops on "away" and she puts the card back in its place on the table, signaling that they are done examining the egg.]

M: [Turning away from the table and looks for her other, younger child who has been playing nearby.] Noah, come back! [She begins getting up to chase the sibling while B puts the egg back in its place on the table.]

M: [Pats the footprint, which is next to the egg, while she stands] And this one, see if you can tell . . . [She pats the footprint again] Look at that one, and tell me what you think. [She runs off-camera after the sibling.]

B: [Picks up the footprint, turns himself half-way away from the table, and starts examining it with a puzzled expression.]

The first thing to notice about the interaction is how the family oscillates between more formal to less formal learning talk. The boy established the agenda by choosing the egg as the first object to examine. It was the fossil farthest away from him, and he had to lean over past his mother to pick it up. He may have been interested in looking at it first because he already thought he knew that it was an egg. His mother's response suggested that she thought he was probably wrong and she began reading to correct him. When she discovered that the boy had been correct, she changes immedi-

[1]For the purposes of this chapter, we have added our interpretive comments into the transcript that were not part of the original transcripts used for coding in the larger study.

ately from her "teacher" voice into a more excited and proud-sounding parent voice, implicitly praising the boy and asking how he knew what the object was.

Three more times in this segment, and throughout the subsequent interaction, the mother goes back and forth between these formal and informal voices. She often marked the transition to formal by turning her face and body toward the table and gesturing toward the fossils and information cards. She marked the transition to informal by turning toward the child, touching him, and hunching over a bit so that their eyes are on a more equal plane. As she asked the boy about his computer game at home, her gestured tapping of an imaginary keyboard occurred away from the table and in the space between her and the boy—offering a physical reinforcement of the connection she was trying to establish between this moment and their prior family learning history.

Another thing to notice is that the mother makes choices about what she highlights for the child. Here is the text that appeared on the information card that accompanied the fossil:

- Replica of a Dinosaur Egg
- From the Oviraptor
- Cretaceous Preriod
- Approximately 65 to 135 million years ago
- The actual fossil, of which this is a replica, was found in the Gobi desert of Mongolia

The mother voiced the words "oviraptor," "egg," and "cretaceous," but paused when she came to "65 to 135 million years ago" and substituted the text "long, long time ago." Similarly, she mentioned "Mongolia," but not "Gobi desert." We are in no position to interpret why she decided to mention some but not all of the card information, however it does serve as a reminder of how parent participation mediates the child's experience—in this case the mother is acting as an online filter for the information available from the exhibit.

Finally, and most importantly with respect to the idea of islands of expertise, the mother makes an explicit connection between the exhibit and the boy's prior learning experience with his computer game which is apparently about different dinosaurs and their eggs.

When the mother returns from chasing the younger sibling, the boy looks up at her:

B: Know what this is? Looks like a footprint.

M: That's exactly what that is! This is a footprint from a dinosaur—we don't know what kind of dinosaur—from the early Jurassic period. Just like, what dinosaur is from the Jurassic period? From your game? Was it the T. Rex? (pause) I think so. Remember I told you there's a movie called Jurassic Park and that's from 200 million years ago. And it comes from. a dinosaur . . . that can be found where we live in North America. There used to be dinosaurs here. And in Europe and in Africa. Okay? And that's the footprint. Okay?

Once again, the mother mixes references to their prior learning conversations—in this case a reference to the movie *Jurassic Park.* This reference is actually something of a stretch with the only connection being that the footprint came from a Jurassic-era dinosaur, with the mother spinning that association back again into one of the child's games. The mother also filters the card information into the statement that dinosaurs used to live where "we live in North America" and then extends that into a list that includes Europe and Africa. And so it goes through several more replica fossils:

M: And this is . . . the hind claw. What's a hind claw? (pause) A claw from the back leg from a velociraptor. And you know what . . .
B: Hey! Hey! A velociraptor! I had that one my [inaudible] dinosaur.
M: I know, I know and that was the little one. And remember they have those, remember in your book, it said something about the claws . . .
B: No, I know, they, they . . .
M: Your dinosaur book, what they use them . . .
B: have so great claws so they can eat and kill . . .
M: they use their claws to cut open their prey, right.
B: Yeah.
M: So that's what that is. And that's from the Cretaceous period. That's a really hard word.
B: Cretaceous period.
M: Good. And that's 80 million (emphasis) years ago which is a really very long time and . . . The real one—this is a copy—but the real one comes from this country which means this dinosaur was in our country.
B: I'm not even afraid of dinosaurs.
M: You shouldn't be because there aren't any.
M: This was . . . we talked about. Aha—this is funny. The dinosaur's name was giganotosaurus . . . Do you think he was really big? Giganotosaurus.

After finishing the replicas, the mother and boy turn to the set of authentic fossils. This time the mother takes the lead, picking up the rib bone fragment:

M: This is a real dinosaur rib bone. Where are your ribs? Where are your ribs? No that's your wrist. Very close.

B: Oh, yeah, right here.

M: Yeah, that's right. Here. Protecting your heart . . . and your lungs. And this was one from a dinosaur from the Jurassic period, also found from our country. In a place called Utah.

M: And this one . . . [M picks up the coprolite] Oh! You're not . . . guess what that is. Look at it and guess what that is.

B: Um, what?

M: Guess. What's it look like?

B: His gum? What? Mom!

M: It's dinosaur poop.

B: Ooooo (laughs)

M: That's real dinosaur poop.

B: I touched it! (laughs)

M: It's so old that it doesn't smell anymore. It turned to rock. It's not mushy like poop. It's like a rock. And that's from the Cretaceous period but we don't know what dinosaur made it. And this was also found in our country in Colorado. I think that's pretty funny.

B: What's this?

M: So this one . . . Oh, that's called . . . that's a stone that dinosaurs . . . remember in your animal book it says something about how sometimes chickens eat stones to help them digest—it helps them mush up their food in their tummy?

B: Yeah.

M: Well, dinosaurs ate stones to mush up their food in their tummy and this was one of the stones that they ate. They're so big, that to them this was a little stone. Right? And that also comes from Colorado.

By now the Boy and his Mother have established a rhythm—he points to a fossil, she tells him what it is, he comments on it, she establishes a link between some aspect of the fossil and the boy's experience, and she provides some information about the geologic time period and where the fossil comes from. The connections for these three fossils have been to the boys own anatomy, to joking references to the smell and texture of feces (the coprolite never failed to delight children and their parents in this way because, except for the fact that it was fossilized, it looked just like what it was), and to a book the boy has that apparently describes chickens and gastrolithes. They finish up with the toe and egg shell fragment:

B: How about this?

M: This one, that's his toe.

B: Toe? (in disbelief)

M: Also from the United States. Utah. And that was one of his toes. Imagine there were probably . . . you know . . . 3 of them, maybe.

B: That looks like it not [inaudible]and that was like this. (pause) And that was up like this (makes silly noises)

M: That's from the Jurassic period.

B: Oh! (yelling and silly) another Jurassic period.

M: They're all from Jurassic and Cretaceous, right?

M: Oh, here's another one we missed. Oh. This is . . . a piece of an egg of a dinosaur from a Saltosaurus dinosaur. I wonder why he was called Saltosaurus. Maybe he was salty.

B: (laughs)

M: This was part of the egg.

B: Well maybe when, where he lived . . . [inaudible]

M: Maybe, maybe. And this is also from South America.

The conversation about the last two fossils is the first place where the mother and boy reveal uncertainty about the fossils. They wonder about the toes ("there were probably . . . you know . . . three of them, maybe) and they pose half-serious hypotheses about why one dinosaur was named Saltosaurus. As they finish this set of fossils, the interviewer moves in to administer the posttest to the boy while the mother fills out the parent questionnaire.

What Parents Said and Children Learned

We now present a quantitative description of what parents in general talked about and what children remembered from the experience. To describe what parents talked about, family conversations while examining the fossils were transcribed from videotape and coded with a line-by-line scheme intended to identify the function of utterances. As shown in Table 10.1, we coded eight different categories of mediation. The first two codes (object label and other ID card information) were for talk where parents provided children details available from the index cards that accompanied each fossil. The next two codes, observable properties and value and authenticity, were for descriptions of the objects' perceptual properties or value. The final group of codes were for four different types of explanations that we encountered in this data set. All coding was conducted by a single rater. Reliabilty, assessed by a second independent rater who re-coded 20% of the transcripts, ranged from 87% to 99% agreement for each category in the coding scheme.

As shown in Table 10.1, the most frequent kind of mediating parent talk was labeling the objects, followed by parents mentioning other information from the identification card that accompanied each fossil. (Families saw a total of nine objects, so the average of 18.2 instances of parents labeling objects works out to parents labeling each object an average of

TABLE 10.1
Coding Categories and Mean Frequencies for Parent Fossil Talk

Coding Category	*Definition*	*Mean Number of Utterances Coded*
Object label	Parent identifies the object, either with a technical term (e.g., "This is coprolite.") or with an everyday equivalent (e.g., "This is fossilized dino poop.")	18.2
Other Identification card information	Parent reads information other than the label of the fossil from the fossil's data sheet concerning where the fossil was found, how old the fossils is thought to be, etc.	7.8
Observable properties	Parent talks about physical properties of the object (e.g., "See these little bumps?"; "It's heavy, isn't it?"; "See this long, pointy thing?").	5.5
Value and authenticity	Parent talks about whether the object is real or replicated or talks about how rare, special, or valuable the object is.	2.4
Explanation		
Compare anatomy	Parent compares the fossil to an analog in human anatomy, most often the child's own (e.g., "See, dinosaurs had ribs just like you do.")	1.5
Connect experience	Parent connects the experience to a previous family experience or to shared prior knowledge (e.g., "Remember when we saw one of these in your book?" or "We went there last year for vacation!", after the parent had read to the child that a fossil was dug up in Colorado.)	1.5
Infer scale	Parent makes an inference about the size of dinosaurs based on the size of the object (e.g., "This dinosaur was probably only as big as a dog.")	2.3
Infer function	Parent makes an inference about the function of the object, based on its properties (e.g., "This was probably used to kill its prey.")	3.1
Total Explanation		8.4
Total Mediation		42.3

two times.) Explanations were quite common, with an average of almost one explanation per object. Among the four kinds of explanation, inferences about function were the most common, followed by inferences about scale and connection to experience and anatomy. Finally, parents described physical properties for about half of the objects and made a few comments about value and authenticity.

What effect did these different kinds of parent mediation have on children's learning? Recall that, at the end of the session, children were asked by the experimenter to identify each of the nine fossils. To determine whether success in identifying fossils was associated with different levels of each kind of mediation, we conducted four ANOVAs on children's recall scores with level of mediation (high vs. low) and child's age group (older [7 to 12 yrs. old] vs. younger [4 to 6 yrs. old]) as between subject factors. The four ANOVAs explored the effect of talk related to the identification cards (labeling and other card information combined); the effect of explanatory talk; the effect of talk about fossil properties; and the effect of talk about value and authenticity. For each analysis children were grouped into high or low mediation categories through a median split on the number of coded instances of each kind of parent mediation. Table 10.2 shows the mean number of fossils children could correctly identify, broken down by age of child and whether parents provided high or low levels of mediation. The table also shows the F and p values for the two main effects and the interaction in each test.

The first thing to notice about Table 10.2 are the significant main effects for age on identification scores in each of the four ANOVAs. Thus, unlike younger children, older children found the task of correctly identifying the nine fossils fairly easy regardless of whether their parents provided higher levels of mediation. The one exception to this was for whether parents provided explanations, where older children who heard more explanatory talk had perfect identification scores vs. the 85% for children who heard less.

The second thing to notice is that younger children generally could identify only half of the objects if their parents provided lower levels of mediation while with higher levels they could identify objects at rates comparable to the older children. This difference is picked up by the interactions for age and mediation level for card information and fossil properties and the main effect of mediation for explanation. Although the difference was in the same direction for value and authenticity, the effect was not significant.

The findings so far support the idea that higher levels of mediating talk by parents was associated with children learning to identify more fossils, particularly for the younger children who jumped from about half correct to more than 84% correct when parents provided more mediation. However, as one can see by reading through the example of the mother and son we presented earlier, different kinds of mediation often occur within the same conversation. We might expect, for example, that a parent who talks often about information from the card might also be a parent who explains often. If that were the case, which kind of mediation might be most directly associated with greater identification scores?

To answer this question we used a step-wise regression, allowing us to identify the variables that accounted for the largest amount of variance in the identification scores. Because the older children's scores were close to ceiling, and thus had little variance, we ran the analysis only on the younger group.

TABLE 10.2
Percent Correct Fossil Identification by High or Low Parent Mediation and Age Group

	Younger (4 to 6 Years Old)		*Older (7 to 12 Years Old)*				
	Low Mediation	*High Mediation*	*Low Mediation*	*High Mediation*	*F(1, 24) Parent Mediation*	*F(1, 24) Age Group*	*F(1, 24) Interaction*
Identification card information	49	86	94	89	3.57	8.16**	6.04*
Explanations	51	84	85	100	8.57**	9.10**	1.29
Observable properties	57	90	93	91	3.39	4.47*	4.60*
Value and authenticity	58	85	91	93	2.62	5.22*	1.78

$*p < .05$, $**p < .01$.

The step-wise regression included 10 variables as potential predictors of children's fossil identification scores. Among the potential predictors were the numbers of coded instances of each of the eight types of mediation that appeared in Table 10.1. We also included two additional variables as potential predictors. Under the logic that parents might offer more elaborate forms of mediation if dinosaurs were already a developing island of expertise for the family, we also included parents ratings of their children's knowledge about and interest in dinosaurs, and parent ratings of their own knowledge about and interest in dinosaurs. Both of these measures were computed from items on the questionnaire that parents completed while their children participated in the posttest with the experimenter. The first-order correlations among all variables in the regression are presented in Table 10.3.

The step-wise regression revealed that object label and connections to prior knowledge were the only significant predictors of the younger children's identification scores. Object label entered in the first step of the regression, accounting for 31% of the variance. This makes sense since children would have been more likely to be able to identify fossils correctly if their parents had labeled them correctly in the first place. What was more interesting was that the next and last variable to enter was the extent to which parents made connections to prior knowledge, accounting for 51% of the variance. Thus, even after accounting for the effect of whether parents had provided children with labels for the fossils, the extent to which parents offered explanations that linked back to prior experience with dinosaurs was associated with higher levels of fossil identification during the posttest. After the effects of labeling and connections to prior knowledge had been accounted for, no other variable accounted for significant variance. The final regression equation was: Correct fossil identification = 2.97 + .56 Identify fossil + .45 Connections to prior knowledge, $F(2, 14) = 7.35$, $p < .01$.

CONCLUSION

Does the mediation parents provide to children in the course of spontaneous conversation make a difference in children's learning? Our findings suggest that it might, particularly when the task is difficult for children. Among the 4- to 6-year-olds in our study, higher levels of parent mediation while examining dinosaur fossils were associated with children identifying more of the fossils on the posttest. The regression suggests that the most important forms of mediation were offering labels and providing explanations that connect back to shared family learning history. Although the older children's responses were close to ceiling and there were no significant effects for most categories of mediation, the one significant effect we

TABLE 10.3
Correlations Between Variables in the Regression Analysis for Families With 4- to 6-Year-Olds

	Fossil Identification Score	*Object Label*	*Other Identification Card Information*	*Observable Properties*	*Compare Anatomy*	*Connect Experience*	*Infer Scale*	*Infer Function*	*Value and Authenticity*	*Child Knowledge/ Interest*	*Parent Knowledge/ Interest*
Fossil identification score	1.00										
Object label	.56*	1.00									
Other identification card information	.44*	.10	1.00								
Observable properties	.54*	.67**	.05	1.00							
Compare anatomy	.38	.50*	.53*	.20	1.00						
Connect experience	.50*	.09	.66**	.16	.42*	1.00					
Infer scale	.22	.05	.54*	–.10	.21	.50*	1.00				
Infer function	.35	.69**	.08	.43*	.69**	.38	–.00	1.00			
Value and authenticity	.36	.19	.48*	.39	.43*	.41*	–.06	.17	1.00		
Child knowledge/ interest	–.01	.03	.29	–.30	.33	.18	.29	.27	–.26	1.00	
Parent knowledge/ interest	.14	.28	.10	.04	.46*	.18	.34	.56**	–.37	.58**	1.00

$^*p < .05$, $^{**}p < .01$.

did observe was consistent with the idea that explanations are associated with greater learning during family museum activity. However, it is important to note that, as with many studies that examine correlations between spontaneous behavior in naturalistic settings, the current findings are consistent with a causal link between parent mediation and children's learning, but they do not, in and of themselves, conclusively support one.

Take a moment to consider the patterns illustrated by the quantitative analyses in relation to the example interaction of the mother and the boy. Among the most frequent kind of parent mediation we coded in the larger study were labeling the fossils and talking about other information from the index cards that accompanied the fossils. As the example of the mother and boy illustrated, these kinds of mediation were important parts of the rhythm the family established as they worked their way through the sets of objects. The mother often used questions about identity of the object as a signal that the pair was moving on to the next object. After the child guessed or the mother told what the object was, she often moved next to provide a few supporting details from the index card while the child continued to handle the object. While she provides such information, the boy can be observed on the videotape turning the objects slowly, sometimes moving them up and down to feel their heft, and, in the case of the velociraptor claw, slashing at imaginary beasts.

Many times we observed that parents stopped with this kind of information and moved on to the next object. However, the boy and his mother often went the next step to engaging in explanatory talk, including talk that connected objects to previous learning experiences—books, movies, and computer games that they had already played. We do not have any good objective measure of exactly how much this pair knew about dinosaurs, but both the content of their interaction and the mother's self-report on the questionnaire suggest that they were already well into building an island of expertise around the topic. Their interaction and the quantitative analyses are consistent with our original claim that much of a child's early domain-specific expertise may be forged from relatively mundane moments where parents and children label, link, and learn through collaborative activity and conversation.

The current study also suggests something about the unique role of museums in building islands of expertise. Although the child and parent may have spent many hours reading about dinosaurs in a book, it is only in the museum that they can attach this knowledge to the authentic objects. Thus, conversations in museums are infrequent events compared to other learning opportunities. We propose that the learning conversation in the museum, precisely because it is rare and thus fairly memorable, may become a particularly powerful example on which further learning can be built. Not in the sense that the child or parent would recall the experience more or less exactly and operate on it to extract new information, but that the general gloss of the situation could be recalled and connected in much the way that the mother did in the story about trains that opened this chapter. It would be much harder to identify an experience that was more common, because there have been many that may need to be distinguished. In other words, the location of the museum "marks" the conversation. Conversations that occur in unmarked spaces, such as around the dinner table, may often be harder to index and recall in joint ways in conversations. A bit of talk that struck someone as particularly meaningful may not strike the other participants that way. When an opportunity to extend children's interest presents itself, and a parent tries to locate an example to build a connective link, it strikes us as somewhat hard to do so by saying, "Remember that one time at dinner when we talked about the T-Rex?" compared to saying "Remember that time at the museum when we talked about the T-Rex?"

Young children are sometimes described as intuitive scientific thinkers with an instinct for seeking out evidence, noticing patterns, drawing conclusions, and building theories. Yet, although children may engage naturally in collecting and organizing evidence in everyday settings, they do so in ways that are not necessarily consistent with formal definitions of good scientific thinking (Kuhn, 1989). As Klahr (2000) pointed out, there is something of developmental paradox here: Despite the fact young children are not systematic, exhaustive, or focused when collecting evidence, they nonetheless appear to do a good job building theories about everyday domains. In this chapter we have advanced the hypothesis that, through joint activity, guided by a combination of children's and parents' interests, families can build deep, shared domain-specific knowledge bases, which we refer to as islands of expertise. As families move across contexts, between the backyard and the museum, between car rides and book reading, between the dinner table and the computer, they trace these interests, looking for opportunities to collect and connect new experiences. These islands can become platforms on which to build advanced conversations about disciplines such as science. In this chapter we have provided an example of how one family in particular, and other families more generally talk about dinosaur fossils in the context of a museum visit. Future research should pursue how these conversations are connected across context and the specifics of whether these well-marked domains support advanced reasoning.

ACKNOWLEDGMENTS

This research was part of the Museum Learning Collaborative and received additional support from a grant from the National Science Foundation to the first author [ESI-9815021].

Thanks to Erin Guthridge and Erin Tully for help with data collection and coding; to Jane Werner, Chris Seifert, and Lois Winslow from Pittsburgh Children's Museum; and, of course, to the families who were kind enough to participate in the research.

REFERENCES

Brown, A. L., & Kane, M. J. (1988). Preschool children can learn to transfer: Learning to learn and learning from example. *Cognitive Psychology, 20,* 493–523.

Callanan, M. A., & Jipson, J. L. (2001). Explanatory conversations and young children's developing scientific literacy. In K. Crowley, C. D. Schunn, & T. Okada (Eds.), *Designing for science: Implications from everyday, classroom, and professional science.* Mahwah, NJ: Lawrence Erlbaum Associates.

Callanan, M. A., & Oakes, L. M (1992). Preschoolers' questions and parents' explanations: Causal thinking in everyday activity. *Cognitive Development, 7,* 213–233.

Chi, M. T. H. (1978). Knowledge structures and memory development. In R. S. Siegler (Ed.), *Children's thinking: What develops?* Hillsdale, NJ: Lawrence Erlbaum Associates.

Chi, M. T. H., Bassok, M., Lewis, M. L., Reimann, P., & Glaser, R. (1989). Self-explanations: How students study and use examples in learning to solve problems. *Cognitive Science, 13,* 145–182.

Chi, M. T., & Koeske, R. D. (1983). Network representation of a child's dinosaur knowledge. *Developmental Psychology, 19,* 29–39.

Crowley, K., & Galco, J. (2001). Everyday activity and the development of scientific thinking. In K. Crowley, C. D. Schunn, & T. Okada (Eds.), *Designing for science: Implications from everyday, classroom, and professional science.* Mahwah, NJ: Lawrence Erlbaum Associates.

Crowley, K., Callanan, M. A., Jipson, J., Galco, J., Topping, K., & Shrager, J. (2001). Shared scientific thinking in everyday parent-child activity. *Science Education, 85*(6), 712–732.

Crowley, K., Callanan, M. A., Tenenbaum, H. R., & Allen, E. (2001). Parents explain more often to boys than to girls during shared scientific thinking. *Psychological Science, 12*(3), 258–261.

Crowley, K., Shrager, J., & Siegler, R. S. (1997). Strategy discovery as a competitive negotiation between metacognitive and associative knowledge. *Developmental Review, 17,* 462–489.

Crowley, K., & Siegler, R. S. (1999). Explanation and generalization in young children's strategy learning. *Child Development, 70,* 304–316.

Dunbar, K. (1995). How scientists really reason: Scientific reasoning in real-world laboratories. In R. J. Sternberg & J. E. Davidson (Eds.), *The nature of insight.* Cambridge: MIT Press.

Dunbar, K. (2001). What scientific thinking reveals about the nature of cognition. In K. Crowley, C. D. Schunn, & T. Okada (Eds.), *Designing for science: Implications from everyday, classroom, and professional science.* Mahwah, NJ: Lawrence Erlbaum Associates.

Gelman, S. A., Coley, J. D., Rosengren, K. S., Hartman, E., & Pappas, A. (1998). Beyond labeling: The role of maternal input in the acquisition of richly structured categories. *Monographs of the Society for Research in Child Development,* 63.

Glynn, S. M., Dult, R., & Thiele, R. B. (1995). Teaching science with analogies: A strategy for constructing knowledge. In S. M. Glynn & R. Dult (Eds.), *Learning science in the schools: Research reforming practice* (pp. 247–273). Mahwah, NJ: Lawrence Erlbaum Associates.

Goncu, A., & Rogoff, B. (1998). Children's categorization with varying adult support. *American Educational Research Journal, 35,* 333–349.

Hayes, J. R. (1985). Three problems in teaching general skills. In S. Chipman, J. W. Segal, & R. Glaser (Eds.), *Thinking and learning skills, Vol. 2* (pp. 391–406). Hillsdale, NJ: Lawrence Erlbaum Associates.

Keil, F. C. (1998). Words, moms, and things: Language as a road map to reality. *Monographs of the Society for Research in Child Development, 63*(1), 149–157.

Klahr, D. (2000). *Exploring science: The cognition and development of discovery processes.* Cambridge, MA: MIT Press.

Krascum, R. M., & Andrews, S. (1998). The effects of theories on children's acquisition of family-resemblance categories. *Child Development, 69*(2), 333–346.

Lehrer, R., Schauble, L., & Petrosino, T. A. (2001). Reconsider the role of experiment in science education. In K. Crowley, C. D. Schunn, & T. Okada (Eds.), *Designing for science: Implications from everyday, classroom, and professional settings.* Mahwah, NJ: Lawrence Erlbaum Associates.

Lovett, M. C. (1992). Learning by problem solving versus by examples: The benefits of generating and receiving information. *Proceedings of the 14th Annual Conference of the Cognitive Science Society* (pp. 956–961). Hillsdale, NJ: Lawrence Erlbaum Associates.

Ochs, E., Taylor, C., Rudolph, D., & Smith, R. (1992). Storytelling as a theory-building activity. *Discourse Processes, 15,* 37–72.

Okada, T., & Simon, H. A. (1997). Collaborative discovery in a scientific domain. *Cognitive Science, 21*(2), 109–146.

Pirolli, P. (1991). Effects of examples and their explanations in a lesson on recursion: A production system analysis. *Cognition and Instruction, 8*(3), 207–259.

Saner, L., & Schunn, C. D. (1999). Analogies out of the blue: When history seems to retell itself. In the *Proceedings of the 21st Annual Conference of the Cognitive Science Society.* Mahwah, NJ: Lawrence Erlbaum Associates.

Siegler, R. S. (1995). How does cognitive change occur: A microgenetic study of number conservation. *Cognitive Psychology, 25,* 225–273.

VanLehn, K., Jones, R. M., & Chi, M. T. H. (1992). A model of the self-explanation effect. *Journal of the Learning Sciences, 2,* 1–59.

Wellman, H. M., & Gelman, S. A. (1998). Knowledge acquisition in foundational domains. In D. Kuhn & R. S. Siegler (Eds.), *Handbook of child psychology: Cognition, Perception, & Language.* New York: Wiley.

Chapter 11

Negotiations of Thematic Conversations About Biology

Doris Ash
University of California, Santa Cruz

This chapter is one of many studies in this text "that puts conversation . . . at the core of museum learning" (Leinhardt & Crowley, 1998, p. 1). My theoretical framework fits well with the organizing principles of the Museum Learning Collaborative, as it relies on the work of Vygotsky (1978), Wertsch (1998), and Wells (1999) as underpinnings for a sociocultural perspective of learning in informal environments.

In this chapter, I have two goals in mind. The first goal is to describe how families talk about and make sense of biological themes at museums. The family, and their interactions with exhibits, are the unit of analysis, and the focus of the analysis is the negotiation of thematic biological conversation, for example, dialogue reflecting the principle of adaptation. I emphasize the complex interplay between thematic content and social negotiation in terms of identifiable significant conversational events (SEs).

Significant events are characterized by distributed expertise, that is, knowledge that is expected to differ and to be distributed among members of a social group (Brown, Ash, Rutherford, Nakagawa, Gordon, & Campione, 1993), and that is negotiated within a zone of proximal development which includes exhibit, individual family members and the family's intellectual, social and cultural background. The zone of proximal development (ZPD) is defined as the "region of activity that learners can navigate with aid from a supporting context, including but not limited to people" (Brown et al., 1993, p. 191; see also Vygotsky, 1978).

The work of the Fostering a Community of Learners (FCL) project (Brown, 1992; Brown & Campione, 1994, 1996) provides a set of underlying design principles that inform this museum research. Other museum family learning research, described in various chapters of this book, supports this view (e.g., the complexity of parent–child scientific reasoning interactions or the role of explanation).

My second and more global goal is to better understand how to apply this theoretical framework to a larger class of research in informal learning settings, a class of work that, to date, has a less elaborated theoretical basis than classroom learning research (Paris & Ash, in press). By providing an underlying theoretical framework for designing research and for analyzing results in informal settings, and by creating a common set of design principles, this new research allows for a comprehensive examination of both classrooms and museums as places where learners actively participate, share expertise, and negotiate meaning. In making conversations a central feature of museum research and by applying a theoretical frame that focuses on the zone of proximal development as a working principle, the larger discipline that has been defined as visitor studies, visitor evaluation or research on visitor learning can be both informed and unified. This current study, then, extends the scope of applying sociocultural theory to family learning in museum settings, and this extension of the application of the theory, in turn, informs learning theory across additional contexts. By translating FCL principles to new contexts, this study extends the scope of applying Vygotskian theory to practice, but it also informs the fundamental design principles as they are altered to fit the practical outcomes of new settings.

Sociocultural theory in general "foregrounds how people's thinking changes as they make meaning of their experiences" (Leinhardt & Crowley, 1998, p. 3), yet would posit that discourse is but one of many semiotic tools of meaning-making, which also include gestures, reading, writing, and drawing, among others. This work relies in part on research from the 1990s that strengthens the notion of collaborative communities of discourse where participants talk, do, reflect, and learn about powerful disciplinary principles, particularly Brown and Campione (1994, 1996) and Rogoff (1995). It acts as a bridge across learning settings, by using consistent design principles (Brown, 1992) to view both classrooms and museums as places where learners do science when they talk science (Lemke, 1990).

THEORETICAL UNDERPINNINGS

The Zone of Proximal Development

Vygotsky's (1978) notion of the zone of proximal development (ZPD) is the theoretical foundation of this work. In FCL classrooms

> ... theoretically we conceive of the community as composed of multiple zones of proximal development (Vygotsky, 1978) through which participants can navigate via different routes at different rates (Brown & Reeve, 1987). A zone of proximal development is a learning region that learners can navigate with aid from a supporting context ... [and] defines the distance between current levels of comprehension and levels that can be accomplished in collaboration with other people or powerful artifacts. The zone of proximal development embodies a concept of readiness to learn that emphasizes upper levels of competence. These boundaries are seen not as immutable, but as constantly changing with the learners' increasing independent competence at each successive level. (Brown, Ellery, & Campione, 1998, p. 12)

In this research, as in FCL classrooms, family conversations are viewed as occurring within multiple overlapping ZPDs, which are established between individuals and between individuals and exhibits, and which provide significant opportunities for meaning-making. Because learners with different kinds of distributed expertise can navigate to new levels of understanding using each other and exhibit materials as supports, there can be multiple routes toward meaning-making among family members within any exhibit or groups of exhibits. Similarly, in FCL classrooms life science was a research focus precisely because it allowed children to use their emergent theories about biology, such as functional reasoning (e.g., sharp teeth are for cutting, long legs are for running) to move toward forming deeper principles, such as adaptation (Ash, 1995, Ash & Brown, 1996).

In adapting Vygotskian theory from an FCL setting to museum settings, I assume that within the zone of proximal development:

1. Family members decide what is worth talking about, including life science interests/themes of the family members individually or collectively;
2. the exhibit itself contributes to the interaction (including interactive tools, signs accompanying the exhibit; and other thematic and factual content materials;
3. interaction with other visitors, explainers or other forms of information can act as scaffolds;[1] and
4. together, all these factors help create the words, ideas and actions that are offered for conversation with others.

---

[1]The gradual shift of responsibility from teacher to learner is a complex one that is at once natural and carefully designed. At first, the teacher/parent/exhibit/docent is directive, acting as a guide until students demonstrate their own abilities to work independently. In a process often referred to as "scaffolding," the teacher gradually fades from control of certain areas as students take on the skills in their own way.

I assume further that, within these overlapping ZPDs, dialogue occurs jointly between family members and the museum exhibits in ongoing, dynamic interactions, so that each can act as a source of support, scaffolding, or mediation. The exhibit, the members of the family, the family negotiation style, and the knowledge they bring to the event can all contribute to the interactions within the ZPD, which include artifacts, books, exhibit labels, computers, audio and video images and text, docent–explainers, as well as children and adults of varying expertise. All are contained within a system of activity that includes the tools and practices of the activity.

Biological Content

It is important to have something of interest to talk about in the family dialogue. In this case both adults and children come to life science conversations with ways of thinking that inform their talk. A growing body of cognitive development research suggests that children's emergent biology has certain systematic and predictable aspects (sometimes called early biology, skeletal principles, constraints, or theories), which include a functionalist or design mode of construal. We know, for example, that even young children use form–function relationships to interpret the living world (Ash, 1995, Ash & Brown, 1996), for example assuming some underlying function when asking parents: "Why does the rhinoceros have that horn?"

Functional reasoning enables a child to look at structures as if they were designed for functional purposes, and to wonder about the design problems they might solve (Keil, 1992). With functional reasoning as a base, children can enter dialogues with a set of expectations and questions about animals, their structures, and how they function[2] (Ash, 1991; Keil, 1992). Such generalizations can lead to larger discussions about adaptation, which can then become thematic areas of interest (cf. "thematic continuities" in Ash, 1995, Ash & Brown, 1996), that can be tracked over time and content. The products of functional reasoning form the platform of knowledge that is later reorganized toward a more mature view of adaptation, a principle central to understanding ecology and evolution.

[2]In other research I have described the initial stages of transition from a functionalist or design perspective (Ash, 1995; Keil, 1992; Springer & Keil, 1988)—the expectation that biological structures have identifiable functions, for example, sharp teeth for tearing—toward a broader adaptionist view—the perspective that modification of living things occurs in order to fit them for their environment (Bates, 1950; Eldredge, 1991; Gould, 1991; Mayr, 1991).

Starts with:

- correlating form to function
  - —for example sharp teeth are good for tearing

Moves toward:

- correlating a variety of structures (and their accompanying functions) with each other.
  - —for example-asserting that sharp teeth are for tearing, sharp eyes for hunting, and long legs for running, are correlated with each other

Moves toward:

- correlating cohesive sets of characteristics with a constraining environment.
  - —for example, otter fur, paws, lungs, skeletal system, and behaviors all combine to fit a certain type of environment, in this case aquatic

Moves toward:

- increasing need to know/understand how adaptations arise and how they are passed on from generation to generation and how they are selected within each generation.
  - —for example, understanding natural selection as a mechanism that is based on existing variation in a population. generates a constant source of variation in populations
  - —need to understand genetic mechanisms
  - —compare above with Divine Order, Lamarckism, or teleological thinking

FIG. 11.1. Steps toward the mature adaptationist stance.

Thematic continuities can act both as generative entry points into deeper learning of core biological principles, and as common threads that link discourse across exposures to scientific information and over time (Ash, 1995, 2000; Ash & Brown, 1996). These larger thematic areas in the sciences, such as adaptation, traits of life, and survival strategies of living things, form content areas for family conversations in museums, and thus are focal points for conversational analysis in this research (Ash & Brown, 1996). These early themes can lead to understanding of deeper principles in biology such as natural selection, as outlined in Fig. 11.1.

Conversation as Methodology

I adopt a Vygotskian perspective of the social origins of mind, which presupposes that language is a negotiating medium for teaching and learning. Purposefully collaborative family conversations are both process and product, and are set within a larger activity system that has multiple purposes, such as having fun and learning new ideas. Because conversations are co-constructed by all family members, meaning changes constantly, is influenced by what came before either proximally or distally, and changes what comes after. Conversation builds on each person's prior knowledge, as well as the content at particular exhibits. As family conversations progress, meanings change as different members influence its direction. Thus meaning is always jointly situated between the family context (past and present), the exhibit context and the ongoing conversation itself. Similarly, family conversations have different sizes and types of segments, from shorter to longer, personal to impersonal, with different thematic content. Conversations reflect family goals (individual and collective), exhibit goals (individual and collective), and the larger historical–cultural context of the museum. In order to better understand these interactions I have developed a four-part analysis tool, to allow for fine-grained analysis while placing family conversations within a larger context. This tool is described in detail later.

The discourse analysis frame in this research is adapted from Wells (1997, 1999) and from Halliday (1993), who assume that discourse is a semiotic tool that fills two functions simultaneously: Language functions as a link to the world of objects being represented, as it also "encodes the speaker's relation to his or her interlocutors" (Wells, 1999, p. 235). Halliday (1993) suggested that language is how experience becomes knowledge. This view matches Leont'ev's, who called language a tool that "mediates activity and thus connects humans not only with the world of objects but also with other people" (Leont'ev, 1981, p. 55). Vygotsky (1978) expressed this succinctly when he called language "the tool of tools."

Distributed Expertise and Mutual Appropriation

Multigenerational family groups, by their very nature, contain varying levels of expertise about concepts, science processes, cultural and social practices, and language. Distributed expertise assumes meaning-making across different ages, because differential knowledge is expected and honored. Each participant in the interaction holds some part of the knowledge and each shares their piece with others; by this process each participant moves according to their own level within the shared ZPD.

Family members need not have a complete understanding of each other's knowing. In the dynamic interaction between adults and children

> children can participate in an activity that is more complex than they understand, producing "performance before competence. . . . While in the ZPD of the activity, the children's actions get interpreted within the system being constructed by the teacher. . . . Just as the children do not have the full cultural analysis of a tool to begin using it, the teacher does not have to have a complete analysis of the children's understanding."[3] (Newman et al., 1989, pp. 63–64)

[3]In constructing a ZPD for a particular task the teacher (parent) incorporates children's actions into her own system of activity.

If one substitutes the word *parent* for *teacher*, and museum setting for school setting, the same can be said of family learning in informal settings.

I assume the multidirectional appropriation (the taking up, use, translation, or change of the words or ideas of others), borrowing, negotiation, and interpretation of distributed expertise and actions, as each member is free to transform them and to offer them back to the group for further negotiation. The term *mutual appropriation* (Moschkovich, 1989; Newman, Griffin, & Cole, 1989) refers to "the bi-directional nature of the appropriation process, . . . [whereby] learners of all ages and levels of expertise and interests . . . [contribute] ideas and knowledge that are appropriated by different learners at different rates, according to their needs and to the current state of the [ZPDs] in which they are engaged" (Brown et al., 1993, p. 193). This mutual appropriation cuts across barriers of experience, age, and the ability to communicate.

Significant Events

Following this reasoning, then, family talk is analyzed both for the nature of the content and also for the ways in which the speakers interact with each other to produce significant events. Significant events (SEs) are sustained conversational episodes with recognizable beginnings and endings. They are interspersed with shorter events, which precede and follow the SEs (in an unpredictable series) but do not share their features. SEs are characterized as having: biological thematic content, distributed expertise among different age members, a variety of science process skills, such as observing, questioning, or predicting; and as being set within zones of proximal development that include family members, the exhibit, and other mediation means.

In this chapter two significant events (SEs) are selected for detailed analysis, as part of a larger system of activity at an exhibit set around the fundamental biological principles of adaptation and natural selection. Both selected SEs are important in several ways. First, they make explicit certain characteristics of family educational discourse in an informal setting. Second, they allow analysis of both thematic content and mediational styles and the interaction between these two factors. Third, these particular SEs allow insight into the way conversations start, are maintained, and are enhanced or limited by particular mediational means. Fourth, they give insight into how conversations are controlled.

Two prior research projects by the author inform this research design. The first project was the "thematic continuities" research in Fostering a Community of Learners (FCL) classrooms, in which children used thematic areas to propel their learning forward as groups and as individuals (Ash, 1995; Ash & Brown, 1996). A second series of studies, set within the context of family visits to life sciences museums, revealed an assortment of content themes; including color and its uses in nature for protection, feeding and its function, camouflage and its relationship to prey protection, taxonomic relationships and life cycles (Ash, 2000; Ash et al., 2000).

Early analysis of the current research has suggested that family members use age-related, domain-specific themes in their conversations. Some examples are given in Fig. 11.2. An in-depth explication of thematic content is in preparation. In addition, concurrent studies using similar methodologies are underway, by the author and colleagues, at life science museum locations across the country, including the Los Angeles County Natural History Museum in California, The Museum of Science and Industry in Tampa, Florida, The Museum of Science in Boston, Massachusetts, and The Monterey Bay Aquarium in California.

METHODOLOGY

Location

The analysis in this chapter is based on research done at the California Academy of Sciences in San Francisco, specifically at the *Life through Time*

Younger children

Feeding:	"It just keeps eating and eating."
Babies:	"They are just trying to protect their babies."

Older children

Color, camouflage:	"The color tells you it is poisonous."
Protection from enemies:	"If you lick him, he is poisonous."

Adults

Taxonomic relationships:	"Is that more like a velociraptor?"
Life cycles:	"See these guys right here. These are called tadpoles and they turn into frogs. Let's see if we can find any with legs yet?"
Anatomy relationships:	"It is a really interesting comparison. If you see the frog anatomy by itself, having the comparison to the human really makes it more interesting."

Prior experiences with science (e.g., dissection)

"In my biology class I dissected my own frogs . . . This brings back fond memories for me . . . Did you dissect frogs? . . . I can still remember the formaldehyde."

FIG. 11.2. Some typical family themes.

exhibit. This was the first phase of a several year study at multiple locations. The analysis scheme used here is being refined and changed with each stage of research in the subsequent work.

The *Life through Time* Gallery represented the sequential story of evolution from the first evidence of life to the present. It consisted of 63 exhibits designed to take visitors 3.5 billion years back through time to discover how plants and animals on earth changed over the millennia. These exhibits encouraged visitors' exposure to large thematic areas in science such as adaptation, survival strategies, and natural selection. The gallery was organized into six chronological content areas—Lines of evidence: Introduction, Early life in the Sea, Transition to Land, Age of Dinosaurs, Age of Mammals, and Lines of Evidence: Summary. It included life-size model dinosaurs, giant insects, a model of a "dig"; and a variety of scenes from the planet's past. Exhibits included a hologram of *T. rex* and tanks with live animals such as the horseshoe crab, as well as a series of realistic dioramas progressing from the earliest life in the oceans, thorough the ages of dinosaurs, to the first mammals. There were also a series of interactive video units spread throughout the gallery.

DATA COLLECTION

Two Grain Sizes: Baseline and In-Depth Analyses

As a predecessor to the more detailed analysis provided in this chapter, several families, visiting this particular exhibit independently, were videotaped, over the course of weeks, as they walked through the exhibit at their own pace and according to their own selection criteria.[4] These visits lasted from approximately 5 to 25 minutes per family. This baseline pilot study helped determine that sufficient thematic material was available for family conversations; that free movement through the exhibits was desirable; that parents with children from ages 1 to 9 tended to talk more often to their children than parents with older children; and that the noise levels needed to be mitigated by audio recording techniques. Analysis of these visits provided a broad overview of the types of phenomena families found interesting, gave a sense for the idiosyncratic nature of visits, and provided a baseline from which to undertake the second, deeper and more detailed phase presented here.

After the baseline phase, three new families were solicited for in-depth visits to the exhibit. They were approached in different ways: two already in mu-

[4]Twenty-two families were observed overall, of these 11 were videotaped as part of the baseline study.

seum settings; one family was acquainted with professional colleagues and agreed to come to the museum. These families were selected on the basis of: appropriate configuration (parents and children aged 1 to 9); availability and interest over time, and willingness to participate in a longitudinal study that included visiting at least three sites; and taking part in several interviews and in stimulated recall sessions (watching themselves on video and reflecting on their thinking and actions).[5] Several different forms of data were gathered, including recorded family conversations at and between exhibits, pre and postvisit family interviews, and written questionnaires.

These families were both videotaped and audiotaped. In the latter case, lavaliere mikes and belt holders were provided for both parents or for one parent and one child. Because children often speak softly and many galleries have loud background noise, video was used primarily for timing; gesture analyses, and for cues only attainable visually. All audiotapes were transcribed. If families split into small groups as part of the visit, both parts were audiotaped. This technique allowed for maximal data collection and minimal interference for families with small children. Families chose their own course through exhibits. Duration of visits was variable[6] and methodological interruptions (change of tapes, etc.) were kept to a minimum, so that families could experience their visit naturally.

ANALYSIS

The Nature of Significant Events

Two significant events, each selected from a different family, are discussed in relation to an analytic frame adapted from Wells (1999) and in relation to the larger context of research on museum learning. Each significant event:

1. Had recognizable beginnings and endings, generally, but not always, centered on one part of a particular exhibit;

2. were sustained conversational segments that differed from short interactions, which can precede and follow SEs. One example of a short interaction is:

Child: What is that called?
Mother: It's a prehistoric tiger; it's called a saber-toothed tiger.
Child: Why is it so big?

---

[5]Stimulated recall interviews are currently underway as are the visits to a third site.
[6]Visits varied in length from 40 minutes to almost 2 hours.

Mother: I'm not sure;

3. illustrated different sources of knowledge, that is, distributed expertise; and

4. illustrated the use of various inquiry strategies, such as questioning, inferring, or predicting.

Four-Part Functional Analysis Frame for Conversations

I analyze SEs using a four-part functional tool, adapted from Wells (1999). Wells proposed an analytic grid of four categories:

exchange (the sequential organization of spoken discourse);
move (of each exchange within the sequence of Initiation, Response, Follow-up, or IRF);
prospectiveness (the ability of an utterance to narrow down or broaden the range of possible responses, such as Demand, Give, and Acknowledgment); and
function (which is the function of the utterance within the discourse sequence).

I have maintained the four-part structure but have radically changed two of Wells' analytic categories in order to address my particular research questions. I do not look closely at the particular arrangement of the discussion, as does Wells. Instead, I focus on thematic content and the mode of mediation of content. My categories thus include:

1. *biological thematic content*;
2. *inquiry skills*, such as questioning, or observing; and, from Wells, the notions of
3. *prospectiveness* (as described by Wells); and
4. *discourse function,* which tracks how a particular utterance affects subsequent utterances.

1. Biological Themes. Children and adults have certain ways of reasoning about the living world. As discussed earlier, these ways of reasoning, especially in relation to adaptation as an underlying principle, can fall into certain larger and predicable thematic areas. In FCL, for example, children expected form to follow function when they asked: "Why does that animal have horns?" (Ash, 1995; Ash & Brown, 1996). In this case, the application of form-function reasoning (Ash, 1995; Keil, 1992) builds the foundation from which children can begin to move toward an adaptationist mindset, a stance that both recognizes and expects complementarity between organisms and their environment. Using functional reasoning as the foundation, children begin to move toward understanding simple themes, such as: *protection from predators*, ways of *feeding and breeding*, or *protection from harsh environmental elements*. In the analysis scheme, each of these is differentiated as a separate thematic area.

*2. **Inquiry Skills.*** As family groups visit a museum and interact with the materials, I note the particular inquiry skill(s) that is (are) actively modeled by parents or used between children in their interactions. The inquiry cycle, which consists of observing, questioning, hypothesizing, predicting, investigating, interpreting, and communicating (Ash, 1999; Ash & Klein, 1999), can occur completely or partially at any exhibit.

*3. **Prospectiveness.*** Analysis of conversation includes identification of the "prospectiveness" (Wells, 1999) of an utterance. *Propectiveness* is Wells' term for the range of possible responses afforded by a particular utterance. Wells divided these into three main categories: Demand, created with questions; Give, created as the answer to a question; and Acknowledgement. Using prospectiveness as a measure is a useful way to determine the potential discourse range of a particular utterance. Here are two very simple examples of this category, from Wells (1999, p. 246).

a. Demand—Give—Acknowledge
   D: Did you hear the forecast today?
   G: They said there'd be snow later.
   A: Ugh.

b. Give—Acknowledge
   G: The forecast says there'll be snow today.
   A: Oh.

As Wells (1999) suggested, and as we can clearly see from these interchanges, "in normal conversations, however, such minimal sequences are the exception rather than the rule" (pp. 246–247). Wells argued that discourse participants "step up the prospectiveness" by changing the nature of the follow-up response, for example by providing another Give or another Demand where an Acknowledgment is expected. "This exploitation of possible follow-up within a sequence" allows a more knowledgeable participant to contribute to the learning of the less knowledgeable in ways which nevertheless incorporate and build on the latter's contribution" (pp. 247–248).

*4. **Discourse Function.*** The discourse function category refers to the role each utterance plays in moving forward the thematic content, the inquiry skill, and the prospectiveness. This was Wells' adaptation of Sinclair and Coulthard's (1975) term. Wells used function to refer to the negotiation functions of a follow-up to a Demand or Give move. These functions can include expand, justify, exemplify, explain, or reformulate a response. Such discourse moves can amplify or "step up" the range of prospectiveness, and can serve as strategies for sustaining conversation beyond the simple I R F (Initiation, Response, Follow-up) structure, a format Lemke (1990) called the triadic dialogue. In the following text I have indicated where the speaker "steps up" the conversation in order to expand the possible outcomes. These step ups are valuable in maintaining conversations and in helping to clarify the participant's intent for the next speaker.

Two Significant Events

I have analyzed two significant events for this chapter. I precede each SE analysis with background material for the family. The visit by Family 1 lasted 68 minutes, within which there were 4 significant events out of 19 discernable events. For Family 2 the total visit lasted 50 minutes, and there were 4 significant events out of a total of 24 discernible events. An event typically centered on a discrete piece of exhibitry. The length of events varied considerably from two short sequential utterances, to many pages of transcription.

Parents in both SEs performed several shorter interactions before the selected SEs. For Family 1 this SE occurred after 7 short events and 1 significant event. For Family 2, the SE came after 9 short events and 1 other significant event for the mother and boy aged 9, and also 9 short events and 1 significant event for father and boy aged 7 (they had split up into dyads and reconvened at this exhibit as a family).

FAMILY 1

Background Information

Three family members, a mother and two children (boy 5, and girl 1½), were thoroughly familiar with museum settings. They were members of many Bay Area museums and visited some museums on a weekly basis. The mother came from a family with a long history of museum going and had herself frequented museums weekly with her parents and siblings. The mother's philosophy was to spend as much time as necessary on any exhibit and to revisit it regularly, while letting the children lead. They knew how to "do museums."

> I used to go to the museum when I was a kid too. She (my mother) said that as a child, she and her girlfriend (also) would take the bus to the museum . . . and we did that every weekend.

> I think it (museum going) is in my history. . . . She (daughter) was practically born here. . . . We come here a lot. We come for lunch and a lot of times, I will just pop in for an hour. A lot of times I will come for the whole day, it just depends. My favorite thing is to come and not have to worry about the time.

Episode

This episode was captured at a diorama designed to suggest that the viewers think about how early (familiar looking, but now extinct) mammalian animals might have looked, hunted in packs, and menaced animals larger than themselves. This was in direct contrast to the large dinosaurs in the preceding halls. This particular exhibit showed a social group of large, prehistoric, flightless birds, surrounded by smaller, more ferocious early mammals. The exhibit's message suggested that animal size is important but that it does not insure success against social groups of predators. It implicitly asked the visitor to think about change over time, an overarching exhibit theme, and to compare and contrast modern and ancient times. It was situated in the Age of Mammals section. It was large (approx. 8′ × 10′), well lit, and situated at an angle so that one could view it from several sides. It was a good example of newer types of dioramas that do not contain glass barriers, and that portray realistic scenarios intended to trigger curiosity.

In the following interaction, the mother is the central figure around which conversation evolves. The 5-year-old is fully engaged and the 1½-year-old is active throughout, although she utters only one word. In the video she can be seen pointing and running toward the exhibit. She tries to climb into it and touch the babies. The four-part functional analysis contains listings for theme, inquiry skill, prospectiveness, and discourse function, as the example illustrates:

Theme	Skill	Prospectiveness	Discourse Function
(Biological theme)	**(Inquiry skill)**	**(Demand D Give G or Acknowledgment A)**	**(amplify reinterpret extend etc.)**

Meta comments are included in the right margin to indicate particular turns that either 'step up' the conversation, model certain skills, introduce new themes or provide other important markers. These are indicated by boxes,

as indicated here: → **Step up prospectiveness**

Son maintains theme of sexual differences

A segment of conversation of Family 1: California Academy of Sciences
Life through time, Mom, Boy 5, Girl 1 1/2

Utterance	Theme	Skill	Pros	Function	Meta comment
MOM: Girl, **look**, wow, is that cool.		**Observing**	**G**	**engaging G**	
BOY: What is it?					
MOM: What are they? Man is that cool. They look like kitties. **They are protecting their babies. There is no fiercer animal than a mommy threatened.**	**Protecting babies**	**Observing**	**G, G**	**extending**	**The mother introduces the Theme—Protection from Predators and advances it in several moves**
BOY: Why are they trying to get them?	**Protecting babies**	**Questioning**	**D**	**engaging**	
MOM: I bet they are hungry and the babies are nice and small and tender, yummy for eating.	**Protecting babies-**	**Hypothesizing**	**G**	**amplifies theme**	

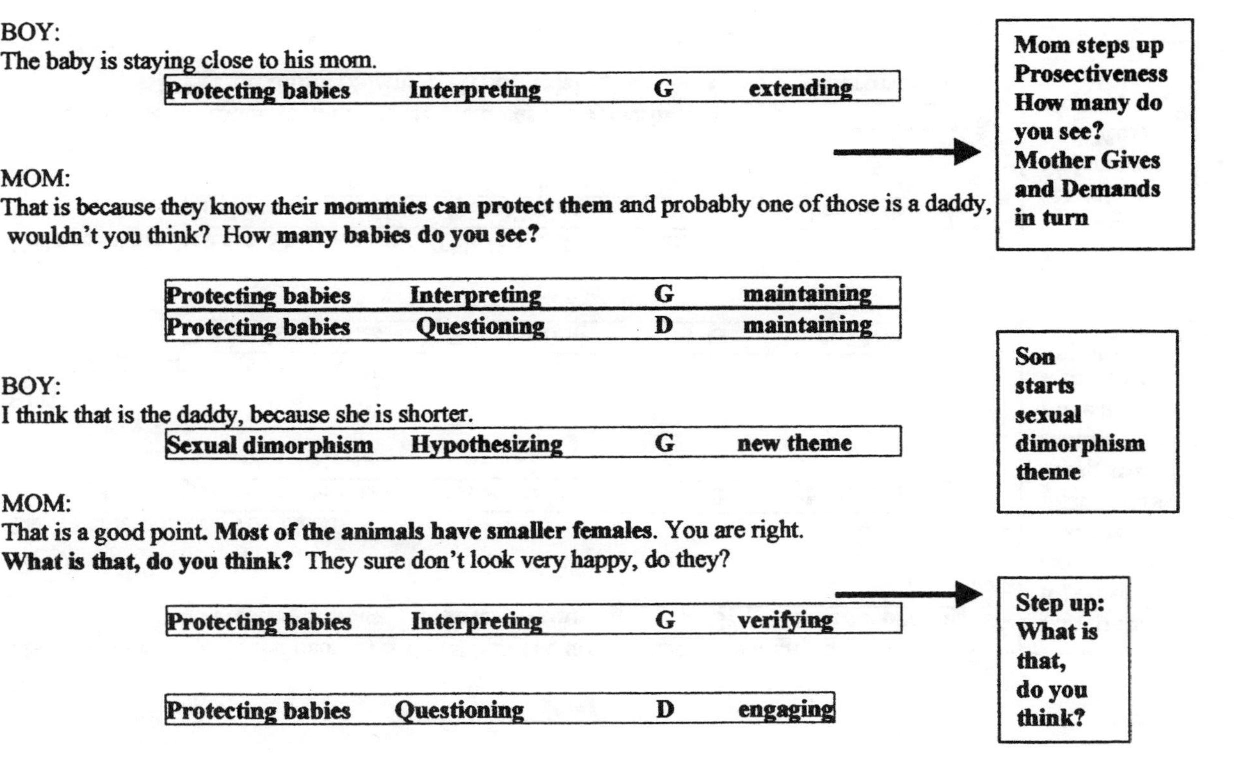

BOY:
The baby is staying close to his mom.

Protecting babies	Interpreting	G	extending

→ **Mom steps up Prosectiveness How many do you see? Mother Gives and Demands in turn**

MOM:
That is because they know their **mommies can protect them** and probably one of those is a daddy, wouldn't you think? How **many babies do you see?**

Protecting babies	Interpreting	G	maintaining
Protecting babies	Questioning	D	maintaining

Son starts sexual dimorphism theme

BOY:
I think that is the daddy, because she is shorter.

Sexual dimorphism	Hypothesizing	G	new theme

MOM:
That is a good point. **Most of the animals have smaller females**. You are right.
What is that, do you think? They sure don't look very happy, do they?

→ **Step up: What is that, do you think?**

Protecting babies	Interpreting	G	verifying

Protecting babies	Questioning	D	engaging

BOY:
The dad is heading for the baby over there, because the dad knows that the baby can't get it.

Protecting babies- Interpreting G re-interpreting

MOM:
Can't get it, what do you mean?

protecting babies- Questioning D clarifying

BOY:
That the baby can't fight very well.

Protecting babies- Interpreting G amplifying

Son puts together protection and sexual differences using size of female and male and weakness of baby

MOM:
Let's see what they are. Shall we see? This is a wolf like mammal

Taxonomy Questioning G change theme

BOY:
Yeah, because the mom, look mom, the mom has big eyelashes.

Sexual dimorphism- Hypothesizing G re-interpreting

Boy expands sexual differences and Mom steps up

MOM:
Yeah, Maybelline. This bird can't fly, but …like an ostrich. It probably used its strong beak to crack nuts, but some scientists believe he was a meat eater. It doesn't look like he has very sharp feet. We can't go in there. It is just for looking.

Feeding	**-**	**Observing**	**G**	**new theme**

Girl speaks One word— identifies bird saying duck

GIRL:
Duck.

Taxonomy		**Identifying –**	**G**	**re-interpreting**

MOM:
It looks a lot like a duck. What does a duck say?

Taxonomy		**Questioning**	**G, D**	**verifying**

→ **Step up to girl**

BOY:
You know what Mom, that is the daddy, that is the daddy and that is the Mom because the Dad has a longer neck.

Sexual dimorphism-		**Hypothesizing**	**G**	**re-interpreting**

Son maintains theme of sexual differences

Overall Analysis of SE 1

General. This segment of discourse meets the criteria for SE, in that there is: a co-constructed ZPD, distributed expertise, conversation over an extended time, thematic content, and a variety of negotiating strategies. The conversation is fast paced, mother-directed, and intentional. Knowledge is distributed between boy, mother, and the signs. The mother models how to use museums; encourages her son to interact with the information; and encourages her daughter's ability to speak words. The mother typically leads interactions with a *Give,* such as "look at this," or a *Demand* such as a question; both hold the expectation of a response, so that more than a brief *Acknowledgment* is required to complete the turn.

The mother introduces the universal notion of protecting a family from harm; this resonates with the son who builds on this by reasoning about the roles of various family members, male and female, leading to sexual dimorphism (larger male, smaller female). The larger theme (protection from predators) has the ability to engage each of the participants in different ways and to lead them into their own areas of interest. The mother looks for guidance to signs, which is only partially helpful; the son maintains the notion of sexual dimorphism; and the little girl falls back to identification, a good strategy when nothing else is known or can be said.

The mother maintains a running commentary, interspersed with questions. She also frequently opens up the conversation by using responses that step up the prospectiveness, for example, by asking "What do you think?" She teaches both the boy and the girl how to get the most out of museums, in short how to "do" museums, and how to do "learning conversations" more generally. Following is more analysis of the thematic content and mediation styles of this SE.

Thematic Content—Protection From Predators. Content is a necessary ingredient in learning how to "do conversations" in museums or other arenas. The underlying universal content theme of this significant event (and throughout the visit) was protection from enemies. This theme was suggested by the exhibit and then appropriated in different ways by family members. The boy initiated a related theme, sexual dimorphism, and the mother amplified this by saying "maybelline" to refer to the long eyelashes of the female bird. The boy used *personification,* or person analogy; that is, using perceived similarity to the human as a referent for predicting the existence of certain characteristics in living things (Carey, 1985; Inagaki & Sugiyama, 1988), when reasoning about birds and humans. He suggested that the same type of dimorphism he was familiar with, that is Mom and Dad, male and female, would also function for birds. In doing so he was partially correct, as raptor females are larger than males but typically male birds are the same size or larger than females. Personification is a common emergent biological principle that both children and adults use in the absence of detailed content knowledge.

Clearly, the boy identified with the birds and wanted to help protect them. He also used *form–function reasoning* by indicating that, for example, being shorter is equivalent to being female. He projected human characteristics onto both male and female birds. Together the mother and the boy attempted to make sense of the notion of protection from predators; the mother sought and got support from the written text, so that she could guide the children's thinking, saying:

> *Mother:* Let's see what they are. Shall we see?
>
> Mother reads from the sign at the exhibit:
> This is a wolf like mammal (predator) . . . This bird can't fly, but . . . (is) like an ostrich. It probably used its strong beak to crack nuts, but some scientists believe he was a meat eater.
>
> She adds: It doesn't look like he has very sharp feet.

The mother used the information in the sign to expand her and the children's knowledge, yet it was not consistent with the line of reasoning they had been pursuing, protection from predators. The sign verified that these birds probably could not defend themselves easily. Meanwhile, the little girl tried to be part of the conversation and valiantly attempted to speak, finally saying the word duck, indicating that she understood that these were, in fact, birds.

Mediation Styles. Content forms the subject of conversation but modes of mediation define how content is negotiated. By mediation I refer back to Wertsch, Cole and Wells, who have each suggested that people individually and collectively use tools to navigate the ZPD and that these tools can take a variety of forms, including artifacts or language. In this SE there are a variety of mediational means; for example, this mother constantly "stepped up" the conversation using guided or directed questions, such as "What do you see?" or "What do you think?" She especially relied on a variety of alternatives to the Give response to extend both the content and the use of the skills, such as observing. These moves stepped up the prospectiveness and encouraged a wider variety of answers. For example, she said:

> That is because they know their mommies can protect them and probably one of those is a daddy, wouldn't you think? **How many babies do you see?**

In the following short episode, which took place at an earlier exhibit, that dealt with a similar theme, the interactional control was in the son's hands. In that case the boy led, while the mom followed. That pattern reversed back and forth throughout the family's visit to the entire gallery.

BOY: Cool. Wow, look. Look giant teeth. Mom, look at his giant teeth.

MOM: He looks like a saber tooth. **Do you think he eats meat or plants?**

BOY: Mom, look at his giant little tooth, look at his teeth in his mouth, so big.

MOM: He looks like a Saber tooth, doesn't he. **Do you think he eats plants or meat?**

BOY: Ouch, ouch, ouch, ouch. (referring to sharp tooth)

MOM: **Do you think he eats plants or meat?**

BOY: Meat.

MOM: **How come?**

BOY: Because he has sharp teeth. (Growling noises).

Even though the boy led the way to this exhibit, the mother had an educational agenda: the structure and function of a predator's teeth. She prompted three times, with repetitive questions, to determine if he understood the correlation between sharp teeth and predatory lifestyle. In this case, the learning direction was in the mother's hands, who, although she stepped up the Prospectiveness regularly in other contexts, did not do so here. She did not let the boy off the hook with an Acknowledge response, or even a Give, as she repeatedly followed his Give with a Demand, another question.

Learning How to "Do" Museums. Throughout the exhibits, the mother regularly included the girl, who was preverbal, but who readily interacted with the exhibits. The mother modeled the use of words for the girl, as well as how to ask questions and how to observe carefully. In this next segment, the bold portions indicate when the boy talked directly to the girl, acting as her learning guide, similar to the mother. The mother modeled for the boy, and the boy, in turn, modeled for the little girl. The girl spoke again in the middle of the segment, saying that a giant clamshell is teeth.

MOM: Girl, look up. Get on the floor and look up at the bird. Straight up, see the bird.

BOY: It is a pterodactyl. Can we go in there?

MOM: Yes we can, we have to wait for your sister.

BOY: (talking to sister) **We are going to go in somewhere scary.**

MOM: Man this is really neat. Look, a big shell.

GIRL: Teeth.

MOM: Are those teeth? I think that is a big shell. It looks like a snail, doesn't it? **Where would its head be, do you think?**

In this episode, which occurred after the SE, the boy modeled looking and questioning to the younger sister, even though he was only five himself.

Clearly he had picked up the style and language of "doing" museums. Still, most information entered the dialogue through the mother, who artfully used questions and repetitive verbal structures to keep the children engaged. She mediated the experience for the children at different levels. She met multiple goals in attending to the exhibit and to the two children in terms of content and language interaction.

In sum, the properties of this SE included: central mediation by mother, using questioning and observing as skills that tended to always "step" the talk; full verbal engagement and attention of the boy; as well as preverbal engagement of the youngest child, the girl. The conversation had strong thematic content centered on sexual dimorphism and the protection of babies. The conversational style included ongoing questioning as an inquiry strategy, accompanied by narrative accounts of the exhibits. The mother and son both modeled how to "do museums."

FAMILY 2

Background Information

The second family, a mother, a father, and two sons, age 7 and 9, frequented museums often and viewed these times as family events for enjoyment and as times to be together. The sons differed in their areas of interest, the older son being more interested in the physical sciences, like the father, and the younger son being more interested in the life sciences, like the mother.

> *MOM:* Okay, in our family Dad works and talks a lot with the kids a lot about physical science and chemistry, that kind of stuff. . . . My background is in art but, I also studied medical illustration, . . . They don't want to hear about dissecting
>
> . . . Boy (age 9) tends to be very uninterested in the biological sciences. . . .
>
> But Boy (age 7) is very curious about what is going on around him and the frogs and the different animals and different shapes. So they are two very different kids.

During an interview on the family's museum going habits:

> *MOM:* I think they (museums) are fun experiences for us, as a family, so the learning comes with that, but it is a nice thing to do together, that is the way it seems.

DAD: Sometimes some concept comes up, you can go back and say remember such and such that we saw and sometimes that works.

MOM: Boy (age 9) went with his class to the aquarium and then we went a week later, and I was so impressed with the amount that Boy could tell me about what he had seen. There is a lot going on individually, that maybe it doesn't come as part of the family experience. His independent learning, I think it is different than the family experience. And it is impressive too.

As the mother talked about the value of museums as a social event that brings them all together, rather than being an overt learning event, she was very clear on the goal for this event. The children wanted to enjoy themselves and the Dad seemed interested in both a fun event and in learning, as well. This was a family used to learning in a variety of different contexts. The following SE illustrates a fun event that doubles as learning.

Episode

This SE was recorded at an interactive video display (15" television screen) where decisions needed to be made within a certain time period. There was a male voice that explained the rules and indicated when choices were to be made. The end goal was to survive. Along the way several rules of natural selection were revealed, based on survival traits such as: size, eating patterns, egg laying, metabolism, carnivore/herbivore and their efficiency over time. If a nonselective trait was chosen, the voice indicated "too bad"; if the choice was correct, there were then further choices. If one did not choose within a certain time, one lost. As species supposedly evolve from aquatic to land animals in this display, there were several choices to be made about size, speed, and overall metabolism, as well as reproductive strategies. When choices were made that resulted in the death of the experimental species, the game was again over. The duration of the game varied from a few minutes to more than 15 minutes. This family had two turns, first with the father and the younger son, and later with all four members together. This SE was taken from the whole family conversation.

The interactive display was in the Hall of Dinosaurs, near the Hall of Mammals. Its main points related to tradeoffs in making the transition to land, and in being warm-blooded and mammal.

The family had been in dyads before this episode, mother with older son, and father with younger son. The father and the younger boy explored this exhibit as the mother and older boy came along to join the other dyad. This SE was recorded as the family re-united at the video interactive. In this segment of conversation all four members joined as a group to make meaning together.

A segment of conversation of Family 2: California Academy of Sciences
Life through time, Mom, Dad, Boy 7, Boy 9

DAD: They keep evolving. Move onto bigger food.

Feeding	Questioning	D	intro theme

Feeding theme is established. Both parents encourage the children within the context of several turns of interaction. Protection from predators is thematically maintained

(Video dialogue in caps)

A LOT OF YOUR FOOD GIVES YOU THE ENERGY YOU NEED TO GET AWAY. IT ALSO HELPS YOU BUILD STRONGER, BIGGER BODIES, USUALLY AT THE EXPENSE OF SMALLER CREATURES. THE NASTY REALITY IS THAT THERE IS ALMOST ALWAYS SOMEONE BIGGER THAN YOU.

Protection, feeding	Explaining	D	amplify

DAD: Do you want to defend yourself or head for the hills?

Protection	Questioning	D	challenge

→ **Step up with challenge**

DO YOU DEFEND YOURSELF OR ESCAPE?

BOY 9: Escape (watching)

Protection	**Interpreting**	**G**	**makes a choice**

Mom gives praise to younger boy's actions

MOM: Good choice.

Protection	**Interpreting**	**A**	**verifies choice**

A WISE CHOICE. THAT ONE HAS ITS ADVANTAGES AND THE MAIN ONE IS THAT YOU ARE STILL ALIVE. THERE IS ONE PROBLEM HERE, THOUGH,. MOST ARE NOT BUILT TO RUN AND BREATHE AND THAT MEANS A LOT OF REST STOPS AND AS YOU CAN SEE, SITTING AROUND REFUELING IS NOT SO HEALTHY.

Metabolism	**Explaining**	**D**	**challenge**

DAD:
Lunchtime, uh oh. He changes.

Feeding	**Explaining**	**G**	**expand theme**

THERE IS A WAY OUT THOUGH. STEP UP AND CLICK DINO DOOR OR MAMMAL DOOR, BECAUSE DINOSAURS OR MAMMALS CAN BREATHE WHILE RUNNING.
I KNOW YOU ARE TIRED.

Feeding/metabolism	**Questioning**	**D**	**challenge**

→ **Step up**

DAD:
Mammals.

Feeding/metabolism	**Interpreting**	**G**	**hint**

WHOA, LOOKS LIKE A CHANGE HAS COME OVER HERE? THE HAIR, THE FLOPPY EARS, AND RUBBERY NOSE, WOULDN'T WORK ON MOST ANIMALS, BUT IT DOES ON YOU; BUT THOSE WHISKERS JUST FINISH OFF THE WHOLE OUTFIT. YOU KNOW THAT CHANGE MUST HAVE MADE YOU PRETTY HUNGRY; LET'S EAT. IT HAS ON ITS MENU, PLANTS OR MEATS, SO WHAT DO YOU HAVE A HANKERING FOR?

Family seeks answer

Feeding **Questioning** **D** **challenge**

Carnivore herbivore

DAD:
Carnivore or?

Feeding **Questioning** **D** **challenge**

The young boy is getting advice from both the father and the older brother yet is holding his own in control of the event.
The three males attempt to figure out the correct move

BOY 9:
I know which one it is

Carnivore/ herbivore **Observing** **D** **hint**

DAD:
I don't think either one is necessarily right. It gives you ten seconds.

Carnivore/ herbivore **Observing** **D** **hint**

BOY 9:
Can I try?

Carnivore/ herbivore **Questioning** **D** **bid/ maintain**

DAD:
I think it assumes that you have walked away, we were still trying to figure out what to do.

Carnivore/ herbivore Observing G hint

Dad is intrigued intellectually

BOY 9:
Can I try?

Carnivore/ herbivore Questioning D bid/ maintain

DAD:
In the earlier ones, this time it didn't say.

Clarifying G hint

Older boy wins bid to try

BOY 9:
Can I try?

Questioning D bid

DAD:
Yeah.

G support bid

Boy 7:
There was one wrong choice, and it (voice too low),
I'll tell you which one to do.

Step up with hint

Clarifying G hint

MOM:
Press the red button.

Clarifying G hint

DAD:
You get to make evolutionary choices for these guys.

Clarifying G hint

GENTLEMAN, AMAZING

BOY 7:
I made it go on land.

Change over time Clarifying G hint

MOM:
That is a good choice.

Change over time Observing G gives praise

BOY 7:
I know, we got turned into a lizard.

Evolving clarifying G verifying

MOM:
That is the way it happened, isn't it?

Evolving questioning D verifying

BOY 9:
Evolving takes time.

Evolving clarifying G verifying

Young child acts as expert gets praise from Mom who also verifies the evolutionary process

Family gets answer

A lesson learned

Overall Analysis of SE

General. This family brought its own learning style to the interaction. They were highly interactive, both with each other and with the machine. They were accustomed to computers and intelligent devices and with interacting socially with them as a social group. The parents worked hard to pay attention, to let the kids lead and to make the most of the themes that were presented.

The game used a series of challenge activities that built upon each other, and led the learner, rather than asking direct questions. The father adopted the same style. During the portion of the transcript that has the vertical line to the right, the entire family got lost in the game, yet they worked together to try to understand it. The father didn't take over but he allowed the younger son to give up control to the older one. The boys advised each other at the machine and competed for turns, while the parents, primarily the father, interacted with the boys and with each other opportunistically. The interactive video acted as a fifth member of the family and mediated much of the ongoing activity.

Thematic Content—Protection From Predators and Others. The themes included feeding, protection from predators, survive or die, carnivore/herbivore, and change over time/evolving. The thematic material was largely determined by the video display. It included discussion of eating and being eaten and the importance of maintaining a metabolism at an efficient rate, the notion of escaping and modeled the trade-off between various mammalian characteristics. The video actively introduced the themes but also allowed choice over timing and selection. It emphasized that different characteristics conferred advantages and disadvantages for survival, and that survival itself was a balancing act.

Consistent with her background, the mother was interested in themes such as evolutionary time and classification. In this segment of conversation which preceded the SE, for example:

MOM: Interesting. Did you see this chart Boy 9?

BOY 9: Yeah I did. Look at these birds.

MOM: Oh my gosh, that is outrageous. That looks like someone's imagination. It is called a diorama. This is what happened when the dinosaurs became extinct and then other animals filled the gap, the dinosaurs, and so this is a. . . .

BOY 9: This is an in-between stage, between present and dinosaur era.

MOM: It says here, new birds and mammals filled many of the niches vacated when non-Avian dinosaurs became extinct. I think there was a long gap between when the dinosaurs became extinct and now. So the middle is kind of iffy.

The father typically helped provide information for the children, often using the signs at the exhibit, for example, in this segment after the SE:

DAD: . . . I think that is, is it a fish, or does it say? It says it is a lungfish, this one. A real fish. That guy on the bottom, is he a real fishy?

BOY 7: I don't know, he sure looks like it.

DAD: You are right, he is alive. He is breathing, he is alive. Horseshoe crab, those are relatives of scorpions and extinct sea scorpions. Horseshoe crabs have existed relatively unchanged for 100s of millions of years, so these guys look a lot the same like they did 100s of millions of years ago.

Mediation Styles. Both the father and the machine provided a series of hints that moved the interaction in new directions. The father seemed to copy the style of the machine in giving timely prompts, yet he left the boys to make most of the decisions. Because the material was also intellectually appealing to adults (change over time or evolution) the parents seemed genuinely intrigued by the exhibit and didn't always have the right answer. In the marked section (vertical line along the right border of the SE) the three males were unsure of the next move and the father seemed genuinely confused. Each member attempted to help the others understand.

DAD: **I think it assumes that you have walked away, we were still trying to figure out what to do.**

BOY 9: Can I try?

DAD: **In the earlier ones, this time it didn't say.**

BOY 9: Can I try??

DAD: Yeah.

BOY 7: (giving advice) Boy 9, there was one wrong choice, and it (voice too low), I'll tell you which one to do.

MOM: **Press the red button.**

DAD: **You get to make evolutionary choices for these guys.**

MACHINE: GENTLEMAN, AMAZING

BOY 7: I made it go on land.

MOM: That is a good choice.

The episode ended with the mother's comment, "That's the way it happened, isn't it?", meaning evolving and the older son saying: "Evolving takes time." The mother was less engaged overall, giving praise several times, but she also looked around at other exhibits while the three males were interacting. Yet she clearly enjoyed the family interaction. Both parents smiled and laughed and spoke to each other in asides. Their posture was relaxed and unhurried.

Learning How to "Do" Museums. The parents were relieved of much of the work of interpreting complex material for their sons; thus they were able to step back and opportunistically comment on the action in either a peripheral or central way. Their role was to be supportive and to act as secondary mediators, except where they advised particular directed moves. This style of doing museums or of doing conversations seemed very familiar to them. Having now watched this family in other settings over time, it seems clear that this slower, more hint-laden approach was and is typical for them. The older boy and the Dad understand and like physical machines, while the Mom and the younger son appreciate the life sciences. The particular interactive of this SE happened to intersect all their interests. It was not accidental, then, that they spent the bulk of their time at this exhibit; they gravitated to it naturally, unlike most families. Of the 11 families viewed overall, only 3 selected this exhibit.

This style of "doing" was less direct, less fast-paced, and seemingly more relaxed than the directed observing and questioning skills modeled in the first family. Yet a lot of conversation about survival strategies and natural selection happened along the way. As the older boy said at the end of the game, "Evolution takes time."

In sum, then, this SE was set within complex and overlapping ZPDs between family members and an interactive machine. Knowledge was distributed between the members of the family and the interactive machine, with the machine acting as expert and the mother, father, and two sons acting as learners, sometimes on equal footing. The primary mediator was the computer, accompanied by more peripheral mediation by the parents (dominated by the Dad) and some hints by the younger son, who had played part of the game before. There was full engagement by all participants with more physical activity by the boys but mental engagement by the parents as well, again more actively on the part of the Dad. The Mom seemed to step back and to enjoy the interaction of the rest of her family. She smiled often and seemed to understand that the guys were into this video game as a unit. There was strong thematic content that included protection from predators, carnivore/herbivore, and egg-laying versus live birth. The overall style of mediation was characterized by hints and prompts rather than by direct questioning by the parents, and by more direct didactic information-laden prompts from the machine.

DISCUSSION

There have been two goals for this chapter. The first has been to describe how families talk about and make sense of biological themes at museums, using Vygotsky's zone of proximal development as a central organizing feature and FCL principles to inform methodological design. The second has been to gain insights into understanding the application of this sociocultural theoretical framework to a larger class of research in informal learning settings, in order to inform learning theory across different contexts. Let us review the results of the analysis from the perspective of these two goals.

Goal 1: To Determine How Families Talk and Make Sense of Biological Themes at Museums, Using Vygotsky's Zone of Proximal Development as a Central Organizing Feature

In these SEs, families played an active role in constructing understanding, by contributing their own expertise, collaborating in reasoning, and negotiating complex thematic material. At a very fundamental level, the analysis provided in this chapter was able to highlight three important aspects of family conversations. First, it seems apparent that powerful thematic content is the underpinning for meaning-making conversations. In order to construct understanding, families need something interesting and complex to discuss and this complexity needs to bridge differences in age and expertise. Second, this analysis has demonstrated that there are distinct mediation styles that families adopt in negotiating content. These ways of doing museums are both subtle and powerful, and include how conversations are maintained and controlled. Third, this research has verified that the ZPD and distributed expertise are powerful organizers within which to explore the structure, function, and meaning-making of family conversations. These issues are explicated next.

Thematic Content

Both families cued into important biology themes, such as feeding, breeding, and protection from the elements, all themes introduced in a variety of ways by the exhibits. The family members, individually and collectively appropriated the themes and made meaning in different ways. In both families, the themes seemed to "drive" the dialogue and to maintain interest. For example, in Family 1 both mother and son wondered about sexual dimorphism; in Family 2 all members weighed and balanced decisions such as metabolic rate. In both cases the material was sufficiently challenging for all members, so that no one member had complete understanding. In each case parents "ran out" of existing information, and needed to rely on the materials presented in the exhibit.

For Family 1 the universally engaging theme of protection from predators engaged first the mother, then the 5-year-old son. The exhibit, however, presented only the broad outlines of the theme itself; the meaning was made by the participants in their interactions with it. The three participants (mother, son, and exhibit) were in a joint zone of proximal development. The mother led, using the *mother as protector of young* theme, while the son later introduced form-function reasoning, as well as personification. These are entirely appropriate interpretations given the age and role of each player. No one of the three "owned" the idea. Each contributed different information and moved in different directions.

For Family 2, the evolution interactive pushed on themes of survival strategies and the advantages these gave evolving animals as part the ZPD that included all family members as well as the machine. The interactive advanced the notion of change over time, while foreshortening the time frame. The themes provided stimulating content for multiple levels of learners. The challenge of finding answers to the game engaged first the younger son, then the rest of the family. The increasing difficulty of providing correct answers engaged all three males actively and the mother peripherally. When confusion took over, all members tried to make sense and to arrive at some acceptable resolution. It was at this point that all players were equal as learners and the collaboration was mutual.

Even though the two families had different modes of negotiation and were at different exhibits, the underlying theme of protection from predators was quite similar in both cases. Although this had been predicted earlier, based on the nature of children's form–function reasoning, this tangible outcome is quite convincing. Families do use themes to make meaning and they seem to like themes to be complex rather than simple. Both families, using different kinds of animals as setting and context, used similar forms of reasoning toward similar ends.

One cannot know for certain which particular exhibitry will pique the interest of one or more visitors. In this and other analyses of different families, though, using different exhibits, the underlying thematic content material was remarkably similar. In both families studied here survival strategies, such as protection, eating, and escaping predators, were central to the content of family discourse. If we can predict that certain themes will most likely trigger certain kinds of conversations, then we can design for this. If we know that certain areas of complexity are naturally attractive to learners of all ages, then we can design for that, as well. In short, there is a great advantage for museums to understand the nature of themes that will most predictably "drive" conversations. Thus, regarding content, the larger task for museums and for designers of exhibits is to both ensure that there is complex thematic material available at a variety of levels, and to make this complex material transparent to multiple ages and expertise. Underlying these two design principles is the finding presented here and elsewhere that powerful themes such as protection from predators appear to be universal biological antecedents for such big ideas as adaptation, and that these themes can be carefully orchestrated to build understanding within related exhibits, such as Change Through Time.

Learning How "to Do" Museums: Mediation Styles

Both families have enculturated their children into the genre of museum talk. Both SE sequences illustrated that although interesting thematic content is a fundamental component of the family conversation at science exhibits, complex themes need to be mediated in conversations. The two families accomplished this in different ways. Both used the museum setting as a family learning opportunity, but after allowing the children to select particular exhibits, the parents modeled reasoning and the negotiation of conversations. The families used different styles of negotiating, both with each other and with objects, as they selectively interacted with the exhibits.

For Family 1 the active mediator, the mother, modeled the repetitive and constant use of verbal prompts. She used questioning (and observing) to continually re-engage the children and to maintain their interest. One interpretation of her behavior is that she was exploiting and expanding possible follow-ups and was allowing "a more knowledgeable participant (herself, or the sign) to contribute to the learning of the less knowledgeable (son) in ways which nevertheless incorporated and built on the latter's contribution" (Wells 1999, pp. 247–248). Another interpretation is that she had learned from her own family museum-going history how to provide an ongoing synoptic conversational line as a way of maintaining engagement and monitoring understanding. Using either interpretation, this mother used a distinct style of negotiating conversations that is at the high frequency polarity of mediation styles, using many utterances over a period of time, initiated by the adult.

The mother's use of questioning, in and of itself, can have a variety of mediational interpretations in the social context. For example Wertsch (1991) refered to the use of authentic versus test questions by teachers in classrooms. Authentic questions, according to Nystrand (1997), "are questions for which the asker has not pre-specified an answer . . . in which the students' thinking is genuinely solicited rather than simply responding with a predetermined response. Authentic questions invite students to contribute something new to the discussion . . . (while a) test question allows only one possible right answer, and hence is monologic" (p. 38).

In Family 1 the mother used questions in both authentic and in test ways. Asking, for example: "What do you think?" allowed many possible answers. In asking: "What is the difference between carnivore and herbivore?" the mother expected a particular answer. The more open-ended or authentic questions act to step up or expand the range of prospectiveness, thus potentially directing the follow-up of the IRF into new areas. This happened often in Family 1, for example, when this mother asked, "How many babies do you see?" An authentic question allows for several answers to potentially contribute something new to the discussion. This opens up the space for conversation to evolve toward new thematic areas, such as the roles and physical attributes (sexual dimorphism) in mothers and fathers.

For Family 2, the interactive video machine was the primary mediation agent, while the parents acted as secondary supports to the main theme of adaptive changes over time. The machine established the tone, yet the family's style matched it well. Overall, the conversation moved forward at a slower, more hint-laden pace. The machine modeled such skills as observing and questioning, and the parents actively supported these skills. Much of the cognitive load was taken by the machine, leaving the parents free to support the boys' conversation. In providing hints and challenges, rather than direct questions or answers, there was a subtle expansion of the zone of proximal development, allowing many different possible ways an answer might be directed.

This approach is similar to dynamic assessment where zones of competence are explored (Ash, 1995, Ash, Campione, & Brown, 1996). Dynamic assessment, also based on Vygotskian ZPD theory, is a term used to characterize "those approaches that guide learning as well as determine a learner's potential for change" (Palincsar, Brown, & Campione, 1987, p. 76). Dynamic assessment can both unveil students' potential for learning and "provide insightful suggestions for teaching" (Bransford et al, 1987, p. 479). The manner in which the parents of Family 2 guided their children contained aspects of an informal dynamic assessment, which generally provides hints in order to determine how far the learner can progress.

Learning How "to Do" Museums: Conversational Control Strategies

In these SEs, family members either knew the rules of conversation or they were actively practicing them. Although the conversational leader changed, in most cases the central control was in the hands of the most active parent or the machine, not the children. Subtle and not so subtle mediation occurred during the co-construction of thematic understanding. Mediation strategies included the use of inquiry skill prompts (such as questioning), attempts to step up the talk (such as opening up the response to a Give or Demand), and multiple rounds of appropriating others' ideas and reformulating them from different perspectives. As family members talked, they were subtly and not so subtly appropriating, changing, and reinventing meaning.

In Family 1, for example, the mother, by asking questions, redirecting, amplifying, constantly stepped up the potential for richer conversation as she managed the talk. She held the daughter, pointed to the exhibit, actively looked the son in the eyes, knelt on the ground, and contained the group in a co-constructed mutual safe zone for conversation. The result sounded like good dinner-table discussion in a museum setting, with real objects as prompts. As the kids responded, touched, asked questions, pointed, looked, and talked to each other and to the mom, they were learning the structure of museum talk.

The same was true with Family 2; one family goal appeared to be to teach the two boys how to engage with each other in fair ways, whereas another goal was staying alert to a series of difficult questions. The parents' hints and prompts allowed for more learning success than either child could have achieved alone or together, without the parents' help. This was an episode of ongoing social scaffolding, played out between four members. In this case neither the parents nor the children had all the knowledge necessary to complete the task. They were practicing the rules of social meaning-making so that each could participate and be heard.

Observing these disparate conversational control strategies leads us to the insight that these I R F functional moves act as gatekeepers for further conversation (Newman et al., 1989, p. 125). If a child is trying to talk about something, they may not be able to continue unless and until the adult follows the child's opening utterance with a response that encourages the child to continue. Within the general rules of social discourse this is also how people are either ratified or not ratified to participate. Thus gatekeeping, in the nature of the follow-up response, is a general mechanism for including or excluding individual speakers or groups of speakers in conversation or social interaction altogether, and these analyses offer us an opportunity to observe the learning and application of these strategies in process.

Goal 2: To Gain Insights Into Understanding the Application of This Sociocultural Theoretical Framework to a Larger Class of Research in Informal Learning Settings, in Order to Inform Learning Theory Across Different Contexts

The implications of this family conversation research touch upon larger issues of research involving social groups, their activities, and dialogue in informal settings using sociocultural theory. Research on theories of learning in informal settings creates tensions, as I call them, as we use theory to design practical methodologies, and then use the practical methodologies and research results to inform our theory—in short, we intertwine theory and practice. These tensions exist within the larger world of informal learning settings—contexts that involve social interactions, content material and meaning making. I argue that there are many larger lessons to be learned and questions to be answered in applying this particular research theory methodology to informal learning.

These tensions include both:

Choosing an appropriate level of analysis, and
The intertwining of content and mediation processes.

Choosing an Appropriate Level of Analysis

In looking closely at dialogue in formal or informal learning settings, there is always the issue of choosing the appropriate grain size of the unit of analysis. In this work I chose the Significant Event as the unit of analysis. Maintaining the tension between looking closely at any particular segment(s) while maintaining the integrity of the whole is paramount in microanalysis. This work has illustrated that even though portions of conversations can be selected for analysis, these must be set within the larger framework of social activity—in this case the family museum visit.

There are two extreme approaches for analyzing conversation, the first being a broad or wholistic approach, and the second being a finer grained analysis. In either approach something important can be lost. In doing a fine-grained analysis it is easy to lose the larger context; in focusing on larger context, it is easy to miss critical detail. By selecting a carefully defined Significant Event I have deliberately chosen a more intermediate level of analysis (White, 1989, 1993) in lieu of either of the extremes, the top-down or bottom-up approaches. I argue that by using SEs as the unit of analysis, I have chosen an area between the two extremes, and can thus combine features of both approaches in important ways. I can provide some fine-grained analysis, while retaining the context within which the analysis is situated. These chunks of conversation are large enough to be self-contained examples of meaning-making in action, yet they ultimately make sense only within the scope of the larger activity. The SEs can, if desired, be broken into smaller segments, for an even finer analysis. By using the intermediate level, we imply that events arise from other events and that they affect future outcomes; thus no single SE is final. An SE is merely a marker of progress to date, with the understanding that meaning made at this moment will be subsequently changed.

If one thinks of conversations as made up of different-sized events, from minimal to large, SEs will always remain a significant intermediate category; but they are also part of a larger activity system that has an overarching set of rules. Thus the Significant Event fits within a larger activity. It does not exist "as an end in itself, rather as a means for carrying out some activity in which the participants are jointly involved" (Wells, 1997, p. 3).

Using this intermediate level view, then, it remains crucial to place the object of analysis within a broader context—in this case, the entire museum visit, which has a larger cadence and organization within which any particular SE fits. In both families analyzed in this chapter, the families began the exhibit visit with exploratory behavior. This was quite reasonable as the gallery was new, they were being taped, and they were motivated (with differing goals) to provide an educational/interesting/fun/modeled museum experience for their children and themselves. This exploratory phase may have been a convenient way to become acculturated to the setting. Typically the adults used the first few exhibits in this gallery to "calibrate" or gauge the exhibits both for level of difficulty, for type of content presented, to determine the level of interest of the children, to read a few signs, to gauge the match with themselves and their children, and generally to reconnoiter. As the parents became familiar with the exhibit by reading signs and listening to the children, they seemed more able to determine what might make the experience more interesting. And so, too, did the children.

Furthermore, throughout each family visit there was an interactional rhythm, marked by multiple short interactions punctuated by significant events. In both SEs considered here, the discourse was part of the larger interactional scheme that included moving, interacting with a video, pointing, showing, nodding, facial expressions, all of which complemented the ongoing talk. The shorter events lay the foundation for subsequent in-depth SEs, that invariably encompassed multiple factors acting simultaneously (participants' prior knowledge, exhibit content, family conversational styles, etc.); and that occurred in different dimensions of meaning (socially, individually, written or spoken, etc.). Each SE, then, is an episode of discourse that acts as a means to achieving larger activity goals (Wertsch, 1998) for the family—for example learning or having fun together.

Intertwining Content and Negotiation

A larger issue for research into meaning-making at informal settings is the interplay between content and negotiation style within a broadly interpreted zone of proximal development. According to Wells (1997):

> Meanings are also strongly influenced by the connection made by participants to related experiences, both personal and collective. These exist on several time scales: within the current activity/discourse; within the participants' individual and collective' experience of similar or related activities in their community; within the history of the activity in the culture more generally. Some of these connections concern the 'content' of the activity; others relate to the 'ground-rules' for participation. (p. 5)

In the family discourse there is a delicate intertwining of content and the method with which it is negotiated. In the discourse considered in this chapter, the SEs arose in the interplay between mediation style and thematic content. In these examples, the families talked about content they found familiar and conceptually comfortable; yet this was only half the story. For both families, conversations became a merging of each individual's interests, so that no one individual entirely owned the discourse. In the interplay between content and the negotiation styles, either can become more prominent at any given time, yet both are always essential reference points for the analysis. At any given moment the discourse emphasis can be placed on content or mediation, each of which have different dimensions of meaning (socially, individually, now or future-oriented, written vs. spoken vs. drawn, among others).

Good exhibits, then, are the jumping off points for thematic conversations, by providing strong themes that pervade family conversations in engaging ways. The family members I observed subtly chose areas for conversation, based on a variety of factors. Initially they appeared to have chosen objects that attracted their children's attention, and these objects were often related to an enduring theme, such as survival of living things. The themes, in turn, were based on ways of reasoning typical of young children, who are predisposed to recognize survival adaptations by referring to functional reasoning or to personification. Parents typically entered the conversation as "experts" to guide their children's thinking. Themes can also be challenging for adults, in the best of cases, putting the whole family on a more level playing field, as happened for Family 2.

There is no way to predict in advance exactly which themes will be included in particular family conversations and where the interactions might lead. Yet, clearly, the particular context influences the thematic content of dialogue, while the dialogue is also dependent on the specific knowledge base, experience, and negotiation strategies that particular families bring with them. In the two analyzed SEs, it appears that each chosen negotiation style interacted seamlessly with the content presented by the particular exhibit. Most importantly, the learning agenda was jointly negotiated by all the members. Returning to the work of Newman et al. (1989) it seems clear, that in family discourse, the children's actions get interpreted within the system constructed by the parent. Although the child initiates, the parent refines and amplifies, asks for clarification etc., so that "Just as the children do not have the full cultural analysis of a tool to begin using it, the teacher (parent) does not have to have a complete analysis of the children's understanding" (Newman et al., 1989, pp. 63–64).

In their conversations then, "children undergo quite profound changes . . . by engaging in joint activity and conversations with other people" (Edwards & Mercer, 1987, p. 19). But parents also change by interacting with children. Wertsch (1998, p. 73) suggested that "language is a cultural tool and speech is a form of mediated action." He relies on the Bakhtinian notion that speech genres and utterances—as part of our everyday life—provide an irreducible tension between the agent (the speaker) and the mediational means (the utterances) because the "the word in language is half someone else's. It becomes 'one's own' only when the speaker populates it with his own intention, his accent, when he appropriates the word, adapting it to his own semantic and expressive intention" (Bakhtin, 1981, p. 294). This was true for both SEs analyzed. Whenever the parents' knowledge was not sufficient to resolve the child's questions, the learners grappled together with the difficult thematic content.

CONCLUSION

The results of this research support the assertion that much can be gained by using methodologies based on sociocultural theoretical principles in designing informal learning research. In the past, much museum research has focused on individual learners with single exhibits in mind, often leaving the cultural and social patterns out of the analysis. Yet, families bring age-related/domain-specific content themes and social mediation styles to conversations in museum settings; they act as a collaborative social group; and they choose conversational topics that can be significantly influenced, both positively and negatively, by the exhibits themselves. Thus museum research would do well to begin to think in terms of larger units of analysis.

In my analysis I have used common FCL design principles across classrooms and museums, viewing both as contexts where learners actively participate, share expertise, and negotiate. The results, therefore, provide powerful practical feedback to general learning theory. The lessons learned from this study suggest that different kinds of research questions need to be asked regarding museum learning. These more appropriate questions would address the issues involved in designing better exhibits that use and promote deep and complex thematic content, as well as in anticipating and encouraging the ways that social groups and individual learners collaboratively construct meaning.

This research has also tested several powerful methodological innovations for the analysis of learning in informal settings. These tools are well matched to sociocultural theory, and allow discourse analyses to be firmly embedded in the larger museum context. The four-part analysis tool allows for fine-grained analysis, while remaining clearly within a larger contextualized surround. Using a scheme that looks at individual utterances as well as the role of the discourse within the broader setting allows the analyst to take into account the complex historical and epistemological beliefs of the family, the institute, and the exhibit. The well-defined intermediate unit of analysis, the Significant Event, is characterized by definable beginnings and endings, distributed thematic content, and inquiry skills, which together provide a vehicle for participants' meaning-making as part of a larger cultural activity, and for analysis of this process of meaning-making, after the fact. Finally, the complex interaction of content and process are set within a broadly interpreted zone of proximal development, out of which the particular significant events arise, as any person or object can act as a source of topic stimulation or elaboration for others. These methodological innovations, which are well grounded in theory, can be adopted in any learning setting, and are particularly appropriate for research in informal learning.

ACKNOWLEDGMENTS

The research reported here was supported in part by the Museum Learning Collaborative (MLC), Learning Research and Development Center, University of Pittsburgh. The MLC is funded by the Institute for Museum and Library Services, the National Science Foundation, the National Endowment for the Arts, and the National Endowment for the Humanities. The opinions expressed are solely those of the author and no official endorsement from the funders should be presumed.

REFERENCES

Ash, D. (1995). *From functional reasoning to an adaptationist stance: Children's transition toward deep biology.* Unpublished thesis. University of California, Berkeley.

Ash, D. (1999). The process skills of inquiry. *Inquiry, Foundations* (Vol. 2). Washington, DC: NSF.

Ash, D. (2000, April). *Social negotiation of life sciences thematic content in family talk: Mapping design principles form community of learners classroom research to museums.* Paper presented at the AERA Annual Meeting, New Orleans.

Ash, D., & Brown, A. L. (1996, April). *Thematic continuities guide shifts in biological reasoning: Children's transition towards deep principles of evolution.* Paper presented at AERA, New York. Manuscript submitted for publication.

Ash, D., Campione, J. C., & Brown, A. L. (1995, April). *Measuring children's shift toward adaptationist reasoning: The guided clinical interview.* Poster session presented at the annual meeting of the American Educational Research Association, San Francisco.

Ash, D., & Klein, C. (2000). Inquiry in the informal learning environment. In J. Minstrell & E. Van Zee (Eds.), *Teaching and learning in an inquiry-based classroom* (pp. 215–240). Washington, DC: AAAS.

Ash, D., Ostrenko, M., Steier, F., & Borun, M. (2000, August). *Analyzing inquiry through visitor conversation.* Symposium at Visitor Studies Association, Boston.

Bakhtin, M. M. (1981). *The dialogic imagination.* Austin: University of Texas Press.

Bates, M. (1950). *The nature of natural history.* Princeton, NJ: Princeton University Press.

Bransford, J. D., Declos, V. R., Vye, N. J., Burns, M. S., & Hasselbring, T. S. (1987). Approaches to dynamic assessment: Issues, data and future directions. In C. S. Lidz (Ed.), *Dynamic assessment: Foundations and fundamentals.* New York: Guilford Press.

Brown, A. L. (1992). Design experiments: Theoretical and methodical challenges in creating complex interventions in classroom settings. *The Journal of Learning Sciences, 2*(2), 141–178.

Brown, A. L., Ash, D., Rutherford, M., Nakagawa, K., Gordon A., & Campione, J. C. (1993). Distributed expertise in the classroom. In G. Salomon (Ed.), *Distributed Cognitions* (pp. 188–228). New York: Cambridge University Press.

Brown, A. L., & Campione, J. C. (1994). Guided discovery in a community of learners. In K. McGilly (Ed.), *Classroom lessons: Integrating cognitive theory and classroom practice* (pp. 229–270). Cambridge, MA: MIT Press.

Brown, A. L., & Campione, J. C. (1996). Psychological theory and the design of learning environments: On procedures, principles and systems. In L. Schauble & R. Glaser (Eds.), *Innovations in learning* (pp. 289–325). Hilsdale, NJ: Lawrence Erlbaum Associates.

Brown, A. L., Campione, J., Metz, K., & Ash, D. (1996). The development of science learning abilities in children. In A. Burgen & K. Harnquist (Eds.), *Growing up with science: Developing early understanding of science* (pp. 156–178). Dordrecht, NL: Kluwer Academic Publishers.

Brown, A. L., Ellery, S., & Campione, J. C. (1997). Creating zones of proximal development electronically. In J. Green & S. Goldman (Eds.), *Thinking practices in math and science education* (pp. 149–201). Hillsdale, NJ: Lawrence Erlbaum Associates.

Brown, A. L., & Reeve, R. A. (1987). Bandwidths of competence: The role of supportive contexts in learning and development. In L. S. Liben (Ed.), *Development and learning: Conflict or congruence?* (pp. 173–223). Hillsdale, NJ: Lawrence Erlbaum Associates.

Carey, S. (1985). *Conceptual change in childhood.* Cambridge, MA: Bradford Books.

Crowley, K., & Callanan, M. (1998). Describing and supporting collaborative scientific thinking in parent-child interactions. *Journal of Museum Education, 23*(1), 12–20.

Edwards, D., & Mercer, N. (1987). *Common knowledge: The development of understanding in the classroom.* London: Routledge.

Eldredge, N. (1985). *Unfinished synthesis: Biological hierarchies and modern evolutionary thought.* New York: Oxford University Press.

Eldredge, N. (1991). Santa Rosalia: Or why there are some many different species. In *The miner's canary: Unraveling the mysteries of extinction.* Englewood Cliffs, NJ: Prentice-Hall.

Gould, S. J. (1991). *Bully for Brontosaurus.* New York: W. W. Norton.

Gould, S. J., & Lewontin, B. C. (1979). The spandrels of San Marcos and the panglossian paradigm. *Proceedings of the Royal Society, Series B: Biological Sciences, 205* (pp. 582–598).

Halliday, M. A. K. (1993). Towards a language-based theory of learning. *Linguistics and Education, 5,* 93–116.

Inagaki, K., & Sugiyama, K. (1988). Attributing human characteristics Developmental changes in over- and underattribution. *Cognitive Development, 3,* 55–70.

Keil, F. (1992). The origins of autonomous biology. In M. R. Gunman & M. Marasotos (Eds.), *Minnesota symposium on child psychology: Modularity and constraints on language and cognition.* Hillsdale, NJ: Lawrence Erlbaum Associates.

Leinhardt, G., & Crowley, K. (1998). *Museum learning as conversational elaboration: A proposal to capture, code and analyze museum talk* (pp. 115–142). Museum Learning Collaborative (Tech. Rep. # MLC-01). http://mlc.lrdc.pitt/mld

Lemke, J. L. (1990). *Talking science: Language, learning and values.* Norwood, NJ: Ablex.

Leont'ev, A. N. (1981). The problem of activity in psychology. In J. V. Wertsch (Ed.), *The concept of activity in Soviet psychology* (pp. 37–71). Armonk, NY: Sharpe.

Mayr, E. (1988). Is there an autonomous biology? In *Toward a new philosophy of biology.* Cambridge, MA: Belknap Press.

Mayr, E. (1991). *One long argument: Charles Darwin and the genesis of modern evolutionary thought.* Cambridge, MA: Harvard University Press.

Moschkovich, J. (1989, April). *Constructing a problem space through appropriation: A case study of tutoring during computer exploration.* Paper presented at the meetings of the American Educational Research Association. San Francisco.

Newman, D., Griffin, P., & Cole, M. (1989). *The construction zone.* Cambridge, England: Cambridge University Press.

Nystrand, M. (1997). *Opening dialogue: Understanding the dynamics of language and learning in the English classroom.* New York: Teachers' College Press.

Palincsar, A. M., Brown, A. L., & Campione, J. (1987). Dynamic assessment. In L. Swanson (Ed.), *Handbook on the assessment of learning disabilities* (pp. 115–142). Austin, Texas: Pro-ed.

Paris, S., & Ash, D. (2002). Reciprocal theory building inside and outside museums. *Curator.*

Rogoff, B. (1995). Observing sociocultural activity on three planes: Participatory appropriation, guided participation, and apprenticeship. In J. V. Wertsch, P. del Rio, & A. Alvarez (Eds.), *Socio studies of mind* (pp. 139–164). Cambridge, England: Cambridge University Press.

Schauble, L., & Bartlett, K. (1997). Constructing a science gallery for children and families: The role of research in an innovative design process. *Science Education (Informal Science Education—Special Issue) 81*(6), 781–793.

Sinclair, J. McH., & Coulthard, M. C. (1975). *Towards an analysis of discourse: The English used by teachers and pupils.* London: Oxford University Press.

Springer, K., & Keil, F. C. (1991). Early differentiation of causal mechanisms appropriate to biological and non-biological kinds. *Child Development.*

Vygotsky, L. S. (1978). *Mind in society: The development of higher psychological processes.* Cambridge, MA: Harvard University Press.

Wells, G. (1997). A sociocultural perspective on classroom discourse: Appendix A, Coding scheme for the analysis of classroom discourse. In B. Davies & D. Corson (Ed.), *The Encyclopedia of Language and Education, Vol. 3. Oral discourse and education* (pp. 3–5). Dordrecht, NL: Kluwer Academic Publishers. (with E. Measures and C. Quell).

Wells, G. (1999). *Dialogic inquiry: Towards a sociocultural practice and theory of education.* New York: Cambridge University Press.

Wertsch, J. V. (1991). *Voices of the mind.* Cambridge, England: Cambridge University Press.

White, B. Y. (1989, December). *The role of intermediate abstractions in understanding science and mathematics.* Eleventh Annual Conference of the Cognitive Society, University of Michigan.

White, B. (1993). Intermediate causal models: A missing link for successful science education. In R. Glaser (Ed.), *Advances in instructional psychology.* Hillsdale, NJ: Lawrence Erlbaum Associates.

Chapter **12**

Finding Self in Objects: Identity Exploration in Museums

Scott G. Paris
Melissa J. Mercer
University of Michigan

How do museum visitors understand the objects they encounter? The diverse and complex answers to this question are embedded in larger issues about epistemology, learning, museum education, material culture, and human development. A traditional answer to the question characterized visitors as apprehending information about the objects by careful viewing, discussions with others, and reading labels. *Passive reception* and registration of information was predominant in this reactive model. More recent views of the experience focus on the *active construction* of meaning by visitors depending on their prior knowledge, interests, and social situation. This interactive model emphasizes how visitors' unique interpretations result from the interactions of their physical, personal, and social contexts (e.g., Falk & Dierking, 1992). These two models reflect traditional approaches in learning theories derived from psychology and education.

A third model, and the focus of this research, emphasizes *transactions* between people and objects in the meanings imbued upon objects and the effects that objects have upon people. Transactions with objects might evoke tangential, unintended, or novel responses and might change the knowledge, beliefs, or attitudes of the visitor. Learning about the object in a unidirectional manner from viewer to object is not as important as creating personally relevant transactions with objects that allow bidirectional influences. A transactional model reflects an object-based epistemology that transcends the actual object by virtue of the cognitive constructions and the social experiences engendered by the object (cf. Conn, 1998; Paris, 2002). We want to apply this transactional view of museum experiences in our research on personal identity and museum experiences. Our guiding hypothesis is that visitors search for features of their personal lives, both actual and imagined selves, during their explorations of objects and museums, and their searches may lead to confirming, disconfirming, or elaborating understanding of their own identities.

CONSTRUCTING AND FINDING SELF

At the outset, we should limit the scope of our hypothesis and acknowledge the incompleteness of a transactional model. We do not believe that visitors deliberately search for meaning about their own lives every time they visit a museum or view an exhibit. Nor does every object elicit important personal reactions. Because visitors have diverse goals before they arrive, and the plans and expectations change during their visit, learning about one's self may be occasional, incidental, or fleeting more than deliberate and persistent. There may be one object out of hundreds or one conversation during the entire visit that strikes a personal chord, resonates with a deeper meaning about self, and elicits feelings that underlie reflections about "who I am and how I got here and what I believe." It is these reactions that are the focus of our hypothesis, regardless of their frequency or intensity. To the extent that some visitors have many of these reactions during visits to museums, self-exploration may lead to larger, transformative experiences with objects. This might be expected, for example, in special museums and exhibitions that focus on significant social and historical events such as the Holocaust, the African diaspora, Ellis Island immigration, internment of Japanese-Americans during World War II, and similar collections that evoke responses from visitors about features of their own identities.

Consider the psychological "self" as a starting point. There are at least two fundamental aspects of self-knowing relevant to museum experiences. The first is the self as learner or agent, and the second is self as a bundle of defining features, traits, and personal experiences. Susan Harter (1999) described these two meanings of self according to a distinction made originally by William James (1890). The self as subject, the I-self, is an active knower with:

> (1) self-*awareness*, an appreciation of one's internal states, needs, thoughts, and emotions; (2) self-*agency*, the sense of the authorship over one's own thoughts and action; (3) self-*continuity*, the sense that one remains the same person over time; and (4) self-*coherence*, a stable sense of the self as a single, coherent, bounded entity. (Harter, 1999, p. 6)

In contrast, Harter uses the term Me-self to describe the self as object, with components that include the "material me," the "social me," and the "spiritual me." The Me-self is the result of observation and analysis, the object of thought whereas the I-self is the analyzer and agent of thought. As a person gazes at a painting on a wall, she may think about how she analyzes the art and what she feels while simultaneously noting how the painting relates to previous experiences or aspects of her own personality. The I-self examines and searches the object guided by references to the Me-self. Various reactions, such as, "It makes me feel . . . ," "It reminds me of the time . . . ," or "I see myself . . . ," are all indications that the visitor has found something in the object that sparks memories, self-discoveries, and prior experiences that are personally meaningful. Not all objects evoke such reactions, but we suggest that visitors are often guided implicitly to recognize or search for personal connections with objects, the Me-self features of their own identities. Indeed, the casual cruising or "museum shuffle" so typical of visitors may reflect their searching for objects in exhibits that are familiar or have any kind of recognizable connection to the person. Finding the connections provides pleasure, nostalgia, and relevance in objects that is not inherent in the object but part of the transactional experience with the object. In our view, finding aspects of the Me-self in objects depends greatly on the kinds of analyses that the I-self conducts, which in turn depends on the cognitive abilities, motivation, mood, and social situation of the visitor.

Defining all the possible dimensions of the self is beyond our scope, but it is worthwhile to note some of the dimensions of the Me-self that are elicited in museums. For example, there are personal characteristics such as gender, age, and race that are often regarded as categorical features of individuals and the bases for personal identification. In fact, special exhibitions are often devoted to these features of people to foster popular appeal. Whether an exhibition focuses on women in sports, African Americans in the military, or Islamic art, part of the drawing power is based on the personal identification that visitors can make with the objects. We think that visitors are sensitive to personalized reactions to objects, especially when their reactions are strongly confirming or contrary. During a visit to a gallery, some visitors may interpret objects as negative stereotypes, biased representations, or pejorative. Others may regard some objects as inappropriate or uninteresting for them because they perceive the objects to appeal to someone older or younger or of a different gender or different race. They may fail to see any relevance to their own lives and thus discount or ignore the exhibit. Such reactions are evident when visitors dismiss or derogate objects in an exhibit or simply walk by at a fast pace. On the positive side, others might remark how much an exhibit reminds them of their own gender, race, or generation with feelings of pride and satisfaction. Exhibitions with popular appeal often reinforce positive reactions to features of visitors' social identities such as gender, race, and cultural heritage.

There are also qualitative, relative characteristics of self such as tall, pretty, smart, or musical that might be stimulated by particular objects and experiences. Appreciation of objects may be deeper when the visitor perceives the objects to mirror their personal characteristics in a positive manner. Of course, there are idiosyncratic dimensions of the Me-self that include interests, hobbies, and expertise—features of self that may give rise to feelings of pride and competence because they are self-made through effort and talent. We contend that people often think of these features of themselves when they encounter objects on public display, not that they necessarily seek them actively, but that they may be prompted to think of them by a memory, conversation, label, or overheard remark. We think that objects that evoke personal connections have both attraction and holding power, that is, visitors are drawn to them by recognition and are likely to view them carefully, read the labels, and talk about them with other people more than objects without connections to the Me-self. Because visitors vary widely in their personal characteristics, interests, and expertise, we should expect objects to vary equally widely in the transactions that they elicit.

The Me-self also includes features that embed Me in society, social connections that define each individual according to group membership and group characteristics. Family is the foremost social group. In a national survey of how American adults related the historical past to their lives, Rosenzweig and Thelen (1998) found that family was the most often reported connection to the past and the most important source of identity.

> Through good experiences and bad, moments of conflict and moments of harmony, bonds of deference and obligation, through feelings of closeness and distance from particular individuals, respondents made their families the starting places in their quest for identity. Within the peculiar familiarity of family life, where individuals observed others trying to become bright angels and overcome dark demons, families developed a sense of common destiny. Respondents not only identified this sense of shared destiny at the center of their identities but also saw it as a buffer against the world beyond the family. At home, family members learned and transmitted the values that set them apart and propelled them forward. (p. 50)

We think the strength of family identity is evident outside the home as individuals recognize and craft their identities in schools, churches, museums, and communities. Family identity merges with more expansive identities, social connections that further define the Me-self. There are generational cohort features of identity that people carry as, for example, American Baby Boomers or survivors of the Great Depression. Identity may also include feelings associated with nationalism, ethnicity, and cultural heritage. Rosenzweig and Thelen (1998) said,

> The most powerful legacies that individuals brought from the larger society for families to engage—to include or exclude—were those of their cultures. Like families, cultures created narratives that described where their members had come from and were heading, what they had overcome and what they aspired to—all basic issues in defining identities. (p. 53)

The twin aspects of the I-self and Me-self are evident in museum visitors as they simultaneously process new information and relate it to their multiple senses of Me-self, including personal and social features. We believe that museum visits can be understood more deeply in reference to other events in an individual's life so that meaning making is not limited to the object and does not depend only on prior knowledge about the object. These analyses are cognitively insular and map meaning only from viewer to object. Instead, we think that visitors regard the objects in reference to their own lives and experiences because the transactions with objects can be self-referenced and socially referenced with thoughts and emotions. Our approach is related to other interpretive frameworks that are grounded in autobiographical interpretation such as self-regulated learning (Paris, Byrnes, & Paris, 2001), life-course theory (Elder, 1998), and narrative analyses (Bruner, 1986). We focus on the visitors' sense of who they are and who they want to become because these are important features of their actual identities as well as their identity strivings or possible selves (Markus & Nurius, 1986). Because narratives are so fundamental to the process of meaning making in museums, we discuss how stories can be at the core of referencing and constructing personal meanings.

MAKING MEANING THROUGH PERSONAL NARRATIVES

Suppose a visitor to a museum encounters objects from Polynesian culture and gazes at samples of tapa, cloths made from pounded mulberry tree bark and decorated with dyed, repeated designs. Information about the tapa may be acquired by reading the label or listening to a description, but this seems like static knowledge, impersonal and unlikely to be used, compared to the personal understanding of the object that museum educators would like to foster. The more dynamic aspect of knowing that museum educators want to nourish embeds understanding in the visitors' lived experiences, such as, "This reminds me of the tapa that we saw in our visit to the Polynesian Cultural Center in Hawaii." These personal experiences include stories about people and objects. Some stories are shared by visitors with other people, and some remain private narratives and memories.

Bruner (1986) distinguished the paradigmatic and narrative senses of knowing precisely to capture this difference between the scientific and personal ways of knowing. Narratives give priority to the stories that connect people with objects and events. The transactional view of museum visits also emphasizes the importance of the stories that visitors create. Visitors typically recall objects and exhibits in museums in narratives about the people who were part of the visit, about the humorous or emotional events that happened along the way, or about singular, moving reactions to objects. Elaine Huemann Gurian (1999) suggested that objects are not important as artifacts alone, filled with meaning, but rather as stimuli for visitors to create their own meanings. This is consistent with a transactional perspective that views museums as more than storehouses of objects or meanings. Viewing the objects allows visitors to recreate and embrace their personal memories, to express their ownership of the experiences, and to share the stories with others.

> Not meaning to denigrate the immense importance of museum objects and their care, I am postulating that they, like props in a brilliant play, are necessary but not sufficient. This paper points out something that we have always known intuitively, that the larger issues revolve around the stories museums tell and the way they tell them. Objects, one finds, have in their tangibility, provided a variety of stakeholders with an opportunity to fight over the meaning and control of their memories. It is the ownership of the story, rather than the object itself, that the fight has been all about. (Gurian, 1999, pp. 165–166)

Narrative accounts can be referenced in three distinct ways to a person's life experiences. First, they can be relevant to one's autobiographical sense of self, to experiences and events in one's life, whether actual, imagined, or potential. These stories usually have the Me-self at the center and describe how the object is relevant to the person by virtue of past encounters, interest, or expertise. For example, the tapa may remind an individual of a specific experience and then stimulate additional memories that surround that story. Second, narratives can be referenced to shared social experiences, values, and potential futures. These stories have the individual as a participant or observer with others. For example, families may reminisce collectively about their reactions to a specific object, perhaps the tapa that they sat on or looked at during their travels. The third type of narrative is a vicarious experience of others. These stories are second-hand experiences because the visitor did not participate in them directly. For example, a docent might describe the life circumstances of an artist who painted a specific picture to enliven the visitors' understanding. Here the narrative of the artist's life makes the painting more memorable and vivid.

The locus of narrative reference may help to differentiate different types of stories and the contexts in which they arise and are retold. Autobiographically referenced stories may be more poignant to the individual as markers of significant yet private events. Socially referenced stories, we think, are more likely to be retold, reinterpreted, and shared over time with significant others as informal stories that bond the group together. Vicarious stories may have the least emotional investment because the listener is not part of the story. Indeed, the focus of the remote, vicarious narrative involves stories that center on the object, rather than the person. Degree of participation distinguishes the three types of stories. The person is at the center of the autobiographical narrative and further from the center in socially shared stories or object-based narratives. Lave and Wenger (1991) described "legitimate peripheral participation" as a social practice of moving from the periphery to the center of a group and part of that movement is promoted by sharing the stories of oldtimers in the group. In a parallel way, we think that visitors move from a peripheral to a central, personal understanding of objects as they become directly involved with stories about objects. Thus, one derived hypothesis is that visitors will find autobiographical connections to objects more poignant, emotional, and memorable than more peripheral narrative connections to objects.

We believe that museum visitors understand objects that they encounter in relation to their own histories and anticipated futures, through self-referenced and socially referenced narratives (Rosenzweig & Thelen, 1998). Looking forward and backward in one's own life shapes the meanings attached to objects and experiences, as interpretation involving both the I-self and Me-self takes place. The narratives may be personalized and idiographic to reflect one's own personal cognitive development (Ferrari & Mahalingam, 1998). Narratives need not be actual, accurate, or authentic. Markus and Nurius (1986) suggested that people envision multiple selves that are possible: "Self-schemas are constructed creatively and selectively from an individual's past experiences in a particular domain. They reflect personal concerns of enduring salience and investment, and they have been shown to have a systematic and pervasive influence on how information about the self is processed" (p. 960). Museum visitors discover bits and pieces of their own lives in the objects they encounter as they browse, cruise, and examine museum spaces. The information becomes meaningful through reference to representations of who they are and who they want to become. Harter (1999) considered such analyses to be critical for identity formation.

> In developing a self-narrative, the individual creates a sense of continuity over time as well as coherent connections among self-relevant life events. In constructing such a life story, the I-self is assigned an important agentic role as author, temporally sequencing the Me-selves into a coherent self-narrative that provides meaning and a sense of future direction. (p. 334)

We might add our conjectures about the development of socially referenced narratives that provide shared past experiences and shared directions for the future. The stories that families create with objects in museums solidify the connections among people and reaffirm their roots and values. When stories reference national events such as wars, they reaffirm feelings of national pride (or shame). When stories connect visitors to legacies of religion, diaspora, or ethnic celebrations, they enculturate the participants and mark their similarities. In this way, narratives go beyond stories of individuals to become significant badges and symbols of identities that locate the person in society, culture, and history. In recognition of the power of stories, museums are beginning to change their approach to exhibit design. Roberts (1997) traced the historical development of museum education and concluded that museums no longer have simple "knowledge-telling" missions. Today, museum educators create narratives about objects and design exhibitions that encourage visitors to construct their own narratives.

We think that the objects encountered by visitors usually elicit three types of reactions relevant to narratives. First, the object may be recognized as a confirming instance of a previous story, that is, the visitor recognizes and re-affirms a prior understanding (e.g., "yes, that looks just like the tapa I saw in Tahiti" or "We saw one like this in the museum in London"). Second, the object may elicit a disconfirming reaction in which the visitor recognizes that the story elicited, read, or heard does not corroborate previous understanding. The visitor's prior experiences may contradict the story presented by an object. This occurrence may become an antagonistic narrative or the basis for future reconciliation of the old and new stories. Third, a visitor's reaction to an object may elaborate and expand the previous narrative by embellishing it with new information or updated autobiographical information (e.g., "aha, now I see that Fijian tapas have different patterns and more black dye than Samoan and Tahitian tapas"). All three kinds of reactions "make meaning" in the sense of personally constructed knowledge, but we hypothesize that distinguishing among these three kinds of reactions helps us to understand how visitors transact with objects that they encounter and how new information can be assimilated into visitors' narrative understanding. In particular, we think that visitors are biased to recognize and generate connections that confirm their prior understandings and stories, a search for affirmation of their previous stories. They may be willing to elaborate their knowledge but less likely to recognize or value contradictory reactions to their stories. Thus, in the research described next, we examined how museum visitors confirm, disconfirm, and elaborate their beliefs about their own identities. There are many features of the Me-self that might be considered, but in this research we focused on race, gender, culture, generation, family, and individual sense of self.

DESIGNING METHODS TO ELICIT SELF–OBJECT CONNECTIONS

This brief introduction to a transactional view of learning through objects during museum visits provides the rationale for our study on visitors' identity reactions. We believe that visitors in museums seek and recognize features of themselves in the objects they encounter, and these searches lead to confirmations, contradictions, or discoveries about various aspects of their Me-selves. These searches are not necessarily directed and deliberate but they may be implicit and unconscious orientations to familiarity. Visitors may be biased to find and recognize characteristics of objects that make sense to them. This is evident in the spontaneous remarks and memories of visitors and it prompted us to elicit the personal stories and recollections of visitors in an historical museum to determine directly if they recognize features of identity in exhibits. The first study reports how adult visitors to some of the exhibits at the Henry Ford Museum & Greenfield Village (HFM&GV) reacted to objects on the basis of five features of identity; gender, ethnicity, historical generation, self, and family. The second study employed a card sorting technique to examine how adults perceived elements of identity in photographs of museum objects. Both studies were initiated in collaboration with the Museum Learning Collaborative at the University of Pittsburgh as part of their research agenda. As such, the studies complement other research reported in this volume in both (a) the search for new methods to use in visitor research in museums, and (b) the quest for deeper understanding of how visitors elaborate their own identities through museum experiences.

PILOT STUDY

We began with a pilot study to help refine the data collecting procedures and to gauge responses of visitors. Twenty-one adult visitors were recruited and shown a random set of 5 to 8 photographed objects (from a total of 38 different exhibits) in the museum. Participants were asked to look at each photograph individually and give a rating of 1 to 5 on the following dimensions:

- How much does this object make you think of either males or females?
- How strongly does it make you think of a period in time or generation of people?
- How strongly does the object make you think of an ethnic or racial group?

- How much does it make you think of yourself?
- How strongly does it make you think of your family?

A rating of 1 indicated *no reaction to the identity feature* and a rating of 5 was considered *a very strong reaction to the feature.* Participants were clearly able to evaluate objects in terms of the five dimensions of identity. Eleven of the 21 participants spontaneously supplied comments such as: "My dad worked on it," "I remember that," "That reminds me of White people," and "That [object] was my great uncle's." Not all reactions were positive, however. On the first day of pilot testing, a 54-year-old White woman was asked to look at a photograph of a handgun and respond to the questions. When the researcher asked, "How strongly does this object make you think of yourself," the woman suddenly became emotionally distressed. She explained that her father had killed himself with a handgun, and although she had walked through the gun displays and examined several of the revolvers earlier in the day, that experience had not evoked the memory. It was only when she was prompted to think of the object in personal terms that she recalled the connection to her own life. After this incident, weapons were removed from the photographed objects and other items were critically examined in order to avoid prompting potentially traumatic experiences. It is worth noting that ethical considerations may inhibit researchers from asking questions about objects that may elicit emotional identity reactions. Although research may not illuminate gut-wrenching and moving responses about one's personal struggles or tragedies, many objects in museums can precipitate exactly these feelings. We speculate that people visit some museums and exhibitions in order to be moved by these objects, not because they want to relive unpleasant memories, but because the transactions with the objects are therapeutic for the individual. Visits to cemeteries and war memorials are examples of such somber reminders of one's own family, nationality, and identity.

Wording of the third question regarding ethnic identity was revised based on the pilot study. Many visitors reacted to it with statements such as, "I'm not prejudiced," and 14 of 21 respondents gave more than 80% of objects a score of 1 on that dimension. We changed the question to, "How strongly does the object make you think of an ethnic, a racial, or a cultural group" with the interviewer emphasizing the word "cultural." With these modifications, we felt the procedures and photos would elicit personal responses from visitors about five distinctive features of identity.

Study 1

The 100 participants were English-speaking adult visitors to the indoor museum building of the HFM&GV in Dearborn, Michigan, during August and September 1999. The participants were volunteers from various social groups: families (55%), friends (12%), couples (24%), and visitors who were alone (10%). Further, 48% were female, 52% male; 77% were Caucasian, 23% other; and 26% were ages 18 to 35, 47% were 36 to 55, and 27% were over the age of 55. One or two adults in a single social group were invited to participate.

A table and two chairs were provided for visitor comfort, and the testing materials were placed on the table. The six standard photographs and two alternates—chosen because they elicited strong responses from visitors on one or more identity dimensions in the pilot study—were turned upside-down in order to avoid cueing participants for the free-recall section of the interview. The six standard photographs depicted the Kennedy car (the limousine in which John F. Kennedy was assassinated), a wooden butter churn, a Buick Riviera from the mid-1960s, an early Holiday Inn sign, a Singer treadle-powered sewing machine, and a late 19th-century horse-drawn sleigh. The alternates showed a train engine and the chair in which Abraham Lincoln sat when he was assassinated. Also placed on the table were a tape recorder, informed consent forms, and two signs stating "Visitor Reaction Study: Help us learn more about visitors' reactions to objects."

Visitors were asked to recall two objects or exhibits in HFM&GV that made a strong impression on them. Their responses were recorded, and the 1 to 5 response scale was explained. Then the interviewer presented a card on which the participant could read the five questions while the interviewer read each question for the first recalled object.

- How much does the object make you think of either males or females?
- How strongly does it make you think of a period in time or generation of people?
- How strongly does the object make you think of an ethnic, racial, or cultural group?
- How much does it make you think of yourself?
- How strongly does it make you think of your family?

Next, visitors were questioned about the second recalled object or exhibit and then shown the six photographed objects. About 17% of our participants were administered one of the alternate photographs because one or both of their freely recalled objects were among the six standard photographed objects. Visitors' ratings regarding the five identity questions were recorded for each object. Finally, the participant could choose to end the session or continue with a recorded interview. Those who opted to continue (46%) were administered a scripted set of questions. These questions were designed to assess whether visitors confirmed, disconfirmed, or elaborated aspects of their own identity in their encounters with objects within the museum that day. A visual reference was provided on a card in which the words confirm, contradict, and discover were shown together with a pictorial representation of the HFM&GV building. The researcher pointed to each word, watched participants for signs of confusion or understanding as she gave the following explanation, and adjusted the wording depending on participants' level of understanding.

> Sometimes we have experiences with people, objects, or events that make us think about ourselves. Some of those experiences help us to *confirm* what we already knew about ourselves. They remind us of who we are, where we come from, or what we believe, perhaps. When we see them, we might say, "That reminds me of myself." Other experiences *contradict* what we thought about ourselves. They make us think, "I thought I knew this about myself or my history or my place in the world, but seeing this makes me need to re-think things." Still other experiences lead us to *discover* altogether new things about ourselves—new interests, new connections to people, events, or objects. They make us think, "I never knew that about myself," or "I had no idea how fascinated I would be by . . ."

The three prompts—discovery, contradiction, and confirmation—were administered in random order. After all three prompts had been given, a final question was posed and the responses were recorded: "Finally, what did your experience today at the museum do for you?" This concluded the interview, although about half of the participants stayed longer to talk with the interviewer. We were surprised, but pleased, to hear many participants say how much they enjoyed the interview. They were eager to have an opportunity to talk about their experiences with someone else and to share their personal reactions. This confirmed for us the power of their transactions with the objects and the pleasure derived from sharing their stories with others, stories that were infused with autobiographical and social references.

What Did Visitors Say? The characteristics of the two objects that visitors recalled as meaningful varied by age on the dimensions of Self and Family. Adults over age 55 were most likely to identify aspects of themselves and their families in the recalled objects. This may mean that older adults recalled objects they had seen during their museum visit precisely because they reminded them of their own personal lives. Younger adults did not rate their recalled objects as highly, which may indicate less Self and Family identification in general than elderly visitors in a history museum.

The dimensions of Self and Family were also significant in the analyses of visitors' ratings of photographed objects. For the Self dimension, some objects (Holiday Inn sign, sewing machine, Kennedy car) were much more likely to elicit feelings of self-identity than others (sleigh, butter churn, Buick Riviera). Gender influenced the ratings of objects; women gave higher identity ratings to some objects such as the sewing machine and lower ratings to others such as the Buick Riviera. Age also affected the ratings; older adults gave higher ratings to the Kennedy car, Buick Riviera, and the sewing machine, presumably because all these objects were more likely to have been directly experienced by the older participants in their own lives 40 to 50 years ago.

The Family dimension revealed similar effects. Some objects such as the sewing machine received high ratings compared to low ratings of the sleigh. Age influenced ratings because the oldest participants rated the sewing machine, butter churn, and Buick Riviera higher than the other three objects on the family dimension. There was a significant influence of Ethnicity on object ratings, because non-Caucasian Americans and non-Americans rated the sewing machine higher than Caucasian Americans, yet rated the Holiday Inn and Riviera lower.

Visitors gave many examples of identity-confirming objects in the HFM&GV. Indeed, 32 of the 46 visitors who remained for the extended interviews said "Yes" to the confirming question. This indicates that visitors are nostalgic as they view objects at HFM&GV and have feelings that affirm their own personal experiences, feelings, and Me-selves. In contrast, 6 of the 46 participants (13%) said they experienced feelings of self-contradiction as they viewed exhibits. These feelings do not appear to indicate an underlying negative experience though, because 4 of the 6 participants who recognized identity-disconfirming objects also said they had confirming and discovery experiences with objects too. Do museums help visitors learn new things about themselves? Yes, 21 of the 46 visitors said that they had encountered objects that made them re-think aspects of their Me-selves. The following excerpts illustrate each type of visitor comment.

Self-Confirming Reactions. Subject 6, a 47-year-old White male visiting with his family said, "The Kennedy car—looking at that stuff, it's like listening to a radio and listening to old music and you can date back. I can even date back to where I was standing when he [President Kennedy] got shot. It was sixth grade. (To his wife) Remember the day he got shot? We was in school."

Subject 20, a 47-year-old non-White male visiting with his family said, "Back here in the machine tools. All my whole family have been machinists. Half of them are auto workers. (The machine tools remind me of) what I did, what I learned in high school, trade school, what I did for a long time, what I still do, what I'm gonna do for another 10 years."

Subject 22, a 46-year-old White female visiting with her family said, "Yeah—in the gift shop. They're selling these little shoes. Wanna see it? (Shows the shoe to the interviewer and another visitor at the table.) Isn't that neat? That's me. That shoe is me."

Subject 23, a 43-year-old White female visiting with her family said, "Everything that's metal and black confirms that I have no interest in the gears and machines and anything like that. As soon as I saw it, my mind shut down. I could not look at it. It was too much of that stuff in one spot, and I steered completely away, and I know that next time I come in here, I'm moving directly to the left where the furniture and all of that, kitchens, dollhouses . . ."

Subject 55, a 69-year-old White male visiting with his family said, "All in all, I would go away feeling like I'm a part of America, and I'm a part of this. And I enjoyed it and I'd come back again."

Self-Contradicting Reactions. Subject 9, a 43-year-old White female visiting with her family said, "When I see the advancements of technology that goes against the environment, I always like the convenience of the train, the plane, and all that, but now I think about how it pollutes the air and all that, so it makes me not so sure I want to have it. Yeah, that's a contradiction."

Subject 100, a 34-year-old White male visiting with friends said, "And I don't like what I . . . (to his colleague also sitting at the table) Close your ears. (Laughs.) What I'm not comfortable with is knowing what I do as an engineer and what I do for a living, I'm not comfortable with it, as how it promotes a certain way of life that I think is detrimental overall."

Self-Discovery Reactions. Subject 15, a 40-year-old woman visiting with German exchange students said, "Showing it to people from another country, so there are some things that I see in a different way this time than I've seen before, because America is a very new country. What we consider old isn't what they would probably consider old. So it's interesting to see the differences in what we see as our pasts."

Subject 17, a 70-year-old White male visiting with his wife said, "There was something that I wanted to start collecting when I saw it here . . . the pamphlets with the cars, like, instructions and brochures. I wish that I could have saved some of those or bought them recently at garage sales."

Subject 23, a 43-year-old White female visiting with her family said, "Well, talking about the Declaration of Independence: we were looking at those signatures again. . . . It was really obvious to me how egotistical the men must've been who signed that. Because the signatures are so . . . well, for instance Benjamin Franklin and John Hancock's signatures are so flourishy. And other signatures are pretty straightforward, but there were a lot of flourishy signatures there. Those men must've thought highly of themselves to have such a signature."

Summary. Study 1 revealed that a simple interviewing method can be used to elicit a wealth of information about how visitors connect their experiences with aspects of their identities. We asked visitors to recall meaningful objects and to rate photographs of objects according to specific dimensions of personal identity that we think are important in a history museum. These dimensions of identity included references to personal (e.g., gender) as well as social (e.g., family, culture) aspects of identity. It would be easy to revise the dimensions that are examined for different types of museums or features of self-referencing. For example, if one wanted to assess how visitors find their own identities in art museums, one could create a survey based on dimensions of creativity and self-expression. If one wanted to examine how visitors to religious shrines or museums connect objects to their own sense of identity, then the dimensions might include spirituality and morality. We believe the method, that is, prompting recognition of features of identity via pictures of objects, can be adapted easily to a variety of settings and dimensions of self and, thus, is valuable as a research tool. The Likert scale method of rating features of identity can also be combined with other research methods, for example, qualitative analyses of conversations and recalled stories, to add quantitative dimensions about the self-perceived relevance of objects.

The findings of this study show that visitors find and recognize aspects of their own identities in exhibits. Self, family, and historical generations were salient in HFM&GV, as one might expect. Older visitors noticed the significance of these dimensions more than younger visitors, but it may be because the older visitors sought out the museum visit and objects for that purpose. Alternatively, older visitors may have been more open to the recognition of the self–object connections or had more familiar first-hand experiences with the objects. Perhaps older visitors are more practiced in sharing and telling stories in museums. The many spontaneous anecdotes shared by visitors illustrates the importance of stories in their transactions with objects. We think that these hypotheses deserve further scrutiny and that this study simply opens the door to many more questions about why some visitors find aspects of self in objects more than other visitors.

Study 2

The purpose of Study 2 was to design and test another method that might illuminate how visitors find self in objects. We sought to examine if visitors associate and group objects in museums according to their own dimensions of personal identity. In other words, we designed a method that did not presuppose the dimensions of self or identity that adults might recognize in objects. Participants were shown 24 photographs of museum objects and asked to group them in whatever manner they chose. The main question we explored was whether adults would group the objects according to the five features of identity in Study 1. In order to identify a standard for evaluating the free sorting patterns, we asked the same adults after the free sort to sort the photographs into piles of exemplars and nonexemplars based on the identity components studied previously: gender, ethnicity/culture, history, self, and family. In this manner, we could identify the spontaneous dimensions that adults used to group photos of objects as well as the likelihood that adults could sort objects into the preassigned categories that we used in Study 1.

Adult visitors to exhibits at the indoor museum building of HFM&GV during December 1999 and January 2000 were invited to participate. Our sample included 40 (78%) Caucasians and 11 (22%) non-Caucasians; 24 (47%) females and 27 (53%) males; and 14 (27%) visitors aged 18 to 35, 25 (49%) aged 36 to 55, and 12 (24%) over the age of 55. A table was set up with a basket of candy prominently displayed and signs reading "Visitor Reaction Study: Help us learn more about visitors' reactions to objects." Groups of visitors who passed by were asked if one adult might like to participate. After obtaining informed consent, the researcher offered pieces of candy or chocolate to everyone in the group as gratitude for their cooperation. The 24 photographs of objects in the museum collection included the six standard and two alternate pictures from Study 1. They were displayed in random order and covered most of the table. A tape recorder was used to serve as a backup record-keeping device, and a 10-sided die was used to randomly assign the two identity prompts that visitors would be given after their free sorts.

Participants were asked to sort the pictures of objects into groups. They were instructed to use whatever sorting scheme they wished to use and make any number of groups other than 1 or 24 pictures. When this task was completed, visitors gave each group a name and read aloud the numbers assigned to each photograph in each group so the researcher could record the grouping. Next, the visitor rolled a die and was randomly assigned one of the identity prompts based on the result. This was done by assigning a pair of numbers on the die to each of the five identity components. For example, if visitors rolled a 1 or 2, they were assigned to the gender category for sorting. The researcher directed the visitor to consider each photograph again and separate objects that reminded them of the identity component (such as "a gender," "yourself," or "a racial, cultural, or ethnic group") from those that did not. Following that sort, a second among the four remaining identity components was randomly selected using the 10-sided die. When the second roll of the die fell in the same identity component as the first, visitors were asked to roll the die again. Then visitors were given instructions to separate the objects into one pile of exemplars and one of nonexemplars.

Free Sort. Did the sorting method reveal features of identity? The first question is whether visitors could sort photos into reasonable groups. We found that most visitors approached the sorting task with a utilitarian schema in mind. For instance, "transportation" was a theme that 75% of the visitors used in their classifications, which is not surprising given the many exhibitions of cars, trains, and other modes of transportation. Another third of the visitors made "household" and "tools" groups. The groupings they made often mirrored the way HFM&GV organized and exhibited objects: decorative arts and home products located together; Presidential cars in a row; and objects related to farming and pioneer life in one part of the building. Overall, more than 80% of visitors sorted objects by form and function, and often their groupings reflected the major exhibition themes within HFM&GV.

The remainder of the visitors, however, used much more idiosyncratic but personally meaningful methods of sorting. The individual's level of interest in objects was a common theme among these visitors. "Nostalgia near and dear to me," "History that's meaningful," and "Things I don't care about," was how one 53-year-old non-White male divided objects and then named his groups. A 22-year-old White female named her groups, "Things I'm most interested in," "OK things," "Things that remind me of being a little kid," and "I don't care about these things."

On closer inspection, many visitors who sorted by utilitarian methods also made reference to one or more of the five identity components that we were investigating in their sorting and naming of sorted piles. "Things people used to use," "I don't know what these are," "Stuff I would find in my husband's garage," "Bad things," and "American nostalgic things," are some examples of categories that reference gender, ethnicity/culture, generational history, self, and family. Although most of the visitors approached the task pragmatically, they used themselves as reference points in passing judgments and assigning group ownership over objects. Visitors used personalized language in communicating categories, even when they did not design those categories to be self-referenced.

Prompted Sort. Our second question, whether adult visitors could sort photographs by the five identity components, was partially addressed in our analysis of the free-sort data. The 51 adults who were prompted to sort specifically with these identity components in mind had no difficulty in doing so. Some objects were classified in the same way by many visitors. For example, the sewing machine was identified by 100% of the adults as reminding them of gender whereas 0% of adults who viewed a pitchfork judged that it reminded them of themselves. Half of the objects were identified as gender-related, including President Reagan's limousine, the 1960s Buick Riviera, and a typewriter. Not surprisingly, almost two thirds of the objects reminded people of specific periods in time or generations of people, such as the horse-drawn sleigh, Lincoln chair, and tractor. Far fewer objects reminded visitors of ethnic or cultural groups—the butter churn, pitchfork, and hatchet each chosen by less than two thirds of visitors—or family—the Holiday Inn sign and sewing machine. There was little agreement on what objects reminded visitors of themselves, the Holiday Inn sign being the only object chosen by at least 70% of visitors. More agreement could be found in what did not remind visitors of culture, self, or family. Many of the objects in our photographed set elicited no feelings of personal identity. We were struck by the extreme variation among visitors in their reactions to the same objects. For example, the same photograph elicited excitement, resentment, and boredom from different visitors. The explanations revealed that visitors who had no narrative connections to objects often rated them very low on our scales of identity. Thus, visitors could sort objects according to features of identity but their ratings varied in idiosyncratic ways among visitors.

DISCUSSION

The results of these two studies show clearly that visitors recall meaningful objects during museum visits that elicit feelings relevant to their own personal identities. The dimensions that we examined included gender, ethnicity, historical generation, self, and family. Naturally, feelings of time and history were elicited in HFM&GV, a history museum, but there were also feelings of gender, ethnicity, self, and family for specific objects. The specific dimensions of identity and the particular objects used in these studies were selected to represent the thematic emphases of the HFM&GV but the methods are adaptable to other settings and other features of self-object transactions. For example, other dimensions of the Me-self could be examined, and we could study the impact of objects on feelings of expertise, artistic expression, manual skill, and so forth. It seems likely that visitors select museums based on personal profiles of interests and talents that in turn reflect their own identity strivings. In the same way that museum goers browse exhibits looking for things that they have experienced or would like to know more about, perhaps they select the overall environments to confirm and extend their own senses of I and Me. In other words, some days you might really feel like visiting a science museum and other days you seek the serenity of a garden because each setting reinforces aspects of your own self in distinctive ways.

These two studies employed a variety of methods including free recall, stimulated recall, structured interviews, free sorting of photographed objects, and directed sorting of photographs by identity dimensions. Part of our purpose was to develop and test new methods that can be used to study aspects of identity in museums. Our intention was to create methods that allow quantification of visitors' responses, along with their own narrative accounts of the objects, as well as methods that can be used in any type of museum. We think all these methods show promise for revealing personal and meaningful reactions of visitors. They may be especially valuable for comparing contexts and exhibits because some settings more than others include objects that evoke highly charged emotional and personal responses. Recollections of identity confirming and disconfirming experiences could be powerful in museums devoted to war, ethnicity, religion, and similar topics that have great personal meaning for some visitors. Likewise, the methods may be valuable for comparing the conditions under which objects are experienced. Perhaps touching objects, hearing audio accompaniments while viewing, or listening to someone tell their personal story while viewing an object would heighten the visitors' awareness of dimensions of their own identities. The methods introduced here could be useful in such studies because (a) they focus on the transactions between visitors and objects, (b) they can be grounded in different theoretical orientations, and (c) they can be used for quantitative hypothesis testing.

Additionally, participants in this study generally enjoyed talking about the objects encountered during their visits. In Study 1, approximately half of those interviewed stayed to talk with the researcher after the interview and they clearly enjoyed engaging in self-related discourse in the museum setting. In several instances, the researcher wished that the tape recorder had not been stopped because of the fascinating stories that came up in postinterview conversations. Indeed, it was not unusual to have a visitor linger at the researcher's table until the rest of the visitor's group had disappeared into another section of the building or the museum was closing down. In Study 2, the researcher often heard comments about how fun or how interesting the sorting task was. Often, other visitors observed the participants because they wanted to hear the conversations. In some cases, a friendly repartee arose around underlying psychological implications of their friends' sorting choices. Thus, an unexpected advantage of these methods is the visitors' enjoyment and reminiscence provided by the conversations. In terms of our own perspective, such conversations move the visitors' stories from the periphery of the museum experience to the center. Their narratives are validated in the conversations through the acts of sharing, embellishing, and explaining their own personal reactions and their perceptions of the significance of objects.

The fact that the research occurred in the museum is important. Visitors frequently gestured to nearby exhibits as they talked about the importance of the place. A 73-year-old White female said, "We appreciate somebody, you know, taking care of all these things." A 44-year-old White female said, "It's the first time I've been to this museum since I took this job at a historic education center. Looking at things in the museum is different." Talking about objects in their presence is probably important for eliciting vivid recollections and reactions. Therefore, we think our methods are most likely to be effective when administered during or after a museum visit and within the physical space of the museum. Visitors recognized the museum as a "place to remember" and they valued this function, as exemplified in these comments of a 73-year-old White male visiting alone:

Interviewer: What did your visit to the museum do for you today?

Visitor: Brought back memories. Yes, most of all.

Interviewer: Is that a good thing?

Visitor: I think it is. I live on memories. You get older, when you get older, people always say older people talk about the past. Something about old men dream dreams, and young men. . . . What does the Bible say about that? "Old men dream dreams and young men have visions." So maybe my visions are mostly gone. But I saw so many things that brought back memories, and I think memories are good. Everybody tells me I have a wonderful memory. If I meet somebody I went to school with, first thing, we'll be talking about something, (and they'll say) "You remember that?" (laughter) Things that they can't remember we did in school, happened in school, it never impressed them, I guess. But it stuck in my mind. I can remember those things. Sometimes, I even write a little bit, and I'll write about things that I remember. So memories are, I think, real important in our lives. I think we should always keep them. Unless you have bad memories. I don't have any of those. All my memories are rather pleasant. I think memories are healthy. It's your conscience. You don't have a conscience, you're hard-hearted.

In conclusion, we want to emphasize the following points. First, museum visitors recognize features of themselves in the objects they encounter. More specifically, visitors to a history museum showed that objects often provoked them to think of aspects of their personal identities and their social group memberships. These referenced transactions with objects are often idiosyncratic because the objects are embedded in narrative accounts that are personal. Such stories are transactional in the sense that visitors reinterpret and retell stories engendered by objects and objects can provoke people to confirm, contradict, and discover something new about their own previous understandings of the objects. In this manner, transactions between objects and people are part of an object-based epistemology (Conn, 1998) in which the natural history and cultural history of objects are constructed, retold, and embellished.

A second point that emerges from our research is that visitors differ in the ways that they find self-confirming experiences. Some may seek museums and objects expressly for the purpose of searching for meaning about their past and present selves. Others may bump into such realizations unwittingly. Our participants showed wide variations in responses to the same objects. Some people thought a specific object reminded them a great deal about family, culture, or self whereas others saw no hint of the dimension in the object. What leads to such wide differences in the apperception of identity dimensions? We think the answer lies in the transactional analysis of the experience and is revealed only by reference to the visitors' narrative accounts (Clandinin & Connelly, 2000). These life stories reference the object in personal and social contexts and give meaning that cannot be discerned by analyses of the object or visitor in isolation. That is why autobiographical and transactional frameworks provide useful lenses for viewing the impact of museum visits.

As one illustration of how transforming museum experiences can be, consider the case of Myla, an African-American girl who felt alienated in a science classroom (Beane & Pope, 2002). As an eighth-grade student, Myla was recruited to be a science explainer as part of the new YouthALIVE! Program of mentoring in Minneapolis. Science was not part of her identity then but she developed an I-self identity as an inquisitive scientist and a Me-self identity as a teacher over a period of 10 years working in museums. She said,

> I truly believe that my greatest works can be accomplished through teaching. I love working with inner city populations. I went into my undergraduate studies with the idea of working on the prevention of delinquency. I wanted to intervene in young people's lives in a positive way. Now I plan to teach! In the graduate program, it seems so strange—yet so divinely orchestrated—that everyone in the program, my instructors, other students, and even I have concluded that I would be a wonderful science teacher. The museum has served as my playground for science learning since the eighth grade. I no longer see science as a foreign subject! I see it as an area of study where one can play, explore, devise theories, test ideas, and recreate. It really does not matter if I am right or wrong. What matters is that I know how to find the answer! I really like the idea of teaching science to primary students, and bringing inquiry and a hands-on approach to the classroom. (p. 345)

A third point of our research is that new methods are needed to uncover the deeply personal reactions of visitors to objects. We showed that interviews, stimulated recall, ratings of photographed objects, and sorting photos of objects into groups can all reveal the subjective connections that visitors make with objects. There are many other methods described in this volume such as diaries, journals, experience sampling, and conversational analyses. The rich variety of potential techniques illustrates how psychological methods may be applied to answer questions about visitors' experiences in museums. These methods go well beyond traditional surveys of consumer satisfaction or maps of visitor movement in museums because they are theoretically motivated and designed to answer fundamental questions about the transcendent qualities of museum visits. Making meaning with objects can transform understanding and the stances one takes with objects, but more than that, the transactions with the objects provoke reflection and reconsideration of one's beliefs that extend one's knowledge (Mezirow, 1991). The enthusiastic reactions of our participants indicates their desire to explore and share their stories, stories that may have roots in specific museum experiences and branches that connect objects with their own lives in unique ways over long periods of time. These stories reveal fundamental aspects of a person's life and cumulative development, stories that reveal the I-self and Me-self to the reflective visitor.

ACKNOWLEDGMENTS

The research reported here was supported in part by the Museum Learning Collaborative (MLC), Learning Research and Development Center, University of Pittsburgh. The MLC is funded by the Institute for Museum and Library Services, the National Science Foundation, the National Endowment for the Arts, and the National Endowment for the Humanities. The opinions expressed are solely those of the authors and no official endorsement from the funders should be presumed.

REFERENCES

Beane, D., & Pope, M. (2002). Leveling the playing field through object-based service learning. In S. Paris (Ed.), *Perspectives on object-centered learning in museums* (pp. 325–349). Mahwah, NJ: Lawrence Erlbaum Associates.

Bruner, J. S. (1986). *Actual minds, possible worlds.* Cambridge, MA: Harvard University Press.

Clandinin, D. J., & Connelly, F. M. (2000). *Narrative inquiry.* San Francisco: Jossey-Bass.

Conn, S. (1998). *Museums and American intellectual life, 1876–1926.* Chicago: The University of Chicago Press.

Elder, G. H. (1998). The life course as developmental theory. *Child Development, 69*(1), 1–12.

Falk, J. H., & Dierking, L. D. (1992). *The museum experience.* Washington, DC: Whalesback.

Ferrari, M., & Mahalingam, R. (1998). Personal cognitive development and its implications for teaching and Learning. *Educational Psychologist, 33*(1), 35–44.

Gurian, E. H. (1999). What is the object of this exercise? A meandering exploration of the many meanings of objects in museums. *Daedulus, 128*(3), 163–183.

Harter, S. (1999). *The construction of self.* New York: Guilford Press.

James, W. (1890). *Principles of psychology.* Chicago: Encyclopedia Britannica.

Lave, J., & Wenger, E. (1991). *Situated learning: Legitimate peripheral participation.* New York: Cambridge University Press.

Markus, H., & Nurius, P. (1986). Possible selves. *American Psychologist, 41,* 954–969.

Mezirow, J. (1991). *Transformative dimensions of adult learning.* San Francisco: Jossey-Bass.

Paris, S. G., Byrnes, J. P., & Paris, A. H. (2001). Constructing theories, identities, and actions of self-regulated learners. In B. Zimmerman & D. Schunk (Eds.), *Self-regulated learning and academic achievement* (2nd ed., pp. 253–287). Mahwah, NJ: Lawrence Erlbaum Associates.

Paris, S. G. (2002). *Perspectives on object-centered learning in museums.* Mahwah, NJ: Lawrence Erlbaum Associates.

Roberts, L. (1997). *From knowledge to narrative.* Washington, DC: Smithsonian Institution.

Rosenzweig, R., & Thelen, D. (1998). *The presence of the past: Popular uses of history in American life.* New York: Columbia University Press.

Chapter 13

Supporting Science Learning in Museums

Leona Schauble
Mary Gleason
Rich Lehrer
Karol Bartlett
Anthony Petrosino
Annie Allen
Katie Clinton
Evelyn Ho
Melanie Jones
Young-Sun Lee
Jo-Anne Phillips
John Siegler
John Street
University of Wisconsin, Madison

LEARNING IN MUSEUMS

Although it is usually assumed that learning means cognitive or conceptual change, learning in the broad sense also includes outcomes like an expanded sense of aesthetic appreciation, the development of motivation and interest, the formation and refinement of critical standards, and the growth of personal identity. This sense of learning is consistent with sociocultural theory's focus on meaning-making in the broad sense, which emphasizes social interaction and cultural symbols and tools as crucibles for appropriating and adapting forms of knowledge, values, and expression. Under this interpretation, visitor learning is an objective shared by a wide variety of informal learning contexts, including science and children's museums, art museums and galleries, historical museums and reconstructions, and zoos and botanical gardens.

Motivated by a focus on learning, many museums are seeking to develop a range of opportunities that encourage visitors to step beyond the "browse mode" that they typically adopt in museums. Accomplishing this goal involves inventing and testing approaches to get visitors to process information more deeply, reflect about prior conceptions on the basis of new information, and engage in systematic study or exploration. Yet developing opportunities for deeper learning is no easy feat. Visitors—especially youngsters—may require assistance and support, both to identify these learning opportunities and to understand how to take advantage of them. Accordingly, there is growing interest in how to provide effective *assistance* of learning in museums, especially the kinds of learning that families and other visiting groups can provide for each other (Borun et al., 1998; Crowley & Callanan, 1998). With few exceptions (e.g., Gelman, Massey, & McManus, 1991), the primary focus to date in this research has been on identifying strategies for learning and assisting that are domain-general, that is, independent of any particular content or task.

For example, in one influential program of museum research, the emphasis has been on identifying "performance indicators" of learning, such as asking a question, answering a question, commenting on or explaining an exhibit, reading text silently, and reading text aloud (Borun, Chambers, Dritsas, & Johnson, 1997). The assumption is that whenever these behaviors are observed learning is occurring, whether the target exhibit is about science, history, or anthropology. All episodes of question posing (and, for that matter, questions about all kinds of topics) are regarded as equally indicative of learning.

Yet, the past 30 years of cognitive psychology demonstrate that thinking and problem solving are always modulated by the content domain and task at hand. Although it is possible to describe general strategies for supporting learning, general strategies are relatively prone to error and are not very well tuned for developing knowledge about qualities of particular domains. Therefore, if one wants to *improve* reasoning or problem solving, it helps to understand how teaching and assistance can best be tailored to the subject matter, the particular task, and the learner's current level of understanding.

This by no means suggests that domain-general studies of learning in museum contexts have not made important contributions. To the contrary, they have helped to turn our collective attention from what gets *presented* in museums to what gets *learned.* This focus on "what gets learned," in turn, suggests related questions about the forms of learning assistance that are tailored more specifically to visitors' thinking *about particular domains of content.* In this chapter, we describe research that begins to address these questions in a museum setting.

In this chapter, we focus specifically on science learning in a museum gallery targeted especially for elementary school-aged children. Our first objective was to get a sense of how adults—both parents and museum staff—generally understand (or misunderstand) children's learning in this kind of context, including children's opportunities to learn and adults' opportunities to assist. To find out, we conducted a series of interviews with parents and staff about learning and assistance in specific target gallery exhibits. Our second objective was to conduct an empirical study of parent–child interaction as dyads worked together on an experimentation problem modeled on one of the museum exhibits.

THE CONTEXT FOR THE RESEARCH

The context for this research, described in detail in Schauble and Bartlett (1997), is ScienceWorks, an 11,000 square foot gallery in the Children's Museum of Indianapolis. The gallery, intended for 6- to 10-year-old visitors and their families, is designed to enhance understanding of thematic ideas about science that are exemplified in familiar, everyday contexts, like a child's back yard, a construction site down the road, and a neighborhood pond. Like most museum galleries, ScienceWorks presents a broad array of materials, resources, and activities. This breadth provides multiple entry points for visitors of diverse ages, experiences, and interests. However, along with these advantages comes an associated weakness: Ironically, the very wealth of possibilities tends to discourage visitors from spending substantial time and concentration on any one activity. When there is a lot in one place to do and see, visitors tend to wander from place to place, interacting with each exhibit for only a few moments. This kind of browsing is fun and sometimes sparks new interests, but it does not necessarily lead visitors beyond entry-level awareness of a topic or the acquisition of a few facts.

To address this problem, which we believe is a general challenge of museum learning, the designers of ScienceWorks adopted what we came to call a "funnel approach" to learning. That is, the gallery provides a wide array of options at entry level for browsing visitors, but also includes successively narrower (because it is expected that fewer visitors will take them) and deeper learning options for visitors who choose to spend more time and concentrated participation in parts of the gallery.

One exhibit, The Creek, is a long stream table where visitors can experiment with principles of turbulence, flow, mechanics, and buoyancy. The Creek attracts large numbers of visitors to an array of easy-entry exploratory activities: building and racing boats of various designs; exploring a set of working canal locks; assembling and operating systems of pipes and valves; moving water from one part of the stream to another with buckets, pumps, paddlewheels, and an Archimedes screw; and manipulating the contours of the stream, including its depth, width, curvature, and obstacles. Visitors often spend an hour or more "messing about" with these features. To provide for the more systematic learning in the narrower and deeper part of the "funnel" metaphor, The Creek is flanked by an adjacent "Dock Shop," where visitors go beyond "attract mode." Similar quieter, restricted spaces are included in the other major museum exhibits, too. In each of these spaces, visitors engage in more sustained exploration of the scientific concepts that are introduced at "acquaintance level" in the exhibit.

The Dock Shop is a setting for investigating the relationships between boat design and performance in The Creek. Visitors can construct boats with hulls of different shapes or sizes and then examine how varying these features affects the boat's capacity to carry loads of metal washers. They can design sailboats with different shaped sails and then compare the racing speed of the boats when they are tested with a powerful wind machine. They can also make paddle-wheel boats and hovercrafts, among other options. Boxed kits provide instructions and materials for preplanned investigations that parents and children can pursue together. In addition, each discovery area provides a range of materials and tools to support more open-ended exploration. For instance, the Dock Shop has shelves of kits and a variety of prefabricated kinds of boats to try out in The Creek, but it also has bins of rubber bands, Styrofoam bowls, cardboard, balloons, and other materials, plans, and blueprints for designing a boat "from scratch." Finally, at the deepest portion of the "funnel," the museum offers activities and experiences for repeat visitors, like family members or children from the local neighborhood. These activities extend concepts first encountered at the museum into wider contexts, such as the child's home, school, or neighborhood. Visitors can borrow materials and activity kits from the museum through Rex's Lending Center, an information center that is housed within the museum (materials can be returned to any local library). Children participate in home-based investigations and mail back "Science Postcards" to the Museum, where their results are added to databases that visitors can manipulate and query. With staff supervision, a visitor can design and conduct a research project using museum collections or in nearby Ritchey Woods, a nature preserve owned and managed by the museum.

LEARNING CHALLENGES IN MUSEUMS

As these deeper kinds of learning opportunities increasingly become incorporated into museums, a corresponding challenge emerges: How do visitors become aware of them? How, for example, do they find out that experimenting with boat hulls is a good thing to do at The Dock Shop—equally important, how do they get "hooked" into pursuing these deeper forms of learning? What forms of mediation are required to make these opportunities fruitful? What are appropriate and effective roles for museum staff and visiting parents and other adults? What kinds of knowledge will best equip these mediators to explicitly support and assist children's learning?

In the case of ScienceWorks, we are interested in identifying the kinds of knowledge about children's thinking that would be most useful for adults who wish to assist children's *science learning*, acknowledging that parents and museum staff cannot and probably should not be emulating what professional classroom teachers do. In a museum context, that goal would be neither feasible nor desirable. Yet, our thinking about adult assistance in museums has been strongly influenced by research on parent–child learning, exemplified in work conducted by Lehrer and Shumow (1997). Lehrer and Shumow's close observations of parents assisting their children as they solved mathematics problems demonstrated that *the right kind of knowledge about children's thinking can provide a significant increase in the effectiveness of adults' attempts to support learning*. Accordingly, for this different domain (science) and context (a museum gallery), one goal of the current research is to identify both the kinds of knowledge that mediators would find most helpful and its appropriate level of detail (which may well be different for parents than for professional museum staff).

In this chapter we describe two studies that we regard as the beginning of this program of investigation. We close the chapter by describing near-term next plans for the program of research.

Study 1: Museum Staff's and Parents' Views of Domain-Specific Learning Opportunities

We began with an investigation of how uninstructed parents and museum staff think about the learning opportunities available for children in target exhibits in ScienceWorks. We intended this study to serve as a source of information concerning adults' typical thinking about how to help children learn more effectively, and also as a baseline in subsequent research for evaluating the effectiveness of more structured forms of adult assistance. In this study, we conducted a series of interviews with parents and staff on the museum floor directly in front of target exhibits of particular interest. Our purpose was to find out what participants thought not about museum learning in general, but about the kinds of learning that a child could ideally achieve in exhibits designed to target specific science concepts and forms of scientific thinking. Because we knew in detail about the learning that each exhibit was constructed to afford (described in Schauble & Bartlett, 1997), we were in a good position to identify whether and to what extent staff and parents recognize these concepts. Accordingly, we focused explicitly on adults' domain-specific knowledge of the learning opportunities at hand. We also asked what forms of assistance they believed could best support children's learning at the target exhibits.

The study was designed and conducted by the authors of this chapter, all participants in a graduate seminar in Educational Psychology on out-of-school learning. Key contributors to both the seminar and the research were made by Leona Schauble and Rich Lehrer, faculty members in the Department, Anthony Petrosino, a postdoctoral fellow, and Karol Bartlett, the Educator–Curator of ScienceWorks at The Children's Museum of Indianapolis. In particular, Lehrer and Schauble were codevelopers of the final form of the interview used in this study. The remaining authors were graduate students enrolled in the class. The data were collected during a single weekend in May at the Children's Museum.

Participants. There were two groups of participants, museum staff and parent visitors. The 16 *museum staff* members were those scheduled to work in the gallery on the weekend that the research was conducted. These staff, who all voluntarily agreed to participate, held a range of assignments and were judged by the gallery curator to be representative of the staff assigned to work regularly in ScienceWorks. Ten of the participants were males and six were females.

The *parent visitors* were adults who came to the ScienceWorks gallery during the weekend of the research with one or more children. Parents accompanying children who appeared to be between 6 and 10 years old were stopped at the entryway to the gallery and invited to participate. If they agreed, they filled out a permission form and a brief screening sheet and were given an identifying sticker to wear (a procedure developed by Crowley and Callanan, 1998). The sticker was labeled with a number keyed to the screening interview.

A total of 94 parents completed screening sheets before entering the gallery. Review of the screening questionnaires confirmed that ScienceWorks attracts an unusual proportion of repeat visitors. Only 33, or about one third of the parents were first-time visitors to ScienceWorks. An additional 18 said they were visiting for a second time; 8 for the third or fourth; 9 for the fifth through ninth visits, and an astonishing 17 parents (nearly one fifth of those screened) reported that they had already visited the gallery more than 10 times. Moreover, eight additional adults identified themselves as repeat visitors but failed to specify how many previous visits they had made. These high levels of repeat visits in the gallery suggested that as a group, these parents had frequent opportunities to reflect about the teaching and learning opportunities in ScienceWorks, issues that were the focus of the study.

Of the 94 adults who gave permission, 32 were subsequently interviewed in the gallery, approximately half males and half females. Sixteen of these parents came with one child, 14 with two children, and 2 with three children. Precisely half of the 6- to 10-year-old children in the participating family groups were girls; half were boys.

Target Exhibits

Two exhibits in the gallery, The Creek and The Construction Zone, were selected as targets for the research. The Creek, described in detail earlier, supports exploration of concepts about hydrodynamics and hydrostatics. The Construction Zone is a simulated construction site where visitors operate a bulldozer, wheelbarrows and ramps, a dump truck, a rock sorter, a giant crane, and a variety of buckets, rollers, pulleys, and other devices to move construction materials (made of foam) from place to place. The large machines are designed to make principles of simple machines apparent. For example, the bulldozer (the "Kiddy-Kat") is operated via hand-levers that are connected to gears, which are clearly visible through a transparent housing. As children attempt to drive the Kiddy-Kat, the direction and speed of the turning gears are apparent as passengers attempt to drive the vehicle forward and backward, turn, and push loads from place to place. This exhibit was designed to encourage children's sustained fantasy play in a setting where the operation of simple and compound machines would be central to the ongoing activity. A particular concern was to provide opportunities for children to experience repeated examples of mechanical advantage, a concept that is often read or talked about in school, but rarely if ever experienced (Lehrer & Schauble, 1998).

These exhibits were identified as targets because (a) they elicit parent-child interaction in settings where assistance could support children's learning, and (b) these exhibits afford multiple levels of learning, from relatively unstructured play to systematic inquiry and experimentation.

Procedure for Museum Staff

A list of museum staff who volunteered to participate was forwarded to the research team before the visit, and each staff member was randomly assigned to one of the two target exhibits, The Creek or The Construction Zone. An interview schedule was arranged in advance by the Educator–Curator. At the appointed time, one researcher conducted a semistructured interview (mean duration 30 min, although a few interviews took up to an hour or more) while the other took notes and operated an audiotape recorder. The interview opened with general questions about the staff member's job and its connection to ScienceWorks. Next the staff member was prompted to enumerate and describe the educational strengths and then, the weaknesses of the target exhibit. He or she was asked to suggest ways that an adult might work with a child in that exhibit to enhance learning. The staff member also was asked how the exhibit might be changed to enhance its educational potential. Finally, the interviewer asked what it takes to make hands-on activities valuable for children. In each case, participants were prompted to continue until they indicated that they had no more information to volunteer.

Procedure for Parent Visitors

Pairs of researchers (rotated on a regular schedule) were stationed in front of each of the target exhibits. Researchers were instructed to scan the crowd (the gallery was very crowded during the weekend when the research was conducted) and identify adults wearing stickers (i.e., those who had completed a permission form). An adult became a candidate for an interview if observed either participating or attending closely as his or her child played at a target exhibit for more than 5 minutes. The 5-minute criterion was established to ensure that parents would have at least minimal familiarity with the exhibit in question.

The questions posed to adult visitors paralleled those asked the museum staff. Parents, like the museum staff, were asked explicitly about the educational potential of the target exhibit. Recall that we wanted participants to talk specifically about the exhibit in question, not to tell us their general theories about learning. The first question concerned the educational potential of the exhibit in question.

> I've been watching your child play in this exhibit. One thing we've been very interested in is how parents think about the educational potential of exhibits. We'd like to know what you think the learning possibilities of this exhibit are. So I'm going to ask you about the strengths and weaknesses of this exhibit for helping to educate children about science. I'll start off with the strengths.

Visitors were prompted to add and explain ideas until they indicated that they had no more to say. Then interviewers asked about weaknesses. Parents were also asked how adults might work with a child in the target exhibit to make the child's participation more educational. Then the parent was asked what it takes to make hands-on activities valuable for children.

Coding the Interviews

All interviews were transcribed for later analysis, and the parent interviews and staff interviews were analyzed separately, because we expected (and found) differences in the beliefs reported by these two groups. We used the data for a subset of half the interviews to generate two frameworks for analysis, one reflecting the concerns of the museum staff and the other summarizing issues raised by the parents. To develop the frameworks, researchers worked in pairs with their own interview notes and transcripts to identify the major themes mentioned in reply to the interview questions. As a group, interviewers then collated these themes into a comprehensive list used to categorize the comments about learning and assistance that participants made during this first subset of interviews. The themes do not comprise mutually exclusive category systems, inasmuch as each participant typically mentioned several themes during the course of the interview.

The candidate list of themes was then used to categorize replies from the second half of the interviews. Final adjustments to the scheme were made during this second round of coding. At that point, all the interviews were again recoded independently by a second set of raters. As a final check, and to ensure consistency in rating, all the interviews were checked one final time by the first author.

The themes coalesced into two overarching "supercategories." The first supercategory (Beliefs about Learning) included comments and replies that provided insight into participants' beliefs about learning, including how learning occurs and the factors that affect its outcome. The second supercategory (Assisting Learning) included respondents' ideas about how best to assist and encourage children's learning. Some of these comments mentioned actions that adults can take; others on how exhibits might be redesigned to optimize children's learning.

Results: Parent Visitors

Table 13.1 lists the major themes that parent visitors mentioned when they were asked to talk about the educational potential and weaknesses that they perceived in the target exhibits, and indicates the percentage of the

TABLE 13.1
Parents' Stated Beliefs Strengths/Weaknesses in the Target Exhibit

Theme	*Percent Adults Endorsing*	*N (of 32)*
Do/make/participate/experience	44	14
Go beyond do or play	28	9
Mentions specific concepts	25	8
Fun, entertainment, excitement	22	7
Interest	22	7
Show/see/observe	19	6
Play value	19	6
Specific exhibit components mentioned	19	6
Variety, lots to do	19	6
Learning, unspecified further	14	5
Teamwork	13	4
Experiment, cause/effect, what happens if	13	4
Work, career	13	4
Ambivalence about learning vs fun	9	3
Imagination, creativity	9	3

parents (total *n* of 32) who spontaneously mentioned each theme during the course of the interview.

These results seem consistent with two different perspectives about learning. Nearly half of the parents described learning in the target exhibits primarily as doing, playing, observing, or having fun. In contrast, a slightly smaller group of parents talked about learning as something *more* than doing. This second group often struggled to try to pin down what they meant by learning, proposing alternatives like experimenting, noting cause and effect, and acquiring particular science concepts. Our conjecture is that the informal museum context suggested "do" and "play," whereas the clear association with science content suggested "learn" and "understand." As we explain shortly, some of the parents (and also the museum staff, whose responses are presented in a later section) expressed ambivalence about how the gallery ought to balance or trade off these two agendas.

Of the 32 parents interviewed, 44% suggested that the value of the target exhibit was in the wide variety of *activity* possible there: doing, making, or participating in some relatively undefined way. In the parents' responses, these ideas about participation were relatively unspecified, and they did not typically contain much justification for why "doing" was considered valuable. For example, Parent 67 explained, "Okay, well, I think it's good in that it lets kids do things on their own. They can just go and do whatever interests them, they can do." To the extent that a few parents did justify *doing*, their justifications centered around the claim that experience is important for children's learning because children learn best by using their senses. As Parent 78 claimed, "First they have to experience it. Children learn, of course, by their senses, feeling, touching, and so on. And when they do it they remember it and then I think they are ready to read about it, and so I think the hands-on experiences are very necessary." Having "lots to do" in the gallery was considered a plus, especially if children could participate on their own with little parental involvement.

These parents tended to mention with favor the fun and excitement that their children experienced at ScienceWorks. Some suggested that fun might eventually spark more enduring interests. As one parent said, "Oh, the stream exhibit . . . the boys seem to enjoy it, seem to have fun. . . . I just bring them here and kind of let them run. I think the best way for kids to learn is just to find what interests them and play with it."

These parents who emphasized doing and having fun typically reported that the best role for adults was simply to stay out of the way. As Parent 67 explained, "I just let them run. If they need help, I'm here, but it's best for them to do it on their own." When these parents did envision a helping role they might take, their view of assistance seemed to center around helping children interact effectively or appropriately with the exhibit. For example, Parent 57 said, "The exhibit is so simple it doesn't take much interaction

TABLE 13.2
Parents' Stated Beliefs About Effective Adult Assistance

Theme	*Percent Adults Endorsing*	*N (of 32)*
Suggest, show how, help do	53	17
Participate	34	11
Explain	31	10
Hands off/stand back	31	10
Be enthusiastic, patient, encouraging	28	9
Expresses ambivalence about assistance	25	8
Teach	21	7
Ask how or what if questions	13	4
Provide follow-up resources	13	4
Model	9	3

with a parent. Maybe show how something works . . . encourage them to use the entire exhibit." Table 13.2 lists the themes that parents mentioned when asked about ways that adults could assist children's learning.

The contrasting perspective, held by the remainder of the parents, was that play alone was not enough to satisfy their expectations about the gallery. Instead, these parents most valued their children's opportunities to learn. However, some expressing this view seemed unsure about what else besides play or participation would be needed to make a learning experience valuable. As Parent 21 asked, "Are they really learning anything or they just playing in water? If someone was here to help direct them a little bit, they might learn something as well as have fun." Parent 13 agreed: "It's fun, but I'm not seeing a whole lot of learning here . . . but I don't think everything has to be learning." Parent 75 commented, "I think it would be a great benefit to maybe put up exactly the different principles at work here. There aren't really any signs." Other suggestions included having more volunteers in the gallery who could deliver "short talks, so children can also be learning something from adults" (Parent 79).

Some participants expressed the view that parents need to take major responsibility for their children's learning. For example, Parent 83 recommended that the parent go through each exhibit with the child, providing explanations at each step. Parent 14 also ratified parental explanation: "Parents can explain why and how come so they will understand." Parent 16, an engineer, described his role as being to talk "about how mechanics, wheels, axles, pulleys work."

Parent 26 thought that rather than providing explanations, parents ought to ask good questions. "I ask questions. 'Are you going to try ____?' 'How do you think ____?' " Parent 78 agreed: "I question him constantly about how things work." Moreover, several parents mentioned building on the museum experience by locating follow-up learning resources: books or library materials (also available at the museum), kits, or other related experiences in the child's life outside the museum. Parent 89, for example, emphasized the importance of "taking it beyond play" by helping children ". . . relate it to other experience. We don't come here for an educational lesson; they have a lot of fun. But when we get home, I look for books and other things that will help them relate and remember."

Some parents made comments that suggested they were unsure how to negotiate what they perceived as a trade-off between learning and fun. One parent argued, "You can just have fun and don't constantly try to be learning." When asked about the value of the exhibit, Parent 88 first said, "I'm a hands-on parent, working with my kids and trying to teach." However, a few sentences later in the conversation, she said, "I know a good parent would say, 'Oh, the educational experience,' but to me, as long as the kids are happy . . ." Parent 48 expressed mild skepticism that the open-endedness of the exhibits would result in learning. However, when asked whether the target exhibit's educational potential could be improved, he demurred, "You'd have to introduce some structure, and I don't know if that would be good."

In summary, parents were equally divided between "museum as a site of 'doing' " and "museum as an incubator for learning." Parent views of learning were oriented primarily toward general strategies for assisting learning, like asking questions or providing explanations. Most did not focus on particular concepts, nor did most see the exhibits as model systems that referred to larger scientific conceptions, like buoyancy or mechanical advantage. Some parents expressed potential tensions between "fun" and "learning" views of activity.

Results: Museum Staff

Table 13.3 presents the themes that the museum staff mentioned when they were asked about the educational strengths and weaknesses that they perceived in the target exhibits, along with the percentage of the museum staff (*n* of 16) who spontaneously mentioned each theme during the course of the interview.

The conceptual organization of most science museums is reflected in spatial organization. That is, a single exhibit is typically the locale for activities and demonstrations about a common scientific idea or related set of ideas, usually identified by labels and other explanatory text. In contrast, ScienceWorks embeds science content in everyday contexts and distributes activities and illustrations about a concept across multiple locations. For example, simple machines are concentrated in the Construction Site, but are also found at the Rock Climbing Wall, The Creek, and the Ball Machines at

TABLE 13.3
Staffs' Stated Beliefs Strengths/Weaknesses in the Target Exhibit

Theme	*Percent Staff Endorsing*	*N (of 16)*
Logistical weaknesses (noise, mess, crowding, misbehavior)	69	11
Mentions specific concepts	62	10
Doing/participating/hands-on	62	10
Experiential learning	56	9
Ambivalence about learning vs fun	56	9
Teamwork, communication	50	8
Misconception	44	7
Encourages observation/focus	32	5
Play, good time	25	4
Promote exploration, discovery	25	4
Develop recognition schema	25	4
Imagination, creativity	25	4
No right/wrong, fear of failure	25	5
Variety, lots to do	19	3
Constructivism	19	3
Learn without effort/recognition	19	3
Appropriate for ability, developmental level	19	3
Open-ended	12	2
Narrative, story	12	2
Work, career	6	1

the entrance to the gallery. There are relatively few signs or blocks of textual information about the scientific underpinnings of the exhibits and activities. The exhibits are designed to encourage visitors to interact with (usually, literally to play with) materials and items that behave in accordance with the focal science concepts of interest. There is a deliberate lack of emphasis on scientific terms and declarative facts.

In the interviews, the staff readily pointed out that these design choices created challenges for their role as interpreters. As a result, they perceived their jobs to be different from those of interpreters in the other galleries in the museum. These challenges can be summarized in a series of questions that staff puzzled over: How do we know what counts as learning? Is it necessary for visitors to be able to verbally describe the science concepts in the exhibits, or are patterns of activity sufficient evidence of learning? If so, which patterns are desirable? Are there effective ways of making the embedded science recognizable to visitors?

Approximately one third of the staff (5 of 16) proposed that visitors might be learning even though they might not be consciously aware of doing so. This was apparently not an idea that occurred to the parents, because none of them suggested it. Some of the staff proposed that visitors were familiarizing themselves on an informal level with ideas that would later serve as the basis for concepts encountered in formal education. For example, Staff 3 said, "They might not understand it now . . . later on these experiences are going to be in their memory, so that when they start studying simple machines, they're going to remember." This proposal seems similar to claims made by diSessa (1973) and others about the value of laying down schemas for recognizing phenomena (like Newtonian motion) that may not otherwise be clearly observed, and that might be foundational for later physics instruction.

More than half of the staff members interviewed (9 of 16) advanced some form of the claim that experiential forms of learning are the ones that are most valuable—particularly for young children. As Staff 1 explained, "Kids can experience it. All this stuff people can read in books—those are great books. I'm not putting them down, but here they can actually do it. You remember it more if you play with it. Years later, you might [remember it]. What would you enjoy more, I mean, reading in a book or actually doing it?" This claim, of course, is identical to the one advanced by some of the parents (i.e., that children learn best by doing). Staff 2 concurred: "Early childhood educators, they have the right model. And sometimes it gets lost. As soon as they hit six, let's stop the experiential learning and let's put them on a book and give memorization." Experiential learning was typically equated with discovery by the staff and was contrasted with transmission forms of learning. Staff 15 claimed, "I can give them the information and it will stick for awhile. If they discover the information for themselves, it stays with them a lot longer." More than one third of the staff members volunteered that they felt their role was to assist children's learning, but this did *not* mean direct teaching. Staff 15 is a good example: "My personal philosophy is, we don't teach kids anything here. We help them discover it. When I first came, I thought we were going to be teachers. That is not the way it works."

Consistent with their emphasis on experiential learning, most (i.e., 75%) of the staff members proposed that the best way for adults to assist children in the gallery was to play with children or "get involved" in children's activities—as Staff 10 advised, "Quit acting like an adult and become a part of what's going on there." This view contrasts sharply with that of the parents endorsing "participation." Recall that these parents suggested that adults could best be helpful by keeping out of their children's way. In fact, several staff members explicitly mentioned that they disliked what they perceived as this passive role on parents' part. As Staff 13 explained it, "A lot of parents . . . will sit down on the bench and say, 'Go play with boats,' or they will kind of stand there and watch. . . . What they need to do is just play with them [the children] at each place in the exhibit and maybe ask some of the same kinds of questions: 'Gee, I wonder what this does? Oh, I see, you turn it this way. Oh, look, the water's coming out of the center. Wow, what is this thing?' " However, other staff members noted that it can also be counterproductive for parents to take an overly "teachy" role. Staff 15 said, "What the parents do wrong is try to be the teachers. They come in and they try to tell the kid what they are supposed to do, what they are going to learn, what they are going to see. I try to get the parents to say, 'Let them discover.' " Many of the staff admitted that it is not always clear even to professional staff what they should do to help children—no wonder parents do not necessarily know how to be helpful in the gallery! They noticed, for example, that many parents feel uncomfortable asking their children questions when they themselves do not know the answers. As Staff 2 explained, "Some parents are uncomfortable with, well, let's figure it out together."

In the face of this sense that some parents were disengaged and others were too didactic, museum staff were not always sure about the best way to solicit parents' active involvement. One strategy described was to use the design of the gallery design to bring parents into the action. An interpreter said, "You have to create an environment where the parents feel that they have to come in." She went on to explain that one way to do so is to include a few activities that are too difficult for children to operate physically on their own. When describing the buckets-and-pulley system at The Creek, she said, "We left it difficult because we wanted parents to step in. We have areas in here that are designed to have parents step in." Other staff members perceived their role as filling in when parents failed to take on these roles: "We act as the absent parent. There are quite a few parents that don't want to get involved." See Table 13.4 for a summary of the staff's views about adult assistance.

Although the majority of staff ratified the importance of experience and self-discovery, some staff members—occasionally even the same individuals who were most emphatic about the importance of discovery—expressed uncertainty about how one could know whether and when learning was actually taking place in galleries like ScienceWorks that emphasize experience over the acquisition of facts. Like the parents, staff often talked about what they perceived as a conflict between *playing* (usually described as the children's agenda) and *learning* (presumably the museum's agenda). Staff 2 expressed this ambivalence in her interview—perhaps unwittingly, because she clearly approved of the gallery's nondidactic approach: "It's (The Creek) a great, fabulous demonstration; wonderful fun. It engages them. Are they learning? Yes, they are learning. What are they learning? I couldn't tell you. But they are learning something." Staff 9 had a similar kind of bemused reaction: "They are playing, they are having a good time and they're experiencing a different way of transporting something from one spot to another. Whether that sinks in is your guess." Staff 6 described this contrast between play and learning in a somewhat darker vein. "The kids are just try-

TABLE 13.4
Staffs' Stated Beliefs About Effective Adult Assistance

Theme	*Percent Staff Endorsing*	*N (of 16)*
Participate, play with, get involved	75	12
Explain, talk to	62	10
Ask questions	56	9
Pose goal or challenge	50	8
Propose redesign	44	7
Different kinds of learning	44	7
Importance of gallery facilitators	38	6
NOT teach	38	6
Signs	38	6
Help kids operate exhibit	19	3
NOT direct, control, dictate	12	2
Comfort level of adults	12	2
Teach	6	1
Scaffold and fade	6	1
Notebooks, pictures in gallery	6	1
Relate to "real" life	6	1

ing to run through and not really notice what's going on. Sometimes I'll talk to them and it's like, "I don't wanna, I know what I'm doing. I'm playing and don't bother me."

This perceived "pull" between the agendas of play and learning resulted in considerable active discussion and sometimes disagreement among staff about how to be most effective as mediators in the gallery. Comparing Table 13.2 with Table 13.4 shows that staff produced a list of ideas about adult assistance that was both longer and more differentiated than that generated by parents (in spite of the fact that twice as many parents as staff members were interviewed). This is presumably because staff, unlike parents, were involved every day in deciding how to mediate visitor experiences. In spite of the fact that collectively, they produced an extensive repertoire of ways for helping children learn, staff talked about the difficulties of knowing how best to negotiate a balance between play and learning in ScienceWorks. Staff 4 was especially articulate about this dilemma. "How much do I corral kids and try to challenge them and teach them? They don't like that. That is for school, and they want to be here to play. How much do I leave them alone? And that is probably one of my biggest dilemmas in every single area, is what should my role be?"

Although staff had many questions about how best to facilitate, they were adamant about the importance of mediation, especially in this gallery. Many of them claimed that effective mediation was the major factor responsible for tipping the gallery experience from unstructured play toward valuable learning experience. They noted that its reliance on human mediation made this gallery especially resource-demanding in comparison to other galleries in the museum, and they expressed worry about whether the museum administration would sustain the long-term commitment to what they perceived as the required level of staffing. Staff described a number of strategies that they used for facilitating learning in the gallery. As described earlier, the most frequently mentioned was to play actively with children, sometimes simply to encourage them to begin. "Some of the kids said, 'What do you do here?' I am, like, "Push it and find out.' It is the oddest thing that we have to tell kids, 'Push the button, turn the handle.' "

Unlike the parents, who talked frequently about more logistical forms of help, staff did not describe assistance primarily as helping children to operate the exhibits. Instead, staff emphasized talking to children or explaining how things work (62%) or asking provocative questions (56%) like the ones described by Staff 13. "If somebody's just playing there, I'll say, you know what that is? No? Well, this is what makes water go up. What do we call a thing that makes water go up? It's the world's oldest pump." Half the staff members volunteered that an effective way to spark learning is to pose a goal or challenge that can provide structure and direction to play that otherwise might become aimless. Staff 6: "We'll walk by and ask them, 'Have you tried, now that you've got your boat down here, can you get it back up?' "

Staff 2, a programmer in the gallery, described two general styles of mediation, which she called "helpers" and "big kids," respectively. According to this staff member, the helpers ask questions and set goals, as just described. In contrast, the big kids primarily participate—indeed, instigate—children's fantasy play in productive ways. Staff 15, who probably falls into the big kid category, described how he accomplishes this in the Construction Zone. "I would like to spend more time with the smaller kids down there with the sleds. We need to have those sleds down, pile them, pile up the blocks, carry the blocks over. Put them on the sled. Drag that sled back. It is obviously easier to drag that sled than it is to carry the blocks, you know, two at a time or one at a time. Then put them on the sled with the runners. Easier still. And then we put them in the gantry basket and let them float down, see."

When asked about the learning potential in a target exhibit, most of the staff responded first by describing specific science concepts that could be encountered in the exhibit. In general, as one might expect, the staff were far more knowledgeable about the science potential in the gallery than the parents were. Indeed, many of the staff (7 of the 16) went beyond talking about the science in the *gallery* to talk about science understanding in the *visitors.* That is, they explicitly discussed interesting forms of thinking that they had observed in children and adult visitors.

For example, several staff members noted that children have a tendency to enthusiastically crank handles on the Archimedes screw and waterwheel in the Stream, but sometimes fail to attend to the results of the handle-turning. When children attend primarily to their own efforts rather than to the way the machine works, they miss the intended messages about efficiency. As one of the interpreters pointed out, "Machines are designed to make work easier for a person. Unless the kids like to just go right into it, really aggressively, very fast, very strong. And they learn from seeing that it doesn't work. The machine stops working for them." A second staff member said that he deliberately tuned his interpretation of this exhibit differently for younger and older visitors: "For the little kids, they can understand . . . once they start turning, so they are pumping water, they are moving a lot of mass. For the older kids, we talk about efficiencies. Every mechanical process has an efficiency curve." Like this respondent, several staff members talked about *ranges* of comprehension that they typically observed in an exhibit. For example, a staff member remarked, "I think that gears are hard for children to comprehend. The second and third graders, I'm not sure [they] grasp some of the more in-depth concepts about what gears do. However, I think they have a basic understanding of how they can turn. If one gear is turning this way, which way will the other gear go? They can . . . figure out which way the gear way down here after all this will turn, which is really cool, but they don't understand mechanical advantage. . . . And I don't think that they necessarily understand how it makes work easier." Staff also described strategies for learning more about children's understanding. One said, "The problem is that the adults tell them [children] to sit on their hands until they get directions. And I tell them, 'No, let's go ahead and let them play with it.' Every once in awhile, I learn something new out of this." This staff member then went on to recount how simply observing children's play sometimes leads to surprising information about how they think about the exhibits.

In sum, parents tended to primarily value *either* play or learning, but a staff framed the task of adults as being to negotiate a *balance* between play and learning, or between open-endedness and structure. Some staff explicitly stated that it would be a mistake to turn these two agendas into an either–or issue. For example, Staff 2 said, "I don't think we can cue everything and I don't think we should. At first I thought they needed to signal everything in the gallery. But, you know, all you would have is a bunch of arrows and signs and lights and flashers and buttons and Christmas lights, and it would be overwhelming. I think having these nice little hidden secrets is kind of nice."

Summary: Study 1

Taken together, the interviews of the museum staff and parents suggest that adults in the museum are challenged and sometimes even openly puzzled about how to help children learn in a gallery that affords multiple levels of investigation. Staff and parents clearly appreciated children's spontaneous fascination and sustained engagement with the exhibits, but were not always confident how they could know that children were really learning. Many of the parents and a few of the staff seemed ready to accept that hands-on engagement alone might be sufficient evidence of learning. A few of the museum staff, in particular, had a tendency to interpret "constructivism" as being synonymous with unguided discovery learning. On the other hand, some of the parents (and at least one staff member) felt that children were not learning unless they were acquiring declarative facts about identifiable science concepts. Most of the staff, however, embraced neither unguided discovery nor the acquisition of facts. For the most part, they were interested in figuring out how to optimize the educational potential of children's activity by directing it toward finding out, making comparisons, closely observing, or systematically exploring, rather than aimless fiddling *or* acquiring terms and labels. Many adults—some parents, but especially staff—expressed ambivalence or confusion about how one could go about identifying learning in this museum context, how one could be confident that learning was occurring, and how adults could offer effective assistance without intruding in clumsy ways on children's self-directed activity. As a group, the staff seemed to embrace this as an interesting challenge of their job, one they felt optimistic about mastering as their experience and knowledge of the gallery grew. However, they clearly wished they could rely more confidently on parents as allies in this enterprise. Too often, they thought, some parents were passively disengaged whereas others tended to be overcontrolling and didactic. The interviews suggest that much could be gained if staff and parents could work more smoothly together toward common directions.

Study 2: Parents' Assistance of their Children During Self-Directed Experimentation

Study 1 focused on adults' self-reports and beliefs about best ways to assist children's learning. In Study 2, we turned to an empirical study of the way that parents actually assisted their children in a scaled-down version of one of the learning opportunities in the museum's *The Creek* exhibit. In this study, which is reported in detail elsewhere (Gleason & Schauble, 1999), parents worked with their children to run a series of experimental trials with a set of small boats and a 6 foot model replica of The Creek. The dyad's goal was to try to figure out which of several manipulable features (including depth of the channel and boat size, shape, and weight) affected the boat speed, and how. Recall that at The Creek in ScienceWorks, visitors can construct boats of various designs and time their progress down The Creek. These experiments can also include manipulations of The Creek itself, which can be reconfigured with plastic flanges to change the breadth, depth, and curvature of the channel. Thus, visitors can investigate what features of their boats and the stream affect the speed of the boats. Our attempt was to capture some of these aspects of this activity in the model used in the study.

The boat-racing task that we chose to model and study empirically is only one of the many in The Creek or elsewhere in the museum that could support study of adult assistance. However, we selected it because it invites participants to work interactively with exhibit components to figure out how they work, a general feature of many museum exhibit activities. Moreover, because neither children nor parents were likely to know in advance the solution to the problem, we felt it would be a good choice for eliciting parent–child interaction.

As we planned this study, we were building on a base of knowledge from previous research in scientific reasoning that has been developing over the past two decades (Kuhn, Garcia-Mila, Zohar, & Anderson, 1995), Schauble (1996), and Klahr and colleagues (Dunbar & Klahr, 1989; Klahr, 2000; Klahr & Dunbar, 1988) Koslowski (1999). Cumulatively, this research describes how adults and children coordinate their theories and beliefs with new evidence in a variety of scientific reasoning contexts. Although we cannot provide an extensive review of this research here (however, see Klahr, 2000; Kuhn et al., 1995), its goal is to identify the strategies that adults and preadolescent children typically use when working in self-directed experimentation contexts that share many similarities with hands-on museum exhibits.

Some of these studies compared the reasoning processes used by adults to those spontaneously used by children while these individuals solved multivariable experimentation problems, like the ones that we studied in The Creek (Dunbar & Klahr, 1989; Klahr, Fay, & Dunbar, 1993; Kuhn et al., 1995; Schauble, Klopfer, & Raghavan, 1991). Typically, participants worked on these problems over multiple sessions—sometimes for weeks at a time. The participants were asked to try to find a "rule" that describes the operation of some device, or to generate a description of the causal interactions in a complex system, for example, by determining which of several candidate variables affect an observable outcome, and how. The participants solved these problems by manipulating the variables, measuring and recording the outcomes, and interpreting the growing database. Several cycles of trials usually needed to be planned and conducted by each participant.

These studies found considerable variability within individuals of the same age group, and some overlap in performance between adults and children. However, in all of them, adults systematically outperformed children, both in making the target discoveries and in using experimentation strategies that are effective and efficient. For example, in comparison to adults, children often tended to overfocus on some of the variables (typically, those that they believed to be causal) as they generated evidence and ignore others (Schauble et al., 1991). They frequently generated experiments that were not informative because they did not include comparisons at all, or alternatively, incorporated experimental confounds (Dunbar & Klahr, 1989; Kuhn et al., 1995). Their predictions about experiments were often unrelated to the interpretations that they made after observing the results, suggesting that they tended to forget the purpose of their experiments midstream (Kuhn et al., 1995; Schauble, 1990). In general, children's performance suggested that they were having difficulty coordinating the embedded goal–subgoal hierarchy that characterizes experimentation (e.g., Klahr & Dunbar, 1988; Schauble et al., 1991).

Children also showed characteristic difficulties in interpreting the evidence that they generated. Children were likely to make interpretations based on only one or a few salient cases, rather than considering the patterns in the entire body of data that they generated (Klahr & Dunbar, 1988; Lehrer & Romberg, 1996). That may be why they often overlooked evidence that was inconsistent with their prior theories (Kuhn, Amsel, & O'Loughlin, 1988; Schauble, 1990, 1996). In comparison to adults, children more frequently drew conclusions that were not supported by valid evidence, and more often neglected to prune the search space by identifying variables that do not play a causal role (Kuhn & Phelps, 1982). Finally, children seemed to pay little attention to keeping, reviewing, or otherwise using written or other records of their work, even in situations where they were conducting multiple trials that were difficult to interpret without notational support (Schauble, 1990).

Given the generally superior performance of adults at generating and interpreting evidence, we suspected that parents would be in an excellent position to assist their children in these tasks, which are similar to activities that are frequently featured in museums. In Study 2, we investigated whether, in fact, parents seem to be aware of children's strategic weaknesses that we summarized, and if so, whether they understand how best to help.

Participants. The participants were 20 volunteer parent–child dyads recruited in the Children's Museum of Indianapolis (11 dyads) and through education courses at the University of Wisconsin (9 dyads). The children were between 8 and 12 years of age, that is, at the preadolescent age most frequently investigated in the scientific reasoning research. Their parents, who ranged in age from 35 to 49 years, were highly educated: 3 PhDs, two MAs, 5 BAs, 2 trade school degrees, 5 currently in college, and 3 high school graduates. We selected such highly educated parents because we hoped to observe an optimal snapshot of adult–child assistance. The sample included all combinations of mothers, fathers, sons, and daughters.

Procedure

Dyads worked together for 45 minutes on the scale model of The Creek, a model originally designed by Klopfer and Schauble (Schauble et al., 1991). The system that we used employs a model canal filled with water and six small, wooden boats of different sizes and shapes. The purpose is to determine which features in the boat-and-canal system affect the time that it takes for a boat to be towed down the "canal" by a weight-and-pulley system. Features that can be manipulated include the canal depth, boat shape, boat size, and boat weight. Participants were asked to design and interpret experimental trials by varying the manipulable features in the system, repeatedly running trials, and interpreting the outcomes. Each of the parent–child dyads worked together for 45 minutes with the model problem. Although the interviewer remained present throughout the session to turn on and monitor the video camera, she moved to an area on the other side of the room and avoided intervening in the dyads' ongoing work or conversation.

As they conducted their trials, the dyads filled out data cards to serve as records of the design and results of their trials. Participants were asked to fill out a card for each trial, circling the levels of features selected and recording predicted outcome, observed outcome, and any conclusions that they wished to make. The interviewer suggested that the completed data cards would be helpful for organizing results and supporting claims about the features that affect speed in the boat–canal system.

All the sessions were video recorded and transcribed, and we coded the dyads' strategies for generating and interpreting evidence, their interaction patterns as they solved the problem, and the forms of assistance that we observed. Before and after their session, the dyad members were individually interviewed about their current understanding of the boat–canal system, so that we could learn whether and how the parent and the child might have changed their beliefs during the session about the variables that affected the boat speed.

Results

In many ways, the highly educated parents in this study delivered an impressive performance with their children. Almost all of the dyads systematically generated readily interpretable patterns of evidence. In fact, 85% of all the inferences that the dyads made were supported by valid patterns of evidence. It is worth noting that this result is in marked contrast to previous studies of scientific reasoning, which repeatedly found flawed experimentation design and interpretation heuristics used by preadolescent children and even by many adults (Kuhn et al., 1995; Schauble, 1996). In contrast to the participants in these previous studies, who often jumped to conclusions long before the data actually supported such inferences, the dyads in Study

2 also tended to reserve making inferences until they had sufficient valid evidence. Finally, the dyads also showed considerable sophistication in data recording and organizing (e.g., by arranging the data cards in ways that supported comparisons, i.e., all the large boats lined up in one column and all the small boats in another). These results suggest that if they get involved in doing so, parents are quite capable of assisting their children in museum-like experimentation activities.

The picture was not altogether rosy, however. We found that in general, the dyads spent far more of their time and attention on designing and conducting the trials than on interpreting the results. For example, there was typically very little conversation about the outcomes that the dyads observed, or about the judgments they were presumably making about the various features and their effects on boat speed. Parents made most of the conclusions (86%), and 14% of the conclusions were simply written by parents on the data cards, and never verbally stated at all. We conjectured that parents might not have discussed data interpretation with their children because they were not really aware how complex it actually is for children to keep track of and incorporate multiple observations into a conclusion. Instead, the parents seemed to regard the meaning of the outcomes as self-evident—to their children as well as themselves. Parents knew, of course, that their children had access to the same information they did. If seeing is taken unproblematically as knowing, then parents might well have assumed that their children were making the same inferences that they were. We knew from previous research, however, that children often overlook much of the data, focus on recent or very salient cases, and tend to overlook evidence suggesting that some variables do *not* play a causal role. Perhaps because these interpretive challenges are less difficult for adults, the adults may not have represented them explicitly, and therefore, may have failed to understand that their children were not necessarily sharing their evolving understanding of the model system as the session progressed. Consistent with this possibility, we found from the postsession interviews that parents made considerable progress at figuring out how the model system actually worked, whereas most of their children did not make progress. That is, parents improved in their capability to correctly identify the features that did and did not affect boat speed. In contrast, over the 45-minute session, children as a group did not show such gains (although a few individuals did).

We found this surprising, given that parents and children were working together smoothly and did not argue or disagree about the meaning of what they were observing (only 2% of the conclusions elicited any disagreement or request for clarification). The transcripts, however, shed light on this dilemma. We noticed that the dyads talked very little about data interpretation—to express either disagreement, agreement, or puzzlement. Instead, almost all of the conversation was about how to design and actually conduct the trials, not how to interpret them. In other words, parents' stance toward helping their children in Study 2 seems somewhat analogous to the ideas parents expressed in Study 1, that is, with respect to the emphasis on helping children attain access to or physically operate the activities in the gallery. The emphasis upon doing rather than thinking or learning seems to carry across both contexts. It is possible that in both contexts—during the empirical study and on the museum floor—parents believed that doing is both a necessary *and* sufficient condition for learning.

Consistent with this possibility, we noticed that parents were more likely than their children to take on important conceptual roles in getting the work done. That is, they were typically the ones who recorded information on the data cards, consulted the data records, and verbalized inferences. These tasks comprise much of the "head work" in this task. Children, in contrast, assumed more of the logistical or mechanical roles, for example, choosing features to test, releasing the boat in the canal, and operating the stopwatch. One might have expected that over the course of the 45-minute session, parents would gradually cede some of the more challenging conceptual tasks to children, but this rarely occurred.

As one might expect, parents assisted their children more frequently than children provided assistance for parents. Assistance occurred more frequently during the evidence-generation phase of the trials, again suggesting that the dyads paid far more attention to evidence generation than to evidence interpretation. Although parents frequently pursued opportunities to help their children design and conduct the trials, they seldom helped their children interpret the evidence, by asking questions ("What do you think about how it came out?"), turning children's attention to the database ("Maybe we should look at the data cards from the earlier trials and compare them to this one"), or suggesting informative comparisons ("How have the little boats been doing compared to the big ones?"). This is not to say that parents did not provide any effective forms of assistance; in fact, we observed several forms of assistance similar to those reported in the earlier Lehrer and Shumow (1997) study. We observed parents helping children manage the goals and subgoals of the experimentation problem, reminding children of the problem structure, encouraging children to justify their predictions, and discouraging the generation of invalid evidence. However, parents missed important opportunities to assist their children in interpreting evidence, or taking on the recording and analysis of the data.

Summary: Study 2

When parents were empirically observed working with their children on a model experimentation problem, they provided forms of assistance that seemed sensitive to children's capabilities with the task. In particular, parents did an admirable job of helping their children design and run experiments; however, they did comparatively little to help their children interpret experiments. Recall that these parents were highly educated, and that the dyads were observed in a situation that would be likely to optimize parents' desire to be helpful (parents were told that the purpose of the study was to learn how parents and children solve a problem together, and the interviewer remained present throughout the session). Therefore, we do not believe that parents failed to assist in data interpretation because they did not care to spend the time and energy. Nor do we believe that parents failed to assist because they were having difficulties in data interpretation themselves (recall that parents made progress in learning how the model system worked, even if their children did not). Rather, we suspect that parents did not understand what their children did not know, and failed to provide assistance because they were not aware that it was needed.

DISCUSSION AND NEXT STEPS

Alas, this has been a chapter about problems rather than solutions. Our beginning work on domain-specific forms of parent–child assistance has focused on developing a better understanding of the nature of the problem, information that we will use in developing and systematically investigating alternative solutions. Next steps will entail putting together what we know about children's thinking with what we are learning about assistance, to design and study effective ways for adults to help support children's learning.

We have suggested that as we "up the ante" on learning opportunities in museums, we must also up the ante for adults who are responsible for helping to support children's learning, whether they are professional museum staff or adults who accompany children on the museum visit. Our observations and interviews suggest that unless careful attention is paid to helping the helpers, the energy and resources devoted to deepening museum learning may be wasted, or at best, underexploited. Museums are contexts where designers give considerable explicit thought to assisting learning via symbol systems and tools, including built environments, texts, activity structures, even colors and traffic patterns! However, less thought has been spent on thinking about how to engineer the role of people, including parents, museum staff, and other visiting children. There is as yet no widely shared vision of professional practice in museums that includes the objective of gaining proficiency in diagnosing and capitalizing on knowledge about typical children's thinking (or the thinking of visitors of any age, for that matter). "Capitalizing" may include a host of strategies, from designing better exhibits, to inventing and testing ways to help parents assist their children's learning, to developing and sharing together a public base of knowledge about scientific thinking.

We believe that to engineer better forms of assistance, it will be necessary to go beyond general-purpose suggestions about participating or asking questions or reading text with children. General solutions, of course, are attractive precisely because they apply across a wide range of situations. However, the museum staff in Study 1 knew that they should ask questions, for example, but they were not sure what questions to ask, or when to ask them. Parents in Study 2 asked insightful questions during the evidence generation phase of their trials, but neglected to ask questions during the evidence interpretation phase, presumably because they were not aware that their children were not finding evidence interpretation to be self-evident. In both studies, it seemed easy for adults to be satisfied with getting children to successfully carry out the activity at hand, trusting that if children were engaged and active, learning would surely follow.

We think that museum research is now at the point where it is confronting issues similar to those encountered over two decades ago by researchers of classroom teaching. Earlier research on teaching focused on the classroom moves that teachers make that are not particular to any domain or content. Increasingly over the 1980s and 1990s, however, it became clear that focus needed to shift from what teachers do in general to *what teachers do about student understanding*. Moreover, the focus is not on identifying how teachers assist students' learning and understanding in some abstract, general sense, but how they support learning of particular ideas in mathematics or science or history. For example, in the Lehrer and Shumow (1997) study of mathematical problem solving, teachers not only helped students elaborate the problem space of the mathematical problems, but also helped students make sense of the mathematical contexts. Contemporary research on teaching emphasizes the importance of building a detailed model about children's typical ways of thinking about important concepts, including typical pathways of development for those understandings (e.g., Carpenter & Fennema, 1992; Lampert, 1998; Lehrer & Chazan, 1998). As a teacher contemplates how and why a child thinks about an idea, it can be extremely helpful to understand where that idea might have come from and where it is likely to be evolving to next.

Some may consider it daunting to consider that good mediation will depend on detailed knowledge of how visitors think—not about one or two important ideas, but about the range of ideas and topics that museums attempt to present. However, if the museum community comes to understand that this goal is at the right level to make progress, at least we will have a shared sense of the kind of research agenda that can lay the groundwork for effective mediation. Tackling this kind of agenda systematically, one piece at a time, is the kind of task that a research field is equipped to tackle. Such a strategy has been the key to impressive progress in fields like mathematics, science, and reading instruction. There is good reason to believe that the same approach will be the key to making progress in museum mediation and learning, too. However, this will require that museums take visitor learning more seriously than they typically have in the past; agendas of this scope cannot be seriously addressed as a side concern in an overburdened education director's schedule. This suggests that more people need to get involved in tackling this agenda. For example, learning researchers will need to take a broader look at learning and learning contexts: learning doesn't happen only in school.

ACKNOWLEDGMENTS

The research reported here was supported in part by the Museum Learning Collaborative (MLC), Learning Research and Development Center, University of Pittsburgh. The MLC is funded by the Institute for Museum and Library Services, the National Science Foundation, the National Endowment for the Arts, and the National Endowment for the Humanities. The opinions expressed are solely those of the authors and no official endorsement from the funders should be presumed.

REFERENCES

Borun, M., Dritsas, J., Johnson, J. I., Peter, N. E., Wagner, K. F., Fadigan, K., Jangaard, A., Stroup, E., & Wenger, A. (1998). *Family learning in museums: The PISEC perspective.* Philadelphia, PA: The Franklin Institute.

Borun, M., Chambers, M., Dritasas, J., & Johnson, J. (1997). Enhancing family learning through exhibits. *Curator, 40*(4), 279–295.

Crowley, K., & Callanan, M. (1998). Describing and supporting collaborative scientific thinking in parent-child interactions. *Journal of Museum Education, 23*(1), 12–23.

Carpenter, T. P., & Fennema, E. (1992). Cognitively Guided Instruction: Building on the knowledge of students and teachers. *International Journal of Educational Research, 17*(5), 457–470.

DiSessa, A. A. (1993). Toward an epistemology of physics. *Cognition and Instruction, 10,* 105–225.

Dunbar, K., & Klahr, D. (1989). Developmental differences in scientific discovery. In D. Klahr & K. Kotovsky (Eds.), *Complex information processing: The impact of Herbert A. Simon* (pp. 109–144). Hillsdale, NJ: Lawrence Erlbaum Associates.

Gelman, R., Massey, C., & McManus, M. (1991). Characterizing supporting environments for cognitive development: Lessons from children in a museum. In L. Resnick, J. Levin, & S. Teasley (Eds.), *Perspectives on socially-shared cognition* (pp. 226–256). Washington, DC: American Psychological Association.

Gleason, M., & Schauble, L. (1999). Parents' assistance of their children's scientific reasoning. *Cognition and Instruction, 17*(4), 343–378.

Klahr, D. (2000). *Exploring science: The cognition and development of discovery processes.* Cambridge, MA: The MIT Press.

Klahr, D., & Dunbar, K. (1988). Dual search space during scientific reasoning. *Cognitive Science, 12*(1), 1–55.

Klahr, D., Fay, A. L., & Dunbar, K. (1993). Heuristics for scientific experimentation: A developmental study. *Cognitive Science, 25,* 111–146.

Koslowski, B. (1999). *Theory and evidence: The development of scientific reasoning.* Cambridge, MA: The MIT Press.

Kuhn, D., Amsel, E. D., & O'Loughlin, M. (1988). *The development of scientific thinking skills.* San Diego, CA: Academic Press.

Kuhn, D., Garcia-Mila, M., Zohar, A., & Anderson, C. (1995). Strategies of knowledge acquisition. *Monographs of the Society for Research in Child Development, 60*(4).

Kuhn, D., & Phelps, E. (1982). The development of problem-solving strategies. In H. Reese (Ed.), *Advances in child development and behavior* (Vol. 17, pp. 1–44). New York: Academic Press.

Lampert, M. (1998). Studying teaching as a thinking practice. In J. Greeno & S. G. Goldman (Eds.), *Thinking practices* (pp. 53–78). Mahwah, NJ: Lawrence Erlbaum Associates.

Lehrer, R., & Chazan, D. (Eds.). (1998). *Designing learning environments for developing understanding of geometry and space.* Mahwah, NJ: Lawrence Erlbaum Associates.

Lehrer, R., & Romberg, T. (1996). Exploring children's data modeling. *Cognition and Instruction, 14*(1), 69–108.

Lehrer, R., & Schauble, L. (1998). Reasoning about structure and function: Children's conceptions about gears. *Journal for Research in Science Teaching, 35*(1), 3–25.

Lehrer, R., & Shumow, L. (1997). Aligning the construction zones of parents and teachers for mathematics reform. *Cognition and Instruction, 15*(1), 41–83.

Schauble, L. (1990). Belief revision in children: The role of prior knowledge and strategies for generating evidence. *Journal of Experimental Child Psychology, 49,* 31–57.

Schauble, L. (1996). The development of scientific reasoning in knowledge-rich contexts. *Developmental Psychology, 32*(10), 102–119.

Schauble, L., & Bartlett, K. (1997). Constructing a science gallery for children and families: The role of research in an innovative design process. *Science Education, 81*(6), 781–793.

Schauble, L., Klopfer, L. E., & Raghavan, K. (1991). Students' transition from an engineering model to a scientific model of experimentation. *Journal for Research in Science Teaching, 28*(9), 859–882.

Author Index

Reference pages are denoted by *italic* face.

L

M

N

O

P

Subject Index

S

V-Z